CHINESE AMERICA

CHINESE AMERICA

The Untold Story of

America's Oldest New Community

Peter Kwong and Dušanka Mišcević

THE NEW PRESS

NEW YORK
LONDON

Requests for permission to reproduce selections from this book should be mailed to:
Permissions Department, The New Press, 38 Greene Street, New York, NY 10013

Published in the United States by The New Press, New York, 2005
Distributed by W. W. Norton & Company, Inc., New York

LIBRARY OF CONGRESS CATALOGING-IN-PUBLICATION DATA

Kwong, Peter.
    Chinese America : the untold story of America's oldest new community / Peter Kwong
and Dušanka Mišćević.
        p. cm.
    Includes bibliographical references and index.
    ISBN 1-56584-962-0 (hc.)
    1. Chinese Americans—History. 2. Chinese Americans—Social conditions. I. Mišćević,
Dušanka Dusana. II. Title.

E184.C5K88   2005
305.895'1073'09—dc22
                                                                        2005049550

The New Press was established in 1990 as a not-for-profit alternative to the large,
commercial publishing houses currently dominating the book publishing industry.
The New Press operates in the public interest rather than for private gain, and is
committed to publishing, in innovative ways, works of educational, cultural,
and community value that are often deemed insufficiently profitable.

www.thenewpress.com

Composition by Westchester Book Composition

Printed in the United States of America

2   4   6   8   10   9   7   5   3   1

Contents

PART III: THE COLD WAR SHAPES
CHINESE AMERICA (1946–1965)

PART IV: FROM CIVIL RIGHTS TO
IDENTITY POLITICS (1965–1980s)

PART V: CONTEMPORARY CHINESE AMERICA

PART VI: SUBURBAN AND SYMBOLIC POLITICS

Acknowledgments

The authors would like to thank André Schiffrin for his confidence in signing up this rather lengthy and ambitious project.

Our navigation through the more than 160-year-long history of the Chinese in America has been guided by the incomparably talented and skillful editor Andrew Hsiao, who is an expert on Asian America in his own right. He deserves more credit than he will get, but, in the event of controversy, merits no blame.

Finally, we would like to express our sincere appreciation to the supportive New Press staff for making the writing of this book a rewarding, collaborative experience in more ways than one.

Introduction

In recent years a blasé attitude has taken hold about Chinese Americans. Many point out that though the Chinese were victims of racial violence and exclusion in the past, they never suffered as much as African Americans. Besides, say others, European immigrants, too, had to endure hardship and discrimination when they first came to America. They made it. Now the Chinese are making it. End of story.

Statistics to prove this are readily available. The median family income of Chinese Americans is higher than that of Caucasians. Chinese Americans complete college at a rate twice as high as that of white Americans. A larger percentage of them live in upper-middle-class suburbs. Their children are overrepresented in the best schools. The problems they *still* have, such as the glass ceiling at the workplace, ethnic stereotyping, profiling as disloyal aliens, and exploitation in Chinatown ghettos, are chalked up to "paying their dues" for membership in the exclusive club that is America. Most members of the affluent white opinion-making class can even produce a relative or friend who is married to a wonderful young Chinese woman, or at least an acquaintance who has just adopted a beautiful baby girl from China. In short, not only are the Chinese a beloved model minority; their example can be used to show that the American paradigm of immigrant assimilation works universally.

The emphasis on recent success stories obscures the fact that

Chinese are one of the oldest immigrant groups in this country. They came long before the "new immigrants" (eastern and southern Europeans, who didn't begin to arrive until after the 1890s), at about the same time as the "old immigrants" (Germans and the Irish), in the late 1840s. They were greeted with animosity by competitors for jobs and opportunities, who battered and segregated them until they forced the passage of the Chinese Exclusion Act in 1882. Very few Chinese were legally allowed to enter the United States after that; those who were already here were attacked and pushed out of the workforce, until the only place most found a way to survive was in isolated ghettos. American laws prevented them from becoming U.S. citizens; they were not allowed the right to vote. In legal terms, they were protected even less than African Americans. American society, in short, wanted them to go away, die off, or disappear from view. When normal Chinese immigration resumed in the mid-1960s, after a new U.S. immigration act eliminated racial and ethnic barriers in the law, the Chinese had to begin again as "new immigrants." Most Americans still see them, collectively, as "foreign"—even those whose families that have spent several generations on this continent. In the meantime, the people who came here after them—Poles, Greeks, Italians, Russians, Hungarians, and Jews—were assimilated in fewer than fifty years.

It is easy to attribute this attitude toward the Chinese to racism. American understanding of racism, however, is infused with the specifics of the historical experience between African and European Americans, with slavery at its core and continued discrimination as its legacy. Minority experience is expected to follow one of two paradigms: either the African American experience of racial exclusion or the ethnic European experience of assimilation. The Chinese are often reduced to props in the battle over responsibility for the continued problems faced by African Americans and in the debate over whether the American system works. Arguing against this line of reasoning is like getting involved in a family squabble between African Americans and whites. This perhaps explains why narratives about Chinese American experience all too often focus on one of the two dominant themes: victimization, with authors seeking redress for past injustice, or celebration of success despite the hardships. The experience of the Chinese in America cannot be fully understood if presented from either of those two angles. The specificity of their racial and ethnic encounters in America, like those of other Asians, Latinos, and Native Americans, must not re-main subsumed by the dominant black/white debate.

Asian American, Hispanic, and other minority movements that emerged in the late 1960s as offshoots of the civil rights movement, placed race at the center of their awareness of themselves as minorities and used it to define their place in American society. Chinese, who pre-viously had little in common with Japanese or Filipinos, merged with the two groups in a new construct—the "racialized" category of Asian America. Before then, white America saw all Asian immigrants as an in-distinguishable "Oriental" mass; now the activists among them hoped to use this given identity as the basis for a broad coalition of national groups from Asia, and to use this new, American, pan-ethnic identity to fight against racism. To maintain unity, unfortunately, the activists of-ten avoided addressing class, gender, and national divisions within the Asian American community. At the same time, by focusing on discrim-ination, the minority movement continued to participate in the squab-ble between the two dominant races (as a not very effective junior partner, at that). The tactic created a culture of victimhood and pro-jected an unintended image of group passivity and lack of individuality.

This book wants to break through the confines such inadequate models have placed on the interpretation of the Chinese experience in America and look at the people who came to the New World in the light of their ambitions, passions, conflicts, unique solutions, and all the roads they took or could not travel. It wants to understand their weaknesses and contradictions on their own terms—not judge them as victims or as failures of assimilation. It wants to present their experi-ence in America as a function of their own motivations and objectives, not just within the parameters of what white America wanted of them and what it gave them. (The book, however, deals only with the expe-rience of Chinese immigrants to the continental USA; their experi-ences in Hawaii were different on account of the islands' unique history.) The biggest challenge of this approach is finding the voices of Chinese Americans to tell the story; especially when it comes to the nineteenth century, only a few snippets are preserved, while there is no shortage of records that deliver the sting of a prejudiced, largely misinformed, white perspective.

Another challenge is the application of different "tools" in taking measure of Chinese experience. Discrimination against the Chinese was rooted in white America's westward expansion and its encounter with people who did not quite fit existing categorization. American lawmakers struggled to define the exact nature of the Chinese "race" until economic, social, and political forces determined the Chinese immigrants' place within the social hierarchy imposed by white America. One of the factors that influenced this decision was white America's perception of China as a nation, which changed from admiration for the mighty civilization to scorn when the collapsing Qing Empire could no longer protect its borders from foreign intrusion. By the time Chinese started immigrating to America in large numbers, China was a weak, subjugated nation.

It was another misfortune for the Chinese, though no coincidence, that they began arriving in America at the height of the national debate on slavery that led to the civil war, having been recruited from across the Pacific to supply the workforce needed to develop the West. This was the time when the advent of large-scale manufacturing and unprecedented industrial development pitted monopoly capital against an emerging labor movement. White employers, in desperate need of reliable workers for the rapidly growing economy, looked to the Chinese as a replacement for the coercive type of labor that was disappearing with slavery, while also using them to undermine white workers' growing militancy. What emerged was an early form of a "guest worker" program for the Chinese, enforced through laws that allowed them to come to the United States without granting them the right of citizenship, and thus depriving them of all legal and labor protection.

Instead of welcoming working-class Chinese into the fold of the American labor movement, white labor leaders fought the employers on the grounds that Chinese were "coolies" working under conditions of indentured servitude. They accused the Chinese of undermining the value of white labor and demanded that employers not hire them. Their racial prejudice trumped their class consciousness, but it helped them unite among themselves and win the battle against their employers. The white labor movement became so strong, in fact, that it succeeded in pressuring the U.S. Congress to pass the Chinese Exclusion Act, which banned further immigration of Chinese laborers.

The factors that brought on the exclusion legislation reveal that the basis for discrimination the Chinese experienced in America was far more complex than just race. By the same token, the exploitation they endured as working-class people was often not directly inflicted by white society. During the nineteenth century, the shipping of poor Chinese immigrants to America was big business, and Chinese merchants quickly jumped in to make profits from advancing the cost of tickets, contracting jobs, or acting as subcontractors and supervisors of Chinese workers for white employers. While the laborers entered into this arrangement with Chinese contractors voluntarily, they had to pay dearly for the contractors' services. It also made their fight against exploitation difficult, because they had to confront both Chinese subcontractors and white employers.

Despite the odds, Chinese workers in America in fact continuously fought for their rights. Class conflicts within the Chinese community simmered throughout Chinese American history and flared up sporadically, especially during the Great Depression of the 1930s. They are currently on full display in the sweatshops and workplaces inside Chinese urban enclaves. That they have been largely unnoticed by the society at large and kept submerged under the rubric of internal Chinese affairs is an index of the indifference of white society.

It would be a mistake, however—and this is frequently a problem with minority studies—to look at the ethnic and racial experiences of the Chinese only within the domestic American context. It is a common misconception that new immigrants happily abandon cultural and institutional attachments to the country of their origin soon after they arrive in America. In the case of the Chinese, where they came from and what happened in China had an enormous impact on their life in America. Because of the hierarchy among nations, as citizens of a weak state that could offer them no protection, they were treated poorly. America would not let them assimilate. As aliens ineligible for citizenship and unable to vote, they could not fight for their rights like Irish or Italian immigrants did with their ethnic voting blocs. The only political action they could take was to help make China into a strong and prosperous nation, so that an influential China would make their life in the United States easier. Instead of giving up on China, they supported a score of reform movements and modernization efforts with generous contributions.

At times this strategy paid off. China stood up against Japanese aggression in the late 1930s and became an ally of the United States after the Japanese attack on Pearl Harbor. The image of the Chinese in this country improved dramatically; almost overnight they were transformed into brave fighters for righteous causes. Their community was no longer seen as a hotbed of indecency, immorality, and juvenile delinquency. More to the point: Congress saw fit to repeal the sixty-year-old Chinese Exclusion Act, while Japanese Americans, 75 percent of whom were American-born, were sent to America's very own concentration camps.

At other times, a connection to the motherland was understood as a direct affront to American principles. During the cold war, especially after direct military confrontation between American and Communist Chinese troops in Korea, the loyalty of Chinese Americans became suspect. During the McCarthy era, Chinese known for progressive or liberal views were investigated by the FBI as possible communist sympathizers or even as enemy agents. A harrowing "confession program" was instituted to induce Chinese Americans to inform on their relatives, friends, and acquaintances. The experience of that period silenced a whole generation of Chinese Americans politically for decades to come.

Having been in America since the 1840s, Chinese have witnessed its many changes—from a divided nation torn by the question of slavery to a confident, westward-expanding continental power, a budding trader with Asia, a dominant industrial post–World War II superpower, and now, a global empire. At each step of the transformation, America has imported immigrants to serve its needs. At each step, the Chinese have played a significant, occasionally even critical, role. This book will chart the effects that the changing needs of American economic development and foreign policy have had on the shaping of Chinese American history.

In America's conquest of the West, Chinese provided the necessary muscle power: they mined its riches, built dikes and dug ditches, reclaimed wilderness, and built the transportation infrastructure that enabled the leap into the industrial age. After World War II, when the United States ascended to the position of the leader of the free world, Chinese scientists and engineers provided the brainpower so it could compete against the Soviet Union. America's shortage of high-caliber specialists was so acute that for the first time it relaxed immigration restrictions to allow "colored" professionals with needed skills from third world countries, such as India and China, to become citizens. The superbly educated, urbanized, English-speaking representatives of the upper stratum of Chinese society who availed themselves of this opportunity formed an Uptown Chinese community, at the opposite end of the social hierarchy from the early working-class immigrants from rural southern China. The liberal 1965 immigration reform opened the door to a two-pronged migration of Chinese from both ends of the spectrum: the professionals at the top, and relatives of early immigrants at the bottom. The latter provided cheap labor for the service and declining industries, particularly garment manufacturing. Chinese America became a distinctly bipolar entity. The two groups, the Uptown and the Downtown Chinese, have little in common. Their different experiences make classification under a single model of integration in America meaningless.

In the early 1990s, at the end of the cold war, America emerged as the only global power with the ambition to dominate the rest of the world. To exercise this ambition and maintain supremacy, it has had to import foreign capital and talent. In addition to immigrant scientists and engineers who give it an advantage in high-tech industries, America now enlists the best in almost every field from all corners of the world—including entrepreneurs, managers, intellectuals, artists, entertainers, and even athletes. It also sends its emissaries abroad in search of cheap resources and acquisition opportunities. Because of the familiarity Chinese immigrant professionals have with Asia and because of their contacts there, they now play a vital role in helping American corporations establish production facilities in Taiwan, mainland China, and elsewhere in the region. They serve as agents and subcontractors enabling American businesses to gain access to the huge China market.

Investment from Hong Kong and Taiwan has been migrating to the United States since the 1970s, with financiers looking for shelters against Asia's political uncertainties and an opportunity to diversify their portfolios. This capital has helped revive America's failing industries, revitalize decaying urban centers, and create jobs. Since the end of the cold war, Chinese financiers have taken on new responsibilities, as America endeavors, in its assumed role as chief defender of freedom in the world, to defend the freedom of finance capital. All nations are encouraged to take part in this free movement by opening up their markets and natural resources in exchange for foreign investment and trade opportunities. Those who refuse are effectively locked out of the international community and denied access to international loans, capital investment, and low-tariff trade relations through the actions of American-dominated international organizations, such as the International Monetary Fund, the World Bank, and the World Trade Organization. Chinese American investors and entrepreneurs, along with those from Hong Kong and Taiwan with considerable capital holdings and know-how, have become transnational partners in this American enterprise. Other Chinese Americans act as advisers and educators to Taiwanese and Chinese government and institutions, advancing free-enterprise ideology and American values. Chinese Americans have, in fact, become a vital instrument of American expansion into Asia.

Their affluence and increasingly important role in American society have given Chinese professionals and entrepreneurs new self-confidence. Not only do new immigrants of this profile move straight to the suburbs these days; they also transplant the amenities of the metropolitan lifestyle they were used to in Hong Kong, Taipei, or Shanghai. Chinese concentrations with Chinese supermarkets and bilingual services have transformed American suburbia. No longer just bedroom communities for urban centers, the neighborhoods they move into, even when they are not the majority, sprout clusters of ethnic businesses—high-end mall versions of Chinatowns. Sociologists call these new suburban ethnic enclaves without strictly defined space but with clear ethnic character "ethnoburbs."

Chinese ethnoburbs are but one manifestation of the selective adaptation that marks the new Chinese American immigrant experience: conforming to certain American ways and values, but rejecting others—particularly in the areas of education and child rearing. Chinese-language schools, for instance, are used to create a community of like-minded families that emphasize hard work and discipline. Alumni associations and professional associations are used to promote business contacts and to erect Chinese versions of old-boy networks, better to confront problems of discrimination and the glass ceiling. Chinese churches, Chinese opera, mahjong and social dancing clubs, as well as the widely circulated Chinese-language papers—many of them published regionally—give shape to the residentially scattered groups and their activities.

With the great strides in economic and social development achieved recently by many Asian countries came America's increasingly tolerant view of "Asian values" and a growing consumer taste for Asian products. Also, its ambition to remain in the forefront of globalization means that it can no longer insist on the same level of conformity that it expected of its immigrants in the past. This calls for a reevaluation of the traditional assumption that all immigrants eventually follow the same trajectory of assimilation in America. What constitutes a successful model of integration may now, more than ever, be an open question.

Whatever model of integration Chinese Americans are currently evolving, the state of the relationship between China and the United States continues to be an important but uncertain factor. The current U.S. administration has used minority political appointments to enhance America's influence abroad. Should Chinese Americans and other minorities rejoice in political appointments that serve America's aggressive, unilateral foreign policy? Or should they continue to struggle to find a voice that truly represents their community interests, safeguards the rights of all minorities, and works to transform America from an imperialist power into a true model of democracy for all nations? Chinese Americans can easily give in to the temptation to bask in the glow of the model-minority myth, but they can also remember the xenophobic hostility experienced by their ancestors and work to ensure that it does not happen to others. They can remember that not so long ago their community was collectively suspected of disloyalty, and speak out against the similar predicament of others. At the beginning of the twenty-first century, they are in a position, more than ever before, to leave a mark on America. This book, of course, hopes to suggest what kind of a mark it might be. Framed as a narrative that asks the question, "Where are you going?" rather than, "Have you arrived?" it leaves the story of Chinese America open-ended, for it is a history in the making.

CHINESE AMERICA

PART I

The Chinese Encounter America
(1840–1882)

Chapter 1

Pioneers

In the romantic version of the Wild West, white pioneers are the only heroes. They wield pickaxes, corral the herds, and ward off attacks by savage natives to bring the frontier under submission. The Chinese get only a bit role to play. Hollywood portrays them as miserable, slave-like creatures laboring under the evil eye of Chinese gang bosses: digging ditches, tending to hot stoves, and bending over washboards as they provide domestic service to the hard-drinking, revolver-packing cowboys.

The truth is that early Chinese immigrants in California and the rest of the West were no different from white Europeans. They embarked on the transpacific journey with ambition that a contemporary Chinese folk song called "as deep as the ocean and as high as the sky."[1] They were just as resourceful and just as willing to try anything. And they just as avidly took part in frontier "leisure activities"—prostitution, gambling, drinking, drug use, and gun fighting—that marked the legendary lifestyle of white frontiersmen. In October 1853 *Alta California* carried the following news item: "Four Chinamen were arrested yesterday morning charged with riding furiously through Dupont Street on horseback. They excused themselves by saying it was a feast day with them. They were fined $10.00 each."[2]

In the census records of the Western frontier between 1860 and 1880 a number of Chinese are regularly listed as gamblers, alongside their countrymen with the more mundane professions of miners, laundrymen, cooks, restaurant owners, merchants, and domestic servants.[3] One gambler, Lip Shee, became quite notorious along the route from San Francisco through the Mother Lode, where he ran more than one small Anglo gambling parlor out of business while posing as a servant, courier, or small-laundry owner; he always played carelessly and complained loudly about his bad luck until, appearing quite drunk, he came down to the last bit of his money or gold dust and vowed to kill himself if he lost what remained of a fortune entrusted to him by a dying relative. Then his luck suddenly changed.[4] A game of chance, pak kop piu (white pigeon ticket), that the Chinese brought to the frontier was eagerly embraced by American gamblers and spread through the country under the name keno.[5] So did mahjong.

Quong Gee Kee personally knew Virgil, Wyatt, and Morgan Earp, Doc Holliday, Curly Bill, and other legendary characters of the Wild West.[6] He himself was something of a legend in Tombstone, Arizona. He had started as a cook's helper in Virginia City, Montana, when it was a boomtown, moved along as the construction of the Union Pacific Railroad progressed, and opened a restaurant in Stockton, California, shortly after the railroad reached the town turning it into a teeming metropolis. He briefly returned to China in 1875, got married, bought a house, and fathered a son, but within eight months he was back in the American West opening restaurants in emerging cattle centers and silver mine towns such as Willcox, Pearce, and Charleston in Arizona, and co-owning the famous Can-Can eatery in Tombstone. Cowboys were known to descend on Can-Can after months of isolation on the range and completely demolish it, but Quong never had a single one of them arrested or taken to court. "When cowpunch sober up, he solly for cause trouble. He come back and pay up," he reportedly reasoned. "In court, lawyer take money. Then Quong have no money, no friends."

Quong had the psychology of the Old West down right. Cowboys always did come back to pay for the damage, and both the Earps and the Clantons of OK Corral fame were "nice fellas" to him and ate at his establishment all the time. At his funeral in January 1938 at Tombstone's Boothill Cemetery, where he was laid to rest alongside his famous gun-slinging customers, the Episcopal minister summed up the life of the town's ninety-six-year-old and by then destitute but beloved last Chinese denizen by saying, "We might call the life of Quong Kee the parable of the Good Chinamen for this man we burry has lived a life of service to the needy. Quong Kee turned no one away hungry. There is a Chinese proverb that reads 'A Chinese lies without regret if there is one man in all the world who calls him friend.' Quong must have died happy knowing that he had many friends." A state senator read the eulogy. The town's only other old-timer who still remembered the good old days remarked on the size of the crowd of more than five hundred that had gathered at the cemetery: "I guess old Quong had just about the biggest funeral ever held on Boothill."

Quong's amicable approach to life in the West, however, may have been unique. Recent archaeological excavations in several mining areas in the Rockies have revealed that many Chinese dwellings contained veritable arsenals of firearms, including Smith & Wesson revolvers and Springfield army rifles, and models that used .22-, .32-, .38-, .45-, and .50-caliber bullets.[7] Contemporary accounts describe mean-looking, hot-tempered young Chinese males carrying Bowie knives and Colt revolvers on their hips in public.[8] The most common causes of arrest of the Chinese in southern Idaho during its frontier days were battery, assault, showing deadly weapons, and disturbing the peace.[9] A fistfight, which was generally accepted in China as a method of settling disputes and which violated no law in America unless one party was severely injured, was the recourse of choice in confrontations among the Chinese themselves.[10] But, as occasion demanded, they were ready to retaliate with arson or to employ firearms, even against their white neighbors and Native Americans. In one altercation in Virginia City, which became the territorial capital of Montana in 1865, having grown to a bustling town of ten thousand after the discovery of gold, a Chinese succeeded in blacking an eye of his Caucasian opponent and was winning the fight when his queue slipped, providing the Caucasian with a grip that ended the fight. Many white bullies in the capital were, however, reportedly discouraged by the reputation the Chinese had for fighting with a knife in one hand and a hatchet in the other.[11] In Idaho Territory in 1870, three Chinese men shot Edward Cahill through the neck, execution style. Cahill had been mining next to a Chinese company on Mores Creek six miles from Idaho City and started a dispute over water usage. The three were acquitted due to "insufficient evidence."[12] In another ongoing neighbors' dispute in 1877, a hot-tempered Irishman, John McGuiness, shot at seven Idaho Chinese miners whom he accused of running sand into his flume. Two Chinese were fatally wounded, one was badly injured, and the remaining four overpowered McGuiness and stabbed him to death.[13] "A Chinaman is slow to deeds of desperation but when he starts in he generally means business," observed *Idaho World* in 1891.

On the other hand, the Chinese were "quick to deeds" when they smelled a good prospect. Among the first to reach Sutter's Mill—only one month after James Marshall accidentally discovered gold there, on January 24, 1848, setting off the gold rush to California—were two Chinese men who had arrived in San Francisco as servants of Charles V. Gillespie on the ship *Eagle* in 1848. Having heard of the discovery, the two immediately deserted their master and headed for the mines. The first wave of prospectors in the Sierra Nevadas also included an enterprising merchant by the name of Chang Ming.[14] He was probably one of a number of merchants engaged in the Manila galleon trade between the Philippines and Acapulco who jumped ship upon learning of better opportunities, and had been in California since 1847.[15] After he found gold and became a rich man, he wrote a friend back home about the glittering nuggets just waiting to be picked up. The friend spread the news around their native district outside the city of Canton (Guangzhou) and booked passage on the next ship.[16]

News of the discovery of gold traveled quickly around the Pacific Rim, due to excellent transoceanic communications long established by Chinese, Spanish, and other European traders. It followed the trade route from California to Peru, across the ocean to Australia, then north to Manila, Hong Kong, and on to China. The city of Canton, which is just up the Pearl River from Hong Kong, learned of the discovery in October 1848—only a few days later than did American cities on the East Coast.[17] That fall, a young Cantonese man wrote to his brother engaged in the tea trade in Boston, "Good many Americans speak of California. . . . I hear good many Americans and Europeans go there. Oh! They find gold very quickly, so I hear."[18] By the summer of 1849, a Danish visitor to Hong Kong noted, there was a "ferment" among the people, and even "gentlemen of the legal profession" who were "doing extremely well" were "induced by the exciting news, which every incoming ship brought from California, determined to seek their fortune there."[19]

The first to sail across the ocean were the merchants. Having always been the class that sought and recognized opportunities overseas, they were among the few who had the money to undertake the trip. A contemporary observer noted that "in the fall of 1849 the Chinese in San Francisco number several hundred. They were not laborers who came, not of the coolie class at least."[20] Records show that of the 57,787 people who arrived in California in 1850, only 500 were Chinese.[21] But that year the news went back to China that California not only was rich in gold and silver, but also had plenty of land, timber, and honey—plenty for many more countrymen to come and make use of. Ever since then, California became known as "Jinshan" (the Gold Mountain) to the Chinese, and, until the Chinese Exclusion Act put an end to it in 1882, some 370,000 young men, most in their twenties or even younger, made their way to it hoping to better their lives.

MINERS

Realizing the amount of enthusiasm the idea of the Gold Mountain generated among the Chinese, American shipowners and labor brokers converged on Hong Kong, feverishly promoting their services. Placards and posters inundated the city: "To the countrymen of Ah Lung. Laborers are wanted in the land of California. Great works to be done there, good houses, plenty of food ... The ship is good."[22] A printed circular was distributed through the surrounding countryside: "Americans are very rich people. They want the Chinaman to come and make him very welcome. There you will have great pay, large houses and food and clothing of the finest description.... It is a nice country, without Mandarins or soldiers. All alike; big man no larger than little man. There are a great many Chinamen there now, and it will not be a strange country.... Come to Hong Kong, or to the sign of this house in Canton, and we will instruct you."[23] Many availed themselves of the services right away.

The Chinese were first brought to California's mining districts in noticeable numbers by the mining companies that hired them as laborers. From there, a few began mining on their own.[24] In 1852, the year some twenty thousand Chinese passengers paid an estimated $1.5 million for passage to California,[25] witnesses reported seeing a great many Chinese along the Yuba River, rocking cradles used to separate gold from rock and sand. They were making from $3 to $8 a day.[26] A few lucky ones struck it rich and returned in triumph to China. One such returnee bought land the size of "four city blocks," built a "palace" on it, and threw a lavish banquet serving one hundred roasted pigs and uncountable chickens, ducks, and geese to impress his fellow villagers. The ostentatious display made such an impact on a wide-eyed sixteen-year-old, Lee Chew, as he recollected half a century later in his contribution to a 1906 collection, *The Life Stories of Undistinguished Americans as Told by Themselves*, that he resolved to one day make his way to America, too.[27] Many young, able-bodied men were similarly inspired to emigrate throughout the 1850s.

By the end of the 1850s, about a quarter of California's miners were Chinese.[28] But those who worked their own claims risked being driven off once they struck a rich deposit, because a California law passed in 1852 prohibited the Chinese from making mining claims. Many bypassed the law by quietly purchasing claims abandoned by white miners when the shallow deposits were exhausted and the mining became less profitable. Since they came from China's wet-rice farming region, they were familiar with water management and were able to develop a sophisticated system of dams, ditches, and long flumes, which they used to divert streams from their natural beds through a series of sluices to flush out gold from deposits that had already been worked over.[29] They were so methodical, in fact, that many of the carefully lined rows of displaced rocks, piled one on top of another, can still be seen today at abandoned mine sites throughout the American West. The locals refer to them as "Chinese walls."

Some of the Chinese had been miners in Southeast Asia. (Chinese, mainly of Hakka origin, were mining tin in what is today Malaysia long before the British acquired it as a colony in the early 1880s.)[30] Their skills did not escape the attention of their contemporaries. At many mines, "China John" became as respected as "Cornish Jack," the immigrant miner from Cornwall, considered to be the best of the European miners.[31] The pluckiest among them prospected on their own, even beyond California's mining region. In 1856, a small party of Chinese miners took off from Fresno, California, into the northern Rockies, following the old Oregon-California Trail—this at a time when the area was still largely unknown to most miners. With help from

Shoshone and Bannock tribes, they managed to get as far as the Boise Basin in what is now southern Idaho. One of the party, Wong Ying, told the story of their exploits to an *Idaho Statesman* reporter in 1931, when he was ninety-four years old and still living in Idaho.[32] A Native American chief in Boise Basin showed them a placer "where you could see heap gold after rain," Wong remembered. But members of his party had already placered "plenty bags gold," and simply filled their deerskin bags with heavy nuggets, marked the spot, and moved on to "more better find." They built log cabins at what would become Idaho City, and after panning for weeks in a rich field, discovered the method of building ground sluices and formed a company. Even after some seventy years Wong could still quote the prices of necessities and luxuries his company paid for in gold nuggets: $34 for a sack of rice, $30 for a sack of flour, $5 for a pound of tea, and $3 for a dozen Chinese salted duck eggs. And he claimed that plenty of gold still remained in Idaho City. The best digging ground, in 1931, was under the county jail.

Another Chinese mining party visited the Boise Basin in 1859. (The first white miners did not begin to venture into the area until after gold was discovered in northern Idaho in 1860.)[33] Other groups of Chinese miners moved up the Rouge River valley in southern Oregon to look for gold as early as 1852, and along the Carson River in what would become Nevada, in 1855. They mined silver in Virginia City, where the richest deposit in the world was discovered in 1859, on the Comstock Lode.

On the eve of the civil war, Chinese mining camps had spread north through Washington Territory, British Columbia, and as far as Alaska, westward throughout the Rocky Mountains from Idaho, Utah, Colorado, Wyoming, Montana, and, in the 1870s, as far east as the Black Hills of South Dakota, where the last of the gold rushes took place and this fabled era of American history ended. Chinese mining was at its peak in the late 1860s and early 1870s. By 1870, Chinese miners, numbering 17,069, made up more than 25 percent of all miners in the West, and an even higher percentage of miners in individual states: 58.5 percent in Idaho, 61.2 percent in Oregon, and 60 percent in California.[34] In Idaho, which according to the 1870 census had a population of 14,999, nearly one-third (4,274) were Chinese.

During the idle season (in the dead of winter and bone-dry summer) some of the Chinese miners took to logging, fishing, and hunting.

Many became leading providers of fresh fish, firewood, and building material. In some places, such as Virginia City, Nevada, Chinese wood peddlers came to completely dominate the wood retail business by displacing the competition—in this case the Paiute Indians. When, in winter, the regular wood supply could not come through because the roads were bad or the snow too deep, Virginia City's white residents welcomed Chinese wood peddlers, who brought a small quantity of firewood to every family's doorstep.[35] Paiutes, on the other hand, resented the Chinese for taking their jobs away and for aggressively making use of natural resources, including the roots of pine-nut trees. They enjoyed ridiculing the Chinese, and the two groups frequently came to blows on the city streets, to the amusement of white residents. The Chinese retaliated by selling Paiutes "expansive whiskey"—ignoring white laws that prohibited the sale of intoxicating liquors to Native Americans—which was in fact a horrible concoction known as "China gin." When the Paiutes became too belligerent, the Chinese simply cut off the supply.[36] The effectiveness of the Chinese cutting timber in the Sierra Mountains also rankled other competitors. Frustrated Irish and French Canadian immigrants in Carson City, Nevada, attempted to drive them out of town and out of the state in 1868, in what became known as the Woodchoppers War.[37]

MINING THE MINERS

The most enterprising among Chinese immigrants did not, in fact, bother to become laborers in the gold mines. Since white migrants to California were almost exclusively interested in mining for gold, there was a shortage of workers in all other occupations. The Chinese knew that good money could be made from the miners, who were willing to pay high prices for goods and services—in other words, from "mining the miners." Soon after the beginning of the gold rush, in early September 1849, there were already three Chinese restaurants in San Francisco and one Chinese hotel in Monterey. Just two weeks after San Jose, the earliest incorporated city in California, became the first state capital, in March 1850, *New York Tribune* reporter Bayard Taylor observed, "the shrewd Celestials had already planted themselves there, and summoned men to take their meals by the sound of their barbaric gongs."[38] Chinese restaurants were very popular with Americans, he admitted, "on account of their regard to quantity." The "barbaric" Chinese restaurateurs were also shrewd enough to retain attorney Selim E. Woodworth as counselor in their business transactions.

Some months earlier, when returning to San Francisco from the gold mines in late 1849, Taylor "saw a company of Chinese carpenters putting up the frame of a Canton-made house."[39] Another contemporary observer, the British writer William Ryan, wrote, "The houses they brought with them from China, and which they set up where they were wanted, were infinitely superior and more substantial than those erected by the Yankees."[40] Importing ready-made houses and building material from southern China for easy assembly in North America was a quick way to solve the housing problem at the beginning of the gold rush. According to Ryan, "Houses that cost $300, sell readily for $3,000; and the demand is constantly increasing. At least 75 houses have been imported from Canton, and are put up by Chinese carpenters." As fires frequently ravaged the wooden structures of San Francisco in the early 1850s, Chinese stonemasons and laborers built the impressive Parrott Building on the corner of California and Montgomery Streets in 1852, with granite shipped from China.[41]

Equally in demand and just as expensive were laundry services. A New Yorker visiting the California frontier complained, "The greatest privations that a bachelor is in this country exposed to consist of not being able to find himself with clean linen when he desires, as domestic service is so difficult to be kept up here for want of working women."[42] Census figures show that there were twelve men for every woman in California in 1850, mainly because few gold rushers brought their womenfolk along with them. As a result, it cost as much as $8 to have a dozen soiled linen pieces laundered in San Francisco. A cheaper alternative, incredibly, was to have the laundry shipped to Canton and Hawaii (called the Sandwich Islands at the time) for washing and pressing. This transoceanic laundry service, though it seems extravagant by today's standards, left much to be desired, as it took several months to get the clean laundry back. The residents of California must have been greatly relieved when enterprising Chinese immigrants started operating hand laundries to provide service on the spot for $5 a dozen pieces.[43] Not only was the service cheaper; it meant that people needed fewer pieces in their wardrobe to tide them over between washings. Beginning in 1851, when Wah Lee opened the first laundry in San Francisco, most of the washing and ironing in California was done by Chinese.[44] By 1870, there were 2,899 Chinese laundrymen in the state—72 percent of all workers in the occupation.[45]

The Chinese hand laundry has been a fixture of American life ever since. People have often wondered how is it that Chinese men so quickly and easily took to women's work, exhibiting none of the reluctance of European immigrants; was it something they were used to doing in China? The "Chinese laundryman" was an American phenomenon. Lee Chew, the sixteen-year-old who had seen the wealth of one lucky returnee on display in his village and came to America in the early 1860s dreaming of striking gold himself, ended up working in a laundry servicing the miners. "The Chinese laundryman does not learn his trade in China; there are no laundries in China," he explained in "The Life Story of a Chinaman." "The women there do the washing in tubs and have no washboards or flat irons. All the Chinese laundrymen here were taught in the first place by American women just as I was taught."[46] The choice of this particular occupation was not a matter of custom, particular suitability, or preference for Chinese immigrant men; it was merely the opportunity that presented itself in America. "No, they do not love it any more than any other kind of labor," bilingual journalist and social activist Wong Ching Foo wrote in *The Cosmopolitan* in 1888. "Laundry work in China is invariably done by women, and when a man steps into a woman's occupation he loses his social standing. They become laundrymen here simply because there is no other occupation by which they can make money as surely and quickly."[47]

The same sense of practicality drove the Chinese immigrants who introduced commercial fishing to the West Coast. They brought fishing gear native to Guangdong Province—gill nets, trawl lines, small wood sampans, and large junks for offshore fishing—and set up some thirty Chinese fishing camps up and down California's shoreline in the early 1850s. Monterey Bay, with its Cannery Row, now a big tourist attraction, was the location of the first Chinese processing plant that dried, packed, and shipped abalone for consumption in China, while the shells were sent to the East Coast and Europe for processing into jewelry and buttons.[48] Chinese fish peddlers became a regular sight in the Santa Cruz–Watsonville region during the 1870s, and after the construction of local railroads, Chinese fishermen supplied great quantities of fresh-packed halibut, flounder, rock cod, shellfish, and sturgeon for the San Francisco and Los Angeles fish markets. But their most lucrative business was the export of dried shark's fins, sea cucumbers, and kelp to China, where such products were highly prized and considered great delicacies.[49]

Other Chinese immigrants, having hailed from commercial farming communities around the city of Canton, found a niche growing fresh produce for miners and California's budding urban centers. Although the conditions were very different from what they knew, they quickly adjusted. They built terraced fields, applied manure, and irrigated the arid hillsides. They labored waist-deep in water to drain the lowland marshes. They almost single-handedly converted the existing farming from wheat to more profitable crops, such as grapes, fruits, and vegetables, and turned central California into the "salad bowl of the world."[50] Later, they followed the miners to the most inaccessible parts of the Pacific Northwest and set up terraced gardens in such improbable places that their vestiges have been turned into tourist attractions and protected historical sights. China Mountain Terraced Gardens Interpretive Site, a National Register property at the Payette National Forest some eight miles east of Warren, Idaho, is accessible only during the snow-free period from spring through early fall.[51] It lies a mile and a half down the steep southeastern slopes of the South Fork canyon of the Salmon River. Yet, as the archeological analysis of the site shows, its cultivator, Ah Toy, managed to grow a variety of vegetables, strawberries, grapes, and rhubarb and haul fresh produce by mule daily across the Warren Mining District.[52] Nearby, on a ranch at the very bottom of the Salmon River canyon, a Chinese woman who went by the name Polly Bemis and was one of Idaho's most famous pioneer women grew apples, cherries, pears, peaches, grapes, tomatoes, blackberries, gooseberries, raspberries, strawberries, muskmelons, watermelons, and currants, in addition to an even greater variety of vegetables, which she sold to people who floated down the river or came down the eighteen-mile trail from Warren.[53]

ENTREPRENEURS

In more favorable climes Chinese horticulturalists made an even greater impact. A grafting expert, Ah Bing, introduced a hybrid cherry tree to Oregon in 1875, whose succulent, plump fruit became America's favorite cherry and to this day bears his name. In De Land, Florida, Lue Gim Gong developed the frost-resistant orange in 1888 that gave birth to Florida's citrus industry.[54] A Chinese squirrel trapper known as "Poison Jim" discovered that the mustard plant, which was highly valued in China as well as Europe, grew weedlike in the Salinas Valley, where California's grain growers considered it a nuisance. The farmers were delighted by Jim's offer to remove the seeds after he cut the plants down. He contracted a few dozen Chinese workers for the job, paid them with what he sold in San Francisco, and bagged the rest. He hit the jackpot when the mustard crop failed in both Europe and South Africa that year, and a French buyer bought his seed for an unheard of $35,000 in gold. Not only did Jim become rich; he unintentionally turned mustard into a commercial crop. When the news of his mustard-gold fortune spread through the region, farmers started employing Chinese crews to harvest the wild seed. Between 1865 and 1882 their effort was so thorough that wild mustard became almost extinct in the area; from then on, it was planted intentionally, at great profit, as the demand for mustard grew in the eastern United States.

Those who profited the most among early Chinese immigrants were, of course, the merchants. In 1852 two Chinese merchants, Hab Wa and Tong Achick, from Sam Wo & Company and Ton Wo & Company, wrote a letter to California's governor Bigler in response to his accusations that Chinese came to America only to dig gold and take it back to China. Many, they wrote, "invest their money in merchandise and bring it into the country and sell it at your markets. . . . You may not be aware how great this trade is."[55] They pointed out the gains of taxation on Chinese imports and the real estate investments Chinese traders had made in San Francisco. "In this city alone there are twenty stores kept by Chinamen, who own lots and erected the buildings themselves."[56] The stores were supplying ethnic foods and provisions to Chinese miners before they headed for the mines, but also American goods—"especially boots, of which every Chinaman buys one or more pairs immediately on landing." Kerosene lamps were another item in high demand. San Francisco's Chinese merchants also acted as distributors for China imports sold by white-owned retail stores. One such broker in 1852 claimed to sometimes sell $10,000 a day of Chinese goods.[57] The most successful among Chinese merchants owned emporia and sold luxury imports—tea, silk, and porcelain—themselves. An English visitor to San Francisco wrote in 1851 that large business was done "in Chinese shawls and various Chinese curiosities. It was greatly the fashion of men, returning home, to take with them a quantity of such articles, as a present to their friends. In fact a gorgeous Chinese shawl seemed to be as necessary for a returning Californian as a revolver and bowie-knife for the emigrant."[58] "Nowhere else in America could one find such exquisite material as the silken bolts in the Chinese merchant shops," noted another. "Many a miner recklessly laid golden nuggets on the counter in return for a silk sash or a dainty fan for the hard working frontier women who had given up the frills of the East."

The volume of Chinese-owned businesses only grew as the number of Chinese immigrants increased. Like the Chinese laundries, restaurants, and truck gardens that sprouted wherever miners and, later, railroads had reached, Chinese-owned grocery stores spread throughout the frontier—to places such as Silver City, Idaho; John Day, Oregon; Walla Walla, Washington; Evanston, Wyoming; Ogden, Utah; and Deadwood, South Dakota. The first Chinese grocery store in Mississippi was established in 1872 or 1873, a year or so after Southern planters imported Chinese laborers to work on plantations.[59] Chinese laborers did not stay on plantations for long, but Chinese groceries took hold in the Mississippi Delta, serving largely poor African American customers. Many Chinese immigrants became merchants as soon as they made enough money in other professions to open their own stores. Between 1870 and 1900 approximately 40 percent of the Chinese in San Francisco and Sacramento were businessmen such as shopkeepers and merchants.[60] Those who procured merchandise through an international supply network headquartered in Hong Kong were the wealthiest.

But the real unsung heroes of the American West were the Chinese physicians. Prior to the scientific and pharmaceutical revolutions of the twentieth century, Euramerican medicine was largely ineffectual in dealing with chronic diseases and many injuries and traumas that plagued the frontier. Chinese medicine, on the other hand, had been using molds to treat infections long before the discovery of penicillin. In America, Chinese physicians discovered the use of baking soda in treating skin infections caused by poison ivy. Every major Chinese mining camp had at least one or two Chinese doctors, who had an herbal shop in town, often combined with the general store serving the community, but who also traveled even to the most remote areas to attend to patients. The herbal medicines were regularly supplied throughout Chinese settlements in America by the commercial networks headquartered in San Francisco and Hong Kong. As a result of good medical care and a diet rich in vitamins from fresh vegetables, Chinese mortality rates were, as shown by the census figures for 1870 and 1880, lower by half than those for the white population in the mining states and territories of California, Idaho, Montana, and Nevada.[61]

Many white Americans held Chinese doctors in high regard. Doctor Ing Hay of John Day in eastern Oregon treated white patients from Walla Walla, Washington, in the north to the Nevada border in the south, from Portland in the west to Payette, Idaho, in the east, where he was known as "Doc Hay," the most respected medical man for hundreds of miles.[62] Idaho's most famous Chinese doctor—a physician, apothecary, and acupuncturist all wrapped in one—was Chuck Ah Fong, who left his father, a doctor, in San Francisco in 1866 to open his own practice in the mining town of Atlanta in Idaho. He traveled the mining region seeing patients for twenty-three years before moving to Boise City, where his reputation brought Idaho's most prominent businessmen, legislators, and at least one governor to his doorstep, and where he continued to work until his death in 1927— after practicing medicine in Idaho for sixty-one years. The respect of his fellow citizens was such that his first wife's funeral in 1902 brought out a procession of more than a thousand people—the largest in Boise City's history—and was attended by the governor, congressmen, and numerous community leaders.[63]

The news of their countrymen's successes, of the opportunities, and of the latest discoveries in the American West was transferred quickly by word of mouth as far as China, through the constant flow of migrants back and forth. Also, a burgeoning press on both sides of the Pacific began to serve the far-flung expatriate community. English-language newspapers published in South China, such as the *China Mail*, frequently carried reports from San Francisco's chief publications, the *San Francisco*

Daily Herald, the *Daily Alta California,* and the *Daily Journal of Commerce.*[64] On the American side of the Pacific, a Chinese-language periodical, the *Golden Hill's News,* which began publication in 1854 in San Francisco, and a bilingual weekly, the *Oriental,* started in 1855—both published by American missionaries targeting a Chinese audience—were among the first news publications in any language to appear in California. They carried basic information about America for their new immigrant readers, including how not to get cheated and mistreated in the unfamiliar environment. They also covered major political events in China and in America and carried price lists and business information. The first Chinese-run Chinese-language daily in America, the *Chinese Daily News,* began publication in Sacramento, California, in 1856.[65] Many other Chinese-language dailies and weeklies—some with hundreds of regular subscribers—sprang up as the Chinese spread wide across the Western frontier.

In all the information that flowed back to China there was rarely mention of the émigrés' troubles, and never of their failure. Those who were unsuccessful, for whom the dreams of the Gold Mountain did not materialize, were too embarrassed and too poor to return to China. They remained in America to pursue other opportunities—always displaying a high degree of entrepreneurship and resourcefulness, regardless of whether they were ultimately successful.

Chapter 2

The World They Left Behind

The type of enterprising acumen displayed by the early Chinese immigrants is not usually associated with people of humble rural origin. Indeed, the background and circumstances of these enthusiastic fortune seekers have generally been misrepresented and misunderstood.

The overwhelming majority of nineteenth-century Chinese immigrants to the United States came from the small area comprising eight counties on the west side of the Pearl River Delta, west and south of the City of Canton (Guangzhou). The eight counties are divided into three subgroups, each speaking a closely related but distinct dialect. The San Yi ("three counties"—Nanhai, Panyu, and Shunde) district consists mostly of flat and fertile farmland, and due to its closeness to the city of Canton, had long been engaged in a high degree of cash-crop production. The Si Yi ("four counties"—Taishan, Xinhui, Enping, and Kaiping) district lies farther to the west and is a relatively poor area of hilly terrain and small farms. The eighth county, Xiangshan (later renamed Zhongshan), is located between the city of Canton and the once Portuguese colony of Macao. The largest portion of the Chinese in the United States hailed from just one of the eight, Taishan County—approximately 45 percent in 1876 and as many as 50 percent after the passage of the 1882 Chinese Exclusion Act, which blocked further large-scale immigration from China.[1]

To put this in perspective: Taishan County is one of ninety-eight

counties in Guangdong Province. At three thousand square kilome-
ters, it is about half the size of Rhode Island. Yet this very small and
distinct part of China was the ancestral home of the majority of the
Chinese in the United States before the 1960s. It was connected by inland waterways to the city of Canton, long an important port in international trade, and was located within an easy two-day walking distance
from the then foreign-controlled ports of Macao and Hong Kong. Far
from being ignorant country bumpkins from some backward agrarian
backwater, these émigrés to America were well aware of the effects of
global trade and highly skilled in finding opportunities in the cash
economy.

Guangdong Province as a whole has been one of the wealthiest
provinces in China for centuries, and the delta region around the city
of Canton has always been the most prosperous. As early as the Tang
dynasty (618–907), Canton was a thriving international seaport, and by
the eighth century its population of two hundred thousand included,
besides the ethnic Chinese, many Arabs, Jews, Singhalese, Indonesians,
and Persians, who were all busy feeding the exotic tastes of China's
elites with gems, raw woods, drugs, and incense, in exchange for Chinese silks, slaves, and porcelain.[2] As China's maritime trade expanded
during the Ming dynasty (1368–1644), the city became a part of a profitable global trading network supplying export goods to the Philippines, Japan, South and Southeast Asia, the Middle East, Europe, and
the Americas. Much of the export products were procured locally, especially in the eight counties, where the growth of foreign trade caused
the shift from rice production to commercial crops. A Ming dynasty
county gazetteer describes "profitable mulberry-tree fields and fish
ponds. Natural silk is produced annually. Men and women live by their
own exertion. The poor lease their land from the rich, who collect the
rent. . . . Others specialize in different kinds of crafts and occupations
that are found throughout the townships."[3] By the seventeenth century,
up to half the arable land in all of Guangdong Province was given to
commercial farming, while traditional crops such as rice had to be imported from the neighboring province of Guangxi and even from
Southeast Asia.

The Ming government, and later the Qing government (1644–1911)
as well, tried to ban the participation of private Chinese citizens in

foreign trade and designated the port city of Canton as the only city in China where international trade could be conducted. From 1757 to the end of the Opium Wars (1839–42), Canton remained the sole port of entry for foreigners and for the export of Chinese goods. Its waterways, according to visitors during this period, were teaming with thousands of "native vessels" of all description: cargo boats from the interior, passenger boats, floating residences, and up-country craft.[4] The volume of products traded at Canton left Chinese merchants with huge surpluses from foreign traders' payments in silver.[5] Some of the local merchants, particularly the *hong* merchants belonging to the *co-hong* guilds designated by the central government to do business with the Westerners, became fabulously wealthy. The general prosperity of the province at this time was reflected in its population growth from 6.8 million in 1757 to 21.1 million in 1842. But it was the Pearl River Delta, whose population had long been exposed to foreign traders, Christian zealots seeking converts, and even black slaves, widely used as house guards by rich families in the city from the time of the Tang to the Ming dynasty, that remained the focal point of Western contact with China and "China's window to the outside world."[6]

By the time of the Opium Wars, when the Pearl River Delta residents began to emigrate to the United States, the area's economy had been integrated into the global economy for quite some time. The more prosperous San Yi residents engaged primarily in commerce and crafts production, supplying the global trade. The somewhat poorer people of Si Yi worked their land and supplemented their income through jobs on neighboring commercial farms and in handicraft workshops. Even the farmers of Taishan, the poorest of the eight counties, were involved in the cash economy supporting international trade, because they all lived within a hundred miles of the area's three international trading ports, Canton, Macao, and Hong Kong, and could easily travel there during farming's slow months to work as menial laborers and longshoremen.[7]

Without a doubt, the exposure of early Chinese immigrants to South China's commercial farming and to Canton's role in the global economy accounts for the ease with which they adjusted to the new environment and for the remarkably enterprising spirit they displayed once they decided to seek their fortune in the New World.

CHINESE MIGRATION

Migration had always been an important strategy in ensuring family survival and prosperity in China, where family property is traditionally divided equally among male siblings. To avoid bitter conflicts among brothers, whenever they could, or whenever they were forced to by circumstances, families tried to diversify their options. The more affluent sent their boys off to study for examinations that might lead to positions in officialdom. The harder pressed looked for work as farmhands in neighboring villages or as laborers in nearby towns. Migration was thus both a family strategy for upward mobility and a way to keep the family finances solvent. People in the coastal provinces of Fujian and Guangdong, especially in the areas where tall mountain chains barred easy access inland, often had to resort to going overseas to find their fortunes.[8]

This practice started with the Han dynasty (206 B.C.–A.D. 8), when Chinese ships first began reaching Japan, the Philippines, and Southeast Asia, propelled by seasonal monsoons. The official Han history notes that many individuals "entered the sea" ("*xiahai*"), implying that they abandoned respected professions as government officials, farmers, and craftsmen to become merchants. Merchants were officially the lowest social class in Confucian China, but many who "entered the sea" to look for the fabled treasure islands in Southeast Asia did return laden with treasures.[9] During the Tang dynasty, because of Arab encroachment in central Asia and the resulting blockade of overland trade routes, the imperial court helped build large oceangoing vessels that carried Chinese traders as far as Baghdad and Aden. Many decided to stay in ports along the sea route and established trade settlements, but they maintained their old way of life. To this day, Chinese call overseas Chinese *Tang ren* ("the people of the Tang") and their communities, the Chinatowns, *Tang-ren jie* ("the Tang-people streets").

Chinese overseas trade and settlement reached a peak during the Ming dynasty, which had the largest navy in the world: 400 large war junks stationed at the first Ming capital, Nanjing; 1,350 warships and river and canal patrol boats stationed elsewhere; 3,000 merchant vessels that could be converted into fighting ships if needed; 400 huge grain transports; and 250 "treasure ships"—overseas warships that were used for far-flung trade and diplomatic missions. The second

Ming emperor, Yong Le, sent these treasure ships on seven voyages through Southeast Asia and into the Indian Ocean, with the objective of projecting the might and technology of the Chinese Empire and securing relations with China's main trading partners on its own terms. All ships were more than two hundred feet long; some even exceeded four hundred feet in length. They were armed with cannon, rockets, and guns and equipped with watertight doors, a magnetic compass, a primitive sextant, and quartered maps. They carried on deck huge tubs of earth planted with fruit trees and vegetables, to prevent scurvy. A Chinese historian who witnessed the first expedition likened the ships to houses. "When their sails are spread they are like great clouds in the sky."[10] All seven westward expeditions, which took place between 1405 and 1433, were headed by the Grand Eunuch of Three Jewels, Zheng He (Cheng Ho), whom the emperor had appointed Admiral of the Western Seas.

Admiral Zheng He was surprised to discover many émigré Chinese merchants and craftsmen in the Kingdom of Champa (in the southern part of today's Vietnam), who had been living there since the time of the Tang dynasty. They had helped spread Confucian ideals, and Champa's ruler willingly offered tribute to the Chinese emperor in exchange for lavish gifts and protection. With a fleet of more than twenty-seven thousand men; Muslim religious leaders and Buddhist monks brought along to serve as diplomats in lands where people practiced those religions; and the coveted gifts of blue-and-white Ming porcelain dishes; fine silk, intricately printed cotton, and durable "Nankeen" cloth; gold, silver, iron, and copper ware; and perfume, Zheng He did not fail to favorably impress any of the rulers along the trade route to the Arabian peninsula and East Africa. He brought back medicinal herbs, dyes, spices, gems and pearls, rhinoceros horns, ivory, amber, incense, dragon saliva, and live animals—lions, gold-spotted leopards, ostriches, and zebras. Of particular interest to the court was the giraffe. The Chinese thought that it was a heavenly creature, like the mythical unicorn, whose appearance signaled that a sage of utmost wisdom and benevolence was on the throne. Emperor Yong Le was understandably pleased. After he died, however, his successors became more conservative and inward-looking.

By the time Zheng He returned from the seventh expedition, in 1433, imperial policy had changed. The Mandarin elite feared that the new class of merchants, who were profiting handsomely from international trade, could undermine its preeminent position in society. In order to maintain the social hierarchy, the Ming government forbade its subjects to trade with foreigners or go overseas. The succeeding Qing dynasty (1644–1911), established through the Manchu conquest of China, also banned overseas trade, because the strongest challenge to its rule came from the coastal communities in Fujian that remained loyal to the Ming. The leader of the longest-lasting anti-Manchu resistance was Zheng Chenggong, better known under the Dutch Romanized version of his popular name, "Lord of the Royal Surname": Koxinga. His father was a Fujianese overseas trader, described by Chinese official records as a "buccaneer." His mother, in testimony to the father's overseas connections, was Japanese. Koxinga fought the Qing forces in the coastal areas of Fujian and Guangdong between 1646 and 1661; in 1658 he lead 170,000 amphibious troops on a campaign to capture Nanjing. In an effort to cut off Koxinga's supplies of food, men, and financial resources, the Qing court ordered all coastal regions evacuated and the population moved several miles inland. This in the end forced the anti-Manchu patriots, as well as many villagers stripped of their homes and land, to move overseas.

Koxinga took Taiwan from the Dutch in 1661, intending to make it his base for further anti-Qing resistance, but he died within a year. He is celebrated to this day by Chinese nationalists everywhere: in mainland China for fighting the Manchus; in Taiwan for expelling the Dutch and establishing Chinese rule over the island. Chiang Kai-shek invoked him as a model of a fighter who retreats to Taiwan to launch attacks on the mainland. Even the Japanese, during their occupation of the island, used him as a symbol of the bridge between Taiwan and Japan, on account of his mother. But his most significant legacy may have been a series of Qing laws that continued to discourage emigration. An imperial edict of 1712 requested "foreign governments to have those Chinese who have been abroad repatriated so that they may be executed."[11] Another decree of 1799 stipulated, "All officers of government, soldiers, and private citizens, who clandestinely proceed to sea to trade, or who remove to foreign islands for the purpose of inhabiting and cultivating the same, shall be punished according to the law against communicating with rebels and enemies, and consequently suffer death by being beheaded. The governors of cities of the second and third orders, shall likewise be beheaded when found guilty of combining with, or artfully conniving at, the conduct of such persons."[12]

Despite the restrictive laws, trade and emigration continued. From the late Ming to 1840, 1 million Chinese went to live abroad, mostly in Southeast Asian countries.[13] Most never returned. Many genealogical records of southern Fujianese families come to an abrupt stop: Ch'en Jung-tse, born in 1549, later moved to Luzon, died and was buried there in 1592; Ch'en Shih-hsu, born in 1643, proceeded to Jakarta to trade, died and was buried there in 1687; K'o Ching-chou, born in 1627, proceeded to Japan, died and was buried there in 1690.[14] Had they tried to return, they would have been subject to a government regulation that read, "Those who find excuses to sojourn abroad and then return clandestinely, if captured shall be summarily executed."[15] Particularly affected were the four Fujianese prefectures, Funing, Xinghua, Zhangzhou, and Quanzhou, where, as Provincial Governor Chen Hongmou explained in his appeal to the throne in 1754 pleading for imperial benevolence toward the law-breaking overseas Chinese merchants and their right to return home, "the cultivable land is narrow and the population is dense. The cultivated fields do not produce enough to feed even half the people. Their livelihood is therefore sustained by maritime shipping."[16]

In an estimate of another government official from Fujian, Lan Dingyuan, a noted geographer and an expert on southeast coastal affairs, "five or six of ten people" in the coastal provinces of Fujian and Guangdong were poor and made their living from the sea. "When cheap Chinese goods are carried to barbarian lands, they are regarded as treasure. . . . Every year silver and goods worth ten million flow from those barbarian islands into China," he pointed out in a letter to the emperor, yet these people "were driven to become criminals because of the overseas prohibition (*hai jin*), which was wrong in the first place due to misinformation on the part of ranking officials and the throne far away in the North."[17] Lan Dingyuan could venture to contradict the wisdom of the court because he had been personally involved in the campaign to suppress anti-Manchu rebels on the island of Taiwan whose activities were disturbing coastal communities on the mainland, and his opinion was respected by the emperor.

Chinese merchants, who had been trading with and emigrating to the Philippines, Japan, and Southeast Asia without the benefit of government sponsorship or the backing of the imperial military power, found an umbrella for their activities when European colonial powers started their expansion into Asia in the late 1580s. The Spanish, the Dutch, and the Portuguese depended on the experience of Chinese traders and their entrenched position in the area. When the Spanish, having conquered the Philippines, started regular trade between Manila and Acapulco, the Chinese provided the goods for the Spanish galleons. Fujianese junks carried goods between Manila, Fujian, and Hong Kong, and even after they slowly became displaced by European sailing vessels, the Chinese, as the producers of all traded goods, continued to enjoy an enormous trade surplus in silver.[18] When the rising colonial powers of England and France began to make their presence felt in the Pacific in the nineteenth century, they too recognized the Chinese experience and dominance in the region. As they struggled to secure their colonies against Spain and Portugal, they sought the help of the Chinese and invited them to settle in Indochina, Malaya, Siam, Java, Sumatra, Borneo, and the Pacific islands, giving them, in exchange, monopolies in gold mining and sugar planting. In 1891 the Chinese consul general at Singapore reported to the throne that "on the islands of the Southern Seas" (Southeast Asia), "coastal trade, real estate and other business is three tenths in the hands of Europeans, Arabs and Malays; and seven tenths in the hands of Chinese."[19]

Though dominant in Southeast Asia, Chinese merchants were not interested in North America, which was at the time backward and undeveloped compared to China. At the time of American independence, the sharp contrast between the two nations was to China's advantage, and the founding fathers were well aware of the fact.

Chapter 3

The China Trade and the Trade
in Chinese Labor

HOW THE IMAGE OF THE CHINESE
WAS TIED TO THAT OF CHINA

The United States of America was a nation founded on slavery and white supremacist ideology. In theory, since the Chinese were not white, they could not become citizens and could not be considered equal. Nevertheless, due to the young nation's relative backwardness compared to China and in the absence of any considerable number of Chinese on the East Coast, at the time of American independence the social and racial status of Chinese people was far from firmly established. George Washington, for one, expressed great surprise in 1785 when told that the Chinese were not white. He had previously thought them merely "droll in shape and appearance."[1]

The ambiguous perception of the Chinese was a reflection of China's geographic remoteness and the fact that very few Americans had had any contact with them. Until significant numbers of Chinese arrived on the West Coast, the idea Americans had of them was based not on an established racial attitude, but on the image Americans had of China as a nation. How the Chinese fit into the American social hierarchy was based on China's rank in the hierarchy of wealth and power among the nations, and on the relative strength of China and the United States.

At the founding of the American republic, China, then under the rule of the Manchu Qing dynasty, was a prosperous empire with a highly developed civilization that even the most advanced nations of Europe looked up to. (In contrast, despite its whiteness, America was an emerging, weak agrarian nation that had yet to develop commerce and industries.) Americans' first exposure to China came through China's luxury exports: tea, silk, and porcelain. Influenced in their tastes by the mid-eighteenth-century European craze for things Chinese (chinoiserie), wealthy American families coveted Chinese embroidered silks, rugs, art objects, and porcelain tea sets to show off when entertaining guests. Consumption of Chinese goods was a sign of cultural distinction. George Washington took a Chinese porcelain tea set along on his independence campaign to impress his men and officers with his refinement—and to reinforce his status and authority.[2]

China figured prominently in the imaginations of the American founders as a place of advanced civilization and innovations. Jefferson was fascinated by Confucian moral statecraft and envied China's political and commercial isolation—a position he wished the United States could assume vis-à-vis Europe. James Monroe drew inspiration for his famous doctrine from the view of China as a nation "perfectly independent" of world powers.[3] Benjamin Franklin (despite his view that Asians were "tawney") was mightily impressed by Chinese census taking, silk production, windmills, and heating systems, and particularly admired the Chinese value of hard work. In the same way that Voltaire celebrated China as a stable and prosperous agricultural civilization that should be emulated in the West, Franklin admired the Chinese emperor's ability to impose Puritan Protestant values of collective hard work onto his people and wrote, "Could we be so fortunate as to introduce the industry of the Chinese, their arts of living and improvement in husbandry . . . America might become in time as populous as China."[4]

But what really drew the young American nation to the old civilization was an interest in the China trade. One of the most compelling economic reasons for the American Revolution was the desire of American merchants to wrest control of the China trade from the British. Soon after independence, the first New York–registered merchant vessel, *Empress of China*, set sail for China, signaling the new nation's desire to follow the European mercantile capitalist model of global expansion in seeking its own economic prosperity. That China was expected to play the major role in America's global wealth-seeking scheme was made clear by the early appointment of Major Samuel Shaw to the consulate at Canton in 1786. It was the first American consulate established beyond the Cape of Good Hope.

Not only did American traders anticipate great wealth in the China trade; they even fantasized that America's abundant supply of ginseng and pelts would solve the problem of trade imbalances that plagued all other Western nations. John Fairbanks, America's preeminent scholar of China, once observed, "American commercial interest in China has always had a large admixture of imagination and hope."[5] At the same time, in an effort to wrest the lucrative trade away from European nations, American leaders also wanted to impress upon the Chinese that the Americans were better than the Europeans. John Adams warned the merchants to behave with "an irreproachable integrity, humanity, and civility to conciliate the esteem of the natives" so that America would "have a great advantage" over the European nations. Jefferson tried to be extremely accommodating to the Chinese government so that it would "understand at length the differences between us and the English and separate us in its policy."[6] This readiness to oblige reflected China's initial advantage in the unequal relationship between China and the United States.

DESPOTIC GOVERNMENT AND SLAVISH PEOPLE

Once direct trade between the two nations began, American traders and diplomats had a chance to form firsthand impressions of the Chinese. The traders quickly discovered how difficult it was to satisfy their new partners. Selling low-priced furs and ginseng did little to offset the imbalance of the luxury trade; as soon as the Americans flooded Chinese markets with ginseng, there was a dramatic drop in demand. U.S. merchants were forced to travel around the world in search of goods that would interest the Chinese, such as seal pelts from the Falkland Islands, sandalwood from Hawaii, and spices from Indonesia. Yet despite all the effort, before 1840 the China trade never amounted to more than 6 percent of total American foreign trade.[7] In their disappointment, the traders grumbled about the restrictions placed on their activities by the Chinese government and relieved their frustration with tales about the peculiarities of Chinese people, describing them as ridiculously clad, ridden with superstition, and possessed of bizarre habits, such as making medicine from rhinoceros horn and soup out of birds' nests.[8]

Christian missionaries, who typically follow in the footsteps of expansionistic Western traders, soon made their own contribution to the negative image. Having imagined China, in the words of Rev. William J. Boone, as "the most desirable field in the world for the church to enter in her missionary capacity," they discovered that the job of converting the Chinese was extremely difficult and quickly began expounding on the "evils" of Chinese culture to justify their lack of success and make the conversion of the "ignorant heathen" appear all the more important. "Ignorance and barbarity," announced the *Baptist Missionary Magazine*, "would place China on a level with the rudest tribes of mankind."[9] Underneath "a very polished civilization," warned an editor of the *Methodist Quarterly Review*, the Chinese were "morally a most wretched people. Sin had spread its deadly venom throughout the whole body politic."[10]

Diplomats joined the chorus, reporting on the existence of idolatry, gambling, and prostitution, and, what's more, polygamy and infanticide. "Almost daily," wrote Edmund Roberts, who headed President Jackson's mission to Asia in 1832, "placards are posted in the principal places about Canton and its suburbs, giving accounts of murders and insurrections, robberies, shocking and unnatural crimes of kidnapping, infanticides, suicides, and all the beastly and unnatural crimes of which the world ever heard or read."[11] W.S.W. Ruschenberger, a surgeon who took part in the same diplomatic mission, concurred: "They are a people who destroy their own tender offspring; a nation wherein the most infamous crimes are common . . . where a chain of beings, from the emperor to the lowest vassal, live by preying upon one another."[12] Their views might not have become widely held by Americans had it not been for the emergence of the "penny press" during the Jacksonian populist 1830s, when the advances in printing and papermaking technology made it possible to produce a newspaper that could be sold for just a cent a copy. The explosion of newspapers that thrived on war, scandals, and xenophobic and sensational news in an attempt to attract as wide a readership among the uneducated working class as possible was crucial in popularizing the scornful reports and bolstering American prejudices against the Chinese that would endure for a very long time.[13] But perhaps the most important factor in convincing the American public that the Chinese were an inferior people was the depiction of the power of the Chinese emperor—so supreme that upon his words thousands could be put to death. Arriving in the middle of America's growing controversy over slavery, it led Americans to conclude, in a peculiar twist of logic, that the emperor could be so oppressive because the common people slavishly accepted authoritarian rule. The association of slavery with racial differences made the reporting all the more brash, emotional, and titillating, and a debasing perception slowly took hold that Chinese people "voluntarily submitted to slavery."[14]

Once impressed by the refinement and high achievements of Chinese civilization, Americans were now convinced that the Chinese were a lesser people compared with Europeans. China would appear ever more backward as American national self-confidence grew following the War of 1812 and as technological invention and industrial development gathered pace. By 1824 Ralph Waldo Emerson could cockily proclaim China a "disgustful . . . booby nation," its civilization "a besotted perversity," and its people distinguished by "their cheerless . . . stupidity."[15]

Accusations against China's despotic government, vindictive legal system, and pervasive social injustice had been previously raised by European commentators, but they now acquired an entirely new meaning in the emerging American context. With the first democratic system in the world—government of the people, by the people, and for the people—Americans were beginning to feel more enlightened than Europeans, who still lived under the rule of aristocracy. U.S. independence gave rise to the concept of a "new man"—making radical changes in politics, economy, and society, based on individuality, hard work, and rational self-interest, fortified by the right to "life, liberty and the pursuit of happiness." In this light, China began to look like America's antithesis: its government was despotic, its people slavish. While Americans were given to self-determination, the Chinese people were cowardly and not able to grasp the concept of democracy.

Given this context, the U.S. government's early expressed interest in colonial expansion to the Pacific was cynical, coming on the heels of the 1823 Monroe Doctrine, which had declared the nations of the American continents off-limits to European interference. (It was particularly ironic since Monroe had admired China as a nation "perfectly independent" of world powers.) But this was the time when the idea of manifest destiny began to take hold in the Union as a result of the young nation's westward expansion, and John L. O'Sullivan, the journalist and diplomat who had coined the term, boldly announced, "Our national birth was the beginning of a new history, the formation and progress of an untried political system, which separates us from the past and connects us with the future." Declaring the United States "the nation of human progress," he asked, "Who will, what can, set limits to our onward march?" It soon became evident that China's imperial government could not.

OPIUM AND COOLIES

By the 1830s, America had joined European colonial powers in trying to pry open China's economy to "free trade." The United States' self-declared moral superiority did not prevent its merchants from emulating the British in trading opium. (By 1830 opium accounted for two-thirds of the total value of British imports to China.) But while the British grew opium in their colonies on the Indian subcontinent, American merchants had to look for it farther afield. The most prominent among them, John Jacob Astor, found a source in Turkey. Since Turkish opium was inferior to the British product from Bengal and far from the market, he was able to compete successfully only by introducing much faster clipper ships into the trade, and soon opium became the major American export to China. An American merchant could buy a pound of opium in Turkey for $2.50 and sell it in Canton for $10. An article in the British journal *Quarterly Review* observed in 1840, "With one or two exceptions, every American [trading] house in China was engaged in the [opium] trade."[16] The opium trade, in fact, created the enormous wealth of the old Yankee trading families the Cushings, the Cabots, the Delanos, and the Perkinses. It financed the Industrial Revolution in the northeastern United States. It enabled Astor to make one of the largest fortunes in American history.[17]

So important was this trade to the United States that the young, freedom-loving nation established the Asiatic Squadron of the U.S. Navy in 1835, which after 1842 maintained a constant presence off China's coast. In the meantime, thousands of Chinese were becoming dependent on opium and were wasting away. Until 1826, the balance of trade had always favored China. By the late 1830s, Chinese consumers were spending more than a hundred million taels of silver each year on opium. The drain on China's silver reserve was so serious that Imperial Censor Huang Chung-mo proposed that the entire foreign trade in Canton, the only port open to foreign ships, be based on barter.[18] In 1838 Emperor Daoguang appointed a brilliant fifty-four-year-old civil official from Fujian, Lin Zexu (Lin Tse-hsu), as imperial commissioner in charge of ending the opium trade. Commissioner Lin ordered the roundup of addicts for treatment in specially established sanitariums and the arrest of Chinese drug dealers. He also dispatched a letter to Queen Victoria, cosigned by the governor-general and governor of the area that included Canton, to plead for her assistance:

> We are of the opinion that this poisonous article is clandestinely man-
> ufactured by artful and depraved people of various tribes under the
> dominion of your honorable nation. Doubtless you, the honorable
> sovereign of that nation, have not commanded the manufacture and
> sale of it. . . . And we have heard that in your nation, too, the people
> are not permitted to smoke the drug, and that offenders in this partic-
> ular expose themselves to sure punishment. It is clearly from a knowl-
> edge of its injurious effects on man, that you have directed severe
> prohibitions against it. But in order to remove the source of the evil
> thoroughly would it not be better to prohibit its sale and manufacture
> rather than merely prohibit its consumption?[19]

Commissioner Lin appealed to Queen Victoria on moral grounds. How could the English have the heart to pursue profit by exploiting an unbridled craving, he asked, when the Chinese provided them with nothing but indispensable and useful commodities?[20] "Now we have al-ways heard that Your Highness possesses a most kind and benevolent heart. Surely then you are incapable of doing or causing to be done onto another that which you should not wish another to do unto you."[21] Failing to receive a reply—opium was in fact considered less harmful than alcohol in Britain at the time, and was not prohibited—the commissioner resorted to force. He ordered that all opium and smoking paraphernalia on Chinese ground be turned over to Chinese authorities without compensation. Some 350 foreign traders in Canton who refused were blockaded in their warehouses, called "factories," for six weeks in 1839 until they gave up more than twenty thousand chests of opium, which the commissioner, praying to the Spirit of the Southern Seas for forgiveness for contaminating the waters, proceeded to flush into a creek and send off to sea.

Unfortunately, his actions did not solve the problem. Opium use in China continued; by 1842, the annual consumption expanded to 5 million pounds. Moreover, British China-trade lobbyists prevailed on Parliament to send a full fleet to Canton in 1840. More ships followed in 1841, seizing towns along China's coast and taking control of inland river traffic by blocking estuaries as far north as Tianjin, while fleet commanders pressed for "free trade." America joined in by sending its own diplomats and gunboats—this despite the fact that selling opium was considered immoral by many in the United States. John Quincy Adams, while having no love for the British, supported the war in the name of commerce. "The moral obligation of commercial intercourse between nations is founded entirely, exclusively, upon the Christian precept to love your neighbor as yourself."[22] Trading is one of "the natural rights of men," he declared, as "there is no other way by which men can so much contribute to the comfort and well-being of one another as by commerce."[23] Following his logic, the trafficking in opium was "emphatically enjoined by the Christian precept." But Adams claimed that the "quarrel over certain chests of opium" was "no more the cause of war, than the throwing overboard of the tea in Boston harbor was the cause of the North American revolution. The cause of war is the pretension on the part of the Chinese, that in all their intercourse with other nations, political or commercial, their superiority must be implicitly acknowledged, and manifested in humiliating forms."[24]

The "arrogant China" was defeated by the British and forced to sign the first of many unequal treaties with Western powers, ceding Hong Kong to Great Britain and opening five seaports farther north up the Chinese coast for Western trade.[25] In no time, American diplomatic envoy Caleb Cushing demanded concessions from the Chinese as well and, to underscore his demand, dispatched a frigate up the

Pearl River from Hong Kong toward the city of Canton. The resulting Wangxia Treaty of 1842 formally inaugurated unequal relations between the United States and China, granting America most-favored-nation status and guaranteeing that any new treaty gains by Britain or other foreign nations would automatically accrue to American interests in China as well.[26] The treaty also gave Americans who committed crimes in China the extraterritorial right of not having to face the Chinese judicial system.

COOLIE TRADE

The end of the Opium Wars coincided with the end of the international slave trade. It also coincided with new Western colonial expansion, pressing British, French, Dutch, and Spanish plantation owners into a desperate quest for some new type of equally compliant workforce. They first turned to the British Crown colony in India, and, soon after the Opium Wars, to China. As America and other Western powers followed the British in demanding their own concessions from China after the Opium Wars, the Chinese imperial government effectively lost control of China's borders and could not stop its citizens from being coerced to work abroad. Laborers thus became China's latest and most sought-after export, and the notorious "coolie" system of long-term indentured labor quickly took shape to replace slavery. It was a system expressly different from slavery, yet in the minds of many Americans it did not seem that different at all.

The system took its name from the Tamil word *koli*, which means "hireling" or "transient laborer." According to this system, laborers were hired for a set number of years under strictly binding contracts that were often signed under conditions of coercion and fraud.[27] Sometimes the coolies were sold at auctions in open markets to the highest bidder, who then held them as virtual slaves for the duration of their contracts.[28] Unlike slaves, however, coolies regained their freedom if they outlived the eight or more years of servitude mandated by their contracts. Yet, because of the abuse and the hardships the South Asian and Chinese laborers endured, the word "coolie" quickly came to signify unfree labor, more akin to slavery than to normal contract labor.

The Opium Wars devastated the economy of southern China. The city of Canton lost the foreign trade monopoly it had enjoyed for some centuries. The tea trade, for instance, became evenly split between the cities of Shanghai and Canton, and one hundred thousand porters and boatmen in the city of Canton lost their jobs. Many were driven by desperation to sign coolie contracts. The British acquisition of Hong Kong and trading rights in other treaty ports along China's coasts made contracting easy and led to an exodus of Chinese laborers. They first appeared in the British colony of Guiana in 1844. Most of the coolies were recruited by the Spanish to work on plantations in Cuba (starting in 1847) and Peru (starting in 1849). American shippers provided most of the transportation, carrying six thousand Chinese laborers to Havana each year between 1847 and 1862.[29] At the peak of the coolie trade, between 1852 and 1858, more than thirty-two American ships were involved, transporting some forty thousand Chinese laborers to the Western Hemisphere.[30]

American coolie clippers were built like the old convict and African slave ships, with iron grates bolted into each hatchway. Thousands died in transit. One survivor, Li Zhaochun, later described a voyage: "We were confined in the hold below; some were even shut up in bamboo cages, or chained to iron posts, and a few were indiscriminately selected and flogged as means of intimidating all others; whilst we cannot estimate the deaths that, in all, took place, from sickness, blows, hunger, thirst, or from suicide by leaping into the sea."[31] The conditions on the ships were so bad that one voyage in every eleven had a mutiny.[32] Villagers in Guangdong Province still remember how their ancestors were tricked with worthless contracts, then loaded onto coolie ships, with the letters P for Peru, C for Cuba, and S for the Sandwich Islands (Hawaii) painted on their bare chests. "My grandfather and two great uncles were bought and sold like pigs," recounts Lau Chung Mun. They were sent to work in Cuba. Those imported to dig guano on islands off the coast of Peru were given physical examinations upon arrival in Lima and auctioned off, much like the African slaves. Working conditions on the plantations have been described as a "new system of slavery." "We labor 21 hours out of 24 and are beaten. . . . On one occasion I received 200 blows, and though my body was a mass of wounds I was still forced to continue labor," a Chinese plantation laborer testified to the China-Cuba Commission sent by the Chinese government to investigate reported abuses in 1874. "A single day becomes a year. . . . And our families know not whether we are alive or dead."[33] Just as African slaves before them, many Chinese coolies, too, rebelled, protested, committed suicide, and ran away.[34] During the 1860s, the rate of suicide for Chinese in Cuba was 500 in 100,000, compared to 35 in 100,000 for slaves and 5.7 in 100,000 for whites.[35]

Once these reports reached China, few individuals accepted coolie contracts voluntarily. Recruiters had to use deceptive methods and even resort to kidnapping. Both the Spanish and the English were involved in attempting to capture coolies in Chinese ports. In one incident, Shanghai residents believed that a group of Europeans walking down a street were kidnapping people to serve as coolies, and a riot ensued.[36] Sometimes recruiters were luckier. They were, for instance, able to purchase the captives of the Hakka-Punti war that broke out in Guangdong Province after the Opium Wars and pack them off to Peru or Cuba.[37] Debtors provided another source. Those unable to pay off their debts got sold to "crimps" (contract labor recruiters).

The horrific reports eventually led to the international prohibition of the coolie trade. The British Act for the Regulation of the Chinese Passenger Ships (adopted on August 14, 1855, and better known as the Chinese Passenger Act) called for passenger ships between China and the Americas to be searched for bonded Chinese laborers. All American presidents from Pierce (1853–57) through Grant (1869–77) criticized the practice in their annual messages to Congress. In 1862, Congress enacted the Prohibition of Coolie Trade Act, forbidding American shippers to participate in the illicit enterprise.

The coolie system could operate only if a control mechanism supported by the state was in place to enforce the contracts—as was the case in the well-established Portuguese, Spanish, and English colonies. Without state sanction, managing involuntary labor was impracticable. That is why out of the millions of Chinese who migrated overseas in search of work, only 11 to 12 percent labored under coolie conditions—mostly those who had been sent to Cuba and Peru.[38] The coolie system could have hardly been expected to work in the freewheeling lawlessness of America's Wild West. Still, when the Chinese first started arriving on U.S. shores in large numbers, many greeted them as coolies. The perception of the Chinese as coolies had arrived on the

North American continent even before the Chinese themselves. With American traders and missionaries to China having already primed the American public with stories of Chinese cruelty and submissiveness, Americans thought the Chinese well suited to replace the outlawed African slaves. White Americans felt licensed to look down on the Chinese as inferior and many saw the term "coolie" as synonymous with the Chinese immigrant—in spite of the facts to the contrary.

Chapter 4

Race

AMERICA'S WHITE SUPREMACIST VISION

The founding fathers had defined the United States as a republic committed to the principles of liberty, equality, and self-government. Yet it was from the start a white supremacist nation. Article I of the U.S. Constitution dismissed Native Americans, whose numbers European immigrants had ruthlessly decimated in the process of acquiring their land, as "foreign nationals," and reduced each enslaved African involuntarily brought to the New World to "three-fifths of a free person" in national population enumerations that were to be held every ten years. The U.S. Congress confirmed the unchallenged position of "whiteness" in American society by the 1790 Naturalization Act, limiting the right of citizenship in the new nation to "any alien, being a free white person."[1]

The sharp color line between black and white did not exist in the early colonial days. During the time of the early European settlement of North America, the most urgent goal facing the colonists was to bring the land under cultivation and make their American venture self-sufficient and profitable. For this they needed a plentiful labor force. But the new continent seemed too rough and primitive a place to attract a steady supply of voluntary farmhands and workers, and it remained underpopulated for quite some time.[2] Instead, the chartered foreign trade companies that drove the settlement of new lands recruited among the indebted, the desperate and the dispossessed in the over-crowded urban centers in Europe, and included convicts—"rogues, vagabonds, whores, cheats and rabble of all descriptions, raked from the gutter," in the words of Abbot Emerson Smith[3]—mainly from England, but also from Germany and Ireland. The Irish were frequently kid-napped and brought on board ships in bondage, much like the African blacks. Having been spirited to the colonies by unscrupulous labor recruiters, all these involuntary migrants were reduced to the status of indentured servants. They worked together and shared the same conditions of harsh labor, exploitation, and abuse—whites and blacks alike, being unfree, were beaten and tortured the same way. When they ran away together, they received the same punishment.[4] The problem of whites and blacks escaping together was serious enough to prompt the Virginia legislature to complain of English servants running away with Negroes. Equally troubling was the habit of cohabitation, with plenty of men and women, both black and white, being punished by whipping or public penance for having sexual relations and conceiving children.

Worse, the colonial society was shaken by a series of revolts between 1660 and 1683 organized jointly by blacks and whites. The most signif-icant was Bacon's Rebellion of 1676. Nathaniel Bacon, himself a mem-ber of the English colonial elite who had led the colonial assembly to a series of democratic reforms addressing the issue of freemen's right to vote, found himself in a dispute with the governor of the Virginia colony and rallied a large number of African American and white ser-vants and slaves to his cause by promising them freedom. Bacon's sup-porters burned Jamestown to the ground and forced the governor and his allies to flee. More than one hundred black and white followers con-tinued to fight together even after Bacon's death from dysentery jeop-ardized the outcome of their revolt.[5] Feeling threatened by this apparent unity of black and white servants, the masters began to separate them and single African Americans out for special treatment. Initially this of-ten involved longer periods of indentured service when servants were caught running away. It eventually ended up with the punishment of labor for life—in effect, slavery. Namely, unlike their European coun-terparts, who were brought to the New World as unfree laborers and who were becoming free after their contracts ran out, by the mid-seventeenth century the African captives were increasingly being turned into slaves. By the 1650s, 70 percent of the blacks in Virginia were serving as slaves.[6] In 1661, the Virginia Assembly began to institutionalize slavery, and in 1669 its legislature defined a slave as property—a part of an owner's estate.

Since by the late 1680s rural revolts and threats to the social order from lower classes had all but disappeared, it can be argued that the delineation between black and white in American society evolved as a pragmatic solution to a labor-management problem. Plantation owners first discouraged the two groups from forming class-based coalitions by making lower-class whites feel superior to blacks, and then used white servants in militias as a means of social control over blacks, turning them into a buffer between the white ruling class and the most exploited black laborers. Only later was the extreme exploitation of African laborers framed in the context of differences between the "civilized" and the "savage," "Christian" and "heathen," and "free" and "bonded" or "slave," which became the standard by which all other groups were to be judged.

By the time of independence, the composition of the nation was fairly simple: there were the whites and there were the nonwhites, which meant blacks (slaves in the South and a small number of free blacks in the North) and Native Americans (described as "tawny"). With the concept of race arrested at this primitive stage and the racial structure of American society set up as more or less bipolar, many issues remained murky, such as the status of free blacks, mulattos, and other types of "colored" people, such as the Chinese, who were yet to appear on the continent in any noticeable number. That crude white supremacy could not define all social relationships became particularly obvious when the white settlers began their land expansion westward. With each new group they encountered, the whole system of social hierarchical relationships had to be adjusted.

THE CHINESE AND THE AMERICAN CONSTRUCTION OF RACE

The arrival of the Chinese in California in large numbers called for one such adjustment. Previously, the presence of the Chinese in the New World did not garner much attention. It is noted only in scattered

records. Some of the seamen who traveled on Spanish galleons between Mexico and Manila (a Chinese community has existed in Mexico
since the late sixteenth century)[7] got stranded in the stopover port of
Monterey Bay on California's coast years before the gold rush. When
the ship *Pallas* developed a problem in 1785, its Chinese crewmembers
were forced to take up temporary residence in the city of Baltimore.
They sailed away within a year. Other records show Chinese sailors entering and leaving East Coast ports from the very beginning of America's China trade. The first permanent Chinese settlement in North
America, however, emerged in New York City after it became the most
important seaport on North America's East Coast, in the early 1800s,
serving as an international port of call connected to all places around
the world as well as to the American hinterland via the Hudson River.[8]

Individual cases of Chinese living in New York are known of as early
as 1808. In 1840, Chinese rooming houses appeared on Cherry Street
below Chatham Square, becoming the core of a Chinese community
that began to emerge in a three-block area along Doyers, Cherry, and
Mott streets. The New York State census of 1855 registered 39 Chinese
in the city's Fourth, Fifth, and Sixth wards of lower Manhattan, along
with 42 boarders on a ship docked off the west-side piers. The same
year the *New York Times* estimated the city's Chinese population at 150.[9]
In addition to sailors and boarding-house operators, the community
included cooks, domestic servants, adventurers, peddlers, Chinese opera
singers, merchants, doctors, clerks, and cigar makers who had been
trained in Cuba. Many of the residents appeared to be former indentured laborers who had escaped from Cuba and Peru. A few had learned
to read and write English and had adopted Anglicized names, such as
John Huston and William Brown, who married Irish American women,
became American citizens, and raised American-born children.[10] But
the Chinese population on the East Coast was small and grew slowly. By
1880, there were only 747 Chinese in New York City, and even fewer in
Philadelphia, Boston, and Baltimore.

Even fewer resided on the West Coast—seven, to be precise, were
known to be living in California when surface gold was discovered at
John Sutter's mill in Coloma in January 1848.[11] (At the time, California
still belonged to Mexico.) It was the gold rush that brought the first
large-scale Chinese migration to North America, and the Chinese population on the West Coast increased quickly. By 1852 there were

twenty-five thousand Chinese in California.[12] Although California was annexed to the union of American states only after the defeat of Mexico in 1848—the annexation being in part driven by the news of the discovery of gold—white Americans who went to the West Coast looking for gold, many recent immigrants from Europe, treated the people they found there as outsiders. New Irish Catholic immigrants who were themselves unwelcome by older white immigrants on the Atlantic Coast joined other Europeans on the Pacific Coast to vent their prejudices at "foreigners"—"Indians" and Spanish speakers native to the area, as well as other "colored" adventurers from Latin America and the Pacific Islands.

The California state legislature enacted the Foreign Miners License Tax in 1850, requiring all miners who were not U.S.-born citizens to pay a tax of $20 per month. Although it was nominally directed against all foreigners, tax reports show that the law was enforced only against Hispanic Americans and Pacific Islanders, while white foreigners of European origin were left alone.[13] (It was applied to the Chinese, too, but at that time only a small number of Chinese miners had arrived.) Tax collectors received $3 on each license tax collected. When "foreigners" refused to pay, they were surrounded and driven off by force. In July 1850, after a riot and an attempt at lynching, all Mexicans in Sonora were ordered to leave the country within fifteen days. Soon most Spanish speakers left the area.

African Americans, who were denied state citizenship and the right to vote, did not fare any better.[14] Local miners passed a law denying "Negroes" the right to work in the mines, and a criminal statute in 1850 barred them from testifying against whites in court. Other laws denied them the right to homestead on public land and prohibited marriage between whites and blacks.[15] Most African Americans ended up with menial tasks in trades that whites didn't want—"nigger work," as the occupations were henceforth called.

Chinese fortune seekers arrived in California's mines in significant numbers only after the Mexicans were forced out, and at first the general public in California did not know how to classify them. They were treated as foreign nationals, lumped together with the domestic races of color, and on occasion even thought of as worthy citizens. The enthusiasm expressed by the *Daily Alta California* in 1851 was probably due to California's seemingly endless opportunities and insatiable appetite for services and labor at the peak of the gold rush: "[The Chinese] are amongst the most industrious, quiet, patient people among us. . . . [They] seem to live under our laws as if born and bred under them, and already have commenced an expression of their preference by applying for citizenship."[16] In 1852 California's governor McDougal went so far as to recommend a system of land grants to induce further immigration and settlement of the Chinese, whom he called "one of the most worthy of our newly adopted citizens."[17]

The view of the Chinese as industrious, quiet, and patient workers reflected the perspective of California employers. The development of California depended on cheap and plentiful labor, but white migrants from the eastern United States were singularly tempted by the prospect of getting rich by panning gold and could not be counted on to stay in regular employment unless they were paid extremely high wages. Employers wanted workers who could not pick up and leave on a whim. Their natural choice would have been Southern blacks, if not for the emotional national debate on emancipation that was raging precisely at that time. California had joined the Union as a free state. Besides, transporting large numbers of laborers across the continent before the existence of the transcontinental railroad was not viable.

A much easier trip away by ship, across the Pacific, the Chinese—who had already acquired their reputation as coolies—seemed a perfect solution. Not only did they work for low wages; importing them under contract would effectively place them in the position of quasi-coerced labor. California employers were so enthusiastic that state senator George Tingley introduced a bill to enforce in California the long-term, fixed-wage labor contracts that would be made in China between a Chinese laborer and a Chinese contractor—to in fact use state power to enforce coolie contracts. He encountered stiff resistance from the white working-class people who had migrated from the rest of the country to the frontier to get away from cutthroat competition. California, it was argued, was a free state, and the bill was defeated.

An indentured coolie system was not realistically operable in California at the time. Most Chinese arrived on the so-called ticket-credit system, with shipping companies or labor recruiters advancing the cost of their passage across the Pacific. The Chinese would pay back the fare after they started working in the country. Once in the United States, theoretically, they were free to work anywhere they liked as long as they were paying off their debts. But many recruiters abused the system by charging such high costs that it took years to pay them off, and some used violence to extract payments, giving the impression that the debtors were indeed forced into coolie-type labor. Still, the lack of government sanction set a limit on how far this abuse could go. Also, the ticket-credit practice was common among immigrants from Europe.

But white working-class immigrants to California saw the "industrious, quiet Chinese" as unwelcome competition and set about finding ways to eliminate it. The first anti-Chinese riot took place as early as 1849, when no more than a few hundred Chinese resided in California. At a Chinese camp in Tuolumne County, a party of white miners drove some sixty Chinese who worked for a British company off the mine.[18] By 1852, the year in which rapid immigration brought the Chinese population of California to twenty-five thousand, things had gotten much worse. White miners held conventions demanding that all Chinese be expelled from the mining region, and the newly elected Democratic governor John Bigler took on the position of white labor. Addressing the state assembly, he asserted that most of the Asian laborers were servile contract laborers and that "the concentration within our State limits of vast numbers of Asiatic races" threatened "the well-being of the mining districts."[19] He proposed that measures be taken "to check this tide," and pushed through a new foreign miners license tax law in 1852—this one explicitly favoring European immigrants by exempting foreigners who intended to become naturalized. The Chinese, who were precluded from naturalization by U.S. laws, were its clear targets. The law mandated a monthly fee of $3 per miner. While it was in force, until 1870 when it was voided by the Civil Rights Act, this tax extracted $5 million from Chinese miners, supplying between 25 percent and 50 percent of all state revenue.[20]

In the spring of 1853 the *Daily Alta California* made a complete turnabout from its earlier favorable attitude and published a series of editorials in which it called the Chinese "debased and servile coolies, inferior to the negroes morally—more clannish, deceitful and vicious and immeasurably lower than the Indians." Racial qualities previously assigned to African Americans quickly became "Chinese characteristics," and white workers began to refer to the Chinese as "Nagurs." The anti-Chinese sentiment peaked because, as the rich surface mines became scarce and both the mining wages and profits fell sharply, only large mining companies could afford the equipment for the new quartz and hydraulic mining technologies to continue deep excavation. They hired Chinese. Instead of taking menial jobs in mining companies, white miners blamed the Chinese for helping the large companies drive them out of work.[21] Knowing the business community's appetite for some form of unfree labor, white miners condemned the Chinese as unfree coolies who were willing to accommodate capital's design by undermining free white labor. Even though the Chinese were no particular threat to white miners, from this early stage on the anti-Chinese sentiment of the white working class fused with its anticapitalist ideology and racial prejudice overtook class consciousness. When sixteen thousand Chinese contract laborers arrived in 1854, white miners saw them as the specter of an imminent Asian invasion.

That year, the California Supreme Court confirmed the inferior racial standing of the Chinese in its decision in *People v. Hall*. George W. Hall had been found guilty of murdering a Chinese man in Nevada County and was sentenced to death. But he appealed the conviction to the California State Supreme Court on the grounds that the testimony of Chinese witnesses—three Chinese and one Caucasian had testified against him—should have been excluded under an 1850 statute providing that "no Black, or Mulatto person, or Indian shall be allowed to give evidence in favor of, or against a White man." In repealing the conviction, the Supreme Court assigned the Chinese to the category of people who were not allowed to testify against white Americans.[22]

To fit the Chinese within the category of "Black, Mulatto, or Indian," the court resorted to some curious anthropology. Christopher Columbus had mistakenly identified America as India, the judges reasoned, and Indians had originally come from Asia across the Bering Straits. "The name Indian, from the time of Columbus to the present day, has been used to designate, not alone the North American Indian, but the whole of the Mongolian race." Then, as if not satisfied by this assertion, the court went on to argue, "Even admitting the Indian of this Continent is not of the Mongolian type, the words 'Black Person' must be taken as contradistinguished from White, and necessarily excludes all races other than the Caucasian."[23] Chief Justice Charles J. Murray went a step further. Even if "black" had not been used by the framers of the statute as a generic term, he offered, "I would decide against the testimony of Chinese on grounds of public policy."[24] The court's highly contorted line of reasoning reflects the lack of clarity and consistency in white Americans' construction of Chinese racial identity at that time.[25]

But soon after the decision, the intensity of racial attacks against the Chinese petered out in California because the declining mine deposits and general hostilities led to a dramatic decline in Chinese immigration, and by the late 1850s those who were there had already begun to leave for other states. By 1863 some twenty thousand Chinese miners left California to take part in a rush to newly discovered mines in Oregon, Nevada, Idaho, Montana, and as far east as the Black Hills in South Dakota. Compared to the peak immigration figure of twenty thousand in 1852, between 1854 and 1855 only thirty-five hundred Chinese entered the country. Between 1864 and 1867, according to census figures, Chinese departures outnumbered arrivals.

CHINESE ON THE EAST COAST

During the time of numerous anti-Chinese incidents in the West, there was no overt hostility on the East Coast, perhaps because there were so few Chinese there. Most Americans outside California at this time were preoccupied with the rush for economic growth and territorial expansion. The nation was expanding westward, adding territories purchased from France, Britain, and Spain, robbed from Native Americans through a series of "Indian removal" programs, and acquired through wars with Spain and Mexico. Settlement and development of those territories became the primary concern. There was a demand for increased production of commercial crops in the South, demand for increased production of manufactured goods in the North, and demand for immigrant labor to satisfy both. Somebody would also have to build all the new roads and canals.

The controversy over black slavery had split the country apart. The Mason-Dixon Line (the border between Maryland and Pennsylvania) became the dividing line between the South and the North, between the slave and nonslave states,[26] and the boundary to preclude the northward migration of African Americans. The main targets of hostility in the northern U.S. cities, therefore, were neither African Americans nor Chinese, but those who found themselves at the bottom of the social pecking order there—mainly new immigrants from Europe. The United States had received 3,153,198 immigrants between 1790 and 1850, but the five years between 1850 and 1855 alone accounted for a huge influx—1,879,828 people—and during this period the anti-immigrant sentiment was directed against Catholics and Catholicism. Italians were called "the Chinese of Europe," French Canadians "the Chinese of the Eastern States."[27] The poor, unskilled, and overwhelmingly Catholic Irish, who immigrated in unprecedented numbers on account of the infamous potato famine, ended up inspiring the worst of the ire.

The Irish provided the flexible labor needed for the construction of roads, railroads, and docks on the East Coast, and like the Chinese in California, they were accused of overstocking the labor market. They were described as "a race of savages" at the same level of intelligence as blacks and were quite commonly referred to as "Irish niggers."[28] Since they worked the same jobs and lived in the same neighborhoods as free African Americans, people took to calling them "niggers turned inside out," while the African Americans acquired the nickname "smoked Irish."[29] In one joke, a Negro complains: "My master is a great tyrant. He treats me as badly as if I was a common Irishman."[30]

The popular press referred to all Irish as "Paddy" and made them look apelike, with hideously low brows and jutting lower jaws. In the political arena, anti-Irish attacks were spearheaded by the American Party, known as the Know-Nothing Party, which gained so much popularity that it elected eight governors, more than a hundred congressmen, and numerous local officers throughout the northern states. (It held more seats than the Republican Party in 1854.) The greatest scorn for the Irish was based on the fact that they belonged to a colonized nation, and in this sense they were very much like the Chinese, whose nation, too, had been defeated by European powers and partly colonized by the British. There was fear that, as Catholics, the Irish could subvert American Protestant democratic values by creating large "un-American" voting blocs under the dictate of an authoritarian foreigner, the pope, and thus threaten "the very life of the nation from within."[31] Chinese subversion was feared, too, on account of their lack of any sense of democratic ideals as demonstrated by their passive submission to the rule of tyrannical emperors. To a New Yorker, the two groups seemed not much different. "Our Celtic fellow citizens are almost as remote from us in temperament and constitution as the Chinese," he wrote in his diary.[32]

The Irish and the Chinese were relegated to the lowest rung of East Coast society, where they had more than casual contact. At least one-quarter (about fifty) of all Chinese men who lived in New York between 1820 and 1870 were married to or lived with Irish women.[33] The "polite society," which abhorred "amalgamation," expressed shock at the practice, but many of its members in fact rated the Chinese favorably compared to the Irish, who were considered the true lowlifes of the city on account of their hard drinking and unruly conduct. A *New York Times* article asserted that "John" (the common appellation for the Chinese) was "a better addition to our society than Paddy."[34] Constituting one-fifth of New York City's population, the Irish naturally attracted more resentment than the handful of Chinese, who, generally perceived as "hard-working, non-drinking and intelligent," posed much less of a "menace" to society.

This attitude became manifest during the trial of a successful Chinese tea merchant, Quimbo Appo, who was accused of killing his Irish landlady when she intervened in a domestic quarrel he had had with his Irish wife. Appo was at first convicted of murder and sentenced to death. At the retrial, however, prominent Anglo white men testified in his defense, characterizing him as "an active and enterprising person—sober and honest, and sociable, quiet, and peaceable in his intercourse with his fellows and neighbors." Several police officers, on the other hand, provided testimony that the deceased, as well as Appo's Irish wife, were well known to be clannish and prone to "excessive use of intoxicating liquors."[35] Appo was acquitted.

Other respectable East Coast Chinese who had done well financially and spoke English received similarly favorable treatment. Several of them were awarded U.S. citizenship by the federal district courts, even though the 1790 Naturalization Act stipulated that only white free persons could become naturalized. Yung Wing, who was sent by a missionary school in China to be educated in America and was the first Chinese to graduate from Yale University, became a Christian and an American citizen and married a white woman. Chang and Eng Bunker, the "Siamese Twins," retired to North Carolina after a successful circus career and married two sisters, Sarah and Adelaide Yates. Due to their world fame and great wealth, they were fully accepted as members of the white community and even owned black slaves. One of their twenty-one children served in the Confederate army during the civil war.[36] (In fact, more than forty-seven Chinese served in either the Confederate or Union armies.)

Before the war, the concept of race was not applied to the Chinese in the United States with any clarity or consistency. When the eighth census was taken, in 1860, the only state that classified the Chinese as a separate group was California. Elsewhere, there was no category to separate Chinese from whites. In Louisiana, up to the 1870 census, Chinese were expressly counted as white.

Up until that time, the position of the Chinese in American society was ambivalent at best. On the one hand, all kinds of Americans found common cause with them and were willing to entertain their presence—employers touted their malleability and assimilability; workers on the East Coast mingled with them as class allies. On the other hand, others found reasons to separate themselves from them—workers, especially those newly transplanted to the West Coast, regarded them as competition, and elites saw them as a threat to American social order. At the same time, educated, wealthy, or upper-class Chinese were largely tolerated and even accepted outside of California. Such discrepancies in American views of the Chinese were possible because until then the American racial construct had not yet assigned them a definite position in the social hierarchy. And the ambivalence continued until it was more or less resolved by the rise of the American labor movement and its dramatic battle with American capital, when, in response to capital's drive to supplement black bonded labor with Chinese bonded labor, white labor took a stand against the Chinese and used racism to knit itself together into a coherent movement. The Chinese emerged from this movement as unequivocally racially distinct—people of color—and separated from the mainstream of American labor.

Chapter 5

Labor

Chinese immigrants, who began to arrive in the United States in large numbers after 1850, were thrust into the midst of a contentious national debate over race, inflamed by the issue of slavery, which led to the civil war. Then, to complicate matters further, they found themselves the focus of a profound conflict over the freedom of labor in America. In the years following the civil war, American business interests, having lost a superexploited labor force because of the end of slavery, scrambled to find a substitute, and, having no confidence in the reliability of white workers to perform harsh menial labor, they fastened onto the Chinese. At the same time, the nascent labor movement, growing at a blistering pace and trying to put an end to bonded labor altogether, likewise fastened on the Chinese—as stooges of capital and threats to their organizing. Labor's opposition soon flowered into an all-out national movement to push the Chinese out of the country and block more from coming. And yet, the saddest and perhaps the least understood fact about this historic backlash is that the Chinese would have made willing comrades for organized labor in its early years.

THE IMPORTANCE OF CHINESE LABOR

The need for labor became a serious concern when the western states became part of the Union and only intensified during the civil war. Since slavery was out of the question, policy makers were forced to turn to immigration, which has shaped American history continuously from the colonial period on, and looked to Europe for recruitment. In 1862 Congress passed the Homestead Act, granting free land during the war to people who would settle and develop it, to encourage European immigrants to take part in the government's determined effort to clear away Native Americans. Prominent capitalists, bankers, lawyers, and railroad presidents formed the American Emigrant Company (AEC) in 1863 to lobby for the procurement of "miners, mechanics, weavers, and agricultural, rail-road and other laborers . . . in any numbers and at a reasonable cost."[1] The same year Congress approved an Act to Encourage Immigration, giving official sanction to imported contract labor.

The practice of importing contract labor for indentured service had been common at the beginning of the European settlement of the continent. At least 50 percent of the labor force prior to American independence was brought in under indentures or as slaves. With the growth of African American slavery, however, the import of contract labor from Europe declined. The passage of the 1863 law brought AEC recruitment offices and agents to England, Scotland, Wales, Prussia, Scandinavia, Belgium, and France as, once again, American employers hoped to counter the problems of cost and dependability of the domestic free labor market by reintroducing contract labor. The fight against the practice, along with the demand for the eight-hour workday, would become the central issue of the American labor union movement, which began to emerge after the civil war as the nation embarked on a period of exuberant postwar reconstruction and expansion, and serious labor shortages made it abundantly clear that even massive immigration from Europe could not compensate for the loss of slavery.

In 1862 President Lincoln pressured Congress to finance construction of a transcontinental railroad with government bonds. Even before the civil war such a railroad had been deemed critical for the exploitation of resources from the newly incorporated West. The railroad's importance as a potential link between the North and the West against the South became even more apparent during the war. Construction began in 1863. It was to start simultaneously from the two coasts, under separate management, with the two railroads working toward each other until they met. The western portion, under the management of the Central Pacific Railroad Company of California, was more difficult to build, as it had to cut through the rugged mountains of the Sierra Nevada and across the parched Nevada and Utah deserts. Furthermore, white railroad workers were difficult to recruit and even harder to keep in the West, especially after the discovery of silver and quartz in Nevada. The Central Pacific's superintendent, James Strobridge, complained that those he could get were "unsteady men, unreliable. Some would stay a few days . . . until pay day, get a little money, get drunk, and clear out." In addition, white workers demanded high wages and threatened to strike. It was only after European workers began to organize for higher wages that the Central Pacific and American capital in general turned to the Chinese as an alternative.

Some policy makers had advocated the use of Chinese labor even before this critical moment. As early as 1848, when there were hardly any Chinese in the United States, Aaron Palmer, a policy pundit and onetime counselor of the Supreme Court of the United States, had sent a plan to Congress forecasting that San Francisco, once connected to the Atlantic states, would become the "great emporium of our commerce on the Pacific." He proposed that Chinese laborers be imported to build a transcontinental railroad and domesticate the fertile lands of California for agricultural use.[2] Under the influence of like-minded opinion makers, a general view gradually emerged that the Chinese could be to the West "what the Negro was to the South and Celt to the East."

Interestingly enough, when someone initially suggested to Strobridge that he use Chinese laborers, he protested that he would "not boss Chinese," as he considered them too delicate for the job.[3] Still, the Central Pacific engaged a gang of fifty Chinese on a trial basis when white workers threatened to strike in early 1865, and the results were gratifying.[4] The Chinese proved to be cheap, fast, and innovative and—used to working in teams—caused few management problems. The company wasted no time in trying to employ more. It engaged labor recruitment companies in the Far East and inundated emigrant communities with promotion placards and circulars that advertised a simple plea: "Come over, help us. We have money to spend but no one to earn it."[5]

The Central Pacific at first used the Chinese only as nonskilled graders, but they quickly became trained to work as masons and provide other types of skilled labor,[6] and company president Leland Stanford noted that they were "nearly equal to white men in the amount of labor they perform," and "much more reliable."[7] White workers refused to work alongside the Chinese and demanded that the Central Pacific stop hiring them, but one of the four company founders, Charles Crocker, who personally supervised the entire building project, minced no words in responding: "If you can't get along with them, we have only one alternative. We'll let you go and hire nobody but them."[8] Out of resentment, white workers nicknamed the Chinese "Crocker's pets." The company's rationale was simple. A white worker received $35 a month plus free board and lodging for the exact amount of work for which a Chinese laborer was paid between $26 and $35—without food and housing. When the Chinese were put to work on one of the most difficult segments of the railroad in the High Sierras, boring a tunnel through the granite rocks of the Donner Summit, they were pitted against Cornish miners, who had the best reputation in the world for that kind of work and were therefore paid extra wages. "We put them on one side of the shaft," Croker stated in his account of the experiment, "and we had Chinamen on the other side. We measured the work every Sunday morning; and the Chinamen without fail, always outmeasured the Cornish miners."[9] And since the Chinese worked in segregated crews under the control of co-ethnic labor contractors, they were perceived as posing no danger of striking.

By the time the two sections of the railroad met at Promontory in Utah in 1869, fifteen thousand of the seventeen thousand workers who had worked on the railroad from the West Coast were Chinese. Superintendent James Strobridge, who was once reluctant to "boss them," ended up believing that the Chinese were the best workers in the world.[10] Leland Stanford attributed the railroad's early completion in large part "to that poor despised class of laborers called the Chinese—to the fidelity and industry they have shown."[11]

The productivity of Chinese laborers was not a result of some special endowment, nor were they trying to do more for less than others.

They were coerced into accepting conditions worse than those given white workers and prevented from seeking recourse. In one well-documented incident on June 25, 1866, while engaged in difficult tunneling work in the High Sierras, some five thousand Chinese workers walked off the job "as one man," demanding higher pay and the same workday guaranteed to white workers. "Eight hours a day good for white men, all the same good for Chinamen," the strikers declared.[12] They also demanded that overseers not have the right to whip them or stop them from looking for other work. The railway company had clearly been handling the Chinese in a fashion closer to the treatment of black slaves than to the management of free labor, giving substance to white labor's claim that the Chinese were unfree coolies. To break the strike, the railway company attempted to transport ten thousand African Americans to replace the Chinese. When the attempt failed, Crocker stopped the provisions to the strikers and, stuck in their camps in the Sierras like virtual prisoners, without food, they were forced to give in within a week.

The experience of the Central Pacific in employing Chinese workers was deemed so successful that every large-scale company in America began casting its eyes on this bargain-basement labor. As American entrepreneurs began to envision more railroads and rapid economic expansion across the West, they stepped up pressure on the American government until the administration of Andrew Johnson began unprecedented negotiations with the Qing imperial government to secure Chinese labor at the source. In the resulting Burlingame Treaty of 1868, both countries recognized "the inherent and inalienable right of man to change his home and allegiance" and also "the mutual advantage of the free emigration of their citizens . . . respectively for purposes of curiosity, of trade, or as permanent residents." The treaty obliged the Chinese government to allow its citizens to migrate to the United States. At the same time, it assured that "citizens of the United States visiting or residing in China . . . and, reciprocally, Chinese subjects visiting or residing in the United States, shall enjoy the same privileges, immunities, and exemptions in respect to travel or residence, as may there be enjoyed by the citizens or subjects of the most favored nation." The objectives of the treaty were to safeguard America's interest in expanding international trade with China under conditions given most favored nations, while at the same ensuring an ample supply of Chinese laborers under conditions over which Chinese government would have no control.

Leaders of the business community were so jubilant that a poem written by the celebrated poet and essayist O.W. Holmes was read at the dinner given to honor the Chinese embassy in San Francisco on the occasion of the signing:

> Open wide ye gates of gold!
> To the Dragon's Banner-fold!
> Builders of the mighty wall
> Bid your mountain barriers fall!
> So may the girdle of the sun
> Bind the East and West in one.[13]

The Democratic *New York World* heralded the treaty's "vast commercial importance." The Republican *New York Herald* declared its impact equal to Columbus's voyage to America.[14]

Anti-Chinese labor groups called the Burlingame Treaty a "cheap labor treaty." Californian newspaperman and labor sympathizer Henry George forecast a "coolie invasion," warning that the thousands entering the American West for the time being were only "a thin end of the wedge which has for its base the 500,000,000 of East Asia."[15] The number of Chinese entering the United States in fact increased from a low of 2,682 in 1864 to more than 14,990 in 1869. The *New York Times*, which was initially enthusiastic about the treaty's anticipated benefit to American trade with China, published an editorial one year after the treaty cautioning that the magnitude of Chinese immigration, even "before the affairs of the 'white man' and 'black man' are settled," was ushering in "the negro question all over again."[16]

Indeed, during the post–civil war congressional debates leading to the adoption of crucial Reconstruction-era legislation, the "Chinese question" had been invoked alongside the more pressing "Negro question." After Congress passed the Thirteenth Amendment, ending slavery, in 1865, it moved on to the issue of extending citizenship rights to the emancipated slaves. It was a seemingly uncontroversial subject, and the proposed legislation was to give "all persons born in the United States"—not only African Americans—the benefit of U.S. citizenship. But many senators expressed fear that extending citizenship to "all persons" would have the grave consequence "of naturalizing the children of Chinese born in the United States." At the time there were fewer than thirty-five thousand Chinese in the United States, whose total population was 30 million. Because of the decline in mining, Chinese immigration had slowed. Senator Cowen of Pennsylvania, for instance, while admitting that he represented a state "infested with Gypsies" but with hardly any Chinese (there were in fact only 305 Chinese on the East Coast),[17] said that he had no doubt that the Chinese presented a singular menace to the nation and particularly to the Pacific Coast. If the Chinese were given political rights as citizens, he warned, California would soon be overwhelmed by the Mongolian race. President Johnson subsequently vetoed the bill on the grounds that by including what he called the "excepted races"—the Chinese of the Pacific states, Indians subject to taxation, the people called Gypsies, as well as the entire race designated as black—it would favor all the colored races against the white race.[18]

Ironically, it was California's Republican senator John Conness, reputedly the most hostile to the Chinese, who had to remind his colleagues that the amendment would benefit only the children born in the United States to Chinese parents and not Chinese immigrants themselves. Since very few Chinese men brought their wives to this country, Conness reassured his colleagues, children born in the United States of Chinese parentage constituted a very small portion of the population in California.[19] Without wives, the Chinese were bound not to remain in this country for very long. It was Conness who introduced the idea that the Chinese in the United States were "sojourners." It was also he who convinced Congress to override the presidential veto and pass the Fourteenth Amendment, which read, "All persons born or naturalized in the United States and subject to the jurisdiction thereof, are citizens of the United States." The amendment was ratified in 1868.

Evidently, Conness was not troubled by the presence of the Chinese, as long as they left the United States after the work they were hired to do was completed. The American business community was looking for ways to harness the "racially inferior" but "industrious" Chinese as effectively as the outlawed slaves. American policy makers were charged with ensuring that the Chinese did not become a permanent problem, as African Americans had, by seriously altering the racial order of American society. The congressional debates were used to define the place the Chinese would be allowed to occupy in American society, and they produced a brilliant formula: the Chinese would never become a problem if made ineligible for U.S. citizenship. Business interests could bring the Chinese to the United States for a set period of time. The legislative branch, by depriving them of full legal protection, tried to make sure they would leave the country before settling down, as soon as their services were no longer needed.

The Burlingame Treaty was designed to provide exactly that. Although most commentators, including historians sympathetic to the Chinese, praise its liberal nature because of the reciprocity invoked by the treaty, they ignore one important provision, which states, "Nothing herein contained shall be held to confer naturalization upon citizens of the United States in China, nor upon the subjects of China in the United States." At this very time, the United States government signed naturalization protocols with a number of European nations (Belgium, Denmark, Great Britain, Germany, Sweden, and Norway), guaranteeing their citizens the right of naturalization in the United States. It is obvious that the Burlingame Treaty deprived Chinese citizens of the same treatment by deliberate design.[20]

Members of the Chinese community in America saw the treaty for what it was: an empty promise. In 1869, prominent merchant Fung Tang delivered testimony on behalf of the Chinese community in front of the House Ways and Means Committee, which was debating new civil rights legislation. Tang first praised the intent of the one-year-old Burlingame Treaty but then complained that the Chinese were still waiting for the just and equal protection the treaty was supposed to guarantee them. The treaty, for instance, did not put an end to the unfair miners' and other taxes aimed specifically at the Chinese in the western states. It did not affect laws that excluded Chinese testimony in courts. Tang pointed out that the Chinese were still defenseless with respect to their life and property and "unable to obtain justice" either for themselves or for others.[21] Their vulnerability was borne out by the case of one Ah Wang, who in 1869 brought a complaint in a California court that he had been robbed and plundered by one George Washington. Ah Wang quickly found himself hemmed in by an 1854 California ruling that "a yellow Chinaman of Mongolian descent" could not testify in court against a white man. George

Washington, on the other hand, although he was of African descent, got full legal protection under the Fourteenth Amendment, ratified in 1868, and the Civil Rights Act of 1866. The Fourteenth Amendment gave him, as a person born in the United States, the status of a U.S. citizen; the Civil Rights Act guaranteed him, as a U.S. citizen, "full and equal benefit of all laws and proceedings for the security of person and property, as is enjoyed by white citizens." In the absence of non-Chinese witnesses, George Washington went free. The Chinese discovered that their legal status was ranked below that of African Americans.[22]

The Chinese were similarly singled out for unequal treatment over the question of voting rights that would be addressed by the proposed Fifteenth Amendment. Until its passage, suffrage had been controlled by the states, allowing many to bar African Americans from voting. Congressional debate once again centered on the issue of whether to grant "all citizens" the right to vote. It hardly involved the Chinese, since their numbers were small and almost none were citizens. Nevertheless, here, too, the concern surfaced that if rights were granted to African Americans, they would have to be extended to other nonwhites. "Unbridled suffrage," given the large and ever-growing numbers of Chinese, could threaten to determine any election in California, presaged Congressman Roscoe Conkling, a Republican from New York.[23] Republican senator James R. Doolittle from Wisconsin contended that the Chinese were known "as far in advance of the African in point of civilization" and questioned the sense of not extending the same privileges to the industrious Chinese as those extended to the "African."[24] But many senators and congressmen used the specter of "Chinese takeover" to deny extending voting rights to the blacks.

The debate foreshadowed the congressional rejection of the amendment to the Naturalization Act of 1790 that Massachusetts Senator Charles Sumner introduced in 1870. By then one of few remaining advocates of the post–civil war Reconstruction programs and a consistent believer in the rights of man, Sumner suggested that the naturalization statutes should be color-blind and that they should apply equally to "all persons." The ratification of the Fourteenth Amendment necessitated an adjustment. In the heated debate that ensued, many of Sumner's colleagues argued that the words "persons of African descent" should be added to the "free white persons" of the old legislation but that the Chinese should remain ineligible for naturalization. Senator Fitch of Nevada wanted to substitute "any aliens except natives of China and Japan" for "any alien, being a free white person." Senator Sargent of California warned Sumner that his amendment would destroy his own state of Massachusetts, because the Chinese would weed out not only the white laborers but also their schools, churches, and all other characteristics of New England life.[25] Sumner insisted that denying naturalization to the Chinese would be "the greatest peril to this republic" because it would be a betrayal to the "great ideas" of this nation, such as those in the Declaration of Independence.[26] His view was defeated. Chinese were declared "aliens ineligible for citizenship," and this ruling would remain the basis for statutory discrimination at both the federal and state levels until the naturalization laws were changed in 1952.[27]

The Burlingame Treaty, the 1870 Naturalization Act, and all subsequent government policies delivered exactly what the American business community wanted. By denying Chinese immigrants U.S. citizenship, they deprived them of full legal and therefore also labor protection. The setup allowed white employers to use coercion and treat the Chinese as disposable "guest workers."

COOLIES AS A SUBSTITUTE FOR NEGROES

By the late 1860s, encouraged by the experiences of the Central Pacific and by the favorable legislation, employers elsewhere in the country became interested in Chinese labor as well. In the post–civil war South, former slaves asserted their rights through federal Reconstruction programs and began to demand higher wages and lighter work schedules. They refused to work in gangs. White owners came to believe that the survival of the Southern plantation economy depended on their finding an alternative source of labor that they could subject to some degree of coercion, and they turned to the Chinese.

By then, it was already well known throughout the South that Chinese coolies had been instrumental in raising the agricultural output in Cuba. As early as 1854, the editor of the journal *Southern Cultivator*, Daniel Lee, had sung praises to the economic advantages of hiring Chinese, because they would accept wages less than the "interest on the cost of Negro field hands."[28] Along with J.D.B. De Bow, a lawyer and opinion maker from Charleston, South Carolina, who started publishing *De Bow's Review* after he moved to New Orleans in 1846, Lee was instrumental in publicizing the experiences of British and French plantation owners in the West Indies, who praised Chinese laborers for their reliability and reputation that they "never strike or form combinations."[29]

Southern newspapers began discussing the possibility of importing Chinese laborers in earnest in 1865, the year the civil war ended. In July, the Galveston *Daily News* described Chinese workers as "docile and thrifty, taking good care of themselves, and doing their work without reluctance"—in marked contrast to the "idle and thriftless peon, such as the Mexican, the native of Central America, and the negro."[30] The Chinese, the argument went, could be a factor in forcing "the freeman either to starvation or to industrial rivalry." "Emancipation has spoiled the Negro," the editor of the *Vicksburg Times* reasoned. "We therefore say let the Coolies come, and we will take the chance of Christianizing them."[31] *De Bow's Review* ran the editorial headline "Coolies as a Substitute for Negroes." Looking back on this early postwar enthusiasm in 1869, Frederick Douglass aptly observed that in "pride, bitterness and revenge," the Southerners had hoped that the "loss of the Negro is to gain them, the Chinese."[32]

This attempt did not go unnoticed by the federal government. A report to Congress in 1866 by the commissioner of the Bureau of Immigration called the employment of "new races" a violation of the 1862 Prohibition of Coolie Trade Act.[33] But the government could not prove that the small group of Chinese who were brought from Cuba in 1867 to work in Louisiana, Mississippi, and Arkansas were not voluntarily contracted laborers, because the State Department did not consider a contract, "however sullied," a violation of the law as long as a laborer did not enter into it fraudulently or involuntarily. Similarly, charges had to be dropped against a ship captain and a labor contractor accused of violating the same law by bringing twenty-three Chinese from Havana to New Orleans. Their employer insisted that the contracts were similar to those of thousands of Chinese laborers employed in California of their own free will. The North was importing Europeans under contract profitably, and railroad companies had saved millions by importing contract laborers from China. Why could the

South not do the same? Even the *New York Times* claimed that to prevent Americans from using Chinese labor anywhere would be on par with attempts to destroy newly introduced machinery.[34]

In 1869, the Memphis Chamber of Commerce organized a Chinese labor convention to formulate the "best and cheapest means of procuring Chinese laborers."[35] A featured speaker, the San Francisco labor contractor Cornelius Koopmanschap, told the two hundred assembled delegates from Alabama, Arkansas, Georgia, Kentucky, Louisiana, Missouri, South Carolina, and Tennessee that his house had employed thirty thousand Chinese in California to work on railroads, in mining, and in agriculture. The Chinese could be induced from California to the South at $20 a month, he claimed, but could also be obtained in China on five-year contracts at $8 to $12 a month.[36] An invited "Chinese gentleman whose enunciation was very clear," Tye Kim Orr (also known as O Tye Kim), was there to provide his expertise and answer questions. He was a Chinese Christian born in the Straits Settlements of the British East India Company, educated in a London Missionary Society school at Singapore, and sent from London to preach the gospel to the Chinese in British Guyana. While in Georgetown, he founded a congregation of Chinese Christians and in 1865 established a Chinese agricultural settlement on a tributary of the Demerara River. He entered Louisiana with a group of Chinese from Cuba in 1867. He told the assembled planters that they may be the means of evangelizing the Chinese. "The Chinese are a docile, patient, susceptible people and will follow . . . and love those who try to teach and benefit them." But he advised the prospective employers not to rely on "speculating agents, but to send agents to China and pick them up there." He also warned, "You must not get the wharf rats; you must get them from the rural districts of China where people are agriculturalists."[37]

The promises of promoters were tempting, but most Southerners remained leery about importing the little-known outsiders. "Soon," a Democratic newspaper in Montgomery, Alabama, had predicted as early as 1866, "the negro question will be lost in the Chinese question, and then will come up the perplexing question of [the] status [of the Chinese] in the community, his contracts, and his privileges."[38] Sure enough, the few planters who did experiment with using the Chinese became sorely disappointed when they discovered that the Chinese, far from being docile, patient, and susceptible followers, had the habit of challenging their bosses' power. The Louisiana Millaudon estate, which was in 1868 purchased by a group of investors from Massachusetts that included a former governor, a four-term member of Congress, and a retired member of the Boston bar, Amos B. Merrill, brought 141 Chinese from San Francisco in 1870 to help the retained emancipated slaves continue to cultivate sugar. Merrill contracted the Chinese for $14 in gold for twenty-six working days a month, plus two pounds of meat, two pounds of rice, and a quarter ounce of tea per day.[39]

Several newspapers noted the arrival of the Millaudon Chinese and commented on their quarters in a two-story wooden building (a former distillery), where two or three of them did the cooking, while one served tea to the laborers in the fields. The Mobile *Daily Register* reported that they put in an "exceedingly and good average day's work with no signs of fatigue, despite the boiling sun."[40] "Do they like the climate?" asked a *New York Herald* reporter, who visited the plantation. "Yes," responded their interpreter, Lee Fock Wing. "It is what they are used to." "Are they contented?" "Yes."[41] But less than a month after they began work at Millaudon, the Chinese discovered that the emancipated slaves employed on the plantation stopped work at twelve o'clock on Saturdays, while they stopped at the end of the day. Lee Fock Wing went to see Merrill to demand equitable hours. Merrill eventually offered them five- and six-day alternating weeks. A much worse conflict arose when their white overseer pushed a Chinese worker for acting "sullen." The Chinese struck him back. The overseer shot the offender in the arm and through the body, and the wounded man died soon afterward. The Chinese all armed themselves with clubs and knives and demanded that the overseer be turned over to them. Merrill let the white man escape, telling the Chinese that he was turned over to the police, but the relations on the plantation were soured forever. A year after their arrival at Millaudon, only twenty-five of the original one hundred and forty-one were still there. Most had gone off to work elsewhere, enticed by better conditions and better pay, and more than forty had run away.[42]

Experiences of other Southern employers were similar. In 1870, all the Chinese employed on railroad construction in Calvert, Texas, ceased work and entered suit against their employers for withholding wages and "for a failure of compliance with contract."[43] Others, employed on the Cedar Grove Plantation in Louisiana, struck in outrage after the whipping of a Chinese servant in 1871. The ensuing riot led to the killing of one Chinese and the wounding of two others; the rest requested court protection and left the plantation.[44] Due to such labor problems, compounded by the high cost of transportation and other related expenses, the Chinese workers turned out to be far more costly than initially calculated. Besides, many were less effective than the emancipated slaves in "handling mules, working with plows, or using cotton gins." Most had no intention of remaining sharecroppers or field hands for long.[45] The newspapers began calling them "unfaithful."[46]

As a result, the early Southern enthusiasm for contracted Chinese laborers waned quickly. Unfortunately, the way in which the plantation owners had hoped to use them gave ammunition to those who wanted to cast a dark shadow over Chinese immigration to the United States. Employers did try to exploit the legal ambiguity between indentured servitude and contract labor. This ambiguity would be used for many years to come and would eventually lead to a highly publicized national debate on the nature of Chinese labor. And although the Chinese made it abundantly clear that they were no more willing to be coerced or mistreated than anyone else, they found themselves reviled and rejected by the emerging labor movement, which ended up accusing them of colluding with the bosses.

AMERICAN LABOR VERSUS THE CHINESE

In the years following the civil war, America's economy was transformed. Not only did the South lose the war; its plantation economy was defeated by the technological innovation–driven manufacturing economy of the North. Large industrial companies shoehorned American laborers into factories as a wage-earning proletariat, giving birth to a vibrant labor movement. Between 1865 and the onset of the depression of 1873, several hundred thousand wage earners joined unions. A greater proportion of American industrial workers were organized during this period than at any other time in the nineteenth century. It was against this tide, in 1870, that Calvin Sampson's shoe factory in North Adams, Massachusetts, decided to hire Chinese workers to break a strike organized by the Knights of St. Crispin—the largest organization of working men in the United States at the time.

The factory's white workers had been striking regularly since 1868 to stop the company from importing European strikebreakers. The new strike was for higher wages, an eight-hour day, and access to the company's account books in order to fix wages in accordance with profits.[47] But Sampson was a new type of large-scale shoe manufacturer whose operation depended on machines to increase productivity and no longer required highly skilled workers. He decided to declare war against the Crispins by introducing the Chinese as a "wedge." He signed a three-year contract with the Chinese emigrant agency Kwong, Chong, Wing and Company in San Francisco for workers who would labor eleven hours a day in spring and summer, and ten and half hours in fall and winter, and who would be paid less than half of what Sampson had offered to the white workers.

The small Berkshires hill town of North Adams greeted the arrival of the seventy-five "pig-tailed, calico-frocked" Chinese to the "model shoe factory" with hostility. *Scribner's Monthly*, on the other hand, hailed them for the steadfastness of their laboring—"losing no blue Mondays on account of Sunday's dissipations nor wasting hours on idle holidays."[48] The antiunion press believed that the Chinese had no labor unionizing tradition and could thus, possibly, be the "final solution of the labor problem."[49] Sampson's experiment in North Adams was considered a success and inspired other employers to follow it. Before long, sixty-eight Chinese were brought from San Francisco to replace Irish women in the Passaic Steam Laundry near Belleville, New Jersey, and rumors began to circulate that more were headed for the potato fields on Long Island and a cigar factory in New York City. When one hundred and sixty-five did arrive to work in a cutlery factory in Beaver Falls, Pennsylvania, the alarmed townsfolk petitioned Congress, complaining that the introduction of Chinese labor "shows a manifest attempt to revive the institution of slavery."[50]

Headlines proclaiming "The Chinese Are Coming!" spread panic across the East Coast. Before the "Chinese question," the focus of the labor movement had been on the fight for an eight-hour workday and against cheap labor from Europe. In 1864, for example, the St. Louis stove maker Giles Filly imported twenty-five Prussians on one-year contracts to break a strike. But the members of the Iron Molders' Union were able to mobilize their entire trade; they even persuaded the Prussian workers to break their contracts and join the union, frustrating management's strategy. The hiring of Chinese by the North Adams shoe factory shifted the focus of labor's attention. The leader of the Knights of St. Crispin, Samuel P. Cummings, at first urged the union to organize the Chinese so as to undermine Sampson's "wedge" strategy, declaring "John Chinaman a gentleman far superior to Mr. Sampson." The contract the Chinese signed with Sampson was published in the *Springfield Republican*, so it was plain for all to see that their terms were not that different from any standard contract laborer's. White workers, however, rejected Cummings's appeal. At a mass meeting in Boston, they turned against the Chinese, as well as Sampson, for reducing "American labor" to the Chinese standard of "rice and rats." Unlike the Iron Molders' Union, the Knights of St. Crispin did not consider the Chinese fellow workers and did not want them in their union.

The American labor movement drew the line between Chinese and European imported labor. A resolution issued at the 1870 labor convention in Troy put it this way: "We are inflexibly opposed to all attempts on the part of capitalists to cheapen and degrade American labor by the introduction of a servile class of laborers from China or elsewhere; while we at the same time, heartily welcome all voluntary emigrants from every clime, and pledge them our sympathy and encouragement in efforts to secure for themselves and their children homes on American soil."[51] The distinction between "servile" and "voluntary," between "importation of coolies" and "voluntary immigration," became the oft-repeated mantra of organized labor. But the labor movement had already tied the definitions of contract labor, coolies, and slaves to race. Slavery was reserved for African Americans. Contract labor, the least objectionable of the three, was set for European immigrants. The status of the Chinese, even if they came under voluntarily signed contracts like any other imported contract laborers, was fixed by the white workers' belief that they were subservient and inferior. No evidence to the contrary could persuade them otherwise, and anti-coolie clubs sprouted within many unions.

The Knights of St. Crispin organized anti-Chinese, not anti-contract labor, rallies in Boston and New York. The agitation of the white labor movement was so vigorous that the New York state legislature considered banning the use of Chinese laborers in the state. At a convention held right after the North Adams incident, members of the National

Labor Union, the most progressive union at the time, overturned a resolution—passed just the year before—that had supported the right of "voluntary Chinese emigration." "The presence in the country of Chinese laborers in large number is an evil," they now declared, "and should be prevented by legislation." Strong sentiment against immigrant laborers was not new in America. However, no one had ever seriously considered legislation to exclude objectionable groups from Europe, no matter how "undesirable" they may have been deemed. Heeding the National Labor Union's call, Representative William Mungen of Ohio delivered a speech to the House in which he called the Chinese "a poor, miserable, dwarfish race of inferior beings" and China "a nation of abject slaves." He was the first to introduce Chinese exclusion legislation, in 1871.[52]

THE DRIVE FOR CHINESE EXCLUSION

The push to build the exclusion of the Chinese into a national movement once again came from California. After the completion of the transcontinental railroad, the thousands of Chinese laborers who had suddenly become unemployed began to spread all across the West Coast and the Rocky Mountain states in search of jobs. Thousands more arrived, spurred by active recruitment by shipping companies and labor-contracting agencies. In the 1870s, the Chinese constituted about one-twelfth of California's total population and, since they were mostly male, one-quarter of its able-bodied labor force. In other western states the proportion of Chinese was as high if not higher. They began to move into cities to work in textile mills and in small-scale factories: rolling cigars, sewing garments, producing silk, and making gunpowder. San Francisco reported that half the men employed in the city's manufacturing plants were Chinese. By moving beyond the unskilled menial jobs and service trades into the skilled labor market, the Chinese were truly becoming a part of the American working class.

Their conspicuous presence in new West Cost industries coincided with a large influx of white workers, whose migration from the East was facilitated by the completion of the railroad. In the early 1870s, the ranks of California's unemployed—twenty-five thousand railroad workers alone—were swelled by a wave of 1 million migrants from the

East Coast, forced west by the 1873 economic depression. These hopeful new arrivals found that jobs in California were scarce and the land already claimed: the giant stock companies had taken over a large number of mines, the railroad companies had received extensive land grants along the tracks from the government, and other areas were held by earlier immigrants. The disappointment of the destitute turned against the Chinese, who were blamed for the economic slump.

The first major spontaneous outbreak of anti-Chinese violence took place in Los Angeles in 1871, when a white policeman was accidentally shot while responding to a feud between two Chinese clans. A white mob of several hundred malcontents surrounded Chinatown, blocked every exit, and began to shoot, burn, and loot. After the mob dispersed, the sheriff found fifteen Chinese hanged, four shot, and two wounded. In a similar incident in Chico, a small town in the Sacramento Valley, a white mob tied four Chinese up and burned them to death. Nowhere in California was a Chinese person safe, nor was Chinese property. "In broad daylight in San Francisco," Mark Twain observed in 1872, "some boys have stoned an inoffensive Chinaman to death, and although a large crowd witnessed the shameful deed, no one interfered." The outburst of anti-Chinese violence was reminiscent of what had greeted freed African American slaves in the industrial cities of the North.

An even more systematic attack on the Chinese was carried out in the courts through a spate of anti-Chinese legislation. One 1870 San Francisco city ordinance required that every house or room contain at least five hundred cubic feet of air space per person. Violators "shall be fined not less than ten nor more than five hundred dollars, or imprisoned in the city prison not less than five days nor more than three months, or both such fines and imprisonment," it decreed. The ordinance effectively outlawed all Chinatown tenement living—or made it very costly for the Chinese and profitable for the city. The so-called queue ordinance ordered that the hair of every male prisoner be cut to within an inch of his scalp, which was a direct attack on the Manchu-prescribed Chinese hairstyle of the time. A laundry ordinance required $15 per annual quarter in license fees from all laundries that did not use horse-drawn vehicles, and it was quickly followed by another that made it illegal for any person on a sidewalk to carry baskets suspended from two sides of a pole placed across the shoulders. Instead of submitting to these punitive discriminatory laws, the Chinese challenged them in federal courts, and most of them were struck down.

White workers in California came from very diverse backgrounds, and not all of them held anti-Chinese views. Some were recent immigrants who had fled political persecution in Europe; others had been victims of economic dislocation. Many were highly skilled and came straight from Ireland and Cornwall in Britain, where mining had been an important occupation for generations. Others were skilled craftsmen born and trained on the East Coast, whose jobs had been usurped by mechanization and the use of unskilled labor, or small midwestern farmers pushed farther westward by the encroachment of a more complex and commercialized system of agricultural production. Politically, too, they were a diverse bunch that included Republicans with abolitionist or free soil sympathies; Democrats, some of whom came from the South and whose belief in the work ethic was coupled with notions of racial superiority; and socialists who came from a strong European working-class tradition.[53] Thus fragmented, the white working class in California found little in common to unite around. The issue of Chinese labor became central to the labor movement because labor leaders discovered that zeroing in on the Chinese was the most effective way to mobilize white workers and organize them into a unified force.

The most unrelenting in their attack on the Chinese were the craft unions, whose leaders sought to maximize their bargaining power through union-controlled competition for skilled jobs. This they achieved by limiting the number of people entering the trade, through rigorous apprenticeship and hiring.[54] In their infancy, in the 1870s, craft unions used anti-Chinese campaigns as an organizing tool and a way to expand political power. The actual threat of Chinese encroachment on skilled trades, such as cigar and shoe manufacturing, was initially minimal, but the idea of that threat became the most powerful means of unifying white skilled labor into unions. The anti-Chinese campaign also enabled the craft unions to forge coalitions with other groups that controlled California politics, such as the Democratic Party, which was desperately trying to rehabilitate itself from the ashes of defeat after siding with the Confederates during the civil war, and now claimed to champion the cause of the hard-pressed working people. As leaders of the anti-Chinese movement, the craft unionists extended their influence beyond the small membership in any particular trade.

What was the rallying point that unified white workers against the Chinese? The Chinese were accused of forcing all workingmen to accept lower wages and of siding with the monopolies—the large mining companies and land grabbers, such as the Central Pacific Railroad. The result was "to make the rich get richer and the poor poorer; to make nabobs and princes of our capitalists, and crush our working class into the dust," wrote Henry George, a New York journalist turned California Democratic Party campaigner and pamphleteer, whose views were eagerly absorbed by the anti-Chinese campaign.[55] The tactic was used to convince the unskilled workers that the Chinese were to blame for their unemployment and other economic hardships. The focus on the Chinese was intended to divert the demands of the unskilled for apprenticeship in specialized trades, to deny them membership in the craft unions, and to gain their support at the same time. Without the challenge by the unemployed and the unskilled, the craft unions could deal with the employers from a position of maximum strength, achieved on the backs of the Chinese.[56] English immigrant Samuel Gompers, who would in 1886 become president of the American Federation of Labor (AFL)—the largest and most powerful trade union in America at the turn of the twentieth century—had his start as a labor organizer of cigar makers and campaigned to have cigar boxes labeled "Made by White Men," to encourage consumers to boycott those that were made by the Chinese.

The use of racial attacks in labor organizing was not new. White labor leaders had long equated freedom with whiteness and slavery with blackness to exclude African Americans on the grounds that the American labor movement could not include unfree labor. By being made to believe that they were members of the privileged group, white workers could be organized to defend their caste status and fight to improve their conditions as the working class at the same time. Civil rights leader W.E.B. DuBois would later write that the creation of "The Black Worker" as an antithesis to "The White Worker" manipulated the white working class into defining itself by its whiteness, which allowed it, even when it received a low wage, to feel compensated in part by a "public and psychological wage." "They were given public deference . . . because they were white. They were admitted freely, with all classes of white people, to public functions [and] public parks. . . . Their votes selected public officials and while this had small effect upon the economic situation, it had great effect on their personal treatment."[57] White labor did not just receive and resist racist ideas, DuBois famously argued, but embraced, adopted, and at times murderously acted upon them.[58]

In this respect, Irish labor leaders had taken the most aggressive racial stance. When the Irish first arrived in the United States, they were despised by the Protestant majority as Catholics colonized by the British. Thrown to the very bottom of the American social hierarchy, where they competed for jobs with African Americans, they were often treated as an inferior race, ambiguously close to the blacks with whom they fought, socialized, and occasionally married. As the people whom witty members of the mainstream society were apt to call "niggers turned inside out," the Irish had the highest stakes not only in forcing African Americans out of job competition, but in insisting on their own whiteness. In 1851, the *African Repository* reported, "In New York and other Eastern cities, the influx of white laborers has expelled the Negro almost en masse from the exercise of the ordinary branches of labor. You no longer see him work upon buildings, and rarely is he allowed to drive a cart of public conveyance. White men will not work with him."[59] That refrain—"white men will not work with him"—became the magic formula of American trade unionism.[60]

In 1862, a largely Irish mob attacked a tobacco factory in Brooklyn, where the employees were mainly black children and women. They drove the workers upstairs and set the factory on fire. It was allowed to reopen only when the employer promised to dismiss the blacks and hire the Irish. The Irish figured prominently in the infamous New York Draft Riot of 1863 against the Conscription Act that exempted the rich. Turning their anger against the black community, frenzied rioters attacked every African American they encountered on the street, chasing down and killing families, lynching unfortunate individuals, and taking an orphanage under siege. Physical attacks on and off job sites became such a habit that African Americans started referring to the brickbats hurled at them as "Irish confetti."[61]

In New York City, Irish immigrants shouted, "Down with the Nagurs!" and "Let them go back to Africa where they belong."[62] In California, they took the lead in the anti-Chinese movement. The most vociferous among them, Dennis Kearney, coined the slogan "The Chinese Must Go!" It was the Irish, whose own status as "white" had hardly been established on the East Coast and who arrived in California after the Chinese, who were instrumental in demanding the exclusion of the Chinese from the competition for jobs and from the country altogether, and who turned the exclusion of the Chinese into a national movement. In California, too, Irish ruffians took the matter of expulsion into their own hands. A Chinese man told a reporter on the East Coast that he left California to escape from the "Ilishman."[63] The American delegation dispatched to Beijing to renegotiate the Burlingame Treaty was told by Chinese ministers Bao Zhun and Li Hongzao that, based on their information from Chinese sources in America, "the Irish" were to blame for advocating exclusion "and that the better class of Americans thought mostly the other way."[64]

Irish agitation against the Chinese was not limited to the West Coast. The five most prominent Irish newspapers in New York during the 1870s expressed unanimously anti-Chinese views. Ironically, the Sinophobic arguments of the Irish press frequently resembled those directed at Irish immigrants by the nativists: the Chinese were incapable of understanding the principles of democracy; they subverted Christianity, committed crimes, and were immoral. Lest his readers get confused, the editor of the *Irish Citizen* reminded them that, in contrast to the Chinese, immigrants from the Emerald Isle had greatly benefited the United States. "We want white people to enrich the country, not Mongolians to degrade and disgrace it."[65]

The Irish used African Americans and Chinese to establish their identity in white America. White workers, whether Irish or not, chose their racial identity over class consciousness to maintain their privileges as members of white America and the white American working class. The labor leader and AFL president Samuel Gompers, who once argued that "the superior whites had to exclude the inferior Asiatics, by law, or, if necessary, by force of arms," years later wrote in his autobiography, "It is my desire to state emphatically that I have no prejudice against the Chinese people." By way of justifying his positions, he continued in the next paragraph, "I have always opposed Chinese immigration not only because of the effect of Chinese standards of life and work but because of the racial problem created when Chinese and white workers were brought into the close contact of living and working side by side."[66] Race was the vehicle of empowerment for white American laborers, which helped them to gel into a vibrant working class that could do battle with American capital.

Chapter 6

The World of Chinese Immigrants

The most unfortunate aspect of American organized labor's push to purge the American working class of the Chinese was that it ignored class divisions within the Chinese community. Had they bothered to look, American labor leaders would have found plenty of class allies among the Chinese. Ironically for people trying to forge unions, white unionists objected to the Chinese workers' ability to function as a group. "I don't object to their coming here," a Knight of St. Crispin complained. "Let 'em come single-handed, like other emigrants, and take their chance. But they come banded together. That isn't right."[1] The unwillingness of the white labor movement to look past Chinese laborers' "Chineseness" obscured the fact that they were far from "banded together" with Chinese labor contractors and merchants. They were forced to depend on the contractors and merchants to travel across the Pacific, to get jobs in America, and to negotiate a racially hostile environment. But the contractors and merchants turned a profit providing these services. They also played a significant role in shaping the manner of the workers' arrival, the form of debt payment, the type of jobs secured, the working conditions, and even the lifestyle the workers in their charge enjoyed in America. But even if the laborers voluntarily entered into this interdependent relationship, it did not mean that the relationship was not riven with class contradictions and conflict.

CHINESE EMIGRATION NETWORKS

To better understand the divisions among the Chinese in America, it helps to look more closely at the mechanisms that brought them to the United States. Despite the scrambling of white employers to hire Chinese laborers for as little as possible and repeated attempts to nip prospective migrants at the very source, Chinese migration (except for the destinations in Peru, Cuba, and Hawaii) was managed and controlled by the Chinese themselves. When significant migration to North America began, at the start of the gold rush, individuals had to find their own means to cross the Pacific and often relied on relatives and familial networks to provide it. Once the original migrant "made it" in a new location, he would sponsor other family members. They in turn sponsored others as soon as they were able, creating a chain migration.

As more folks emigrated, however, the strains on kinship-based networks began to show. Soon enough Chinese merchants began paying for the passage to California of enthusiastic gold rushers in exchange for half their future profits. Then American shippers and labor brokers jumped in to turn the shipping of laborers into a moneymaking enterprise. With tickets costing $40 to $50, a fortune for most farmers and laborers in southern China, Chinese emigration brokers took over the procurement of tickets, and for a 5 to 10 percent commission often chartered entire vessels. American shippers were so satisfied with this arrangement that they required no cash from the brokers up front. "If a Chinaman came down and wanted a hundred tickets to ship tomorrow, we gave him a hundred tickets, and when we wanted the money we sent for it," boasted the general agent of the Pacific Mail Steamship Company, Henry Hart. "And we never lost a cent."[2]

A surviving example of a typical transaction, the Agreement Between the English Merchant and Chinamen, concluded in 1850 and now in the possession of the Wells Fargo Bank, spells out the conditions:

> The *Tseang Sing* Hong having now hired The American ship called the Ah-mah-san for voyaging purposes, the mechanics and labourers, of their own free will, will put to sea, the ship to proceed to Ka-la-fo-ne-a, and port of Fuh-lan-sze-ko, in search of employment for the said mechanics and labourers. From the time of leaving Shanghae, the

expenses of provisions and vessel are all to be defrayed by the head of the *Tseang Sing* Hong. On arrival, it is expected that the foreign merchant will search out and recommend employment for the said labourers, and the money he advances on their account, shall be returned when the employment becomes settled. The one hundred and twenty-five dollars passage money, as agreed by us, are to be paid to the said head of the said Hong, who will make arrangements with the employers of the coolies, that a moiety of their wages shall be deducted monthly until the debt is absorbed: after which they will receive their wages in full every month.[3]

The whole business operated on credit. Each migrant promised to pay the broker $100 to $125 for a ticket that cost no more than half that amount. The markup included the broker's commission and interest charges, which more than compensated him for his "trouble." Although the price was more than an immigrant could pay off in a year, the prospect of doing well in the New World was so high that brokers were never short of takers. American shippers made more than $1.5 million from Chinese passengers in 1852 alone, and the task of chasing after ticket-credit debts, which had proved too burdensome for them, fell to Chinese brokers, who typically held the migrants' families left in China as "human security."[4]

Chinese brokers' services gradually expanded into finding jobs for the migrants and, later, to providing for all their daily needs. As the migration to California became fully commercialized, overseas Chinese traders formed networks to control all aspects of the business. Eventually, the networks branched into capital ventures and banking and became sophisticated enough to handle the transportation and trading of any amount of money, goods, services, and people. Although their roots were in China, their span reached across the entire Pacific Rim region. They went wherever there was money to be made and were especially well established in Southeast Asia, which had the longest history of Chinese immigration. To be competitive, they set up a keen communication system to exchange information on where and what kinds of services were needed at any given time.

The economic crisis that engulfed China after the Opium Wars and caused the great Chinese diaspora in the second half of the nineteenth century gave Chinese overseas commercial networks an opportunity to make a fortune. First they made profits from transporting migrants to the New World, and then they acted as middlemen between white employers seeking laborers and adventuresome Chinese looking for jobs. When employers looked for labor contractors to oversee the work of the Chinese they had recruited, the merchants provided that service, too. Needless to say, the new Chinese settlements overseas gave them new outlets for China's export consumer goods.

White employers understood that success in employing and retaining Chinese laborers ultimately depended on the active participation of Chinese businessmen and their agents, the labor contractors. Leland Stanford and his business partners at the Central Pacific secured the fifteen thousand Chinese workers used to complete the western section of the transcontinental railroad through subcontracts with the Chung Wah Kongsi.[5] The Houston & Texas Central Railway Company's procurer General John G. Walker signed a contract with Chew Ah Heang, a Chinese labor contractor, in San Francisco in 1869 for the service of three hundred Chinese workers.[6] In all these cases Chinese brokers were used not only to recruit workers but also to manage them on their jobs, to provide daily necessities, and to dispense wages to the working crews. In fact, of the seventy-five "steady, active and intelligent Chinamen" Calvin Sampson hired through Kwong, Chong, Wing and Company of San Francisco for his North Adams shoe factory, seventy-two were laborers, two were cooks, and one was a foreman, who doubled as the translator, known as "Charley" Ming.[7] Charley's salary was $60 a month—double what the other workers were promised in their three-year contract.[8]

Some American employers found such wages too high and tried to bypass San Francisco by recruiting directly in Hong Kong, but they still ended up contracting Chinese merchants to broker the hiring, shipping, and labor management. In 1869, for instance, Captain George Washington Gift, acting as labor-procuring agent for Southern planters, found out not only that no Chinese laborer would sign on with him out of conviction that he was looking for slaves; American consular authorities also believed that "it would be illegal and improper to make contracts with Chinese subjects in China, for labor performed in the United States."[9] In the end, he engaged the services of a Chinese merchant in Hong Kong who, for the sum of 25 cents per month per man, agreed to find the laborers, persuade them to emigrate, accompany them to the United States himself, continue to reside among them, look after them, and act as their interpreter—with an understanding that he would get an additional $10 per man after the termination of the labor contract.[10] This type of subcontracting was also used in hiring Chinese workers for large agricultural projects such as wheat harvesting and for the canneries.[11]

Sometimes the hiring of Chinese laborers went through several subcontractors. Desperately looking for workers for the Houston & Texas Central Railroad in 1869, Captain R.P. Boyce went through Chinese labor advocate General John George Walker and labor contractor B.J. Dorsey before learning that "chiefs" of a Chinese "league" or "union" in California conducted all negotiations and took care of all the interests of the men he intended to hire. The "chiefs" wanted "side contracts and private bargains, just as a Southerner or a Yankee politician does before he can comprehend the true interests of his constituents."[12] He had to agree to establish a Chinese store with $3,000 in stock, which Chinese contractors supplied with dry goods, clothing, and writing and accounting supplies. The *St. Louis Democrat* printed the list of the procured goods with some fascination:

> Narrow leaves, 500 pounds; bamboo brushes, 5 dozen; foo chuck, or been curd sticks, 10 boxes, or 400 pounds; 10 boxes vermicelli, 500 pounds; 200 pounds of ginger root; 50 pounds orange peel; 200 pounds cuttle fish; 10 boxes soy; 10 jars ketchup; 20 reams Chinese writing paper; 200 Chinese pencils; 10 daily accounts books; 5,000 Chinese visiting card papers; 5 pieces paper (for lights); 300 pounds California abalones; 40 pounds red melon seed; 2 dozen frying pan shovels; 4 dozen copper spoons, (large); 100 pounds pak ko; 10 pairs crape suspenders; 50 pounds sugar candy: 50 pounds red dates; 6 counting boards; 1 pound Chinese ink . . . Additional Goods for Chinese New Year.[13]

As the need for Chinese labor grew elsewhere in the country, representatives of San Francisco trading houses set up shop near the emerging markets for their services and goods. Fou Loy and Company operated a general store in New Orleans selling groceries, teas, and a variety of Chinese goods, including firecrackers, Chinese smoking tobacco, Chinese shoes, and, according to the *New Orleans Times,* "thousands of Chinese curiosities." The *Times* called it a "stock company, each member of which takes a part in the management of affairs," and it had a $20,000 policy from the Salamander Insurance Company on its stock. Fou Loy and Company also provided food and supplies to Chinese laborers working on nearby plantations, charging them $1 per head per month. In 1871, the firm announced to the local press that it would add the service of recruiting Chinese laborers from California for the sugar planters at $22 per month in gold, with the laborers furnishing their own food and clothing. (Those, of course, would be supplied by Fou Loy.)[14]

But it was the rapid growth of large-scale manufacturing enterprises on the West Coast that led to the heaviest recruitment of Chinese laborers. The number of Chinese admitted to the United States between 1870 and 1880 was 123,201—double the number for either the decade before (64,301) or the decade after (61,711). During the previous two decades, immigrants from China included a good number of merchants, producers, craftsmen, and professionals (druggists, doctors, interpreters, gamblers, actors, etc.), but after the Burlingame Treaty the Chinese migrant population became visibly proletarian.[15] Most Chinese laborers worked for white employers under the supervision of Chinese labor contractors in all manner of industries. (By 1880, 70 percent of the Chinese in Sacramento and 67 percent in Marysville depended on white employers.)[16] Some, however, wound up employed in sweatshops run by Chinese, who in many cases rose from the ranks of subcontractors and supervisors to become capitalists themselves. Since they could be competitive in the kinds of manufacturing that required low initial investment on account of their easier access to the Chinese labor market, they eventually came to dominate San Francisco's three main industries—clothing, with 51 firms; shoes, with 61; and cigar manufacturing, with 120 firms—employing 7,500 Chinese workers.[17]

Chinese commercial networks quickly turned every aspect of migrants' needs into a profit-making opportunity—not just providing consumer goods such as rice, tea, processed food, herbs, medicine, clothing, and sundries from China, but, even more important, maintaining links with the home country through mail and news delivery at both ends, as well as money remittances to family members in China. The heart of their operations was in Hong Kong—a port city protected by the British legal system from Chinese officialdom, yet located near the migrant villages and well integrated into global finance and trade. It served as the base for thousands of migrant businesses: banking houses (*yinhao*), which bought and sold gold and doubled as loan associations; letter offices (*xinju*), which shipped and delivered mail, but also provided letter-writing and currency-remittance services; and public companies (*gongsi*), operated by regional associations, which organized the movement of goods, people, and money between China and various overseas Chinese communities through their branch offices in places such as Singapore, New York, San Francisco, Mexico, Havana, Vancouver, and Lima, Peru.[18]

"Gold Mountain shops" (*Jinshanzhuang*) specialized in service to America. They began to emerge in the 1850s, to take orders and arrange shipments of rice, dry oysters, preserved ginger, water chestnuts, flour, and herbal medicine for Chinese grocery stores and restaurants in San Francisco and across North America. Later they added books, newspapers, and magazines. The original meaning of the word "*zhuang*," used here as "shop," is "hamlet" or "village" and implies the center of a community linked by kinship where commercial activities take place. Many of the "shops" scattered across America operated on the same principle. As their owners and customers often came from the same village, they extended established social ties to the migrant communities in the United States. In doing so, they turned local kinship systems into transnational trading networks. Gold Mountain shops reached wherever the emigrants had dispersed to—even places as forlorn as Warren, Idaho, where even now in our digital age the U.S. Postal Service delivers only twice a week. They offered loans, transferred currencies with favorable and stable exchange rates, and administered savings plans that paid for the living expenses of the migrants' families in China through the disbursement of interest.[19] They delivered to areas in Guangdong Province where no comparable service was provided by the Chinese government. They even provided reading and writing services to their illiterate customers.

Chinese migration contributed to the creation of Chinese wealth on both sides of the Pacific. So when the movement to exclude Chinese from the United States gained momentum in 1880, a group of Hong Kong and Guangdong merchants sent a petition to the Qing government urging strong action to protect the right of Chinese emigration. "We have operated Gold Mountain grocery stores for years and maintained intimate relationships with Chinese stores in San Francisco. We are mutually dependent. Only when Chinese, most of whom are laborers, can leave and enter the United States freely can the grocery business flourish," they wrote. "There are many emigrants from Guangdong who earn the province millions each year because it is easier to make money in America. Virtually every single item used by Chinese laborers in their daily life—silk, clothes, shoes and socks, medicine, oil, liquor, tea, sugar, seafood, sauces—is imported from China. This represents millions of dollars' worth of business. Customs revenue is also huge. Thus, the more Chinese who go to America, the more money Chinese merchants will make. This is not just about people's livelihood; it also affects the national economy."[20]

With the profit motive driving the migration, Chinese business had the incentive to help recruit an ever-larger number of migrants. This, in turn, created more efficient and sophisticated services. When American steamship transpacific passenger service was introduced, for instance, the once excruciating two- to three-month-long passage on crowded sailing ships was cut to two weeks. But the success of migrant businesses ultimately depended on their continued access to home villages in China and close contact with Chinese communities in the United States, and on their ability to ensure that the migrants continued to trust them. How did they prevent a migrant from running off to find another job, or from shopping in non-Chinese-owned stores? What means did they use to ascertain that debts and responsibilities accrued through their numerous business transactions were honored? Since American legal authorities were not willing to enforce Chinese contracts, the merchant elite had an interest in creating a power structure within the Chinese American community that would enforce their deals and maintain their control over the migrants.

CHINESE AMERICAN ASSOCIATIONS

Life in overseas Chinese communities was dominated by associations much like the ones in China. Guangdong Association (Guangdong Huiguan) had long existed in Beijing and Shanghai, for instance, to provide scholars from Guangdong Province who resided there a "home away from home." Similar associations were later created by merchants, and even rural migrants, and existed on the regional, county, village, and clan levels. The structure of overseas associations was not an exact duplicate of those found in home villages, but it nevertheless followed the basic organizational principle of traditional Chinese native-place and kinship organizations.

In their most basic form, Chinese American organizations were collectives of men from the same village and lineage who had come together for friendship and mutual support. Since their association usually revolved around a store or shared rented rooms, such organizations were called *fong*, meaning a house or a room. They gave the newcomers a place to stay, the old-timers a place to receive mail, and everybody a place to purchase supplies, exchange the news from home, and gossip. As more people arrived, a more formal version of the village or surname association with officers and charters emerged, called *tongxianghui*. It provided people from the same village or of the same clan or family name with help caring for the sick, raising funds for famine relief, and purchasing weapons for defense against bandits for relatives at home. These better-structured organizations also ran credit unions based on the rotating credit principle and were, not surprisingly, led by store owners and labor contractors, who could provide jobs and loans.

The most powerful migrant associations in overseas Chinese communities were the *huiguan*. Often called "companies" by white observers, they were formed along geographic, district-based lines. In 1868, *Harper's Monthly* carried a pretty rosy description of one company house in San Francisco:

> The smaller apartments below are occupied by the managers and servants of the Company. The largest room or hall is pasted over with sheets of red paper covered with writing. These contain a record of the names and residence of every member of the Company, and the amount of his subscription to the general fund. The upper story and the attic, with the outbuildings on the upper side, are, it may be, filled with lodgers, nearly all of whom are staying but temporarily, on a visit from the mines, or on their way to or from China. A few sick persons be on their pallets around, and a group here and there discuss [over] a bowl of rice, or smoke and chat together. In the rear is the kitchen. All is quiet, orderly and neat.

The same article remarked on the "Masonic" character of a similar *huiguan* association in New York. "What is apparent on the surface is an earnest of the beneficent character of its work. It furnished, in the first place, a pleasant meeting room, in which to while away a leisure hour. Chinese games are played. The Chinese orchestra practices here; and the poetical contests, which are a feature of Chinese amusements are held in its large meeting rooms."[21]

The *huiguan*'s claimed purpose of existence was to provide services and protection to members, and they did hire lawyers to challenge discriminatory U.S. laws that affected the entire Chinese American community. In 1853, they sent a letter to Congress on behalf of Chinese miners to complain about California's foreign miners' tax.[22] But the *huiguan* were mainly concerned with business issues, reflecting the interests of their governing boards, which were composed entirely of merchants or representatives appointed by merchants.[23] They arbitrated business disputes among members and served as credit and employment agencies. The power of a *huiguan* was based on the number of its members, the size of its home district, and, most important, the clout of its merchant oligarchs and the size of their bank accounts.

The six district *huiguan* in existence in the 1860s in San Francisco formed a federation, which became the most powerful political organ in the Chinese community. The federation was known to the American public under the collective term the "Six Companies" and epitomized *the* overseas Chinese establishment. The leaders of the Six Companies, the *qiaoling*, were usually successful businessmen who spoke some English and often served as liaisons between the Chinese and American communities. Up until 1900 most of them came from the wealthy San-Yi region on the outskirts of Canton and dominated the import-export trade through their business connections in Hong Kong and China.

Chinese associations tried to build a sense of shared community between merchants and average migrants, but membership in them was not voluntary. During the nineteenth century, every Chinese immigrant disembarking on San Francisco pier was automatically registered with the appropriate association based on his surname, kinship, and place of origin, and membership dues were added to the debts he already owed for the passage from China. One of the most important functions of the associations was to act as a general collection and creditor agency for its more affluent members. Migrant brokers and merchants holding credit-ticket debts transferred their contracts to migrants' associations, giving the associations significant control over their fellow countrymen.

No Chinese immigrant was able to purchase a return ticket to China without a certificate issued by his association. It was to be presented to the captain of the Pacific Mail Steamship Company or the Oriental Lines at the time of the ticket purchase, according to an agreement with the Six Companies.[24] The associations even sent their own inspectors to the docks to collect exit permits from the departing Chinese, to ensure, as Rev. Ira M. Condit noted, that "they are not running away from debts or claims against them, and that they have paid the dues."[25] Late in the nineteenth century the departure dues were $9 per passenger, and they went up to $11 early in the twentieth century, constituting a major source of revenue for the associations.[26]

Early on, the associations used force on those who defied their rules. The most common punishment was flogging. Ah Ti, an association leader, was known for cutting off his countrymen's ears, and keeping them chained. Such practices certainly enhanced the credibility of charges that the Six Companies were involved in trafficking coolies, although they stopped once they were exposed by the San Francisco County Grand Jury in 1853.[27]

China's consul-general in San Francisco from 1882 to 1885, Huang Zunxian, registered his overall disappointment with the associations in a report to the Qing throne: "According to my investigation each *huiguan* has comparatively large incomes. Yet they have not provided for the welfare of the membership with this money collected from them. None of the *huiguan* can escape criticism on this point."[28] Among the few social services the *huiguan* did provide was to maintain a cemetery. They paid for medicine and the burial expenses of the poor and donated passage money for the return of the infirm and the indigent elderly to China.[29] For a fee, they also shipped the bones of the deceased that had been temporarily buried in graves in Chinese cemeteries all across the western states back to their native villages in China for final interment. Other than that, their chief role was to facilitate transpacific migration and trade by acting as a link for the moneymaking business networks.

Another type of association that played an important role in policing overseas Chinese communities was the *tong*. *Tongs* were fraternal organizations based on their members' sworn "brotherhood" loyalty. They were patterned after secret societies, the triads, whose original goal in China was the overthrow of the foreign Manchu (Qing dynasty) rule and the restoration of the Ming dynasty. Long persecuted by the Qing government as subversives, they tended to attract elements of the Chinese underworld. In the United States, their function was not that different from that of the *huiguan*, except that, lacking comparable financial and "legitimate" means of dominance, they were more willing to use force in defending their interests.

The first *tong* in America was established in San Francisco in 1848 by members of a triad from southern China as a fraternal organization for laborers. Then, after a secret society in Guangdong Province, the Red Turbans, led a failed revolt in 1855, many of its members arrived in the United States to escape Qing authorities. Some of the *tongs* were labor gangs, controlled by labor contractors who doubled as *dailos* ("big brothers") of the *tongs*. Such labor gangs functioned extremely well as teams, since the *dailos* who supervised them got them their jobs.

The power of the *tongs* was quite marginal at first. It grew only after discrimination and exclusion limited the number of jobs that Chinese immigrants could get, causing antagonism among regional and clan associations, when Chinese community leaders often found themselves unable to count on the Six Companies to resolve the intergroup animosity by peaceful means. The *tongs* maintained trained fighters for the protection of their members—one of the reasons migrants who did not belong to powerful associations sought to join them. Rich merchants with powerful affiliations employed them to fight out their unresolved issues. The associations, in a bid to preserve their public image as nonviolent arbiters of community peace, worked out secret deals, using them to extract profits from gambling, prostitution, and the opium business.

Community peace came to depend on the "division of labor" between the *huiguan* and the *tongs*. *Tongs* acted as arbitrators of right and wrong at the bottom. Merchants joined them to reinforce their position at the top. The resulting alliances were beneficial in diffusing the absolute power of the rich few, as ordinary folks drew strength from membership in a *tong*, in addition to their village, surname, and district associations.

Early in the twentieth century, China's exiled reformer Liang Qichao marveled at the fact that there were more than eighty Chinese associations in San Francisco,[30] and Mary Coolidge, the first American scholar to publish a book on Chinese exclusion, in 1909, noted that "every Chinaman is enmeshed in a thousand other relations with his fellows."[31] The abundance of social and political organizations reflected the many needs of Chinese migrants in the hostile U.S. environment. Unfortunately, it was also an indication of the differences that, when they could not be resolved through peaceful means, and without the recourse of appealing to the American legal and judicial system, led to outbreaks of violence among contending groups. In 1869, a fight broke out between two rival Chinese gangs of railroad workers near Camp Victor in Utah over a $15 debt owed by a member of one *tong* to a member of another. They faced off, firing from every conceivable type of weaponry, until the superintendent of the Central Pacific Railroad intervened to prevent serious bloodshed.[32] Battles by rival groups or factions over business turf or control of illegitimate operations could last for years.

Feuds of this type regularly paralyzed the whole Chinese community, and they threatened to undermine its entire control structure. In a bid to maintain dominance, major associations sought the blessing of the Chinese government and in 1883 formed an umbrella organization, the Chinese Consolidated Benevolent Association (CCBA), which was to act as the ultimate arbiter of internal disputes—the "unofficial mayor's office of the Chinese community." Out of habit, English speakers continued to call the new "mayor's office" the "Chinese Six Companies," while new CCBA organizations soon sprouted in other cities, including Los Angeles, Sacramento, Seattle, Portland, and New York. To gain respectability, they imported scholars from China to act as their presidents. From the 1880s to the end of the Qing dynasty, the San Francisco office, being the most powerful organization of Chinese Americans in the country, invited the Qing consul to San Francisco to sit as a member of its advisory board to further enhance its legitimacy.

Once their power was firmly established, the associations and the Six Companies, dominated by wealthy businessmen, became generally indifferent to the concerns of the average immigrant, and the Chinese American community became clearly divided into a mass of ordinary working people and the wealthy few with institutional power. No organization arose to represent the interests of the laboring class.

INTERNAL CLASS CONFLICT

The interdependent relationship between Chinese merchants and laborers had always existed at a very heavy cost to the latter. "Our country has enormous resources but our people," lamented the reformer Liang Qichao, noting that Chinese migrants needed several years to pay off their debts to the merchants, "would pay such a price to live abroad as slaves to another race."[33] Even more problematic was the "package deal" that came with the credit-ticket system, providing work under Chinese labor subcontractors. Conveniently, such jobs did not require any English-language skills, but in the long run they erected insurmountable barriers for immigrants to break into American society. The system, leaving co-ethnic subcontractors in charge of the workers' living quarters and provisions, made it much more difficult for migrant workers to negotiate an improvement in their working and living conditions.

Chinese workers were perfectly capable of standing up for their rights, but when they worked under Chinese labor subcontractors, they were put into double jeopardy. The employer and subcontractor could act jointly to apply pressure, or they could blame each other for being the source of the laborers' complaints. As any demand on their employers led to conflict with their Chinese overseers first, the workers' frustration in many instances ended up in bloody intra-ethnic disputes. At the large Booth Company salmon cannery in Astoria, Oregon, in June 1875, some 150 Chinese workers refused to work when their Chinese contractor failed to pay their wages on time. The following year, when their demand for higher wages failed, they turned their anger against Chinese foremen.

In 1876, a strike of Chinese workers at the shoe factories Einstein Brothers and Buckingham, Hecht, and Company in San Francisco failed to produce results, and the workers recruited fellow *tong* members to fight it out with the *huiguan* association their contractors belonged to. The conflict shook San Francisco's Chinatown for weeks. It was so bloody that, when the Chinatown police detail sent for reinforcement, the wounded had to be carried away in an express wagon.[34] Similar disputes were regularly referred to by outside observers as "the inscrutable *tong* wars" or "Chinese gangland warfare," but they were in fact class conflicts.

Surrounded by the white labor militancy of the 1870s, Chinese workers were becoming increasingly class conscious. The historian of California's labor movement, Ira B. Cross, remarked that "the Chinese learned to use the strike as a means of exacting higher wages and improved conditions of employment" and that this became "another source of irritation for the white employers."[35] During the labor uprising of 1877 among the New York cigar workers, the majority of whom were Germans and Bohemians, the Cubans, Spanish, and Chinese also walked off the job. "Even Chinamen," the *New York Labor Standard* observed, "have asserted their manhood in this strike" demanding higher wages.[36] In 1884, the Chinese employed in San Francisco's tobacco industry conducted a successful strike for a wage increase and formed a union, Tang Dak Tong, or Hall of Common Virtue. Though a Chinese union—the first formed in North America—it was first and foremost a labor union. It struck later in the same year to demand the dismissal of two Chinese workers who were not members of the union. There were plenty of other instances showing that the Chinese were as class conscious as any other immigrant group, and ready to put their class interests above ethnic solidarity. Sadly, however, they received no support from white labor unions. White leaders of the Cigar Makers' International Union criticized the Tang Dak Tong for beginning "to feel overbearing in their strength" instead of making an attempt to incorporate them.[37] Isolated by the subcontracting system and by the racism and scorn of white unionists, Chinese workers were reduced to fighting uphill battles that usually failed, and the world knew nothing of their struggles.

Chapter 7

The Anti-Chinese Movement

Working-class African Americans had a similar experience when they tried to join the American labor movement, although they were not burdened by the intra-ethnic subcontracting system and informal political structure the way the Chinese were. African Americans came directly face to face with their employers. Nevertheless, American craft unions were reluctant to organize them. The National Labor Union (NLU), founded in 1866 as the first nationwide institution linking wage workers from different locations and from different trades, stated at its founding congress that "the interest of labor are one; there should be not distinction of race or nationality." NLU leaders expressly noted the need to "seek the cooperation of the African race in America."[1] Yet most of the trade unions affiliated with the NLU held on to the policy of excluding African Americans from membership. NLU caved in and followed the policy of exclusion, which African American leaders called "an insult of God and injury to us, and disgrace to humanity." They subsequently formed the separate Colored National Labor Union.[2]

CHINESE MUST GO!

The exclusion of the Chinese would be an even greater disgrace. From 1870 on, virtually every labor newspaper and organization in the

United States supported the ban on Chinese immigration, proclaiming loud and clear that white workers stood not for class solidarity but for racial hostility. They demanded the right to "white men's wages," not the "starving slave wages" fit for the Chinese. Even the International Workingman's Association, which Karl Marx had founded in Europe, passed an anti-Chinese resolution only one year after it had called for "complete political and social equality for all, without distinction of sex, creed, color or condition."[3] African American delegates at the first Colored State Labor Convention in Baltimore in December of 1869, too, had passed a resolution in favor of excluding the Chinese. Many African Americans apparently held the belief that the hordes of Chinese were willing to work for much lower wages, which would force them to labor for "the starvation prices of the beggars in London and the serf[s] of Moscow."[4]

The Knights of Labor, which had been founded in 1869 and was during the 1870s the largest craft union in the country, with fifteen thousand local assemblies representing between seven hundred thousand and 1 million members, initiated new members with the words "On behalf of the toiling millions of the earth, I welcome you to the sanctuary." They even tried to organize farmers, unskilled laborers, women, and Negroes. But they drew the line when it came to accepting the Chinese. An article published in their mouthpiece, the *Journal of United Labor*, maintained that the Chinese "bear the semblance of men, but live like beasts . . . who eat rice and the offal of the slaughter house." It called them "natural thieves" and referred to all Chinese women as "prostitutes."

The Irish-born demagogue Dennis Kearney built a political career riding on the crest of the anti-Chinese sentiment he had stirred up among white laborers. His California Workingmen's Party, organized during the depression of the mid-1870s, called for far-reaching economic reforms, including the destruction of "land monopolies," on the assumption that the rich and the Chinese were engaged in a conspiracy to oppress white workers. In 1877 the party coined the slogan "The Chinese Must Go" and advocated direct acts of violence "to rid the country of cheap Chinese labor as soon as possible and by all means in our power, because it tends still more to degrade labor and aggrandize capital."[5] Kearney's impact on American politics, however, went beyond his ability to galvanize white workers against Chinese labor in that he helped forge Chinese exclusion into a national movement that went beyond class.

Kearney started by rallying unemployed crowds with his supporters on the vacant sandlot opposite the San Francisco city hall. The Sand-Lotters, as they were called, threatened to burn and pillage Chinese quarters. With support from the unemployed, the California Workingmen's Party managed to elect a third of the delegates to California's Second Constitutional Convention, which met in 1878–79, and prescribed a course for the state that embodied most of its anti-Chinese ideology. Kearney's battle cry, "Now we are ready to come right to the scratch, and expel every one of the moon-eyed lepers," resulted in the enactment of stringent laws, which, though obnoxious and revolting to some participants, were deemed necessary to make California less attractive to the Chinese. The new California Constitution of 1879 denied suffrage to the Chinese (along with "idiots," the "insane," and "persons convicted of an infamous crime") and specified that no corporation operating under the laws of California nor "any state, county, municipal, or other public works" would be allowed to employ, directly or indirectly, any Chinese, except in punishment for a crime. It also declared the presence of "foreigners ineligible to become citizens" dangerous to the well-being of the state. The state legislature was directed to pass legislation to enforce their exclusion.[6] The popular opposition to the Chinese was so intense that no Californian in public life dared counter it lest he risk his political career.[7]

The Chinese government, previously indifferent and uninformed about the problems of Chinese in the United States, finally became alarmed. It instructed Chen Lan-pin, the head of the Chinese mission in San Francisco, to retain the law firm McAllister and Bergin for the purpose of challenging the constitutionality of the anti-Chinese legislation passed in California. The case was heard in the United States Circuit Court for the District of California, and, after hearing the evidence, both presiding judges ruled that any state constitution that purported to restrict the rights of the Chinese and not of other classes of aliens was in clear violation of the Burlingame Treaty, the equal protection clause of the Fourteenth Amendment, and the Civil Rights Act of 1870.

In response to this defeat, Californian leaders of the anti-Chinese movement upped the ante: they mounted a well-organized political campaign designed to bring their agenda to the national level. The state legislature placed anti-Chinese lobbyists on the state government payroll and authorized funding for voicing California's grievances in Washington. In reality, however, politicians everywhere had already taken note of Kearney's success and understood the popular appeal of an anti-Chinese agenda. By the mid-1870s all major newspapers and most public figures across the nation supported some sort of restrictions on the Chinese. Even President Ulysses Grant, delivering his sixth annual message to Congress during a lingering depression in 1874, vowed to enforce any regulation that Congress passed to legislate against the evil of the coolie trade. (Later, after his presidency ended, he urged Chinese policy makers during a trip to China to stop "the slavery feature" of Chinese emigration, which he deemed the cause of problems in the United States. In the same breath he also pleaded for restrictions on free emigration.[8])

The Democratic Party, which had championed slavery in the South and lost the civil war, exploited the Chinese problem to build new grassroots strength in the West. In 1870, it took the lead in advocating federal legislation to discourage Chinese immigration. During the 1876 election campaign, Democrats attacked the Republican Party for doing nothing for "our brethren of the Pacific coast" who were exposed "to the incursions of a race not sprung from the same great parent stock."[9] The Republican Party, which traditionally advocated free soil and was dedicated to equality, found it difficult to maneuver around the Chinese issue. Public support for its championship of black rights was waning by the mid-1870s, while the Democrats managed to stage a resurgence by invoking Jacksonian ideas of race, which saw nonwhites as intrinsically inferior and incapable of participating in American democracy. The Republican Party's subsequent retreat led to the end of the liberal Reconstruction era, as the old coalition of abolitionists, free soilers, suffragettes, and freemen gave way to a free and white Democratic America.

The Republicans faced a tight national presidential election in 1876, amidst the continuing economic depression. Being the party in power, they were unable to ignore the demand of their West Coast constituents to take on anti-Chinese positions. Delegates to the party's national convention in Cincinnati agreed to Congress's request to "investigate the effects of the immigration and importation of Mongolians on the moral and material interest of the country."

That same year, a joint congressional committee was sent to California to investigate "the character, extent, and effect of Chinese immigration." The committee was dominated by Californians and was overwhelmingly anti-Chinese. Among its members were the two senators from California, William Piper and Aaron Sargent, both honorary vice presidents of the Anti-Coolie Union of San Francisco. Representing the city of San Francisco before the committee was Frank M. Pixley, a former state attorney general who held that the Chinese were "the inferiors of any race God ever made" and who had publicly declared that he would "gladly stand on Telegraph Hill and see all of them hanged from the yardarms and the ships bearing them burned as they came into the harbor."[10] Among all the hostile testimonies given to the committee against the Chinese by lawyers, judges, doctors, journalists, labor leaders, and self-styled sociologists, the issue of slavery was preeminent. The hearings focused on how the Six Companies conspired to traffic "quasi-slave coolies" into this country. Many equated Chinese immigration with a "modern slave trade system."

INFERIOR AND INASSIMILABLE

By the mid-1870s the American discourse against the Chinese was, on the whole, moving away from economic considerations and toward a more general indictment on cultural and racial grounds. Like the Negroes, the argument went, the Chinese were incapable of attaining the state of civilization of Caucasians. But while the number of Negroes in the country was fixed, the number of Chinese might increase indefinitely, and that had to be stopped.[11]

This racist worldview was supported by new pseudoscientific racial studies, which emerged during the takeoff period in America's economic growth and rapid industrial transformation. Equating change and technological innovation with progress, America's new bourgeois industrial elite found in race a convenient justification for its unabashed sense of accomplishment. Until 1850, most American intellectuals subscribed to the concept of monogenesis—a belief, in religious terms, that all humans were the children of Adam and Eve and therefore equal (as the Constitution had declared in 1776). The monogenesists were well aware of racial differences in American society, but they considered them a function of environmental variances and were thus confident that the reordering of the environment could alter humans both physically and culturally. The idea of the melting pot grew from this point of view.[12] By the 1850s, however, a number of ethnologists, phrenologists, craniologists, and linguists had stepped to the fore to pander to the need of America's confident new elite to project itself as somewhat more elevated than the rest of mankind.

As early as 1862, in a report to the American Medical Association (AMA) entitled *Chinese Immigration and the Physiological Causes of the Decay of a Nation*, Dr. Arthur B. Stout presented his list of "hereditary diseases" known to exist in China—"phthisis or consumption, scrofula, syphilis, mental alienation and epidemic diseases"—and warned that they posed the main threat to American society. In 1876, the president of the AMA himself, world-renowned gynecologist J. Marion Sims, alleged that "Chinese slaves" used for the purpose of prostitution bred "moral and physical pestilence" and that "even boys eight and ten years old have been syphilized by these degraded wretches."[13]

With the American scientific community given to such pseudo-theorizing, it is small wonder that the *New York Tribune* would sound an alarmist note in 1870, when the columnist John Swinton wrote, "Can we afford to permit the transfusion into the national veins of the blood more debased than any we have known? Can we afford to offer the opportunity for this sort of mongrelism?"[14] By 1877, Edwin R. Meade could stand confidently in front of the crowd assembled for the annual meeting of the Social Science Association of America and insist that the Chinese—only fit to be coolies on account of the size of their brain—would also be rejected from participating in free government on account of their social characteristics.

Racial arguments for the exclusion of the Chinese from the United States—be they genetic, medical, anthropological, or ethnological—were but one side of the multifaceted attack launched against the Chinese on the eve of exclusion legislation. Even more insidious in the long run was the argument that the Chinese themselves did not want to be part of the American nation—that by coming to the United States under contracts to work for a limited number of years they demonstrated that they had no intention of staying in America and integrating into its society. "Sojourners"—a term used by Senator John Conness of California to describe the nature of Chinese residence in America during congressional debates over the Fourteenth Amendment, in 1865—would stick and remain the label for the Chinese experience in the United States for almost an entire century. The proponents of the sojourner theory claimed as evidence to support it the fact that 233,136 Chinese arrived in San Francisco between 1848 and 1876, while 92,273 left through the same port during the same period. Even more damning was the fact that few Chinese who came to the United States brought their wives. The gender gap among the Chinese in the United States in 1870 was huge; for every woman there were 12.75 men.[15]

But most of the Chinese lived in California and in a few other even less developed territories of the western frontier. Before the completion of the railroads, this was a predominantly male society. Chinese were not the only group who went to the Wild West planning to make money quickly and return to family life in an environment better suited for it. Also, the fact that they were now accused of a sojourner mentality was ironic, because they had previously been sought as laborers precisely on the assumption that not many would stay after their contracts expired. The most enthusiastic proponents of Chinese labor had even claimed that returning laborers would take back, in addition to saved capital, the seeds of Christianity and a taste for American goods. The flow of Chinese workers back and forth across the Pacific had been expected to have short- and long-range benefits for both nations.

Immigrants typically do not settle down permanently until they find conditions to support a family. Most European immigrant groups also delayed starting families. Irish and Italian immigrants, too, had high return rates. A *Harper's* magazine article in 1889 observed that immigrants from southern Italy almost always came with the intention of returning to Italy as soon as they gathered "enough out of the plenty of this country to suffice for their simple wants at home."[16] Between 1910 and 1914 as many as 75 percent went home. The mining and railroad jobs that early Chinese immigrants performed were hardly conducive to setting up a family, but by 1870 the number of

Chinese children in California—198 girls and 192 boys, 283 of them born in California—indicated that the Chinese were slowly beginning to establish families and that they were planning to stay.

This trend, however, would not be supported by white American society. Chinese women in California had long excited much controversy. At first very few women arrived with the first gold miners, and those who did were mostly prostitutes. During the late 1850s almost 85 percent of the Chinese women in San Francisco were engaged in prostitution. By 1870, however, as the number of Chinese women slowly increased, it is estimated that half were not. Many of the Chinese women thought to be prostitutes were in fact merchants' wives or domestic servants, shoe binders, seamstresses, laundresses, or gardeners.[17] Nevertheless, the growing anti-Chinese sentiment portrayed all Chinese women as degenerate and dangerous on account of their "hazardous potential of infusing foul, contagious and poisonous disease in Anglo-Saxon blood."[18] This was the kind of toxic opinion mongering that entered into the California statutes of 1870 (all Chinese men were "inveterate coolies," all Chinese women "degenerate prostitutes") and was used by Congressman Horace F. Page to push through a resolution in 1875 prohibiting importation of Chinese women "for immoral purposes."[19] A 1877 report to the congressional Joint Special Committee to Investigate Chinese Immigration prepared by a specially appointed California senate committee included an "Address to the People of the United States upon the Evils of Chinese Immigration" and charged that Chinese prostitutes were cheaper and more immoral than their white counterparts, "having not the decency to refuse the patronage of young boys."[20]

The Page Act, which also prohibited importation of Chinese coolies, passed without opposition, but it had almost no impact on Chinese male immigration, while it certainly proved an effective measure in limiting the entry of Chinese women. From 1876 to 1882, every Chinese woman traveling to the United States was interviewed by zealous officials: first in Hong Kong, by the representatives of the British colonial government, and then at the point of disembarkment, by the U.S. Port Authority. The aggressive enforcement of the Page Act made most Chinese wives and daughters reluctant to go through the process.[21] Between 1876 and 1882 emigration of Chinese women to the United States decreased by 68 percent compared to the previous seven-year period, while it increased to other popular migration destinations, such as Singapore, Southeast Asia, and Hawaii, at the same time.[22]

NATIONAL POLITICS AND CHINESE EXCLUSION

Democratic Party candidate Samuel Tilden won the popular vote in the 1876 presidential election but was one electoral college vote short of victory. Through a compromise, Republican candidate Rutherford B. Hayes assumed the presidency—in exchange for the end of Reconstruction programs and the federal government's role in protecting the rights of African Americans in the South. With the "Negro problem" thus off the front burner, the focus was squarely on the Chinese. The federal courts became quite forward in their decisions, ruling in 1878 (in *re Ah Yup*) that the Chinese were not white—based on scientific evidence, common knowledge, and congressional intent.[23] The momentum of the national campaign against Chinese immigration could no longer be stopped.

In January 1879, the House Committee on Education and Labor, which was handling all anti-Chinese initiatives and legislation, recommended an anti-Chinese resolution in the form of a "fifteen passenger bill," that would restrict to fifteen the number of Chinese passengers, male or female, that any master of a U.S. vessel could take aboard with the intent of bringing to the United States. It passed easily, but President Hayes vetoed it. "Experience has shown that the trade of the East is the key to national wealth and influence," he explained, and "the policy which we now propose to adopt must have a direct tendency to repel Oriental nations from us and to drive their trade and commerce into more friendly lands."[24] At the same time, however, mindful of the fact that he had only narrowly retained Republican control of the White House in the disputed 1876 election, he was quick to express his frustration with the failure of these "strangers" and "sojourners" to integrate into American life, and he promised to attempt to renegotiate the Burlingame Treaty, which the "fifteen passenger bill" would have violated.[25]

In face of another close election in 1880, the Republican Party took aim at Chinese immigration to win critical Californian votes. Its platform included the position that unrestricted immigration of the

Chinese was a matter of "grave concern" requiring federally imposed limits—so long as they were "just, humane and reasonable." Within a decade, the political will toward the Chinese had shifted to the degree that pressure was now put on the Chinese government to agree to Chinese immigration restrictions.

When renegotiations of the Burlingame Treaty started, it turned out that the Chinese side, although angered by the indignity imposed by American hostility, was not that concerned about its emigrants. Historically, the Qing government had ignored the overseas Chinese, who in its view had broken its laws and ethical codes by emigrating. Besides, as lowly merchants and laborers, they were hardly deserving of imperial protection.[26] When informed of the massacre of thousands of Chinese in the Dutch East Indies in 1740, for instance, the Qing official who received the information replied that they had deserved it. The emperor's response was that "the court would not want to hear from them."[27] This indifference had made the coolie trade, which had over three decades carried off hundreds of thousands of Chinese laborers under varying degrees of coercion, pressure, and false promise, possible in the first place.

It was only during the economically troublesome 1870s, when some Chinese officials realized that China's difficulties could be ameliorated by donations from overseas communities, that the Qing government decided to pay more attention to its emigrants. The first Qing minister to the United States was sent in 1878.[28] The first diplomatic protest regarding the treatment of Chinese in the United States was lodged in 1880, in response to the anti-Chinese riot in Denver, where white men broke windows and doors in the Chinese quarters, shouting "Kill the Chinese! Kill the damned heathens! Burn their houses! Run them out!" One Chinese was killed, many others were brutally beaten, and property with an estimated value of $53,655.69 was destroyed. As the final straw, all the Chinese were taken by the police to the city jail "for safety." The U.S. government refused to press for the arrests of the guilty, claiming limited federal power over local issues, and it refused to compensate the victims.[29] With China's power weakened, the United States could afford to ignore its official protest, prompting a Chinese scholar to comment wryly, "If a single American was treated in China as were the victims of the anti-Chinese riots at Denver, the United States would send 100,000 missionaries to civilize the heathen."[30]

In reality, at the peak of the American anti-Chinese movement, the Qing government was too distracted by its internal economic crisis and external colonial infringement to handle problems on the American continent. Its top priority was maintaining China's territorial integrity, and to that end, in fact, it hoped to get U.S. help in resolving its dispute with Japan over the question of Korea. It was not in a position to quibble with the U.S. government over the treatment of Chinese under American jurisdiction. It easily succumbed to pressure to modify the Burlingame Treaty, as long as the American side agreed that the exclusion of the Chinese not be total. The resulting Angell Treaty of 1880 conceded to the United States government the right to "regulate, limit or suspend" but "not absolutely prohibit" the "coming and residence" of Chinese laborers. It also stated that "Chinese subjects, whether proceeding to the United States as teachers, students, merchants, or from curiosity, together with their body and household servants, and Chinese laborers who are now in the United States shall be allowed to go and come of their own free will and accord."[31]

The highest-ranking Chinese official, Li Hongzhang, sent a memorandum to the U.S. government, insisting on the maintenance of the spirit of the Burlingame Treaty, but the Qing government was interested only in saving face and protecting the classes of people who were of consequence in its own social hierarchy. The plight of Chinese laborers did not matter much. The Qing government's willingness to de-link immigration issues from trade paved the way for the U.S. exclusion of Chinese laborers.

CHINESE LABOR EXCLUSION ACT

The Chinese Exclusion Act, when it was passed by the U.S. Congress in 1882, honored the main provisions of the Angell Treaty. It suspended the entry of Chinese laborers, both skilled and unskilled, to the United States for ten years but exempted merchants, scholars, teachers, and officials from such restrictions. It also specified that state and federal courts were not allowed to naturalize the Chinese.

At the same time, the American government extended a welcoming hand to Europe. European immigration to the United States reached 5.2 million in the 1880s and surged to 8.2 million in the first decade of the twentieth century. Between 1882—the year the Chinese laborers were barred from immigrating—and 1914—the year World War I broke the pattern, approximately 20 million European immigrants came to the United States. When the Statue of Liberty was dedicated in 1886, Cuban revolutionary José Martí wrote, "Irishmen, Poles, Italians, Czechs, Germans freed from tyranny or want—all hail the monument of Liberty because to them it seems to incarnate their own uplifting." That year 334,203 European immigrants arrived in the United States.[32]

The Chinese Exclusion Act marked a revolutionary shift in the course of American immigration history. The pluralistic ideal of a melting pot (a cauldron, rather, in which the immigrants would be cleansed of their foreign ways), already challenged by the presence of African and Native Americans in the country when it first attempted to define a vision of itself, now came with a lid. It brought to a close the era of free immigration and signaled that the new nation was prepared to enact exclusionary legislation in order to maintain white racial purity. The Chinese had the distinction of being the first nonwhite immigrant group in the United States singled out for exclusion. (Native and African Americans already in the country would be either isolated on the plantations or corralled into reservations, in an internal exclusion of sorts.) The exclusion of the Chinese forecast the way in which other undesirable immigrant groups would be dealt with in the future. Japanese immigration would eventually be blocked by the "Gentlemen's Agreement" between the U.S. and Japanese governments in 1908. The Immigration Act of 1917, also known as the Asiatic Exclusion Act, excluded all other Asians—from Arabia to Asiatic Russia and the Polynesian Islands. Filipinos, being colonial subjects of the United States, were for a time allowed entry, until the passage of the Tydings-McDuffie Act in 1934.[33]

The policy of immigrant exclusion was eventually extended to certain less desirable white immigrant groups from southern and eastern Europe as well, when the Anglo-Saxon majority felt threatened by further immigration. The National Origins Act, passed in 1924, set future immigration quotas based on 2 percent of each national group's numbers in the 1890 U.S. census—before the eastern and southern European migration took place. It was a victory for American nativism, and the triumph of the doctrine of Anglo conformity, which unabashedly used immigration laws to shape the country into the kind of nation Anglo-Saxon Americans wanted.

PART II

The Transnational Ghetto:
Life During the Exclusion Era
(1882–1945)

Chapter 8

White Dominance at Home
and Abroad

The period between the passage of the Chinese Exclusion Act in 1882 and the onset of World War II is usually known to Chinese Americans as the Exclusion Era or the Silent Decades. During this time the idea first brandished by the anti-Chinese labor agitators, that the Chinese were inassimilable, was debated, denied, and fought over by Chinese and non-Chinese Americans alike. Those who most fervently espoused this idea helped to make it true, by furthering racist exclusion and harassment of Chinese Americans and their banishment to ghettos. Those who most avidly argued for Chinese integration in America, including many second-generation Chinese Americans and sympathetic intellectuals, found themselves cut off from the majority in the community and, ironically, often buying into some version of the anti-Chinese view. But the most ironic thing about the supposedly Silent Decades is that throughout this time the marginalized Chinese vociferously carried on with all kinds of activism—cultural, political, and economic—in a manner that is quintessentially American and that belied their image as inassimilable or silent.

"OPEN SEASON" ON THE CHINESE

The Chinese Exclusion Act was the capstone of years of anti-Chinese agitation, but it did not end it. The original bill introduced by Senator John Franklin Miller of California, which was to have put a twenty-year embargo on the admission of Chinese laborers, was approved by the Senate and passed by the House of Representatives in late March 1882, but even as it awaited the president's signature, the Representative Council of Trades and Labor Unions (Trades Assembly) was moving to take the matter into its own hands. As soon as President Arthur vetoed Miller's bill on April 4, the Trades Assembly voted to call a convention of "trade and labor unions, local assemblies of the Knights of Labor, Grangers, Caucasians, and all organizations of a bona fide labor character" to "unitedly deliver this Coast from Chinese competition."[1]

The West Coast was in an uproar. At parades and mass rallies in several towns in California, President Arthur was hanged in effigy and burned at the stake. From the East, New York Tammany boss John Kelly and Chicago Mayor Carter Harrison raised objections to the presidential veto; the New York Central Labor Union and the Washington Federation of Labor condemned it. The Philadelphia boss of the Knights of Labor, John Kirchener, assembled ten thousand workers to protest. Milwaukee cigar makers marched with a banner that read "Coolie Labor the Curse of Civilization."[2]

By April 17, Congress was considering the revised exclusion bill, introduced by California's veteran anti-Chinese legislator, Horace F. Page, which reduced the length of exclusion from twenty to ten years. The bill passed Congress, but while the Senate was deliberating its vote, the Trades Assembly convention met in San Francisco on April 24. Three days later, on April 27, the convention established a permanent structure, the League of Deliverance, which was to operate in the area of the North American continent west of the Rockies, from the Mexican border to British Columbia. It would be open to all persons eligible for U.S. citizenship who were willing to pledge their honor not to "employ or patronize Chinese directly or indirectly" or "knowingly patronize . . . any person who does employ Chinese."[3] The league planned to finance itself by a 10 cent initiation fee for individual members and adherence-to-the-pledge cards issued to shops upon inspection for a fee of $1 a month. More important, it planned to divide the Pacific West into districts and order all Chinese to depart from them within a specified period of time. In the case of noncompliance, the districts would be declared "dangerous," and it would become "the duty of the Executive Committee to call upon the League to abate such danger by force. This abatement to be done with as little violence as is compatible with a certain enforcement of the order. That such course be adopted in regard to every district until no Chinese remains on our shores."[4]

A day later, on April 28, the Senate passed the Chinese Exclusion Act with a vote of 32 to 15, with 29 abstentions. Eight days later, on May 6, President Arthur signed it. It is commonly understood that he did so because another veto would have spelled the end of his political career. The role of the government and national leaders, he was told by Senator James Blaine, was to preserve order, not justice. His party needed the western vote and had convinced him that the bill was an expedient way to put an end to the growing agitation of the leaders of the labor movement.[5]

Needless to say, the anti-Chinese agitators were not appeased. The Chinese Exclusion Act was to temporarily stop the Chinese from immigrating; they wanted the Chinese completely and permanently eliminated from the country. An article in the union magazine *Truth* called the exclusion law "practically worthless" in ridding the state of the Chinese and argued, "Whatever California wants done, she must do herself."[6]

It was as though the Senate vote had sent a signal to the vigilantes for an "open season" on the Chinese. The League of Deliverance members unleashed their "abatement campaign" to drive the Chinese from mines, ships, and lumber camps. Employers in San Francisco were told to replace Chinese workers with white union members.[7] General John Bidwell, owner of a soap factory in Chico, was forced to fire all Chinese employees under threat of boycott and burning.[8]

Mob violence and forced expulsion of the Chinese from their homes followed. In the next few years, there were thirty-four incidents in California alone, and many more throughout the western states. Millions of dollars' worth of property was plundered and burned in mining towns all across Oregon, Washington, Colorado, Nevada, South Dakota, and even Alaska. White laborers at the coal mine owned by Union Pacific in

Rock Springs, Wyoming, had been complaining of the company's hiring and "favoring" of the Chinese ever since the Chinese were first hired in 1875, although the Chinese earned less and had to pay more for services, such as housing, provided by Union Pacific. A minor work assignment dispute on September 2, 1885, which had led to blows between a few Chinese and white miners, ignited a major riot. White mobs, egged on by members of the Knights of Labor, marched toward the Chinese workers, blocked all escape routes, and began to fire at them. As the un-armed Chinese fled, white vigilantes shot them down; others searched them for valuables. Homes of seventy-nine Chinese were set ablaze and the bodies of many of the dead and wounded thrown into the flames.

When the final reckoning was made, it was found that twenty-eight Chinese had been killed, fifteen wounded, and that dozens were miss-ing; a hundred houses were burned down.[9] Hundreds of survivors had fled into the surrounding desert. The National Guard had to be called in to maintain peace. But the team appointed by Wyoming authorities to investigate the massacre was dominated by members of the Knights of Labor. Witnesses were intimidated and the grand jury brought no indictment. In the words of Chinese diplomats, the process was turned into a burlesque. Knights of Labor leader Terence Powderly, however, pointed the finger at the government for failing to enforce the 1882 exclusion act. "Had steps been taken to observe the law," he charged, "the workmen of Rock Springs would not have steeped their hands in the blood of a people whose very presence in this country is contami-nation."[10] The federal government initially refused all responsibility, but President Cleveland was eventually persuaded "solely from senti-ment of generosity and pity" but not under "obligation of treaty or principle of international law" to indemnify the Chinese with a mere $150,000.[11]

Coal mine towns throughout Washington Territory drew inspira-tion from Rock Springs. Public meetings were held in town after town to applaud the violence and draw plans to drive their own Chinese out. Less than a month after labor activists organized an anti-Chinese con-gress in Seattle, the Chinese section of the city was burned down. Of-ficials in Tacoma, Washington, ordered the city's Chinese residents to leave by November 3, 1885, when a riotous mob of several hundred—led by the mayor, the sheriff, and several judges—invaded the Chinese community. Evicted from their homes and businesses during a heavy rainstorm, the Chinese were "peacefully escorted" out of the city to the train station, where they spent the night without shelter before being put on freight trains to Portland, Oregon. Two men died from exposure and one woman went insane as a result of her ordeal.[12] Two days later, the Chinese settlement in Tacoma was burned to the ground. The "Tacoma model" was adopted by many others. In Carbon County, Utah, the Chinese were herded into a boxcar. After the doors were fastened, the car was sent down the railroad tracks, and, as a local eyewitness said, "They have not been seen from that day to this."

The federal government hardly intervened to stop the vigilante actions, claiming it had no jurisdiction over local affairs. In the few cases when it clearly did have jurisdiction—the cases that spanned two or more states—it still did nothing, claiming lack of funds. In the infamous Snake River massacre of 1887, thirty-one Chinese miners who had been mining gold in Hells Canyon on the Oregon side of the river were brutally killed by a group of white robbers and horse thieves. The murder was discovered by friends of the murdered miners who had been mining at a camp upriver. Led by Lee She, they had come down by boat to pay Chea Po and his group a visit and instead found tools, blankets, and cooking utensils scattered on the sand bank, Chea Po's boat destroyed, with holes chopped into its bottom, and three bodies still straddling the riverbank. Horror-stricken, Lee She and his companions sped downriver as fast as they could and reported the crime to the authorities in Lewiston, Idaho. But the murders had been committed on the Oregon side of the canyon and had to be prosecuted there. Oregon authorities claimed that the criminals had fled across the river into Idaho, so they had no jurisdiction to pursue them. Idaho was still a territory, not a state, and the sheriff of Lewiston, though willing to arrest the guilty, claimed they were in Oregon, and he had no authority to make an arrest there. No pursuit took place until the Chinese consul-general in San Francisco offered a reward of $1,000 for the murderers' apprehension and asked the Sam Yup Company, to which the victims had belonged, to dispatch an agent and hire a special investigator—a U.S. commissioner—to track them down. Even then, it took a letter to the secretary of state by the Chinese minister to the United States, and several letters between the State Department and officials in Oregon and Idaho, before any authority resolved to act.

When, almost eleven months after the massacre, four of the seven accused murderers were finally caught, one turned state's witness and blamed everything on the three absent members of the group; the other three were found not guilty. George S. Craig, who owned the cabin in Hells Canyon that the killers had used as the staging ground for their attack on the miners and who had attended the trial, told an interviewer, "I guess if they had killed 31 white men, something would have been done about it, but none of the jury knew the Chinamen or cared much about it, so they turned the men loose."[13] One of the perpetrators, Robert McMillan, who had just turned sixteen, died of diphtheria soon after the trial and on his deathbed confessed to his father that all seven men were guilty, but not a single person was ever sentenced for the crime. McMillan's confession and all documents pertaining to the trial were filed away in the county offices in Joseph, Oregon, where the trial took place, and disappeared. They were discovered accidentally almost a century later when a new county clerk undertook the reorganization of the office and found them locked away in a safe.[14]

"They call it exclusion; but it is not exclusion, it is extermination," is how Chan Kiu Sing, a Los Angeles social commentator and police court interpreter described what was happening to the Chinese in the West.[15] As a result of the "open season," most Chinese decided to leave small and isolated areas of the western frontier and move into larger cities, where a concentration of other Chinese could offer some protection. It is arguably during this period that the established Chinese communities on the West Coast in cities such as San Francisco, Los Angeles, and Sacramento became entrenched as permanently segregated Chinatowns. Other Chinese refugees from the hostile Wild West set up Chinatowns in metropolitan areas in the Midwest and on the East Coast, such as in Chicago, St. Louis, Boston, Philadelphia, and New York. "Every Saturday night, we never knew whether we would live to see the light of day," a Chinese who once operated a laundry near a mining camp recalled after he moved to New York. "Saturday was the night for the miners to get drunk. They would force their way into our shop, wrest the clean white bundles from the shelves and trample the shirts which we so laboriously finished." One time, after a miner accidentally hit his face against the flat side of an iron, he "came back with a mob who ransacked our shop, robbed us of the

$360 that was our combined savings and set fire to the laundry. We were lucky to escape with our lives, so we came east."[16] Between 1880 and 1890 the Chinese population of New York almost tripled, to 2,048.[17]

While American law enforcers kept turning a blind eye to anti-Chinese crime, the lawmakers took additional legal steps to curtail the Chinese population in the country. A federal court ruling in 1884 denied the wives of Chinese laborers the right to join them in the United States, thereby reducing many Chinese laborers in America who already had wives in China to a life of virtual bachelorhood. The situation was further aggravated by the Scott Act of 1888, which prohibited the return to the United States after they visited China of Chinese laborers properly certified as U.S. residents. The law affected at least twenty thousand Chinese who were visiting China when it was passed; some six hundred were already on their way back to the United States and were not allowed to land. One of the six hundred was Chae Chan Ping, a resident of California from 1875 to 1887, who had obtained a return certificate before departing for China.[18] He returned to San Francisco one week after the Scott Act took effect, and the port officials declared his certificate annulled. Chea took his case to court, backed by the Six Companies, which raised $100,000 on his behalf. He argued that his expulsion and the Scott Act violated earlier treaties between the United States and China. The Supreme Court agreed but ruled that Congress had the power to act as the final arbiter when it came to the nation's borders.

The decision gave the nod to the U.S. immigration authorities to detain all Chinese ship passengers arriving in San Francisco in a two-story shed at the Pacific Steamship Company wharf until their papers were examined. Often as many as five hundred were locked up in the small building. Upon visiting the facility, the Reverend Ira M. Condit wrote, "Merchants, laborers, are all alike penned up, like a flock of sheep, in a wharf-shed, for many days, and often weeks, at their own expense, and are denied all communication with their own people while the investigation of their cases moves its slow length along."[19] Newspapers described the conditions as "worse than for jailed prisoners."[20] But an even worse long-term consequence was that it effectively sentenced the Chinese laborers who wished to remain in the United States to a lifelong separation from their families. Combined

with the antimiscegenation laws adopted by most states to prevent interracial marriage, the additional legal measures were clearly intended
to ensure the disappearance of the Chinese from American soil after
one generation.

White labor kept pace with the legislature by turning the screw a
notch tighter to permanently force the Chinese out of the U.S. job
market. Through their abatement campaign and certification of no-
Chinese businesses, the Knights of Labor and the League of Deliverance were forcing all California employers to replace Chinese workers
with white union members.[21] Their effort was successful because
white employers did not want to arouse the anger of the well-organized
white working class. By 1910, the Chinese completely disappeared
from the labor market. They were forced to retreat to self-employment
in laundry and restaurant trades or to doing domestic work for white
patrons. Yet even there they were not left alone. In Utah, miners organized a boycott of Chinese laundries and restaurants as they campaigned to end all Chinese employment and prohibit the sale of
Chinese-made goods.

In Butte, Montana, which by 1890 had one of the largest Chinese
communities in the Rocky Mountains, the Trades and Labor Assembly, made up of more than thirty labor unions, endorsed a boycott of
all Chinese and Japanese restaurants, tailor shops, and washhouses in
January 1897, with a notice in a local newspaper that declared, "American manhood and American womanhood must be protected from
competition with these inferior races."[22] The labor press called Chinese laundries "pest houses" and Chinese laundrymen "leporous [sic]
and mouth-spraying." Wagons bearing pictures of Chinese laundrymen spitting foul fluids over white shirts were driven around town.
Banners advertising the boycott hung all across the city. So did banners calling for the boycott of white businesses that employed Chinese. "Members and Friends of Organized Labor," announced one,
"Notice is hereby given that Mrs. Geo. Althoff, proprietress of the
Will Lodging House, defies organized labor. Guide Yourself Accord-
ingly. By order of Silver Bow Trades & Labor Assembly." The Will
House was employing one Chinese cook.[23]

Some of the most enthusiastic perpetrators of the boycott were
Butte's white women, who accused Chinese men of taking jobs away
from Irish laundry women. They picketed Chinese stores, and stopped

other customers from entering.[24] Butte's business leaders supported them because, as *Home Industry*, the publication of the Butte Chamber of Commerce, claimed, "the girls of our town were unable to secure employment of any kind, except prostitution." Getting rid of the Chinese laundries was hailed as a way "toward giving employment to the unemployed white girls of Butte."[25] In Helena, Montana, a local newspaper editorial claimed that "Mongolian hordes" were preventing "Helena women from making a living washing clothes."[26]

There were still white employers in the West who wanted to use Chinese labor despite the abatement drives, the boycotts, and the exclusion, but usually for temporary work as migrant farmhands, in fish canneries, on construction crews, or doing punishing menial work at isolated sites where they would remain unseen by white workers. In 1883 Harmony Borax Works hired Chinese to work in its mine at the bottom of Death Valley in California's high desert, where temperatures easily hover around 123 degrees during the day and fall below freezing at night. (Death Valley is one of the hottest places on earth, having attained the second-highest temperature ever recorded, 134 degrees, in 1913. It claimed the lives of many gold rushers who tried to cross it, giving it its name.) The Harmony Works' Chinese gained notoriety for operating twenty-mule-team wagons and for the fact that nobody but them (and the mules) was capable of withstanding the conditions. But such job opportunities were rare and the numbers of Chinese in the country were declining. Between 1880 (roughly when Chinese exclusion began) and 1930, the Chinese population in the United States dropped from 105,465 to 74,954. (At one point, in 1920, it fell to as low as 61,639.) During those same decades, some 28 million Europeans immigrated to the United States.

Regardless of the facts, the anti-Chinese forces continued to claim that the Chinese were still coming into the country by the thousands, infiltrating its borders from Mexico and Canada. In 1883, the *Labor Enquirer* from Denver and the *Truth* from San Francisco published articles about Chinese smuggling prostitutes into the United States through Victoria, British Columbia. The unions continued to put pressure on the government to pass ever-more stringent laws. In 1892, Congressman Thomas J. Geary of California introduced a bill (the so-called Geary Act) that, when passed, extended the Chinese Exclusion Act of 1882 for another ten years. It also required the Chinese living in the United States to carry a certificate of residence, without which they were subject to deportation or imprisonment and a year of hard labor. The anti-Chinese lobby was still not satisfied. In 1897 the well-known anti-Chinese agitator and former leader of the Knights of Labor Terence V. Powderly was appointed commissioner general of immigration and immediately set out to check the flow of the Chinese by plugging all the "loopholes." His zeal extended to attempts to stop the "exempted classes," such as merchants and students, from coming into the country, and even to exclude Chinese diplomats.

Powderly's successor, Frank P. Sargent, a onetime official of the Locomotive Firemen, tried to outdo him. Miss Luella Miner, a Presbyterian missionary to China who was bringing two Chinese students admitted to Oberlin College in 1901, had occasion to do battle with both. Her protégés Fay Chi Ho and Kung Hsiang Hsi had risked their lives to save American missionaries during the Boxer crisis and carried student certification from China's viceroy Li Hongzhang himself, but they were stopped upon arrival in San Francisco. After various interventions, Powderly allowed them to remain in detention "as a special act of executive clemency" (rather than being sent back on the next ship), and Miss Miner visited the infamous facility several times, of which she wrote in the *Independent*: "Suicide is common, death is not infrequent."[27] She pulled strings to have the two students moved to a hospital and have them released, but they remained detained on the West coast for a whole year. Then, after she took them to Oberlin via Canada, they were detained again in North Dakota. This time it was Sargent who insisted that his bureau was "at a loss to suggest any means by which the two students . . . could be afforded relief."[28] It was only after many interventions, involving the president of the United States, the secretary of state, and the secretary of the treasury, that the two finally arrived at Oberlin in 1903. One of them told Miss Miner: "I am glad that the Kingdom of Heaven is not so hard to enter as America." The other wrote: "Now I know that it is easier for a camel to go through the eye of a needle than for a Chinaman to enter the United States."[29] Kung Hsiang Hsi would later become minister of industry and commerce (1928–31) and minister of finance (1933–44) of the Republic of China, and governor of the Central Bank of China (1933–45).

In 1902, in Boston, Sargent's officers raided a Chinese party of 250 without a warrant and arrested them all. While in prison, all 250 were humiliated, many received physical injuries, and 50 were deported, although in the end only 5 were proven not to have had legal resident status. One of the arrested was a student, Feng Xiawei, with perfectly legal status, who wrote a book about his unhappy experience in America. After he returned to China, Feng committed suicide in front of the American consulate in Shanghai in an act of protest and became a martyr of the growing anti-American sentiment in China. Thousands of Chinese across the country held demonstrations in his memory.[30]

In an even more notorious incident, Sargent ordered the strip search of members of the Chinese delegation arriving for the Louisiana Purchase Exposition in St. Louis in 1904, which was headed by His Royal Highness Prince P'u Lun. The "Bertillon system of identification," lauded as a "scientific way of identifying criminals by the accurate measurement and inspection of the naked body" and developed in France to facilitate police classification of hardened criminals and spotting of repeat offenders, had been adopted by the U.S. Immigration Bureau in 1903.[31] The bureau used it indiscriminately on incoming Chinese merchants, students, and travelers, claiming suspicion they might be laborers. Prince P'u Lun was cordially received at the White House by the president of the United States, yet Sargent treated his delegation of official emissaries of the Qing throne, as the *New York Times* pointed out, "practically as intending criminals." Sargent's action created so much ill will in China that it ignited a nationwide anti-American movement and boycott of American goods.[32]

By this time the U.S. government clearly didn't care what the Chinese thought. In 1901, a year before the Geary Act was to expire, the head of the American Federation of Labor Samuel Gompers, had testified in Congress in support of yet another ten-year renewal of the Chinese Exclusion Act. The essay he submitted as "evidence" was entitled "Some Reasons for Chinese Exclusion: Meat vs. Rice. American Manhood Against Asiatic Coolieism. Which Shall Survive?" The Chinese Exclusion Act was extended by another ten years in 1902, but the anti-Chinese pressure continued to mount. In 1904, with only minimal debate, Congress finally passed a resolution to extend the exclusion of the Chinese indefinitely.

"COLORED PROBLEM" CONTAINED

Chinese exclusion represented only one phase of America's coordinated attempt to resolve its "colored" minority problem. In 1876, the two political parties had struck a historic compromise—giving the presidency to the Republican candidate, Rutherford B. Hayes, in exchange for leaving the South in the hands of the Democratic Party. The move ended the radical Reconstruction programs aimed at establishing economic and political equality for African Americans after the civil war, which were becoming increasingly unpopular and difficult to enforce. The U.S. government withdrew its troops from the South and tacitly abandoned federal responsibility for enforcing the civil rights of freed slaves. The gains African Americans had made during Reconstruction (1865–77) were quickly dismantled as Jim Crow laws began to proliferate throughout the South, systematically codifying the subordinate position of African Americans in U.S. society.

By 1910, the system of legalized segregation and disenfranchisement that predated the civil war was fully in place once again in every state of the former Confederacy. In addition, as if the laws were not brutal enough, white supremacists regularly resorted to lynching to "keep the Negroes in their place." By the end of the nineteenth century, there were on average more than two lynchings a week somewhere in the South. They were often witnessed by huge mobs, which, on occasion, burned the victims alive. In one incident in 1921, white onlookers waited around while a black man burned sufficiently for his bones to be picked up as souvenirs.[33]

As for the Native Americans, they had been driven off the western plains for good after the civil war, and the remaining tribes were forced onto reservations. Most of the violence against them was committed by government troops, charged with pursuing those who tried to escape from captivity. Four hundred years of violence against Native Americans, which began with Columbus, came to a climax in 1890 at Wounded Knee when U.S. army soldiers massacred Sioux chief Big Foot and some 350 of his followers. Big Foot had promised his followers that they would soon be freed from the reservations and once again roaming the ancestral plains surrounded by plentiful buffalo. The massacre put an end to that dream. To add insult to injury, the barren reservations the Native Americans were forced to live on were administered by the

Federal Bureau of Indian Affairs. Without jobs or resources, many tribes became plagued by poverty, low life expectancy, high infant mortality, rampant alcoholism, and suicide, and the bureau that oversaw it all became the symbol of mistrust, fraud, and cultural destruction.

Well before the end of the nineteenth century, the master plan for America's "colored" minorities was thus completed, with African Americans pushed back to southern plantations, Native Americans locked up on reservations, and Chinese blocked from further immigration and reproduction on U.S. soil. In December 1904 writer W.S. Harwood observed that the Chinese population of San Francisco had dropped from fifteen thousand to ten thousand. The old, tubercular, and wifeless Chinese in America, he predicted, would become extinct by 1930 or 1940.[34] America's "colored problem" was contained.

AMERICAN IMPERIALIST EXPANSION

The tyranny over domestic "colored" minorities was consistent with America's policies of imperial expansion into "primitive lands" overseas. In 1890, the year of the massacre at Wounded Knee, the U.S. Bureau of the Census officially declared the internal frontier closed.[35] In 1891, William McKinley, who would six years later become the twenty-fifth president of the United States, having promoted himself "as the advance agent of prosperity," summed up the future design for the country in simple terms: "We want a foreign market for our surplus products."[36] By 1893 American foreign trade was larger than any other country's in the world except England's, and with its oil, steel, and farm production exceeding domestic needs, America was ready for a major push into new markets through colonial expansion.[37]

Alas, it came to the global competition for raw materials and new territories too late. Most of the world was already divided up by the long-established European imperial powers, so, like the other latecomers, Germany and Japan, the U.S. had to fight for the redivision of old empires. As soon as he became president, McKinley took to the task. While France, Germany, Belgium, Italy, and Spain fought for the redivision of North Africa and the Congo, he embarked on what he would call the "splendid little war" with Spain for the control of Cuba in 1898—splendid because, once Spain was defeated, the United States went on to annex its colonies in Guam, Puerto Rico, and the Philippines. The Philippines, long at the center of the transpacific trade, were of course the crown jewel, with "China's illimitable markets" waiting just beyond.

The American media greeted McKinley's global grab with enthusiasm. "A new consciousness seems to have come upon us—the consciousness of strength," said the *Washington Post* on the eve of the war. "Ambition, interest, land hunger, pride, the mere joy of fighting, whatever it may be, we are animated by the new sensation. . . . The taste of Empire is in the mouth of the people even as the taste of blood in the jungle."[38] The war may have been splendid, but having stripped Spain of its Caribbean and Asian colonies, McKinley soon found himself having to deal with a Filipino insurrection against American rule. In response, he vowed that he would bring democracy to the Philippines, that America was to "educate the Filipinos, and uplift and civilize and Christianize them."[39] To boost public morale, several American magazines published Rudyard Kipling's poem "The White Man's Burden" with a running commentary: "The emerging global order demands an enforcer. That's America's burden."

The resulting three-and-half-year war cost some five hundred thousand Filipino lives. Charles Warren Fairbanks, the senator from Indiana who would later be elected vice president of the United States on the Republican ticket with Theodore Roosevelt, justified America's imperial expansion as "the mission of our race, trustee, under God, of the civilization of the world. God has not been preparing the English-speaking and Teutonic people for a thousand years for nothing. He has made us the master organizers of the world to administer government among savage and senile people."[40] Thus, the new argument for American imperialism came to rest on the unique qualities of the superior Teutonic and Anglo-Saxon races that had made America strong.

Chapter 9

Anglo-Conformity

The spirit of Anglo-Saxon supremacy was equally on display at home through contempt for the inferior races entering America. At the beginning of the twentieth century, the United States entered a period of even more rapid industrialization, with an ever-increasing need for labor. Almost 20 million people immigrated to the United States between 1890 and 1920; 8,795,386 arrived during the decade of 1901–10 alone. The ratio of foreign-born among the U.S. population reached 14.7 percent in 1910—the highest in American history.[1]

Deprived of labor from Asia, American employers had by now turned exclusively to Europe and had found an enormous source of cheap and vulnerable workers among immigrants from economically underdeveloped eastern and southern Europe. Eighty-one percent of all immigrants who came to America between 1893 and 1907 were Catholics, Jews, and Eastern Orthodox Christians from Italy, Russia, Austria-Hungary, Spain, Portugal, Poland, Bulgaria, Romania, Serbia, Greece, and Montenegro, displacing Protestants from western and northern Europe as the chief source of U.S. immigration.[2]

To Protestant Anglo-Saxons these newest immigrants suddenly became the symbol of everything undesirable. Attributes of contempt were heaped upon them, as the "weak, broken, and mentally crippled" races from the Mediterranean, Balkans, and Poland who brought crime and vulgarized the American way of life.[3] In comparison, older "new

immigrants" from Ireland and Germany, who had started arriving in
America in the 1840s, now seemed frugal and industrious—"substantial
citizens" capable of assimilation. The *Baltimore News* wrote, "The Italian immigrant would be no more objectionable than some others were
if not for his singularly blood thirsty disposition and frightful temper
and vindictiveness."[4] The Italians were called the "Chinese of Europe"
and "guineas." The Greeks were labeled the "scum of Europe." A restaurant in California advertised its services: "John's Restaurant. Pure American. No Rats. No Greeks."[5] And, according to New York City's police
commissioner, Theodore A. Bingham, "half of the criminals" in New
York City in 1908 were Jews. "They are burglars, firebugs, pickpockets
and highway robbers . . . but though all crime is their province, pocket-
picking is one to which they take most naturally," he wrote in the *North
American Review.*[6]

A nativist movement emerged to combat the "evils," such as violent
industrial strikes and crowded slums in the rapidly growing cities,
which were now designated the province of immigrants from southern
and eastern Europe. Even social reformers believed that they were the
source of corrupt urban political machines.[7] Though European and
white, they were categorized as racially distinct from the northern
Europeans—the only race deemed capable of "self-governing." These
"ethnics" were also not seen as promising material for assimilation.
Prominent educators such as John Fiske, chairman of the New York
Zoological Society, believed in the racial superiority of the Anglo-
Saxon race as a product of natural selection. The proof? The English
and the Americans had already covered a third of the globe and had
spearheaded progress in the form of democracy and capitalism. With
the influx of so many non-Anglo-Saxons, however, Fiske warned, the
superior races in the United States were in danger of being swamped
by inferior immigrants.

The popularization of Fiske's application of social Darwinism to
racism resulted in the growth of the grassroots Immigration Restriction
League, founded in the 1890s by elite Bostonians bent on limiting the
influx of "inferior breeds." The most illustrious member of the league
was Senator Henry Cabot Lodge from Massachusetts, a close friend of
President Theodore Roosevelt. On behalf of the league, Lodge introduced a literacy bill that would require immigrants to demonstrate that
they could read and write in some language before being admitted to the

United States. "The literacy test will bear most heavily upon the Italians, Russians, Poles, Hungarians, Greeks, and Asiatics," he argued, "and very light, or not at all upon English-speaking emigrants or Germans, Scandinavians, and French."[8] The league was powerful enough to pressure Congress to pass the literacy test bill in 1897, but President Grover Cleveland vetoed it. In 1917 Congress succumbed to the league's pressure due to wartime hysteria and passed the bill once again. This time it was vetoed by President Woodrow Wilson. After the second failure, members of the league lost interest in the issue and the organization declined in influence.

During World War I, German immigrants became the league's most prominent target. After the war, its aim turned against immigrants from Russia when, because of the victory of the Bolshevik Revolution in 1917, the fear of foreign agitators, especially communists, reached epidemic proportions. The Red Scare lasted from 1918 to 1921, during which time Palmer Raids (Palmer was the U.S. attorney general under President Wilson) went after Jewish immigrants, since they were seen as tied to Bolshevism, but also after Italian immigrants and all labor agitators and political dissidents. "Aliens" suspected of "radicalism" and "leftism" were often illegally arrested, detained, or deported as a result.

As the only power that survived the First World War unscathed, the United States during this period began to project a sense of American supremacy to the rest of the world. The U.S. government no longer cared about what the rest of the world thought about its policies. If it needed Europe at all, it was only on its own terms, which were spelled out in the 1924 immigration law, the National Origins Act, which set immigration quotas at 2 percent of the 1890 population figures. By using a year that predated the great wave of immigration from southern and eastern Europe, it clearly favored the old immigrant groups from the British Isles, Germany, and Scandinavia, while putting a tight lid on future immigration from other, less desirable nations. President Calvin Coolidge, who signed the act into law, had in fact published an article when he was vice president entitled "Whose Country Is This?" in which he professed his belief in Nordic supremacy and the idea that intermarriage between "Nordics" and other groups produced deteriorated offspring.[9] With the agenda of the Immigration Restriction League and other nativists thus embedded in the nation's statutes, 65,721 new immigrants from Great Britain were permitted into the United States every year after 1924, but only 5,802 from Italy, and 2,712 from what had by then become the Soviet Union. Asians were almost completely excluded.

The nationwide movement to restrict immigration that had been initiated in 1882 finally produced an all-encompassing legal framework to make America not only white but also mainly Anglo-Saxon. Soon after the passage of the National Origins Act, in April 1924, the *Los Angeles Times* ran a headline: "Nordic Victory Is Seen in Drastic Restrictions."[10] Congressman Albert Johnson, the chief author of the 1924 law, said three years later, "The United States is our land. . . . We intend to maintain it so. The day of unalloyed welcome to all peoples, the day of indiscriminate acceptance of all races, had definitely ended." Historian Roger Daniels has called Johnson's racial theories, which played into the hands of most Americans of his day who wanted restrictions on immigration, only slightly different in form from what became the official ideology of Nazi Germany.[11]

New immigrants were expected to adapt to Anglo-American culture as quickly as possible. President Theodore Roosevelt, while willing to accept Europeans of diverse origins, insisted, "We must Americanize them in every way, in speech, in political idea and principles," and wanted to oblige them "not to bring in their old-World religions and national antipathies."[12] The president shared the view of his contemporaries who stood "only for 100 percent Americanism, only for those who are American and nothing else." Americanism basically meant Anglo-conformity. The coercive Americanization campaigns denied immigrants even a nostalgic affection for their homeland and attempted to make them speak English only.

Many states passed laws prohibiting the teaching of foreign languages in schools. Those who spoke them at home were seen as a threat to national unity. In the Midwest and the South, old-stock Protestant groups spawned the Anti-Saloon League, which led the attack on the "criminal tendencies" of "ethnic" Europeans by supporting Prohibition—all in the belief that a great social reform would bring the nation once again under the sway of solid Protestant moral values, touted as, "the traditional American values." Since adherence to the old Protestant standards was a precondition for access to better jobs, higher education, and other opportunities, the un-Americanized "ethnics" were left out of the competition. A number of states instituted laws that explicitly prevented aliens from practicing medicine, surgery, pharmacy, architecture, engineering, and surveying, or from driving buses.[13] Other laws and regulations established quotas for admission of Jews to colleges and professional schools. New York University started the trend in 1919—the year World War I ended. It was followed by Columbia University. In 1922, the Harvard University president justified the quota set for Jews as a way to keep the university from becoming a "new Jerusalem." In his view, based on "experience," the acceptable proportion was "about 15%."[14]

Even where not regulated by quotas or laws, discrimination was common practice. Ninety percent of the gentile firms in New York City refused to hire Jews. Jews were not allowed to live in certain buildings and neighborhoods. The Ku Klux Klan sprang back into action, adding anti-Catholicism, anti-Semitism, and anti-foreignism to its traditional hatred of African Americans. Its new agenda attracted five million new members. Violence against immigrants was rampant. In one incident in West Frankfort, Illinois, in 1920, hundreds of Italian immigrants were burned out of their homes, clubbed, and expelled from town.[15] The fear of intimidation and violence caused many immigrants to Anglicize their names, adopt Protestantism, and purge offensive ingredients and flavors from their kitchens. What remained of the so-called ethnic foods conformed to the blend Anglo taste of the "traditional" American diet.

INADMISSIBLE, INELIGIBLE, AND EXEMPTED

If ethnic white immigrants found assimilating into Anglo-Saxon America daunting, what could be said of the experience of the Chinese? The Chinese were never given a realistic chance to even try. The exclusion act singled them out as inadmissible for immigration. Those who still tried to come in were assumed illegal and treated as criminals. The few who entered legally, such as merchants and scholars, were categorized as "exempted" and "aliens ineligible for citizenship."

Women became the focus of the U.S. government strategy to minimize the proliferation of the Chinese who had been admitted before the restrictive immigration laws took effect. A statute of 1878 denied the privilege of admission to and citizenship in the United States to foreign-born children of Chinese women born in the United States, while granting it to descendents of American-born men. An extension of the 1882 exclusion act barred the wives of Chinese laborers already in the United States from joining their husbands, because the American courts decided that a woman should be accorded laborer status upon her marriage to a laborer, even if she had never worked outside the home.[16] (In the decade following the passage of the 1882 act, the female to male ratio dropped to 1:27.) The Cable Act of 1922 deprived female American citizens of the right to bring in their husbands if they were from countries that made them "aliens ineligible for citizenship." More alarmingly, it also stripped them of their own U.S. citizenship.

Florence Chinn Kwan met her husband when both were studying at the University of Chicago. They married in 1923 and went to live in China. After five years they returned to America. Florence's husband had foreign student status and was admitted without a problem. Florence and their two children were detained on the boat. "The immigration officer said, 'It's because you're married to an alien and you lost your citizenship,'" she recalled five decades later in an interview for the *San Francisco Journal*. "And that was the first time that I knew I had lost my citizenship when I married." She was eventually released on bond, $2,000 for herself and $2,000 for her children, when a friend who worked for the Immigration Service vouched for her identity. Florence vowed never to come back. But she did. The Cable Act was rescinded in 1930, and she applied for naturalization and regained her citizenship in 1936.[17]

Others were less lucky. Fung Sing of Port Ludlow, Washington, was taken to China by her parents in 1903 and got married there. She came back to the United States in 1925, after the death of her husband, but was not allowed to land in Seattle. Like Florence, she was not aware that she had lost her citizenship through marriage. She sought release under a writ of habeas corpus, but the district judge ruled that by marrying a citizen of China, she, too, became a citizen of China. Since Chinese citizens were not eligible for U.S. citizenship, and ineligible aliens were denied entry to the United States, she should be barred from entering the country.[18] Most American-born women fought hard for their citizenship, and not necessarily because of the privileges, if any, they might derive from it. As Flora Belle Jan, another University of Chicago student married to a Chinese classmate, described in a letter to her best friend, Ludmelia Holstein, in 1932, as she pushed to have her status adjusted before she left for China, "I must go through this before I ever dare leave America because once I am out of the country, as an alien, I'll have a devil of a time trying to get back. And I know that I will always want to come back because it is my home."[19]

Because the provision in the 1924 National Origins Act that made persons ineligible for citizenship inadmissible barred even the foreign-born wives of U.S. citizens of Chinese descent from entering the country, it caused an uproar in the Chinese American community. The Chinese Consolidated Benevolent Association got together with the Chinese American Citizens Alliance (a national organization that started out as the Native Sons of the Golden State, the first group formed by American-born Chinese) and the Chinese Chamber of Commerce to raise money and retain lawyers to challenge the law in court.

The first appeal the Committee to Challenge the 1924 Immigration Act brought in 1925, for the admission of merchants' wives, was successful. In *Cheung Sum Shee et al. v. Nagel*, the Ninth Circuit Court of Appeals judge determined that wives of resident Chinese merchants, although they did not come to carry on trade, should by "necessary implication" be admitted with their husbands under the treaty with China. The second appeal, on behalf of the citizens' wives, however, was not successful. In *Chang Chan et al. v. John Nagle*, the same judge ruled that the wives of U.S. citizens did not become citizens by their act of marriage and, since they remained incapable of naturalization, could not be admitted under the Immigration Act. He did instruct the plaintiffs, however, that, "the words of the statute being clear, if it unjustly discriminates against the native-born citizens, or is cruel and inhuman in its results, as forcefully contended, the remedy lies with Congress and not with the court."[20]

The Chinese American Citizens Alliance quickly mounted a second campaign and in 1926 appealed to the Committee on Immigration and Naturalization of the House of Representatives for a "remedy for the hardship under which the American citizen of the Chinese race suffers in his separation from his wife." Several alliance members appeared before the committee, many World War I veterans among them. George Fong, Peter Soo Hoo, and Wu Lai Sun argued that "Chinese

American citizens should be entitled to no less protection than alien Chinese merchants." And if *they* could bring their wives to live with them in America under the treaty between China and the United States, the same should be allowed to American citizens. But members of the House were less interested in the right of the Chinese American citizen to his wife's companionship than in the alarming report from the immigration commissioner raising fears that a greater number of Chinese women might try to enter the country as merchants' wives as the result of the *Cheung Sum Shee et al. v. Nagel* ruling. They refused to act.[21]

The consequences were drastic. Whereas 2,848 Chinese women had come to the United States as wives of citizens between 1906 and 1924, not a single one was allowed to enter between 1924 and 1930.[22] The law remained in effect until the Chinese Exclusion Act was repealed, in 1943.

That courts deferred grievances over anti-Chinese immigration legislation to Congress is a clear sign that immigration was regarded as a matter of national sovereignty. Regardless of contradictions brought out in legal cases, Congress retained the power to exclude those it considered "injurious or a source of danger to the country," which it defined as a "right of self-preservation." Dr. Joseph Hill, a statistician at the Bureau of the Census and chairman of the Quota Board charged with deciding on the number and percentage of immigrants that would be allowed from different nations, had asserted that "the stream that feeds the reservoir should have the same composition as the contents of the reservoir itself"; otherwise, the American stock would degenerate. An influx of Asian immigrants was viewed as a form of aggression on U.S. sovereignty. The Supreme Court deliberation on *Fong Yue Ting v. United States*, in 1893, had included the assertion that "the government of the United States . . . considers the presence of foreigners of a different race . . . to be dangerous to its peace and security."

American-born Chinese, although U.S. citizens, were a minority among the Chinese who were resident aliens ineligible for citizenship and were regarded by the rest of Americans as foreign. In a master's thesis at the University of Southern California entitled "A Study of the American-born and American-reared Chinese in Los Angeles," Kit King Louis's interviews revealed a prevalence of alienation. "I thought I was American, but America would not have me," said one interviewee.

"In many respects she would not recognize me as American. Moreover, I find racial prejudice against us everywhere. We are American citizens in name but not in fact." Another complained, "I am an American citizen by birth, having the title for all rights, but they treat me as if I were a foreigner. They have so many restrictions against us."[23]

A major restriction affecting all American-born Chinese was in access to education. The city of San Francisco and many other places on the West Coast instituted an educational policy based on the principle of "equal but separate," forcing the Chinese, although they were regular taxpayers, to send their children to overcrowded, understaffed, and underfunded segregated schools.[24] Those who excelled in school despite discrimination and went on to college discovered that higher education offered a false promise, because Chinese college graduates simply could not find work. "Many firms have general regulations against employing them; others object to them on the ground that the other men employed by the firms do not care to work with them," a Stanford University placement officer explained to a research scholar in 1927. "Just recently, a Chinese graduate of Stanford University, who was brought up on the Stanford campus with the children of the professors, who speaks English perfectly, and who is thoroughly Americanized, was refused consideration by a prominent California corporation because they do not employ Orientals in their offices."[25] The few who bothered to obtain doctoral degrees in physical medicine found work only in Chinatown or in China.

Regardless of their means, Chinese Americans were forced to live in geographically segregated neighborhoods by "restrictive covenants"— a legal device used in the South to keep African Americans from white neighborhoods. Eva Lowe, who grew up in Fort Bragg, California, where other kids threw horse manure and rocks at her and called her, "Ching Chong Chinaman," went looking for an apartment to rent in San Francisco with a white girlfriend in the early 1930s. They were rebuffed several times. Landlords would say yes to her girlfriend but would change their mind when they saw Eva, explaining, "We don't rent to Orientals." A landlord finally accepted them on Russian Hill because Eva pretended to be her friend's maid.[26] In other neighborhoods that had no restrictive covenants, lynching mobs often helped the brazen Chinese looking for an apartment decide to move to "where they belonged."

As a result, most Chinese were trapped in crowded and dilapidated tenements in Chinatown. In his contribution to the unpublished "History of the Gan Family," a family memoir, David Gan writes of the apartment he grew up in during the 1930s in San Francisco's Chinatown: "It had two rooms and a closet-sized kitchen with a window facing other apartments. George and I slept on a sofa bed. Ma and Pa slept in the bedroom with Virginia, Norman and Hank, I think. . . . There was no bathroom. Each floor had a communal bathroom, consisting of a tub and a toilet, shared by four or five apartments' tenants."[27] To add insult to injury, Chinatowns were considered "a sort of a human zoo," a sociologist wrote in the *Journal of Applied Sociology* in 1925, "which becomes a point of attraction for tourists."[28]

To this day, cities across the United States view their Chinatowns as a commercial asset. Tourist companies bill them as places where visitors can indulge their exotic fantasies and see locations where horrible crimes were once perpetrated by vicious hatchet men and unfortunate innocents were induced into a life of vice. The San Francisco Tourist Chamber's 1914 tour guide called its Chinatown "the most fascinating city of America" but also stressed that "nowhere is the white visitor more secure in property or person." In New York, busses still bring sightseers to Manhattan's Chinatown on weekends. During the 1930s, these bus excursions were an everyday occurrence. Decorated with Japanese paper lanterns, they bore huge signboards announcing feature visits to "clandestine opium dens," "gambling halls," "hidden dungeons," and "mysterious underground tunnels."

White Americans found exotica in residential segregation and economic deprivation of Chinese Americans because of the imagery long cultivated by Hollywood films. Celluloid Chinese men were physically weak, small, and genderless and thus perfectly suited for the "feminine" occupations of washing, cooking, and housekeeping. Two of the earliest feature-length American movies—Cecil B. DeMille's *The Cheat* (1915) and D.W. Griffith's *Broken Blossoms* (1919)—suggested that Chinese people of both sexes were given to sexual deviancy and as such posed a threat to white civilization.[29] Another fabricated Chinese cultural trait was perpetuated over the span of almost five decades through thirteen popular pulp novels (the first was published in 1913, the last in 1959), countless radio programs, and many films about the diabolical Dr. Fu Manchu. Created by Arthur Ward (under the pseudonym Sax Rohmer), Dr. Fu Manchu was the archetype of "oriental villainy"—coldly intelligent, yet possessed of no soul or emotion and thus inherently sinister and menacing. Even Charlie Chan, whose Harvard-educated author, Earl Derr Biggers, later attributed his creation of the clever, amicable detective—the "good" ally of the white people—to the effects of Hollywood ("I had seen movies depicting and read stories about Chinatown and wicked Chinese villains, and it struck me that a Chinese hero, trustworthy, benevolent, and philosophical, would come nearer to presenting a correct portrayal of the race"[30]), was made to appear inexplicably subservient and ludicrously asexual on the big screen.

The images had their impact. Several white Americans whom the sociologist Paul Siu interviewed for his doctoral dissertation looked back to their childhood and recalled thinking of the Chinese as "criminal" or "villainous" people who would slit throats without remorse. Most of them attributed these impressions to the movies.[31]

WHENCE ASSIMILATION?

Amidst racist laws and attitudes that so openly ostracized Chinese Americans, it is rather strange that the topic of their assimilation should even arise. Yet this is exactly what happened. American Baptist, Methodist, and Presbyterian missionaries had a long-lasting agenda of converting Chinese "heathens." They believed that the civilizing effects of Christianity rendered Chinese converts into perfectly socially acceptable members of society and took pride in promoting the standing and professional advancement of their protégés. They also actively participated in efforts to counter the effects of anti-Asian agitation and consistently spoke out against unfair American laws. There were also some liberal academics sympathetic to the Chinese, who subscribed to the concept of culture as a way of getting away from biological and racial determinism. Both groups conducted their ministrations and research out of a desire to help or at least understand the Chinese. Nonetheless, they still saw the Chinese in the light cast by the anti-Chinese movement—as fundamentally different. Where the liberal friends of the Chinese race differed is that they didn't want to exclude the immigrants—they wanted to change them.

This was the milieu that produced the most authoritative academic analysis of immigration in the early years of the twentieth century— the analysis proffered by the so-called Chicago School of professors and students who gathered under the aegis of a sociologist named Robert Park. Park grew up in the rural Midwest and, after spending some time working as a reporter for newspapers in Minneapolis, Chicago, and New York, came to work at the University of Chicago's Department of Sociology and Anthropology, specializing in the study of human collective behavior and interaction. In the 1920s he articulated a theory of immigration that would come to be widely influential, and is still, arguably, the basis for how Americans continue to understand immigration today.

Robert Park argued that immigrants "adjust" to America in a discernable pattern, which he called the "assimilation cycle." In his view, contact between any two well-formed social groups follows a series of progressive stages of social interaction: competition, conflict, accommodation, and, eventually, assimilation. Although he allowed that external factors, such as customs, regulations, immigration restrictions, and racial barriers, could slow down the process or even halt it completely for a time, he maintained that they could not change its direction. Moreover, Park argued against the biological basis of social differences and believed that the "assimilation cycle" could be applied equally to African Americans and to Asians. This liberal view was probably influenced by Park's experience working as a press secretary for Booker T. Washington at Tuskegee Institute in Alabama, before joining the University of Chicago. He viewed racism as a matter of "subjective attitudes," which societies could be rid of through development of "mental consciousness." He and his followers were convinced that racial conflict would disappear if all men just stopped thinking about race. Once that happened, they argued, any group, regardless of its race or ethnicity, was bound to eventually become integrated into the mainstream.

The main problem in achieving this end, as Park saw it, was that "Japanese, Chinese and Negroes" were segregated from other Americans. And since prejudice could only be overcome by sharing experiences and memories, their prejudice-caused "isolation" only perpetuated prejudice, because it cut off their communication with society at large. The "Negroes and Orientals" could not achieve the last step of the assimilation cycle because of the "race consciousness" among whites, but this did not invalidate the assimilation theory. It did not mean that they could not and would not achieve it in the end, once the vicious cycle of isolation and prejudice was broken.[32]

Park and his followers were particularly interested in the "Orientals" because they presented a double challenge to their theory, both as immigrants and as a distinct racial group. The initial findings of a number of Park's followers suggested that the Orientals who became conscious of their distinctness and were willing to reject their Oriental identity in the attempt to assimilate were rejected by the white society. A twenty-year-old University of Chicago student, Kazuo Kawai, described how in high school he strongly identified with America and resented a "Japanesy" fellow student who made him feel self-conscious about his race. When he entered college, however, he was made to feel "Japanese." Although "in language, in thought, in ideals, in custom, in everything, I was American," he wrote, "America wouldn't have me."[33] Unlike European immigrants, whose second or subsequent generations could ignore their European past and merge with the mainstream, an Oriental who rejected his origins would be marginalized by both sides and caught in a no-man's-land.

To Park, however, the predicament of a man caught in this situation—whom he called the "marginal man"—was the most fascinating aspect of the racial and ethnic experience in America. Park thought that the marginal man, being a product of increased migration and cultural contact, had broken off his bonds to traditional societies and was thus freer and more creative—a higher form of human being. His cosmopolitan ability to navigate among different cultures placed him in a position to lead others to a higher form of "civilized" society.

Under Park's mentorship, a number of his Chinese American disciples tested his ideas of the marginal man and assimilation cycle through field research in Chinese American communities. Paul Chan Pang Siu was born in China and studied at an American missionary school in Canton before coming to St. Paul, Minnesota, in 1927, to join his laundryman father and enroll in Macalester College. Without funds to complete his education as a full-time student, he moved to Chicago, where he could take courses at night and work as a waiter in a Chinese restaurant during the day. In 1932, Robert Park's colleague Ernest Burgess "discovered" him and offered him funding for graduate studies in sociology at the University of Chicago. Like most of Park's students, Siu was sent back to do fieldwork in the community he came from. He lived with relatives in a suburban laundry and worked as a laundry supply agent. It took him two decades to complete the dissertation "The Chinese Laundryman: A Study of Social Isolation." He was forty-seven when he defended the dissertation, but he had created the richest and most detailed portrait of Chinese America the Chicago sociologists would ever produce.[34] It was a bleak depiction of immigrant life marked by loneliness, desperation, and maladjustment.

What made Siu's work particularly significant was the number of Chinese in America who led the life he so vividly depicted. Chinese hand laundries had remained fixtures of the American urban landscape for decades, their lonely owners and operators seemingly frozen in isolation across the nation. By 1930, there were 3,350 Chinese hand laundries in New York City alone, 430 in Chicago, 160 in St. Louis, and 52 in the Boston area. Almost 40 percent of the entire Chinese population in the United States during the 1930s was engaged in laundry-related trades. In New York City, laundrymen constituted 60 percent of all Chinese.

The apparent success of this enduring Chinese American enterprise was based solely on the hard work and sweat of people who had been squeezed out of the labor market and who lacked capital to make a living any other way. To compete with modern American laundries, which employed black women laborers and used washing and steam ironing machines, they had to charge low prices and work long hours to compensate for the lack of equipment. In 1897, a New York reporter observed, "The Chinaman works from eight o'clock in the morning until one or two o'clock at night. Sometimes he washes, sometimes he starches, sometimes he irons; but he is always at it, not tireless, but persevering in spite of weariness and exhaustion. Other laborers clamor for a working-day of eight hours. The Chinaman patiently works seventeen."[35] In 1935, Tung Pok Chin, who at the time worked for a laundry in Boston that employed five people, still had the same work schedule, although the laundry was equipped with modern shirt-pressing machines. "Our workday lasted from seven o'clock in the morning until two o'clock the next morning, day in and day out, six days a week. We ate supper at two o'clock in the morning and slept at two-thirty. We had only four and one-half hours of sleep daily," he wrote in his memoir. He also noted that the owner of the laundry "himself worked harder than any of the others."[36]

With that kind of brutal work schedule, laundrymen usually ate and slept in the laundry shop, rarely leaving the premises, except on Sundays, when they would travel to Chinatown to visit relatives and friends and buy food for the coming week.[37] On some days they hardly had time to eat. The son of a New York laundryman recalls that his father used to joke about having a flexible stomach—"like rubber bands." He could skip meals for a couple of days. Others reportedly hung pieces of bread in front of them on strings from the ceiling and took a bite whenever they had a moment to do so.[38] Most were saving money to send back to their families in China, who were largely unaware of their hardship. "In China, people were talking about going to the 'Flowery Flag' [America], and I was dreaming, too, about coming over," a laundryman told Paul Siu in 1939.[39] "Now I am here. What I see in this country is just like this: working day and night." "When I heard about chance to come to America, the hardship just don't occur to me," another said, adding the inevitable refrain: "Now I am here, I began to feel America is work, work, work."[40]

Most laundries were located in non-Chinese neighborhoods, where Chinese laundrymen typically had very little contact with their neighbors. Since they were obliged to throw themselves into work just hours after they arrived in the United States in order to start paying back their immigration debts, they had no time to get English instruction, and their chances to learn the language through contacts with their white customers were minimal.

For the laundrymen who maintained one-man operations, the isolation was almost complete. The little socializing they did was when they went to Chinatown on Sundays—dressed up in suits and wearing ties, so as not to be looked down on by whites.[41] But instead of attributing their isolation to the prejudice they encountered, which precluded them from "progressing" to the final stages of the assimilation cycle, as Park would have done, Siu argued that Chinese laundrymen developed a "sojourner's mentality" because they wanted only "to do a job and do it in the shortest possible time," so they could return home quickly. It was an insightful challenge to Robert Park's idea of the marginal man. These were not men who straddled two cultures, having broken off home ties and "reaching for the integration into a new social order." Siu's sojourners were trapped in perpetual isolation through personal choice and the prejudice of the host society.[42]

Yet Siu, although he understood that the inability to assimilate was not entirely the laundrymen's choice, still blamed it for the misery of their lives in America. Other disciples of Robert Park's, most notably Rose Hum Lee, went so far as to blame the stubbornly tradition-bound Chinese for their failure to integrate. Insistence on assimilation as the primary measuring stick for immigrant life in America inevitably dooms the Chinese experience to be seen as a failure. Even more unfortunately, it can end up, contrary to the original intentions of the liberal Chicago School social theorists, blaming the victim. The experience of the Chinese in America, even during the exclusion era, when they were shunned, was much richer than the focus on their inability to assimilate implies. If one steps around to the opposite side of the lens and looks at it from the point of view of those who continued to come to America at great personal risk and high cost—if one considers their objectives and their motivations—the same experience begins to look like a life of great accomplishment, even fulfillment, despite the hardships and the sacrifices.

Chapter 10

The Chinese Build Their Community

THE STRATEGY BEHIND CONTINUED CHINESE IMMIGRATION

Although obviously unwelcome, the Chinese continued to find every possible way to come to America during the period of exclusion because they were in fact quite aggressively pursuing their own agendas—of which assimilation was not a central concern. They were willing to come to America, where they would be wifeless and alien, because their entire extended families in China expected to benefit from their sacrifice.

In China, migration has always been a family strategy. All family members pool resources to help the individual chosen for the mission. The migrant understands that in heading to work overseas he is participating in a rational distribution of family responsibilities. (His responsibilities of tending to the land, caring for the elders, and maintaining a wife and children fall on others who are left behind.) Once he has established a foothold—usually after paying off the debts he incurred to make the journey—he sends for other relatives so that the entire extended family can share in his economic gain. The more difficult the domestic situation in China and the more efficient an emigrant in earning income overseas, the more family members get dispatched, setting off a family-based chain migration. As the Chinese moved around the United States in search of work, this model of migration brought about the preponderance of particular family groups in various locations: Ongs in Phoenix, Moys and Chins in Chicago, Lees in Washington, D.C., and Yees in Pittsburg.

Naomi Jung, who grew up in Albany, New York, remembers the frequent arrivals of "cousins" at her parents' doorstep when she was a little girl:

> [T]here would always be somebody coming from the old country. And as he would come over, the cousin would be taken downtown and he'd be bought one good suit from a good, conservative store. He'd get a Stetson hat. He'd get Florsheim shoes. . . . He would be given money to start a business. Whether it would be business with them or for himself. There was always room for one more when he came from the old country. It was always good to see someone come from your village because they brought stories of everybody from the village. And when you come from the same village, with the Chinese this is kinfolk. That's why people would say all the Lees are here. One would come and settle in New York. Before you know it they'd write back and more Lees would come.[1]

The more Lees there were, the more powerful the Lee clan became, improving the chances of all the Lees to do better.

By improving his family's standard of living, a migrant helps his family ascend in the social and economic hierarchy within the clan and its native village. The comfort of living with his wife, children, and other family members takes second place. If by sticking it out alone, even for a long time, he can buy choice land and build a new home for the family, he has succeeded and can expect the respect of people who had known him from birth when he returns home. Even the most ambitious Chinese—the traditional scholars who became prominent officials—at the end of their careers returned home. The objective of modern fortune seekers who venture abroad remains the same.

The responsibility of repaying family and clan members for their unlimited support locks most Chinese emigrants in an endless cycle of mutual dependency. In many parts of China, as in Guangdong Province, the system extends from family to clan, and even to the village. This can be an advantage, since the larger size of the collective can provide a potential migrant with more options. A struggling restaurant owner in America can get the cheapest labor possible by asking relatives to come and help. Far from being passive victims, as Paul Siu implied, Chinese migrants succeeded in making a life in the United States in spite of the difficulties, and even achieved a measure of collective well-being through ethnic solidarity. Of course, ethnic solidarity is precisely what Rose Hum Lee condemned as the cause of the Chinese inability to be part of the mainstream. But without it—without the traditional social networks and associations, regardless of how undemocratic and oppressive they may have been—the immigrants could not have achieved anything, not even coming to this country.

The first order of business for traditional associations after the exclusion laws were passed was to find a way to get around them in order to maintain the chain migration. The only Chinese allowed into the United States after 1882 were merchants, scholars, and diplomats, but the majority of those interested in immigration were the poor working-class people. They could enter only by being smuggled in, or by being sponsored by legitimate Chinese merchants with already-established businesses in the United States who could vouch for them as business partners. But would-be merchant immigrants had to produce not only documents showing investment and partnership in a U.S. business but also two white witnesses to testify that they were on the premises of the said business "reasonably often." According to the U.S. Treasury Department Annual Report for 1903, "It is a notorious fact that many small grocery establishments have twenty or more professed firm members, each claiming an interest of $1,000 therein, and at no time can the business done furnish support to more than a small minority of such partners, nor frequently can more than four or five members, and sometimes fewer, be found at the business stand. In many instances the other partners are found to be merely laborers, whose callused hands show plainly the nature of their occupation."[2] Nevertheless, once certified, a Chinese with merchant status could travel back and forth between China and the United States and bring a wife into the country. This was the high road that few immigrants had the finances and the connections to take.

The less well-off opted for a system of entry based on false parentage claims, which was developed immediately after the passage of the 1882 exclusion act, when merchants and their wives already legally in the United States began claiming as their American-born offspring children, usually boys, who were brought over from China and smuggled into the country. The practice came to the attention of the Bureau of the Census by 1900, when the twelfth census found that 6,657 of the 9,010 Chinese who claimed to have been born in the United States were males, and only 2,353 were females. This would suggest that 73.9 percent of the Chinese born in the United States were male.[3] Equally suspect were the overall birth numbers among Chinese Americans, which suddenly mushroomed during the 1890s. A federal judge noted in 1901 that "if the story told in the courts were true, every Chinese woman who was in the United States twenty-five years ago must have had at least 500 children."[4] But the fire that followed the 1906 earthquake in San Francisco destroyed all immigration records, and from that point on all Chinese already in the country could claim that they were born here. This made them U.S. citizens.

The fire also granted numerous new immigrants a quasi-legal way of entry. A Chinese American citizen could take advantage of the Fourteenth Amendment provision granting the right of citizenship to anyone born in the United States and his foreign born-children, go back to China, and claim to have gotten married and sired a child. The child would be registered with the immigration office under a specific name and given a "slot," making that child eligible to enter the United States legally as a citizen. Thousands of these slots were sold, and thousands of Chinese entered the United States "legally" as registered children of American citizens, since without DNA testing or some similar method of verification, there was no way for the immigration office to disprove any such claim. The "paper son" method became the most prominent means of entering the United States after 1906.

In his memoir, *Paper Son: One Man's Story,* Tung Pok Chin describes how he arrived in Boston in 1934, at the age of nineteen, with a paper purchased on the Chinese black market. "My real father, already in Gold Mountain as a paper son himself, made my passage to America possible. He informed me of the availability of this particular paper and then, in a manner befitting a spy novel, I obtained it from the agent in my village. My father also managed to borrow enough money from a distant cousin to finance my trip. My paper, at a cost of $100 for each year recorded—that is, each year of my age—cost me $2000 with fee, excluding transportation. This I was able to purchase on credit and would repay when I arrived and found work."[5] Chin's father could not bring him as his own son, because his paper stated that he was "single" when he arrived. Likewise, Chin's paper stated that he was single. Such papers involved less complicated identity adjustments and were cheaper to obtain, since they guaranteed entry to only one generation.

Early on, the U.S. immigration service realized that three to four generations of paper sons stood to benefit from each false claim and promptly tightened the citizenship verification process. Chin studied "facts" about his paper identity for months before leaving China: his paper name, his paper father's name, his paper mother's name, his age, their ages, his place of birth, their places of birth, their occupations, and so on. "This wasn't easy," he writes.

> I had to completely block out my real and immediate family: my parents who raised me and arranged a marriage for me at the age of thirteen, my wife, my two young sons, aged four and five at the time of my arrival in Boston, and all else that related to them. One slip during the interrogation and I would be sent back on the next boat to China! And the methods they used were tricky. Questions were asked nonstop, one after another under a glaring light, and the key questions were repeated over and over again to catch any inconsistencies.

Unfortunately, the innocent Chinese with perfectly legitimate papers had to suffer through merciless interrogations, too. Every Chinese entering the country was detained at Angel Island in San Francisco or Ellis Island in New York and questioned over a long period of time. A blameless Chinese immigrant penned in at Angel Island wrote a poem in the early 1900s: "American laws are fierce like tigers: People are jailed inside wooden walls. Detained, interrogated, and tortured, birds plunged into an open trap. Fed up with this treatment I regret my journey here. I am innocent, yet treated guilty; how can I take this?"[6] Indeed, when it came to the Chinese, the most basic principle of American jurisprudence was turned upside down: Chinese immigrants were considered guilty until proven innocent. "Alas, yellow souls suffer under the brutal force of the white race," wrote another detainee. "We are not even the equal of cattle and horses."[7] The living conditions were deplorable, the treatment subhuman, but the worst were the interrogations. They could last several days and were often conducted after an immigrant had spent several months in detention. Although supposedly designed to weed out individuals with fraudulent claims, the questions asked could be so absurd that even legitimate immigrants frequently were stumped.[8]

Law Shee Low, who arrived in San Francisco with her husband, was separated from him when their ship docked and taken to Angel Island for physical examination and interrogation. Disrobing in front of male doctors and presenting a stool sample was shocking enough. Then, after days of waiting, Low heard what happened to a woman in her fifties who had been questioned all day. "She said they asked her about [life in China:] the chickens and the neighbors, and the direction of the house faced," Low told Judy Yung in an interview for *Unbound Feet: A Social History of Chinese Women in San Francisco*. "How would I know all that?" Low, a legal entrant, had not been prepared for such questions. The woman had been deported, and Low was scared. "When the interpreter asked me whether I visited my husband's ancestral home during the wedding, I said no because I was afraid he was going to ask me which direction the house faced like the woman told me and I wouldn't know." Low's husband, who was being interrogated at the same time in the same room, had evidently said yes, because, after she denied it for the second time, he said, "You went back; why don't you say so?" This made the immigration officer hit the table with his hand, and Low, scared to death, quickly said, "Oh, I forgot. I did pass by but didn't go in." Fortunately, they let her land.[9]

In response to these intense interrogations, Chinese who were selling slots prepared elaborate family genealogies to avoid detection. When the immigration office began exacting greater details, the applicants were coached in ever-more elaborate particulars of family life. When immigration officers attempted to use information obtained from various family members or co-villagers to trick the respondent into making errors, Chinese smuggling networks countered by amassing a database of consistent and fraud detection–proof responses, down to the minutiae, such as what side the bathroom window faced the river on, or which members of the family had had chicken pox. The system worked. The collective effort, with the professional assistance of the smuggling networks, enabled the Chinese immigrants to back up the claimed slots with evidence, and more of those who applied gained entry than not— 90 percent, according to both the immigration office and the assertions of the Chinese themselves.[10] "People might say," a Chinese interpreter on Angel Island commented, "we might have come under fraudulent papers but we got in here legally."

It is certain that much of the success was owed to the involvement of the organized smuggling networks, for whom the new immigration scheme was a profit-making business. They had the incentive and the means to beat the system. The cost of false papers was determined by the immigrant's age and was generally set at $100 per year of age. Someone entering at the age of twenty would have to pay $2,000, which amounted to approximately two years of average earnings in the United States. For the price, the smuggling operators found individuals willing to sell the paper son slot, matched the details of age, gender, and dialect, and, most important, supplied the coaching books, or prompt books.

The Chinese Exclusion Act of 1882 thus brought about a fundamental shift in the method and means of Chinese immigration. With the large-scale labor recruiting and contracting of the decades preceding the act over, immigrants were now entering the country on an individual basis. The large, powerful migrant networks of the past were now replaced by smaller profit-based groups, whose most impressive feature was their ability to acquire and disseminate the information needed to outsmart American immigration authorities. Their ability to beat the immigration service at its own game was perhaps most apparent when it came to aiding Chinese who were entering the United States in a third way—without status or proper papers, by crossing the border illegally.

BEATING THE SYSTEM

Prior to the Chinese Exclusion Act, the issue of illegal entry into the United States did not exist. There were no border controls to speak of. After 1882, special "Chinese Inspectors" were placed at the ports to enforce the exclusion act, and only some years later, in 1891, did the U.S. government set up the Office of the Superintendent of Immigration within the Treasury Department to carry out inspection, admission, rejection, and processing of *all* immigrants seeking admission to the United States. Federal immigration stations were established on Ellis

Island, off the coast of New York, in 1892, and on Angel Island, off San Francisco, in 1893, to enforce a more rigorous immigration policy.

Despite the new controls, the Chinese found ways to enter the United States from Canada and Mexico. In 1891—the first year all immigrants were subjected to inspection—a journalist for *Harper's New Monthly* magazine observed that there was scarcely any part of the northern border where a "Chinaman may not walk boldly across it at high noon."[11] The government's inability to control Chinese immigration was affected by the multiple division of responsibilities and by the lack of unity in interpretation of laws among the vast array of offices in charge: the State Department, the Internal Revenue Service, federal courts, customs collectors, and so forth. And while the enforcers of the law lacked coordination and understanding of proper procedures and struggled over jurisdiction, the Chinese used the bureaucratic confusion and inefficiency to exploit the loopholes.

In 1885, in its own bid to curb Chinese immigration, the Canadian government imposed a head tax of $50, which was to be collected by ship captains at the point of departure on each Chinese headed for Canada. Chinese immigrants headed for the United States, however, were allowed to spend ninety days in Canada without paying the head tax before crossing the border into the United States. Chinese immigrants amply availed themselves of this loophole. Elaborate smuggling networks were set up to bring them across the U.S.-Canadian border, either into the state of Washington, for a fee of $23 to $60, by boat, or into the state of New York, where the border was even less guarded, after sending them across the continent on the Canadian Pacific Railroad. The Vancouver–Puget Sound area, where the smugglers used the boats and routes already established for the opium trade, was known as the "smugglers' paradise." In 1909, local newspapers reported that two to four Chinese were brought into Buffalo weekly at a price of $200, while groups of two to seventy-five were frequently taken to Boston and New York City.

According to Mexican statistics, during the rule of President Porfirio Díaz (1876–1911) an estimated one thousand to two thousand Chinese per year migrated illegally into the United States, and 80 percent of all Chinese arriving at Mexican seaports eventually reached the U.S. border. They arrived at Ensenada, Manzanillo, Mazatlan, and Guaymas, where they either changed to other boats or took trains north, disembarking well before the U.S. border to cross it on foot. A Mexican guide for the crossing cost between $25 and $75 in the 1890s, depending on the location of the crossing. The price increased to $200 by the 1930s. El Paso, Texas, was well known as the "hotbed for the smuggling of Chinese" headed for the western U.S. states, while those headed for the eastern states often took the sea route to Florida, Louisiana, and Mississippi.

The Chinese illegally crossing U.S. borders from the north typically took on the guises of Native Americans. The *Buffalo Times* reported in 1904 that white smugglers commonly fitted their clients with "Indian garb" and baskets of sassafras and sent them rowing across the border.[12] Those entering from Mexico often wore the most picturesque Mexican dress and were taught to say, "Yo soy Mexicano." Immigrant inspector Marcus Braun, who traveled to Mexico under cover to investigate illegal immigration to the United States in 1907 was amazed, when he examined the photographs on fraudulent Mexican documents used by the Chinese, that it was "exceedingly difficult to distinguish these Chinamen from Mexicans."[13] In Louisiana, U.S. immigration inspectors reported on a group of Chinese, painted black to look like the crew of a ship arrived from Cuba, who "walked off the steamer in New Orleans without trouble." In Mobile, Alabama, an inspector revealed a project to "disguise the Chinamen as negroes." Mobile had become a popular destination for Chinese coming from Mexico because a Chinese man known as "Crooked Face" excelled in providing his countrymen with this disguise.[14]

In the end, the exclusion act did not stop the Chinese from coming to the United States, but it did make their immigration considerably more difficult and significantly reduced their numbers. By shifting the emphasis from large-scale importation of laborers to family-based migration, the act dramatically altered the social and economic structure of the Chinese American community. It made those who came illegally dependent on the criminal networks that could provide the means for successful migration. Also, it forced the would-be immigrants to rely more than ever on the extensive networks of relatives, friends, and fellow villagers already in the United States, as anyone hoping to pass through the gates as a merchant had to produce ironclad proof of business partnership with someone already established in the country, and paper sons depended on the valid identities provided by the earlier immigrants. It is American policies that forced Chinese immigrants to retreat into their communities and depend on their ethnic and traditional networks instead of "choosing integration."

STRENGTHS OF TRADITIONAL CHINESE NETWORKING

As Chinese American society became transformed into a community of small family-based owner-operated service businesses, the need for traditional associations only increased. The associations provided a safe and reliable environment in which to facilitate business transactions, set rules and regulations for economic transactions, mediate conflicts, restrict hostile competition, and set conditions for profit sharing among partners, as well as arbitrate in Chinese on Chinese labor disputes. Although steeped in the feudal traditions of rural China, the associations provided stability, and their structure proved flexible enough to promote commercial activities in a "modern" society. Certain groups within the community, however, benefited from their activities more than others.

One of the chief functions of traditional networks was to pool financial resources to help members start a business. In the early decades of the twentieth century, a number of ambitious laundry, restaurant, and mom-and-pop grocery operators established stores that sold mainstream American groceries, meats, and produce to the white population. No American bank would lend them money, so, aside from using their own savings, they usually looked for investors and partners among fellow members of their surname, village, or county associations. Investors with bigger shares or with skills critical for the business, such as butchers, became major partners. They controlled bookkeeping and carried greater weight in decision making.

Lee Gim came to America in 1916 at the age of sixteen. After working as a kitchen helper in San Francisco and a cook on a ranch in northern California, he accepted an offer from his old friend Lee Toy, a successful laundry operator in the town of Colusa, to take over a grocery store that two Japanese brothers had abandoned with some merchandise in one of Lee Toy's buildings. With nearly zero dollars in capital, the Chung Sun Grocery was born in 1921. Pretty soon, Lee Gim invited another friend, a former cook, to join him as a partner and hired several employees to help with the expanding business, some of whom he sponsored to immigrate from his native village, and who were all either related or friends. They all slept in the basement and shared meals cooked there, which reinforced their real or surrogate familial ties. When some of the employees saved enough money to form partnerships, Lee Gim helped them open their own stores in nearby towns of Marysville, Oroville, and Woodland by investing in them as a major shareholder. From the late 1920s to the 1950s, through partnerships and pooled resources, profits from Chung Sun Grocery helped finance a network of markets in northern California that shared wholesale suppliers and delivery trucks, earning Lee Gim the reputation as the father of Chinese American supermarkets.[15]

In Lee Gim's and similar operations, all partners put in long hours to save on labor costs. The relatives and friends, recruited as necessary, worked hard without complaining out of personal loyalty, gratitude for the opportunity, and understanding that the harder they worked the sooner they too would become partners. These kinds of arrangements enabled Chinese businesses to easily extend service hours at minimal additional cost, giving them an advantage over their white competitors.[16] There was little potential for labor trouble. Even if there were, all the business transactions, partnership arrangements, and labor relations were regulated by the traditional associations, whose structure always favored the owners.

Traditional networks helped propel a number of Chinese businesses to expand into supermarkets and eventually chains. The best known among them were Farmers Markets (with forty branches), Giant Foods (with four), Centr-O-Marts (with nine), Jumbo Markets and Dick's Markets (with eleven each), Bel Air (with seventeen), and Famous Food Markets (which was a cooperative of several supermarkets connected to Lee Gim's Chung Sun Grocery by common partners and shareholders—Lee Gim being the chief among them—whose number varied over time).[17] There were many others as well. By the 1950s, there was a Chinese-owned supermarket in nearly every northern Californian community. In the city of Sacramento, Chinese Americans operated 91 of 223 supermarkets and grocery stores.

In much the same way, Chinese farmers in California attracted ethnic investment as early as 1891 to start the Pacific Fruit Packing Company. It was the largest fruit-packing factory on the West Coast at the time, and due to its success, many other Chinese canning and packing companies followed, packaging vegetables and tomatoes.[18] National Dollar Store, a department store that sold clothing and household furnishings, was established in 1921 in San Francisco on similar organizational principles, with branches all over California, as well as in Nevada, Oregon, and the state of Washington. By the 1940s, it was recognized as the largest Chinese American business in the United States, and, with forty branches, had expanded to places as far-flung as Kansas City and Hawaii.[19] Similarly successful large Chinese American enterprises were the Bank of Canton, established in San Francisco in 1906, which drew its major stockholders from within the Chinese community, and the China Mail Steamship Company. The steamship company was initially formed in 1907 by a group of investors brought together by a Chinese American merchant, Kwong Chu Chin, in response to China's nationwide boycott of American goods and sailing on American ships. Its services became very popular among the Chinese because the crews of its ships were mainly Chinese, and they serviced Chinese customers with respect, in contrast to the demeaning treatment Chinese passengers received on American and Japanese vessels. With Japan's increasing territorial designs on China, patronizing the China Mail Steamship Company became a patriotic act as well, helping to wrestle Chinese transpacific traffic away from Japanese carriers.[20]

All business transactions involving borrowing, investment, and forming partnerships required a system of fixed rules and regulations that only the well-established traditional associations' structure could provide. Rose Hum Lee's wish that the Chinese rid themselves of their traditional attachments, however logical from an integrationist's point of view, would have left them without the resources or protection to counter the hostile American society. In addition, the traditional associations and immigrant networks were the only institutions that offered the semblance of a normal social life to the Chinese stuck in their segregated communities.

ENTERTAINMENT

In the dreary lives of Chinese laundrymen in America, Chinatowns provided a much-needed and rare emotional outlet. Despite the negative image of vice and corruption that white Americans associated with them, Chinatowns were safe havens for the otherwise isolated Chinese Americans. They were a home away from home, where the immigrants could find familiar foods and meet fellow countrymen. Even in the smallest of Chinatowns, they could sip tea at a grocery store operated by fellow villagers, hear the gossip, and exchange news from home.

Larger Chinatowns, aside from grocery stores and standard restaurants, boasted meat shops, fish peddlers, bakeries, teahouses, herb stores, barbershops, temples of worship, calligraphy offices with letter writers, and theaters. Chinese doctors could prescribe what to white Americans seemed like strange medicinal brews, prepared from dried herbs, tree bark and roots, preserved centipedes, scorpions, and snakes, animal claws, bones, horns, and the like, but which were in fact based on homeopathic principles and were very effective in curing the ills of Chinese people. Despite the ridicule typically accorded Chinese doctors by the white press, which called them quacks, they were doing a good job. They attracted many wealthy white patients, and the death rate in San Francisco's Chinatown was lower than in any other part of the city.[21]

Although short on women and children, so central to Chinese culture, Chinese communities in America did their best to maintain age-old customs and practices. Several holidays were faithfully celebrated as if entire families were there. Chinese New Year's Day, replete with lanterns, firecrackers, and lion dances, was the day when friends exchanged greetings and everyone paid respect to ancestors and gods of good fortune by burning incense. Children, the few that were there, were indulged with candy and little red envelopes containing money. Debts were forgiven, enmity forgotten, and white friends and acquaintances invited to participate in the festivities. In the spring, during Qing Ming memorial day, people visited family graves. In the fall, for the mid-autumn Full Moon Festival that marks the traditional Chinese harvest day, everybody ate moon cakes.

The favorite amusement of the Chinese was the theater. Professional troupes from China were touring Chinese communities across the United States almost as soon as Chinese mass migration to the country began. The first Chinese theater performance was given at San Francisco's American Theater in 1852, when the city's Chinese population officially stood at not much more than three thousand. The Hong Took Tong (Associated Theatrical Benefit Society)—a Chinese company of

123 performers—was so popular that it remained on tour for several months. All the performers were brought by booking bureaus and actors' managers from China, usually on a straight hire-and-fire basis, as were the plays, costumes, musical instruments, and stage props. The New York State census of 1855 registered an entire troupe of touring Chinese opera singers and actors stranded by a contract dispute as residents of New York City. By the end of the 1860s, three Chinese playhouses existed in San Francisco, giving nightly performances. All were "profitable to the stockholders."[22] Chinese Royal, the most popular of the three, had the reputation of being "visited by every stranger from the east of the Rocky Mountains who comes to see the wonders and curiosities of California."[23]

The productions were based on traditional Chinese themes and historical events, depicting striving scholars, righteous officials, and situations resulting from that quintessentially Confucian conflict: the irreconcilable tension between filial piety and loyalty to the throne. They followed the established conventions of China's most popular theatrical forms: three main characters had singing roles, a few minor characters spoke their lines, comics provided tongue-in-cheek commentary on the events, acrobats created drama, a small orchestra added simple musical accompaniment, and wooden clappers set the rhythm of the music, singing, speaking, as well as some of the action. The theaters usually opened early in the day, with performances running until late evening, allowing members of the community to drop in and out at leisure and catch up with friends while sipping tea, eating snacks, and smoking at tables set up below the stage. The chatter stopped only when a performer's rendition of a famous passage was particularly noteworthy, and the audience rewarded it with shouts of "*Ho!*"—the Cantonese version of "bravo."

During the holidays, theaters opened their doors at seven in the morning. Except for one intermission at noon and a couple of hours, from five to seven o'clock in the evening, that gave performers time for dinner, the play went on until late into the evening.[24] Its "din" was so "loud and frequent that the district . . . is nightly disturbed far into the small hours of the morning," complained nearby San Francisco residents, requesting that the theaters be closed at ten o'clock by ordinance from the city's board of supervisors. The Committee on Health and Police responded by setting the closing hour at 1 A.M. But when police arrived at one o'clock to break up a benefit show given in 1878 at a Chinese theater near Washington Street, the eighteen hundred Chinese who were attending broke into a riot that resulted in smashed benches, a battered box office, and one arrest.[25] If anything, the passion of Chinese audiences for opera only grew, because by the 1890s there were six theaters that regularly produced Chinese plays in the city.

Chinese theaters were also established in Portland, Oregon, Los Angeles, and New York. In Portland, which had the second largest Chinese enclave in America, two Chinese theaters "ran throughout the year."[26] New York had its first Chinese theater at 12 Pell Street in the heart of Chinatown, which, after it was remodeled in 1890, became known as the Chinatown Music Hall. It had a fifty-actor resident company.

Wherever they sprang up, Chinese theaters never failed to arouse considerable curiosity among the non-Chinese public. Though most unaccustomed viewers found Chinese productions noisy, strange, and incomprehensible, many white avant-garde artists drew inspiration from them. At the invitation of the great actor and director Harry Benrimo, playwright George C. Hazelton wrote *The Yellow Jacket*. It was the first play based on elements of Chinese opera to be staged by a white theater company, and it became an enormous success.[27] *The Yellow Jacket* was a montage of several Chinese plays and told a rather melodramatic tale of one Wu Hoo Git, the first son of a Chinese provincial governor, who was banished from home when he was still an infant so that his father could install his younger brother, the son by a concubine, as his official heir. Wu Hoo Git, raised by a farmer, grew into a fine and elegant gentleman who eventually won back his rightful position in his birth family. The play opened at New York's Fulton Theatre in 1912, moved, restaged, to Broadway, where it played for many years,[28] and also found a home at San Francisco's Grand Opera House. It traveled across the country and throughout Europe. In 1916 the great Spanish dramatist Jacinto Benavente, a Nobel Prize winner, translated and adapted it for the Spanish stage, where it met with popular success; it later traveled to Cuba and all over South America. Before it's global run ended, *The Yellow Jacket* held a world record: no American play had ever traveled so far and been performed in so many cities.

The New World's appreciation for this old Chinese art form reached its peak in 1930, when the greatest living Chinese actor, Mei

Lan-Fang, toured America performing in Chinese theaters. Mei Lan-Fang, renowned for his uncanny portrayal of female roles, is probably the most famous Peking Opera star of all time. He acted as China's official ambassador of the arts, touring constantly throughout his career and entertaining dignitaries from around the world at his home. Bertolt Brecht, who believed that physicality had more integrity than speech, saw Mei Lan-Fang's use of pure movement to transform himself into a woman while wearing male civilian attire as a revelation of the body's true mutability.

VICES

Despite the rich cultural life of the Chinese American community, in the eyes of white American society Chinese American "cultural identity" remained forever wedded to opium dens, reckless gamblers, and lewd Susie Wongs peering from behind every curtain in Chinatown—images that inspired vicarious excitement and, at the same time, drew Christian moral condemnation. Unfortunately, the isolated and shunned Chinese often gained their only exposure to the outside world through contact with local police departments, where reports on their activities demanding criminal prosecution were filed. As a result, for much of the outside world vices were the only recognized activities of the Chinese in American society.

In 1876 Senator Oliver P. Morton had in fact concluded, based on the testimony presented to the joint Special Committee of the U.S. Congress on Chinese Immigration, that the Chinese engaged in prostitution relatively less than white men, that they gambled extensively but certainly not more than white settlers under similar conditions, and that the number of Chinese who used opium was smaller than the number of whites who abused alcohol.[29] But after years of forced isolation and bachelorhood, gambling, opium use, and prostitution did become more pervasive in Chinese American communities than in mainstream America—as may well be expected of any predominantly male society, with men working extremely long hours and lacking family ties. It is also true that many Chinese entrepreneurs, aware of the weaknesses of their compatriots stuck in such conditions, were on the ready to indulge them for huge profits.

Many Chinese stores sold opium and advertised it extensively in Chinese newspapers. A report by the American Opium Commission, presented at an international conference in Shanghai in 1909, estimated that about one-third of Chinese Americans were habitual and heavy users. A regular user consumed about six pounds a year.[30] At the mid-1870s wholesale price for the best two grades of opium, which was about $1.36 an ounce, a regular user would be spending $150 a year—more than the cost of passage across the Pacific.[31] It is small wonder that many a Chinese immigrant saw his hard-earned savings evaporate and the dream of returning to China delayed.

There did seem to be an unspoken tolerance of prostitution in the Chinese American community. Much has been made of the sale of women and forced prostitution, which was quite common among the desperately poor in China, and the underlying male supremacist system of values. On the other hand, patronizing prostitutes was not condoned by Chinese society. Plenty of cautionary tales and poems published in Chinese-language newspapers have been left behind by inhabitants of Chinatown as a warning to their countrymen looking for physical gratification and escape. "My life's half gone," wrote one. "I've erred, I'm an expert at whoring and gambling. Syphilis almost ended my life. I turned to friends for a loan, but no one took pity on me. Ashamed, frightened—Now, I must wake up after this long nightmare."[32] There are many versions on the same theme—stories of hardworking Chinese who lost all their savings in gambling and prostitution and, unable to return to China, ended up dying as bachelors in America. Yet all understood that "turning around" was next to impossible. Sociologist Paul Siu noted that the overwhelmingly oppressive conditions, compounded by the lack of emotional outlets, led Chicago's Chinese laundrymen to self-destructive behavior.[33]

Addiction to opium generally met with stronger disapproval in the Chinese community because not only was it viewed as a ruinous habit for an individual and his family; it carried with it the added stigma of China's "national shame." China had fought and lost a war against Britain, aided by the United States, over British imports of opium, and its military loss had led to an overall political and economic decline. Opium addiction took such a toll on the Chinese population that it earned the entire nation the sobriquet "the sick man of Asia." Writing about it in America, Chinatown balladeers struck a warning note:

"Opium is most poisonous. Ruining families, weakening the race. Once you are addicted to it, your life is gone to waste. . . . O, strike the warning bell—Shape up, don't be an addict any more!"[34]

Ultimately, much of the responsibility for the flourishing of vices in the Chinese American community can be laid at the feet of the merchants and their organized crime enforcers. Profits from vice industries were their main source of income, and their stranglehold over the community was so overwhelming that very few individuals dared to oppose them. One rare exception was Rev. Hie Kin of New York, who carried on his crusade against vices in Chinatown on several fronts. He founded the Chinese Students' Christian Association to educate the young generation of Chinese immigrants. He personally went to gambling halls, where he and his followers, dressed like ordinary workmen, stood at the entrance "persuading patrons who were being strapped of their meager earnings" to get out of the unhealthy games.[35] His efforts, in fact, damaged the gambling business so much that attempts were made on his life. At the same time, his efforts were backed by the Society for the Prevention of Crime and recognized by the White House, which invited him to meet with President Harrison.

Unfortunately, America's public attention generally remained limited to condemnation and moralizing. Although outside observers played up the extent of the Chinese menace to public morality, local police departments were loath to intervene. They were known to take payment not to raid, or to raid the payer's competitors. After police raids, the most powerful establishments reopened as if nothing had happened.[36] The police in New York were known for informing certain establishments in advance of raids, so that they could recruit a few gamblers to sit in the jails overnight. The arrangement was beneficial to all involved: professional jail sitters got paid, no damage was done to the gambling businesses, and the police department could take credit for effective law enforcement with impressive arrest records.[37]

ACHIEVEMENTS

The overall experience of Chinese American communities may have been difficult, but it was not singularly marked by deprivation and grief. Many hardworking individuals in fact took pride in their ability to seize on the opportunities life presented them with and counted their blessings. Lee Chew started his life in America as a house servant in San Francisco, but he also attended Sunday school to learn English. "I was getting $5 a week and board, and putting away about $4.25 a week," he later recalled. "I worked for two years as a servant, getting at the last $35 a month. I sent money home to comfort my parents . . . saved $50 in the first six months, $90 in the second, $120 in the third and $150 in the forth. So I had $410 at the end of the two years."[38] With that he was able to purchase a laundry and settle in New York.

Whereas the laundrymen worked hard for a pittance by U.S. standards, what they were able to save and send home was a fortune in China. Families in China continued to encourage young men to go to the Gold Mountain to make money, and while those already here may not have been exactly happy about their lives, they nevertheless put up the money as down payment for the transport of new immigrants. The lucky ones were able to save enough to purchase new laundries in more desirable neighborhoods, where high-income customers and higher prices enabled them to save even more. The really lucky ones were able to purchase "merchant" status, which allowed them to bring their wives, have children, and settle permanently in the United States.

The collective results of Chinese American contributions to their homeland were impressive. By the 1890s, the livelihood of the majority of residents of Taishan County in Guangdong Province was sustained almost exclusively by remittances from émigrés overseas. By the turn of the twentieth century, remittances from overseas exceeded the region's agricultural output.[39] *Paper Son* author Tung Pok Chin recalls how in his childhood, in the 1920s, Taishan was the least productive district in all of Guangdong Province, but was, ironically, financially the richest, "because more than half its population of 1 million received U.S. dollars for their daily living expenses."[40] In the 1920s and the early 1930s, remittances to Taishan from the United States alone constituted one-eighth of all money China received from abroad.

A survey of American banks in Hong Kong concluded that more than 50 percent of all remittances sent to China through Hong Kong in 1930 and 1931 came from the United States and Canada, which is amazing, considering that the Chinese population in North America accounted for just 1.7 percent of all Chinese overseas.[41] North American Chinese laundrymen's hard work enabled their relatives in China to pay off family debts, purchase more land, and thus increase crop yields better to sustain the family, purchase weapons to defend against banditry, build new homes, educate their young, and generally live better. Money left over from overseas remittances after the family needs were met was used to build schools, hospitals, and orphanages. It also paid for new roads and electricity in the area.

Everywhere in the Pearl River Delta region one still finds the remnants of houses built by the "Gold Mountain guests" as showcases of their American success. Many of the "foreign" houses built in the 1920s of tough gray oven-fired brick are decorated with Western motifs and have marble floors, Greek columns, and stained-glass windows. Many are built like minicastles, with towers soaring above the villages and with gun holes on the lower floors, better to withstand bandit attacks and sieges. Inside, one finds ornate chandeliers, bas-relief moldings, Western tile, and American stoves and refrigerators. Women in China dreamed of marrying the "Gold Mountain guests" when they returned for brief visits home. The "Gold Mountain wives" (*jinshanpo*) and their sons, "Gold Mountain young masters" (*jinshanshao*), were the topic of gossip and envy, with receipts of remittances from overseas rolling into their coffers and no husband in the house to order them around.

Aside from the money sent to their families and their villages for education and pubic works, working-class Chinese Americans contributed impressive amounts to all manner of China's domestic political causes and supported various efforts to reform, strengthen, and modernize China as a nation. That their contributions were having an effect was manifested by the fact that many young people who came to the United States under the slot system had more education and held more liberal views then the older working-class immigrants.

Chapter 11

In Search of Respect

NATIONAL DIGNITY

The degree of success an immigrant group achieves in integrating into American society is generally judged by the extent of its involvement in electoral politics. In the case of the Chinese, such measure was by and large not possible, because for the first hundred years of their life in America the Chinese could not be naturalized and could not vote. Yet they were far from politically passive. They were very much involved in the politics of China, because they believed that the mistreatment they suffered in America was to a large degree the result of China's being a weak nation.

An oft-repeated refrain among Chinese Americans has always been, "If only China were modern and powerful, we would be treated better!" To demonstrate the point, a Chinese could always point out that Chinese laborers were excluded from the country by a humiliating congressional act in 1882, while Japanese laborers, although excluded as well, were barred from the United States by a diplomatic accord allowing the Japanese government to handle the restrictions without invoking American authorities—the so-called Gentlemen's Agreement. Besides, Japanese farmers were permitted to immigrate along with their spouses. Also, when the ships docked at the port of San Francisco, Chinese old-timers could watch the prescribed order with envy: the white passengers disembarked first, followed by the Japanese, and only then the Chinese and all the other people of color.

Japan, whose people were "Orientals," too, had been forced to open its borders to the West by the U.S. Navy under the command of Commodore Matthew Perry in 1854. But, although humiliated, Japan quickly instituted a series of Western-style Meiji reforms and in less than four decades rose to become a Pacific power that could no longer be pushed around. In fact, Teddy Roosevelt, known for his chauvinistic views, had a grudging respect for the Japanese on account of their stunning annihilation of the Russian army in 1905 and did not want to antagonize the Japanese government on the issue of treatment of Japanese in the United States. Chinese in America wanted to help China become prosperous and modern like Japan, so that Americans would respect it more and treat them better as well. It was a high-risk strategy, because their "pragmatic nationalism" could be interpreted as evidence of their unwillingness to integrate and at times even led to charges of disloyalty to America.

Also, the indifference of the Qing imperial government toward the overseas Chinese was notorious and long-standing. As early as 1858, American naval captain Samuel F. Dupont approached a high-ranking Qing official to suggest that a Chinese consulate be established in the United States to handle the affairs of Chinese migrants. The reply he received was, "When the emperor rules over so many millions, what does he care for the few waifs that have drifted away to a foreign land?"[1] Other Qing officials justified the government's noninvolvement by pointing out that Hong Kong contract companies made a profit of $120 on each Chinese laborer sent to the United States—a total of more than $500,000 annually, divided between the contract merchants in Hong Kong and the Chinese secret societies in the United States. They saw no reason to extend government protection to that kind of business. In the end, given that only two types of Chinese went abroad—"the most stupid and the most wicked" (meaning the laborers and the merchants)—there was hardly a compelling need for the involvement of the Qing government.[2]

Only an international scandal eventually forced the Qing government's hand. In 1872, a Japanese naval patrol stopped a Peruvian ship attempting to smuggle 230 Chinese nationals, many of them minors, to Peru. The amount of publicity generated by the press coverage in all major Chinese cities was so overwhelming that it brought the Qing government's reputation into question and prevailed upon it to change its policy and set up legations in foreign countries, including the United States.[3]

Another incentive for the change of heart came when the Qing government realized the true economic power of the Chinese who lived abroad. As it experienced an increasingly serious economic and political crisis at home, it finally began to listen to arguments, long advanced by its officials in Fujian and Guangdong provinces, that it should take advantage of the financial assets and technical strength of the overseas Chinese to modernize China and thus counter the colonizing efforts of the Western powers and, by then, even Japan.[4] In 1875 Minister Li Hongzhang, the most powerful official of the Qing court, proposed sending diplomats to Peru with a mission to protect Chinese laborers there, because, as he explained, if the government was trying to elicit overseas Chinese contributions to modernize China's naval forces, "how can we ask for their help . . . if we do not care about them in peaceful days?" In his opinion, it was important to let the overseas Chinese know that the government did care about them, because only then would they "be loyal to the Qing," which he deemed "very important to our grand strategy."[5]

Such diplomatic efforts fit into the category of the proverbial "too little, too late." At every crucial junction during the anti-Chinese movement in America, the Qing government had been unable or unwilling to stand up to the United States, nurturing the illusion that if it acquiesced to American demands "the Chinese residing in the United States will be immune from mistreatment."[6] In the end, it only took it upon itself to defend the rights of the moneyed upper class—the people who were of consequence in its own social hierarchy—while it conceded to the American government the right to keep out the "objectionable class" of Chinese.[7] By signing the Angell Treaty of 1880, the Qing government gave the United States the right to "regulate, limit or suspend" the entry of Chinese laborers. The tactic did not sit well with Chinese merchants in the United States (the very people the Qing government chose to protect), because without Chinese laborers they stood to lose the main source of their income and profits.

During the last two decades of the nineteenth century, there would be no reason for overseas Chinese to want to support the Qing government either. It had brought China to the verge of becoming fully colonized: forced into signing unequal treaties, ceding territories to foreign control, allowing the Chinese Maritime Custom Service to be managed by foreigners, and consenting to the presence of foreign troops on Chinese soil—not just in treaty ports but inland, along major waterways. Just as it began to suffer a series of humiliating defeats at the hands of the Japanese army and navy, a medical doctor from Xiangshan County, outside the city of Canton, one of the chief overseas émigré communities, formed the Revive China Society (Xingzhong hui), in 1894, with the aim of overthrowing the Qing dynasty and establishing a republic. The doctor's name was Sun Yat-sen. He had been trained in Hawaii and had established the revolutionary party in Hawaii. He would eventually become known as the father of the Chinese Republic.

The new organization's primary objective of raising money for an army to carry out the overthrow was still too radical for the Chinese in the United States at the time, and Sun Yat-sen was able to attract only a modest number of followers among people from his home district and of his Hakka origin. Much more successful were Kang Youwei and Liang Qichao, the leaders of China's failed One Hundred Days' Reform. They had escaped from China after the Guangxu emperor, who had instituted many of their reform plans to turn the Qing Empire into a constitutional monarchy, was dethroned in 1898. A year later, they founded the Imperial Reform Party (Baohuang hui, also known as the Chinese Empire Reform Association, Chinese Constitutionalist Party, or Save the Emperor Society), in Victoria, British Columbia, to continue the effort of establishing a progressive constitutional monarchy by restoring to power the dethroned emperor. They received huge support in North America because they advocated the use of Western techniques to supplement Chinese tradition and proposed a program by which Chinese modernization could be accomplished within the framework of the Chinese imperial system.

In no time Baohuang hui claimed a membership of one hundred thousand in the Americas, with 11 regional headquarters and 103 chapters—of which 25 were in Oregon and 12 were in Montana. By collecting hundreds of thousands of dollars from ordinary Chinese across America, it was able to set up commercial corporations, which sold hundreds of thousands of dollars' worth of stocks to members.

The proceeds were then invested in its own banks, mines, restaurants, book publishing, and even streetcar lines in places as far apart as Panama, Mexico, China, and Southeast Asia, but also in New York, Chicago, and San Francisco. Profits from commercial corporations were channeled to party programs, such as education, and newspaper publishing (*Wenxing bao* in San Francisco, the *Chinese Reform News* in New York, the *New China Daily* in Honolulu, the *Chinese Times* in Vancouver, British Columbia). Military schools called *Gancheng xuexiao* (known as Western Military Academies, or The Vanguards) were established in twenty-one U.S. cities, including Los Angeles, San Francisco, Oakland, Fresno, Chicago, New York, and St. Louis.[8] They were put under the command of Homer Lea, a onetime West Point cadet and self-styled military theorist, who was appointed commander in chief of the Chinese Imperial Reform Association Army and who taught modern drill, troop deployment, and logistics.[9] The instructors consisted of Chinese volunteers and retired U.S. Army personnel. Chinese youth were trained to be capable of military action in China to restore the deposed emperor back to power. Similarly, the so-called Patriotic Schools (*Aiguo xuexiao*) were set up to indoctrinate future leaders in Baohuang hui politics. The most appealing aspect of Baohuang hui politics for Chinese in the United States was the party's position against exclusionary laws.

THE 1905 CHINESE BOYCOTT OF AMERICAN GOODS

The pro-China patriotism of Chinese Americans received a boost from the parallel rise of nationalistic sentiment in China itself, which for the first time led to an expression of public concern for the Chinese who lived overseas. In 1905, merchants in Shanghai initiated a nationwide boycott of American goods to express their outrage at increasingly humiliating immigration policies and mistreatment of the Chinese in the United States. News of mass raids on Chinese quarters, with U.S. immigration officials entering Chinese restaurants and private homes without warrants and roughing up innocent people, had spread like wildfire after the wrongfully arrested student Feng Xiawei wrote a book about his unhappy experience and committed suicide in front of the American consulate in Shanghai in protest.[10]

Equally notorious were the draconian methods employed by the pro-labor Sinophobic Commissioner-General of Immigration, Frank P. Sargent, intended to harass and humiliate every Chinese who showed up at the U.S. border, including the classes legally exempted from exclusionary restrictions. Mai Zhouyi, a missionary from Canton and the wife of a Chinese merchant, was locked up for more than forty days in the notorious shed on the Pacific Mail Steamship wharf while her papers were examined. "All day long I faced the walls and did nothing except eat and sleep like a caged animal," she told a public gathering in Chinatown after her release. "Others—Europeans, Japanese, Koreans—were allowed to disembark almost immediately. Even blacks were greeted by relatives and allowed to go ashore. Only we Chinese were not allowed to see or talk to our loved ones and were escorted by armed guards to the wooden house." Mai ended her speech by calling on her compatriots to work together to make China strong, and her appeal was carried by the *Chung Sai Yat Po* on June 10, 1903.[11]

Two high-profile cases were even more alarming. First was the experience of a military attaché of the Chinese legation in San Francisco, Tom Kim Yung (Tan Jinyong). During a raid in 1903 in San Francisco, police officers tied his queue to a fence and beat him up. He was later handcuffed and thrown into prison, despite his diplomatic status. He, too, took his own life once released.[12] Second was the already mentioned humiliation of the Qing court dignitaries, led by Royal Prince P'u Lun, who were stripped and subjected to the Bertillon system of measurement and inspection of the naked body when they went to the United States to attend the opening of the St. Louis Exposition in 1904.[13]

In the eyes of the Chinese public, the shame brought on individuals through such acts of personal degradation was topped only by the collective humiliation created by the resolution passed by Congress in 1904 (after renewing the exclusion act in 1902 for the second time for another ten years) to extend the exclusion of the Chinese indefinitely. Reflecting America's new clout among colonial players in the Pacific after victory in the Spanish-American War, Congress had buried the resolution in a general appropriations bill and hurried it through without any consultation with the Chinese government and, as reported by the *San Francisco Chronicle*, "without a single vote being cast against it and without a word being said against it by anybody."[14] The cumulative effect of the mounting anti-Chinese measures left Chinese Americans in fear that any further concessions by the Qing government would leave them totally unprotected. In 1904, Chinese merchants in the United States began to use their well-established business ties with bankers and merchants in Shanghai, Canton, and other treaty ports to urge a boycott of American businesses. The editors of *Sun Chung Kwock Bo* (New China News), a Chinese-language newspaper in Hawaii, openly advocated a boycott of American goods. Other Chinese Americans sent telegrams with private appeals.[15]

The urban, educated people in China took up the issue of the wretched treatment of Chinese in America because they saw it as yet another signal of the fundamental crisis swallowing China—a sign that it was time to wake up and build a movement to save the nation. The Shanghai Chamber of Commerce was the first to respond, calling for a nationwide boycott. Other groups followed. A slogan coined by a Fujianese merchant, "When our government proves itself unable to act, then the people must rise up to do so," was adopted for the national campaign, which quickly spread across China, especially the coastal port cities. Chinese communities in Hong Kong, Japan, and Southeast Asia joined in as well. At the peak of the boycott, Chinese citizens everywhere refused to purchase American-made cigarettes, flour, and kerosene supplied by Standard Oil. Chinese boatmen in Guangdong Province refused to ferry American goods across the Pearl River. Students demonstrated in major cities, civic groups organized highly emotional rallies in support of the boycott, and all newspapers carried articles condemning American exclusionary measures aimed at the Chinese. The exact impact of the boycott was not clear, though the Standard Oil Company in Canton did report a steady decline in sales during this period.[16] The Qing government at first tried to use the boycott as leverage to force the U.S. administration to modify its immigration policies, but it soon became alarmed at its potential to foment unrest similar to the Boxer Rebellion (1900), which almost brought down its rule.

In view of the reactions in China, President Theodore Roosevelt publicly condemned the abuses in the way the exclusion laws were administered and issued an executive order to "put a stop to the barbarous methods of the Immigration Bureau." Secretary of State John Hay, a proponent of the expansion of trade and cultural ties with

China, thought that the harsh exclusion laws were undermining his Open Door Policy, which he hoped would act as a deterrent to the bid of other colonial powers to divide China territorially. In the aftermath of the boycott, in 1905, the Department of State and the Department of Commerce and Labor instructed their personnel to be courteous in the treatment of all Chinese immigrants who were not laborers and threatened with dismissal any immigration bureau official caught in noncompliance.[17]

THE TRANSNATIONAL NATIONALIST PROJECT

The boycott of American goods in China further encouraged Chinese patriotic activities in the United States. After all, Chinese Americans were living in and had personally witnessed and understood well America's dynamic, technologically advanced, and democratic system. Why not act as an informed voice of advocacy for modernity and Western-style political reforms at home?

Perhaps the most important role the Chinese American community played in shaping the future of China came through the dozens of Chinese-language newspapers published in America. The papers articulated political programs, engaged in debates about alternatives, and criticized Chinese officials and policies—something that could be done only outside China. Chinese American positions were filtered back to China as "opinions of outsiders" and were as such subjected to less scrutiny and censorship. Chinese politicians, in fact, often borrowed and manipulated this channel to express their true feelings. They also unabashedly courted the overseas Chinese, visiting all major association headquarters across America with hands extended for donations and with promises of "official recognition" and government titles as rewards as soon as they came to power. This form of flattery exists to this day and has certainly contributed to making Chinese American leaders feel all the more self-important.

After the death of the reform-minded Guangxu Emperor in 1908, the hope for reform of the Qing imperial system faded, and the overseas Chinese community shifted its support from the Reform Party to the Tongmenghui (the Revolutionary Alliance, also known as the United League). Originally set up by Sun Yat-sen in Japan in 1905 through unification of his Revive China Society with other revolutionary groups, its stated political platform was "to overthrow the Manchu barbarians, to restore China to the Chinese, to establish a republic, and to distribute land equally." (It would provide the nucleus for Sun's future Nationalist Party, the Kuomintang.) Sun's vision for China reflected the fact that he was from the region of "overseas villages" in Guangdong Province, had been educated in the United States, and had been exposed to advanced political theories, all of which became embodied in his Three People's Principles: anti-imperialist nationalism, democracy, and socialism. It borrowed liberally from Western political thought, including French Fabian socialism, the American republican system of separation of power, and the British parliamentary system.

The Three People's Principles became the official ideology of the new Republic of China, established after the Qing dynasty was finally overthrown on October 10, 1911. October 10 became the official National Day of the new republic, and a provisional national assembly elected general Yuan Shikai as its first premier. In November of that year, New York's Young China Association organized a festive rally of two thousand people in Chinatown to celebrate the occasion. Boy Scouts and music bands led the parade. Floats decorated with the new national flag rolled down Mott Street. The crowds shouted, "Long live the new republic!" Barbershops remained open day and night, cutting off men's queues, which had been imposed on all ethnic Han Chinese men as the mandatory hairstyle by the ruling Manchus during the Qing dynasty.[18]

THE KMT AND OVERSEAS CHINESE

The elation about the new republic was short-lived. In 1913–14 General Yuan Shikai dissolved the National People's Party (better known as the Nationalist Party, i.e., the Kuomintang, or KMT), suspended the national parliament and provincial assemblies, and promulgated a new constitution that made him president for life. In 1915 he reinstituted the monarchy, had himself "elected" emperor, and sold out China's territorial interests to Japan. Mass protests erupted across China, and overseas Chinese gave generous support to Sun Yat-sen once again, when he called for a Second Revolution.

Although Yuan Shikai announced that he would cancel the monarchy in 1916, province after province declared independence as a handful of ambitious military leaders vied for power. When Yuan died later that year, the country plunged into a decade of warlordism. China's weakness on the international stage was fully exposed in 1919, when a provision of the Versailles Treaty that ended World War I ceded China's Shandong Province to Japan, although China had been among the victor nations. China's outraged intellectual elites spearheaded the May Fourth Movement of new national awakening, forcing a public reevaluation of traditional Confucian values and institutions. In this hour of crisis, Chinese nationalism emerged in full force to replace the narrow concepts of family and clan loyalty. Almost all segments of the population began to demand national unity to counter foreign imperialist aggression.

The only Western nation sympathetic to the predicament of China was the Soviet Union, which had itself just emerged from its own revolution against an authoritarian Czarist regime that was under European imperial domination. (Even Woodrow Wilson, the notorious campaigner for the right of self-determination of all nations, had ignored China's pleas to stop Japan from seizing Chinese territories.) China's Nationalist Party (KMT), under the leadership of Sun Yat-sen, accepted the Soviet Union's political and material support. Under Soviet influence, the KMT formed a "United Front" government with the Chinese Communist Party (CCP) against warlords and imperialism. It dispatched trained party cadres to mobilize the people into broad-based political activism. Although Sun's government grew stronger from the new mass-support base it found among China's workers and peasants, Sun never forgot the importance of the overseas Chinese in his effort to build a national government. The nation revered him as the "Father of the Republic," but he credited his overseas supporters as the "Mother of the Chinese Revolution." During the 1920s, in addition to actively soliciting their support by traveling to many Chinese communities around the world, Sun set up a special Overseas Chinese Affairs Bureau within the KMT.

The KMT began a systematic recruitment of cadres in the United States and emerged as an institutional power, with branch offices in all Chinese communities across America. It published newspapers to promote the party line, spread its anti-imperialist and antifeudal ideology, and enlist financial and spiritual support. It set up study groups to keep Chinese Americans abreast of the latest developments in China and tap into their energy. New York's Chinese community, for instance, contributed extensively to the military Northern Expedition under-taken by the KMT to reunite China under its party rule. In 1928, the party mobilized thousands to demonstrate against the Japanese mas-sacre of Chinese civilians in the city of Jinan in Shandong Province.

Chiang Kai-shek, who had assumed the leadership of the KMT after the death of Sun Yat-sen in 1925, set up a Nationalist government in Nanjing and decided to end the party's alliance with the Chinese Com-munist Party in 1927. He ordered a bloody purge of Communists, and when he finally occupied Beijing and unified the nation at the end of 1928, his government rejected many of the party's social programs insti-tuted under Sun Yat-sen. He suspended the implementation of demo-cratic practices promised by the Three People's Principles under the pretext that China needed "order" and "party tutelage," since it was not ready for democracy. The KMT was transformed into a party of offi-cials, persons wishing to enter the government service, and representa-tives of the dominant economic groups.[19]

The KMT's departure from the causes of the common people in China had an effect on the operations of its overseas branches as well. Initially many Chinese in America saw the KMT as the powerful new force capable of transforming the feudal and undemocratic practices of the traditional associations. Now, as the party undertook a wholesale purge of its progressive elements, it put an emphasis not on politicizing the overseas population but on educating it to preserve traditional Chi-nese culture. The Nationalist government viewed overseas Chinese communities as the chief source of financial support and investment in China. The party began to cultivate relations with the wealthy, influen-tial elites and traditional associations rather than with the general pub-lic, leaving the feudal structure within Chinatowns undisturbed. The association leaders, for their part, rendered full support to the National-ist government in China because they could use this connection to proj-ect an air of legitimacy and further their control of the community. Thus began a close alliance between the KMT and the traditional asso-ciations in dominating the politics of Chinese American communities.

The popularity of the KMT in the United States declined once it began to concentrate on fighting a civil war for domestic dominance and toned down its opposition to foreign aggression in China, particularly after it adopted a conciliatory position toward Japan. As the party splintered in China, with different cliques supporting Chiang Kai-shek, his "liberal" opponent Wang Ching-wei, and the archconservative Hu Han-ming, similar splits occurred in New York and San Francisco. Eventually, the liberal and radical factions abandoned the party. Some of them ended up forming political coalitions with non-Chinese groups.

CHINESE ANTI-IMPERIALIST ALLIANCE

A number of Chinese university students came to the United States for advanced education during the 1920s. Some had been politically active in China and were, like most intellectuals of their generation, highly idealistic and interested in mobilizing the masses. But they had no political base in the United States and had little direct contact with Chinese American communities. Chinese Americans, in any case, leaned toward moderate, pragmatic, and pro–free enterprise positions. Since many of the students had belonged to the left faction forced out of the KMT in 1927 after the breakup of the CCP-KMT alliance, they actually found a friendlier reception among American leftists and in the labor unions outside the Chinese community.

Historically, American leftist and labor organizations did not greet the Chinese warmly. In the nineteenth century, the reception had been outright hostile. (At that time, even Marxist groups supported "unconditional exclusion of Chinese, Japanese, Koreans, and Hindus" from the country.)[20] For a long time only the anarcho-syndicalist Industrial Workers of the World (IWW) held the belief that fraternal bonds existed among all wage earners regardless of racial divisions; only they made an attempt to enroll Asian workers, including the Chinese, into the union on equal terms. The attitude won some Asians over. Chinese followers translated IWW literature into Chinese and, as early as 1914, founded a Chinese Socialist Club in San Francisco's Chinatown for "sympathizers to gather together to study the doctrine." The club's founder was a political refugee, Jiang Kanghu, who originally founded the Socialist Party in China but had to escape when China's president Yuan Shikai banned the party because of its radical doctrines. IWW efforts to organize the Chinese did not go very far, however, because the group was targeted for suppression during the Red Scare of the 1920s. A number of Chinese activists affiliated with the organization were deported, while a police raid on New York's Chinese Workers' Club resulted in the confiscation of alleged IWW literature and the arrest of four individuals who claimed to be students.[21]

During the twentieth century, most leftist groups in America began to adopt positions against U.S. and European imperialism. They also came to believe in the importance of organizing colored minorities, in line with their strategy of trying to recruit the most exploited and most oppressed—potentially the most militant sector of the working class. In the eyes of the American Left, China was a victim of Western imperialist aggression and the Chinese people in the United States came to symbolize the victims of racial oppression, in addition to being exploited as workers. As such, they seemed a promising target for organizing. Many Chinese leftists were recruited and became active in the Red International Union, the Communist Party, the anarchist movement supporting the cause of Emma Goldman, and Trotskyite organizations.[22] A group of Chinese anarcho-syndicalists organized the Unionist Guild (also known as the Workers' League of San Francisco, Sanfanshi Gongyi Tongmeng Zonghui) in San Francisco in 1919, but their attempts to organize workers at Chinese shirt factories met with only marginal success, because they were too intellectual, with a penchant for abstract discussion and dogmatic adherence to set positions.[23]

The Third International, founded by the Soviet Communist Party in 1919 to coordinate the international communist movement, took the position that communist parties could form a united front with bourgeois nationalist forces, such as the KMT led by Sun Yat-sen in China, to fight against imperialism. Following this political line, the Communist Party in the United States (CPUSA) also actively supported the Chinese revolution against imperialism through a front group, the All-American Anti-Imperialist League (AAAIL), whose program was to organize a united front of organizations of workers and poor farmers against capitalism. It naturally took an interest in attracting progressive Chinese into its circle.

When Chiang Kai-shek split the KMT from the Chinese Communists in 1927, a number of Chinese American KMT leftists drifted toward the CPUSA. Among them was Chi Chao-ting, a KMT student leader in Chicago, who had already been recruited in 1926 by Manuel Gomez, head of the AAAIL. He was the first among Chinese Americans to join the party. As others followed, they formed a new radical group, the All-American Alliance of Chinese Anti-Imperialists (AA-CAI), and established branches in San Francisco, New York, and a number of other cities. Its Philadelphia branch seized the local KMT office and used the premises to publish *Chinese Vanguard*, the official organ of the AACAI. One of the first public manifestations organized by former KMT supporters in the United States was an anti-KMT protest. Held simultaneously in New York, San Francisco, and Los Angeles in July of 1929 by members of the radical Chinese Students Alliance, CPUSA, and AACAI, it led to near riots and several arrests.[24]

The first task of the AACAI was to rally the Chinese American community to its anti-Japanese position. It did so by pointing out that Chiang Kai-shek, despite his verbal commitment to resisting the Japanese, was dragging China into civil war, and that a true nationwide effort against the Japanese could not take place as long as he was in power. The leaders of the Chinese American community responded by accusing the AACAI of being partisan and anti-Chinese, and banned the *Chinese Vanguard* from Chinatown newsstands. From that point on, anyone reading the paper was to be denounced to the immigration office as a communist.

The alliance's second task was to organize Chinatown workers—no mean task. The Chinese did work long hours at very low wages, but most were self-employed owner/operators of laundries and restaurants. Where there were employees, they were related to the employers by kinship and village ties. Attempts to organize them along class lines won the alliance very little support. In San Francisco, the alliance members set up a Revolutionary After Working Hours Club, targeting disaffected workers in Chinatown's food industry who were paid low wages and worked fourteen- to sixteen-hour days without time off for holidays and vacation. But the members showed great insensitivity to local conditions when they pushed the workers to dogmatically demand an eight-hour day.

A very serious problem for the alliance was the fact that most of its members were Chinese university students who became radicalized in the United States. Most of them spoke the northern Chinese Mandarin dialect and were thus separated from the Cantonese-speaking workers in both class and language. Their attempts to educate the masses through outdoor rallies designed to raise the "consciousness" of the people met with considerable objections from the traditional associations. But it also made them easy targets for traditional community leaders, whose "information," given to the police, often led to their arrest and imprisonment on a variety of charges, such as disturbing the peace, illegal gathering, obstruction of traffic, and harboring subversive material. A few were deported in the process.[25] In April 1930, two student leaders of the Kung Yu Club (Worker's Association), Xavier Dea and Xie Jue, were arrested by police while making street-corner speeches in San Francisco. They were brutally assaulted at the station house before being delivered to Angel Island for deportation. They were released on bail posted by a leftist organization, the International Labor Defense.[26] On other occasions, alliance members were roughed up by local gangs.

The AACAI's worker-organizing effort in the end produced one conspicuous result: an admission of failure. Leaders of the AACAI published a number of self-critical articles in the *Chinese Vanguard* in 1933 acknowledging among other things that (1) the alliance cadres, with their overbearing abstract and theoretical concerns, ignore the concrete problems that face the masses; (2) the cadres look down on the masses and are not willing to educate them politically; and (3) the cadres mouth slogans and yet provide no concrete leadership for the people to follow.[27] Since the "rank-and-file leaders of the party were not from Chinatown masses," they "did not know or appreciate the problems and sufferings of the masses." Instead of working out "careful plans and strategies," which was difficult, they admitted, the organizers "chose the easy way out by shouting revolutionary rhetoric and condemning the backwardness of the masses."[28] The leaders of the alliance concluded that they had depended too heavily on theories derived from other people's experiences. They would have to develop their own politics based on work in their own community.

Chapter 12

American-Born Aliens

As the result of tight restrictions on female immigration, the number of children born to Chinese parents in the United States was extremely low. Nevertheless, the number of those who claimed to have been born in America grew steadily in the twentieth century, particularly after immigration records were destroyed in the 1906 San Francisco fire. By the 1930 census, the number had risen to 30,868 (or 41 percent of all Chinese in the country) and by 1940 to 40,262 (or 52 percent of all Chinese), surpassing the number of foreign-born Chinese immigrants.[1]

Since the only Chinese men legally permitted to bring wives to the United States were from the merchant class, most of the American-born Chinese (commonly referred to as ABCs) belonged to the elite within the Chinese American community. They never had to experience poverty in the old country, the horrors of steerage, the dreaded detention and questioning by immigration officers, or the struggle to make a living. At the same time, they were quite different from their foreign-born parents in that they were U.S. citizens, had political rights, and could speak English. They were educated in American public schools, which taught them about democracy, liberty, and individualism, and were fully exposed to American popular culture and mass media. They were also influenced by the myth of assimilation. Not surprisingly, they had reservations about Chinese culture and their parents' insistence on the virtues of hard work and frugality. While brought up eating Chinese food and celebrating Chinese holidays, they were less willing to speak Chinese and be controlled by the Chinese traditions of unquestioning obedience to elders and the prescribed and formal ways of relating to relatives and acquaintances.

The second generation of Chinese Americans also developed their own concepts about education, marriage, career choices, and leisure time. "When I was a little girl, I grew to dislike the conventionality and rules of Chinese life," university student Flora Belle Jan, a subject of Robert Park's survey of race relations, wrote in the mid-1920s. "My parents have wanted me to grow up a good Chinese girl, but I am an American and I can't accept all the old Chinese ways."[2] Chinese tradition was harder to swallow for American-born and educated girls than it was for boys. Parents expected girls to be compliant, marry the person of their parents' choice, and serve their in-laws. The girls wanted to go to college and make their own way in the world. The American mainstream exerted its own pressure. It expected the children of various immigrants to throw out the foreign cultural baggage that their parents had brought with them and to assimilate, or, in the case of the Chinese, to conform to the American way—or suffer increased discrimination. Under this pressure, Chinese American youth did everything it could to be as American as possible.

In 1922, the owner of the San Francisco paper *Chung Sai Yat Po* noted that his city's Chinatown had been completely transformed: "The younger generation of the Chinese people are so thoroughly Americanized. Most of them are well educated, receiving a high school [diploma] and many a college education. They are very ambitious and patriotic in the extreme. They take important parts in everything pertaining to the duties of American citizenship. . . . There is nothing Chinese about them except their complexion which is only skin deep."[3]

Their complexion, however, was all that mattered in the eyes of American laws and institutions, which treated the Chinese not much differently from African Americans. Outside Chinatown, Chinese Americans were customarily refused service in restaurants. David Young, who eventually became the Chinese vice-consul of Seattle, retained a vivid memory of trying to purchase a theater ticket. "They would only sell me tickets in certain parts of the show. . . . We were forced to go upstairs, when the lower floor was only half full."[4] Like

African Americans, the Chinese were not welcomed at public swimming pools, for fear that they might "contaminate" the water. Likewise, they were expected to attend segregated "Oriental" schools.
Since, San Francisco aside, the Chinese population in many cities was
too small to warrant a separate school, some Chinese children were
admitted to white schools, but they were barred from taking part in
extracurricular activities and social clubs. If they wanted to play
sports, dance, or debate, they had to form their own clubs.[5] Moreover,
the harassment they had to endure was often so devastating that it
forced many not to attend.[6]

Despite all that, Chinese American children, without exception,
showed a strong preference for American culture and a readiness to be
Americanized—to speak and think freely. Unfortunately, they ran into
a stone wall once they reached puberty, when their Euro-American
peers began to ostracize them. So they ended up alienated from their
parents by the virtue of refuting their Old World culture, and at the
same time rejected by their white peers, to whom they would remain
permanently foreign. This betrayal by their native country caused
young American-born Chinese to be confused about their identity and
to feel ashamed of China and of being Chinese. In fact, many abandoned learning Chinese—even though they were attending Chinese
schools. In an essay contest organized by the Ging Hark Club in New
York, the second-place winner, Kaye Hong, who was a student at the
University of Washington, wrote, "The ridicule heaped upon the Chinese race has long fermented within my soul. I have concluded that
we, the younger generation, have nothing to be proud of except the
time-worn accomplishments of our ancient ancestors, that we have
been living in the shadow of glories, hoping that these arts and literature of the past will justify our present. Sad but true, they do not."[7]

The problem that plagued Chinese youngsters in America even
more than alienation and rejection was that of career choice and mobility. They were the product of American schooling and, at the same
time, their parents' belief in scholastic attainment as a road to respectability and social mobility. The parents' Confucian conviction
that "if a man is raised to officialdom, even his dogs and chickens will
be promoted," sadly, failed to produce the desired results in American
society. Even with advanced degrees from American colleges in the
1920s and 1930s, American-born and raised Chinese could not get

jobs. Two Chinese engineers wrote to fifty engineering companies and, having received nothing but rejections, gave up. Even a graduate of the Massachusetts Institute of Technology ended up working as a waiter in a Chinese restaurant.[8] C.C. Wing, a magna cum laude graduate of St. Ignatius School of Law (now part of the University of San Francisco) was told that he could not make a living practicing law on account of his race. He barely managed to eke out a living as the only lawyer in San Francisco's Chinatown.[9] The well-known writer Jade Snow Wong received the following advice from a placement officer just before she graduated from Mills College: "If you are smart, you will look for a job only among your Chinese firms. You cannot expect to get anywhere in American business houses."[10] Indeed, American society gave its most educated citizens of Chinese ancestry "a China-man's chance."

Unlike their immigrant parents, who did not expect much beyond making a living in America, the second-generation Chinese Americans expected to enjoy the rights and privileges of all American citizens. Blatant racism, however, confined them to inferior jobs set aside by white society for members of their race. An alternative was to seek work in China, and many parents encouraged their children to do just that, believing that "a Chinese could realize his optimum achievement only in China." They were often told to "get an education and go back to help the people in China," because they were not wanted in the United States.[11]

China in the 1930s was enjoying a rare period of relative stability. Having embarked on extensive modernization programs, it was in desperate need of skilled professionals, especially in the fields of engineering, medicine, education, and research. Because of it, the choice for American-born Chinese to help China was actually a real one. The Chinese government encouraged the choice through several recruitment campaigns advertised in Chinese American publications. The Shanghai Aviation Association placed an advertisement in the *Chinese Digest* seeking Chinese students with aviation skills. The Chinese Ministry of Industry used the Chinese embassy in Washington, D.C., to urge engineers who specialized in iron and steel smelting to apply for jobs in Shanghai. The Chinese Department of Agriculture, too, actively disseminated the news of employment opportunities for skilled Chinese Americans. The campaigns were effective enough to lure an estimated 20 percent of the American-born Chinese to China in the 1930s.[12]

Sam Chang, a scion of a prominent Cantonese family with a government career in China who became a pioneer asparagus grower in Southern California, sent his American-born children back to China. He also urged his younger brothers to remain there. He believed that their knowledge would be wasted in America and that, as "America is the most racist society and very prejudiced against the yellow race of people," they would never become respected citizens. "Chinese in America have achieved downward mobility rather than upward mobility," he explained.[13] In reality, forcing China into their children's consciousness was for most Chinese American parents a way to put an honorable face on the pragmatic quest for decent jobs. "Serving the old country in need" was meant to help the youngsters come to terms with their ethnicity without acknowledging defeat in the face of the discrimination they encountered in America.

Going back to China was not easy for the American-born. They were too American for the people in the old country, too materialistic and free with money—particularly the young women. Still, marriages between native Chinese and American-born Chinese were not uncommon. Chinese American parents advised their sons to get wives in China, expecting native Chinese girls to be more obedient, more willing to work, and less wasteful with money. Young American-born women, on the other hand, had a better chance of catching a decent spouse among Chinese foreign students who were attending American universities and dreaded returning home to prearranged marriages with uneducated, homebound women. Modern young Chinese American women who followed their Chinese spouses back to China after their graduation found themselves among China's upper classes. In China, even a daughter of a humble Chinatown restaurant owner exuded the allure of a foreign princess. Such allure aside, most American-born Chinese found out that their Chinese-language skills were not good enough and that they were not sufficiently versed in the cultural practices and subtleties of Chinese ways to interact smoothly with people in China. In China, they were simply not quite Chinese. But what made settling there particularly difficult were the conditions. War with Japan was looming, and with the continued civil war against Chinese Communists; endemic floods, droughts, and famine; general civil disorder; and infirm government structures, establishing a career in China depended on whom you knew rather than what you knew and what you could do.

The experience of the American-born descendants of Loke Kee, a true Chinese pioneer in the West who had come to the Boise Basin in Idaho in 1863 to work as a gold miner and then used the earnings to open a general store in Idaho City, is a case in point. As his fortune and family grew to more than thirty members spanning three generations, Loke Kee decided in 1906 that he'd had enough of the discrimination in his adoptive country and that he would take his entire family back to China. Not everyone wanted to go, but the patriarch left them no choice. His teenage granddaughter, Cue Di Sang, was dragged from her hiding place on the day of departure and forced into the adventure of her lifetime, which she would always regret. Loke Kee died in Hong Kong, before getting to his home village, leaving his American-born offspring to fend for themselves in a land they had never seen. "When we reached China and found how the country was, our heart became very sad," Cue Di Sang wrote to her friends in Idaho, with whom she would remain in contact for the rest of her life. "I have seen many new things here but nothing that can beat what the United States has."[14] As the civil war raged throughout the 1920s and 1930s, the wealth accumulated by Cue Di Sang's grandfather was depleted and the family struggled to survive. "How foolish my father is, to bring such a crowd of native born children back to China," she complained, blaming her father and grandfather for ruining her life. She ended up teaching English in a private school and dreaming of returning to America one day. Her friends from Idaho kept writing and sending money to assist her, so that none of her family members were ever starving, but neither were they "a bit happy, nor satisfied" being where they were. Luckily, most Chinese in America realized that, regardless of how unwelcoming the racial environment in the United States, going to China was not a good option for their American-born offspring.

The second-generation Chinese in America took to shaping their social environment by developing their own organizations, such as San Francisco's Chinese Cultural Club, Chinese Arts Club, Chinese Musicians Associations, Ging Hawk Club, and Chinese Athletic Club. They all encouraged educational and cultural activities, and many promoted understanding of Chinese culture among Chinese Americans, but their ultimate objective was to help the American-born gain confidence to seek access to the American mainstream. Even more bent on Americanizing Chinese youth were the Chinese YMCAs (established in 1912 in San Francisco, in 1916 in New York, in 1921 in Oakland, and in 1923 in Seattle) and the Chinese YWCA (established in 1916 in San Francisco), whose expressed goal was "less to convert souls than to Americanize the foreign-born."[15] They all became very active during the 1920s, encouraging community and social responsibility beyond roles prescribed by Chinese tradition, particularly among young Chinese American women. They also worked closely with other Chinatown organizations and sponsored fund-raising benefits and disaster-relief activities for China.

Seven American-born teenage girls were inspired by the Chinese axiom "In deeds be square and in knowledge be all-round" to form the Square and Circle Club in 1924 in San Francisco—the first purely Chinese American women's organization—in response to the news of devastating floods in China. They wanted to do something to help, so they organized a jazz dance to raise relief funds for the victims. A similarly American approach was taken by the CCBA and the Chinese Hospital Association in 1925, when, following the model set by the first Miss America beauty contest, held in Atlantic City in 1921, they organized a Chinese beauty contest to raise money for the Chinese Hospital in San Francisco. Sixty Chinese American women took part in the contest, and the fund-raising was a great success. The crowning of the beauty queen (chosen not for her physical or intellectual attributes, but based on her ability to sell fund-raising tickets) by the Caucasian mayor of San Francisco turned into a community showcase of Americanization and modernization,[16] with everyone eager to show that they were just as liberal and free-thinking—and as apt in dressing, singing, and dance stepping—as any American.

In New York, a bunch of former Chinese members of the Columbia University student band formed a musical group called the Cantonians in 1932 to perform Cantonese music. While primarily providing entertainment for the largely Cantonese Chinese community, the group also received several invitations to perform on Broadway. In a somewhat different approach, the Chinese Musicians Club, in addition to performing Chinese theatrical music, learned and practiced American music, as it saw the importance of introducing American music, especially jazz, to the Chinese community. Its members translated jazz songs into Chinese to make them easier for the Chinese to understand.[17]

Such activities may seem frivolous on the surface, but they were an attempt by Chinese youth to break through the isolation of Chinese American communities, which was both self-imposed and enforced by the mainstream. The kids were out to show America that the Chinese were just as human as other Americans. In 1936, when, following the new trend of the nightclub era that blossomed after the lifting of Prohibition in 1933, two "legal" cocktail bars opened in San Francisco Chinatown, young Chinese women found a new type of well-paying job, as cocktail waitresses. In 1938 the first Chinese nightclub with live entertainment, Forbidden City, opened on the outskirts of Chinatown.[18] Its owner, Charlie Low, dreamed of following the model set by the famous Cotton Club in Harlem, New York, and showing the Chinese brand of "colored minority talent" to mostly Caucasian audiences. "Why, Chinese have limbs just as pretty as anyone else!"[19] he declared, presenting Chinese American women in modern jazz, tap, soft-shoe, ballroom, and chorus line routines. White audiences thought Chinese girls performing Cole Porter and Sophie Tucker or parodying western musicals in cowboy outfits were cute and funny. But they saw them only as amusing imitators, not as artists to be taken seriously. Many marveled at the fact that these "Orientals" could even speak English, let alone perform Western song and dance.

By and large, the Chinese community condemned the brazen young women for un-Chinese behavior. "Dancing just was not a part of the Chinese culture," explains Mary Mammon, one of the Forbidden City dancers.[20] Jadin Wong, who escaped from home through her bedroom window to join the chorus line, recalls, "When I started to dance, people thought our family went to the dogs." Instead, Jadin went on to Hollywood. (Now in her nineties, she is the doyenne of Asian American performers and entertainers and runs a talent agency in New York.) But the girls were delighted with the opportunity to show off their American-style talents and make some money at the same time.[21] Some, like Bertha Hing, supported themselves through college by kicking up their heels at the Forbidden City. The club was so popular that it counted senators, governors, and Hollywood types such as Ronald Reagan among its customers. It inspired C.Y. Lee's best selling novel *Flower Drum Song*, which was made into a musical by Rodgers and Hammerstein.

Chinese communities in New York and Los Angeles followed suit by opening Chinese nightclubs catering to white clientele. Chinese performing Chinese Frank Sinatra or Chinese Ginger Rogers routines were conscious that they were selling their ethnicity and often adjusted their hairstyle, dress, and even names to conform to the expected image of the exotic Oriental. Yet even while doing so they were subverting the expectations of both Chinese and American society by not playing the real-life roles of obedient sons and daughters, demure maidens, laundrymen, and houseboys. Like the flappers of the 1920s Jazz Age who rejected convention, Chinese nightclub girls were rebels. Unfortunately, their defiance of the racial order and the limits that it set upon them could carry them only so far. Even the most successful Chinese American performer of all time, Anna May Wong, was ultimately unable to break through racial stereotypes and typecasting.

Born in 1905 to a Los Angeles laundryman, Anna May Wong became infatuated with "flickers" as a child and became a Hollywood star while still a teenager. She made more than a hundred films in a remarkable forty-year career that spanned the silent, sound, and early television eras. Due to antimiscegenation laws that were still in effect in the United States during the first half of the twentieth century, relationships between races were forbidden on-screen, including kissing. Wong was thus relegated to supporting, stereotypical roles that embodied prevalent racist notions of Oriental exoticism and villainy, but she fought hard throughout her career to make her roles more positive and authentic. Her thoughtfully crafted, nuanced performances and her powerful, alluring screen presence often upstaged the top-billed white leads. Despite the raging racism in the society around her, American audiences loved her, and she was a household name.

Her inability to break out of the Hollywood mold, however ultimately took its toll. Anna May Wong moved to Europe in 1928, as did many nonwhite American entertainers of her time, seeking a more racially tolerant climate. She made a number of films and appeared in stage productions in England, Germany, and France. "I think I left Hollywood because I died so often," she later explained her decision. The ultimate insult, however, was the decision of studios to pass over her authentic talent and cast Caucasian actors in "yellowface" in the few available leading Asian roles. When she did not get the coveted role of O-lan in 1936 in the film version of Pearl S. Buck's *The Good Earth* about peasant life in China, in which all of the characters were Chinese (the role went to the German-born Luise Rainer, amidst a cast of other Caucasian actors), this most modern and most American of Chinese American women, disillusioned, went to China, where the Chinese government berated her for portraying the Chinese in a negative light. "Because I had been villainess so often in pictures, it was thought that I had not been true to my people," she later explained.

Anna May Wong's story would be tragic if it were not also so remarkable. The slender, 5-feet-7-inch-tall Chinese American beauty, more than anyone, embodied the defiant spirit of her time and almost single-handedly carried the mantle of racial, feminist, and artistic challenge to the rules imposed by America's social order, Hollywood's conformity, and Chinese tradition.

Chapter 13

Inroads to American Politics

THE GREAT DEPRESSION THE CHINESE AMERICAN WAY

America's Great Depression began in 1929, and by the spring of 1933, 15 million people in the United States were unemployed. Minority groups and foreign-born workers suffered the most. Unemployment among African Americans was 30 to 60 percent greater than among whites.[1] "The depression brought everybody down a peg or two," Langston Hughes observed, "and the Negroes had but a few pegs to fall."[2] More than a thousand Chinese merchants lost their savings in bank failures, and many of them went bankrupt. In 1930 alone, more than 150 Chinese restaurants in New York City were forced to close for lack of business.[3] By 1931, 25 percent of the Chinese in America were jobless.[4]

With the rise in general unemployment, fewer people could afford to use Chinese laundries. Those who did brought in fewer items requiring less expensive work. Quite often, customers failed to retrieve clothes they had brought to be laundered because they had no money. In the restaurant business, which was hit even harder, the establishments that remained in business were forced to fire workers and cut prices, as well as contend with customers who refused to pay after eating.[5]

Yet, according to a Federal Emergency Relief Administration

report in 1933, only 1.2 percent of New York's Chinese residents sought relief, as opposed to 9.2 percent of whites and 23.9 percent of African Americans. The real Chinese unemployment figures were much higher, but they remained hidden behind strategies developed by the Chinese American community to get through the crisis. Many Chinese, for instance, split full-time jobs with fellow association members, or received temporary room and board at their *fong*, or associations, for free. Although the traditional mutual-aid system was able to mitigate the worst effects of the depression on the community, after several years of economic hardship the depression began to take its toll. Stories of tenant evictions for nonpayment of rent, of old men starving to death in their apartments, and of suicides caused by prolonged unemployment became quite common. The struggle for survival in America, in fact, became so tough that many Chinese left the country, either to return to China or to migrate to South America.[6]

It was during the height of the Great Depression that the "dogmatic leftists" finally found an issue on which they could connect with the Chinese community. In both San Francisco's and New York's Chinatowns, members of the AACAI set up Chinese Unemployed Councils (Huaren Shiyi Hui), following the lead of similar organizations in other communities. In Harlem, for instance, the Unemployed Councils had mobilized the community into rent strikes and helped tenants forcibly evicted by city marshals to move their furniture back from the street into their apartments. Their appeals to community members, neighbors, and passersby to resist marshals and police if the evictions were repeated proved to be popular and very effective, buying beleaguered tenants time to solve their financial problems.

The Chinese Unemployed Council in New York started a project to fight the illegal eviction of Chinese tenants. It also appealed to local businesses to make relief donations. It accepted clothing, rice, and newspapers from individuals, and called for help from the government. It thus became the first Chinese organization in America to demand federal and municipal assistance. At the same time, it encouraged Chinese unemployed workers to participate in activities organized by the American labor movement. It sent a delegation to a national demonstration in Washington, D.C., to show its solidarity with all unemployed workers. Within months, membership in the Chinese Unemployed Council in New York climbed to several hundred.

The Chinese Unemployed Alliance of San Francisco organized several hundred unemployed Chinese workers in 1931 to march on the Chinese Consolidated Benevolent Association to demand relief. The alliance criticized the indifference of the CCBA to the plight of the community at a time when, according to its studies, there were 3,000 to 3,500 unemployed Chinese in the city. Twelve percent of the unemployed were women. More than 1,000 were heads of households with an average of three dependents.[7] At the mass meeting that concluded the march, the only female member of the Chinese Unemployed Alliance—the indomitable Eva Lowe, who used her early experiences with racism (she was the young woman forced to pretend she was her Caucasian girlfriend's maid so that the two could rent an apartment together on Russian Hill) to forge herself into a tireless campaigner for the disadvantaged and champion of the underdog—presented the CCBA with its demand for shelter, food, and free hospital services for the unemployed, education for unemployed women, and establishment of an employment office. Afterward, many of the participants in the march joined a massive demonstration of the unemployed in San Francisco's financial district.[8]

Under pressure, city hall finally opened a Chinese-staffed family relief office and established a Chinese Single Men Registry in the building of the Chinese Consolidated Benevolent Association so that bachelors, who were the hardest hit, could also apply for relief. As the economic conditions worsened, the CCBA, working with the city government, opened a forty-bed shelter and a reading room for unemployed men, while the Chinese YMCA provided free showers and a soup kitchen serving two meals a day for two hundred people. The unemployed could get free medical care at San Francisco's Chinese Hospital.[9]

The CCBA in New York was less responsive. After a demonstration similar to the one held in San Francisco, it declared in an editorial posted in *Chinese Nationalist Daily*, a KMT newspaper, that the right way to resolve the unemployment problem was to "continue to follow the traditional way" and threatened that "all those Chinese who participate in political organizations may be in danger of 'being deported' by the Immigration Office."[10]

Unfortunately, the internal system within Chinese community could not handle the worsening situation. Like everyone else, when desperate, the Chinese swallowed their pride to accept relief. By 1935, approximately 2,300 individuals (18 percent of the Chinese population) in San Francisco were on government assistance, including 350 families, 25 unmarried women, and 500 unmarried men. Initially, the government supplied Chinese stores with free groceries for the needy, but by 1934 it issued weekly checks that families could use to pay for rent, food, utilities, and clothing.[11] Significantly, the Chinese (along with the Filipinos) on assistance received a food budget that was 10 to 20 percent lower than that given to white Americans, because the relief agencies believed that Asians could subsist on a less expensive diet.[12]

This inequity notwithstanding, the fact that so many Chinese joined the unemployed movement shows not only the extent of their hardship but also their realization that the economic system, not an individual, was responsible for unemployment. This understanding, shared by the majority of the working people in America, had turned unemployment from a local issue into a national movement. It had persuaded a growing number of people to question the validity of the capitalist system. With the political stability of the country threatened, the federal government had initiated New Deal programs in 1933 to support public works projects and provide a social security net for the unemployed and the poor, to blunt the edge of the movement.

As part of the New Deal, the U.S. Congress passed the National Industrial Recovery Act, granting organized labor the right to collective bargaining. This shifted the labor movement's emphasis from unemployment to organizing industrial workers to fight for improved job security and better working conditions in the workplace. By the end of the 1930s, industrial labor had gained the right to join unions, the right to collective bargaining, minimum wage protection, social security, and a whole range of other social benefits and safety nets, but the Chinese, who were not part of the industrial labor force, were left behind.

LIMITED UNION MOVEMENT WITHIN
THE CHINESE COMMUNITY

Although there were a number of attempts to organize the Chinese into labor unions, the problem was that very few Chinese worked in industries that were being organized. In New York, for instance, members of the AACAI did claim to have organized twenty Chinese restaurant workers into the Restaurant and Food Production Union, a branch of the radical International Labor Union, but these individuals turned out to be working neither in Chinatown nor in Chinese restaurants. The only employees of a Chinese-owned restaurant unionized by a U.S. union—the Cafeteria Employees Union—worked for New China, a restaurant near city hall.

The unionizing effort did not spread elsewhere partially because the unions were not able to recruit Chinese organizers. The American Federation of Labor (AFL) set up a Chinese organizing branch under its Local 211 in 1939, under the name Chinese Restaurant Workers Federation. Its avowed aim was to "promote unity among the Chinese and American workers."[13] In a "Letter to the Restaurant Workers," it condemned harsh conditions in Chinatown restaurants and called for a $5 minimum daily wage for waiters (not including tips), 15 cents per hour overtime pay, a $1.25 per week raise for cooks, and a sixty-hour week for all workers. If management rejected these demands, the workers were urged to picket the restaurants. Chinese restaurant owners became alarmed enough to appeal to the Chinese community for "unity" and a "friendly relationship between workers and management," against "outsiders." In the end, the AFL was unable to win sustained support from the Chinese workers; the few that joined soon dropped out, in part because those associated with the union were fired and blacklisted in restaurants throughout the Chinese community.

In San Francisco, the organizing effort focused on the Chinese garment industry, which employed the largest group of factory workers in the community. In the early 1930s, a handful of radical community leaders attempted to set up a Chinese branch of the left-wing Trade Union Unity League's (TUUL) Needle Trade Workers Industrial Union and lead the notoriously overworked Chinese garment workers to a strike. But because they merely copied the militant organizing style of the mainstream American labor movement, their radical approach gained them no support among the Chinese. The much more powerful International Ladies Garment Workers' Union (ILGWU), which entered the arena in 1934, was similarly unsuccessful for several years until it finally managed to lead the dissatisfied workers at the National Dollar Store factory, the largest in San Francisco's Chinatown, to a 105-day strike in 1938. The three-and-a-half-month work stoppage forced the employer to recognize a Chinatown union local.[14]

Ultimately, Chinese union activists failed in building a labor movement because there were few Chinese who worked under classical wage-labor conditions. Their biggest failure was their inability to recognize the plight of the most important segment of the Chinese working population, which labored in the hand-laundry industry. When the Great Depression brought a true and enduring labor movement to the Chinese community, it was organized not by the Chinese leftist activists but by the laundrymen themselves.

CHINESE HAND LAUNDRY ASSOCIATION

During the 1930s, there were 3,350 Chinese hand laundries in New York City, where 60 percent of the Chinese population was engaged in the laundry trade. The laundry work was intense but the Chinese had no choice. They were competing against the large mechanized laundries, which since World War I had been using cost-cutting washing machines and steam presses, operated by cheap black and immigrant female labor. The Chinese were forced to fight for customers by providing extra service, such as free mending, pickup, and delivery. They kept their prices 1 or 2 cents lower than the competition's. The strategy was successful, since a writer for the trade journal *Progressive Laundryman* complained in 1932 that Chinese free pickup and delivery was taking a large chunk of business from the mechanized laundries.[15]

New York's non-Chinese laundries responded to the challenge by forming a citywide trade organization. The organization established industrywide minimum prices that all laundries were supposed to abide by, but Chinese laundries refused to comply. The trade organization retaliated by organizing a massive anti-Chinese boycott. The attack was highly racial: a cartoon poster depicting a bucktoothed Chinese laundryman, sporting an old-fashioned queue, which no Chinese wore after 1911, and spitting on the clothing to wet it for ironing, appeared in store windows throughout the city. The non-Chinese laundries took the campaign a notch higher by convincing New York City's board of aldermen to pass a laundry ordinance that required one-person laundries applying for a license to post a $1,000 bond. Under the pretext that the bond was meant to cover possible loss of customers' property, it was clearly designed to force the Chinese out of business, because the small, unmechanized, one-person hand laundries averaged only $400 to $500 in profits per year, and could never raise the bond money.

The shocked Chinese laundrymen turned to the CCBA for help. The CCBA was supposed to represent Chinese laundries when they were confronted with legal problems because it had been regularly collecting $4 in annual registration fees from every Chinese laundry plus a $5 certification fee for every transaction relating to laundry ownership, so as to make it "legal." It had been making good income from the fees, since each year hundreds of laundries changed hands as their owners returned to China, purchased better stores, or downscaled to settle gambling debts. But the money went straight into the pockets of CCBA officials, making CCBA posts so lucrative that candidates were willing to pay as much as $50 for a single delegate vote during CCBA elections.[16] When the crisis struck, neither the CCBA nor any other traditional Chinatown association showed any interest in fighting the new ordinance. During a communitywide meeting to discuss the $1,000 bond issue, attending CCBA officials responded to a group of pleading laundrymen that more fees needed to be collected before they would even look into the matter. The few laundrymen who attempted to voice protest were cut off; one of them was bodily removed from the meeting by CCBA "goons."[17]

The encounter convinced most laundrymen of the need for their own organization that would transcend traditional village- and kinship-based ties. Most were so isolated from others in their trade that they found out about the city ordinance and CCBA's response only through a few articles in the Chinese-language newspaper *The Chinese Journal*. A reporter for the journal, Y.K. Chu (aka Zhu Xia), who had been critical of the CCBA leadership for years, regularly covered issues concerning the Chinese laundry business because he had many acquaintances among New York's Chinese laundrymen. He became instrumental in promoting the idea of a "laundry alliance for the laundrymen," open to "all Chinese engaging in hand laundry trade, regardless of political persuasion and sex."[18] Traditional community leaders were so alarmed by the possibility of defection by such a significant portion of their dues-paying "membership" that the CCBA, the *huiguan*, and the *tongs* all posted public notices around Chinatown to send a warning to their respective members: "It has been known that a group of self-serving rotten elements hope to use the laundry crisis to make private gain. . . . All Chinese laundrymen are hereby forewarned not to be fooled by these elements. If you ignore this advice, you should expect to suffer the consequences."[19]

Despite the threats, plans for the Chinese Hand Laundry Alliance (CHLA), spearheaded by the American-educated Lei Zhuofang, who immigrated from Taishan as a child (the son of a U.S. citizen) and therefore had a good command of both Chinese and English, went ahead. On the day of the inaugural meeting, called for April 1933, several thousand people poured into the basement of the Catholic church on Mott Street in Chinatown, representing two thousand laundries from throughout the city. To avoid family, clan, geographic, and secret fraternal divisions that could plague their alliance, the creators of the CHLA gave all members the right to elect their leaders. Three hundred members oversaw the counting of the first ballot, done by mail, which elected fifty officials of the organization—thirty-five to the executive committee and fifteen to perform the supervisory function.[20] The CHLA became the first democratic mass organization in the history of New York's Chinese community.

Paradoxically, since the laundrymen were self-employed, leftist labor organizers including members of the Chinese All-American Anti-Imperialist League had thought of them as members of the petite bourgeoisie—a class that in orthodox leftist view lacks working-class consciousness, oscillates in opinion, and has no determination to struggle. The laundrymen were therefore believed to hold little organizing potential.[21] Yet, even if petit bourgeois in theory, they were engaged in backbreaking menial work. If they hired assistance to help during busy periods, there was little division of labor within each laundry that would separate the work of an employee from that of an employer.

While there was little class conflict among laundrymen within shops, they did feel oppressed by the traditional associations, which taxed them, defined laws and regulations for doing business in the community, and claimed to speak for them without their consent. Once the CHLA was established, its first order of business was to hire Caucasian lawyers to challenge the proposed bond ordinance. Accepting the lawyers' argument that the ordinance was discriminatory, the city's board of aldermen reduced the bond amount to $100. The CHLA victory secured its position in the Chinese American community. Its leadership structure, democratic decision making, transparency in accounting, and stable annual dues attracted a membership of more than 2,400. The organization maintained contact with local government, applied for yearly city licenses, and dealt with police, health, housing, and immigration authorities on behalf of its members at no extra cost.

At first, the CCBA disallowed dual membership in traditional associations and the CHLA. The On Leong Tong, for instance, ordered the resignation of any member who joined the CHLA to be announced in a Chinese newspaper. The next round of attacks targeted CHLA allies, such as *Chinese Journal* reporter Y.K. Chu. Owned by an American publisher, Barrow Mussey Company, the journal had been taking independent positions that made it the most popular Chinese-language paper, with a daily circulation in the thousands. The CCBA initially tried to stop it from being sold on Chinatown newsstands, then sued Chu for slander. Finally, the CCBA tried to form a laundrymen's association of its own. None of these tactics succeeded in weakening the position of the CHLA. It stood up successfully against the traditional associations as an alternative vision for the future of Chinese Americans, ushering in the confrontation between old and new that would end up polarizing the Chinese community for years to come.

NEW DIRECTIONS IN POLITICAL ACTIVISM

Once the CHLA got caught in a long-term battle with the Chinatown establishment, it had to look for allies—and it had to do so by venturing beyond the Chinese community to an area that most laundrymen were not too familiar with. Up to that point, the only groups in the Chinese community with extensive outside connections were the leftist groups.

The issues of racial discrimination encountered by Chinese laundrymen within the industry and the tyranny of feudal forces within the Chinese community that most concerned the CHLA had a great appeal for the larger U.S. radical movement, which was at the time launching a drive to organize the unorganized into industrial unions

in factories. Helping the laundrymen's struggle seemed a logical extension of the Left's commitment to organize unskilled and immigrant
workers.

Meanwhile, after the CHLA emerged as a powerful mass movement, a group of Chinese radicals, having understood their mistake in
underestimating the laundrymen, wrote yet another self-critical article in the *Chinese Vanguard*. Members of the CHLA were now designated as the "poor laboring class" fighting against the exploitation of
the "evil gentry and local despots of the CCBA."[22] For its part, the
CHLA, although wary of the Left, recognized that it needed outside
help that only the leftist activists could provide contacts for. It is
through the leftists, who were generally better educated and had a
more informed view of the world, that the CHLA members learned
about American politics and gained contacts, legal help, and political
support.

Another issue on which the CHLA received the support of progressive labor organizations was its anti-Japanese stance. When during
Chiang Kai-shek's Northern Expedition in 1927 to crush China's
northern warlords the Japanese army sent troops to the northern Chinese city of Jinan and massacred nearly four thousand Chinese civilians, local KMT branches in New York and San Francisco organized a
Chinese Citizens' Patriotic League. The league sent a cable to President Coolidge, urging him to take a stand against the Japanese aggression as a threat to world peace. But when Chiang Kai-shek embarked
on a quest for KMT hegemony over China through civil war (aimed
mainly against Chinese Communists) at the expense of mobilizing the
country to counter Japanese aggression, the overseas Chinese communities were outraged. The only group that consistently called for resistance against the Japanese was the AACAI—a leftist group that most
Chinese Americans shied away from. But as the threat of Japanese aggression intensified, the Left's position became more popular.

When the Japanese Kwantung Army invaded and occupied Manchuria in 1931, a local military leader, General Ma, who had disobeyed
Chiang's order not to resist, was hailed by the Chinese public as a national hero. The only Chinese-language paper that reported Ma's
story in the United States was the *Chinese Journal*. As a result, the circulation of the *Chinese Journal* doubled to 10,500. Yet the local
branches of the KMT wanted the traditional associations to suppress

both the sentiment and the paper. Similarly, General Cai Ting-kai refused the order to withdraw the Chinese Nineteenth Route Army from the Chinese section of Shanghai in 1932 and held his ground for many months against the overwhelmingly superior Japanese troops and weaponry. Although he was later dismissed by Chiang Kai-shek, he became a national hero, and when he visited the United States every Chinese community he went to greeted him as royalty. By this time, the CHLA had emerged as the leader of the anti-Japanese movement among Chinese Americans.

As a result of Chiang Kai-shek's politics, a full-fledged opposition to the CCBA and the traditional associations, which were aligned with the KMT, took hold in Chinese American communities. The CHLA represented the working people, who sided with the Chinese Left, the American progressive and labor unions, and forces calling for resistance against the Japanese occupation of China, many of whom were sympathizers of the Chinese Communist Party. Consequently, without necessarily intending to do so, the CHLA began taking increasingly specific positions consistent with the feelings of its membership, its allies, and even the enemies of its enemy. By mid-1934 it was powerful enough to assume the role of spokesperson for all manner of progressive projects and groups, giving them space and nurturing them to grow under its wings.

The CHLA became openly critical of many venerable community customs and leisure-time activities, such as wasteful banquets, weekday all-night gambling, and expensive, unending mutual gift giving during New Year and birthday celebrations that only obliged recipients to give more. Under its auspices, study groups were organized to discuss current events in China, while a flying club trained volunteer pilots to fight the Japanese. Due to its efforts, a new social environment was emerging in the community, giving the people long accused of having a sojourner mentality an optimistic attitude about their life in the United States. One of the most successful social clubs in Chinatown was the Quon Shar (Mass Club), organized by CHLA members. It sponsored trips, dances, lectures, and other social and educational programs.

New clubs and social groups gave rise to a new Chinese American identity, breaking loose from the confines of the family, clan, village, and *tong* ties. The Chinese were no longer content to struggle in isolation and wanted to reach out to American society. A few joined the

International Workers' Order (IWO), a cooperative health-insurance organization whose other major aim was to sponsor social and political functions where members of different ethnic groups could meet. There was so much interest in it that a Chinatown branch, IWO Lodge No. 678, was formed, and at one time it had more than eighty members.[23]

Chinese youth clubs sprouted in both New York and San Francisco to give young people their own space for healthy recreation and socializing. By joining the progressive American Youth Congress, Chinese youth clubs participated in various movements and events of American society at large, such as the May First Labor Day parade.

UNITED FRONT

Second-generation Chinese Americans, long grappling to find their own identity and make a path for themselves different from that of their parents, could nevertheless not help but go along with their parents' commitment to support China's struggle for independence. They saw it as the way to free themselves in America. Like their parents, they felt a surge of humiliation when leaders in China failed to stand up to Japan. "If you were a Chinese-American, you certainly felt the fate of China was important," wrote architect James Low, describing the feeling that dominated his Californian youth to Victor and Brett de Bary Nee for their groundbreaking study *Longtime Californ': A Documentary Study of an American Chinatown.* "I remember the teachers would always complain, 'China is weak, and look at the treatment we get here.' "[24]

One of the main frustrations of overseas Chinese was that Chiang Kai-shek, the leader of the Nationalist government, refused to declare war on Japan, insisting he could not do so until he eliminated the Chinese Communists. This policy increasingly ran against the majority sentiment of Chinese people both in China and overseas, to the point that even conservative groups would not support Chiang. Chee Kung Tong, the oldest and most political of the *tongs* in the United States, for instance, issued open letters expressing support for a united front effort against Japan. The notorious On Leong Tong, the largest in New York's Chinatown, also declared its opposition to those "national traitors" who refused to fight the Japanese. But only when warlord

Zhang Xueliang kidnapped Chiang in 1937 to force him to make peace with the Communists did Chiang finally accede to lead a united front against Japan. The Chinese Communist Party joined the national effort under the command of the Nationalist government.

The united front was formed none too soon, because on July 7, 1937, Japanese troops stationed at Lukou Qiao on the outskirts of Beijing fired on Chinese soldiers, to create an incident that would precipitate an all-out Sino-Japanese War. "As soon as the Lukuo Qiao Incident occurred on July 7 1937, the anger and frustration that had been building up for decades in the hearts of the Chinese people finally exploded," the *China Daily News* editorial published on the third-year anniversary of the incident reminisced. "We were able to mobilize the whole Chinese community within several hours."[25] All parties and classes, from top to bottom and across the country, were for the first time united as one. In San Francisco, the Left, the KMT, and all other political factions called for a halt to their quarrels. In New York, the CHLA and other leftist groups visited the Nationalist government consulate to pledge their loyalty to the common cause of anti-Japanese struggle under the government's leadership.

On the night of July 7, an ad hoc meeting of all community groups took place in New York and the General Relief Committee was set up. It was to oversee and coordinate all patriotic activities, particularly fund-raising and propaganda. The committee authorized a compulsory monthly contribution for every Chinese person and business in the metropolitan New York area. The minimum was set at $5; those who failed to make the scheduled contributions were to be fined. In seriously negligent cases, names might be published in local papers, or the storefront windows of delinquent businesses smeared with eggs. Within six months, the committee announced that it had collected $1 million. The CHLA was particularly active. Some of its young members set up a flying school and hired a U.S. Army Air Force major to coach them at a Brooklyn airfield, in the hope of going to China as volunteers. The CHLA also conceived of the idea of soliciting funds through donation boxes, which were to be passed around from store to store. It was from such donations that the CHLA was able to purchase three ambulances to send back to China; each vehicle had the alliance's name printed on the side to boost the troops' morale.

Chinese American women approached the war effort with great

ingenuity and resolve. The dedicated community organizer Eva Lowe, who started protesting against Japanese imperialism while still a member of the Chinese Students Association in San Francisco, had coined the famous slogan "If you have money, give money. If you have muscles, give muscles. I have neither money or muscles, but I can give my voice."[26] After 1931, in direct response to the Japanese occupation of Manchuria, women's patriotic organizations started appearing around the country; first the Chinese Women's Association in New York, and then numerous others in San Francisco, Chicago, Seattle, and Portland. The New Life Association, with ties to Madame Chiang Kai-shek's Women's Committee for the New Life Movement, eventually established chapters in Los Angeles, Sacramento, and Boston, too.

San Francisco was the hotbed of female activism. It boasted seven groups with different cultural and political orientations, but all dedicated to fund-raising and collecting clothing and medical supplies for the troops and refugees in China. There were drama benefits, raffles, sales of patriotic bonds, patriotic scarves, lucky coins, handmade flowers, donated jewelry, and confetti, as well as direct solicitations for war orphans and wounded soldiers. There were speeches, parades, picket lines, and fashion shows that featured historical and modern clothing worn by Chinese American women to the accompaniment of music. The shows proved very popular with Chinese as well as white Americans. "Ticket lines were so crowded that the lines formed around the block on Washington Street," remembers the woman who directed many of the shows, Alice Fong Yu. "As soon as we let one group out, new people were pushing in already—just one show after another."[27] They were great for the war effort in China, and at the same time, they brought Chinese and white Americans closer together.

PEOPLE'S DIPLOMACY

As Chinese Americans pooled their energy and resources to help China defend itself against Japanese occupation, they reached out to other Americans for support, starting a phenomenon that became known as the "people's diplomacy." Until it declared war on Japan in 1941, the United States was officially neutral in the conflict that was quickly spreading through China, although its relations with Japan had remained tense since World War I, when both countries competed for dominance in the Pacific region. Japan's expanding influence in China was certainly a cause for American concern, and in some quarters there was considerable alarm over Japan's close association with the German and Italian fascist governments. The American Left was particularly troubled by Japan's pretext of preventing the spread of communism to justify its attacks on China and its hostility toward the Soviet Union. Consequently, many people in the United States recognized the need to support China in order to check the expansion of Japan and, by extension, to combat the worldwide menace of fascism.

This, however, was not a generally shared sentiment. A strong isolationist trend prevailed in public discourse, while many U.S. corporations, including Ford, General Motors, Kodak, and Singer, maintained joint operations with Japanese firms and therefore had significant commercial and financial interests in Japan and Manchuria.[28] The broad aim of people's diplomacy was to inform the American public of what was going on in China and explain the reasons for war against Japan, in the hope that an educated public would put pressure on American policy makers to move away from their neutral stance. On a more concrete level, Chinese Americans used their contacts with the progressive Left to call for a boycott of Japanese goods. The Aid China rally, sponsored by the U.S. Congress Against War and Fascism and the Friends of China Committee, gathered some 15,000 people in New York on October 7, 1937, including 2,000 Chinese and Congress of Industrial Organizations members, to endorse the boycott. Two months later, under the sponsorship of the New York Friends of China Committee, 2,000 women, 450 of them Chinese, marched down Fifth Avenue with banners that asked American women not to buy Japanese silk stockings. Many movie stars, Loretta Young and Frances Farmer among them, promoted the cause, and many women indeed began to wear cotton stockings, or none at all.

Another challenge for Chinese Americans was to stop the sale of scrap iron by U.S. companies to Japan, as it could be processed for military use. In 1938 Chinese groups organized a picket at the Brooklyn pier to protest the loading of scrap iron onto the Greek freighter *Spyros* bound for Japan. The National Maritime Union gave its support to the picketing of cargo ship piers, both in Brooklyn and in San Francisco, and in one instance the longshoremen refused to load the scrap iron onto the departing ship. Such activities, which enjoyed the wide support of friends in the American labor movement, projected a new image of Chinese Americans. American-born Chinese, fluent in English and well versed in American ways, took the lead in steering the general public awareness away from "*tong* wars" and "docile" Chinese trapped in ghettos riven with internal divisions toward an image of a spirited community united by common purpose, aggressively reaching out for support from the larger U.S. society.

The new quest of Chinese Americans was aided by influential Sinophiles, many of whom were born to missionary families in China and maintained a commitment to the country in addition to having expressed sympathy for the Chinese. Best known among them were the writer Pearl Buck and Henry Luce, publisher of *Time* and *Life* magazines (both born in China), and John Leighton Stuart, a former missionary educator who later became the U.S. ambassador to China. All tried to depict and interpret the Chinese for Americans, none with more impact than Pearl Buck, whose book *The Good Earth*, published in 1931, was awarded the Pulitzer Prize for fiction and was made into a Broadway play and a very popular Academy Award–winning Hollywood movie. In this rags-to-riches tale set in the Chinese countryside, where simple folk struggle with nature to eke out a meager living, Buck made Chinese people feel real for the first time to millions of Americans. She endowed them with admirable attributes of hard work, strength, and perseverance in the face of the most severe adversities. Buck's Chinese were warm and lovable, kind to children, and respectful to their elders. Since her book's publication coincided with the Japanese attack on China, it accomplished a feat that could hardly be matched by any propaganda—it humanized the people who became Japan's principal victims and brought out full-scale American sympathy for the Chinese. Harold Isaacs, a left-wing journalist, MIT political science professor, and China sympathizer in his own right, said that Pearl Buck "created" China for a generation of Americans in the same way that Charles Dickens "created" Victorian England.[29] Others have accused her of inauthenticity and faulted her for her patronizing portrayal of the Chinese. Although her influence may be overstated (some have even credited her with drawing the United States into war with Japan), one cannot deny the shift in American sympathies for the Chinese even before the Pearl Harbor attack and the country's entry into

World War II. American sympathies for the Chinese rose, according to the Gallup poll, from 43 percent favorably inclined in 1937 to 74 percent in 1939.[30] Meanwhile, Chiang Kai-shek and his wife were chosen by *Time* magazine as the International Man and Wife of the Year for 1937.

On June 17, 1938, San Francisco Chinatown held the first of its three Rice Bowl parties, named for the collection bowls that were the most prominent feature of more than seven hundred fund-raising parties and parades held nationwide to support war relief in China. This one was planned as a Mardi Gras, with a parade, dancing, entertainment, and fashion shows lasting into the morning hours. People from outside Chinatown were invited to come, wear a "Humanity button," and "see for the first time behind the veil of mystery with which tradition cloaks this Oriental outpost"—as advertised in the *San Francisco Chronicle*. Two hundred thousand did. At the end of the festivities, the community, whose every member took active part in making the event a success, could take pride in the largest collection of any U.S. city—$55,000—and reporter William Hoy could joyfully announce in the *Chinese Digest*, "All Chinatown has come to agree that it was the most magnificent, heartwarming and spontaneous spectacle ever given in this 90-year community. . . . Chinatownians had always known the sympathy and generosity of the American people toward China. But whereas before they had only read or been told of it, on the night of June 17 they saw it—saw it in the faces of 200,000 Americans as they milled into Chinatown, as they vied on purchasing 'Humanity badges,' as they literally poured money into rice bowls placed everywhere for that purpose. The cause of this active sympathy was very pithily expressed in four Chinese characters written on a strip of rice paper pasted in front of a store which read: 'America Believes in Righteousness'."[31]

On the eve of World War II, the Chinese American community was, for the first time, unified, and its members were for the first time getting respect from the American public.

PART III

The Cold War Shapes
Chinese America
(1946–1965)

Chapter 14

A Window of Opportunity

EXCLUSION ACT REPEALED

When the United States joined the war to fight the Axis powers after the Japanese attack on Pearl Harbor in 1941, the American attitude toward China underwent a dramatic change, from contempt to admiration, because China's antifascist policy coincided with U.S. objectives at the time.[1] Almost overnight the backward and semicolonized country became a valuable ally, and its people were hailed as heroic fighters. The new image affected the status of Chinese in the United States as well.

Before the war, Chinese repeatedly complained about the preferential treatment accorded the Japanese in America. After Pearl Harbor, some 120,000 Japanese Americans—75 percent of them American-born—were incarcerated in internment camps because they were suspected of disloyalty, while an active lobbying effort by a coalition of liberal China scholars, church leaders, politicians, and influential Chinese Americans got under way to pressure Congress into repealing the Chinese Exclusion Act. Clearly, the effort on behalf of the Chinese did not mean a change of American attitudes toward "colored people" because, while Japanese Americans were interned, the loyalty of German and Italian Americans was never questioned. It merely reflected the fact that the treatment of Chinese in the United States became a major concern of the American war effort.

After the United States declared war on Japan, Radio Tokyo began to broadcast to China the information that Chinese in America were "forced to undergo the most humiliating and discourteous treatment and detention at the various immigration stations" and reminded Chinese audiences that "while white people are free to live in China, the Chinese cannot enter the United States."[2] At the same time, the Japanese government used racial mistreatment of all Asians in America in support of its call to all people of Asia to unite in a race war against white America.[3] Japan justified its expansion in Asia by coining the concept of "Asia for Asians" and by claiming the need "to liberate Asian countries from Western imperialist powers" through the building of a Greater East Asia Co-Prosperity Sphere.

A few prominent Americans understood that if America was to carry on its mission as the "arsenal of democracy"—as its leaders claimed when joining World War II—it would have to change its domestic racial policy to silence the foreign critics. Writer Pearl Buck, for instance, suggested that "every lynching, every race riot, gives joy to Japan."[4] Additional pressure for the repeal of the Chinese Exclusion Act came from the rumor that Japan had approached Chiang Kai-shek to offer a separate peace, knowing full well that he was unhappy with the level of support he was getting from the United States, which had been devoting almost all its attention and resources to the European theater after it joined the war. Citing lack of resources to fight Japan, Chiang Kai-shek threatened time and again to reconsider his commitment. Admiral H.E. Yarnell, the one-time commander of the Asiatic Fleet, who was appointed special adviser to the Chinese Military Mission in the Office of the Secretary of the Navy prior to the outbreak of World War II, cautioned that the Chinese Nationalist government might collapse and urged Congress in 1943 to show "by act as well as by word" that China was in every aspect an equal partner with all the United States' other major allies. Repealing the Chinese exclusion law, he argued, would have the impact of "twenty divisions" against the Japanese army.[5]

The motion for the repeal was initiated by a group of China scholars, church leaders, media figures (like Time/Life founder Henry Luce), and politicians (such as Congressman Walter Judd from Minnesota, who had once been a medical missionary in East Asia), who formed the Citizens Committee to Repeal Chinese Exclusion.[6] Their motivations varied. Christian groups always had an optimistic view of China as a land replete with people ready for conversion to Christianity. The politicians subscribed to the business community's vision of the Chinese multitudes becoming active consumers of American products. One of the Citizens Committee leaders went as far as to predict that "in the years just ahead, a free and independent China will turn to us for all the products that American industry and mechanical genius can produce."[7] The Chinese American community joined the lobbying effort to plead its own case. Theodora Chan Wang of the Chinese Women's Association of New York wrote to Eleanor Roosevelt to ask for her support in granting Chinese Americans the privileges enjoyed by "our companions in ideology and arms."[8] The Chinese Consolidated Benevolent Association of New York criticized the exclusionary laws as a violation of the fundamental principles of equality and friendly cooperation between China and the United States.

Finally convinced, President Roosevelt sent a letter on October 11, 1943, urging Congress to "be big enough" to "correct a historic mistake." By repealing the Chinese Exclusion Act, he suggested, Congress could "silence the distorted Japanese propaganda."[9] The repeal was to be a "sweetener" to keep the wavering Chiang in the war on the U.S. side and the Chinese fighting against Japan "with a greater vigor and a larger understanding of our common purpose."[10] Congress passed the Chinese Exclusion Repeal Act in December 1943.

Once the repeal act ended the exclusion, the Chinese were allowed to immigrate, like citizens of all European nations, according to the quotas set by the 1924 National Origins Act—which in the case of the Chinese meant merely 105 people per year. In terms of numbers, the repeal bill brought only a small gain, but it *did* allow the Chinese to become naturalized citizens of the United States. Since most licensing and professional certification required U.S. citizenship, the Chinese in America were for the first time given the opportunity to participate in professional and commercial activities that had previously been denied to them. This proved to be of enormous benefit once the war was over to the thousands of Chinese who served in the U.S. Army. They also gained the right to own land and to form corporations in many states that had barred them from doing so on the grounds that they were "aliens ineligible for citizenship."

The significance of the repeal, however, went well beyond the benefits to the Chinese. It sent a signal that American immigration policy could no longer remain a purely domestic matter and that it would have to take into account national interest as defined by foreign policy. It can also be argued that the repeal opened the door for a series of modifications in immigration policy that eventually led to the 1965 immigration law, which got rid of the discriminatory national origins provisions of earlier legislation.

WORLD WAR II: A RARE OPENING

World War II also opened new horizons for many Americans economically. As the result of a massive mobilization in all industries related to national defense, women and colored minority groups, including the Chinese, found opportunities in new fields of employment.

The opportunities did not come automatically. Rather, they were the result of a militant struggle mounted by African American communities, which at the beginning of the war found themselves in especially dire straits. More than 50 percent of African Americans in southern cities were unemployed. The New Deal programs, although designed to provide a safety net for people in distress, had offered them little relief. The Agricultural Adjustment Administration had been designed to raise agricultural prices by paying farmers to cut production, but the money was given to the landowners and never benefited the African Americans who worked for them. "The AAA was no new deal for the blacks," wrote historian Harvard Sitkoff, as it had effectively shut out the sharecroppers, both black and white, from the funds.[11] The National Recovery Administration had been charged with establishing minimum wages for all workers, but as a result of its policies many employers fired African Americans to replace them with whites. Black leaders decried the acronym NRA as standing for "Negroes ruined again" or "Negro rights assassinated."[12] And while World War II revived the American economy, defense jobs were reserved for white Americans. Seventy-five percent of war industries refused to hire colored people. In 1940, for instance, African Americans constituted only 0.2 percent of the workers in aircraft production.

At the very time the United States was trying to cultivate its image as a beacon of democracy abroad, President Roosevelt signed the Selective Service Act in 1940, prohibiting the intermingling of "colored and white" army personnel in the same regiments.[13] The National Association for the Advancement of Colored People (NAACP), which had been fighting against racial discrimination in the armed forces for years, was outraged. "[D]eclarations of war do not lessen the obligation to preserve and extend civil liberties here while the fight is being made to restore freedom from dictatorship abroad," it warned. "[A] Jim Crow army cannot fight for a free world."[14] All the same, the army remained segregated throughout the war.

Once the war started, African Americans were assigned to the worst camps for training and given menial and dangerous jobs, regardless of their skills. Members of the highly qualified Seventy-eighth Aviation Squadron dug ditches, washed dishes, worked around officers' houses, and waited on officers. Black troops stationed on southern bases were attacked and even murdered by local residents. In April 1941, Private Felix Hall's body was found hanging from a tree near the military base at Fort Benning, Georgia, with his hands bound behind his back. In 1942 in Louisiana, two black soldiers were ordered to go into town near the base to pick up supplies. While one was in the store placing the order, the other was attacked, caught, and dragged up and down the street until he died.[15] These and many other similar incidents prompted the NAACP to issue a "Statement to the Nation," in which it warned that as long as "Negroes in the uniform of the nation" were "beaten, mobbed, killed and lynched," the "Four Freedoms" (freedom of speech and expression, to worship God in one's own way, from want, and from fear) that President Roosevelt had proclaimed to be values worth fighting for everywhere in the world "would be regarded as hypocritical."[16]

Meanwhile, branches of the NAACP organized protests against discrimination in the defense plants of Detroit, Los Angeles, and other cities. Their slogan was, "If we can fight for democracy, we can work for democracy."[17] A female grassroots organizer at a 1941 NAACP meeting in Chicago called for a march on Washington. "We ought to throw 50,000 Negroes around the White House, bring them from all over the country, in jalopies, in trains and any way they can get there . . . and keep them there until we can get some action from the White House."[18] President of the Brotherhood of Sleeping Car Porters A. Philip Randolph suggested that the march on Washington be used to demand an end to discrimination not only in the military but also in the defense industries.

Not only was the prospect of thousands of black marchers descending on the White House alarming; many officials were consumed by anxiety over the negative publicity such an event would create. "What will they think in Berlin?" asked President Roosevelt. Forced to meet with Randolph, he offered to call up the heads of defense plants and urge them to hire African Americans. But Randolph wanted much more. He asked for an executive order that would make it mandatory for Negroes to be permitted to work in these plants. Roosevelt at first refused. One week after the meeting, however, when he was told that the march was expected to bring one hundred thousand protesters to Washington, he signed Executive Order 8802, which read, "There shall be no discrimination in the employment of workers in defense industries or Government because of race, creed, color, or national origin."[19] As a result, almost 1 million African Americans entered the industrial labor force during the war years.

Other colored minorities benefited from the executive order as well, including the Chinese. Previously denied access to industrial and white-collar jobs, 30 percent of young Chinese men in New York almost overnight found employment in defense-related industries, such as the airplane factories on Long Island and the navy shipyards in Brooklyn. Many restaurants in New York's Chinatown had to be closed for lack of waiters. Arthur Wong, who had been working as a laundryman on weekdays and in a restaurant on weekends since he arrived in New York in 1930, went to work for Curtiss-Wright as an assembler and riveter, making airplanes. In Los Angeles, three hundred Chinese hand laundrymen left their shops to work on the construction of the ship *China Victory*. In 1943, the Chinese accounted for 15 percent of the shipyard workforce in the San Francisco Bay Area. Chinese also found employment with the Seattle-Tacoma Shipbuilding Corporation, at the shipyards in Delaware and Mississippi, in arsenal plants in New Jersey, in airplane manufacturing in Texas, and in war-materials manufacturing in Alaska.[20] Even professional jobs in defense industries were opened to college-educated Chinese with engineering and technical skills, the majority of whom were men.[21]

Chinese women found new opportunities, too. The *Chinese Press* reported in 1942 that several hundred "alert young Chinese-American girls" got jobs in defense industries as office workers. Alice Yick was the only Boston Navy Yard's Chinese woman mechanical trainee who could run light lathes, grinders, shapers, planers, and other machine tools. Helen Young, Lucy Young, and Hilda Lee were the first Chinese women aircraft workers in California. They helped build B-24 bombers in San Diego.[22] The pioneer Chinese American writer Jade Snow Wong, then fresh from Mills College with Phi Beta Kappa honors in economics and sociology, was hired as a typist-clerk in a shipyard in Marin County.

Jobs in factories, shipyards, offices, and laboratories gave Chinese the opportunity to learn new skills. At the same time, white employers were able to learn how capable Chinese workers could be. A Mrs. Yam, who had joined the Mare Island Navy Shipyard in Vallejo with her husband in 1942 right after her graduation from San Jose High School, commuted to her job as an electrician's helper in Shop 51 every day by bus from San Francisco's Chinatown. To honor her commitment, the company selected her to christen a Liberty Ship in December 1942, which she did, with the help of six young Chinese American girls, by smashing a bottle of champagne on the hull of HMS *Foley* (built for the British navy), as thousands of her co-workers cheered. She felt that she was "the proudest and happiest girl in the world," she told a *Chinese Press* reporter who covered the event.[23]

Many of these defense-related companies continued to hire the Chinese after the war. The experience helped dispel many prejudices. For the Chinese, getting jobs in the defense industries was a major step in the process of integration into the U.S. labor market.

Another major consequence of the war was that a large number of young Chinese men joined the army. Out of the 77,505 Chinese who lived in the continental United States in 1940, as many as 13,311 served in the armed forces—or about 17.2 percent, as compared to 11.5 percent for the U.S. population as a whole. A smaller number served in the air force, and 500 were recruited as apprentice seamen by the U.S. Navy. Given the gender discrepancy in the Chinese American community, this amounted to almost one-third of all Chinese American males between ages of fifteen and sixty. In New York, approximately 40 percent of the Chinese population was drafted, which was the highest ratio of draftees among any national grouping in the country.[24] Most of the Chinese American men welcomed the chance to join the army, anticipating that the specialized skills they would learn would useful to them later, in civilian life.[25] In New York's Chinatown, boys were so excited about the prospect of joining the army that a number of them tried to enlist early by giving the authorities their Chinese age, which made them appear a year older than the age indicated on their U.S. birth certificates.[26]

Unlike African Americans, the Chinese who joined the armed forces were generally not assigned to segregated units, though they, too, were usually given lowly tasks. Author of the earlier mentioned memoir *Paper Son*, Tung Pok Chin, joined the U.S. Navy three weeks after the attack on Pearl Harbor, taking a loss on the laundry he had purchased to become New York's first Chinese volunteer. "The status the navy allowed minorities was not particularly prestigious," he writes. "We served mainly as waiters for the captains and admirals. At the time the U.S. Navy would not allow any people of color, Asians included, into any other division than the Mess Attendants'. They later changed that classification to 'Stewards' Mates'."[27] Still, a high percentage of Chinese GI's saw combat, either in Europe or in the Pacific. Twenty-five percent of them were assigned to the Army Air Corps. The all-Chinese 407th Air Service Squadron was sent to the China-Burma-India theater with the mission of providing aircraft maintenance for the Fourteenth Air Force (the Flying Tigers).[28]

Hundreds of Chinese women joined the armed forces as well—either the WAC (Women's Army Corps) or the WAVES (Women Accepted for Volunteer Emergency Services, the women's corps in the navy). In San Francisco, in order to pass the hundred-pound weight minimum required of all enlistees, Emily Lee Shek, the first Chinese American woman to join the WAC, lived on a special diet and drank two gallons of water before her medical exam. She became a lieutenant and encouraged other Chinese American young women to enlist, too. A family friend, Jessie Lee Yip, wanted to follow her example, but her family was against it. "Like dancing or anything that was different," she later explained, "all the parents were against it." In the end, after she quit her Western Union job, her more liberal American-born mother blessed her decision. The results were rewarding. Jessie rose to the rank of sergeant, gained confidence, and after the war continued her education, supported by the GI Bill, to eventually become a court recorder.

The most confident of the young Chinese American women were the two fliers who joined the U.S. Women Air Force Service Pilots (WASP), created in 1943 to overcome the shortage of male pilots at home. Hazel Ying Lee from Portland, Oregon, had learned to fly at a program sponsored by the Chinese Consolidated Benevolent Association and received a pilot's license at the age of nineteen, in 1932, when fewer than 1 percent of American pilots were women. (Her intention had been to fight against the Japanese in China, but when she went there with another female and eleven male Chinese American aviators in 1933, the two women were not allowed to join the Chinese Air Force.) In 1944, Hazel became a member of the elite group of women pilots who flew fighter planes for the U.S. Army from production factories to air bases across the continental United States. She was killed in a severe weather collision during the winter of that year, when picking up a new P-63 fighter at the Bell Aircraft factory at Niagara Falls, New York, for delivery to Great Falls, Montana, and eventual delivery to Russia. She was one of thirty-eight U.S. women pilots who died during the war.

The only other Chinese American member of the WASP was Maggie Gee. She had dropped out of college to work for Mare Island Naval Shipyard in north San Francisco Bay but soon realized that she "wanted to do something more, something more exciting" and decided to enroll in flight school. Some 25,000 women applied, 2,000 were accepted, and only 1,074 received wings. Gee was one of them. She flew BT-13s and AT-6s for the WASP and flight-tested damaged airplanes. One of her assignments was to take male military pilots up for qualifying flights to renew their instrument ratings. She also co-piloted B-17 Flying Fortress bombers through mock dogfights staged to train bomber gunners. Years later, although forced out of flying by postwar sex discrimination, Gee recalled the war years fondly. "My horizon had broadened by the friendships I made with active women—doers from all parts of the country." As a result, she believed that she had become a more outgoing and politically aware person.[29]

For most Chinese Americans, men and women alike, joining the army had been their first chance "to see the world." It marked a turning point in their lives.

POSTWAR OPTIMISM

The most important benefits for the Chinese American community came after the war, when a number of the Chinese who had come into the country with nonresident merchant status or illegally were granted citizenship for their military service. Before the war, even Chinese who were American citizens were barred from bringing their alien wives or brides into the United States on account of their ineligibility for naturalization. After the war, the government decided to modify this policy to reward Chinese American veterans for their service. It passed the Chinese Alien Wives of American Citizens Act, which, along with the War Brides Act and the Alien Fiancées and Fiancés Act, allowed Chinese war veterans to send for both their wives and their children. In the five-year period between 1945 and 1950, 7,449 Chinese women immigrated to the United States, representing 80 percent of all Chinese arrivals.[30] Their entry pushed the gender balance between Chinese males and females from 18.9 to 1 in 1900 to a near normal 1.8 to 1 in 1950. The fact that for the first time in Chinese American history women joined men in significant numbers to make the United States their permanent home led to a fundamental change in the Chinese American community from a bachelor to a family-based society.

Another unforeseen consequence of the war was the breakthrough the Chinese made into mainstream American labor organizations. Most notably, the National Maritime Union (NMU) incorporated thousands of Chinese merchant seamen as members. Chinese seamen had long been serving on European and American ships. Many of them were natives of Fujian Province; they were usually recruited in Hong Kong and were generally underpaid and mistreated. The NMU had been one of the most progressive and racially integrated chapters of the Congress of Industrial Organization. When it organized a seamen's strike all along the East Coast in 1936–37, Ferdinand Smith, the black union leader who would later become a vice president of the NMU, was able to convince some twenty thousand African American seamen to join the strike. The union also reached out to Chinese seamen, many of whom were stranded in New York due to the lockdown, promising to negotiate with management on their behalf for equal pay and the right to shore leave if they joined the strike. The Chinese agreed, and the strike was successful.

Beginning in 1939, even before the United States joined the war, some fifteen thousand Chinese seamen were recruited in Hong Kong to serve on Liberty ships. The ships crisscrossed the Atlantic Ocean carrying Lend-Lease supplies to support the anti-German wartime efforts of England and, later, the Soviet Union. These were dangerous missions. Liberty ships were constantly attacked by German U-boats. By the end of 1942, 681 ships had been sunk and 4 percent of all U.S. merchant seamen were dead or missing—four times the combined losses of the army, navy, marine corps, and coast guard during the same period of the war. Among them, hundreds of Chinese also lost their lives. A number of them drifted in the open ocean for weeks before they were rescued. In one case, Poon Lim, a native of Hainan Island in southern China, was the only survivor of a U-boat torpedo attack that sunk his ship. He was able to build a makeshift raft and, maintaining himself with fish caught on a hook he made out of a spring from a flashlight, he survived drifting on the ocean for 133 days (a record to this day) before being rescued by a Brazilian fishing boat. For his heroism, Lim was given the British Empire Medal and authorized by special order to wear the United States Merchant Marine Combat Bar with One Star. After the war, he was granted American citizenship and employed by United States Lines.[31]

Their heroism aside, Chinese seamen who worked on Liberty ships were underpaid and not allowed shore leave on either the British or the American side of the Atlantic for fear that they might jump ship. Some remained on the ocean for months without setting foot on land. Their objections only subjected them to violence. One Chinese seaman who had been so abused that he requested to be relieved of duty and put ashore was shot to death by a British captain for "insubordination during wartime." The Chinese community in New York sought help from the Committee for Protection of the Foreign Born, an organization founded in New York in 1933 to defend the rights of the foreign-born residents of the United States, especially radicals and communists. They persuaded the NMU officials to side with them. Once the crisis was defused and the Chinese gained the right of shore leave, they began to join the union. Soon, the NMU formed a Chinese section and took a strong position in lobbying Congress to end the Chinese Exclusion Act. Later, it also asked Congress to grant the right of naturalization to all foreign seamen who had worked on U.S. vessels for more than three years during the war. Congress did pass a resolution allowing those who had served in the U.S. merchant marine before July 30, 1945, to continue their service. By 1946, the NMU Chinese section had a membership of three thousand, most of them in the New York area, with a branch headquarters in the Red Hook section of Brooklyn.

Gaining membership in a major American union was a critical breakthrough for Chinese Americans. Generally, the period after World War II was promising to be an optimistic one. China, in recognition of her role as one of the major victors over the Axis powers, won one of the five permanent member seats on the U.N. Security Council, and the gain of international status for China directly translated into respect for Chinese in America as well. The influx of women was transforming Chinese America into a family-based community. For the first time since Chinese exclusion started in the 1880s, Chinese had the opportunity to enter American job markets as they continued to work in the fields in which they had acquired skills during the war.

Politically, too, the patriotic movement of the war effort brought unity to the Chinese community. Even though the unity did not last after the war, the climate became more open to diverse political views, and the postwar Chinese community was no longer dominated by feudal district- and kinship-based associations. The traditional associations had already lost influence due to their ineffectiveness in addressing the needs of the Chinese population during the depression. At the same time, China's ruling Nationalist Party had lost support both in China and in the overseas Chinese communities because of its initial unwillingness to resist Japanese aggression. The vacuum allowed for the emergence of new mass-based associations, such as the Chinese Hand Laundry Association in New York City, along with a whole array of political, cultural, artistic, women's, and American-born youth organizations, which offered the community a sense of new possibilities in America.

Chapter 15

Cold War and the Chinese American Community

The hope of the Chinese American community brought on by the promising change in America's postwar domestic affairs was soon frustrated by new international developments. After the war, the United States was left as the lone superpower, with a tremendous industrial production capacity. By the 1940s, one-third of all manufactured goods in the world were made in the United States. It was crucial for the country to maintain high levels of export to avoid economic depression. The main project after the war therefore became reviving the world's major economies so that they could be America's trading partners. In Europe, there was the Marshall Plan, and in Asia, the reconstruction of Japan.

The Asia-Pacific region became important because, in addition to raw materials, its vast not-yet-industrialized population offered a potential source of cheap labor and a huge export market, vital to the U.S. economy. It was also a highly profitable region for the export of capital. American investment in Asia outside Japan brought profit returns of 25.5 percent, and in Japan, 11.3 percent.[1] As the new overlord of the region, America supplanted the European colonial administrations of Great Britain, France, and the Netherlands with local nationalist elites whose economic interests and political allegiances were aligned with its own. The U.S. government formed multilateral military security arrangements with Australia, Taiwan, Japan, South Korea, and the

Philippines, which were later expanded to include Pakistan and Thailand, better to encircle Communist China. In the name of "collective security," the U.S. military began maintaining more than thirty naval bases and airfields in the Pacific to reinforce its military dominance in the region, which started with the occupation of Japan (1945–52) and a series of interventions in China (1945–49), the Philippines (1948–54), and Korea (1951–53).[2] Over the years, the civilian coating would be added through foreign aid, blunt propaganda, and more subtle information programs. The U.S. Information Service operated libraries, published newsletters, broadcast news (mainly through Voice of America), and ran cultural exchange programs in targeted nations throughout Asia to disseminate the American point of view.

Only the rise of the Soviet Union challenged America's global project, but it quickly responded with the policy of containment, designed to stop Soviet communism from spreading beyond Eastern Europe. The United States first took this stand in Greece in 1947, and later in defending the western sector of Berlin. The result was the creation of two relatively stable opposing blocks in Europe. Elsewhere, the two powers were never in direct conflict. Rather, they competed for the loyalty of Asian, African, and Latin American countries—mostly ex-colonies, nonwhite, underdeveloped, and poor—which did not belong to either the socialist or the capitalist block, and which, after the conference of nonaligned nations in Bandung sponsored by India, the People's Republic of China, and Indonesia in 1954, became identified as the third world. The two superpowers then used third world surrogates to fight their battles without getting directly involved themselves.[3]

To woo the third world, the United States once again had to confront its embarrassing racial policies. The seat of the United Nations was located in New York, and leaders of third world nations had problems finding accommodation in the city. When Cuba's Fidel Castro arrived in September 1960 to attend the UN General Assembly meeting, the service his delegation received at a midtown hotel near the UN was so unfriendly that they decided to bed down in the Theresa Hotel in Harlem—to be among "their own people," in Castro's words. The cold-shouldering may have been more political than racial in origin, but Castro aptly used it to condemn American racial policy toward African Americans and threatened to present "a motion in the United

Nations against the racial segregation in the United States."[4] African diplomats in Washington, D.C., were forced into segregated quarters, while not so far away in southern states the lynching of African Americans still went on. In 1961, while on his way to present his credentials to President Kennedy, the ambassador from Chad was refused a cup of coffee at a diner on Route 40 in Maryland. Despite the embarrassment the discriminatory practices were causing the State Department, the desegregation and the dismantling of racist laws and ordinances progressed only very slowly.

The executive branch, even when willing to initiate reforms, could not count on Congress to pass new laws. It had to push for progressive change through the courts. In 1947 it sent a brief supporting the dismantling of housing discrimination in the *Shelley v. Kraemer* case, which challenged racially restrictive real estate covenants in St. Louis, Missouri. In 1948 President Harry Truman issued two executive orders, one instituting fair employment practices in the civilian agencies of the federal government, the other providing for "equality of treatment and opportunity in the armed forces without regard to race, color, religion, or national origin." The second order finally put an end to the racial segregation that had plagued the image of the American armed forces throughout the war. American schools, however, still remained segregated in the early 1950s. In the landmark Supreme Court case *Brown v. Board of Education*, which was the most important postwar desegregation case in the United States, both the NAACP and the Justice Department emphasized the role the case would play in the way the rest of the world would see America. The amicus brief of the Justice Department stated, "Racial discrimination furnishes grist for the Communist propaganda mills and it raises doubts even among friendly nations as to the intensity of our devotion to the democratic faith."[5]

The other cold war battle waged on the domestic front was the result of fear of communism from within, especially of labor militancy. During the war years, union membership had grown from 9 million in 1940 to 15 million in 1945, which was 36 percent of the nonagricultural workforce in the country. The unions had accepted a no-strike policy during the war and had agreed to curb wage demands so as not to damage the war effort, but once the war was over, wildcat and sit-down strikes erupted, resulting in 4,500 work stoppages in 1945 alone. In 1946, after the steel workers' and miners' strikes, the striking fever flared into a general strike in Stamford, Connecticut, and later in a number of other cities. The Truman administration acted aggressively. It seized railroads and put critical industries under temporary federal protection to prevent striking, while businesses all across the country launched a massive attack against labor radicals, particularly Communist Party members. Congress passed the Taft-Hartley Act in 1947, outlawing shop closings and secondary boycotts and thus preventing the unions from calling for general strikes. Also known as the Labor-Management Relations Act, it was passed over presidential veto; Truman had in fact denounced it as a "slave-labor bill." It deprived workers of the right to have communists in leadership positions. The act also gave the president the right to declare an eighty-day cooling-off period, during which labor would be compelled to return to work, in order to slow down strike momentum. As a result, the unions became more moderate and accepting of a cooperative, businesslike relationship between labor and management, which became known as the Fordist Compromise, since it marshaled in the "scientific management" stage of capitalism that had been envisaged by Henry Ford.[6]

At the same time, the country was swept up in a wave of investigations of communists and denunciations of "the Reds." The House Un-American Activities Committee (HUAC), which had been convened in 1946 as a permanent congressional body, spearheaded a broad offensive against "radical agitators," "communist sympathizers," and "fellow travelers." More than 2 million public employees were submitted to the "loyalty oath program" to combat the "communist menace in America."[7] The next step was ridding the country of "foreign" militants and radicals. A 1947 Department of Justice report claimed that out of the 4,984 "more militant members of the Communist Party," 91.4 percent of them were of foreign stock, implying that communists were mainly aliens and foreigners, not Americans.[8] In this context, the Chinese, long seen as aliens and foreigners by mainstream America, became prime suspects for disloyalty. The situation only got worse once China turned communist. As relations between China and the United States soured, Chinese Americans were caught in a serious conflict between the country that didn't want them and the country of their ancestors, which many had never seen.

In China, the Communists and Nationalists had suspended mutual hostility during World War II to unite against the Japanese, but the tension between them never vanished. Throughout the war, the Communists employed the strategy of hit-and-run campaigns against the Japanese, and their guerrilla tactics were successful largely because they enjoyed the support of the peasants, which in turn strengthened their military prowess. The Nationalists used the tactic of limited military engagement against the Japanese in order to preserve strength for the expected conflict with the Communists after the war. Near the end of the war, with help from the Soviet Union, Chinese Communists mounted a powerful attack against the Japanese and gained great expanses of Chinese territory in the north when the Japanese army retreated. As they advanced southward in 1945, the United States, fearing establishment of a communist foothold in Asia, airlifted between 400,000 and 500,000 Nationalist troops to block them. At the same time 53,000 U.S. Marines landed in North China to occupy Beijing, Tianjin, the Kalian coal mines, and, more crucially, the railway lines, in order to hold them in trust for Chiang Kai-shek's KMT government. By 1946, U.S. military assistance to the Nationalists exceeded US$1 billion, and more than 120,000 U.S. troops were stationed in China.[9] But Chiang's army proved no match for the Communists.[10] As it retreated from one area after another, the United States had no choice but to reluctantly push the two sides toward a negotiated settlement.

The Chinese Communist Party, aware that most Chinese people had no stomach for another war after decades of civil war and eight years of war with Japan, called for the formation of a "coalition government" in which the two sides would share power. Chiang Kai-shek refused. In the eyes of most Chinese, the Communists' position was more reasonable, as it reflected their concern with ending the civil war, rather than dwelling on ideology. In addition, Chiang's government was so rife with corruption and incompetence that it had brought the country's economy to the brink of disaster. The national currency, the yuan, was devalued sixty-seven times between 1946 and 1948; it became so unstable that gold and foreign banknotes were increasingly used in its stead. The poor were devastated. In 1948, in just a six-month period, prices soared by a factor of 85,000. A sack of rice, priced at 112 yuan at the beginning of the period, cost 63 million yuan six months later. Consumers had to push wheelbarrows of paper currency to

purchase daily groceries, forcing the government to institute a currency reform to replace the old coinage with gold yuan. A price ceiling
was set, and private hoarding of foreign currency or gold was strictly
forbidden. Two thousand people were executed for violating this law
administered by Chiang Kai-shek's son, Chiang Jing-kuo. But millions
of Chinese people who had converted their liquid assets into gold yuan
found themselves penniless when it, too, collapsed. After that, very few
people, even among the wealthy, remained loyal to the Nationalist government. The general feeling in China at the time, observed American
China scholar A. Doak Barnett, author of *China on the Eve of Communist Takeover*, was, "Any change will be for the better; this can't go on."

The sentiment of the overseas Chinese was similar. Most of the
Chinese in the United States came from Guangdong Province, and
when the *New York Times* reported a serious famine in the province in
late 1943, the news was doubly shocking because the Nationalist papers did not mention it at all. After the *Times* report, KMT officials in
the United States tried to assure the overseas Chinese that the problem was under control, but their relatives were giving a different
story. They blamed the famine on corrupt KMT officials who, by
joining hands with merchants, had caused grave scarcity through
hoarding of food supplies. The price of rice rose precipitously, and
when the Chinese in the United States tried to cable funds to relatives, they found the Bank of China slow and ineffective. Moreover,
while the money cabled home had to be converted at the official rate
of US$1 to 29 yuan, the much more realistic "market value" was $1 to
100 yuan. The overseas Chinese had to spend more than three times
the market value on the official rate, and everyone knew who was
pocketing the difference.

By then, Chinese American communities uniformly favored a coalition government. The Chinese Hand Laundry Alliance (CHLA)
sent telegrams to the Nationalist government and the Communist
Party, calling for serious negotiations and avoidance of one-party rule.
A newspaper owned by the conservative Chee Kung Tong (a leading
triad), which had no love for the CCP, also sent a cable to both sides:
"We are uniformly and absolutely against the resumption of civil
war. . . . We urge the formation of a coalition government based on a
constitution with democratic principles."[11] The KMT responded by

sending agents to overseas communities to suppress such views, which it considered dissent. Liu Leung-mo, a well-known figure in New York's Chinatown and conductor of Chinatown's anti-Japanese Patriotic Chorus, told a *New York Times* reporter that the Nationalist defeats were largely a result of the government's internal problems, and that the government, if it were more democratic, would not be in such trouble. The KMT officials immediately labeled Liu a communist and a traitor, and his chorus was branded a Communist front.[12]

In 1948, Chiang Kai-shek's army lost some five hundred thousand troops and was defeated in the crucial battle of Huaihai. It was only a matter of time before the Nationalist regime collapsed. Still, the United States, under the sway of cold war logic, continued to send millions of dollars in aid to Chiang's government, making Chinese Americans increasingly frustrated with U.S. policy. They saw an opportunity to express their views during the 1948 presidential election campaign, when Henry Wallace, the former U.S. vice president who was running on the Progressive Party ticket against Thomas Dewey and Harry Truman, was the only candidate to come out against American intervention in China's internal affairs. The Chinese Committee to Support Wallace was set up in San Francisco's Chinatown, and many Chinese in New York also backed his campaign. But Wallace received fewer votes than Strom Thurmond, who ran on the State's Rights Party ticket, because his Progressive Party was accused of being infiltrated by communists.

On the eve of the Nationalist government's collapse, even many within the U.S. administration thought that Chiang Kai-shek was responsible for his own failure.[13] The State Department released an official government report to document Chiang's failings—*United States Relations with China, with a Special Reference to the Period 1944–1949*. Commonly known as the white paper, it was intended "to set the American public straight" on the fact that the collapse of the Nationalist government "was beyond the control of the United States."[14] As for Chinese Americans, since they had been taking the Nationalist demise as a given, their concerns quickly turned to what the new Communist government had in store.[15] As they waited for the installation of the new government, many were curious about its future policies—particularly its attitude toward overseas Chinese.

AMERICA'S TURN TO THE RIGHT

From the American point of view, the Nationalist government's loss of China in 1949 was a major setback for the "Free World," critically tilting the global balance of power to the communist side. The United States had secured southern and western Europe against Soviet expansion, but the loss of China was placing American interests in jeopardy. Although the American diehard anticommunists' long unconditional support for Chiang Kai-shek was scarcely rational, given the billions of dollars that were spent to save him to no avail, his defeat at the hands of the communists was viewed as a failure of the Truman Doctrine to halt "Soviet expansionism."

Whatever questions about the rationale for supporting Chiang there may have been, they were quickly put to rest when the Korean War broke out in 1950 and American troops were engaged in fighting under the auspices of the United Nations on the South Korean side against the invading North. In his aggressive pursuit of the North Korean army, General MacArthur maneuvered his troops and the air force close to the Korea-China border, despite warnings from China that it viewed these intrusions as a threat to its national security. As a result, China sent its own volunteers into Korea, pushing the UN troops to retreat in disarray back to the thirty-eighth parallel. At that point, the conflict was resolved in a stalemate and an armistice between the two sides—a standoff unresolved to this day—but 33,651 Americans had lost their lives, and American popular reaction was one of shock and dismay.

Communist China instantly became the most hated enemy of the United States. The American government decided to blame the "loss of China" on those who had betrayed the Nationalists, and unleashed a nationwide witch hunt for communists and their sympathizers in the United States' foreign policy establishment. Anyone who had ever criticized Chiang Kai-shek or did not support him came under attack. A number of State Department officials, journalists, and leading China scholars and experts who had spoken their minds were subpoenaed by the House Un-American Activities Committee for inquisition. Leftists, liberals, and labor leaders were placed on a list to be investigated by the FBI. Several Chinese American organizations made the list, including the CHLA and the *China Daily News* in

New York, as well as the Chinese Workers Mutual Aid Association and the Chinese American Democratic Youth League (Min Qing) in San Francisco.

The first to come under scrutiny were the activities of progressive Chinese foreign students in the United States. *New York Times* columnist James Reston, a Washington-based "journalist with extraordinary access to the White House," wrote in 1951 that many members of the Chinese Students Christian Association (CSCA) and the Association of Chinese Scientific Workers in America (ACSWA) were subversives.[16] Soon after that, the U.S. government issued orders restraining Chinese students and experts in the United States from leaving for the Chinese mainland. Those in the fields of science and technology were particularly hard hit. Even earlier, in August 1950, the U.S. government had barred Tsien Hsue-shen (Qian Xuesen), one of the founders of the Jet Propulsion Laboratory at the California Institute of Technology, from leaving the country. During the same month a group of 126 returnees had left on the USS *Wilson* for China, but when the ship reached Japan, U.S. armed forces personnel detained Zhao Zongyao (a physicist), Shen Shanjiong (a biologist), and Luo Shijun (an aeronautics expert). They were only released forty-seven days later, after strong international protests. In September 1951, when the China-bound ship USS *Cleveland* docked at Honolulu, nine returning Chinese students were detained by Immigration and Naturalization Service (INS) officials and returned to the U.S. mainland, with the explanation that their advanced technical knowledge could be used against the United States by Chinese Communists. Such fears were exaggerated. Most of the Chinese students in the United States at the time belonged to the old regime elite and were not prepared to venture home to test the hospitality of the unknown, new Communist system. Only 120 of more than 4,000 eventually applied for permission to depart for China.[17]

Across the country, intelligence authorities spent thousands of hours investigating suspected groups and individuals. Businesses in San Francisco that were owned by progressive Chinese, such as Oasis Bookstore and World Theater, found their supply sources blocked as U.S. Customs agents impounded any book and film even remotely suspected of having originated in mainland China. The FBI investigated all subscriptions to the *China Daily News*, a popular paper known for its anti-Nationalist and anti–Chinatown establishment views. Its subscribers were warned to discontinue their subscriptions. Some were interrogated, often repeatedly, and pressed to answer questions such as, Why do you read the *China Daily News*? Are you a communist? Whom do you know that is? Tan Yumin, a member of the Chinese Hand Laundry Association, was so distraught by the interrogations that he later jumped off the Brooklyn Bridge.[18]

The campaign was quickly turning all Chinese in the United States into suspects. In testimony before the Senate, J. Edgar Hoover, the head of the FBI, declared, "Red China has been flooding the country with its propaganda and there are over 300,000 Chinese in the United States, some of whom could be susceptible to recruitment either through ethnic ties or hostage situations because of relatives in Communist China." (Hoover more than doubled official population figures.) Some members of Congress were so alarmed that Senator Pat McCarran and Representative Richard M. Nixon sponsored an Internal Security Act (the McCarran Act), which permitted the president of the United States to declare an "internal security emergency" during which the attorney general, by virtue of the suspension of habeas corpus rights, could "apprehend and detain" any suspect. Since virtually all Chinese in the United States were now considered suspects, the act could have been used to incarcerate the entire Chinese American population, just as the U.S. government had done during World War II with Japanese Americans.[19]

The INS used the McCarran Act against various Chinese with radical and progressive views, especially anyone who had associated with the American Left and progressive unions. Kwong Hai-chew, a seaman who had been a legal U.S. resident since 1945, was denied entry upon return from a tour of duty on a U.S. merchant vessel on the grounds of alleged membership in the Communist Party between 1945 and 1948. Under cross-examination, prosecution witnesses were unable to substantiate the charge. Kwong was a union activist, a member of the Chinese section of the National Maritime Union and an elected chairman of a Chinese seamen's association. It took him seventeen years of litigation to reverse the deportation order.[20] Similar cases greatly altered the internal dynamics of Chinese American communities. The witch-hunt atmosphere led many to avoid involvement with leftist and progressive organizations, and gave the conservatives, particularly the KMT, the opportunity to regain their influence.

After the Communist victory on the Chinese mainland, the KMT had retreated to the island of Taiwan, where its survival was secured by the presence of the U.S. military and where it continued to proclaim itself the sole legitimate government of all Chinese people, even though it ruled over only the Taiwanese population of 10 million. (In comparison, 583 million Chinese were under Communist rule, according to the first modern census taken on the mainland, in 1953.) To give some credibility to its claims, the Nationalist government desperately needed the support—or at least the illusion of support—of the overseas Chinese around the world. In the United States, it rode the wave of anticommunism and employed Red-baiting tactics to terrorize the community into submission. With the help of traditional Chinatown associations, it formed the Chinatown Anti-Communist League, which most community groups, eager to keep out of trouble, were quick to join.

Those who refused, such as the CHLA, quickly became targets of attacks. CHLA membership lists were turned over to the Justice Department and the INS for investigation. Its leaders were prosecuted on a variety of charges, including illegal entry. The *China Daily News* got an additional dose of government persecution in 1952, when its editor and president, Eugene Moy, and other officials of the paper were summoned to testify before the grand jury of the southern district of New York in respect to a possible violation of Title 18, No. 371 of the U.S. code—the Trading with the Enemy Act. As the paper had accepted advertising revenue from Nanyang Bank of Hong Kong, which was allegedly owned by the People's Republic of China, the court found the *China Daily News* guilty. It was the only time anyone had been prosecuted under this law since its passage in 1917. The bank had merely advertised a service that Chinese Americans could use to send money to relatives in China, which was not a crime. The paper's editor, Moy, was sentenced to two years in prison nevertheless, and he died shortly after his release. Other defendants were charged and convicted for sending money to relatives and acquaintances on the Chinese mainland through the bank. The indictments and subsequent convictions stunned the community. In their wake, subscriptions to the *China Daily News* declined to the point where the publisher could afford only biweekly issues.

J. Edgar Hoover raised the Red-baiting bar in 1955 when he testified to the Senate, "The large number of Chinese entering this country as immigrants provides Red China with a channel to dispatch to the United States undercover agents on intelligence assignments." His allegations were based on a foreign service dispatch sent by the U.S. consul in Hong Kong, Everett F. Drumright, which accused the Chinese community of operating a "fantastic system of passport and visa fraud." Drumright was an avowed anticommunist and had alleged that the Chinese were culturally inclined to fraud and perjury since they "lack a concept equivalent to the western concept of an oath." When he headed the consulate in the early 1950s, his office was burdened with 117,000 cases of Chinese applicants claiming "derivative citizenship" through fathers who were U.S. citizens. With the fall of China to the Communists, most of those who could, desperately wanted to acquire passports and join their families in the United States. In response, Drumright and his office developed a whole series of special regulations, requiring applicants to answer hundreds of questions and submit dozens of extra forms, affidavits, blood tests, X-rays, and fingerprints. Those without birth certificates were told to produce identifying witnesses, preferably American citizens—a practical impossibility for most applicants. Drumright's office also wanted to subject them to polygraph tests, which were not required of applicants elsewhere. Between 1952 and 1955, more than twelve hundred Chinese applicants claiming derivative citizenship were denied entry to the United States.

Drumright's 1955 eighty-nine-page white paper to the State Department alleged that almost all Chinese in America had entered the United States illegally. Even more sensational was his charge that the paper son system, providing legal entry to fake sons of Chinese Americans, had been perpetrated by the Chinese Communists to send spies to the United States.[21] "Thousands of Chinese in recent years have obtained illegal entry into the U.S. by posing as the sons of Chinese who are American citizens," U.S. News & World Report informed the American public. "Many who entered this way were red agents."[22]

The INS responded by announcing the so-called Confession Program in 1956, for which no official policy or guidelines were issued. Instead, the program was advertised through "informal and unwritten publicity" to civic leaders, asking Chinese Americans who had in the past fraudulently established U.S. citizenship to come forward. The government claimed that it was not interested in entrapment, and that it was the prospective confessors who could gain from the program, but it never promised anything specific.[23] Since no official statute governed the process and no specific legal provisions were made for the amnesty of "confessors," the prospect of going through the program was terrifying. Before making the confession, an individual had to surrender and officially sign all documents of citizenship over to the INS. Officers also required the confessors to state that they were "amenable for deportation" if their confession was denied.

The program affected a good number of people within the Chinese American community. Many families were divided over the decision of whether to confess. If they did, they would implicate others. If they did not, they might still be exposed by others who did. Or they could simply be told that unknown informants had accused them of "leftist political acts" that they had not committed. Worst of all, failing to confess, if detected, could be grounds for deportation. For years Chinese residents lived under a dark shadow, not knowing who was telling what and on whom to the authorities. By 1965, when the program finally ended, 13,895 people had confessed, exposing 22,083 others and resulting in the closing of 11,294 potential paper son slots.[24] Considering that the Chinese American population in the United States (without Hawaii) in 1950 was only 117,629, the impact on the community was enormous.

Most of those who confessed were permitted to stay in the United States, though a few were deported because of their political activities. The situation was complicated by the fact that the United States had no relations with China and could thus deport only those who agreed to go to Hong Kong. World Theater owner Karl Fung, for instance, departed "voluntarily" for Hong Kong when he was charged with fraudulent citizenship and threatened with a prison term. All members of the San Francisco Chinese American Youth Club (Min Qing) were indicted and tried in court. More than half were stripped of their U.S. citizenship because either they or their parents had entered the country by means of fraudulent claims of citizenship.[25] One of the club's leaders, Maurice Chuck, was indicted by a Tacoma federal grand jury in 1962 for procuring citizenship based on false statements. Chuck came to this country at the age of fifteen in 1948 to join his father, Hwong Jack Hong, who was himself a paper son. The two were strangers to each other and often clashed over Maurice's activities in the radical Chinese American Youth Club and articles he wrote for the

China Daily News. During the grand jury proceedings, the court subpoenaed Hong, who had participated in the confession program, to testify against his son. The two stayed in the same room during the trial, where the father cried every night in agony over the government's tactics. Maurice was found guilty, stripped of his citizenship, and served three months of a five-year prison term.[26] The Chinese American Youth Club, which had already been forced by the political climate to refocus its activities exclusively on counseling and tutorial programs designed to help immigrant youth overcome adjustment difficulties and pursue higher education, lost so many members that it had to close down.[27]

Deportation proceedings against suspected communists, the imprisonment of leftists, and the Confession Program taught Chinese Americans a lesson: Keep quiet. The progressive individuals in the community became completely isolated, especially after their outside allies among the liberals, the Left, and the unions came under attack themselves. By the mid-1950s, the only voice that could be heard was that of the anticommunists and the CCBA, and the KMT could claim to represent the whole community. Every year banners at the October Ten Chinese National Day parade proclaimed, "All Thirty Million Overseas Chinese Support the Republic of China" (the Taiwan government), and no one dared to challenge that.

The only Chinese who benefited from the cold war, which had such a devastating effect on the working-class Chinese American community, were the "good Chinese"—the political refugees and the stranded scholars.

Chapter 16

Chinese Professionals Wanted!

POLITICAL REFUGEES AND STRANDED SCHOLARS

After the fall of the Nationalist government on mainland China, thousands of its top government, military, and intelligence officials, as well as the very rich that had to leave Communist China, arrived in the United States as refugees. The most influential individuals in this group were H.H. Kung, the wealthiest financier and onetime director of the Central Bank of China and vice president of the Republic of China, and the Harvard-educated T.V. Soong, the onetime finance and foreign minister of the republic. Soong was perhaps even better known as the brother of the famous Three Soong Sisters: one married to H.H. Kung, one to Chiang Kai-shek, and one to Sun Yat-sen. Although Kung and Soong belonged to the "dynastic family" of the Republic of China, they clearly lacked confidence in the dynasty after its move to Taiwan, and came to the United States instead, bringing with them the millions they stole from the Chinese people. The president of the United States used his discretionary power to grant these high-profile political refugees temporary admission and, eventually, legal permanent resident status.

At the same time, a group of Chinese scholars who were stranded in the United States during the political power change on the mainland decided to stay and apply for political asylum. Since scholars from China were exempted from immigration restrictions (unlike their less fortunate compatriots classified as "laborers" by the 1882 Chinese Exclusion Act), over the decades thousands with exceptional scholarly qualifications came to the United States for graduate education. Very few of them wanted to remain in the country after completion of their studies, since they faced an inhospitable racial environment and could not find jobs, while good positions awaited them in China. According to a study based on the survey *Who's Who in China*, 56.2 percent of the highest-ranking figures in the Chinese government, academy, and military by 1939 had received an advanced education in the United States.[1]

After World War II, the Chinese Nationalist government embarked on an expanded mission to send students abroad, calculating that a critical mass of well-educated young people would speed up China's economic growth, while conveying a sense of national pride and confidence in the future of China. These students were expected to return as several generations before them had done, but with the collapse of the Nationalist government in 1949 this ceased to be an appealing prospect. The options for some 4,000 students who were studying in the United States in 1949 were to return to mainland China under Communist rule or follow the Nationalist government to Taiwan, which could easily fall into Communist hands in the very near future. Being largely from China's most elite families, few of them were procommunist. Most chose to stay in the United States.

This decision involved considerable hardship. For one, many had been scholarship students and would no longer receive any money from the Chinese government. Second, they were jeopardizing their U.S. visa status and would become "stateless." The State Department eventually allowed them to adjust their visas, and as a result some of China's most brilliant scientists and intellectuals stayed and became naturalized. The best known among them are the joint winners of the Nobel Prize for Physics in 1957, Chen Ning Yang and Tsung-tao Lee, the computer industry pioneer An Wang of Wang Laboratories, and the architect I.M. Pei.

The first legislation that directly benefited the political refugees and stranded scholars was the 1948 Displaced Persons Act, which was adopted to help the victims of Nazism and fascism in Europe and to rectify America's failure to help them before and during the war. Congress voted to allow 400,000 displaced persons—their numbers still tied to the quotas set for various countries by the Johnson-Reed Law of 1924—to settle in the United States, but it also added a number of categories that reflected its new anticommunist, cold war orientation. Almost all beneficiaries were Europeans, among them 140,000 Jews. Only a very small fraction were Asians. Among the 3,465 "refugees of Chinese decent" who were given permission to settle, having been vouched for by the Nationalist government in Taiwan, were some of the stranded scholars.

Other acts followed. The Refugee Relief Act of 1953, the Refugee Escapee Act of 1957, the Act of September 22, 1959, the Fair Share Law of 1960, and the presidential directive issued by John F. Kennedy in 1962 all contributed to further admittance of Chinese students already in the country and other escapees from Communist rule.

THE DEMAND SIDE OF U.S. IMMIGRATION

The new attitude toward the Chinese stranded scholars reflected the anticommunist climate of the time, but it also marked a new era in American economic development and a need for a new type of human resource.

Until World War II, America mainly imported poorly educated laborers, and mainly from Europe. One exception was a group of elite Jewish and European scientists who were escaping from Nazi Germany and came to the United States as refugees after the rise of Hitler in 1933. The most illustrious among them were the eight émigrés who had already received the Nobel Prize (Albert Einstein among them) and the three who received it soon after arrival; all became the super-elite of the American scientific establishment. Many other top European scientists also came during this period and contributed to the U.S. war effort. In fact, the ranks of the Manhattan Project, which developed the atomic bomb, were filled with scientists from Italy (Fermi), Germany (Bethe), Poland (Ulam), Hungary (Wigner, Szilard, Von Neumann, and Teller), Russia (Kistiakovsky), and Austria (Rabi). The bomb would never have been built but for immigrant talent. In a radio address in 1945, Eleanor Roosevelt declared that the atomic bomb, developed by "many minds belonging to different races and different religions sets the pattern for the way in which in the future we may be able to work out our difficulties." Foreign scientists fostered a new generation of American scientists and mentored future Nobel laureates, creating a chain reaction that is sometimes referred to as "Hitler's gift to American science."[2] The same designation befits the rocket scientist Wernher von Braun, who was imported along with some lesser Nazi scientists from Germany after World War II. All this resulted in great savings in capital investment in education and time gained in America's bid for global dominance.

The United States emerged from World War II as a mature industrial nation, that no longer needed manual laborers on the scale it did before the war. The American economy now needed technically trained and university-educated professionals who could easily adapt to the growing technological complexity of modern production. American universities could not gear up fast enough to satisfy this demand, and a very large number of trained personnel had to be recruited abroad—not just the first-rate scientists, but also engineers and technicians with an advanced education, who were needed to perform the tedious work in research labs and corporate engineering divisions. The government took a hard look at its immigration laws and decided to modify them in hopes of remedying the shortage. Thirty percent of the slots opened under the provisions of the Displaced Persons Act of 1948 were earmarked for scientists and specialized skilled professionals.

During congressional hearings in 1950 that preceded the revamping of the 1924 Johnson-Reed Immigration Act in 1952, INS officials proposed preferential treatment for specialists who would facilitate American industrial expansion.[3] President Truman's Commission on Immigration and Naturalization concurred that the law "should encourage entry in the United States of persons whose skills, aptitudes, knowledge or experience are necessary or desirable for our economy, culture, defense, or security."[4] One of its subcommittees recommended that 30 percent of the immigration quota be given to this type of person.[5] The final bill, known as the 1952 McCarran-Walter Immigration and Nationality Act, raised the quota for skilled workers to 50 percent.[6] At the time, opposition to increased immigration was very mild, since the United States was experiencing a labor shortage and the general prosperity after World War II did not make an increase in the number of immigrants look threatening to native white workers.[7]

Moreover, American organized labor was cooperating with capital by expanding and exporting its own brand of unionism to the third world, which helped ease whatever organized opposition to immigration there was.

But despite the ambitiously set goals, from 1954 to 1964 less than 6 percent of the "quota immigrants" and only 2 percent of all immigrants were the desired professionals with the needed backgrounds. The problem was that the immigration quotas heavily favored Europeans from the most developed nations, but Europe was enjoying an economic boom under the Marshall Plan, underwritten by the United States, so highly educated Europeans by and large opted to stay at home. The language in the 1952 McCarran-Walter Act was by all accounts racist; President Truman had in fact vetoed it once as "a mockery of the Bill of Rights and of our claims to stand for freedom in the world" because it refused to end the restrictive national-origins quota system which discriminated against immigrants of third world as well as southern and eastern European origins. But the Act gave no race-specific reference as to where the professionals should be from. In effect, anyone who had gained an advanced professional degree and found employment in the field in the United States could apply. As it happened, there was a pool of third world foreign students attending American graduate schools in science and engineering, because the McCarran-Walter Act had also facilitated admission of exchange students from developing countries, in the hope that their exposure to American values would be used to promote the U.S. agenda abroad. They were now eligible to apply for naturalization under the "professional" quota if American firms were willing to hire them and sponsor their application for permanent resident status.

In this way, nonwhite professionals slowly began to replace the unavailable Europeans. A particularly prominent group among foreign students who participated in the educational exchange came from South and East Asia. The number of students from this region attending American learning institutions grew steadily as the cold war competition between East and West heated up—from around 10,000 in the mid-1950s to more than 142,000 by the mid-1980s, mostly in technical fields. The escalation in numbers was driven by a 1956 report by the Joint Congressional Committee on Atomic Energy, which warned that America was experiencing a shortage of scientific staff

workers and engineers and claimed that the USSR would quickly surpass the United States in the field of military technology.[8] The fears
were not purely imagined: the United States was at the time behind
the USSR in the number of students who were graduating annually
with degrees in scientific and engineering fields. Then the Soviets
launched *Sputnik* in 1957. In shock, the U.S. government responded
with a move to improve the nation's science education. The National
Science Foundation started a locally based project known as the "math
bee," and it began giving generous scholarships to anyone who wanted
to do graduate work in science and engineering. An increasing number
of students from Taiwan and Hong Kong took advantage of the situation. Taiwan in fact converted its best colleges to produce thousands
of world-class science graduates to be exported to the United States.
Chinese graduates became the staple of major American universities,
research labs, public health facilities, and the defense industry.

There is no doubt that the recruitment of nonwhite professionals
represented a major racial shift in American immigration policy. It was
institutionalized as a separate preferential quota set aside for "professionals, scientists, and artists of exceptional ability" in the 1965 Immigration Act (the "third preference"), set at 10 percent of each nation's
overall quota.

The influx of political refugees, the stranded scholars, and the
Taiwan- and Hong Kong–trained professionals produced a new community of Chinese Americans. They were well educated and upwardly
mobile. In less than a decade after arrival, a Chinese college graduate
could gain a graduate degree, a professional job, citizenship, an upper-
middle-class income, and residence in a desirable neighborhood.
Moreover, as escapees from Communist rule or products of the anticommunist bastion of Taiwan, these Chinese had impeccable anticommunist credentials—they were the "good Chinese." These "Uptown
Chinese" had very little in common with the early immigrants from
the semirural regions of southern China, who were mainly working-
class restaurant, laundry, and sweatshop employees. They did not even
converse in the same dialect—most Uptown Chinese were from the
North and spoke Mandarin or Shanghainese, while the Downtown
Chinese spoke Cantonese. And they most certainly did not reside in the
same neighborhood. Most Downtown Chinese were isolated in ethnic

ghettos, while the uptown Chinese moved into affluent integrated city neighborhoods or to the suburbs.

THE UPTOWN CHINESE

The preselected group of professional elite Chinese immigrants that started to arrive in the United States in the 1950s from mainland China, Taiwan, and Hong Kong completely threw off the statistics pertaining to the Chinese American population as a whole. While in the 1930s more than 60 percent of all Chinese in the United States worked as cooks, waiters, domestics, and laundrymen and in the 1940s only 1.5 percent had completed a college education, by 1970, according to the U.S. census, Chinese Americans had surpassed white Americans in both median family income and years of completed education. But general hostility toward Chinese Americans remained intense, even after World War II. A 1948 survey reported that 64 percent of white Americans would not want Chinese as kin by marriage, and 28 percent would not welcome a Chinese as a neighbor.[9] This does not mean, however, that the remaining percentage of people would. When a former high-ranking officer in the Chinese Nationalist Army, Sing Sheng, attempted to move into the San Francisco suburb of Southwood in the early 1950s, his new neighbors protested and threatened with both legal and violent action. Unpersuaded, Sheng proposed a ballot on the matter. The community voted 174 to 28 against him. Surprised and mortified, he moved away.[10] So unattractive were the Chinese to other Americans that in a 1954 survey they ranked second only to African Americans as the most unwanted choice for a marrying partner—a second distant by far from all the other groups, such as Jews, Catholics, Irish, and Swedes.

By the mid-1960s, the image of Chinese Americans began to change. A 1966 *U.S. News & World Report* article praised the Chinese in the United States as a "model minority" capable of "winning wealth and respect by dint of its own hard work." Their objective situation changed as well. The 1970 U.S. census showed that the percentage of Chinese Americans employed as service labor declined to 25 percent, while their median family income was $1,000 higher than the U.S. average.[11] Some

27.6 percent of Chinese Americans were college graduates, compared to 12.2 percent of all Americans. Among them were a few who had attained national prominence, including two Nobel laureates. A little over a decade later, the impressive scholastic achievements of Asian Americans, the Chinese most noticeable among them, would cause a controversy about their "overrepresentation" at the best universities in the country.

Popular pseudo-academic explanation attributed this dramatic upward mobility in such a short time to the Confucian values that permeate Chinese culture. This is nothing short of comical, considering that until very recently Asian scholars argued that the very same feudal values perpetrated through Confucian teaching stifled innovation and individual thinking and were the cause of China's stagnation and backwardness. An even more widely circulated cultural explanation has been that the Chinese owe their success to hard work and respect for education. It has taken root and is still loudly embraced by many, including many Chinese Americans. "One of our enduring beliefs is that hard work brings rewards," Susan Au Allen of the U.S. Pan-Asian American Chamber of Commerce testified to the House Committee on Small Business in the 1990s. "That is why so many of us pursue higher education. We also place great value in individual responsibility and entrepreneurship."[12]

Susan Au Allen is herself a middle-class immigrant from Hong Kong. She speaks bitterly about the racism and discrimination she experienced growing up under British colonial rule, yet seems to ignore the racism and discrimination of institutional and legal limitations placed on generations of Chinese immigrants who came to America before her. For more than a hundred years, their hard work and education—such as they were allowed to obtain before the civil rights movement—were never equitably rewarded. Not even the civil rights movement, which had indeed removed legal obstacles to equal access, could have brought the spectacular success touted by the model minority myth so rapidly to the descendants of the early working-class immigrants, no matter how diligent they were at school or how hardworking, responsible, and enterprising they may have been. As African Americans like to point out, the mere passage of the 1964 Civil Rights Act did not provide for a fair competition. In a race between an unburdened individual and another who carries a fifty-pound load on his back, eliminating the load long after the race has begun does not mean that the disadvantaged person has a chance to catch up. The race would be fair only if the two runners were placed in the same position, which would become the starting point of a new race. Based on the earlier example of the impoverished and illiterate eastern and southern European immigrants, it would take several generations to achieve that—one for the move from the laboring class to small business ownership, and at least one more for the move up into the educated professional class. (In the case of eastern European Jews, the integrating effects of World War II and the massive postwar veteran benefits, including public housing, low-interest home mortgage loans, and free education granted by the GI Bill helped to propel them into the mainstream.)

The fact is that during the 1960s an entirely new group of Chinese "runners" began to enter the race—a group unburdened by past injustices and preconditioned to succeed. It was the imported professionals, selected for immigration because of their exceptional abilities and skills, who were able to leap over obstacles placed in front of the earlier working-class "runners" and skip several steps in the proverbial immigrant's ascent into America's upper middle class.

Doctors Ching-ling Chu and May-li Chan, husband and wife, are a good example. They both graduated from Taiwan University and arrived in the United States in the early 1970s. He attended Berkeley and received a PhD in physics; she attended Columbia University and received a PhD in chemistry. Both accomplished this feat in merely four years. By the mid-1970s, both were respected professionals: he a laser specialist for GTE, she a professor at Rockefeller University's Department of Immunology. That's when they met and got married. By the early 1980s, they were having children, had a healthy combined income, and had little time to attend to the details of their children's upbringing. They moved to Scarsdale in Westchester County, to one of the most respectable addresses in New York's suburbia noted for good public schools, and hired a full-time live-in nanny to care for the children. In fewer than ten years they had made the transition from penniless foreign students and would-be immigrants to America's upper middle class—in other words, they had arrived.

The new wave of preselected immigrants, Doctors Chu and Chan among them, became the mainstay of the affluent new class of

"Uptown Chinese" that had taken seed from the very small elite group of stranded scholars from mainland China and grew steadily through the export of elite college graduates from Taiwan.

THE TRANSNATIONAL LADDER OF SOCIAL MOBILITY

Under the Chinese Exclusion Act, which had barred Chinese laborers from entering the United States between 1882 and 1943, students were one of the few categories treated as an exception. Consequently, from the late nineteenth century to 1949, some fifteen thousand Chinese students (20 percent of them female) received advanced degrees at American universities.[13] Very few of them wanted or needed to stay in the country upon graduation.

It may seem curious that America, with its overtly anti-Chinese official stance, was a popular destination for the most promising young Chinese seeking an advanced education. But at the end of the nineteenth century, political leaders and influential social thinkers of the crumbling Qing Empire realized that China had to be modernized if it was to be saved from disintegration under the onslaught of Western colonial aggression. They looked to Europe, the United States, and even Japan for the practical know-how needed to launch a "self-strengthening movement." The United States, despite its hostile attitude toward colored minorities, impressed these Chinese reformers as a young nation with the least amount of imperialist designs on China. Many Chinese in fact credited the easing of the competition "to carve up China like a melon" among the leading European powers and Japan to President Taft's call for an "open-door policy." Most of all, reform-minded Chinese leaders came to view science and democracy as the two primary prerequisites for their nation's salvation. On both counts, America, as it emerged from World War II, stood out as a powerhouse of manufacturing and a nation of constitutional laws, a bill of rights, and an advanced degree of democracy.

Schools in England, France, Germany, and Japan were all held in high esteem, but American educational institutions were valued the most. In addition to taking courses and passing numerous exams, the successful PhD candidate in America had to write a thesis as well. Since most European universities required no such thing, recalls Albert

Liu, a student at the University of Wisconsin in 1927, recalls that "American education was seen as more serious and challenging. A degree from there was recognized as 'gold plated trophies' in China." Returning home with one instantly guaranteed a top administrative or academic position. Ninety percent of all foreign-educated students who went back to China upon graduation became prominent officials. Their list is almost synonymous with the Who's Who of China.

To study in America, Chinese students had to meet strict requirements. Following the 1924 Immigration Act, only those who had already completed a bachelor's degree in China and whose credentials had been accepted by an American institution of higher learning were admitted to the country. In addition, they had to prove that they were financially self-supporting and that they had sufficient funds to pay for their return to China within six months of graduation. They also had to prove that they were proficient in English.[14] Since China was a poor nation, most Chinese, even many members of the elite, could hardly afford to pay on their own and needed a scholarship. The best scholarships were provided from a fund established by the U.S. government with the reparations money that China had been forced to pay the United States after the failed Boxer Rebellion, which President Theodore Roosevelt decided to return to China in 1907. Others were sponsored by the Chinese government, the U.S. government, and missionaries. Getting any of these scholarships required outstanding academic qualifications that were the equivalent of passing the palace level of the old imperial examination system.

Traditionally, imperial Chinese governments had used the education system to prepare candidates for state employment, selecting the best through an extremely competitive examination system. From the government's point of view, the system was used not only to provide people with knowledge to rule, but also to screen out rebels and misfits. From the candidates' point of view, obtaining an education was not so much a pure quest for knowledge as it was a guarantee of a well-paid and respected career in the state bureaucracy and a stepping-stone to upward mobility.

Initial examinations took place at the county level. Those who were successful moved on to compete at the provincial level. Finally, a palace examination was held at the capital. The level at which an individual competed successfully determined the type of office he would be awarded. By controlling the content that the candidates needed to master, every Chinese government, past and present, has been able to shape the values and political thinking of its educated elite. The centrality of imperial civil service examinations in molding Chinese values and culture is borne out by the fact that they are a major theme in traditional Chinese opera. Even folk songs sing high praises to studying as a source of great joy, pride, and honor. Ancient philosopher Mencius is often quoted to inspire youngsters to study harder: "The people are bestowed at their birth with good virtue. But if they are well fed and clothed and live leisurely without education, they become like birds and animals."

The imperial examination system was abolished after the fall of the Qing dynasty. It was replaced by a "modern system" based on the Western model, which channeled those in pursuit of education through elementary, junior, and high schools, and on to college, with the coveted aim of attending school abroad. The ultimate success in the new de facto transnational elite educational system—a graduate degree from an American Ivy League university—is what now guaranteed success in the new Republic of China.

The road to America inevitably led through one of China's few elite universities, the most prestigious of which were Qinghua (Tsinghua), Nankai, and Yanjing (Yenching, which later became Peking, or Beijing, University). Entrance exams to any of these schools were extremely competitive, as altogether they took in no more than 10,000 students annually from a population of more than 300 million during the first part of the twentieth century.

Success in the new system required a major transformation of personal character as well. Those who succeeded in climbing to the top were completely foreign-oriented. They were interested in Western culture and art; they wanted to speak, read, and write English—and this in a sea of compatriots the majority of whom were illiterate even in their own language. These were the people who were happy never to have to write a single classical Chinese "eight-legged essay" again, who gladly abandoned traditional Chinese instruments for Western classical music and Chinese theater for Hollywood movies; to whom Goethe and Shakespeare were far more interesting than the Chinese classics. An Wang, who founded Wang Laboratories in 1951 and later pioneered personal computing, recalls that his favorite readings in

China, before he came to the United States in pursuit of a PhD, were *Popular Mechanics* and *Popular Science*. A less specialized and more commonly appreciated read was *Reader's Digest*. Not surprisingly, the Chinese who ultimately achieved their goal belonged to a very narrow slice of the Chinese social spectrum, and many of them were from Shanghai, which was the most urbanized and Western-oriented community in China. People often referred to these goal-getters as the "white Chinese."[15]

The chief purpose of Qinghua University, built in Beijing in 1911 from the Boxer Indemnity Fund, was to prepare some two thousand Chinese students for studies at American universities—all costs paid by the fund.[16] Its curriculum was identical to that of Phillips Andover Academy in Massachusetts.[17] The schooling involved conversation in English words and phrases, and total immersion in Western values. It drew inspiration from the philosophies of Cicero, Brutus, and Patrick Henry. Its pro-Western emphasis became even more intense after the May Fourth Movement, in 1919, which was led by an ambitious group of highly educated young people who feared their country was about to succumb to Japan's colonial designs. Even more than earlier reformers, they thought that China's problems stemmed from its useless traditional education and conservative social and political philosophy. A few among them, including Mao Tse-tung, called for a total cultural and political transformation. Some favored Japanese Meiji-style reforms; others, centered around Beijing University and Qinghua, invited scholars such as John Dewey and Bertrand Russell to lecture on needed reforms.

Once they had arrived in the United States, these enthusiastic followers of Western ways were protected from the worst effects of anti-Chinese discrimination. Still, many were refused service in "white" restaurants. Chen Guangfu, who would later become a pioneer of Chinese banking, was told by a landlord in St. Louis that "colored" people were not welcome. Another Chinese student in the South complained, "The people here seldom see upper-class Chinese, hence they always mistake us as [sic] Hispanics."[18] Nevertheless, Chinese students in the United States, a class exempted from the provisions of the exclusion act, were protected by American laws and sheltered in the tolerant and polite American educational environment as long as they concentrated on their studies.

They had no contact with the residents of established Chinese American communities, with whom they had almost nothing in common. The two groups were separated by a great social and educational divide and did not even speak the same dialects. Some Chinese scholars in fact blamed the "half-civilized" and ignorant San Francisco Chinese workers for the negative attitude Americans had toward Chinese as a whole. They despised them not just for coming from a "lower class" but for maintaining an "anti-modern" way of life that the students aspired to eradicate from China. In a memoir written in English, Chinese diplomat Wu Ting-fang (1842–1922), who had once been stationed in the United States, argued, "Unchecked influx of immigrants who are not desirable citizens cannot but harm the country. Persons . . . who are ignorant and illiterate, cannot become desirable citizens anywhere. They should be barred out of the United States of America."[19] The American-born sociologist Rose Hum Lee observed cynically that foreign Chinese scholars often referred to Chinese Americans as "low-class" or "chopsuey people" in the hope of currying favor with the whites.[20]

AMERICA'S PRECIOUS IMPORTS

The Chinese revolution in 1949 altered the status of scholars who were attending American universities. Since most belonged to the old regime's elite, their family members had to either leave the mainland (to go to Hong Kong, Taiwan, Southeast Asia, or North America) or stay but face an uncertain future under the new government. Few had confidence in the Nationalist government, which had escaped to the island of Taiwan, to want to follow it there. As a result, they became temporary refugees in the United States, preferring to wait and see how the situation developed in China before deciding what to do; hence the popular term "the stranded scholars."

A few idealistic young men among them responded to the Chinese Communist government's call and planned to return to help with rebuilding China, but the U.S. authorities tried to prevent them from doing so. Eventually, only a hundred and some made it back. The overwhelming majority of the stranded scholars were convinced by the dramatic deterioration of U.S.-China relations and the new government's clear leaning toward the Soviet bloc to accept the American government's offer of refugee and, eventually, permanent residence status. Still, it was a difficult decision to make. The 1957 Nobel laureate Chen Ning Yang recalled years later in an interview the guilt that consumed him when he became a U.S. citizen in 1964. He was afraid that his father would not forgive him, as long as he lived, for the crime of forsaking his country. "Our culture does not accept the concept of long-term emigration to another country. It is seen as a treasonous act."[21] By choosing to stay in America, most scholars had to downgrade their aspirations. Some, who would have become leaders of industries back in China, had to settle for routine research jobs; others, who had majored in social sciences and humanities, had to retool to engineering and other more practical fields to gain employment at all. Instead of being distinguished members of China's small elite, they became drops in the sea of America's huge immigrant refugee community.

TAIWAN: EDUCATION GEARED TO EXPORT

The next wave of Chinese graduate students came from Taiwan, which was officially recognized by the United States as the only China. Although not outright refugees, most of them decided to stay in America after graduation to escape from political conflicts and economic problems at home.

The island of Taiwan had been under Japanese occupation for fifty years. When Japan capitulated in 1945, it turned Taiwan over to the Chinese Nationalist government. In 1949, as the new seat of the Nationalist government, Taiwan was quickly turned into a bastion of anticommunism. It was defended by the United States with economic aid and military assistance, and the Nationalist leaders, who had originated on the mainland, made every effort to model it after the United States. They introduced the American grade structure, curriculum, and even textbooks to replace the existing Japanese education system, believing that its focus on science would play the central role in modernizing Taiwan's economy.

To the average resident of Taiwan, however, the American educational system seemed like a ticket to the United States. Many families who had left mainland China after 1949 did not feel that Taiwan was their real home. Of all those forced into exile by the Communist takeover of the mainland, the truly influential and wealthy had found refuge in the United States as soon as the Nationalist government fell. Others with international connections settled in Hong Kong, Southeast Asia, or other parts of the world. Only those who lacked substantial resources and contacts ended up fleeing to Taiwan. To an educated denizen of cosmopolitan Shanghai, Tianjin, or Beijing, moving to this backwater of civilization was like being sent to a penal colony. Happy as they may have been to escape communism, the sophisticated exiles were neither blind to Chiang Kai-shek's misrule nor necessarily interested in sticking it out with his regime. They waited, and planned their escape.

Once they heard that the United States had relaxed its immigration laws—first through the McCarran-Walter Act, which set aside immigration slots for educated professionals without racial restrictions, and then through the passage of the 1965 Immigration Law, which gave 10 percent of its annual immigration quota of twenty thousand for each nation to skilled professionals—Taiwan's top families became singularly focused on taking advantage of this opportunity. Henceforth, the most ambitious among Taiwan's youth of excellent family background had their future carefully prescribed: the goal was to emigrate to the United States and eventually bring their entire families to settle with them.

The only way one could leave Taiwan for the United States was by becoming a graduate student at an American university, and all the would-be émigrés knew that very few individuals would get an opportunity to do that. An outstanding college degree from a first-rate Taiwanese school was required to even think about applying. In the 1960s, Taiwan's colleges were highly selective: only 3 percent of secondary school graduates went on to an institution of higher learning, and there were only four such institutions to speak of, accepting only 1,666 students per year. Moreover, it was virtually impossible to get into a good college without previously attending a good high school. Getting into such a high school required superior achievement in lower grades, for which, in turn, almost without exception, the prerequisite would have been graduation from the best elementary school.

At each stage of the educational process a select few were picked through open, nationwide competitive examinations, and at each stage the entrance examinations for the next stage became tougher. The end result was a small pool of not just hardworking and smart, but also psychologically toughened and overly prepared graduates. In a well-publicized anecdote, mainland Chinese dissident astrophysicist Fang Lizhi complained to the Taiwanese minister of education during a visit to his ministry that the mainland Chinese examination system taught children to pass exams and not to think rationally. "In order to get into a good school, children on the mainland already start preparing themselves to pass examinations in elementary school." His remark provoked the Taiwanese minister's amused reply: "Oh, here they already start in kindergarten." Steven C. Lo, a science graduate of National Taiwan University and a successful transplant to America, writes in his English-language satirical novel, *The Incorporation of Eric Chung*, that the Taiwan youth were made to believe that there is "either America or the end of the world."[22]

An average Taiwanese high school graduate was, at least in the area of science and general basic knowledge, much better prepared than his or her best American counterpart. But the Taiwanese youngster would not get a chance to put this fact to the test until he or she graduated from college and could compete internationally for a slot to study abroad. Even with their sights firmly on U.S. universities, the successful competitors could still not apply to an American graduate school until they passed yet another exam, because starting in 1954 the Taiwanese government took to administering an additional annual examination for those who wished to study abroad—to determine whether they had fulfilled their military service obligation and could thus be certified as possessing the qualities that would not bring disgrace to "the quintessence of Taiwan's national culture" (*guocui*).[23] The selection process did not end even there. Because Taiwan's living standard and average income were very low, only students who were accepted with a scholarship could afford to attend American schools. In the end, those who eventually did attend were indeed the select of the select, the crème de la crème. And the results, as soon as Taiwan started sending students to the United States in the mid-1950s, were gratifying. Many American universities favored these carefully groomed "splendid blossoms" of the Taiwanese educational system. Their reputation was only enhanced when two Chinese scientists (though educated before 1949 on the mainland) jointly won the Nobel Prize for Physics in 1957.

Soon thereafter almost every science graduate from National Taiwan University left for America. The school became known by a popular jingle: "Come, come, come to Taiwan U. You'll go, go, go to U.S.A." It turned out scientists as if on a factory production line. Their grooming practically became a national export industry.

Taiwanese science majors were exactly what America's science establishment needed. Ever since World War II, the American government, corporate and university laboratories, research institutes, and hospitals had been suffering from a shortage of scientists, in terms of both quality and quantity, because the best and the brightest American students were more interested in better-paying careers in law, business, and management. The numbers of those who opted for the more rigorous training in science and engineering were certainly not large enough to support America's scientific establishment, which turned to foreign imports. The contributions of immigrant scientists have had a direct impact on America's overall technological dominance in the world.[24]

GLASS CEILING

In addition to the scientists America got for its most demanding jobs, foreigners were also recruited for the less glamorous positions requiring tedious research. For the highly preselected Taiwanese scientists and engineers who had to work very hard to get to America, ending up in these less prestigious jobs could be extremely frustrating. It was particularly so when they were confronted with lower pay and lack of promotional opportunities compared to their white peers.

Most of Taiwan's exported scientists in fact found themselves toiling away unrecognized in America's research and academic establishments, excluded from responsible management positions—a phenomenon popularly known as "hitting the glass ceiling." "Whenever a difficult problem comes up, usually only the Chinese experts are able to solve it," Dr. Kuo-chong Chang, a senior scientist at Bell Laboratories in New Jersey, summed up his professional experience during the 1970s and 1980s in a private interview. "When it comes to promotion . . . Chinese can expect moving up to the dead-end 'senior research scientist' status. Whites, on the other hand, go on to management." The accumulated frustration is reflected in a 1987 survey in the San Francisco Bay Area, where 75 percent of Chinese Americans mentioned the lack of "career advancement" as the reason for wanting to change jobs.[25] That is why ambitious scientists such as Dr. Chang opted to establish their own start-up companies in Silicon Valley as soon as they mastered the tricks of the trade of corporate America.

Statistics confirm that even now there is reason for their dissatisfaction. Asians collectively account for 28 percent of the enrollment at the top twenty business schools in America. They comprise 60 percent of Silicon Valley's professional and technical workforce. But according to the Fortune 1000, Asian Americans make up barely 1.5 percent of the top executives in the country.[26] An article in the *Wall Street Journal* observed that "the same companies that pursue them for technical jobs often shun them when filling managerial and executive positions."[27] Some refer to Chinese American scientists as the "housekeepers" who do the actual work, while their Anglo-American supervisors get the credit.

A study by Vivian Louie, an Assistant professor at Harvard Graduate School of Education, based on interviews with children of immigrant Chinese professionals, found that parents almost uniformly complained about the intense sense of racism they experienced in the workplace, yet they felt unable to do anything about it.[28] Discrimination at their level is subtle and difficult to prove. Civil rights laws were established to combat discrimination by granting equal access to jobs and opportunities, and have been used by African Americans to gain college educations and professional jobs. Chinese Americans, on the other hand, are already overrepresented in colleges, professional schools, and highly respected skilled professions, and their problems don't get much sympathy or attention from the American public. Insofar as they are aware of the glass ceiling at all, Americans usually associate it with the experiences of middle-class professional women.

Using only samples that could be perfectly controlled—namely, those where education, work experience, English ability, urban residence, and industry employment, along with other variables such as marital and disability status, were completely identical—the 1988 Commission on Civil Rights found that Asian Americans were clustered in certain jobs, lacked mobility to management positions, were underrepresented in other areas, and received lower financial returns. A

1999 National Science Foundation study found that the median salary for Asian American scientists and engineers between the ages of forty and forty-nine was $53,000, while it was $58,000 for their white counterparts. A look at employees at Pacific Gas and Electric Company (PG&E), one of California's largest employers, revealed that almost all Chinese Americans got stuck in the middle level, just below the responsible junior management positions.

When kept from advancing to the higher echelons of their companies, the Chinese are usually given the explanation that they lack the leadership qualities and interpersonal skills needed on the managerial level. Indeed, a 1994 Federal Glass Ceiling Commission report found that Chinese American scientists and engineers are on the whole seen as "excellent workers, but are not equipped to step into positions that require communicative skills—such as management." However, what the Chinese Americans are told they lack is hardly measurable by objective standards. What is recognized as leadership quality in a white male is often considered bitchy behavior in a female, too aggressive in an African American, and hostile in a Chinese American. Talking to colleagues about the previous night's NFL football game is generally a good way of making interpersonal contacts, but it may put at a disadvantage someone who grew up with soccer.

That the judgment of abilities in interpersonal relations is highly subjective in nature was well demonstrated by the case of five Asian American health inspectors who filed a legal suit against the San Francisco Department of Public Health in 1970, claiming promotional discrimination. All five had passed the written exam but had scored miserably on the oral exam and were denied promotion to the position of senior health inspector. Yet all five had graduated from the University of California at Berkeley School of Public Health and had extensive training and work experience, while none of the Caucasians selected over them had more than high school diplomas. The Chinese American inspector who had scored the highest on the written exam was, in the course of his oral interview told twice, "I suppose you like to play the lotteries like all good Chinamen," by the Caucasian examiner, but it was the "Chinaman" whose social skills were judged as poor.[29]

In this case, the plaintiffs held back by racial discrimination were American-born, as were many of the employees of PG&E stuck in middle-range jobs, none of whom could have been blamed for lacking

English language skills. After many complaints from its Asian American employees, in the early 1990s PG&E decided to revise the Individual Performance Management forms that supervisors had to fill out annually by moving evaluation criteria away from subjective standards such as leadership qualities and interpersonal skills to more performance-oriented standards such as achievement results, ability to communicate mission, and innovation.

The glass ceiling issue becomes more complicated, however, when it comes to the immigrant Chinese American professionals, because of the attitudes they have about themselves. While they may complain of discrimination at work, many foreign-born Chinese engineers and scientists privately lament their own lack of language and communication skills, which renders them incapable of presenting their research findings in a stimulating and exciting way. They recognize this to be a shortcoming of the Chinese education they received back home. In a 1990 interview for an article about this problem, City College of New York professor of physics Chi Yuan, for instance, could not recall ever being asked to write a long essay or a term paper in all his years of education in Taiwan; not at the best high school in the country, or even at National Taiwan University. As a distinguished member of the American academic community, he realized how valuable such an exercise would have been in honing his ability to successfully formulate and present his thoughts. Another problem that gets its share of the blame is the Chinese culture's aversion to self-promotion, which is essential for success in American society. Chinese like to believe that knowledge speaks for itself. They consider the type of performance required at typical American job interviews or presentations as boasting at best and vulgar at worst.

Under the rule of the Chinese Nationalist Party, especially after it moved to Taiwan, political dissent was not tolerated. Parents and teachers alike discouraged discussion of any type, labeling it "idle talk," which was only bound to distract youngsters from useful studies. One government slogan advised, "Use your education to save the country, not to discuss the affairs of state." With China having gone through so many unpredictable political ups and downs, the would-be émigré scientists shunned politics to avoid trouble. In fact, their preference for science was a conscious choice to avoid being connected to ideological issues.

The system did produce a large number of outstanding scientists, but its rigorous system mostly trained students to pass highly competitive examinations; its emphasis on rote memory stifled independent thinking and innovation. Taiwanese-born Nobel laureate Yuan Tseh Lee likened Taiwanese education to "goose stuffing" and made it clear that, had he not received a freethinking education in America, he never would have won the prize. Another Chinese American Nobel laureate, C.N. Yang, pointed out in a speech to students at Peking University that there is a huge difference between passing exams and doing innovative research. While Chinese and Japanese students may have better grades than Americans, they don't do as well in research because they are not encouraged to think independently—they are "high grade, low ability," in his words. The pure pursuit of academic achievement based on the "stuffing principle" and "risk-aversion strategy" promoted by Chinese education does not allow for the full development of individuals. "Build your own future on the foundation of what really interests you," he advised, as a way to personal satisfaction.[30]

This is not the advice Chinese youngsters—whether in China, Taiwan, or the United States—were likely to get from their parents, for most of whom the pursuit of education translates directly into practical consequences. Ambitious parents typically forced their children to major in science, even when they were not interested or particularly talented in it. Filmmaker Peter Wang, who started his career as a filmmaker by charmingly lampooning the unrewarding experience of one such Chinese American science graduate in his film *A Great Wall*, himself studied physics at National Taiwan University and earned a PhD in the field from the University of Pennsylvania, although his greatest talent and interest since childhood had been in the arts. He loved literature and was good with words. His great sense of humor always made him the center of attention at any gathering. But in his family and social circle everyone believed that only the smartest students could major in physics, and he did not want to be seen as stupid, so he chose to major in physics out of pride and under social pressure. Finally, after a fifteen-year academic career, he abandoned science and started making films.

The streamlined scientists and engineers produced in Taiwan for export to the United States were ideally suited to fill the lower ranks of America's scientific establishment as research associates, teaching assistants, and project engineers. Many who entered academe were never slated to reach the rank of professor or research director. They were given postdoctoral grants for as long as the projects they worked on had government funding, and if they performed well they were promoted to research assistants or senior research assistants. Since they had been groomed by Taiwan's educational system and conditioned by Taiwanese society to be "quiet" individuals, the institutions that hired them expected not to have to worry about their demands for equitable conditions. Research conducted by the conservative economist Thomas Sowell suggests that Chinese American university faculty are underpaid, when the quality of their education is taken into account.[31] The 1990 census in the state of California showed that Chinese Americans, after adjustment for differences in education, earned 2.8 percent less than non-Hispanic whites.[32] Some observers have likened the work of imported scientists to that of "white-collar coolies."[33]

THE PROFESSIONAL CLASS FAMILY PROJECT

For most immigrant Chinese professionals in America, careers in engineering, science, and medicine, despite the inequities they experience, have provided the proverbial "door of opportunity" enabling their families' emigration to America. Viewed from that angle, they don't leave the underpaid or sidestepped professional much room to complain—at least not until all the utilitarian goals set for them by their families are met. And this means that they simply have to do whatever it takes to bring their family projects to a desired conclusion.

The blueprint for a classic professional-class Chinese family immigration project was established by ambitious Taiwanese parents in the 1960s. (It is now increasingly followed by the mainland Chinese as well.) After enrolling in graduate school in the United States with the support of a scholarship, the young Chinese science scholar uses the eighteen months of professional training that every student receives as part of graduate instruction to find a job, where he or she has to perform well enough to convince the employer to apply on his or her behalf for U.S. permanent residence status under the "professional preference" clause. Once that is done, the young professional can settle down. With a secured job and citizenship in the pipeline, it is time to get married and start a family. The next step, after having children, is to purchase a home in a neighborhood with good public schools, which typically means the suburbs. This is exactly what Doctors Ching-ling Chu and May-li Chan, the husband and wife mentioned earlier, did. Within ten years of arriving in the United States as penniless graduate students from Taiwan, they were living in an upper-middle-class neighborhood of New York's suburban Westchester County, and they were ready to bring their parents over from Taiwan. The arrival of the parents and in-laws in the United States to care for grandchildren completes the grand family project set in motion decades earlier. The parents' strategizing can now be put to rest. They can rejoice in their grandchildren and savor American middle-class life. If they have retired, they can stay forever, and even enjoy the benefits of Supplemental Security Income (a form of welfare provided to senior citizens who did not work in the United States and are thus not eligible for Social Security).

At no point in the realization of the family project is the immigrant professional allowed to take full measure of his or her own wishes and preferences; any decision not to follow the blueprint is rejected by the parents as destructive to oneself and inconsiderate to the whole family's welfare. The spirit of self-sacrifice is expected to go on after one has settled down with a job, because professional fulfillment cannot be allowed to interfere with the family project. The dutiful sons and daughters tolerate bias at the workplace, telling themselves that they are, after all, the lucky ones who made it to America. The psyche of these immigrant professionals, who carry the burden of their refugee families and are repeatedly told not to get involved with anything political so as not to endanger their parents, is not shaped around individual needs.

Chapter 17

American-Born Achievers

The uniformity of the early wave of immigrant Chinese professionals in terms of aspirations and training has greatly shaped the way they view their experience in this country and the ways they have tried to mold their American-born offspring—the Chinese American Generation X. This is not surprising. After all, they all hail from two small elite groups of graduates from the half dozen best universities in China and Taiwan. They have gravitated to the same neighborhoods and suburbs, known for their excellent public schools. If unable to afford such neighborhoods, they have made sure that their children excel in school so much that they qualify for the most prestigious magnet schools, such as Lowell in San Francisco or Stuyvesant High School in New York City.

Vivian S. Louie, who interviewed a cross-section of American-born children and their immigrant Chinese parents from both classes of Chinese Americans—the Downtown working class and the Uptown professionals—for a study of the second generation's drive to excel, found that middle-class parents knew which were the "good" schools. "When I asked Mrs. Wu how she had learned about Stuyvesant High School . . . attended by her daughter, she was puzzled," Louie writes. "To her, the answer was so straightforward that the question seemed unnecessary. Mrs. Wu had heard of Stuyvesant before even coming to the United States; as she explained, the school's reputation was common knowledge in her native Taiwan."[1]

Equally common among the middle-class parents is their involvement in their children's education.[2] They pay attention to their children's education after school. "My mother was very rigid in terms of my schoolwork when I was younger," Judy Lai, who was a student at Columbia University when Louie interviewed her, said of her experience. "She didn't think the school system was giving me enough in terms of how much I was studying, so she gave me supplementary homework often, and when I had tests or exams, she always expected 100s."[3] If their children don't compete in the top rank of their class, they hire tutors to make sure that they catch up. No effort or cost is spared to make their children's performance at school nothing short of stellar, paving the way to a future entry into an Ivy League school, a Seven Sisters college, or an acceptable equivalent, such as Stanford University, University of Michigan, or University of California at Berkeley. Immigrant Chinese professionals are avid readers of the annual ranking of best schools in the country published in *U.S. News & World Report*, and these days their range of acceptable schools has broadened to include the top-ranked liberal arts colleges, such as Williams and Amherst. But they still insist on enrolling their children every summer in SAT prep classes and Advanced Placement courses to give them a leg up in college admissions considerations.

The parents' involvement in their children's education does not stop there. Taiwanese parents are particularly concerned with the career choices of their children, translating their own experience and somewhat marginal and tenuous position in American society into ironclad strategies designed to protect their children from suffering the same. They insist that their children avoid jobs that require a great deal of interpersonal relating, which might subject them to racial prejudice, and subjective evaluations of their performance. Despite their own experience, they see jobs in science and technology as requiring minimal skills of articulation, where the quality of work is judged by much more objective standards. Social science, humanities, and arts are dismissed as having no foundation in hard knowledge. Business is considered worse because it favors unprincipled, uneducated people who "talk empty" and "lie to make it."

Parental control also extends to leisure time and to the choice of their children's friends. It is a traditional Chinese belief that people become bad through contact with "bad elements." Children are thought of as being born into this world with minds as pure as a white piece of paper, onto which anything can be written. They become contaminated only by their surroundings. So if a Chinese child is to be made to work hard, it has to be around people who work hard. In the eyes of Chinese immigrant parents, American children, white as well as black, have no work ethic because the schools don't give them enough to do and American parents don't bother to teach them discipline. While white kids play sports after school, Chinese kids are typically enrolled in an activity with an academic component.[4] "I think they have too much free time," Taiwan-born stay-at-home suburban mother Mrs. Chang explains her strategy, "and I hate to see kids waste their time. You know, I don't think that life should be like that, you know, waste time. So then I heard some other friends, their children are learning music. And so I think it's good that they can learn music."[5] Her children ended up going to Julliard.

Most second-generation Chinese immigrant kids consequently grow up a yardstick away from "American" temptations and influences. Some of the more typical objections that their parents raise when it comes to their friends are that American kids lack respect for their elders and authority in general, eat the wrong things—particularly too much fried food—and spend too much time pondering deviant sexual behavior that can lead to their own gender confusion. All in all, they constantly worry about the unrestricted lifestyle of American families. Consequently, Chinese kids are not allowed to take part in sleepovers, attend nightlong parties, or start dating too early. These are considered distractions bent on derailing the proper course of the children's education and ruining their plans for the future.

By streamlining the youngsters' lives in this way, Chinese immigrant parents may in fact be doing the second generation a great disservice. Their children are born to, want to, and should assimilate with their natural American environment. They have no interest in maintaining their parents' "Chinese culture." The irony is that the parents themselves were not steeped in Chinese culture when they were young; they wore American jeans whenever not required to be dressed in school uniforms, sang along with Elvis on the radio, rushed to see the latest Hollywood movies, and never ventured to a Chinese opera house or paid any attention to Chinese traditional customs, which they considered backward and superstitious. Most in fact do not know the time and meaning of traditional holidays, such as the Lantern, Mid-Autumn, or Pure Brightness (*Qingming*, the Grave Sweeping Day) festivals. Now, suddenly, they insist on instilling their kids with "superior Chinese values" and reducing their socializing options to other Chinese kids whose parents have the same priorities. In this small circle, regular topics of conversation are whose child got all As and whose children got into Harvard; who just got a job at AT&T or Intel. Associating with other Chinese families and children helps to hammer these goals and values into children at a young age. The children are constantly reminded of positive and negative examples by being told that a who's who child is doing well at Yale, while a so-so kid barely managed to enroll in NYU, and another who'd hung out with the wrong kind ended up at some "playboy school" in the South.

Chinese-language schools, which exist in every community with some degree of Chinese concentration, tend to become the most important venue in reinforcing this regimen of racially exclusionary association. Every weekend, starting from age six, Chinese American children are ferried to one of those schools, which usually operate from rented public-school classrooms, for two hours of language instruction. The outcome is not impressive. Very few American-born Chinese learn to speak Chinese well, much less read it or write it. The truth is that most Chinese parents are not determined to have their children learn Chinese; they merely complain in front of other Chinese parents that their kids were able to speak Chinese perfectly when young but lost the ability once they started attending American schools. Quite often, after a couple of years the kids refuse to continue with classes. After that, when the parents speak in Chinese, the kids answer in English, but the parents allow it because, after all, they consider the mastering of the English language to be of primary importance for success in America.

From the parents' point of view, the main purpose of Chinese-language schools is not making their children learn Chinese but bringing them in regular contact with other Chinese children. It is also an opportunity for the parents to exchange ideas and form social circles around the children. The children hate them, but Chinese-language schools have in fact acted as one of the most important institutional building blocks of Chinese American communities. From there, the parents can expand their ethnic reinforcement projects into setting up

Chinese culture centers to teach and promote Chinese painting, calligraphy, and martial arts, even cooking—something to proudly showcase to their non-Chinese neighbors. Chinese-language schools also typically run youth summer camps and organize Chinese New Year parties and culture tours of Taiwan or China that the parents and the children can take part in together. The objective of all these programs is to create a social environment in which upper-middle-class Chinese professional families can best shape and mold the future generation. None of it is subtle. When children reach the dating age—of at least eighteen—their parents match them into pairs, much to the children's horror and embarrassment. The most blatant attempt to engineer their children's lives, however, has to be the infamous "love boat tour" to Taiwan. Officially called the "Taiwan Study Tour," it is a four-week program sponsored by the Taiwanese government every summer for college-age overseas Chinese men and women to "search for their ancestral roots." Most Chinese American kids don't really want to go, but their parents push them, hoping that the search might unearth not just roots but, even more important, future marrying partners.

AMERICAN MIDDLE-CLASS DREAM

The second-generation middle-class Chinese Americans grow up with the very confused and contradictory value system of their immigrant parents, who want their children to be fully accepted as Americans yet chastise them daily for acting too American. At issue, in addition to the typical points of contention between all parents and children—their clothing, their hairstyle, and the company they keep—is the American lack of respect for elders, loose behavior, and overindulgence in material goods and comforts.

The parents themselves are of course far from immune to the accouterments of the American way of life. To the contrary, they readily succumb to all the customs and outward symbols that give them status as members of the American upper middle class. In doing so, they could be viewed as embodying the American idea of a pluralistic society, responding to various unresolved aspects of their immigrant experience by constructing their own values and their own hybrid world. As hybrid Americans, they are in fact the true practitioners of America's

new multiculturalism, even as they think that they are engaged in preserving Chinese culture while building an American middle-class environment of a bygone era for their children's future. This fractured and
at times disoriented world is hilariously depicted by Gish Jen, a second-
generation Chinese American herself. In her novel *Typical American*, a
family of freshly naturalized American citizens invents a name for itself: Chang-kees, short for Chinese Yankees. The way the Chang-kees
raised their children, Jen writes, "is not at all what the conventional interpreters of Chinese American experience would lead you to think it
is. It is not an incubator designed to preserve Chinese culture." The
Chinese Yankees want to project themselves "as modern and sophisticated human beings able to distance themselves from the superstitions
and backward traditions they associate with Chinese culture," and at
the same time "they want the best of the West for their children: ballet,
tennis and classical music, and if and when an opportunity presents itself, tours for the family to visit the highlights of Western European
culture: museums and opera houses in Paris, Vienna, London and
Rome." So, Jen concludes, "When all is said and done, they want to live
the ideal American middle class life gleaned from Hollywood movies
and *Reader's Digest* (in Chinese translation)—the first sources of information on American culture their generation of Chinese had come in
contact with."

The aspirations of immigrant Chinese professionals are not different from those of other immigrants trying to move into the American
middle class, particularly the Jews, and the similarities are not lost on
them. Both groups have relied on education to acquire status and as
the means to upward mobility. In both cases the parents have displayed
an unusual commitment to their children's education. "The Jew un-
dergoes privation, spills blood, to educate his child," wrote the *Daily
Forward* in 1905, as if to validate the hard work of its readers. "In [this]
is reflected one of the finest qualities of the Jewish people. It shows
our capacity to make sacrifices for our children . . . as well as our love
for education, for intellectual efforts."[6] It is hard to find a Chinese
parent who does not completely identify with this. Moreover, the Chinese like to see themselves, like the Jews, as both a model minority and
victims of discrimination. Both groups were at one time thought of as
unassimilable. And both encountered institutional backlash. In 1922
Harvard president Abbott Lawrence Lowell imposed a quota on the

enrollment of Jewish students in response to the circulated opinion that "Jews are an unassimilable race, as dangerous to a college as indigestible food to man."[7] Similarly, during the early 1980s, unbeknownst to the public, quotas were set to check the dramatic increase of Asian American student enrollment in top American universities. At MIT, for instance, the admission-to-application ratios for Asian students between 1982 and 1986 were 20 to 30 percent lower than those for white students. (There was no breakdown for individual Asian groups, but the majority of college-age Asians were of Chinese origin.) Once the practice was exposed and stopped, the rate of Asian American enrollment shot up immediately at all elite universities.

Currently, 24 percent of the student body at MIT and Stanford and 18 percent at Harvard are Asian Americans. Thirty-nine percent of the students admitted to UC Berkeley in 2003 and 45 percent of the freshmen at UCLA were Asian. It should also be noted that a disproportionate number of these high-performing young Chinese come from upper-middle-class professional families.

The decision of the working-class "Downtown Chinese" to emigrate to America is often brought on by the lack of economic resources to provide for a decent education for their children back home. Yet, although they too encourage their children to perform well so that they can get into the best schools, their children's achievements very rarely measure up to those of "Uptown Chinese" professionals. Deborah Ow, who grew up in New York Chinatown, jumped around several high schools before ending up at the least desirable in the neighborhood, Seward Park High School, known for violence and poor academic performance. Her parents used their networks to learn about better local elementary schools and specialized high schools but were unable to get any additional information when she failed to get into the target schools. They did not have the time, energy, or background to become more involved. "I think that my parents, they want us to succeed and have an education or whatever we choose to do but there wasn't a big push for it because I think they weren't pushed and also they were too busy with their jobs. I mean, there was nobody to sit there and read a book with you or check your homework or stuff like that."[8] Deborah's experience is typical of working-class Chinatown kids. In many cases their parents don't even have a working knowledge of the English language.

The professional-class Chinese have a clear set of advantages. Not only do they have the resources to move to the suburbs or find other ways to send their offspring to schools better than the inner-city schools if they live in the city; their own education enables them to help their children with schoolwork and impart their understanding of how to navigate the educational system. In most families, the mother sacrifices her career to stay at home and supervise the children's education. It is a paradox that in the Chinese American community women with PhDs often don't work (at least not usually until their children grow up), while the untrained women have no choice but to toil long hours earning less than minimum wage.

The concerted and determined effort of professional parents gives their children an enormous advantage over poorer Chinatown kids, while the Chinese-style enforcement of discipline pushes their children to perform better than the children of their social peers from other, less education-oriented ethnic groups. It is not surprising that the overwhelming majority of Chinese who attend elite universities come from "Uptown Chinese" families. It is *their* success that pushes up the statistical average, making all Chinese appear to be one of the most highly educated and professionally successful groups in the United States.[9]

PART IV

From Civil Rights
To Identity Politics
(1965–1980s)

Chapter 18

The Rise of Asian America

THE CIVIL RIGHTS MOVEMENT

By the mid-1960s, a swelling number of American-born Chinese—children of stranded scholars, Taiwanese immigrant professionals, and couples united due to the War Brides Act—reached adulthood and college age. Like other young Americans of their generation, these Chinese baby boomers were swept up by the social and political movements of the 1960s that were questioning the very foundations of America's prosperity and role in the world. But more so than white baby boomers, they found inspiration for their social activism in the civil rights movement of African Americans.

The end of World War II ushered in an era of stability and prosperity. In 1948 the U.S. economy recorded the biggest jump in earnings in history, encouraging African Americans to pursue more aggressively what Adam Clayton Powell (a congressman representing New York City's Harlem) described as "nothing short of complete equality." During the following decade African American leaders worked closely with organized labor to gain access to better jobs and new housing, to gain representation in government, and to end police brutality. But during the McCarthy era, the fight for civil and labor rights was often equated with communism. Loyalty oaths and security programs were set up at every level of government, leading to the harassment and firings of countless activists and nonpolitical people alike. A teacher of crafts at the Department of the Interior was subjected to a barrage of questions: "What were your feelings at the time concerning racial equality? . . . How about civil rights? . . . Do I interpret your statement . . . that maybe Negroes and Jews are denied some of their constitutional rights at present?"[1] In defense of submitting a black employee to similar questioning, a Department of Agriculture attorney stated, "I think it is well known that the Communist Party has adopted . . . plans to secure membership . . . [in] the advocacy of equality for racial and religious minorities."[2] Many of the most outspoken African American leaders were fired from their jobs and silenced.

By equating civil rights activism with communist subversion, the government disabled the most committed and militant activists and organizations. In doing so, it pushed the movement toward more strictly legal demands, such as access to lunch counters, bus service, stores, restaurants, hotels, housing accommodation, and the like,[3] and away from economic demands. Once their objectives were framed as a nonviolent demand for equal rights in the marketplace, it was hard for the government to accuse the African American civil rights leaders of being under the influence of communism, and it was forced to abandon its long-standing opposition to African American activism. Instead, in the *Brown v. Board of Education* case in 1953, the Justice Department issued an amicus brief in support of desegregation in which it assessed that it was "racial discrimination [that] furnishes grist for the Communist propaganda."[4] Lending assistance to the federal government's push for change, the Supreme Court struck down the principle of "separate but equal" that had been used since the end of the Reconstruction era to sanction segregation in the South.

Polls, however, showed that mainstream American public opinion was slow to accept African American civil rights as legitimate. The unchanged status quo pushed the African American leadership to initiate a series of sit-ins in 1955: first on buses in Montgomery, Alabama; then at segregated lunch counters in Greensboro, North Carolina. Because a large number of their participants were middle-class African American college students, the sit-ins quickly mobilized entire African American communities across the South. By 1960 some fifty thousand students were involved in nonviolent actions under the leadership of the Student

Nonviolent Coordinating Committee (SNCC). A year later, the northern-based Congress of Racial Equality (CORE) began to organize Freedom Rides, in which black and white people traveled together on buses through the South in an attempt to break segregation in interstate travel. The civil rights movement reached a peak with the 1963 March on Washington, during which Dr. Martin Luther King Jr. delivered his now famous "I Have a Dream" speech. The massive mobilization of African Americans forced the White House and Congress to pass the 1964 Civil Rights Act.

The Civil Rights Act, however, did not address African Americans' economic demands, and as America entered a period of industrial decline, frustration turned some jobless African Americans stuck in segregated urban ghettos militant and violent. Riots erupted in 1963 in New York. Over the next two years they spread to Philadelphia, Detroit, Washington, D.C., and Newark, culminating in a six-day riot in Los Angeles in 1965, in which large parts of the Watts section were destroyed, costing thirty-four lives. The federal government responded with the Great Society War on Poverty, introducing welfare programs that aimed at defusing urban tensions. But the programs were merely concessions that did not improve the wages, income, housing, and occupational opportunities of African Americans. As Kenneth Clark, a prominent African American educator, pointed out, "The masses of Negroes are now starkly aware that recent civil rights victories benefited a very small number of middle-class Negroes while their predicament remained the same or worsened."[5] Instead, African American leaders demanded full employment and a Freedom Budget, a kind of domestic Marshall Plan for black communities.[6]

Toward the end of his life Martin Luther King Jr. understood the problem of disassociating political from economic issues. Later, Congressman Parren Mitchell (Maryland's first African American congressman, a founding member of the Congressional Black Caucus, and a leading advocate for federal aid to minority small businesses) owned up to the failure of black leadership by admitting, "We made a serious mistake during the 1960s. We should have meshed in our agenda the demands of civil rights and economic parity at the same time. One is meaningless without the other."[7] The failure led a score of younger African American activists to abandon the nonviolent tactics and the earlier struggle for a "race-less society."[8] They wanted the power to change their own conditions—black power, not civil rights—and reached out to the poor and working-class constituencies in the African American communities, trying to organize them from the bottom up—something that the established civil rights organizations were unwilling to do. The role of campaigning for the poor and unemployed fell to radicalized organizations such as the Black Panther Party. A key figure in this transition was Malcolm X, who saw a similarity between black communities in the United States and the oppressed European colonies in Africa and projected the struggle of African Americans in the context of the worldwide movement for decolonization and national liberation. "You can't separate the African revolution from the mood of the black man in America," he announced in 1964, upon returning from a trip to Africa. As the then presidential adviser Daniel Patrick Moynihan observed a decade after the Watts riots, "It was not a matter of chance that the Negro movement caught fire in America at just that moment when nations of Africa were gaining their freedom."[9]

The original vision of the Black Panther Party was to serve the needs of black communities by demanding decent education and health care, employment, and the end to police brutality. It started a free breakfast program for poor ghetto youth. It also gained spectacular notoriety when its members showed up armed at the Capitol in Sacramento and started carrying guns in their surveillance of the police, shouting "Death to pigs!" Suddenly, everybody—and not just in America—knew their Afros, black berets, and take-no-shit attitude. But the party also wanted to raise the consciousness of the people and motivate them to fight for "total liberation" from the "oppression of the system," drawing inspiration from the most radical international revolutionary figures, such as Che Guevara, Mao, and Frantz Fanon. The party's activities were so radical that it was at one time assailed by FBI chief J. Edgar Hoover as "the greatest threat to the internal security of the United States." Global events gave its members and other militant African American groups a sense of invincibility, as the whole world turned against American imperialism by the late 1960s, and it seemed that American global dominance was on the verge of collapse.

The U.S. military presence in Vietnam reached a peak of 542,000 in 1968, and while the U.S. government claimed that the war was turning in its favor, the Vietcong launched the Tet offensive in February and struck at targets across South Vietnam, reaching even the grounds of the U.S. Embassy in Saigon. For most Americans, stunned by televised scenes—this was the first TV war—of U.S. troops fighting to retake the embassy, this marked the turning point in support of the war. Antiwar protests by white youth went into high gear, with marchers shouting, "Hell, no, we won't go!" and "Hey! Hey! LBJ! How many kids have you killed today?" In the New Hampshire primary, the peace candidate, Eugene McCarthy, garnered 40 percent of the vote, leading to Lyndon B. Johnson's decision not to run.

In 1968, in the aftermath of the assassinations of Robert F. Kennedy and Martin Luther King Jr., major riots erupted in urban centers across America. At Columbia University in New York, students opposed to the university's research contracts with the Defense Department, campus recruitment by the CIA and the Reserve Officer Training Corps (ROTC), and the building of a new university gymnasium on the grounds of a public park in Harlem seized administrative buildings. They demanded that the practices that aided America's imperialist policies abroad and at home be stopped, and that university education be reformed. After a standoff that lasted for weeks, the city police were called in to retake the buildings by force; 150 students were injured, and 700 were arrested. But student protests spread to other campuses across the country, with similar demands for the moral accountability of university administrations. Later that year antiwar protesters converged on the Democratic National Convention in Chicago, where Vice President Hubert Humphrey was selected as the Democratic Party candidate for the national election. The site in Grant Park was protected by jeeps laced with barbed wire, evoking for American TV audiences the still-recent images of Soviet tanks shutting down the protests of Prague Spring—the attempt earlier that year by Czechoslovakians to create "socialism with a human face." Chicago mayor Richard Daley's blunt, violent response to antiwar campaigners made no distinction between the Black Panther Party and the Weather Underground, the Yippies, Ralph Abernathy's Poor People's Campaign, Women Strike for Peace, and even the pacifist Quakers. Peaceful marchers were turned back with tear gas. Radical youth battled with the police during the entire convention week, which ended with 668 arrests and 111 hospital-treated injuries.

The convention had several consequences. It made militant

protesters more militant. The Weatherman faction of the Students for a Democratic Society organized the Days of Rage in Chicago as "revenge" for the police brutality during convention week, with pipe-wielding Weatherman coming back in October to race through the streets, attacking police and smashing windows and cars. It also galvanized peaceful protesters into a national antiwar movement. So while in late 1967 the National Mobilization to End the War in Vietnam (MOBE) had drawn only a hundred thousand protesters to a demonstration it organized at the Pentagon, by 1969 an estimated 2 million people from across the country participated in the first Moratorium Against the War.

Nineteen sixty-eight became known as the "Year of the Barricades." Students protested across Europe, Australia, and Japan. In Paris, they were joined by 10 million workers in a strike that drew out ten thousand battle police to the barricades, turning the streets of Paris into battlefields reminiscent of the French Revolution. Radical student movements in the United Kingdom and Germany staged major confrontations with the governments. In Mexico, ten days before the start of the 1968 Olympics, police fired on student protesters against Mexico's lack of democracy, killing anywhere from thirty-eight to several hundred. The spirit of rebellion did not spare communist countries. In June, Yugoslavia's University of Belgrade was taken over for seven days by students demanding the abolition of bureaucratic privileges, further democratization, a solution to the problem of mass unemployment, reduction of social differences, and university reform. China was in the midst of the Cultural Revolution against established party leaders and bureaucrats. Czechoslovakia's communist leadership itself, broadly backed by the populace, briefly defied Soviet orthodoxy before being crushed by Soviet troops.

People protested worldwide—not just against the Vietnam War but also out of dissatisfaction with the absence of values and the empty lifestyle of uncontrolled consumerism of advanced capitalist societies, as well as in frustration with the bureaucracy and rigidity of Soviet-style socialism. Young people around the world were rebelling against their elders and "the system." "The essence of the democratic surge of the 1960s," noted conservative scholar Samuel Huntington, "was a general challenge to existing systems of . . . the family, the university, business, public and private associations, politics, the government bu-

Chinese gold miners in California, at the head of the Auburn Ravine, 1852. *Courtesy of the California History Room, California State Library, Sacramento, California*

Chinese workers building a right-of-way for Loma Prieta Lumber Co., Santa Cruz County, California, ca. 1876. *Pajaro Valley Historical Association*

Hong Neok Woo, an immigrant from Shanghai, arrived in this country in 1855 and became a citizen and served as a private in Co. I, 50th Pennsylvania Volunteer Emergency Militia Infantry, 1863. *Thomas P. Lowry Collection; originally found by Mike Musick*

Chinese workers picking olives on the Quito Ranch, Santa Clara County, California, ca. 1905. *Albumen (?) print, Alice Iola Hare Photograph Collection, No. 445, Unit ID: 1905.04953; courtesy of The Bancroft Library, University of California, Berkeley*

Chinese fishing village, Monterey, California, 1875. *California Historical Society, FN-22407*

Cover of *The San Francisco Illustrated Wasp*, Aug. 1877–July 1878. *Courtesy of The Bancroft Library, University of California, Berkeley*

"Massacre of the Chinese at Rock Springs, Wyoming, September 2, 1885," engraving published in *Harper's Weekly*, September 26, 1885. *Courtesy of the California History Room, California State Library, Sacramento, California*

Chinese women and children at the Angel Island Immigration Station, Marin County, California, early 1900s. *California Historical Society, FN-18240*

The champion Chinese hose team of America, who won the Great Hub-and-Hub Race at Deadwood, Dakota, July 4, 1888. *Courtesy of the South Dakota State Historical Society-State Archives*

Chinese Boy Scouts on parade through Chinatown, Oakland, California, ca. 1925. *Courtesy of the Oakland Museum of California*

Forbidden City, the first Chinese nightclub with live entertainment in America, opened in San Francisco in 1938. *Courtesy of the Gladys Hansen Museum*

A parade sponsored by the New York Overseas Chinese Public School to raise funds for China's fight against Japanese occupation in the Second Sino-Japanese War (1937–1945). *Courtesy of the Museum of Chinese in the Americas, New York*

The U.S. 14th Air Service Group operated out of China, Burma, and India, and was composed predominantly of Chinese Americans. Here Chinese American members of the 14th Air Service Group are seen serving in Burma, 1943–1944. *Courtesy of Corky Lee*

Leah Hing is believed to have been the first Chinese American woman to fly an airplane. Born in Portland, Oregon, in 1907, she received a pilot's license in 1934 (roughly when the picture was taken) and joined the Civil Air Patrol after the outbreak of World War II. She worked as an instrument mechanic at a Portland air base. *Courtesy of the Oregon Historical Society, 148-05*

The Congress passed the War Brides Act in 1946 allowing wives of Chinese who had served in the U.S. military during the war to come join them in this country. This image shows Chinese wives of Chinese American servicemen after World War II in a Chinese Sunday school, Westminster Presbyterian Church, Minneapolis, Minnesota, 1950. *Bing Wong, Minnesota Historical Society*

Two immigration officers interrogate Chinese immigrants suspected of being Communists or deserting seamen at Ellis Island, New York, 1951. © *Bettmann/CORBIS*

Chien Shiung Wu received a PhD in physics from U.C. Berkeley in 1940. Because of the war, she was unable to return to China. Here she assembles an electro-magnetic generator at the Smith College Physics laboratory, where she held her first teaching job (1942).Wu worked on the Manhattan Project (to enrich uranium fuel). She is known to many scientists as the "First Lady of Physics" and the "Madame Curie of China." *AIP Emilio Segrè Visual Archives*

Starting from the 1950s, second-generation and immigrant professional Chinese Americans began to move to less racially restrictive suburbs. *Ken Huie, Minnesota Public Library*

First Asian Coalition march against the Vietnam War, Washington, D.C., 1971. © *Corky Lee*

A victim of police brutality during the Chinatown protest against police brutality—to this day the largest protest in the history of New York Chinatown, 1975. © *Corky Lee*

A garment factory on Mott Street, New York, ca. 1976. © *Corky Lee*

Apprentice carpenter fired due to injury protests in front of 34th Street and Madison Avenue in New York, 1995. She was rehired as the result of the protest. © *Corky Lee*

A gathering of Asian American students at Columbia University, 1997.
© *Corky Lee*

Ang Lee (*Crouching Tiger, Hidden Dragon*) and David Henry Hwang (*M. Butterfly*): commercially, the most successful Chinese American filmmaker and playwright, at the Pan Asian Repertory Theatre Benefit Dinner, New York, 1993. © *Corky Lee*

Chinese Americans protest against racism in the *National Review* coverage of the Democratic Party fundraising scandal labeled "Asiagate," New York, 1997. © *Corky Lee*

Chinese super malls are scattered all across American suburbs where there are significant Chinese American concentrations. © *Corky Lee*

New York City Council Member John C. Liu (the first Chinese American elected to New York City Council) and Washington State Governor Gary Locke (the first Chinese American governor in U.S. history), mobilizing Asian Pacific American voters during the 2004 Presidential Election, walk through the streets of Chinatown, New York. *Courtesy of John Choe, Office of Council Member Liu*

reaucracy, and the military service."[10] The decade ended with the American invasion of Cambodia, in 1970, and the killing by the National Guard of four students who protested against it at Kent State University in Ohio.

EMERGENCE OF THE ASIAN AMERICAN MOVEMENT

It was during this tumultuous and chaotic period that American-born Chinese baby boomers reached adolescence. As dominant assumptions about the nature of American society exploded under the attack of the civil rights and black power movements, groups as disparate as women, gays, lesbians, and other nonwhite minorities were inspired to push for radical democratic participation in every aspect of life.[11] Chinese American baby boomers came into contact with diverse groups of young Americans and their political agendas, usually while attending college, and many took part in the free speech, antiwar, student, and civil rights movements. Struggling along with everyone else to redefine their relationship to the centers of power in American society, they were particularly influenced by the African American movement, which taught all minorities to liberate themselves by rejecting the false white consciousness. But before they could do that, so that they could bring a new brand of activism to Chinese American communities, which had largely been silenced since the cold war, they had to develop a self-identity to rally around.

Americans of "yellow" skin—mostly Japanese, Chinese, and Filipinos—never saw themselves as one group until that time, although they were all "Orientals" to white Americans. Whether "Chinks" or "Japs," they were considered equally inferior and were equally targeted for discrimination. This common experience became the basis from which their consciousness as a single racial group began to evolve. That the term "Asian American" came to denote their new identity was a matter of deliberate choice. According to Yuji Ichioka, one of the founders of the Asian American movement credited with coining the term, Americans of Asian descent regarded the term "Oriental" as reeking of the European colonialism that had defined Asia as "Orient" or "East" in relation to Europe. "Oriental" suggested passivity. In contrast, "Asian American" connoted political activism—an individual who "gives a damn about his life, his work, his beliefs, and is willing to do almost anything to help Orientals become Asian Americans."[12] The movement gelled in 1968 at UC Berkeley, when a group of individuals of divergent Asian descent were called together by Ichioka and his wife, Emma Gee, to take part in the coalition with the Black Panther Party and antiwar groups in support of the new Peace and Freedom Party—an alternative to the two-party establishment. The caucus named itself the Asian American Political Alliance (AAPA). It was the first time that the idea of "Asian Americanism" was used nationally to mobilize people of Asian descent.[13]

Soon AAPA chapters were being set up at San Francisco State University, UCLA, and across the country, while the first New York–based movement organization, Asian Americans for Action, was established in the fall of 1968 by two longtime friends and activists, Kazu Iijima and Minn Matsuda, who had stumbled upon the idea when contemplating a Japanese American group for their college-age kids.[14] The newly found identity energized Asian Americans and gave them license to take part in history in the making with an increased sense of urgency and a sense of belonging to the worldwide movement of liberation.

ASIAN ANTIWAR MOVEMENT

The Asian American identity was not an intuitive construct; rather, it was a reaction to white America's concept of Asians, as well as a pragmatic means of mobilizing people. No single issue brought Asian Americans together and galvanized them into a movement more than the Vietnam War. The mainstream antiwar organization MOBE coordinated thousands of local antiwar groups into massive nationwide demonstrations on a simple program that it assumed everyone could agree with: end the war, withdraw American troops, bring our boys home. The issue of race never came up for discussion.

African Americans, however, had understood the war's racial aspect all too well. As early as 1965 young blacks in McComb, Mississippi, having learned of a classmate's death in Vietnam, printed a leaflet that stated, "No Mississippi Negroes should be fighting in Vietnam for the white man's freedom, until all the Negro People are free in Mississippi."

In 1966 six members of the Student Nonviolent Coordinating Committee, one of the groups in the African American community organizing opposition to the war, were arrested for invasion of an induction center in Atlanta and sentenced to several years in prison.[15] In 1967 Muhammad Ali, the heavyweight champion of the world, refused to serve in what he called a "white man's war" ("I ain't got no quarrel with them Vietcong . . .") and the boxing authorities took away his title. The government took away his passport. Martin Luther King observed that white society, which praised the nonviolence of the civil rights movement and was reluctant to use force to guarantee the rights of African American citizens in places such as Birmingham and Selma, Alabama, almost gleefully sent both white and black young men to Vietnam "to slaughter, men, women and children."[16]

From the very beginning, Asian Americans had a visceral reaction to the war—they could not look at the pictures of carnage at My Lai without noticing that American troops were killing and maiming unarmed, unresisting women and children with faces like their own. During the Winter Solider investigation into U.S. war crimes in Vietnam, which was held in January 1971 in Detroit, Scott Shimabukaro of the Third Marine Division testified that Vietnamese were referred to as "gooks" and that "military men have the attitude that a gook is a gook . . . they go through the brain washing about the Asian people being subhuman—all the Asian people—I don't mean just the South Vietnamese . . . all Asian people."[17] General Westmoreland famously announced from the top of the military establishment, "The Oriental doesn't put the same high price on life as does a Westerner. Life is plentiful. Life is cheap in the Orient." Down in the trenches, GIs echoed the attitude through the expression "The only good gook is a dead gook," often heard by correspondents stationed in Vietnam. Ampo Fusai, a UC Berkeley student, wrote in an Asian American Political Alliance newsletter that the American presence in Vietnam was nothing more than the "perpetuation of the white man's war of colonial exploitation and the bloodletting of Asian peoples." In addition, one could not help but make a connection between the callous American attitude toward the Vietnamese and the treatment of Asian Americans in the United States.

Asian American GIs serving in Vietnam often had to endure racist taunts by officers and fellow GIs because of their racial similarity to the enemy.[18] Scott Shimabukaro was greeted with the comment, "Oh, we have a gook here today in our platoon," when he first arrived in Vietnam.[19] A Chinese American GI who objected to this kind of verbal abuse was assigned to two years of hard labor in the stockade. Others were drawn to identify with the enemy. "I saw how whites were treating the Vietnamese, calling them Gooks, running them over with their trucks," Mike Wanabe told Asian American scholar Yen Le Espiritu in 1989. "I figured I am a Gook also."[20] Studies of Asian American veterans have shown that they were at a much greater risk than other American soldiers of developing post-traumatic stress disorders or other psychiatric problems due to exposure to negative race-related events, such as being stigmatized or targeted as the enemy and being shot at by fellow Americans, or being harassed and physically injured because they were perceived as resembling the enemy.[21]

The MOBE slogan "Bring the Boys Home," in the eyes of Asian American antiwar activists, showed concern only for Americans, not for Vietnamese. It even seemed to support the Nixon administration's call for the "Vietnamization" of the war—for the accelerated training and arming of the Vietnamese, who would take over the duties from the Americans—the objective of which was not ending the war and stopping the slaughter but encouraging Vietnamese to kill Vietnamese. The emphasis of Asian American opposition to the war was summed up in their rallying cries, "We don't want your racist war," and "Stop killing our Asian brothers and sisters."[22] In the fall of 1969, Asian American activists held a symposium in San Francisco, called "Towards an Asian Perspective on Vietnam," and decided to hold their own demonstrations under their own banners, or participate in the third world rallies with African Americans and Latinos.[23] Still, in May 1970, after American troops invaded Cambodia and protests flared up across the nation, members of the Asian American Coalition attended the emergency meeting at the Columbia University student center called by MOBE to plan for citywide action in New York. They pleaded for the broadening of the slogan to include condemnation of the official American policy of the slaughter of Asians, but they were shouted down. Introducing issues other than "Bring the Boys Home" would harm the effort to unite the greatest number of people, they were told, and their request was sectarian and divisive. Because they raised a racial issue, they were accused by MOBE of trying to break up the unity of the antiwar movement. On other occasions, Asian American activists were shunted off to the side at protests and left off the roster of speakers at rallies, leading many of them to conclude that the supposedly progressive white activists were racist.

African Americans activists, on the other hand, were favorably disposed toward Asians because of what they saw as the brave Asians' resistance in Vietnam, Korea, and China against Western aggression and domination. They may not have been knowledgeable about what exactly was happening in China during the Cultural Revolution, but they were impressed by what they heard. Mao Tse-tung was particularly popular as someone who was standing up to Western imperialism and supporting the cause of the oppressed third world. During the African American urban riots in 1968 Mao had declared, "I hereby express resolute support for the just struggle of the black people in the United States," and during that same period sent thousands of Chinese workers to East Africa to help build the railroad between Zambia and Tanzania.

In another Asian connection, when Huey Newton and Bobby Seale first formed the Black Panther Party for self-defense against police brutality toward African Americans in Oakland, California, in 1966, they got their first guns to patrol the streets with from a Japanese American, Richard Aoki. And they drew inspiration from the Red Guards in China, who were leading rebellious youth to challenge the bureaucratic party elite and oppressive state institutions in the Great Proletarian Cultural Revolution. The Red Guards' emphasis on changing college admission standards to benefit the historically bypassed children of workers and peasants seemed particularly akin to their own struggle for affirmative action in higher education in America. One of the first things the Panthers did to raise money for their programs was to sell the "little red book" of quotations from Chairman Mao on street corners and on college campuses.

Asian Americans, for their part, drew inspiration from the Panthers' drive to organize the lowest and most dehumanized stratum of their community, that is, the ex-prisoners, the street gangs, the addicts, and the juvenile delinquents in the ghettos. In 1967, a few of the more politically conscious Chinatown street kids in San Francisco organized a raffle to raise money for a pool hall for neighborhood youth, who otherwise spent their time attacking gawking tourists, fighting with foreign-born Chinese youngsters, or engaging in theft and burglary. The nucleus of their organization, Leway (Legitimate Ways), was influenced by the Black Panther Party. In 1968 the group invited Bobby Seale for a talk, and he encouraged them to form the Red Guard Party in honor of the young revolutionaries in China inspired by Mao Tse-tung's call for rebellion against "the system"—which to Mao had meant the vestiges of feudalism and elitism as well as the bourgeois corruption embedded in China's state institutions. They began to study Mao's quotations, formed the Red Guard Party, and adopted the Black Panther Party's ten-point program with minor changes.

The Red Guards exhibited an audacious and defiant attitude and a total lack of deference toward established Chinatown institutions. They openly advocated allegiance to the socialist politics of China. When the party's office first opened on Jackson Street in Chinatown, long a bastion of anticommunism, it flew the Chinese five-star flag and played the song "East Is Red" (China's equivalent of the national anthem during the Cultural Revolution) into the streets. "We made it clear [to the Chinatown establishment] that we liked Mao," says Alex Hing, one of the Red Guard Party founders. Like the Black Panthers, the Red Guards started breakfast for children and free lunch programs for Chinatown's working poor. They organized tenants against landlords and developers. And they were constantly harassed by the San Francisco Police Department's Tactical Squad, with dozens of officers in full riot gear storming frequently into the Leway pool hall to look for guns and drugs.

In response to intense police harassment, party members saw fit to bear arms for self-defense, just like the Black Panthers. One of the members, Tyrone Won, who was on parole at the time, had an armed standoff with the police. He later escaped and wound up hijacking a plane to Cuba, where he died. But the ultramilitant stance—promoting armed struggle—did not endear the Red Guards to anyone. Much like the Black Panthers, they were soon split by internal dissention; they were later subsumed by another radical organization, I Wor Kuen.[24]

Chapter 19

Struggle for Identity

ASIAN AMERICAN STUDIES

The Asian American movement took full shape at universities, such as San Francisco State College, UCLA, UC Berkeley, City College of New York, University of Wisconsin at Madison, Yale, Princeton, and Columbia University, where American-born children of both working-class and professional Chinese families first gained political awareness. The organizations they formed, Asian American Political Alliance and Asian American Coalition, served not only to nurture and disseminate "Asian American consciousness," but also as vehicles to engage in social and political issues of the day and give support to other groups and movements—the Antiwar Movement, Latino Movement, American Indian Movement, Women's Liberation Movement, etc. Sooner or later, their protests typically turned to challenging the university system.

Asian Americans first got involved in challenging university policy at San Francisco State College (now California State University at San Francisco), where the majority of the students came from working-class families. What started in 1966 as a proposal by African American and other third world students for admission of more economically and culturally disadvantaged students and for a black-controlled Black Studies Department had by 1968 turned into a general student strike. It was called by the Third World Liberation Front—a coalition of African

Americans, Chicanos, Native Americans, and Asian Americans—and demanded relevant and accessible education for their communities, including open admissions, community control and redefinition of the education system, as well as the establishment of ethnic studies and a curriculum that reflected the participation and contributions of groups previously omitted from what was taught as American history.[1] The strike went on for five long months and culminated in the police takeover of the campus when then governor Ronald Reagan declared a state of emergency, sending 650 club-swinging policemen to disperse the student picket line in front of classroom buildings. But the students' demands generated increased community support and their agenda spread to other campuses. In the end, they won the distinction as the first university in the nation to establish an academic program in ethnic studies, including Asian American studies.[2] Several dozen other ethnic studies and Asian American studies programs were created soon thereafter, as administrators ceded to student demands after similar strikes at other schools across the country, including UC Berkeley, UCLA, and the City College of New York.

The launching of Asian American studies programs provided resources and opportunities for all kinds of new research and intellectual breakthroughs, from the unearthing of ethnic histories shoved under the carpet by official mainstream American historiography to the research on Asian American communities persistently ignored by American social sciences. Previously, the presence of Asians in America had been pretty much omitted from the standard precollege school curriculum. A San Francisco Board of Education study of three hundred social studies textbooks used in local elementary and secondary high schools revealed that about 75 percent of them did not mention Chinese at all, while 17 percent gave them only a token representation, barely mentioning their role in the building of the transcontinental railroad. There was nothing in the textbooks about the internment of Japanese Americans during World War II.[3]

The pioneers of Asian American studies at UC Berkeley, UCLA, and San Francisco State University intended to work with African American, Latino, Native American, women's, and gay and lesbian studies to reshape the so-called common knowledge, so as to fully reflect the pluralistic reality of American society. But their work went beyond creating a new knowledge base to the even more important task of giving substance to the idea of an Asian America. Asian Americanism was a pragmatic pan-ethnic identity conceived without—in the term that began to emerge at this point—a "shared history" (a history that the diverse groups that made up Asian America had in common). The hope was that universities would provide an environment where the task could be accomplished and a "soul" could be given to an Asian American movement. It turned out to be a complex and conflict-ridden task.

University administrations fiercely resisted establishing Asian American studies programs, yielding only after unrelenting organized student pressure. Once forced to accept them, the universities viewed the programs as a challenge to their institutional power to define and determine what constituted proper knowledge. They used every opportunity to undermine their operation, to shrink them, claiming lack of funding, or even to freeze them under the pretext that they could not find academically qualified scholars to teach.

Opposition by existing faculty, including most liberal members, was even more intense because they saw these programs, born of political movements, as lacking in intellectual rigor. The new studies would not be accepted as part of their disciplines unless they were subsumed under the existing categories of "race relations" in sociology or "voting patterns" in political science and taught by the existing white male faculty. (Needless to say, the development of various ethnic and women's studies programs threatened white male dominance within the academy.) The problem at the initial stage of the development of Asian American studies was that there was no expertise in the new fields within the academy. But neither university administrators nor established faculty expressed any interest in nurturing the programs or the expertise required to teach them. The funding priorities of the established faculty were for vacancies in the Western civilization, Elizabethan literature, European history, and American electoral politics programs—fields viewed as paramount in maintaining the "integrity of university education." If concessions were made, they were always to African American studies and always as a result of mobilized political pressure. No one was willing to do the same for Asian American studies. The number of Asians attending universities was small, and their demands for separate academic programs were considered to lack merit because, not having experienced slavery, they did not quite share in the history of oppression, which deserved special consideration.

The few Asian American studies programs created under student pressure during the late 1960s and early 1970s were constantly threatened by negative academic reviews, and the position of Asian American faculty made untenable through the withholding of reappointments and denial of tenure. When hired, Asian American studies specialists found themselves housed in hostile departments because no school would allow them to form their own. Each appointee had to receive academic recognition in a mainstream discipline, while at the same time being asked to migrate to Asian American studies and develop a new field of specialization. And this had to be done almost overnight, as these new "experts," usually drafted from among the most recent PhDs or graduate students who had completed their studies but not their dissertation, scrambled for teaching material. Relevant sources had to be "discovered" among obscure and out-of-print novels, such as *America Is in the Heart* by Carlos Bulosan and Louis Chu's *Eat a Bowl of Tea*; among the previously ignored monographs and doctoral dissertations on New York's or San Francisco's Chinatowns; or in personal testimonies of Japanese internment, such as John Okada's *No-No Boy*. Pioneer Asian Americanists set up ad hoc editorial teams to collect whatever relevant material they could get their hands on and fashion them into anthologies (*The Big Aiiieeeee!*), journals (*Amerasia Journal*), and textbooks (*Roots* and *Counterpoint*). These would become indispensable as teaching tools and guides for future research in the field.

DEFINING ASIAN AMERICAN CULTURE

The militancy of the 1960s had also infused a new generation of artists and writers with a rush of energy, paralleling the efforts of pioneers in the Asian American studies programs in their ambitious efforts to define an Asian American cultural identity. Dozens of journals and magazines, such as *Bridge Magazine* (New York), *East/West* (San Francisco), *Gidra* and *Amerasia Journal* (Los Angeles), and *Yellow Rice* (Philadelphia), sprang from college campuses and ghetto communities. Their expressed aim was to challenge the white monopoly on American culture. Like African Americans at the time, Asians too saw their own history systematically marginalized and destroyed. Their "new consciousness" was the wholesale rejection of Anglo-American values and traditions.

The best formulated Asian American polemic of this generation of activists was articulated in *Aiiieeeee! An Anthology of Asian American Writers*, edited in 1974 by Frank Chin, Jeffery Paul Chan, Lawson Fusao Inada, and Shawn Wong. Right off the bat, the editors argued for a native-born Asian American literary consciousness that was not Chinese, Japanese or white Western European, but a native development of American culture. Having been excluded from creative participation in American culture, but also "separated by geography, culture, and history from China and Japan for seven and four generations," Chinese, Filipino, and Japanese Americans "have evolved cultures and sensibilities distinctly not Chinese or Japanese and distinctly not white American." Asian American writers thus see themselves as different from "Americanized" Chinese writers "who were intimate with and secure in their Chinese cultural identity in an experiential sense, in a way we American-born can never be. . . . We were neither one or the other. Nor were we half and half or more one than the other."[4]

These Asian American culture makers regarded the work of pioneer American-born Chinese writers Pardee Lowe (*Father and Glorious Descendant*, 1943), Jade Snow Wong (*Fifth Chinese Daughter*, 1950), and Virginia Chin-lan Lee (*The House That Tai Ming Built*, 1963), who were recognized by the mainstream, with unmitigated disdain. Although Lowe's, Wong's, and Lee's work had explored the Asian American racial experience through stories of East and West conflicts, the generation gap, and interracial marriages, and rebelled against the feudal traditions that had been instilled in the Chinese American community by their immigrant parents, it was also infused by their pursuit of American individualism and desire to show patriotism and loyalty to America. The 1960s activists did not see this as mirroring the authors' lives, which had been governed by intense social pressure to assimilate; it was simply unacceptable.

Similarly, they dismissed the accomplishments of C.Y. Lee, the San Francisco Chinatown reporter who wrote *The Flower Drum Song*—the first bestseller by an Asian American author, which was made into a popular Broadway musical and a successful Hollywood movie with a score by Rodgers and Hammerstein. Lee's slapstick comedy of generational conflicts exposed American racism and blamed it for making assimilation for both immigrant and American-born Chinese difficult. But it was at the same time infused with an optimism that anticipated an America where differences of race, sex, class, and nationality could be erased by the embrace of individualism and modernity. Asian American cultural activists believed that assimilation of colored minorities into the white supremacist society was impossible. In their view, those who subscribed to the myth only gave ammunition to the mainstream to blame the minorities—the victims—for failure to integrate. Lee's nuanced dark humor and forgiving spirit were denounced as a sign of submissiveness. The editors of *Aiiieeeee!* derided his unrealistic and glorified picture of a Chinatown in which ancient Chinese elite culture was preserved as a product of "a white tradition of Chinese novelty literature . . . for the entertainment of Americans."[5]

White Americans who were "sympathetic" to the Chinese fared even worse. Pearl Buck, born to a missionary family in China, was the best known among them. She was a long-time civil rights advocate and outspoken opponent of racism. As a trustee of Howard University, she had raised the issue of black patriotism in the early days of World War II, opposed British colonialism, and spoken against the internment of Japanese Americans (all of which was registered by FBI director J. Edgar Hoover). In her book *The Good Earth* she had endowed Chinese people with admirable attributes, but the unimpressed young Chinese American cultural activists faulted her for being patronizing. Her loudest critics, Frank Chin and Jeffrey Paul Chan, co-wrote an article entitled "Racist Love" in which they called the Pearl Buck–type portrayal of the Chinese a plot by the mainstream to mold minority behavior. "Each racial stereotype comes in two models, the acceptable model and the unacceptable. . . . The unacceptable model is unacceptable because he cannot not be controlled by whites. The acceptable model is acceptable because he is tractable." Those who conform to the stereotype are treated with "love," Chin and Lee maintained; those who refuse, with racial hatred.

As the leading voice among the angry young men of the 1960s, playwright Frank Chin (*Chickencoop Chinaman, Year of the Dragon*) called for Asian Americans to refuse to be good, loyal, and obedient; to refuse to be Americanized. He claimed as his heritage not the culture of China but the ethos of the Chinese railroad workers who had built the transcontinental railroad in the nineteenth century (he himself had worked on the railroads and liked to sport an old railroad standard his grandfather had carried in the railroad's steward service) and as his model, which he believed ought to be the model for all Asian Americans, the protagonist of John Okada's novel *No-No Boy*. The no-no boy, interned in the camps during War World II, refuses to serve in the U.S. Army in order to be free. At the same time, he rejects his pro-Japanese mother's notion that Japanese warships will show up on the West Coast to liberate his family and the rest of the Japanese Americans. He chooses to say no to both America and Japan.

The critical lead the editors of *Aiiieeeee!* took placed them in a role somewhere between Asian American politicos and artists; they wanted to guide the way in which Asian American literature was written and appreciated, and thus contribute to the building of a new Asian American consciousness and collective identity. They acknowledged that the road they were traveling was a tricky one, but they were guided by the belief that "the subject matter of minority literature is social history, not necessarily by design but by definition."

The establishment of Asian American studies programs at several universities provided a ready forum for many of their heated debates. The issues they raised became the teaching points, their output the teaching material in Asian American studies classrooms. Yet, despite their hearty contribution, the challenges faced by Asian American studies programs remained daunting because the pioneers in the field, in addition to performing the contemplative task of theory building and shaping a vision for the future, had to simultaneously struggle with school administrations for funding to survive.

Many students and faculty alike devoted countless hours to the thankless task of setting up programs and transforming the ugly duckling into an integral and recognized part of the academy, and their efforts were not always appreciated. The faculty needed to develop an inclusive curriculum that would help correct American education's Anglo-centric bias. To achieve that, their teaching and research had to conform, at least to some degree, to established academic standards. This did not always meet with the approval of student activists, who expected Asian American academic programs to document accomplishments achieved by Asian Americans and play an advocacy role in promoting a positive image of them. Such expectations, in turn, gave credence to the charge leveled by many critics that Asian American studies was simply a feel-good discipline. Satisfying the activists' demands would effectively take the discipline out of play in the academic arena—the very sphere that the Asian American studies programs had been created to reform and shake up.

Student activists were a complex lot. In the midst of the New Left environment of the late 1960s, a number of them were drawn to the Marxism-espousing anticapitalist revolutionary ideology. They did not see "identity" as the central issue and demanded that the Asian American curriculum emphasize the class dimension of the Asian American experience. Others saw the academic programs they had fought for as a part of larger movements beyond the college campuses and believed that the resources from the Asian American studies programs should be diverted to aid those larger struggles. Student leaders at UC Berkeley wanted to make the Asian American studies program into an authentic "community college," meaning that its "course content, admission standards, and scholastic requirements should be geared to the needs of community youth" and its "research activities should be directed at solving, not contributing to community problems."[6]

At that time, Asian students at UC Berkeley were actually more interested in organizing Chinese women working in the garment industry into the Chinatown Cooperative Garment Factory and defending elderly Asian bachelor tenants at the International Hotel from being evicted by developers, than sweating out a college curriculum of any kind. Activists at UCLA set up a Student/Community Projects unit as a part of the Asian American Studies Center. Warren Furutani, who served for four years as its coordinator, established undergraduate field study courses allowing students to work as interns with different Asian American community organizations in the Los Angeles area. The project's aim was the "empowerment and development of a new generation of scholars, community service workers and organizers . . . to address social and community problems."[7] Generally, community-oriented student activists expected academic programs to train recruits for their activist causes and expected the resources to be directed toward working-class communities through the purchase of material that supported the political work of sectarian groups, through hiring community activists of questionable expertise to teach courses, and through granting academic credits to students doing unsupervised "community organizing." They expected this because they believed that political work produced a higher form of knowledge than purely academic studies.

A more sophisticated group of activists argued that there was a brain drain of Asian students, who were groomed in colleges and universities to assimilate into the mainstream and thus became lost to their own communities—leaving the communities leaderless and steeped in poverty and social problems. The task of Asian American studies programs, according to them, was to give relevant training to such students, so that they would return to their communities to "liberate" them.

The inevitable tension between the academy and the community led to open conflicts. The Asian American studies program at UC Berkeley was repeatedly threatened by coups and takeovers by community activists. More often than not, it ended up serving as the battleground for different factional political groups.[8]

Chapter 20

Radicals and Reformers

BACK TO THE COMMUNITY

Soon after Asian American studies began to emerge as an accepted academic field, most student activists lost interest in campus struggles because they realized that university battles took place in a detached reality, and that the main arena for social change was not on campuses. The most ideologically committed were pulled away by a deep sense of responsibility to their ethnic communities. Once again, the African American movement set an example for the kind of work needed in segregated, poor, working-class ghettos, which it treated as "internal colonies" in need of liberation. The Asian version of the internal colony could readily be found in J-town (Japan-town) in Los Angeles, Manilatown in the San Francisco Bay Area, and numerous Chinatowns all across the country.

Among Asian communities in the United States, Chinatowns came the closest to the African American ghetto model. New York's Chinatown, for instance, was home to unskilled and poorly educated immigrants employed in manual and service jobs. According to a 1969 survey, its residents had a median family income between $4,000 and $4,900, compared to $7,436 for an average family in the United States. They lived in substandard overcrowded dwellings and received inadequate health care, education, and social services.

Conditions in San Francisco's Chinatown were not much better. There, more than fifty thousand people were crammed into only forty-two city blocks, with a population density of 885.1 individuals per residential acre versus 189 citywide. Sixty-seven percent of the Chinatown housing was considered substandard, compared to 19 percent for the rest of the city. More than 21 percent of deaths in Chinatown were caused by tuberculosis, which was three times the rate for the rest of the city. Residents older than twenty-five had received only 1.7 years of formal schooling, and English-language deficiency was widespread.[1] Newly arrived female immigrants could get jobs only in garment factories, where they slaved twelve to fifteen hours a day with pay well below the minimum wage. The community was burdened with impoverished elderly residents who, too poor to get married, had remained lifelong bachelors. Forty-one percent of Chinatown residents lived below the poverty level.[2]

It is easy to see why conditions in Chinatown attracted young Chinese American activists. One of the first groups to emerge from the back-to-the-community movement in New York City was I Wor Kuen (IWK; Righteous and Harmonious Fists), named after the paramilitary organization prominent during the Boxer Rebellion that aimed to expel Westerners from China in the late 1890s using bare fists. It was formed by a small group of college students from Columbia, Princeton, Sarah Lawrence, and City College of New York, several of whom were members of the Weatherman faction of Students for a Democratic Society. Their motto was the popular Chinese Cultural Revolution slogan "Serve the People." They wanted to do what the Black Panthers and the Young Lords did for their people. The Young Lords was a Puerto Rican group founded by "Cha Cha" Jimenez from among street gang members in Chicago and once closely associated with the Black Panthers. It was committed to equal rights and to the liberation of Puerto Rico, but it also set up a number of community programs in New York's East Harlem: free breakfast for children, free clothing drives, cultural events, and Puerto Rican history classes. One of the first community actions taken by its New York chapter was to challenge the city's sanitation department for denial of service to people living in "El Barrio" (the Hispanic ghetto). The Young Lords built barricades of garbage across major avenues and set them on fire.

When firemen and police intervened, they were met with community mobs demanding action in dealing with the garbage problem. As city hall relented, the Young Lords became heroes in the community.

Similarly, IWK started a number of programs run from a Chinatown storefront: a "barefoot doctor" clinic (based on the model set during the Cultural Revolution in China), which administered free testing for tuberculosis and lead poisoning, a day care center, and free English-language classes. It also established one of the first draft-counseling services for Asian youths. Its cultural programs included selling books and showing films from mainland China—activities that had been more or less banned in the community since the 1950s. The weekly parking-lot film screenings—usually propaganda extolling Communist China's achievements—were enormously popular; hundreds of Chinatown residents showed up to watch them. But the militant "internal colony" phraseology adopted by the IWK, reflected in the slogans "We Want Self-Determination for Asian America," "We Want Liberation of All Third World Peoples and Other Oppressed Peoples," "We Want Community Control of Our Institutions and Land," and "We Want a Socialist Society," did not resonate at all.

It did not help that most of the IWK members were middle-class American-born college-age kids with no previous contact with and very little understanding of the power structure within Chinese communities. Most of them did not even speak Chinese. One of their first actions in Chinatown, in 1970, which would set the pattern of their future relationship with the Chinatown establishment, was a demonstration against the tourist buses that brought white out-of-towners to gawk at the Chinese as if they were freaks in a circus. It was organized at the bus stop where the tourists disembarked. Taunting the tourists, the protesters demanded that the bus company end its demeaning and racist tours. It was only after the group received a warning from the Hip Sing Tong—threatening them with violent reprisals should protests continue—that the IWK learned of the arrangement: the bus company had an agreement with the Hip Sing Tong, which acted as the "protector" of the souvenir shop where the tourists were brought to "tour." From that incident, IWK learned that it was dangerous to interfere with the interests of the tongs and the established traditional associations. It stopped the protests, recruited supporters from inside and outside of the community to stand guard in front of its headquarters in anticipation of gang attacks, and from then on quietly stayed away from the turf of the Chinatown establishment.

Nevertheless, other serve-the-people types of student organizations emerged across the country, including Wei Min She (For the People Organization) in San Francisco, Yellow Seeds in Philadelphia, and Food Co-op and Asian Americans for Equal Employment in New York. All wanted to use providing services—free health clinics, cheap food and produce, free legal counseling to tenants against landlords, pro bono lawyers for youth in juvenile courts, and after-school care—as a way to reach the masses. Without exception, they found community residents who were receptive to their help and keenly aware of racial discrimination and exploitation but not impressed by the activists' calls to "revolution," "third world unity," and "socialism." Chinatown residents were apparently interested in China out of nationalistic pride, not because of its principles of socialism. After all, most of the new immigrants had come to the United States in part to escape from China's Communist rule.

Even more problematic was the activists' idea that Chinatown conformed to the model of a third world community. Unlike African Americans, Puerto Ricans, and Native Americans, who arrived at their identification with the third world nations on account of belonging to colonized nations or historically oppressed minorities in America, the majority of Chinese who populated urban Chinatowns by the early 1970s were new immigrants. They could claim discrimination as "colored people," but not as a historically oppressed population.

In the end, such misconceptions resulted in a serious miscarriage of idealistic activism—and a lack of political converts among the targeted community. The activists thought they would find answers for their problems by studying radical ideologies and as a result became theoretically inclined toward Marxism, which emphasized the vanguard role of the working class. Many of them reasoned that the most revolutionary elements in America were the factory-employed "proletarians" and that the real organizing should thus be done in urban industrial centers, among the workers. The American economy was doing poorly at the time, in the aftermath of the oil crisis, and as American industries became less competitive and economic restructuring got under way, a high degree of uncertainty provoked workers' militancy and major labor strikes in the industrial heartland. A number of Asian activists joined newly formed white-dominated Marxist-Leninist party cells to organize the working class outside the Chinese communities. IWK, renamed the Chinese Progressive Association, became part of the League of Revolutionary Struggle; Asian Americans for Equal Employment (AAFEE) and Wei Min She both joined the multiracial Revolutionary Communist Party. Others joined the Communist Labor Party and the Socialist Workers Party. While all maintained a continued presence in the Chinese community, the shift in their priorities meant that they devoted less energy to community programs.

A number of militant workers' strikes did explode spontaneously, but the Chinese American Marxist-Leninists were too far removed from the people they were trying to organize and too inexperienced to confront entrenched union bureaucrats and sophisticated management to make any gains. Their response to organizing failures was, as always, to turn to theoretical studies in search of the "correct political line"—for "if a political line is correct," one political pamphlet of the time claimed, "the people will move."[3] To get the correct political line, they devoted most of their energy to disagreements with fellow Marxist-Leninist organizations on whether Asian American and third world workers should play the leading role in the labor movement, being the lowest paid and most exploited of all. They engaged in an endless polemic on who was upholding the true Leninist line, who was "revisionist," who had the correct line in dealing with African American and minority issues, and which of the two communist parties—China's or the Soviet Union's—was revisionist. By the late 1970s, most of the groups had disbanded and disappeared.

COMMUNITY REFORMERS

As the Vietnam War started winding down during the early 1970s, the energy of the black power and the antiwar student movements began to wane. The raw anger of African Americans was shifting to more concrete ends. The call for self-determination was replaced by demands for relief, especially in the urban centers of the North, where the new movement could draw on people at the very bottom of the black community to stage a rebellion against circumstances that deprived them of both jobs and income.[4]

The African American poor people's movement for relief had been a part of the larger civil rights movement all along, but its demands surfaced in earnest when job opportunities became less promising. The movement's emphasis shifted toward forcing the government to dispense more benefits and services. Unemployment among African Americans was already disproportionately high in the early 1960s, but the ethics of self-reliance had made the civil rights leaders call for jobs, not handouts. The famous Martin Luther King speech, "I Have a Dream," was in fact delivered in 1963 under the banner of the March on Washington for Jobs and Freedom.

It was the federal government, first under John F. Kennedy and later under Lyndon B. Johnson, that decided to institute antipoverty relief programs as a way to evade the serious job demands of the civil rights movement and, as the movement heated up, to cool off some of its militancy. Johnson's War on Poverty comprised a series of programs, such as the Model City Programs, Project Head Start, Job Corps, Upward Bound, Volunteers in Service to America, and Food Stamps, that targeted mainly black inner cities. All were carefully designed and delivered in such a way as to avoid white antagonism. The funding was channeled directly from the federal level to the ghettos, bypassing municipal and state governments, which had in the past often kept it from getting to African American communities.

By emphasizing poverty relief, the federal government avoided the issue of creating jobs for the poor, which would require economic restructuring and redistribution on a national level, and would certainly cause significant white resentment. This approach was propped up by a theory that the condition of poverty was caused by the mental attitude of the poor, who were unable to escape it—which became known as the "culture of poverty." After the 1965 Los Angeles riot that had left thirty-four people dead, Governor Jerry Brown of California explained, "The riot took place in a scene of broken families and broken hearts; lonely children and aimless adults; of frustration and poverty." He made no mention of the lack of jobs and civil rights that had plagued the affected African American community. The future senator Daniel Patrick Moynihan, then in the Johnson administration, carried the cultural approach even further in what became his well-known thesis on the "social pathology" of broken black families.

The federal government based its programs designed to fight pathological poverty on the logic that the poor, if given real power over their own condition, would in time be able to effect meaningful changes for themselves. It encouraged "community action programs" and mandated "maximum feasible participation" of poor people in them. In the words of Lyndon B. Johnson, "The war on poverty is not a struggle simply to support people, to make them dependent on the generosity of others. . . . It is an effort to allow them to develop and use their capacities."[5]

Since the programs completely bypassed Chinese ghettoes, some of the activists who remained there after the Marxist radicals abandoned them seized on the opportunity to seek government relief for the Chinese poor. The Chinese, they believed, deserved it as much as African Americans did. The radicals regarded this type of social welfare activism with contempt, and branded those who practiced it "reformers" and "poverty pimps." By staying, however, the reformers were in fact, unlike the radicals, serving the community.

The reformers' work was no picnic. First, they had to convince government agencies that the Chinese needed help—no mean task considering that official statistical surveys and census data rarely provided meaningful information on Chinese Americans. The U.S. government, in fact, never recognized Asian or Chinese Americans the way it did African Americans, Latinos, and Native Americans—as minority populations traditionally "disadvantaged" and therefore deserving attention. In 1974, Man Bun Lee, the onetime chairman of the board of Chinatown Manpower Project (a social welfare agency in New York's Chinatown), testified to the New York State Advisory Committee to the U.S. Commission on Civil Rights, "Whenever Asian Americans apply for employment, minority scholarships, and community service funds, we are told we cannot apply because we are not a minority."[6] A common excuse for not giving relief was the notion, in part perpetuated by the Chinese community elite itself, that the Chinese took care of themselves and were too proud to accept it. According to Yukon Chang, an editor of the *Chinese American Times*, no government agency seemed interested in Chinatown's problems. "They say, 'Oh you do all right, you take care of your own problems.' "[7]

The truth was that Chinese communities had great needs. The 1970 census showed that in urban areas in New York State there were 2.8 Chinese families in poverty for every 1 receiving public assistance (the national average was 2.1 to 1). Yet New York Chinatown received no funding for job training. Very few senior citizens who were eligible for Medicaid had been reached to enroll in the program, and there was no public health clinic serving the community—let alone one providing bilingual services. The Civil Rights Commission report called the Chinese the "forgotten minority."[8]

It didn't take long for the reformers to realize that the lack of funding and services in Chinatown was due ultimately to the lack of grass-roots pressure on the government. They had to mobilize Chinatown residents in order to attract official attention, and in doing so they in fact subscribed exactly to the line that it took "maximum feasible participation" by the poor to eliminate poverty.

Beginning in the mid-1960s, dozens of Chinese American social welfare organizations sprang up across the country to take part in the Great Society antipoverty programs. In New York, a small group of second-generation Chinese American professionals disenchanted with the indifference of the traditional Chinatown establishment decided to apply for federal, state, and city funds and formed the Chinatown Planning Council (CPC). Their initial efforts failed, but after persistent lobbying and even demonstrations, the desperate poverty of Chinatown residents was finally recognized and the CPC was able to acquire funding for dozens of programs, including day care, senior citizen, youth employment, and jobs training centers.

Once set in motion, activism in the Chinese American community did not stop at obtaining services and relief. Chinese for Affirmative Action (CAA) was established in San Francisco by a small band of college graduates to seek equal access in employment and job opportunities. One of their first actions was to force Cahill Construction Company, which was building a $13-million, twenty-seven-story Holiday Inn in the heart of Chinatown, to hire Chinese construction workers. After much negotiation, they won. As a result of their success, the local government began to put pressure on construction and other industries that receive government grants to consider affirmative action hiring and training programs for Chinese Americans.

By the 1970s, hundreds of Chinese American social welfare pressure groups were active in a wide range of areas. One of them helped thirteen non-English-speaking Chinese American students in 1970 file a class-action suit in federal district court in San Francisco against Alan Nichols, president of the San Francisco Board of Education, on behalf of nearly three thousand Chinese-speaking students, charging that Chinese-speaking children were not receiving the kind of education they were entitled to in the San Francisco Unified School District because they needed help with English. The denial of special help, the suit claimed, "doomed them to become dropouts and join the rolls of the unemployed."[9] During court hearings, the school district admitted inadequate language support but insisted that due to budgetary constraints such special help would be offered only "gratuitously," as personnel permitted, rather than as a matter of principle. The district court sided with the school board, as did the Ninth Circuit U.S. Court of Appeals. But the plaintiffs took the case all the way to the U.S. Supreme Court, and it brought a unanimous decision: "There is no equality of treatment merely by providing students with the same facilities, textbooks, teachers, and curriculum; for students who do not understand English are effectively foreclosed from any meaningful education."[10] As the result of the ruling in *Lau v. Nichols*, bilingual education became the standard offering nationwide in all schools with a significant non-English-speaking population, particularly in Hispanic American communities.

The militancy of social welfare agencies—especially the unrest created by the grassroots welfare rights movement—put the federal government on the defensive. Aid to Families with Dependent Children alone, for instance, jumped from a budget of $1 billion in 1960, covering 745,000 families, to one of $6 billion, covering 3 million families, in 1972.

One of the first measures Congress took to thwart activists' militancy was to amend the Economic Opportunity Act. It now required community action programs to set themselves up as community-based development corporations (CDCs) in order to get funding. The new structure required that community groups work "with the private business community in self-sustaining, economically viable enterprises," thus steering them toward private financing and the logic of the capitalist economy. Mandated cooperation with foundations, labor unions, and universities was expected to curb the excesses of social activism. By 1972, Congress further amended the conditions for CDC funding by narrowing eligibility to three types of endeavors: business and economic development programs; manpower training to supply the needs of the job market; and housing activities "which create new training, employment and ownership opportunities."

The government, after years of looking for ways to cool off mass movements, learned that housing development was the most effective way to do so. By working on public housing developments, community activists had to consult with experts and architects in order to come up with viable construction plans, then woo private developers to act as partners in order to qualify for government financing. With politicians and bureaucrats having to approve all projects before releasing funding, there was no fear of social activism running amok. Since the need for cheap public housing, especially in poor neighborhoods, is always there, in choosing housing development as the core activity, the government was in fact able to permanently shift the energy of community activists away from grassroots community organizing. By 1990, approximately 80 percent of all CDCs were engaged in housing development, and two-thirds of them in the management of the housing they created.[11]

A different but connected strategy the government adopted to mellow community activism was to encourage community leaders to get involved in electoral politics. Grassroots leaders, no matter how confrontational they might have been, once they became community program directors or executives subjected to the restrictions and guidelines imposed by federal funding, began to act as de facto government officials. They became dependent on government support, not just to maintain their organizations, but also to ensure their own political survival. In return for acting as government-sponsored service distributors, they became recognized by the establishment as local political leaders. Organizations such as the Chinatown Planning Council and Asian Americans for Equality in New York or Chinatown Community Development Center in San Francisco ended up with politically well connected boards of directors whose members could use outside recognition as a stepping-stone in seeking appointed or elected political office. The symbiotic relationship between community leaders and politicians allowed the government to institutionalize political activism and absorb its leaders into the political mainstream.

The clearest evidence of the success of this strategy is the large number of former community action program leaders among the nation's most prominent elected African American officials. Its critics could only lament as one after another community leader turned politician became more focused on winning the political prize (often succumbing to corruption in the process) than showing concern for community interests. Los Angeles–based journalist Susan Anderson wrote in the *Nation* in 1989 that "black politicians gained office as a direct result of the civil rights movement," yet African American mayors Tom Bradley of Los Angeles, Marion Barry of Washington, D.C., Coleman Young of Detroit, and William Espy of Atlantic City have all been the subject of scandals, criminal investigations, and charges of conflicts of interest. At the same time, the "widening chasm between the ambitions of black officeholders and the needs of their urban constituents, particularly the poor," led writer and scholar Cornel West to note, "There has not been a time in the history of Black people . . . when the quantity of politicians . . . was so great, yet the quality . . . has been so low."[12]

ASIAN AMERICANS FOR EQUALITY: CLOSE-UP OF AN ASIAN AMERICAN MOVEMENT GROUP

Asian Americans for Equality (AAFE) is one of the most enduring Asian American organizations to have come out of the activism of the 1960s and 1970s. Originally set up as Asian Americans for Equal Employment, it has traveled along with and adapted to each stage in the evolution of the Asian American movement through its three-decade-long existence. It started as a college-based group, became a back-to-the-community service organization, took on a revolutionary Marxist-Leninist front, and finally retreated to the Asian American community to play electoral politics and manage housing as a community development corporation. It is now mainly a nonprofit housing developer claiming to be a community organization.

AAFE began in 1974 as Asian Americans for Equal Employment, when a group of professionals, students, and community residents got together to force a construction company building a federally funded housing project in the heart of New York's Chinatown to hire Chinese workers. In reality, AAFEE was the front for the Asian Study Group (ASG), one of a number of outfits of young radicals guided by what was known then as MLMTT—Marxism, Leninism, and Mao Tse-tung Thought. This dual organizational structure, at once underground and open mass-based, was popular with a number of radical civil rights and student groups at the time on account of the aggressive and some-times violent tactics adopted by the FBI in its own covert campaign against American radicals. (Its COINTELPRO counterintelligence program and a number of other government surveillance operations in the 1970s were set up to harass, disrupt, and neutralize the Black Panthers and other dissidents.) AAFEE/ASG was founded by Jerry Tung, who was born in mainland China and was allowed to immigrate when a teenager to the United States by special permission after his father was lynched by the Ku Klux Klan in 1951 in North Carolina.[13] While studying at the State University of New York at Stony Brook, Tung became a member of the Progressive Labor Party, a pro-China Maoist faction that split off from the Communist Party USA in the 1950s. He was arrested for violent antiwar activities on campus and was imprisoned for a year on twenty-nine counts of conspiracy to riot. Once released, he established himself as a Marxist theorist and a po-litical leader by recruiting college radicals in New York to form the Asian Study Group.

ASG was meant to be a vanguard party for revolutionaries. Its members were carefully recruited among political activists, trained in MLMTT theories, and asked to adhere to a strict centralized party discipline. Its leaders aspired to build a "true," that is, Maoist, commu-nist party that would replace the "revisionist" pro-Soviet Communist Party (the CPUSA)—an ambition shared by many radical student groups of the day. AAFEE was meant to function as ASG's "serve the people" mass-based arm, with its membership open to the community and its programs designed to politicize the Chinese population, but with an eye open to recruiting its most "advanced" elements to be-come members of ASG. The projects and direction of AAFEE were controlled by ASG, though its influence was invisible because ASG members also belonged to the mass organization.

The initial projects undertaken by AAFEE were successful. In early

1974, it approached New York City's Housing and Development Administration to enforce contract compliance by the construction company contracted to build Confucius Plaza—an affordable middle-class housing project with a school and a day care center planned at the heart of Chinatown. To qualify for federal funding, contractors were supposed to provide training and jobs for the local community, and AAFEE obtained hundreds of signatures from Chinatown workers eager to apply for the high-paying union jobs. But the lead contractor, DeMatteis Construction Corporation, refused to hire them, so AAFEE formed a coalition with community groups—Black Economic Survival, Black and Puerto Rican Coalition of Construction Workers, and Fight Back—that had experience in obtaining construction jobs for their communities and breaking into racist unions, and began to organize the Chinese community. The coalition mounted rallies and pickets of the construction site, with some protesters even willing to be arrested. As the demonstrations gained momentum and community support, the *New York Times* observed that the "meticulously organized protest" was a daily occurrence, involving a large number of people, sometimes several hundred, representing a cross section of the community, "from school girls carrying their books to wizened members of the Chinese Golden Age Club," who marched and chanted, "The Asians built the railroads: Why not Confucius Plaza?"[14] Even the Chinese Consolidated Benevolent Association, normally afraid to confront white institutions, spoke out in support of the job demands. In the end DeMatteis Construction Corporation gave in and agreed to hire forty Asian American workers (about 20 percent of all workers at the site), and the city hired an Asian American investigator to monitor employment practices at Confucius Plaza and other sites.

After that, AAFEE started to mobilize the community on more politically sensitive issues. In 1975, twenty-seven-year-old architectural engineer Peter Yew attracted a large crowd of onlookers as he loudly protested a parking ticket to the issuing officer. A group of witnessing policemen, angered by Yew's assertiveness, dragged him forcefully into the Fifth Precinct police station in Chinatown, where they stripped him and beat him. AAFEE quickly organized a community protest against police brutality—to "let the city government know that the Chinese can't be pushed around," as its newsletter stated later.[15] More than twenty-five hundred Chinatown residents joined the demonstration, which lasted for more than eleven hours, and its strength took the police and the city government by surprise. It also forced CCBA to approach AAFEE to jointly hold a second demonstration, and this time, since the CCBA ordered all Chinatown merchants to close their shops and attend the rally, twenty thousand people showed up.

The early successful actions gained AAFEE a great deal of respect, and AAFEE became a magnet for college student activists. These successes were the result of hard work by a number of idealistic Cantonese-speaking leaders and volunteers who were able to attract a grassroots following. Community trust was built on a wide range of AAFEE service programs, such as free English-language instruction and free legal advice on housing issues, and strengthened by AAFEE's fight against service cuts resulting from New York City's budget crisis. It was AAFEE, for instance, that rallied to stop the closing of the Gouverneur Hospital, which was the only one serving the community. But community service-oriented members of AAFEE did not belong to the trusted inner circle of ASG. The ASG leadership saw them as do-gooders and social reformers who, due to their low level of "class consciousness," needed to be placed under "party control." The decisions of the do-gooders were often countermanded by the secretive ASG.

At the same time, persuaded by the rising labor strife gripping the nation that the nature of the political foment had become a nation-wide working-class struggle, the ASG leadership decided in 1976 to change its name to Workers' Viewpoint Organization (WVO), better to identify with the working class at large.[16] WVO became the vehicle for recruitment of a multiracial group of Marxist "revolutionaries," who eventually, in 1979, established the Communist Workers Party (CWP). WVO began to push AAFEE to become more openly political—first, to change its name from Asian Americans for Equal Employment to Asian Americans for Equality (AAFE), to broaden its political agenda, and, later, to reorganize itself into a national organization with chapters in Chicago, San Francisco, and Los Angeles, with a new mission of working with members of the proletariat in general. Community-based AAFE members were told to either unite with the working class and be a part of the revolution or be ousted. There was no time for community reforms; the goal was a socialist revolution.[17] In January 1979, twenty-six people were expelled from AAFE for resisting the plan.

WVO/CWP and the remaining members of AAFE were so convinced that their position was correct—so sure of the impending economic crisis that would bring about a revolutionary situation—that they became confrontational and self-righteous. When the expelled members formed the Chinese American Democratic Rights Association, AAFE loyalists marched into their Chinatown office carrying lead pipes and iron bars, beat up and injured three individuals, and destroyed the office. They demonstrated in front of the *China Daily News* for refusing to publish an AAFE news release related to a dispute it had with I Wor Kuen, and later broke into the office. But their confrontational tactics came to haunt them. In November 1979, at a housing project in Greensboro, North Carolina, the CWP organized a protest against the public showing of the film *The Birth of a Nation*, which glorified the Ku Klux Klan. Their handbill described the Klan as "the most treacherous scum . . . produced by the dying system of capitalism." For weeks before the rally their spokesman had taunted Klan members: "We invite you and your two-bit punks to come out and face the wrath of the people." A caravan of Klansmen and Nazis did show up at the Greensboro rally. They opened car trunks, took out pistols and shotguns, and began firing at peaceful protesters. Five CWP members were killed while chanting, "We shall not be moved."

The massacre was a cruel irony for Jerry Tung personally in view of his father's lynching in North Carolina some decades earlier. Years later, he admitted privately to having misjudged the political situation and acknowledged that the country was not ready for revolution. "We had to work within the system," he explained.[18] Not only did AAFE begin to tone down its rhetoric; it wholeheartedly entered the 1984 election campaign as a member of the Rainbow Coalition supporting the presidential bid of Jesse Jackson. At a convention in mid-1985, the Communist Workers Party formally dissolved itself, and in its place arose a new organization, the New Democratic Movement, devoted to establishing "local power bases." On the occasion, Jerry Tung, general secretary of the dissolving CWP, explained to the assembled that "once you get people elected or appointed to office, you can award contracts to friends. . . . When you can raise money for political purposes, when you do it in the right place . . . then the [mainstream] party bosses . . . take you seriously."[19] He dumped his Marxist convictions and urged his followers to study "futurists" such as Alvin Toffler and John Naisbitt and read the theorists of the corporate world such as ITT chairman Harold Geneen.[20]

Regardless of where Tung wanted to lead it, AAFE had pretty much been discredited within the Chinese community on account of its radical leftist sectarianism. It did, however, have an advantage in the mainstream American political arena because of its previous experience with the Left. Having learned about American politics, absorbed its jargon, and acquired the ability to gain media attention, it was now able to operate easily in the mainstream political environment. Its previous connections were useful in building alliances with liberal, reform, labor, and minority factions within the Democratic Party at the state and local levels. Being young, energetic, and articulate, and displaying some familiarity with the Chinese community scene, AAFE members impressed outsiders as community insiders and as the democratic future of the community.

AAFE began to take moderate, at times even conservative positions to gain the confidence of the Chinatown establishment. In the early 1980s, a new group, the Chinese Staff and Workers Association (CSWA) started a major organizing initiative with garment and restaurant workers to fight for a minimum wage, a forty-hour workweek, health benefits, and job security for the workers—all very basic demands, considered standard for American workers but long denied to the Chinese. At that very same time, Jerry Tung said that "the garment factories, the restaurants, they exploit workers. There is no question about it—how are they going to create money? But they also create jobs. . . . One of the reasons that Chinese immigrants set a foothold in New York, and then raise their kids to go to college, and from there go into the mainstream is because they . . . have their own . . . self-contained economy."[21]

By the late 1980s, AAFE's sights were squarely set on its members' bid for public office. In 1990, when New York City council district lines were being drawn, AAFE went against many in Chinatown by proposing that the neighborhood be included in a district with affluent Soho and Tribeca, rather than the immigrant Latino Lower East Side. Their logic was that liberal whites had backed an AAFE leader, Margaret Chin, for a Democratic Party position. But the strategy backfired. Chin banked on gaining Asian support for attempting to become "the first Asian to be on the City Council in its history," but many Chinatown community groups didn't like AAFE's developer-friendly redistricting position and Chin's closeness to the Chinatown establishment (her family had influence in the traditional associations). Instead, they—along with almost all whites in the district—voted for her white opponent, Kathryn Freed, who was elected.

In the end, however, AAFE got its due. As a reward for supporting Mario Cuomo's campaign for governor in 1988, it first got the New York State Department of Social Services grant of $1 million toward construction of a shelter for the homeless and was later appointed as the first neighborhood preservation company funded by the New York State Division of Housing and Community Renewal to serve the Chinatown area, which effectively launched its new career as a community development corporation. With its main function shifted to housing development, AAFE now works closely with local banks, the U.S Department of Housing and Urban Development, and Fannie Mae to develop low-income housing. A *New York Times* article has described its current executive director, Chris Kui, as businesslike: "He wears dark suits and pressed white shirts. The bookshelves in his office are lined with titles like '*Jack Welch and the G.E. Way,*' and '*How to Think and Act like a C.E.O.*'"

To be sure, there is nothing wrong with providing housing for the poor. But the kind of housing AAFE is involved with is defined as "affordable housing" for those with a minimum of $30,000 in annual income, which excludes a large segment of Manhattan's Lower East Side residents. In the aftermath of 9/11, AAFE obtained funding from the federal Lower Manhattan Development Corporation to work with private developers who would get tax credits to build housing, a part of which would be for low-income residents. Since the rents and costs of ownership would revert to market values after a number of years, Chinese Staff and Workers Association's Wing Lam has accused AAFE of using its "community organization as a façade to in effect usher private housing developers making further inroads in gentrifying the whole of Lower Manhattan, which has traditionally been the home of a multi-racial working-poor community."

Well connected and well financed by federal and state governments, AAFE heeds no criticism; nor is it accountable to the Chinese community. Having gained a new elite status, it has in fact attempted to suppress its 'radical past.' It routinely refuses to discuss it, to the point that even Jerry Tung, the founder, found himself blocked out. He stopped participating in the group's activities when he realized that "they don't want people to know their real history . . . because they are concerned that funding would be affected."[22]

Chapter 21

Culture Wars

BATTLE FOR CULTURAL IDENTITY

The history of AAFE illustrates the ability of the American political system to absorb the political upheaval and mass mobilization of the 1960s. In this respect, the experience of the Asian American movement has not been unique. At the same time, complex internal developments within the Asian American community made it difficult for the movement to cohere. The realities of life were also more complex and nuanced than suggested by the initially unambiguous and unyielding positions taken by Asian American artists and writers as they struggled to define the Asian American identity.

The writing of the most strident advocate of a distinct Asian American sensibility, Frank Chin, is not free of perplexity and introspection. In his best known play, *The Chickencoop Chinaman* (which was staged at the American Place Theater in New York in 1972 and became the first Asian American play in New York stage history), the protagonist, Tam Lum, "a Chinese-American writer and film maker with a gift of gab and an open mouth," rages about wanting to "kick the ass of the establishment," while at the same time feeling hopelessly trapped in a suffocating, paralyzing "chickencoop" of a Chinatown ghetto.[1] In *The Year of the Dragon* (acclaimed as the first Asian American play to be shown on Television), Chin's central character, Fred, a tour guide in Chinatown, desperately wants to get away but can't be-cause of his sense of guilt and responsibility, placed upon him by his dying father and other members of his family. Chinatown is depicted as a place for the dead and dying. In a fit of anger, Fred shouts, "I am shit. This family is shit. Chinatown's shit. You can't love each other around here without hating yourself."[2] Chin often used violent lan-guage to express his own anger and to shock, but his writing is also typically full of irony and self-deprecation. In *The Chickencoop China-man*, Tam Lum looks for a meaningful identity, yet blurts, "I am the natural born ragmouth speaking the motherless bloody tongue. No real language of my own to make sense with, so out comes everybody's trash that don't conceive. . . . I am the result of a pile of pork chop suey thrown up into the chickencoop in the dead of night."[3]

The humility and ambivalence of his characters were rarely evident in Chin's public persona. With an incontestable "gift of gab and an open mouth," Chin took it upon himself to defend the manhood of Chinese men in America (or "Chinamans," as *Chickencoop*'s Tam Lum occasionally calls them), who had been forced into bachelor communi-ties, deprived of a chance to father the next generation unless they re-turned to China, and left with no choice but to do "women's work" in restaurants, laundries, and domestic trades. "We are meek, timid, pas-sive, docile, industrious. We have the patience of Job. We are humble. A race without sinful manhood, born to mortify our flesh," he and Jef-frey Paul Chan, a co-editor of *Aiiieeeee!*, wrote in "Racist Love," pub-lished in 1972.[4] To counter the stereotypical emasculated image, Chin projected a deliberately masculine assertiveness, which was often over-done, better to make a point. His critics have found his bravado to be uncomfortably anti-immigrant and antifeminist, and too frequently redolent of the male chauvinism inherent in the traditional Chinese patriarchal value system.[5]

This male chauvinism was challenged head-on by Maxine Hong Kingston in *The Woman Warrior: Memoirs of a Girlhood Among Ghosts*, an autobiographical account of a young American-born Chinese woman trying to come to terms with her Chinese heritage and the tug of main-stream America. Insofar as she described the world of impoverished immigrants, whose family laundry is being condemned by racist bu-reaucrats so that it can be torn down to make room for a public parking lot, Kingston shared with her male American-born fellow writers the sense of alienation from white America. "White racist boss . . . I easily recognize them—business suited in their modern American executive guise . . . two feet taller than I am and impossible to meet eye to eye," she wrote. But on another level, as a female, Kingston used her heroine to contend with the sexism of the traditional Chinese community— with attitudes that "girls are maggots in the rice" and that "it is more profitable to raise geese than a daughter." Feeling that a Chinese American female is doubly marginalized, by both mainstream America and Chinese American society, Kingston's heroine refuses to submit and becomes, in her fantasy, a woman warrior—the mythical Chinese Joan of Arc–like figure, Fa Mulan—to do battle against both cultures that undermined her self-esteem.

Kingston's book was a sensational success. It won the National Book Critic's Circle Award for nonfiction in 1976. The *New York Times* called it a "brilliant memoir." Newsweek deemed it a "book of fierce clarity and originality." It became a bestseller and, because it had established a new kind of female image in American literature, required reading in schools and colleges nationwide. But many Asian Americans criticized Kingston for "exaggerating" Chinese patriarchal practices and making Chinese society appear void of ethics.[6] Frank Chin in particular accused her of distorting Asian American reality and pandering to Orientalist tastes, calling her a "yellow agent of the stereotype" for participating in white America's emasculation of Asian men. More damningly, he called her a fake. Even her use of the autobiographical form, Chin argued, was fake, since its basis in the Western metaphysical tradition and the Christian confession could never capture the sensibility and the imagination of Chinese America.

Chin's crusade against Kingston culminated in 1991, when the editors of *Aiiieeeee!* published a new volume entitled *The Big Aiiieeeee! An Anthology of Chinese American and Japanese American Literature* to further promote their take on the right kind of Asian American literature. "Every Chinese American book ever published in the United States of America by a major publisher has been a Christian autobiography or autobiographical novel," they wrote, leveling their attack against the acclaimed work by Kingston, Amy Tan, and David Henry Hwang. They called the China and Chinese America portrayed therein "the products of white racist imagination, not fact, not Chinese culture, and not Chinese or Chinese American literature."[7] Chin had long been at odds with "Christian soldiers" and "whitewashed Chinese" who "bought their way into second-class white status by humiliating their whole race and people and history and fucking up the future." According to him, "This is exactly what white race culture has demanded."[8] Instead, he believed that writing should be fighting—a political act by which a writer combats racial stereotypes.[9]

CULTURAL EXCLUSION

As arbiters in the debate about "authenticity" and Asian American identity, *The Big Aiiieeeee!* editors took it upon themselves to create the Asian American literary cannon. Because of their criteria, they largely left out the work of Chinese writers from two diametrically opposed camps: the commercially successful American-born Chinese who wrote in English and were embraced by the mainstream, and the foreign-born Chinese Americans who wrote in Chinese and were better known in Taiwan, Hong Kong, or China than among the American-born Chinese. By leaving out these two categories, their canon effectively excluded the bulk of the creative output of Chinese in the United States.

The exclusion of the literary contributions of the foreign-born Chinese-speaking Americans is not surprising, given that very few of the American-born Chinese who assumed the position of cultural gatekeepers during the Asian American movement of the 1960s and early 1970s could read Chinese. But the work written in Chinese by the foreign-born depicts a far broader span of experiences of Asians miscast, misfit, and misunderstood in America. It has also found venues of expression worthy of note.

Before the 1960s, much of the writing by Chinese immigrants, often referred to as "Chinese sojourner literature," was published in Chinese newspapers and periodicals that had sprung up in major Chinatowns all across the country. Several dailies, such as *Chung Sai Yat Pao* (1900–1951) and *Mon Hing Yat Bo* (1891–1969), were known for the quality of and their commitment to their literary section. "Discovered" by Asian American scholars during the 1970s, most notably Him Mark Lai and Marlon K. Hom, well after the papers ceased publication, it became known as "overseas Chinese writing" (*huaqiao wenyi*). The literary quality of overseas Chinese writing rarely lived up to classical Chinese elite standards. It might best be described as user-friendly to the less educated Cantonese-speaking immigrants. Its themes focused on the struggle of Chinese immigrants for survival and success in the new country. It also stressed traditional values and conveyed a strong sense of nostalgia for the homeland, which was often invoked by the axiom "Falling leaves settle on their roots," meaning that no matter how far one wanders off overseas, eventually everyone returns to one's ancestral land. Because they wrote about the sojourner experience that was shared by their readers, the immigrant writers managed to establish a sense of community and ethnic solidarity.

Among the outstanding products of this overseas literature was a two-volume collection of poems published in San Francisco Chinatown in 1911 and 1915 under the title *Songs of Golden Mountain*. Its Cantonese vernacular rhymes were a departure from the strict classical Chinese prosodic forms, and so was the content. Besides the expected nostalgia for families in China, the amateur immigrant poets used their poetry to express remorse about drug addition, destructive gambling habits, and consorting with prostitutes.[10] One wrote, "Stranded in a lodge: a delay; / Old debts up to my ears: here to stay. / No sign of relief, only a pain stealing through my heart. / And nagged by worry for my aged parents. / I want to go home; / But what can I do without money in my purse? / Determined to shape up and shake loose, I move elsewhere; / But I am still stuck with rotten luck, as life only gets worse."[11]

Another great discovery were the poems written by Chinese immigrants on the barrack walls of Angel Island detention headquarters in San Francisco between 1910 and 1940, which were collected, preserved, and translated in the volume *Island: Poetry and History of Chinese Immigrants on Angel Island, 1910–1940*, edited by Him Mark Lai, Genny Lim, and Judy Yung and published in 1980. Some displayed knowledge of the linguistic intricacies of Chinese poetry: "My grief, like dense clouds, cannot be dispersed. / Whether deliberating or being melancholy and bored, / I constantly pace to and fro. / Wang Can ascended the tower but who pitted his sorrow? / Lord Yu who left his country could only wail to himself." Others betrayed that their authors did not have much formal schooling at all. "I hastened here for the sake of my stomach, and landed promptly in jail," started one. "The doctor extracting blood caused us the greatest anguish. / Our stomachs are full of grievances, but to whom can we tell them? / We can but pace to and fro, scratch our heads, and question the blue sky," ended another. None could contain the frustration, rage, despair, and homesickness that the detainees felt as they awaited jurisdiction on their medical examinations and immigration papers, or for ships to transport them back to China. As vital records of the indignities Chinese immigrants suffered in America, they occupy a unique place in Chinese American literary culture.

In New York, a magazine called *The Bud* (*Xinmiao*), published in Chinatown in the late 1940s, carried a substantial number of short stories that depicted life in Chinatown. It was also the first to run a series on literary criticism in the Chinese language in America. Its *Huaqiao wenyi shinian* (*Ten Years of Chinese Sojourner Literature*) attempted to review the history of the overseas literary output (*huaqiao wenji*) and lay down the criteria for evaluating it. It advocated the use of Cantonese vernacular style, and, as if forecasting the preoccupation of the 1960s cultural activists, encouraged overseas Chinese writers to draw not only on Chinese tradition but also from American culture. Even more significantly, it suggested the need for "trans-generational" work and criticized the Chinese community for not paying attention to the writing of the American-born.[12]

A distinct new phase of Chinese-language literature in America started after 1965, when a new wave of diverse Chinese speakers transformed the profile and the dynamic of the Chinese American community. The Chinese American population increased more than tenfold in less than forty years, mainly from immigration, which included some 150,000 students from Taiwan who arrived for graduate work and stayed. As a result, Chinese-language publications in the country mushroomed. Each publication added a literary supplement (*fu kan*) to promote high-quality creative writing among its well-educated pool of readers. Professional writers among the immigrants could now survive on their craft in the new country without ever venturing into English. The most successful among them, women writers Yu Lihua and Chen Juo-hsi, for instance, both published several novels in serial form in Chinese American newspapers before having them come out as books in Asia. The works of both have been translated into English.

Yu Lihua, interestingly, had written her first short story in English ("Sorrow at the End of the Yangtze River") and even won the prestigious Samuel Goldwyn Creative Writing Award for it in 1956, but she failed to attract the interest of mainstream American publishers in her subsequent work about the struggle of Chinese immigrants. "They were only interested in stories that fit the pattern of Oriental exoticism—the feet-binding of women and the addiction of opium-smoking men," she would later explain in an interview.[13] C.Y. Lee, author of *The Flower Drum Song* (1957), admitted that his success as a bestselling writer in English right about that time depended on just that—"exposing mysterious elements in Chinatown life, because it can satisfy the curiosity of American readers."[14] Yu Lihua did not want to oblige. Instead, she turned to writing in Chinese. Since she adopted many of the Western creative writing techniques, her work gained many fans among the educated immigrant professionals, who were well read in both Chinese and Western literature. Her themes—the glass ceiling experience of a Taiwanese science professor denied tenure, his well-educated wife's growing dissatisfaction with her stay-at-home-mom life, and the poverty and alienation of Chinatown, all explored in her novel *The Ordeal*—made her writing interesting to all segments of immigrant society.

Writing in Chinese, in fact, proved to be liberating for the bilingual immigrant writers. Since they had to seek affirmation and recognition only from within the Chinese-speaking community (as there would be little response from outside), they could pick their topics more freely than the American-born Chinese, who had no choice but to write in English. They could draw attention to crime and poverty in Chinatowns without fear that watchdog Chinese American academics would accuse them of "uglyfying" the image of all Chinese. They could be frank about gender issues, interracial relationships, and racial prejudices without worrying about political correctness. They could talk about sex between Chinese men and white women, criticize affirmative action, question American values, and bust cultural expectations from both ends. In "A Visit at Night," by Zhuang Yin, an immigrant father instructs his son on how to succeed in America: "I tell you, in this country, whether you are right or wrong depends on if you have tough muscle and dare to fight. . . . Be quiet and patient? Forget it! If you are modest and self-giving, others will treat you like trash. The high-sounding Chinese doctrine of endurance, benevolence, and always putting others before you doesn't work at all in this place."[15]

More important, since they observed and presented a very different Chinese American reality from the English-speaking American-born writers, their contribution went to prove that an experience as varied, rich, and complex as that of Chinese in America could hardly be fit into the narrow definition of Asian American sensibility prescribed by the self-appointed canonizers of Chinese American culture. The same is true of the English-language writing produced by the "Uptown Chinese" and their offspring. The ideological context of the Asian American movement mandated a focus on poverty and segregation, and the literature promoted by the cultural activists as the only authentic Chinese American product was in fact "Chinatown literature" (though it was typically written by the college-educated middle class). The experiences of the middle-class Chinese who lived in integrated and often suburban neighborhoods did not qualify. The stories of the second- and third-generation Chinese Americans who traveled to China in search of their roots in the late 1970s, after the United States formally recognized mainland China, could not be part of it. Narratives of suburban kids tracing the footsteps of their pioneer forefathers and generating oral histories of the Chinese in the American West were also unacceptable, because the pioneers with offspring were by definition merchants, and their lives fell into the category of success stories in the best American tradition. They rubbed uncomfortably against the accounts of hardship, discrimination, and rejection suffered by most sojourners and bachelors championed by Asian American studies.

However counterintuitive to the credo of the framers of Asian America, however, all these excluded narratives presented an undeniable piece of the Chinese American experience. Moreover, as the fervor of social activism waned during the unabashedly consumerist 1980s, the interests of the new generation of Chinese Americans shifted to the self-centered agenda of the affluent me generation. By the time *The Big Aiiieeeee!* came out in 1991, complex political positions were no longer registering in the public imagination, while the taste for the "exotic, yet familiar" grew as America began to embrace multiculturalism. David Henry Hwang moved to center stage on Broadway. Maxine Hong Kingston's work remained prominently on college curricula. New women writers, Gish Jen (*Typical American*) and Fae Myenne Ng

(*Bone*) among them, gained critical acclaim. And Amy Tan sold more books than any Asian American ever. Her first novel, *Joy Luck Club*, sold an astonishing 275,000 hardcover copies upon its 1989 publication, and more than 2 million since; it has been translated into seventeen languages and was turned into a movie that was a box-office success.

FROM RACIAL TO CULTURAL IDENTITY

The multicultural turn the mainstream discourse in America took during the 1980s and 1990s gave huge play to Chinese Americans who were interested in celebrating their heritage. Just as the once radical groups such as AAFE became absorbed into the mainstream through the carefully orchestrated government policy of the War on Poverty, the celebrationists of Chinese culture found their way into the mainstream by giving proof to the basic premise of the same policy: that the blame for America's urban minority crisis could be placed on the culture of African American ghettoes—the pathology of poverty.

Just months after the federal government launched the Great Society War on Poverty in 1965, an article by sociologist William Peterson appeared in the *New York Times Magazine* under the title "Success, Japanese American Style" (January 1966). The article praised Japanese Americans for their achievements and used their example to attack what Peterson saw as an erosion of the standards of American life. In the process, he developed the concept of "model minority"—to both celebrate the success of Japanese Americans and encourage the "non-achieving" minority groups with "problems" to "emulate" the model. Later that year an article in *U.S. News and World Report* extended the praise to the Chinese: "At a time when Americans are awash in worry over the plight of racial minorities. . . . At a time when it is being proposed that hundreds of billions be spent to uplift Negroes and other minorities, the nation's 300,000 Chinese-Americans are moving ahead on their own—with no help from anyone else. . . . Few Chinese-Americans are getting welfare handouts or even want them . . . the large majority are moving ahead by applying the traditional virtues of hard work, thrift and morality."[16] Their success was used to blame African Americans for their own failures, and, more important, to reinforce the position that there was nothing intrinsically wrong with the American system.

Since that time, many Chinese Americans have been joyfully embracing the designation "model minority" as a sign that after a long experience of discrimination and contempt, they have finally been granted the respect due them. Proud of their successes, they have begun to espouse the virtues of their Chinese cultural heritage. A *Time* magazine article in 1987 on "The New Whiz Kids," celebrating the scholastic triumphs of Asian American students, quoted Professor William Liu of the University of Illinois, for instance, saying that "the Confucian ethics drives people to work, excel and repay the debt they owe their parents."[17] Accolades to Chinese special qualities began to roll in from all over the world—particularly after the economies of East Asia took off in the 1980s. The role of ethnic Chinese (and the overseas Chinese capitalists) was especially noted in the miraculous rise of three of Asia's "Little Tigers," Hong Kong, Taiwan, South Korea, and Singapore, not to mention the superheated economic growth of mainland China. In his bestselling book *Tribes*, business writer Joel Kotkin built up traditional Chinese family, clan, and kinship networks into the idea of networks based on Confucian principles that he labeled "global tribes," which he pronounced to be a superior form of economic entity when it comes to modern global competition. Famed futurologist and Manhattan Institute founder Herman Kahn observed as early as 1979 that neo-Confucian societies create "dedicated, motivated, responsible and educated individuals and the enhanced sense of commitment, organizational identity, loyalty to various institutions." He even concluded that "societies based upon the Confucian ethic may in many ways be superior to the West in the pursuit of industrialization, affluence and modernization."[18]

The praise for the Asian American "cultural traits" of hard work and self-discipline dovetailed with corporate America's attempt to justify its restructuring of the American economy. Faced with declining profits in the 1970s, American capital was no longer willing to be tied to the "Fordist compromise" with American labor, which had ensured a stable labor-management relationship by giving workers high wages, job security, and union representation. American corporations wanted to be able to move their production and capital freely across national borders as well as from region to region within the United States to wherever they could find a low-wage, unorganized workforce. They justified their outsourcing to Asia and elsewhere by claiming that

American workers, black and white alike, displayed a deteriorating work ethic compared to Asians. Ironically, the "discipline" of the Asian workers was at least in part the consequence of American political and military interventions in the region since World War II. American client states such as Taiwan, South Korea, and Singapore were all ruled by authoritarian regimes that exerted strong controls over working standards and conditions and enforced harsh restrictions on labor movements in compliance with American corporate interests.

America's industrial heartland was hollowed out as production moved overseas. The businesses that remained forced American workers to accept downsizing, lower wages, reduced benefits, and truncated labor protection. American employers continued to import workers to do the work Americans wouldn't, offering jobs only to those immigrants who would work under unregulated labor conditions. While Chinese immigrants, both legal and illegal, were forced to work in low-wage sweatshops, the myth of the Confucian work ethic was used as a standard for Americans to follow and as a weapon to destroy America's social welfare structure. In this context, the model minority myth has the power to promote voluntary conformity. It rewards those who conform and shuts out those who condemn exploitation of their co-ethnics, accusing them of sullying the image of an already browbeaten minority. The only accepted image is that of hard work and unity.

The self-reproducing cultural aspect of the model minority myth is as enduring as that of the black culture of poverty, making social division into groups based on cultural traits as rigid as the previous (and now discarded) one based on biological racial characteristics. Multiculturalism merely puts a different facade on old racial arrangements, providing a new language to maintain social differences without invoking the negative concept of race. The formulation allows white dominance to go undefined and unquestioned, while the entrenched system of exploitation and inequality can remain unchallenged.

The ingenious shift from the objectionable biologically determined "race" to the realm of "culture" has given an impression of open-mindedness and tolerance to the new attitude about differences among American people. Along with it has come the attempt to cast the narrow white-versus-colored racial divide in the framework of a more accommodating "multicultural" society. European colonial authorities once used the similar idea of "pluralism" (originally an anthropological term) to maintain the colonized people in separate groups by celebrating their own culture, religion, and language. As a result, as Frantz Fanon pointed out, "This culture, once living and open to the future, becomes closed, fixed in the colonial status, caught in the yoke of oppression."[19] It may be wise for the Chinese American leaders who have embraced their cultural trump card as an empowerment tool to take a closer look at the multicultural agenda that divides them from other minorities.

PART V

Contemporary Chinese America

Chapter 22

The Rise and Fall of Chinatowns

At the time Asian American identity was conceived, most Asians in America—Chinese, Japanese, or Filipinos—shared a similarly circumscribed economic background and an experience of racial discrimination. This concordance of race and class, similar to the shared experience of African Americans, was conducive to the growth of a common consciousness. But after the 1960s, the Asian American population grew exponentially, from 877,934 in 1960 to 11.9 million in 2000, more than doubling every ten years. As most of the increase came from immigration, the majority (68.9 percent) of the Asian American population today is foreign-born and has had only a limited experience in America. Because of the provisions in the 1965 Immigration Act, these new Asian Americans are from widely diverse national origins and social and economic backgrounds. Some of the groups, such as the Vietnamese, Koreans, and South Asians, had almost no immigrant communities in the United States before the 1970s. The Vietnamese came as refugees. Many Koreans fled political repression. South Asians were motivated by economic and in some cases religious concerns. The diversity within each group is enormous as well. This has made nurturing an Asian American consciousness, originally thought of as the foundation for the Asian American political project, almost impossible.

That kind of unity of purpose has become difficult to achieve even for the Chinese alone. The loosening of immigration laws in the 1950s and the 1965 Immigration Act led to a tenfold increase of the Chinese American population, from 237,292 (0.13 percent of the U.S. population) in 1960, to 2,879,636 (1.02 percent) in 2000. The 1965 immigration quota for the Chinese was set at twenty thousand—the allotment given all other nations—but it included immigrants from both Taiwan and the People's Republic of China, with Hong Kong getting its own allotment of only six hundred. As the People's Republic of China had not been officially recognized by the United States, most immigrants came from Taiwan and from among the Hong Kong residents who were born on the mainland and could therefore be considered for the annual 20,000 national quota based on their mainland origins. With the establishment of formal diplomatic relations between the United States and the People's Republic of China in 1979, the mainland was given a separate quota of twenty thousand. Then, in the late 1980s, as Britain prepared to return the Crown colony to China, Hong Kong got its own quota of twenty thousand, bringing the annual Chinese quota to sixty thousand.

In addition to the sixty thousand who immigrate under the national quota, spouses, parents, and minor children of American citizens can come as nonquota aliens. Then there are the ethnic Chinese from other parts of the world. The largest group of ethnic Chinese immigrants from third countries came from Vietnam or via Thailand from Laos and Cambodia—many of them "boat people" escaping from the area's communist regimes in the late 1970s. Many Malaysian Chinese emigrated around the same time due to their government's affirmative action programs favoring ethnic Malays in business, education, and government. Significant numbers of Chinese also reached the United States through secondary migration from Jamaica, Peru, and Cuba. Lastly, none of the official immigration and census figures show the unusually high number of Chinese illegal immigrants, most of whom originally came from Fujian Province but increasingly come from other parts of China as well, due to the social dislocation created by China's rapid economic development.

The differences among Chinese Americans today are staggering. They include Southeast Asian refugees, with the highest poverty rates and lowest education levels in the country, as well as Taiwanese professionals, with the highest percentage of doctoral degrees and some of the largest capital reserves. One can hardly talk of a Chinese American community. American-born Chinese, whose ancestors immigrated generations ago, present a relatively cohesive group, but the most recent mainland Chinese immigrants are polarized. They include sons and daughters of top government officials, who bring their wealth and their mainland China connections; persecuted intellectuals escaping from likely imprisonment, who arrive with few assets; and thousands of working-class illegals, who arrive with nothing but debts and high hopes. Most mainland Chinese are able to communicate in Mandarin, but the Fuzhounese prefer the Min dialect; the Taiwanese use their distinctive Southern Min, while the Cantonese speak an array of Guangdong dialects. Many Southeast Asian Chinese use the Hakka.

The most fundamental difference within Chinese America comes from the way American immigration laws have created two divergent flows of migration: one based on professional preference and the other on family unity. Family-based migration (besides the nonquota spouses, parents, and minor children of American citizens) takes up most of the annual national quota, with adult children of citizens and permanent residents, as well as citizens' brothers and sisters. It brings in relatives of earlier working-class immigrants from Guangdong Province, whose skills and English proficiency are limited. The professional preference brings in the highly educated upper middle class. These bipolar admission criteria have created two Chinese American subgroups with dramatically different experiences in every aspect of their existence in America, the most visible of which are their different patterns of settlement. The working class is still steered to urban ghettos, while the professionals are able to jump straight to the suburbs.

Working-class Chinese were forced to live in segregated ghettos after they were pushed out of the American workforce by the late-nineteenth-century exclusionary laws. One exception were the laundrymen, who lived behind shops scattered across the nation's metropolitan areas. When white American attitudes toward the Chinese changed after World War II, Chinese slowly began to move away from Chinatowns to less crowded urban neighborhoods considered racially tolerant. The move was led by the American-born children of immigrants who had served in the U.S. armed forces and had taken advantage of the GI Bill to gain a college education and enter the professional class as accountants and engineers. They were followed by those who had gained skills in mainstream jobs outside Chinatown during World War II and continued to be employed in skilled and white-collar jobs after the war. But various laws prevented colored minorities from moving into white neighborhoods. Although in 1948 the Supreme Court struck down real-estate covenants restricting minority homeownership as unconstitutional, the practice continued in much of the country until the civil rights era. By then a few Chinese families could even afford to move to the suburbs, such as Hempstead on Long Island or Monterey Park in Los Angeles. "With money and determination," a report by the Institute of Governmental Studies at UC Berkeley concluded in 1963, "an Oriental-American can usually locate a suitable place" in the San Francisco area. "Whites may occasionally express their resentment, may even take overt steps to prevent Oriental occupancy," the report said, but it no longer deemed such gestures "systematic or sustained."[1]

As American-born Chinese slowly abandoned the ghettos, leaving only the elderly and the bachelors behind, Chinatowns began to shrink. It seemed that they were poised to disappear, the way earlier European immigrant settlements did.

ETHNIC ENCLAVES

When the new wave of working-class immigrants began to arrive in the 1960s, it did not seem that Chinatowns could provide for their long-term settlement. The traditional laundry, grocery, and restaurant trades were in serious decline and were barely supporting the old-timers; it was hard to imagine how they would accommodate the new influx of their working-class relatives. Yet, not only did the population of the old Chinatowns in New York, San Francisco, Los Angeles, Boston, Seattle, and elsewhere grow; the newcomers stayed on in these urban ethnic enclaves long after their European counterparts (following the typical assimilation pattern) would have left.

What set the new wave of Chinese immigration apart was that after 1965 the United States also attracted middle-class Chinese with savings and entrepreneurial skills, mainly from Hong Kong, who wanted to escape the political chaos in Asia. After liquidating their affairs in Asia, they transferred their assets to the United States, where it was easy to start a restaurant or a grocery store in the Cantonese-speaking milieu of Chinatowns. Sewing factories quickly emerged as the most popular business to invest in, because they could take advantage of the large pool of newly arrived female immigrants.

Up until the 1960s, the U.S. garment industry employed unionized Jewish and Italian immigrants, but they were just beginning to retire as the industry encountered threatening competition from abroad. American manufacturers were forced to close down, move their oper-ations overseas, or take advantage of the abundant supply of nonwhite immigrant labor that, without unions, commanded lower wages. Iron-ically, it was the use of immigrant workers, often from countries that were competing with cheap exports, that preserved at least a small sec-tion of the American garment industry in the metropolitan areas of Los Angeles, San Francisco, Miami, and New York. Between 1969 and 1982 the number of jobs in New York's midtown garment district, once considered the heart of the American garment industry, fell by almost 40 percent. During the same period the number of Chinese women workers employed by the industry grew from eight thousand to twenty thousand.

By employing immigrant labor, garment manufacturers not only saved on wages; they also gained flexibility. They shifted production to a system in which Chinese subcontractors rented factory space, leased equipment, and handled the hiring, firing, and management of the non-English-speaking workforce. Chinese subcontractors now had to confront workers' demands for higher wages, although the prices paid by manufacturers for finished goods dictated the wage scale. The arrangement was so perfect for the manufacturers that they encour-aged the Chinese to become subcontractors by giving them advance orders and inexpensive leases for complete machinery—down to boil-ers for steam presses and the necessary electric and gas hookups. By the mid-1960s, 90 percent of the garment factories in New York em-ploying Chinese women were Chinese-owned.

Chinese women liked working for Chinese-speaking employers. (They would have had problems finding jobs elsewhere anyway, given the high unemployment rate in the unskilled sector of America's re-structured labor market.) Chinese bosses gave them flexible hours so they could take care of their young children. They were permitted to bring children to the factories after school for "free day care," and the children were "allowed" to work to help support the family. This meant that most women could work. According to the best estimate, some 80 percent of women in New York's Chinatown were employed.[2] Garment factories also mushroomed in Chinatowns in Los Angeles, San Francisco, Oakland, Philadelphia, and Boston.

The earnings from garment work, though not high, supplemented the income of husbands, who were by and large employed in restaurants. They also gave a boost to the local restaurant trade. Since most Chinatown women now worked and had less time for cooking, they began to rely on neighborhood restaurants' takeout food for lunch and for their evening family meals. If they bought barbecued duck, roast pork, or soy sauce chicken, they needed only to stir-fry some fresh vegetables and cook a pot of rice when they got home. Small home-style restaurants popped up all over the community.

Before the 1970s, Chinese food had a limited appeal for most Americans. Its authenticity had long been eroded by the dictates of American taste. To any serious Chinese chef, dishes such as chop suey, egg foo yung, and chow mein, which dominated the menus, would seem, if not an outright insult to Chinese cuisine, at least a bad joke. But most of the Chinese who operated restaurants in America were not trained in the trade anyway; their food could hardly be expected to be of high quality. After Nixon's visit to China in the early 1970s, however, Americans began to take Chinese cuisine seriously. Who wouldn't, after learning the details of twelve-course state banquets featuring mouth-watering dishes with ingredients the English language scarcely had words for? Nixon's visit started a "China fever" across America, and Chinese food quickly became very popular.

The new interest in Chinese food was also spurred by the boom in ethnic foods of all types, with the newly dubbed yuppies helping to spark a trendy popularization of cuisines such as Japanese and Chinese, once considered exotic. Chinese restaurant owners responded by opening stylish restaurants with well-known chefs recruited from Hong Kong and Taiwan, preparing the best of Chinese regional dishes: spicy Szechuanese food, Peking duck, Cantonese dim sum, Shanghai soup dumplings, and Hong Kong ten-course banquets. Each new restaurant brought an innovation: an emphasis on seafood, a low-fat menu for the health-conscious, or the fusion flavor of the day. Chinese restaurant chains appeared in the suburbs.

With the thaw in Sino-American relations, the status of China rose in the eyes of the American public. So did the self-respect of Chinese Americans. Even the uptown Chinese professionals who rarely ventured to Chinatown began to descend on the neighborhood in search of genuine Chinese ingredients. New supermarkets sprang up to cater to their tastes.

As Chinatowns began to boom again, bilingual services became widely available to residents. Banks, the phone company, the local hospital, and even some municipal offices began employing bilingual staffs. Social services and senior citizen and day care centers were staffed and often run by Chinese. Revitalized Chinatowns also began to attract bilingual middle-class professionals, usually recruited from Hong Kong and Taiwan. Almost every major American city with a Chinese population produced its own *Chinatown Business Directory*, advertising a wide range of professional services: Chinese-speaking lawyers specializing in immigration cases, real estate transactions, property disputes, and tort cases; dentists and internists practicing western-style medicine; Chinese acupuncturists, herbalists, and specialists in the nonsurgical treatment of hemorrhoids; tax accountants, stock brokers, realtors, and travel agents.[3]

Instead of working in sewing factories and restaurants, some new immigrants saw opportunities in a variety of small-scale businesses, selling fresh produce, clothing, and underwear, working long hours on marginal profits and sharing retail space with other vendors in minimalls and sidewalk stalls. Taxi companies began offering services by Chinese-speaking drivers on twenty-four-hour call, ferrying people to and from airports, hospitals, gambling casinos, and wedding banquets. Driving schools appeared, guaranteeing that their students could pass both written and road tests and get a license even with a minimal knowledge of English. Funeral parlors and undertakers sold burial plots in cemeteries with areas reserved for Chinese.

Local Chinese-language daily papers mushroomed; several began to distribute nationally. The largest one, the *World Journal*, today has a nationwide circulation of a hundred thousand. The dailies promoted local businesses and stimulated an interest in Chinese-language entertainment: movie theaters showing popular low-budget Hong Kong films, video rentals carrying Cantonese soap operas, subscription stations broadcasting Chinese radio and TV programs. For those not particularly conscious of tradition, shops provided reminders, selling moon cakes in late September to mark the Mid-Autumn Festival, rice cakes in February for the Chinese New Year, and paper gold ingots in April to be burned for deceased ancestors on Grave-Sweeping Day.

The 1970s were the golden age of urban Chinese communities, with new waves of immigrants providing labor and attracting investment, services, and white-collar jobs, which in turn led to more investment, jobs, and immigrants. The cycle kept repeating, turning Chinatowns into booming, full-service, multi-class communities. The phenomenon, shared by the Little Havana Cuban enclave in Miami, was quickly noted by sociologists and by the popular press as well. A 1967 *National Geographic* article called Cuban refugees the "Golden Exiles" who built a shining city in South Florida. It was a departure from the immigrant model established in the past. New immigrants could now find jobs and opportunities for upward mobility right inside their ethnic enclaves, whose supportive environment, the argument went, enabled them to become property owners and join the American middle class without ever having to venture out to look for jobs or even having to learn English.

This optimistic view exaggerates the degree of upward mobility within ethnic enclaves. The newcomers to Chinatown, who start out as menial laborers working for Chinese bosses at low wages and for long hours, soon learn that in the enclaves standard American labor practices do not apply. The central premise of the enclave economy is cheap labor. The seamstresses who work at piece rates make more money the faster they work. However, the contractors make sure the piece rate is structured in such a way that only experienced and quick, usually young workers can make a reasonable income by working long hours. Waiters and shop clerks are expected to work more than ten hours a day, six days a week, with no compensation for overtime, no holidays, and no sick leave. In some restaurants waiters don't receive wages at all; their income consists entirely of tips. Some of them even have to turn part of their tips over to the management, which divides it among other personnel—not just the bus boys and maitre d', but managers, too.

Once new immigrants start working in the enclave, their opportunities to learn English and find work outside are effectively blocked, which is why employers can lay them off as soon as the economy sours without fear of losing them forever. The workers have no place else to go.[4] The enclave is like a warm bathtub—comfortable to get into, but cold long before you want to get out. After a few years of furious labor, most Chinatown workers suffer from job-induced ailments: foot problems for the waiters, back pain and carpal tunnel syndrome for the garment workers. A seamstress must then request less strenuous tasks, such as cutting threads or folding garments, at even lower wages. A waiter will have to work in a less popular restaurant, where the pace is not as fast. The prospect for immigrants who remain in Chinatown is downward mobility.

THE END OF CHINATOWN'S GOLDEN AGE

The golden age of the 1970s, when many immigrants found new opportunities, did not last long. Old Chinatowns were usually located near city downtowns, so as more immigrants arrived and more residential housing, retail space, wholesale storage, and factory facilities were needed to accommodate them, the enclaves began to fall victim to the urban renewal process. The space available for expansion was limited and land values extremely high.

Chinese garment and restaurant businesses were competitive only because their profit margins were small, and it did not take long for entrepreneurs to realize that as long as immigrants continued to come, real estate was where the real money was. Business owners who had made money in the enclave began to reinvest in real estate. They bought up old loft buildings and turned them into office space, and tore down dilapidated tenements to make way for high-priced residential housing. A Hong Kong immigrant, architect by training, Vincent Tai, secured $21 million from private investors in Hong Kong to purchase a rundown building in San Francisco's China Basin district in 1979. Three years later, after complete renovation, he sold it for $47 million.[5]

The level of activity in Chinatown real estate quickly attracted the interest of financial institutions. Chinese American–owned banks had become prosperous from processing remittances back to China and from the increase in deposits by working-class Chinatown residents—most of whom had no health and life insurance and therefore tended to keep a significant portion of their earnings in savings accounts.

Many of these banks began aggressively extending mortgage loans for the purchase and renovation of Chinatown properties. Moreover, foreign capital began to pour in from East Asian countries that had experienced rapid economic growth in the 1950s and 1960s. During those decades the Chinese in Taiwan, Hong Kong, and Macao, as well as the ethnic Chinese from Burma, Malaysia, Indonesia, the Philippines, and Thailand, had made a great deal of money, and the political uncertainty in Asia during the 1970s encouraged them to diversify their assets by investing in other parts of the world.

A major factor causing the movement of capital from Asia to the United States was the world recession that followed the 1973 energy crisis. Most countries suffered economic depression and currency devaluation, but the United States, being the financial center of the capitalist world, fared better than most. A large volume of capital, including oil money, poured into the country to earn high interest rates.[6] The flow was facilitated by the U.S. government's maneuver to finance its Vietnam War deficit through the sale of Treasury bonds to the international community. Encouragement of direct foreign investment became a mainstay of U.S. policy, as the country struggled to boost its sagging economy and create jobs at home. No longer worried about foreign ownership, the government welcomed Japanese and German automakers planning to set up factories in the United States. European and Japanese investors made significant corporate and real estate purchases in the country. National pride was thrown to the wind and foreigners were invited to buy landmarks such as Rockefeller Center and the Empire State Building in New York City.[7]

Chinese capital from Hong Kong, Taiwan, and other parts of Asia was part of that global movement. It moved aggressively into the real estate market, often taking over properties unloaded by Japanese investors of earlier years. Most top hotels in Los Angeles are Chinese-owned, including the Universal Hilton, the Beverly Wilshire, and the Airport Hilton. With office space in Los Angeles going for one-tenth the price of its equivalent in Hong Kong, Chinese investors have gobbled up prime office towers from downtown to Santa Monica.[8] According to the U.S. Department of Commerce, Hong Kong invested $3 billion in the United States between 1974 and 1988—most of it in real estate, banking, and hotels. One group of Hong Kong investors acquired the Omni Hotels Group; another purchased the Ramada Inn chain for $540 million.[9] In New York, Hong Kong Chinese money poured in to prop up such deals as Donald Trump's Riverside South development, the Hotel Millennium in lower Manhattan, and the Worldwide Plaza condominiums. At the same time, more quietly, Taiwanese money was building a large commercial complex, Evertrust Plaza in Jersey City, New Jersey,[10] and acquiring franchises from Comfort Inn and Quality Inn to 7-Eleven and other retail chains.[11] Taiwanese investment in 1989 alone may have reached $1 billion.[12]

Some of the overseas Chinese investment initially trickled into Chinatown to finance wholesale, supermarket, and restaurant chains. But after the United States deregulated international retail banking in 1981, most of it went into the banking sector, as major overseas banks began to set up branches in the United States—usually in Chinese communities first.[13] In 1986, there were twenty-seven banks in New York's Chinatown, two-thirds of them Chinese-owned. San Gabriel Valley outside Los Angeles, dubbed the "Chinese Beverly Hills" or "Little Taipei," boasted twenty-six bank branches with $1.9 billion in total assets. These banks were getting deposits from Chinese living elsewhere for safekeeping in the United States. It was not only the rich; thousands of middle-class professionals and businessmen in Asia opened accounts in the United States or shifted their money to the care of relatives residing in America to avoid the complicated rules governing nonresidents.

Many banks were set up precisely to facilitate such transactions. They were not strict about client identification or income tax and banking regulations. Chinatown residents of modest income could be found with tens of thousands of dollars in certified deposit accounts earning fixed interest. When the New York City branch of the Gold Pacific Bank (established with overseas Chinese money) was declared insolvent in 1985, federal regulators who examined the books found hundreds of Chinese savings accounts with deposits exceeding the federally insured maximum of $100,000. Chinese newspapers speculated that their owners were simply holding large sums of money on behalf of relatives in the Far East.[14]

With such enormous amounts of capital flowing into the community and being invested in construction and real estate, the basic character of American Chinatowns could no longer be sustained. The rising prices created a speculative fever, encouraging investors and real estate dealers to buy buildings with no intention of improving them. They merely held onto them long enough to sell them at a profit. The next owner did the same thing. The practice was familiar to most Chinese from Hong Kong and Taiwan, where it is called "frying real estate in a wok." The longer you fry it, the hotter it gets. As the stakes got higher, the price of buildings leapt so out of proportion with rental income that landlords had to jack up rents, drive out the original tenants, and shorten the leases, causing uncertainty for residents and businesses in the community.

The resulting disputes wrecked Chinese communities nationwide. There was no longer any reasonably priced housing for the poor. When fifty-five elderly Asian residents of the International Hotel in San Francisco's Chinatown were evicted in 1971 to make room for an office tower—despite a protracted community protest—everyone in Chinatown realized that very soon no new immigrant would be able to find affordable housing in the oldest Chinese community in the United States. In New York, a development corporation financed by ethnic Chinese from Burma applied to the city community board for a special zoning permit to build a thirty-three-story residential apartment complex on a plot occupied by several rent-controlled tenements. The units in the planned building, intended for middle-income residents, were to cost a minimum of $150,000—a princely sum in 1981. To vacate the tenements before demolition and construction could begin, the developers used gang intimidation, arson, and deprivation of basic services to force out the tenants.[15] Similarly, gentrification in Chicago's Chinatown forced young families to move, leaving it with 40.6 percent of its households occupied by the elderly, who could not afford alternative housing.[16]

Businesses suffered as well. As higher rents reduced their profits, restaurants, factories, and neighborhood retailers had to cut deeply into their employees' already low wages. The real estate owners did not care; they were interested solely in recouping the "real value" of what they had paid by getting tenants with higher income. Their agenda forced factories and working-class residents to move out, and along with them went businesses dependent on them. Restaurants changed their names to include Orient-conjuring catchwords such as "dragon" and "empire," introduced white tablecloths and uniformed waiters, added tourist-pleasing but uninspired foods to their menus, and raised prices. Grocery stores turned to selling scarves, rubber snakes, and dashboard souvenirs. A number of Chinatowns, such as the ones in Washington, D.C., Los Angeles, and to some degree even San Francisco, were transformed into mere tourist destinations, but without their Chinese residents and customers, their authenticity was gone, too. Restaurants attracted few customers at night. The prosperity that the San Francisco, New York, and Los Angeles Chinatowns gained in the 1970s vanished. Real estate speculators had killed the goose that laid the golden egg, and the booming Chinatown economy stagnated.[17]

SWEATSHOPS

The influx of speculative capital caused extreme hardship for the working people in Chinatown, particularly those employed in the garment industry. As the export of American manufacturing jobs accelerated and the quality of offshore production improved, ever-more jobs were lost domestically and manufacturers were in a position to force domestic contractors to accept even lower prices. By the 1980s, business insiders in the garment industry were complaining that they were "dying a slow death."[18] Facing the prospect of ever-increasing rents for their factory space, Chinese contractors had no intention of staying in the business for long. Rather, they viewed it as a temporary purgatory, to be endured until they accumulated enough profits to invest elsewhere, so they had no incentive to improve their facilities. The half-century-old factory spaces remained unmodified and the sewing machines still in use were the equally old Singers, though the much more efficient and up-to-date Japanese models could have made work easier.

The disinvestment harmed working people, but there was no fear that jobs would disappear altogether. To produce in the United States meant saving on transportation and customs costs. It meant direct access to designers and consumer markets, allowing for quick, last-minute production adjustments. If retailers found that a particular summer fashion line shipped from China did not match the current taste of American consumers, manufacturers still had time to produce replacements on the spot. Moreover, the manufacturers knew that

Chinese subcontractors were so desperate for orders that they would bid for lots at such low prices that they could not offer minimum labor standards for their workers. Subcontractors would simply present Chinese workers with the fait accompli and offer substandard wages. The rationale for pushing the wages and costs down as close as possible to those prevailing in China and other third world production sites was "Either this, or no jobs at all."

Wages of immigrant Chinese workers declined across the board, which meant longer hours for the same pay. Mrs. Tang, a school-teacher in Guangdong Province who had emigrated to Brooklyn in the mid-1980s, testified at a Senate hearing for anti-sweatshop legislation in 1995 that when she first arrived in the United States she worked eight hours a day and earned $40–$50. A decade later she was slaving twelve hours a day for a paltry $30. She had to work almost twice as long to make the same amount of money.[19] After a decade in the industry, older workers who could get out, got out. The news of difficult conditions in Chinese ethnic enclaves encouraged fewer arrivals from Hong Kong, which was, fortunately, experiencing an economic boom in the 1990s. The conditions in factories there were in fact better than they were in New York. But immigrants now began to arrive from mainland China, mostly from the coastal province of Fujian.

ILLEGAL IMMIGRANTS

Chinese leader Deng Xiaoping began the liberalization of the Chinese economy in the late 1970s by designating several coastal areas in southern China as special development zones to attract foreign investment. The economic expansion that resulted from the investment brought flocks of people from the interior to coastal cities such as Shanghai, Fuzhou, and Guangzhou, causing major social dislocations. Unprepared for the sudden influx, the cities began to experience congestion, overcrowding, pollution, unemployment, vagrancy, and crime. The rural outskirts of targeted metropolitan areas were particularly affected. As the first to have been given a crack at experimenting with a free market economy, their semirural residents became wealthy quickly by selling fresh produce, handicrafts, and light-industry products such as shoes, suits, and weaved carpets to city folk at high prices. But with the country's opening to foreign investment, they could no longer compete with the efficient foreign firms that began to turn out cheaper products. Many, especially those from areas with a long history of emigration—such as the rural counties surrounding the city of Fuzhou, with centuries-old ties to Southeast Asia—decided to once again turn to emigration with financial assistance from their overseas relatives.

The United States, as the powerhouse of the global economy, became one of their favorite destinations. Since few Fuzhounese had immigrated to the States in the past to provide legal immigration links, the new immigrants had to enter the country illegally, with help from human smugglers. Their ever-increasing numbers quickly turned the smuggling of willing émigrés into a major international business, akin to the nineteenth-century transport of coolie laborers sought by white employers or the Chinese merchant–sponsored illegal immigration of the exclusion era. Some of the overseas Chinese organized crime networks involved in the transport of heroin from the Golden Triangle shifted their business to the lucrative transport of illegal immigrants.

In 1989, Lu Jianguo, from Fuqi, a poor village on the outskirts of Fuzhou City in Fujian, paid a "snakehead" (human smuggler) $18,000—the price of passage then—to smuggle him into the United States. At the time, the jocular Chinese term for the Fuzhounese was "the eighteen-thousand-dollar men." A more accurate term would have been "the eighteen-thousand-dollar-debt men," since none of them had the money to pay for the passage—simply the willingness to do whatever it took to pay back the incurred debt after their arrival. Ironically, the more people were successfully smuggled, the more others wanted to follow them—relatives, friends, and envious community members left behind. The higher demand for smuggling services kept driving the prices up. By the time the broken-down steamer *Golden Venture* ran aground on Long Island shore in Queens just a few miles from downtown Manhattan in June 1993, the cost of one passage had risen to $33,000. The abominable condition of almost three hundred unceremoniously discharged illegal immigrants finally called the attention of the American public to the monstrous practice of human trafficking. The incident unleashed a public outcry. CNN's *Moneyline* calculated that thousands of Chinese illegal immigrants entering the United States cost the U.S. 20 billion dollars a year. The outcry was directed more against the immigrants than against the traffickers, and it greatly contributed to the passage of the harsh new 1996 Immigration Reform and Immigration Responsibility Act. Unfortunately, the new law did not stop human smuggling; it only raised the stakes and increased the sophistication of the smuggling networks. These days, illegal immigrants from China usually arrive by plane, either with counterfeit documents or with genuine documents giving them legal status as students, commercial representatives, or temporary workers, at a cost of $55,000 per person.

The repayment of debts is enforced through threats of gang violence, directed not only against the indebted illegal immigrants themselves but also against their family members back in China. Torture, kidnapping, and incarceration have been used to ensure compliance. In 1992, a hysterical Chinese man called 911 in New York pleading for police help. He had just talked on the phone with a kidnapped relative, while the relative was being tortured. The word "kidnapped" quickly brought federal authorities to the case. When they broke into the apartment in Brooklyn that the kidnappers were using, FBI agents found a half-dead man handcuffed to a bedpost, where he had been beaten with crowbars and burned with cigarette butts.

To avoid this kind of violence, illegals are forced to take low-paying jobs and work long hours under any conditions. In 1990, a middle-aged Mrs. Lee, whose three daughters and a son, ranging in age from twelve to fifteen, were all allowed to help in Wai Chang garment factory in Brooklyn, was taking home only $100 a week for the two hundred hours of labor the five of them put in jointly. But they simply had to have steady work to meet the regular scheduled payments to the loan sharks. "Every bit of extra money helped," she said, since her husband had a low-paying job in a restaurant, and the employers had "promised" to sponsor her application for legal immigration. Employers understand the vulnerability of illegal immigrants and like them precisely for that reason. They can lay them off whenever there are no orders and require them to work for seventy-two hours at a stretch to finish a rush order. Without any legal protection, the illegals are subjected to conditions that break every legislated labor protection clause in the country. Yet they can do nothing, because employers threaten to report them to the immigration authorities if they complain.

Employers have in fact become so brazen that they routinely with-hold wages. After weeks of work without pay, the workers have to make the hard choice: continue working, potentially without ever get-ting paid, or walk away and write off the loss. This is exactly what hap-pened to Mrs. Lee. The factory she worked for, after less than two years in operation, owed its seventy workers a total of $170,000. As getting their paltry back pay was a question of survival, the workers be-gan striking. The second time they stopped work, the owners brought in a mean-faced gangster to bully them: "If you want to fool around with the management, step outside to talk with me, face to face." The owners also threatened to report them all to the Immigration and Nat-uralization Service. What the workers didn't know was that the own-ers, Wai Chee Tong and Stanley Chang, had operated a garment factory in Manhattan's Chinatown during the late 1980s, which they had closed down once the workers began demanding withheld wages. When Mrs. Lee and her co-workers sought assistance from the Chi-nese Staff and Workers Association to lodge a complaint with the New York State Department of Labor, the owners closed down Wai Chang, too. The practice is common among Chinatown's subcontract-ing factory owners, but they hardly ever face legal accountability, be-cause federal labor and local corporate laws are too weak to stop this kind of abuse.

In the case of Wai Chang in 1991, the Department of Labor gave up its investigation when it "could not locate the owners" (the two had already closed the factory, of course, and transferred their accounts out of the corporation) and refused to help the workers contact the manufacturers who subcontracted to Wai Chang to ask them to with-hold their payments to the partners until the back wages were paid. Only when the workers went public at a press conference, where they vowed to pursue the case and get their hard-earned pay even if it meant deportation, did the New York State Attorney General's Office respond to the criminal charges they brought against the owners. Tong and Chang were found guilty on forty-one misdemeanor counts for failing to pay wages and ordered to pay more than $80,000 to the workers—the largest suit ever won in New York's garment industry. The victory, in the end, meant nothing, however. The owners declared bankruptcy, and the workers never collected a cent from the judgment.

There is no doubt that American authorities are fully complicit in maintaining this outrageous situation. In the current climate of supply-side economics, they shy away from enforcing mandated labor standards. In 1997, the Department of Labor reported that 63 percent of the garment shops in New York were in violation of the minimum wage or overtime provisions of the Fair Labor Standards Act. Though shocking, the finding did not result in any law enforcement action. By 2000, according to a new report, the number of violators had increased to 65 percent. Legal and illegal immigrants alike have been used to "readjust the balance" in favor of capital at labor's expense. It is ironic that American businesses have been able to export American jobs to gain greater profits and to discipline American labor by importing immigrant labor for the same purpose at the same time.

Unfortunately, organized labor has not been able to counter this global corporate strategy. Most Chinese garment workers in New York's Chinatown have been members of UNITE (formerly the International Ladies Garment Workers Union) since the 1970s, but the union is more interested in maintaining union membership levels than in enforcing union contracts, for fear of driving the shops overseas or to other states. It has devoted more energy to cultivating good relations with Chinese subcontractors than to supporting the activism of the rank-and-file workers. A 1992 internal survey conducted by the union's Sunset Park Garment Center in fact revealed that nonunion workers were in some cases paid better than ILGWU union members. The average gross nonunion wage was $4.97, while the average union wage was a mere $3.73—at a time when the federal minimum wage was $4.25, and the official union contract rate was supposed to be between $6 and $9.45 an hour.[20] Due to the complicity of labor unions, urban ethnic enclaves, far from facilitating upward mobility of their residents through ethnic solidarity, have in fact contributed to the degradation of labor standards for all.

Chapter 23

Into the Suburbs

CHINATOWN DISPERSION: THE END OF CHINATOWNS?

In the 1980s, high rents forced the poorer Chinatown residents to look for cheaper housing elsewhere. In many cities alternative Chinese communities already existed, dating to the time after World War II when Chinese American urban pioneers began to venture into racially tolerant neighborhoods, such as in Flushing, in New York's borough of Queens, and Richmond, in San Francisco. Some new working-class immigrants trickled into these existing middle-class Chinese communities, but by the 1980s the choice of where one lived was governed less by discrimination than by housing costs. In addition to low cost, the other most important prerequisite for new immigrants with English-language difficulties was an easy transportation link to Chinatown.

Sunset Park in Brooklyn, New York, emerged as a popular destination for poorer immigrants escaping from Manhattan's Chinatown. Once a vibrant industrial neighborhood populated by Scandinavian immigrants, it had been designated a federal poverty area in the 1970s, after the loss of manufacturing led to its decline.[1] Sunset Park was an easy commute for non-English-speaking Chinese: all they needed to remember was to get on the N train in Manhattan Chinatown and get off when the train emerged from underground. Initially, it was a bedroom community for people who worked in Manhattan Chinatown, and the two neighborhoods mirrored each other: 7 percent of Manhattan Chinatown residents have degrees above college level compared to 8 percent in Brooklyn's Sunset Park; the average annual household incomes are $24,000 and $23,000, respectively.[2] To better link the two communities, Chinese-owned private minibus companies began ferrying people door-to-door, from the heart of one community to the other.

By the mid-1980s so many Chinese had moved to Sunset Park that many old Chinatown business establishments began to set up branch stores there. Before long, a busy commercial community emerged along the neighborhood's main street, Eighth Avenue. Factories followed, to take advantage of cheaper commercial space and to be closer to the resident workers. The sweatshop conditions, which were also carried over by the factory owners, could thrive in this new community with even less scrutiny from law enforcement.

With time, satellite Chinatowns such as Sunset Park, in New York, or Oakland and Richmond, in the San Francisco Bay Area, inherited all the problems of the old Chinatowns. As more immigrants arrived, more Chinese businesses opened, and the racial diversity of the once mixed neighborhoods began to decline. The Chinese purchased most of the property in and around the area, and within a decade of their arrival the property values quadrupled. Members of an extended Chinese immigrant family might work twelve hours a day to collectively save enough to purchase a quarter-million-dollar brownstone, which, although expensive, would still be cheaper in the end than if they all paid rent separately. But bank loans available to multiple-wage families jacked up real estate values, quickly making the once inexpensive "new" neighborhoods unaffordable to the less fortunate and the newcomers. Thus, by using their labor and hard-earned savings to revive an abandoned urban area, the Chinese, like many other new immigrants groups in the United States, have at the same time played a role in the gentrification process that forces the poorer earlier residents to move on.

The search for cheap housing has sent wave after wave of new Chinese immigrants further afield, creating a series of mini–Chinese communities, scattered among non-Chinese neighborhoods but still connected to the original Chinatowns. With each extension, however, the integrity and intensity of the character of the Chinese community has been diluted, so that some of the outlying satellite Chinatowns that dot the San Francisco Bay Area and the outer boroughs of New York City—places such as Alameda, in Oakland, or Avenue U, in Brooklyn—can be identified only by a small cluster of new Chinese groceries and restaurants.

During the past two decades a new urban economic model has taken hold of cities across the United States, marked by the disappearance of manufacturing and expansion of the "FIRE" sector (finance, insurance, and real-estate), which sells images and services rather than making products.[3] Investment has shifted from the creation of jobs and affordable housing to publicly funded projects that qualify for tax credits, such as downtown restorations, or the building of sports stadiums and museums that attract tourists. Compounded by deregulation, downsizing, and outsourcing, the process has left very little room for working-class communities.

But the most important factor pushing the working-class Chinese to move away from the old urban ethnic enclaves is the continued decline of garment manufacturing due to imports. Finding new alternatives is a question of survival. In both the San Francisco Bay Area and New York, Chinese women have managed to get jobs as hotel room cleaners and as home-care assistants servicing Chinese-speaking people with disabilities and senior citizens, where skills and English-language requirements are minimal. Men have found work in construction. In New York, dozens of private Chinese-run bus companies ferry Chinese customers to gambling and suburban work destinations. Half a dozen of them provide cut-rate long-distance bus service to Washington, D.C. Boston, and Philadelphia, and are beating out Greyhound and Trailways in competition for the general public. Increasingly popular with the general public are Chinese buffet-style restaurants—an invention of Fuzhounese immigrant entrepreneurs—offering a wide array of Chinese (and sometimes even Japanese and Italian) dishes in unlimited quantities at a flat fee. These efficient all-you-can-eat establishments employ thousands of immigrant Chinese kitchen and serving staff in suburbs and even rural areas all across the country. If the trend continues, Chinese immigrants, already on the verge of breaking out of the ethnic enclaves into the general labor market, may well end up repeating the integration cycle of European immigrants. This would seriously cripple the power of Chinese traditional family, kinship, and fraternal associations, and could even spell death to Chinatowns.

Another viable option for working-class immigrants has been to move to the dispersed middle-class suburban Chinese communities to work as supermarket personnel, home-care assistants, store clerks, construction workers, and delivery boys. Thus, the recognizable pattern of Chinese settlements in this country is not exactly disappearing; rather, it is being reconstituted in a much more complex, dispersed way.

DISPERSION OF UPTOWN CHINESE

American-born Chinese and immigrant professionals have had a pattern of settlement in the United States distinctly different from that of the working-class non–English speakers. The professionals tend to reside in integrated urban neighborhoods, away from the ethnic enclaves. Immigrant professionals in particular have been gravitating toward the outskirts of metropolitan areas from the moment of their arrival in the United States; most have never experienced life in the inner city. For American-born Chinese, settling away from the urban core has meant "making it."

Flushing, Queens, for example, was originally a white middle-class neighborhood. In 1946, a small group of Chinese who worked for the United Nations, which at the time operated out of a temporary Long Island headquarters close to Queens, moved there because they were unable to afford housing in the exclusive North Shore communities on Long Island. After the UN headquarters moved to Manhattan in 1951, many diplomats, translators, and members of the administrative staff of the Chinese delegation decided to stay in Queens. They were joined by the stranded scholars who had decided to remain in the United States after 1949. By the time American-born Chinese discovered Flushing, the character of the community had already been set by the Mandarin-speaking professionals—its "original settlers."

No sooner did a discernable Chinese community in Flushing emerge than Chinatown businesses recognized the moneymaking potential of servicing its high-income professionals and opened shops near its transportation hub—the subway station of the number 7 train on Main Street. It became known as the Orient Express because other Asians in the city, most notably Indians and Koreans, were also attracted to the neighborhood. The convenience has continued to draw growing numbers of immigrant professionals from Taiwan, Hong Kong, and, more recently, mainland China, turning Flushing into one of the fastest-growing neighborhoods in New York City.

Flushing's Chinese residents are distinctly different from those populating Manhattan's Chinatown. According to census data, 36 percent of Flushing's Chinese Americans are professionals concentrated in the fields of accounting and computer science, compared to only 14 percent in Manhattan's Chinatown; 38 percent have degrees above the college level, compared to 7 percent in Chinatown; their average annual household income is $36,000, compared to $24,000.[4] The language of Flushing is Mandarin; it's Cantonese in Chinatown. Flushing's businesses and shopping centers are patronized by immigrants from Taiwan and central and northern parts of mainland China, and services are specifically tailored to them: hairstyling and beauty treatments by professionals trained in Taiwan, following the latest trends publicized in Taiwanese fashion magazines; Taiwanese-style teahouses and juice bars serving tropical fruit juices with tapioca beans; karaoke bars featuring pretaped Taiwanese top-forty songs accompanied by video clips; CD and video rentals of Asian films and Taiwanese soap operas.

The Taiwanese flavor of the community is so strong that many Taiwan-based organizations, such as Taiwan TV and several radio stations, have set up their North American bureaus in Flushing. *World Journal*, the largest Chinese-language paper in the country, has moved its headquarters and established a printing plant there. For a long time even political organizations representing Taiwan's independence movement had their North American headquarters in Flushing.

The numerous businesses crowded along the main thoroughfare in Flushing include travel agencies, real estate brokers, discount electronic and computer software stores, piano and music schools, dance classes, and martial arts academies. Flushing's commercial hub provides jobs for thousands of service professionals, and also for Mandarin-speaking low-skill laborers. As a result, the surrounding sections of Queens have attracted even more Chinese of all classes. The 2000 census shows 102,902 Chinese residing in Queens County. They have long moved beyond Flushing into Elmhurst, Woodside, and the more desirable Bayside, which is the home of Benjamin N. Cardozo High School—the number one neighborhood high school in New York City. The school has turned Bayside into a magnet community for affluent Chinese immigrants. Forty-six percent of Bayside's Chinese residents are professionals; 42 percent have degrees above the college level. Their average annual household income is $69,000.

Immigrants and developers from Taiwan, aided by local banks and overseas Chinese financial institutions, have fueled a building boom in the once quiet residential neighborhoods, tearing down blocks of old single-family homes to replace them with multistory apartment complexes. New supermarkets, department stores, and shopping centers are turning sleepy tree-lined streets into crowded and congested commercial hubs. The changes have created plenty of resentment. In 1996, Queens councilwoman Julia Harrison said that many of her elderly white constituents were forced to "feel increasingly out of place in their own neighborhood." She characterized what happened to Flushing in the 1980s as "an invasion." These Asian immigrants "did not come because of a potato famine or because some czar was conducting a pogrom. . . . They were more like colonizers. . . . They sure as hell had a lot of money, and they sure as hell knew how to buy property and jack up rents of retail shops and drive people out."

Despite white resentment, established communities such as Flushing will continue to draw more new settlers as long as Chinese immigration continues. In Flushing's case, its closeness to the suburbs of Long Island and the convenient expressway links to Westchester County, New Jersey, and Connecticut enable suburban Chinese residing there to make weekend visits to shop for Asian food and enjoy a meal at an authentic Chinese restaurant without the traffic and parking problems associated with a trip to Manhattan. Queens has in many ways taken over as the specialized regional Chinese consumer hub for Greater New York. As of 1990, Flushing and Queens have become the preferred destination for new immigrants arriving straight from Asia. The outer boroughs of New York City now house four times more Chinese than does Manhattan. (As late as 1960, Manhattan claimed more than 63 percent of the area's Chinese.)

The dispersion of Chinese from urban centers does not stop at the outer boroughs. Rather, it is currently focused on farther-flung suburbs, many of them associated with universities and high-tech laboratories, such as Stony Brook, on Long Island, which is close to both the State University of New York campus and the Brookhaven National Laboratory, or the Route 1 high-tech corridor near Princeton University. The trend is even more pronounced among the Chinese on the West Coast. The suburban sprawl of Santa Clara County, outside San Francisco, and San Gabriel Valley, outside Los Angeles, today claims larger numbers of Chinese residents than the urban core areas of those cities.[5] Between 1990 and 2000 the Chinese population in the city of Los Angeles dropped by 6 percent. During the same period it grew by more than 34 percent in the counties surrounding the city. Only 2 percent of the Chinese in the Los Angeles area now live in the old Chinatown. Census figures suggest similar dispersion patterns elsewhere in the country. During the 1990s, the number of Chinese residents of New Jersey's three main suburban counties more than doubled. Although in 1993 the majority of Chinese Americans (53.6 percent) still lived in central cities, a very high percentage also lived in the suburbs—41 percent of all Chinese, compared to 33.7 percent of all white Americans.[6]

INTO THE SUBURBS

Since the weakening of the most virulent forms of segregation, Chinese professionals—both the post-1949 stranded scholars and, later, foreign students from Taiwan—have chosen to live near universities, hospital complexes, and the corporate research labs where they work. In the greater Detroit area, for instance, most Chinese work as engineers and researchers for large auto companies or as academics at neighboring universities, and they live scattered across dozens of suburban towns (including Ann Arbor, where the University of Michigan is located). Those who moved to the suburbs in the first wave after World War II were under the sway of the then prevailing assimilation discourse. They wanted to be accepted, and they wanted their children to grow up as Americans. Typically, they maintained only marginal contact with the Chinese community. China's long civil wars had in fact cut off much of their contact with even their families and relatives in China. Their intent was to rebuild their lives in the United States, and they willingly conformed to American ways. To raise their children as Americans, they often spoke very little Chinese at home. As there were few places outside Chinatowns during the 1960s and 1970s that sold ingredients essential to Chinese cooking, many abandoned Chinese dietary habits as well. Their children demanded American food anyway, having quickly learned about it at school, and were even less interested in their Chinese heritage.

This disappearance into white America has been a theme for many second-generation Chinese American writers. Gish Jen grew up in the New York suburbs of Westchester County, immersed in the Jewish culture of her neighbors and friends. The protagonist of her second novel, *Mona in the Promised Land*, a second-generation Chinese American, lives in an upscale New York suburb where she becomes fascinated by the Jewish community that surrounds her and, to the shock of her parents and friends, decides to convert. In an interview about the book, Jen said, "Mona turns Jewish and, in a way, that's my story."[7] Eric Liu, who grew up in Connecticut, was overwhelmed by a feeling of separation from the world of his grandmother after seeing her in Manhattan's Chinatown: "I was dimly conscious of the fact that we, even though we were blood relatives my grandmother and I, that we occupied very different worlds. And, you know, as we drove up from the city and into the suburbs and the kind of surroundings got greener and more spacious and we finally arrived back at our home pretty late at night—and it was quiet in our suburb. Our worlds were so proximate yet so distant in some ways."[8] Others marvel at the fact that they never encountered another Asian at school before attending college.

In the rush to the suburbs, however—and despite their desire to assimilate—many Chinese ended up congregating in the same areas because of shared priorities and concerns: a safe and clean environment in which to raise children; ample living space to accommodate three generations under one roof, since a typical family would include grandparents; good public amenities; low taxes; reasonable cost; and proximity to white-collar professional job sites. The most important requirement was that their suburban home be located in a good school district. Real estate agent Sandi Ohms from Fremont, California, one of the suburbs in the San Francisco Bay Area that Chinese parents target for the sake of their kids' education, says that her Chinese buyers "just look at the test scores." To live in Fremont's Mission area, which includes Fremont's highest-ranking Weibel Elementary School and streamlines its graduates to the school district's top-scoring Mission San Jose High School, Chinese are willing to pay $75,000 to $100,000 more than for comparable homes in other sections of Fremont.[9] The Chinese top-ten list of good public school districts nationwide, in addition to Fremont

Mission in California, includes Scarsdale in Westchester, New York; West Windsor and Princeton in New Jersey; Montgomery County in Maryland, and Winnetka outside Chicago. Even when the top choices are out of reach, the attitude is the same: "I place a great deal of emphasis on investing in my children," a typical Chinese American mother, Heidi Ames, explains of her decision to move from Irondequoit to Brighton outside Rochester, New York, "and everybody knows Brighton has one of the best school systems in the nation."[10]

The accelerated pace at which Chinese Americans have been flocking to the suburbs since the 1980s, however, has produced an unexpected development: many new Chinese suburbanites increasingly resist the assimilation espoused by the generation before them. Many of the new immigrant professionals come from elite social backgrounds, whether from China, Hong Kong, or Taiwan; their education level is twice that of non-Hispanic white Americans. They have posed a real challenge to the established paradigm of the classic American ethnic-enclave-to-suburb pattern of melting-pot social mobility. They have, in fact, set off a reverse re-segregation process of sorts. Seventy percent of the Chinese population today is concentrated in five states: California, New York, Texas, New Jersey, and Massachusetts. California and the Greater New York City metropolitan region (including parts of New York, New Jersey, and Connecticut) claim more than three-fifths of all Chinese in the country, 41 percent and 20 percent, respectively. More specifically, new Chinese immigrants still favor the three main cities and their surrounding suburbs—San Francisco, Los Angeles, and New York—that were the oldest and earliest Chinese settlements in the country.

Chapter 24

Chinese American
Transnationals

A NEW CHINESE AMERICAN

In 1990 the U.S. Congress adopted a series of aggressive measures to expand the immigration of highly educated professionals—it almost tripled the annual quotas set for them, and it broadened the definition of preferred employment skills to include persons of extraordinary ability, professionals holding advanced degrees, skilled professionals with bachelor's degrees, religious workers, former employees who had worked with the U.S. government, and alien entrepreneurs intending to invest in the United States. (At the same time, policy makers contemplated ways of discouraging poor and working-class families from entering the country.) As a result of the new laws, the number of employment-based immigrants between 1991 and 1992 nearly doubled, from 59,525 to 116,198. By 1994 the annual total had climbed to 123,291. To understand the full impact the new laws have had on U.S. immigration, one need look no further than the legal limits set for fiscal year 2004: 204,422 for those entering under the employment-based preference and 226,000 for family-sponsored immigrants. The1965 Immigration Act had set 10 percent of the annual quota for employment-based immigration and 80 percent for individuals coming under family sponsorship.

About the time Congress pushed through new immigration criteria,

President George H.W. Bush responded to the 1989 Tiananmen Square massacre of prodemocracy protesters in Beijing by issuing an executive order that allowed all nationals of the People's Republic of China who were in America on or after June 5, 1989 to stay in the country. In 1992 the Chinese Student Protection Act granted more than seventy thousand mainland Chinese students, most of whom were attending graduate schools in the United States, temporary resident status. They were allowed to adjust the temporary status to permanent resident status in 1993. The impact of these actions on Chinese immigration was huge. In 1994, more than 59 percent of foreigners admitted to the United States with their families under the employment-based immigration preference were born in Asia. China, with 33,559 employment-based immigrants, claimed the largest number of the slots.[1]

Later during the 1990s, major American players in the booming semiconductor industry, including Microsoft, lobbied the government to address the shortage of software engineers in the nation by increasing the number of temporary work visas. Congress raised the annual limit of H-1B visas to 195,000. These were used almost exclusively to hire foreigners with college degrees or the equivalent experience, mainly from Asia, for positions in computer programming and engineering. In 2000, 9 percent of H-1B visas went to Chinese.[2] Offering temporary work status to highly trained professionals was a departure from the spirit of the 1965 Immigration Act, which would have rendered individuals in this category eligible for permanent residence status and eventual citizenship. This significant modification provoked minimal reaction from the immigrant community, however, which was mostly interested in the numerical increase.

A number of other immigration provisions were simultaneously instituted in 1990 to allow more professionals into the country. The L-1 visa allows American multinational corporations to perform intracompany transfers of their foreign employees to the United States. An IBM subsidiary in Taiwan, for instance, can transfer a Chinese engineer to IBM's American headquarters on an L-1 visa without going through regular immigration procedures. In 2000 there were 329,000 foreigners working in the United States on L-1 visas, and 384,000 on H-1Bs. The vast majority of these 713,000 foreign workers were software and information technology engineers of Asian origin.

Arguably, the most significant immigration policy shift was the introduction of an annual allocation of ten thousand spots for (EB-5) immigrant investors and entrepreneurs "seeking to enter the United States for the purpose of investing at least $1,000,000 in a new commercial enterprise that would benefit U.S. economy and create at least 10 full-time jobs." The initial investment could in fact be as little as $500,000 if the business was located in an economically depressed area; the "benefactor" would still gain permanent residence status in return. Foreigners with money were also given the option of entering on E-1 trader visas. Anyone whose company does at least half its business between the United States and the owner's home country in trade or investment is eligible for this status, created solely for the purpose of encouraging foreign direct investment.

The new categories of legal alien admission dramatically increased the number of Chinese with professional skills and capital in the United States. Although they did not affect the number of Chinese immigrating under family-based quotas, the new minimum income requirement for immigrant sponsors, combined with the Welfare Reform Bill's termination of protection and benefits for nonresidents, greatly discouraged poor working-class people from applying, and the vacated slots were taken over by relatives of the professional, Uptown Chinese. The combined effect of all the new immigration programs was to significantly increase the proportion of investors and technically skilled individuals in the overall total of Chinese entering the United States, and this in turn has altered the class balance within the Chinese American community.

The timing of these changes in U.S. immigration policy could not have suited would-be immigrants of means from Taiwan and Hong Kong any better. In anticipation of Hong Kong's return to mainland China in 1997, many pessimistic Hong Kong residents—even those who were not interested in leaving—tried to obtain a foreign passport, just in case the Communist government did not honor its commitment to leave the Crown colony's capitalist system alone for fifty years. Also, the Asian financial crisis of 1997 caused the Hong Kong real estate bubble to burst and led to years of economic recession. Many looked for ways to get L-1 company transfers, and plenty of the wealthy were more than willing to purchase "entrepreneur visas."

Emigration from Taiwan also increased dramatically during the 1990s. According to its Ministry of Internal Affairs, emigration from the island increased more than fourfold between 1990 and 1996, from 25,500 to 119,100, and the majority of people leaving fell into the category of middle-class businessmen, investors, and professionals.[3] The Taiwanese independence movement and China's threats of intervention contributed to a sense of political uncertainty in Taiwan during the 1990s. Combined with social dislocations caused by Taiwan's rapid industrialization and urbanization, it created a classic push factor propelling emigration. But there was more at play than that.

After three decades of rapid economic development, wages in Taiwan went up, labor protection legislation was in place, and environmental standards were greatly improved, pushing businesses to look for production facilities overseas, in places such as mainland China, Vietnam, and Central America. Some even moved production to the United States, their main export destination, not just to gain direct access to its markets, but also to avoid strict environmental controls in Taiwan. Formosa Plastics Corporation, Taiwan's largest petrochemical manufacturer and one of the top producers of polyvinyl chloride in the world, for instance, moved parts of its production to Texas, Delaware, and Louisiana, where the environmental laws are less stringent. According to a report prepared by the Environmental Working Group, Formosa Plastics Corporation, U.S.A., contributes 16.1 percent of all vinyl chloride emissions in the country.[4] Vinyl chloride is a known human carcinogen, and long exposure to it can result in nerve damage and liver cancer.

Integrated production and capital flow between the United States and Taiwan, Hong Kong and, increasingly, mainland China has meant that the owners and managers of transpacific businesses need easy mobility to travel across international borders. In this regard, holding a Taiwanese passport is a disadvantage. Taiwan has not been recognized by most nations in the world since the time when mainland China, newly welcomed into the community of nations, conditioned its relations with other states on their terminating diplomatic ties with Taiwan. The lack of accredited diplomatic representatives makes Taiwanese vulnerable to harassment and extortion. This is particularly the case in mainland China, where local partners and corrupt officials prey on Taiwanese businessmen, aware that they lack effective means of recourse. The same individuals are treated differently, however, when they hold North American or European passports. Not surprisingly, most Taiwanese want "a second nationality." Those with capital have gladly invested in American businesses in order to get American passports.

Not all foreign passport-seeking migrants move a lot of money, but many do. Between the mid-1980s and mid-1990s, Taiwan's foreign exchange reserves grew from $50 billion to more than $95 billion, to become the second largest in the world after Japan's. During the same period, the government allowed each resident to take up to $5 million a year out of Taiwan. The total amount of capital transferred to the United States is estimated to have been between $2 billion and $3 billion a year. Taiwan's Ministry of Economic Affairs has reported that $1.5 billion was transferred to the Los Angeles area alone each year between 1985 and 1990.

In addition to the political and economic considerations that drove residents of both Hong Kong and Taiwan to take advantage of American immigration law, there is of course the benefit of a better environment to raise a family. Many entrepreneur immigrants leave their wives and children in the United States so that the children can get a highly valued American education, while they themselves continue to work in Taiwan or Hong Kong. After getting a doctoral degree in engineering from Stanford University and working in Silicon Valley for a few years, Tsenshau Yang returned to Taiwan in 1993 to become vice president of an integrated circuit start-up company. His wife, Shyun, who is an accountant, and their two children remained in Cupertino. The decision was based on better job opportunities for both ("I didn't want him to come to me in ten years and tell me he regretted not starting his own company," Mrs. Yang explained), but now they see each other only a few times a year, when he comes to California to visit.[5] In the Chinese community, people like Tsenshau Yang are known as "the astronauts." When both parents work in Taiwan or Hong Kong, their children left in the United States to attend schools under the supervision of relatives or nannies are called "the parachute kids."

Years ago Taiwan suffered a brain drain; the best educated among its young people left for America and about 90 percent never returned. Today, after decades of economic growth, it is those who were not so lucky and competitive to gain a berth to study overseas—the ones who stayed behind and built up Taiwan's economy, and in the process made a lot of money—who are, ironically, now leaving for America with cash, creating a capital drain. America wins, either way.

By the 1990s capital began leaving mainland China as well, as sons and daughters of corrupt high-ranking officials took public funds out of the country in the name of investment. Although the $3 billion officially invested in the United States as of the end of 1999 seems like a relatively small sum, the unofficial investment is much larger.[6] During China's 1997 National People's Congress, delegates castigated the government for its failure to halt the massive exodus of $100 billion in funds stolen since 1979. An estimated $17.8 billion left China in 1995 alone.

FROM SILICON VALLEY TO SILICON ISLAND

Immigration policy changes in the 1990s were by no means accidental. The restructuring of the American economy that began in the 1970s sent the country through a number of transformations. Domestic industries were decentralized, and their focus shifted from manufacturing to information technology, while American capital penetrated deeper into the third world, especially in East Asia. Before the restructuring, big corporations carried out research, development, and production on their own premises. Since the restructuring, they have been outsourcing much of those responsibilities.

Classical manufacturers such as General Motors used to do everything in-house: design, parts manufacturing, assembly, sales, and marketing. Today, they focus on investment and financing, and outsource production to subcontractors overseas or to low-cost domestic producers. East Asia has become everybody's preferred center of production. The trend started with Japan, spread to the Little Tigers (Korea, Hong Kong, Singapore, and Taiwan), was followed by Thailand and Malaysia, and has now come to mainland China. But multinational corporations are not known for their skill in establishing efficient production facilities in third world countries, mostly because they lack cultural sensitivity and the knowledge to navigate social mores and bureaucratic barriers. They have to rely heavily on local contacts. Long-existing overseas Chinese networks based on kinship and ethnic association, as well as individual Chinese Americans who have maintained family and social links in Taiwan, Hong Kong, and China, can easily be used as go-betweens for multinational corporations and subcontractors in East

Asia. They have been instrumental in building subcontracting networks that produce products for American manufacturers, such as clothing, footwear, appliances, and electronic goods for export to the United States, to be sold at Wal-Mart, the Gap, and Home Depot.

Moreover, Chinese Americans with friends or family in the Chinese government help multinational corporations tap into the fabled Chinese *guanxi* (connections) system. The system operates on the same principle as the American old-boys' network. The more enterprising well-connected Chinese Americans have of course put their *guanxi* to work for themselves. Since they are familiar with American consumers' tastes and needs, many have set up their own companies with financing from transnational banks.[7] Some of the highly trained Chinese American scientists and engineers, who were once almost exclusively employed by American companies and who complained about invisibility and the glass ceiling, are now able to bypass the American corporate system. The most ambitious Chinese Americans these days get MBAs and law degrees, not doctoral degrees in science.[8] Between 1980 and 2000, Asian American enrollment in law schools in California quadrupled to 12 percent of the total. According to the Association to Advance Collegiate Schools of Business, an organization that accredits business schools, at present 11 percent of full-time MBA students in the country are Asian Americans.[9] Others convert their science training to become hedge fund analysts, or manipulate complex mathematical models for stock-trading companies and financial institutions.

Chinese Americans who remain employed in the scientific fields now often provide technological and scientific know-how as independent contractors. High-tech companies such as IBM depend on small private vendors to provide hardware maintenance and software assistance to their customers. When a stock brokerage company needs to hook up all the computers in the office and phase them into a network using software specially designed for their business, it contracts a consulting firm to do the job and then hires individuals as in-house engineers to troubleshoot as necessary. A film production company needs advice from engineers on what camera systems to purchase and how to phase them in with appropriate editing machines through the latest operating software for graphic design and post-production. Home-computer users need neighborhood computer shops to handle garden-variety hardware repair and technical service calls. Thousands of Chinese information technology engineers have formed their own companies to work in these capacities. They are no longer limited to providing just technical knowledge. They handle client relations, staff hiring and management, company accounting and payrolls, marketing and, above all, the entrepreneurial task of raising capital for future expansion.

The most visible role Chinese American professionals play remains in the field of scientific research, but it now comes with a twist. Since corporations these days rely on outsourced research for technological innovation, much of the innovation in semiconductor, integrated communication, and biotechnology is done by scientists at small, independent research firms with financial backing from venture capital. Everyone involved receives shares in the company. During the 1990s, many scientists became wealthy, particularly when their companies went public (through the sale of IPOs). Quite a few went on to start new companies and projects, or used the financial windfall to back the ventures of others. They are no longer just bit players servicing huge bureaucratic corporate structures as good "techies," considered unfit for any other type of responsibility. Once treated as "good workhorses" but not "racehorses," they have come out at the head of the race—not just in terms of invention, but also in terms of the wealth they have created for themselves.

The list of the top four hundred richest people in the United States published by *Forbes* magazine in 1999 included Charles Wang of Computer Associates, Jerry Yang of Yahoo, Henry Yuen of Gemstar (a major fiber-optics company), and David Lee of Global Crossing (a cybernetics company). The list of Silicon Valley's ten top-ranked high-tech firms that generated $31 billion in revenues in 2002 includes four that are Chinese American: Computer Associates, Solectron Lam Research, AST Computer, and Wang Laboratories. Many of these leading immigrant entrepreneurs started out in Taiwan or mainland China, earned advanced degrees at American universities (40 percent of them hold graduate degrees, compared to 31 percent of their white colleagues), and worked as engineers for five to ten years in established technology companies, learning the business before striking out on their own.

Chinese American scientists involved in independent research and development enterprises can be found in all major cyber-hubs in the country, including Route 128 outside Boston, "Silicon Wannabe" in Seattle, "Silicon Alley" in New York, "Silicon Hills" in Austin, Texas, and, of course, most notably, in the mecca of high tech, Silicon Valley itself. Silicon Valley is known as "the home of the IC" (the integrated circuit), but locally "IC" is used to refer to the Indian and Chinese engineers, most of them immigrants, who make the valley their home. Seventeen percent of all high-tech companies started in the valley between 1980 and 1998 were run by Chinese and accounted for 13.5 percent of total valley product sales. In 1998, Silicon Valley had two thousand Chinese-led firms employing 41,684 people, with sales of $13 billion.[10]

The dominance of Chinese Americans in the valley has only increased since the late 1990s,[11] through two basic types of companies: IC design houses and small firms that sell PC components and handle systems integration.[12] An important ingredient in making the companies successful is the network their founders are able to tap into, starting from friends, family members, and college schoolmates who can help with start-up money, and expanding to Chinese professional associations. One of the oldest is Silicon Valley Chinese American Computer Association, initially founded by Chinese engineers and scientists to combat isolation and the problems of the glass ceiling many were experiencing in their professional lives. The group soon turned into an instrument for sharing information that benefited those who were striking out on their own. Other associations followed. Seminars on topics such as writing a business plan, negotiation skills, and even the very nineties topic of stress management proved extremely useful to their new immigrant members.[13]

It is not unusual for a Saturday conference organized by Monte Jade Science and Technology Association, a Chinese American professional group, most of whose members have immigrated from Taiwan, to attract anywhere from five hundred to more than a thousand participants. "Success in high tech is dependent on cross-cutting institutions and relationships that allow people to learn quickly from one another," explains UC Berkeley professor Anna Lee Saxenian, an authority on Asian immigrants in Silicon Valley. There are currently an estimated two to three dozen Chinese American organizations in the valley, whose membership is broadly based on place of origin and specialized professions.[14] Hua Yuan Science and Technology Association, for instance, is the mainland Chinese equivalent of the Monte Jade Association. There is also the Hong Kong Association of North America, the

Photonic Society of Chinese Americans, the Association of Chinese Scientists and Engineers, the Chinese American Semiconductor Professional Association, the Chinese Software Professional Association, and the Silicon Valley Chinese Engineers Association. The other important function of these associations is to bring members together to negotiate with vendors (such as Microsoft) and service companies (such as UPS) as a group.[15]

Chinese Americans are also playing a vital role in transnational production. While Silicon Valley is the center of development in leading-edge technologies, manufacturing is typically done elsewhere, usually in Asia. Taiwan, for instance, offers world-class manufacturing with quick and flexible production. It is the world's most important producer of computers, monitors, printed-circuit boards, and other high-tech goods. Taiwan's information technology industry took off in the early 1980s, when IBM decided to decentralize its minicomputer production by subcontracting the manufacturing of computer mouses, motherboards, sound cards, and cases to mom-and-pop factories. A short time thereafter, Taiwanese companies won contracts to make computers for other multinational companies, such as Hewlett-Packard and Compaq.

The Taiwanese government has done everything it can to stimulate the development of the high-tech industry by pumping funds into research, giving tax incentives to information technology companies, and establishing science parks to serve as incubators of information and ideas. The American connection remains critical for Taiwan's industry. According to unofficial statistics, one of every five information technology professionals in Silicon Valley is an ethnic Chinese, and most of them are from Taiwan. "It is the black-haired, yellow-skinned Chinese who are always the most eye-catching members of the research and development staffs of American [technology] firms, whether they be giants like Intel, Hewlett-Packard and IBM, or tiny IC design houses," observed Chen Wen-chi, who left Intel in 1992 and returned to Taiwan at the invitation of the Formosa Plastics Group, before becoming the president of VIA Technologies. Since about half of his old classmates from National Taiwan University's electrical engineering department were in Silicon Valley, he joked, it was more convenient to hold a class reunion there than in Taiwan.[16]

Those who returned to Taiwan to establish its high-tech industry have maintained close contact with those who continue to work in the field in the United States to keep abreast of the latest developments in the industry. Silicon Valley is still the technology capital of the world, and Wu Se-hwa, director of the Institute of Technology and Innovation Management of Taiwan, insists that "if Taiwan hopes to continue to advance, it must continue to import people and experience from Silicon Valley."[17] Under contracts with multinational companies, Chinese scientists on both sides of the Pacific have been able to collaborate on design and in production, and with the help of Chinese American scientists, Taiwan has kept its high-tech industry on the heels of Silicon Valley's growth and innovations—often by hiring Chinese Americans to work at Taiwan's well-known Hsinchu Science Industrial Park as consultants.

"Interdependence creating a single whole" is how Taiwan's minister of state Yang Shih-chien describes it. "Silicon Valley does basic research. . . . Taiwan designs and builds these products, and then sells them back to the U.S. market. The two sides are tightly linked and have a synergistic relationship." Mathew F.C. Miau, chairman of the Mitac Group (one of the two largest PC manufacturers in Taiwan) and himself a returnee from the United States, where he had been one of the team of five that produced Intel's first microprocessor, elaborates on the nature of collaboration. "Big firms need only give us their specifications: what kind of machine with what particular capability . . . what kind of look it should have, retro or trendy. We can take such general specifications . . . to design and produce a machine."[18] In the late 1990s, his company made huge profits building machines to order for Compaq, then the world's largest PC maker.

The end products of the Silicon Valley–Taiwan collaborations are earning great returns for the island, now known as Silicon Island, which manufactured virtually all laptops made in the world—32.1 million units—in 2004. Very few customers who buy notebook computers with the brand names Dell, Compaq, Gateway, Apple, HP, IBM, Sony, Sharp, Fujitsu, and Siemens know that they are actually buying products made by the Taiwanese company Quanta, which, though little known, produced around 4 million notebook computers in 2001— one-seventh of all units sold on earth that year. Quanta has five hundred design engineers in Taiwan, and it did about half the design work for Apple Computer's G4 Notebook as well as 60 to 80 percent of the design work for Dell's popular Latitude models. Quanta's revenue for 2001 was estimated at $3.8 billion. Company Chairman Barry Lam claims that HP and Compaq would have been marginal players in the computer realm by 2001 if not for Quanta's help in designing their products.[19]

Such impressive results have been bringing American corporate and private venture capital to Taiwan. At the same time, Taiwanese capitalists, flush with enormous profits, have been reversing the flow by finding lucrative deals and investing in Silicon Valley, where some thirty to fourty Taiwanese venture capital firms have set up branch offices investing $300 million to $400 million in 1999 alone.[20] They are joined by Chinese American scientists turned entrepreneur-investors, and, increasingly, even the mainstream American venture capitalists who, until recently, did not bother with Chinese American ventures. Having realized that they cannot ignore the impact of the Chinese–driven transpacific silicon synergy on the industry as a whole, they now actively seek Chinese American partners to invest in start-ups headed by Chinese.[21]

Since 1999 Taiwan has been moving the emphasis of its research beyond electronics and information technology into optoelectronic (electronic devices for emitting, transmitting, and sensing light) communications, biotechnology, and microelectronics. What's more, the synergy created by the collaboration of American multinational corporations, venture capital, and Chinese American scientists and entrepreneurs with the Taiwanese high-tech infrastructure is now bringing mainland China into the fold as a major player as well. The emerging network has been dubbed the Golden Triangle: the valley (and more broadly the United States) contributes graduate education, new technologies, a market, and global marketing know-how; the Taiwanese side excels at production and quick response to market changes; and the mainland supplies a rapidly growing domestic market and a huge pool of so far mostly inexperienced talent.[22] But things are changing quickly. Many of the mainland Chinese students who earned advanced degrees in science and engineering at American universities during the past two decades and remained to work as "techies" for technology firms in the United States, just as the Taiwanese did before them, are now starting their own companies. At the close of the twentieth century, there were already more than thirty companies in Silicon Valley started by entrepreneurs from mainland China.[23]

Chapter 25

Ethnoburbs

The overall restructuring of the U.S. economy away from manufacturing and toward high-tech industries and finance greatly benefited Chinese Americans, whose education level is higher than that of the average American, and whose emphasis in education had for some time been on science and engineering. Moreover, as American corporations decentralized production and moved it to Asia, Chinese American professionals for the first time had real opportunities in transpacific management and sales, as well as the chance to try their hand at entrepreneurship and venture capitalism.

While the latest statistics still show entrenched poverty among the "Downtown Chinese," the improvement in economic circumstances of well-educated middle-class Chinese Americans has steadily pushed upward the average income figures for the Chinese American population as a whole. Even though the Chinese American population increased by seven hundred thousand (66 percent), mainly through immigration, between 1990 and 2000, and even though the percentage of the foreign-born in the community is as high as 70 percent, the Chinese American family's median annual income continued to grow during this period (from $41,000 to $63,000) and to surpass both the U.S. national average and the figure for non-Hispanic whites. In fact, its lead over the U.S. average increased from 17 percent to 25 percent, and its lead over the white population from 11 percent to 14 percent.

This marked increase is partially the consequence of new immigration laws that have discouraged poorer and less educated Chinese from entering the country legally, while the influx of poor illegal immigrants from mainland China is not adequately reflected in the census. But there can be no mistake about it: the high earning power of new Chinese immigrant professionals has had the most significant impact on the general income average.

These considerably wealthier new Chinese immigrants still gravitate to the desirable suburbs for their good schools, but they are not as eager as the first generation of Chinese suburbanites to bend over backward to favorably impress their white neighbors. In the Weibel section of Fremont, California, (which has the district's best elementary school), their white neighbors describe them as "excessively wealthy" and "elitists" and accuse them of "not assimilating."[1] It is true that most of these new immigrants, who paid premium prices to own homes in this high-ranking school district, would rather play mahjong than bridge and would gladly give up a quiet dinner for two at a fine French restaurant for a boisterous feast at a Chinese restaurant with a contingent of extended family members and friends. The younger ones among them, especially, like to meet with friends at karaoke bars, where they can sing their favorite songs—many of them Western tunes translated into Chinese. Even when they engage in thoroughly Westernized things, such as attending a church sermon, the new immigrants are more comfortable listening to it in Chinese.

As the income gap between Asia and the United States narrows—in 2002, the average annual household income in Taiwan was $32,600 and in Hong Kong $28,888—new Chinese immigrants these days come from highly developed countries with high living standards. The professionals, being members of the upper crust of those societies, are much more confident of their own values when encountering the outside world than Chinese immigrants used to be. Also, like all people of means, they want the creature comforts they are accustomed to—certain services and conveniences, and, above all, good food. They don't crave Chinese food in a provincial sort of way; what they miss is the best that cosmopolitan cities such as Taipei and Hong Kong can offer.

To these middle- and upper-class immigrants, accustomed to high living standards as they are, going food shopping in Chinatown is not an attractive option. The alien feel and sound of the place due to the difference in dialect and class, the nightmarish parking situation, and the need to enter many stores to buy different items—ending up with a dozen small orange plastic bags—while jostling with pushy crowds all make Chinatown a place to avoid. Suburbanites want to maximize their time by shopping at one place and carting everything they purchase into the parking lot to be loaded into their car trunk. They want a large assortment of processed foods and plenty of choice produce—fresh, clean, and well packed. And they want it in their neighborhood, or as close to it as possible. Ethnic Chinese businesses understand these needs and have been indulging them from the beginning of the Chinese move to the suburbs, first with food and grocery stores, then with services that quickly expanded to take over entire blocks or malls and eventually spilled over into ever-larger, visibly Chinese commercial districts.

The earliest and to this day the most prominent example of such a development occurred in Monterey Park in the San Gabriel Valley on the outskirts of Los Angeles, where Chinese Americans had for some time lived scattered across the valley. It was an aging but respectable postwar white bedroom community at the beginning of the 1960s when Latino, Japanese, and later young Chinese American families with children, escaping from the congestion of downtown LA, began to move in. Soon immigrants from Taiwan arrived with money to buy homes, not just in Monterey Park but also in the surrounding San Gabriel Valley, and with capital to start businesses. Before long, Monterey Park's main thoroughfares were peppered with Chinese-owned restaurants, bookstores, banks, and beauty salons. And as Chinese signs and Asian businesses began to dominate all major commercial streets, condos were quietly invading the domain of cozy single-family dwellings.

Monterey Park's developing suburban economy and its need for ethnic Chinese services and workers delivered a timely rescue to the working-class Chinese stuck in LA's stagnant Chinatown. Following their new jobs to the suburbs, they also began to move into the valley, though they could afford only poorer townships where their neighbors were mostly African Americans and Latinos. Their move added the multi-class dimension to the suburban Chinese community of the San Gabriel Valley. It also spelled death for LA's Chinatown. In 1983, about half the Chinese-owned businesses in the Greater Los Angeles area were located in Chinatown, and one-third in the San Gabriel Valley. By 1992 merely 6 percent remained in Chinatown, while 55 percent were in the valley, with 12 percent in Monterey Park.[2]

Not only did moneyed immigrants from Taiwan and Hong Kong look at Monterey Park as their own community, which they proceeded to developed aggressively; they also brought in banking, turning Monterey Park into the focal point of transpacific investment. By 1989, Monterey Park boasted twenty-six financial institutions, most of which were owned and run by Chinese. The combined deposits in local banks amounted to more than $1.9 billion—roughly $30,000 for every man, women, and child in town.

The flow of transnational capital in and out of the region made Monterey Park the largest Chinese business center in California,[3] and, with its sixty thousand residents living in some of Southern California's priciest homes, earned it the title of Chinese Beverly Hills.[4] At the same time, as its new residents transformed its old Mexican and Southern Californian relaxed architecture into a mixture of large shopping centers with Chinese motifs and competing homes built in the latest Asian styles, the city also became known as Little Taipei. Whatever its unofficial name, according to Immigration and Naturalization Service records, Monterey Park was the second most popular destination for new Chinese immigrants between 1983 and 1990, after New York's Chinatown. By 2000, 41.23 percent of Monterey Park's residents were Chinese—more than four-fifths of them first-generation immigrants—and only 21.29 percent where white. New Chinese communities had spilled beyond the original confines of Monterey Park and Alhambra throughout the San Gabriel Valley. The Chinese population of the suburban municipality of San Marino, for instance, increased dramatically, to 41 percent; Arcadia's grew to 34 percent; Rosemead's was not far behind at 29 percent, and growing.[5]

The suburban Chinese community of the San Gabriel Valley is in some ways different from that of a typical American suburb. Geographer Wei Li, who has observed the phenomenon, coined the term "ethnoburb" to denote a suburban area in which one ethnic group, although not its absolute majority, is present in a concentrated enough fashion to appear as a recognizable ethnic residential and business cluster and maintains a high degree of economic activity and social interaction among its members.[6] Such a community—as is the case with Chinese immigrants in the San Gabriel Valley—replicates some of the features of an urban Chinatown. For instance, the Chinese population of San Gabriel Valley as a whole has never exceeded 20 percent, but it is a place where Chinese immigrants both live and work. This makes it very different from a traditional American suburb, where people only live, while their jobs are elsewhere.

Monterey Park is not the lone Chinese ethnoburb in the nation. Several others have emerged around Silicon Valley, as both the home and workplace of Chinese high-tech scientists and entrepreneurs. One of them is Fremont. Many Taiwanese immigrants were lured to it by the reputation of its public school system when they first began to move to the Bay Area in the mid-1980s. Now a five-acre Chinese shopping center at the intersection of Mission and Warm Springs boulevards stands as the most visible sign of Fremont's transformation from a drowsy suburb to a magnet for new immigrants and high-tech businesses spurred by Taiwanese and Chinese American investment. As many as a hundred high-tech firms with Taiwanese connections are located there.[7] According to the city's current official estimate, some thirty-thousand Chinese live in Fremont—about 15 percent of the city's two hundred thousand residents.

The truly wealthy among the successful Chinese of the San Francisco Bay Area live in the most exclusive area of the Santa Clara Valley, at the southwestern arch of the San Francisco Bay, in towns such as Saratoga, Mountain View, and Los Altos Hills, where average home values rival Hollywood's bedroom communities of Beverly Hills, Bel Air, and Malibu. The ethnoburb that serves as the hub for the Chinese of the Santa Clara Valley (the way Monterey Park serves San Gabriel Valley in Southern California) is Cupertino—a city of fifty-one thousand best known as the headquarters of Apple Computer and the home to many highly educated, affluent high-tech professionals. In 1980, 88 percent of Cupertino's population was white. By 1998 its Asian population had grown to 44.8 percent.[8] (Inside estimates put Asians at 20 percent of Silicon Valley's upper management and 40 percent of its professional and technical workforce.) Here, too, the rapidly changing demography has brought Chinese-language signs and opulent homes—in place of apricot orchards. Several giant Asian shopping malls sell Chinese produce and pipe Taiwanese Muzak, and their almost exclusively Chinese customers give one the feeling of being in Taiwan or Hong Kong.

The ethnoburb, as defined by Wei Li, is only one of many variants of Chinese American adaptation to suburbia. With a few exceptions in California, the Chinese population in suburban areas rarely exceeds 20 percent, yet almost all Chinese gravitate to areas where there is some concentration of fellow Chinese, even if the only evidence of it is a small stretch of Chinese shops and restaurants.

One such concentration can be found in Rockville, Maryland, which took shape when Chinese residents of the Washington, D.C., area forsook the traffic congestion surrounding old Chinatown, located near the Capitol, for more leisurely shopping at Wintergreen Plaza on Rockville Pike, near the intersection with Wootton Parkway.[9] "It's the new Chinatown. Everyone is starting to say it," says Jenny Lin, co-owner of Ten Ren's, a stylish shop selling loose tea leaves, traditional and modern Asian teapots, and fashionable bubble tea and fruit drinks made with pearly bits of tapioca. The Taiwanese restaurant Bob's Noodle 66 serves small-plate portions of authentic crisply fried foods and is the in place to dine out. Chinese immigrant families from Hong Kong, Taiwan, and the mainland cities of Shanghai and Beijing have moved to suburban Montgomery County where Rockville is located on account of its excellent public school system, along with other amenities. Its Asian population has increased by 60.5 percent since 1990.[10]

The malls that house these supermarkets also sell ginseng, herbal products, and freshly baked goods. They are likely to contain a hair salon, a skin care center, a bookstore selling Chinese-language books and periodicals, and photo and bridal shops. Optical and cell phone outlets are also a typical feature, making the Chinese malls almost identical to Wal-Marts, except that the majority of goods are imported from China, Hong Kong, Taiwan, and Southeast Asia to suit Asian tastes. "This is the place to meet each other and have a comfortable conversation, just like traditional bowling alleys and movie theaters," explains

Chiao Ku, a student at San Jose State University, who frequents a café adjacent to a 99 Ranch while on class break. "It's basically the life we had back in Hong Kong or Taiwan."[11] On the average, Chinese customers spend three to four hours at a mall before heading home. Wan Loo, owner of Asiamall.com, an online directory and importing company, estimates that there are 50 to 60 supermalls of this type in Southern California, and roughly 140 more around the country.

In some cases, the existence of a suburban Chinese community is not even marked by a telling stretch of shops. The only sign that Chinese reside in an area may be an "oriental supermarket"—a giant establishment stocked as well as the best markets in Asia. There are several major chains, including Hong Kong Foods, Asian Food Markets, and 99 Ranch, which, with twenty-one stores in California alone, is the Goliath of Chinese supermarkets. Under the gleaming fluorescent lights, they all have aisle upon aisle packed solid with dozens of brands of fish, bean, and hot sauces, and various flavor enhancers essential to divergent Asian cuisines—everything from Japanese to Indian.[12] On any given day, there will be ten different kinds of bok choy, seven kinds of eggplant, standard produce found in a typical American supermarket, but also countless delicacies craved by Asians, including sea urchins and sea cucumbers, licorice-infused olives and salted plums.

On the East Coast a number of diffused suburban Chinese communities are located in the vicinity of major high-tech companies and research facilities, in districts with very good public schools. There is a concentration of Chinese scientists in Princeton, New Jersey, for instance, and of Chinese students at Princeton High School (where the average SAT score is 1400) and the nearby West Windsor (with scores close behind). To an unsuspecting outsider, their presence in the community is indicated only by the Chinese-owned Asian Food Market—one in a chain of suburban supermarkets with half a dozen branches scattered in New Jersey and the Philadelphia area. At a superficial glance, it is just a large, clean, bright, and well-stocked supermarket like any other in the country. What gives away its significantly Chinese character is the presence of a huge water tank containing live fish, and the barbecued meat section teaming with soy sauce chicken, roast duck, stewed pork stomach, and ox tongue hanging on the display hooks.

Chapter 26

A Culture of Growing Self-Confidence

Increased numbers and economic strength have given Chinese Americans greater self-confidence. Shopping malls and Chinese-language schools are but two aspects of the determination of the well-educated professionals to maintain their way of life and gain respect for their culture. In some of the nation's best school districts, Chinese parents are petitioning local school boards to introduce Chinese as one of the languages taught in public schools, on par with French, German, and Spanish. "At the current rate of growth, China's GDP (in terms of purchasing power) will overtake the US in twenty years. USA's largest trade deficit is with China. . . . In order to compete in the huge market of China, and in order to bridge the trade gap, the US will need many more workers and business people who are fluent in Chinese. Therefore, it is in the best interest of the US to set up programs to encourage and boost the learning of the Chinese language and culture by students of all heritages," wrote Youxue Zhang, the principal of Ann Hua Chinese Language School, in a sample petition letter he drafted for its pupils' parents to send to the Board of Education of Ann Arbor Public Schools.[1] As a result of this kind of lobbying, a number of school districts across the country have granted credits to students who study at Chinese-language schools. The College Board's Advanced Placement program, for the first time since it was established almost half a century ago, is adding four new languages: first Mandarin Chinese and Italian, and, at a later point, Japanese and Russian. The program, intended to give academically talented high school students a chance to earn college credit, has until now offered only Spanish, French, and German.

There is also a renewed demand for Asian American studies programs at colleges nationwide. Currently there are at least forty-three of them—twice as many as two decades ago. Almost every major campus these days offers some courses in the field, while a few universities grant PhD and master's degrees or certificates in Asian American studies. Unlike the programs driven by the militancy of the civil rights movement of the 1970s that shrank or became defunct with the waning of the movement, today's programs are the natural outgrowth of a phenomenal increase in Asian American student enrollment. At least 150 universities in the nation have more than 10 percent Asian American students. At the 49 most competitive ones, 13.3 percent of the student body is Asian (though Asians constitute only 4 percent of the nation's population). With their numerical strength, Asian American students are putting enormous pressure on university administrations to establish new programs or to strengthen the existing ones. In the 1990s, they took over administrative buildings at Hunter College, Cornell, and Stanford University and resorted to a hunger strike at the University of California, Los Angeles. At Princeton, they took over the president's office to demand faculty hires in Asian American and Latino studies. At Columbia, three students took part in a fifteen-day hunger strike and a five-day sit-in to demand the establishment of an ethnic studies department and an Asian American studies program. In solidarity, minority students at Cornell held support vigils for the fasting Columbia students. Similar protests demanding Asian American studies programs occurred at Harvard, Northwestern, and Smith. Students at Yale and Amherst sponsored Asian American studies activism conferences to develop strategies for mobilization on other campuses.[2]

Many Asian American students consider the establishment of such programs a matter of personal validation. According to Andrew Chin, a founder of the Asian American Cultures Committee at the University of Texas at Austin, "This was a university that in every possible respect saw everyone as three groups: white, African American and Hispanic. Asian Americans were usually left out or treated as 'other'."[3]

The establishment of an ethnic studies program is a symbol of that ethnic group's political clout.

Administrative resistance to the establishment of Asian American studies programs these days is weaker because most universities realize that their Asian students making demands today are their future alumni and promising donors. Potentially, they could give the schools access to rich and successful individuals in Asian communities. An administrator at Columbia University, under pressure, bluntly told agitating students and faculty that, if they really wanted the university to hire more Asian American professors, they could seek out rich Asians for contributions to establish an endowment for Asian American faculty chairs at $5 million per chair. Other administrators have been attempting to channel students' energy to divert scarce "Asian American funds" into equally underfunded Asian studies programs. The resulting combined Asian and Asian American programs are a kind of bait-and-switch scam, designed to pacify Asian Americans students with a handful of Asian language and culture courses.

The increase in the number of Asian American studies programs in the country has not necessarily produced a clearer sense of direction and mission. The early emphasis on racial oppression and discrimination, demanding social activism and justice, has not been able to accommodate the shift in the quality of life the majority of Asian Americans have experienced in the meantime. The model-minority image, as objectionable as it may be, has in fact found confirmation in the undisputable affluence of a large middle class. And it is from this class that the field draws its participants. Unlike African American studies, whose practitioners are still driven by the political agenda of poor black communities—even if at times only posturing for the mainstream or paying lip service to political institutions such as the NAACP—Asian American studies have been largely disconnected from the still poor, working-class immigrant communities and pulled away from their own activist roots into a realm where their main preoccupation seems to be successful communication with peers in their academic disciplines.

This is not to say that there is no merit in scholarly attempts to define Asian American identity and articulate a coherent position; just that the task is more difficult when the scholars draw from and answer to other academics only, rather than the community they are trying to

define. An example: "Here, I show how understanding Asiatic racial-
ization through the language of transnationalism helps us to recognize
the radical and permanent *undecidability*, to borrow from Jacques Der-
rida, of identificatory terms like 'Asian American'."[4] The author's
view, expressed in this way, is not likely to gain broad circulation.
When theorizing is a purely intellectual exercise, it can lead to curious
results. For a time, the majority of Asian American scholars who presented papers at academic conferences were under the sway of postcolonial theories: questioning the validity of dominant American
social mores, cultural practices, and linguistic power, as well as subtler
methods of control over minorities. They proudly took the spotlight
alongside third world scholars from India, Egypt, and North Africa
with direct colonial and postcolonial experiences under French,
British, and Israeli rule. Too often, the postcolonial approach allowed
them to vent grievances vaguely reminiscent of those raised by colonized nations, and yet to ignore their own role in America's neoimpe-
rialist ambitions as the world's only hegemonic power.

Other theoretical approaches have gained a foothold in the field
as well. Feminist theories have brought rewarding results for Asian
American feminists. Transnational scholarship, increasingly fashionable in a world of reduced geographic and national certainty due to
globalization, has been particularly popular with Chinese American
intellectuals because of the heightened transpacific exchanges among
the Chinese, Chinese Americans, and other overseas Chinese. Beginning to see themselves in the light of a Chinese diaspora, they are
questioning the American concepts of assimilation and national loyalty, as well as the idea of an Asian American identity. To them, ethnic identity is increasingly deterritorialized, and it allows for the
unabashed celebration of the successes of ethnic Chinese everywhere.[5] At the same time, few have questioned Chinese transnationalism as the extension of U.S. imperialistic dominance in the
Asia-Pacific region.

Many of these theoretical approaches have dragged Asian American studies even farther away from its origins in social activism and reform, while the proliferation of often unreadable and mostly unread
treatises presented at rarified academic conferences has not produced
a clear narrative of the Asian American experience for the mainstream.

ASIAN AMERICAN CULTURE OF THE MARKETPLACE

The truth is that the ponderous theories produced by Asian American studies are of little help to most Asian Americans in dealing with the complex ethical choices and subtle forms of discrimination they face in their everyday lives. They are even less incisive when it comes to pinpointing the cultural identity of an increasingly numerous and complex group that has become more amorphous than ever. That task, in tune with mainstream American trends of the 1990s, has been removed from the intellectual sphere and placed in the hands of those who see culture as a marketable set of colorful trivia. For these folks, Asian Americans, with expendable income of more than $150 billion in 2000 and the highest median income and education level in the country, are becoming increasingly interesting both as consumers and as originators of new marketable trends. To advertisers, consumer analysts, and market developers, a vaguely defined Asian identity has become a valuable commodity.

One of the first to tap into the marketing potential of Asian Americans was Jeff Yang, who launched *A. Magazine: Inside Asian America* soon after graduating from Harvard University in 1989. The nation's largest publication for English-speaking Asian Americans, the magazine featured stories on prominent Asians in America, news bytes about issues of concern to Asian Pacific Americans, arts and entertainment reviews, interviews, cultural commentary, and flashy fashion spreads highlighting Asian models. It aspired to raise Asian American consciousness but "recognized the need to be inclusive first." Advertisers wanted as large a circulation as possible, Yang said, so "[w]e had to find a common ground among Asian Americans." The result—not pushing any hard agenda so as not to antagonize any group—satisfied almost no one. Critics of its celebrity-driven entertainment focus have called it vapid. Others found its high-end advertising, aimed at younger, more affluent demographics, alienating. Though well known and influential in the Asian American community for over a decade, it was only very briefly profitable, and it went under in 2002 following the dot-com bust.

A. Magazine's demise prompted a panel discussion at a New York City art galley, "Asian American Magazines: Can They Survive in

Today's Market?" It was attended by dozens of journalists and raised a provocative question: Is there an Asian American community with enough commonalities and shared concerns to rally a publication around and rake in Madison Avenue dollars? The jury is still out.

Little India editor Achal Mehra believes that there is no such thing as a coherent Asian American community. "We are talking about constructing a reality that isn't there." Saul Gitlin, executive vice president of Kang and Lee Advertising, an agency specializing in the Asian American market, says the term "Asian American" is a product of the U.S. census and means something to demographers, not people.[6] Rather, he says, Asian Americans don't think of themselves as Asians, but as Chinese Americans, Japanese Americans, and so on. It remains to be seen whether the Asian American identity is relevant enough to make people consume media.[7] But thirty-year-old Sam Lau, advertising manager at *Audrey* magazine for young Asian women, finds agencies like Gitlin's to be a step behind the times. They justify their existence by preaching "in-language advertising," he points out. "They don't recognize my generation." Although most of the advertising money still goes to the more than six hundred in-language publications catering to the six most numerous Asian American groups, many publishers are increasingly willing to bet on the young, American-educated, English-speaking, ethnicity-crossing twenty-something and thirty-something affluent set.

Instead of trying to be everything to all people—to satisfy both readers who hold PhDs and those who don't even know who the president is—many look for niches of like-minded Asian Americans whose identity is defined more by the products they consume than by the accident of birth. A small quarterly Los Angeles magazine, *Giant Robot*, created by Eric Nakamura and Martin Wong, for instance, covers everything from market surveys of instant ramen noodles and energy drink taste tests to Japanese love hotels. It featured Hong Kong movies and celebrities such as Chow Yun-Fat, John Woo, and Jet Li years before they became popular in the United States, but once declined an offer to interview Jackie Chan because he had become too mainstream. "We're just not interested in mediocre Asian actors in mainstream movies," Martin Wong explained. The magazine is aimed at "the punk-rock kids in the corner who didn't get invited to the parties." It is not trying to be politically correct, nor trying to please anybody. Although its circulation of forty thousand is considered modest by publishing standards, it has emerged as one of the chief arbiters of what is cool in Asian American pop culture, and now, more than a decade since its founding, it draws serious advertisers such as Adidas, Sony, and Universal Studios.

Half a dozen other niche and niche-in-a-niche Asian American magazines are banking on the idea that Asian Americans, like everybody else, have a specific outlook and limited interests. At the same time, when attracting advertisers, they like to point out that "Asians represent half [the] world's population," as did Max Lau when he launched *Noodle* in San Francisco in 2002 to cater to gay Asian Americans. (His calculation was also that 10 percent of Asians are gay.)[8] *Yin* magazine, launched in New York in 2004, competes with San Francisco–based *Audrey* and New York–based *Jade* for fashion-conscious young women readers. *Yolk*, published out of Los Angeles between 1994 and 2003, had its sights set on "becoming the definitive Asian American entertainment, lifestyle, and pop culture magazine." In 2000, due to budgetary problems, it was revamped into an electronic journal (*Yolk: Generasian Next 2.0*) and dropped all "political content" other than "Asian Americans in media," but it was still forced to fold. Its evolution illustrated the shift of interest among the young Asian American "Generasian Next" crowd away from identity-circumscribing narrative toward flashy, identity-expanding image, reflecting a world of discerning, informed consumerism, in which one's belonging to a group is determined by the ability to tell apart different varieties of rice from Asia and find the best instant ramen—not one's parents' brand of values and tradition.[9]

A similar kind of nonchalant attitude toward identity was in evidence in the film *Better Luck Tomorrow* by American-born director Justin Lin, which was a breakaway success in 2003. The film follows a group of Asian American high school students from Orange County as they navigate a typical suburban Southern California life full of expected model-minority achievements and extracurricular activities— while also casually engaging in petty crime that eventually leads to murder. It is deliberately void of standard backdrops, such as family pressure (not a single parent makes an appearance in the entire film) and racism, allowing its heroes/antiheroes to hustle and shoplift, sell exam answer sheets, and deal drugs without as much as an afterthought, let alone guilt, as if existing in a universe completely separate from their parents' concerns and values. An angry audience member at the Sundance Film Festival stood up after a screening of the film to attack Justin Lin. "Why would you make a film that is so empty [and] amoral for Asian Americans?" he wanted to know. In private conversations, many Asian Americans, particularly those belonging to older generations, have objected to its senseless violence and negative representation of Asian Americans. But its young director, who financed the film with credit cards, took a calculated risk in exposing the world of youthful alienation and bottled-up frustrations that flourishes in American suburbia, among the high-achieving Asian kids as much as among their Caucasian peers. After all, he himself belongs to this new generation, which is impious, self-centered, and self-confident enough to define its own culture and the way it wants the outside world to see it.

Long gone seem the days when Asian American actors fought for a chance to get a part—any part—in films and plays by Caucasians, who defined the roles for them. When producer Cameron Mackintosh announced in 1990 that he was bringing to Broadway *Miss Saigon*, a musical loosely based on Puccini's opera *Madame Butterfly* that was a box-office hit in London, Asian American actors were interested. For years, Asian American playwrights, actors, and producers had complained of prejudices that limited their opportunities. Regardless of their training and talent, actors typically found themselves typecast in demeaning roles as amoral exotic girls, sinister gangsters, brutish prison guards for America's enemy nations, or, at the very best, asexual sidekicks who never got the privilege of intimacy with the leading characters. Nothing epitomized the problem better than the stunted career of the exceptionally talented actress Anna May Wong. Here at last was a production in which just about every character was Asian! The joy was short-lived. Mackintosh cast the acclaimed Welsh-born actor Jonathan Pryce in the play's leading role as a Eurasian pimp, Engineer. The Actors' Equity Association immediately condemned "the casting of a Caucasian actor made up to appear Asian" as "an affront to the Asian community." The decision, the charge went, was "especially disturbing when the casting of an Asian actor in this role would be an important and significant opportunity to break the usual pattern of casting Asians in minor roles."

A coalition of fifteen Asian American community organizations led by the Pan Asian Repertory Theatre, including the New York Chapter of the Asian American Journalist association and the Asian American

Legal Defense and Education Fund, as well as the well-known actor B.D. Wong and playwright David Henry Hwang, came out to support Actors' Equity's position. What really hit a raw nerve was Mackintosh's claim that there were no qualified Asian actors to take up that role, and that the casting of Pryce was therefore an artistic decision. The coalition did not dispute the right of a Caucasian actor to play Engineer; it simply demanded that the play's producers make a good-faith effort to audition Asian actors for the role. "The main issue is not who gets cast," insisted Pan Asian Repertory Theatre founder and director Tisa Chang, but that Asian American actors should be given a chance to try out. Many qualified and talented Asian actors were never given the opportunity to showcase their craft. To deny them an opportunity to audition, Chang accused, was to "perpetuate and encourage stereotypes at the expense of artists of color, which borders on 19th century imperialism."

Chang knew exactly what she was talking about. She had abandoned a career in mainstream cinema and television and established the Pan Asian Repertory Theatre in 1977 precisely to give talented, classically trained Asian actors like herself a chance to get parts beyond the mainstream's stereotypical roles. But Mackintosh turned the argument against the Asians, accusing them of "reverse racism." When he threatened to withdraw from staging *Miss Saigon* in New York, Actors' Equity backed off, and the Asian organizations were castigated for racist intolerance.

Ironically, *Miss Saigon* contains disturbing racial stereotypes. It is set against the fall of Saigon in 1975, and its heroine—a Vietnamese prostitute who is abandoned by her American GI lover—in the end commits suicide so that their child can go to America to live with him and his Caucasian wife. Like its century-old prototype, it tactlessly portrays Asian women as the sexually submissive Oriental stereotypes born of white male fantasy. Some of its critics, including playwright Frank Chin, have questioned why Asian American actors would fight to play such silly, stereotypical roles. Most actors, however, saw it professionally, as an opportunity to break into a career on Broadway, where actors of all races should be allowed to play both "good" and "bad" parts. The exclusion of Asians from principle roles in *Miss Saigon* was, according to Vincent Tai, a board member of the Asian American Theater Company, a variant of the glass ceiling.[10]

Since then, there has been an explosion of small theaters determined to make true Asian American plays using Asian-sensitive scripts and Asian American casts. Groups with names such as Yellow-Mellow, dueEast, Mango Tribe, Silk Road Theatre Project, Stir-Friday Night!, and Tea Company draw small audiences on both coasts, but increasingly also elsewhere in the country where large Asian American communities have taken root. A 2004 theater festival called Saving Face showcased seven Asian American theater companies at the Studio Theater in Chicago. Of course, it is still the venerable institutions such as East West Players (established in 1965 in Los Angeles), Asian American Theater Company (founded in 1973 as a playwrights' workshop in San Francisco by Frank Chin, and turned into a professional theater company in 1975), and the aforementioned Pan Asian Repertory Theatre of New York that launch the careers of the most visible Asian American artists on and behind the stage. Chinese Americans among them, such as the actors B.D. Wong and John Lone or the playwright David Henry Hwang, have certainly become household names nationwide due to their successful moves to Broadway and Hollywood. Current East West Players resident director Chay Yew's plays have been produced by the New York Shakespeare Festival, Royal Court Theatre (London), Manhattan Theatre Club, Mark Taper Forum, Long Wharf Theatre, and La Jolla Playhouse, among others, but because they cross prejudicial barriers of race and sexuality in less comfortable ways, Chay Yew is not as well known to the mainstream. Perhaps it's a question of time, or a question of the medium. Theater is the least funded of the traditional arts, while big money goes into film, where the product can be marketed globally, and where the draw of Asian audiences combined with the expanding ambitions of Asian investors is beginning to make an impact on Hollywood.

The first feature-length film about Asian Americans with an Asian American cast and produced and directed by Asian Americans was the 1982 black-and-white *Chan Is Missing*. Its writer-director Wayne Wang shot it in 16 mm on an ultralow budget of $22,000, using unpaid actors. It employed a loose plot of two San Francisco cabbies looking for their friend Chan, who disappeared with their $4,000, to poke around Chinatown street corners, restaurants, and homes; its characters frequently spoke Chinese, and no subtitles were provided. It also explored a variety of social issues, such as generational conflict within the community, tensions among residents from Taiwan and mainland China, and the conflicts between those who identify themselves as Chinese American and those who identify themselves as Chinese. Unexpectedly, *Chan Is Missing* became a sleeper on the art-house circuit and paved the way for other ethnic indie auteurs like Spike Lee and Jim Jarmusch to make quality low-budget films. Wang himself went on to make several other low-budget Asian American films, including *Dim Sum: A Little Bit of Heart* and *Eat a Bowl of Tea*, before directing the major Hollywood box office hit *The Joy Luck Club* (1993).

The Joy Luck Club, based on Amy Tan's bestselling novel of the same name, almost didn't get made because no major studio would finance the writing of the script, which called for an all-Asian cast (it was because of the personal dedication of a young Chinese American producer, Janet Yang, that a script written on spec finally found a buyer in Jeffrey Katzenberg at Disney), but it was in the end embraced by the mainstream. It was the one movie that almost single-handedly changed the perception that mainstream movies had to feature Asians only as sinister villains like Fu Manchu or the mafia-types of the Chinatown underworld depicted in the 1985 release *Year of the Dragon* to be successful. Although some critics complained that *The Joy Luck Club* portrayed Asian men in a negative light, there was no denying that it signaled that movies featuring Asians and Asian themes had arrived. It also gave Janet Yang the status of "the head priestess of Hollywood's Asian Destiny."[11] That same year Ang Lee's Taiwanese-produced film *The Wedding Banquet*, about the clash of cultures that ensues when an aging Taiwanese couple visits their New York–based son, was nominated for an Academy Award as a foreign-language film. It proved popular with American audiences, too. Other films with Asian themes followed.

It is no accident that the success of these two films with Chinese/Asian American themes coincided with the economic rise of East Asia and the growing presence of China on the world scene as an economic, financial, military, political, and cultural powerhouse with an ever-expanding appetite and reach. The growing affluence of Asian Americans and the influence Chinese Americans have enjoyed in pulling the strings that strap China's development to the driving engines in America have also meant that it is easier for Asian Americans to find funding, not just for political causes, but for cultural endeavors that reflect the tastes of the benefactors as well. At the same time, Asian markets are increasingly important for the manufacturers of American "cultural products," such as music and film. Nothing reflects the resulting bond better than the Taiwan-born, NYU Film School–educated film director Ang Lee's martial arts fantasy *Crouching Tiger, Hidden Dragon*. Filmed in Chinese (Mandarin) on location in mainland China, it was produced with financial backing from Taiwan, Hong Kong, the United States, and China, and starred actors from Hong Kong, China, and Taiwan. It received ten Academy Award nominations in 2000—in both the best foreign–language film and the best picture categories, which had happened only twice before in the history of the Oscars (for *Z* in 1969, and *Life Is Beautiful* in 1998). Like its two predecessors, it won the best foreign-language film award—for Taiwan. Ang Lee became the third nonwhite director ever nominated for best direction. True aficionados of Hong Kong martial arts films in Asia thought the film was too American; less discerning viewers thought it was one of the most stirring and dazzling martial arts films ever made. Audiences loved it. In the United States, it was, at over $128 million, the highest box-office-earning foreign film of all time.

The box-office success of *Crouching Tiger, Hidden Dragon* made Hollywood take a serious look at the Asian potential in the film industry. Many actors and film directors have been imported from Asia to showcase their craft in Hollywood flicks, while American's non-Asian filmmakers have ventured into Asia in search of locations and themes. The martial arts genre has proven particularly adaptable to the global designs of the industry, with big Asian stars such as Jackie Chan and Jet Li taking on English-speaking roles in movies set in America, while American stars such as Tom Cruise and Uma Thurman dabble in Japanese while they kick butt on Asian turf. Some of the biggest box-office hits at the turn of the millennium have been developed around martial arts: films such as *The Matrix* and its two sequels, *Charlie's Angels* and its sequel, *Rush Hour* and its sequel, *The Last Samurai*, and *Kill Bill* in two "volumes"; even the James Bond films have become more physical in the martial arts vein. In this genre-bending frenzy taking over Hollywood, a homegrown Chinese American actress, Lucy Liu, too, has found fame. Her career, more than any other Asian American actor's so far, suggests that race-based identity bending may be in the offing on the big screen in the not-so-distant future. Liu has auditioned for and gotten parts that were not written for Asian actors; her performances have convinced producers and directors to move her from small race-specific sidekick roles into bigger parts, if only as an equal member of the *Charlie's Angels* lead ensemble.

Like all accomplished professionals, Chinese American artists don't want their opportunities to be limited by their race. The most respected Chinese Americans in creative professions, such as I.M. Pei, Yo-Yo Ma, and Maya Lin, have been so outstanding in their fields that they are always defined by their craft first and almost never by their racial or ethnic identity. Hollywood's Chinese image makers who work behind the camera as directors, cinematographers, and producers have over the course of the past two decades gained the same ground, but comparable acceptance has eluded the actors so far. If anybody can push the envelope that extra inch, it is the up-and-coming generation of new trendsetters in the arts, who, like the transnational inventors, designers, and venture capitalists, confidently use their heritage as an asset but don't apologize for who they are and don't feel that they have to be like someone else to be validated.

Chapter 27

The Limits of the Civil Rights Agenda

The economic gains, increased confidence, and greater mobility of Chinese Americans, whose numbers have grown dramatically since the 1960s, have not translated into political power. One of the main reasons for this has been the separate settlement patterns for the Uptown and Downtown immigrants. In the past, European immigrants who came from the same region, spoke the same language, and shared similarly humble means ended up living in the same poor neighborhoods, where they remained attached to strong social institutions they brought from home, particularly the churches. Their shared ethnic and class backgrounds shaped their political views, too, allowing them, once they became citizens, to vote as a block—something mainstream political parties capitalized on by offering favors and patronage in exchange for votes, until the immigrants realized that they could turn the system to their advantage and elect their own candidates to political office.

Immigrants from China were legally barred from voting and their American-born offspring effectively blocked from making inroads into the American electoral system until the Civil Rights era. Then, as Chinese Americans began to enter the middle-class and move to integrated urban and suburban communities, they became too dispersed to form effective voting blocs. Urban Chinatowns that continue to exist as dense pockets of ethnic concentration are now populated by new immigrants, who are notoriously underrepresented in the electoral process. Many do not speak English and are not familiar with the rudiments of American politics. Many who have permanent resident status have not been naturalized. Most of those who have been naturalized are not registered to vote. (The overall voter registration rate for the Chinese is around 30 percent—the lowest of all Asian ethnic groups in America.) Even those who are registered may not necessarily turn out to vote.[1] A study by the Public Policy Institute of California shows that during the 2000 election, the turnout rate of Asian Americans in California, the majority of whom are Chinese, was 50 percent, compared to 74 percent among Caucasians.[2] And when they do vote, many cast their ballot without a particular party affiliation. According to political scientist Pei-te Lien, as many as 33 percent of Chinese Americans claimed no party affiliation during the election of 2000.[3]

Initially, Chinese American voters favored Republicans, reflecting the influence of Chinese American elites with close ties to the anticommunist KMT and government of Taiwan, who had a long history of supporting the Republican Party. But since the mid-1990s, the vote has shifted markedly toward the Democrats. (A poll taken by the Asian American Legal Defense and Education Fund, AALDEF, during the 2004 election showed that 51 percent of Chinese American voters were registered Democrats, 14 percent Republicans, and 32 percent had no party affiliation; 72 percent voted for the Democratic presidential candidate John Kerry, and 24 percent voted for the Republican incumbent, George W. Bush. During the election of 2000, according a CAVEC exit poll, Bush got only 16 percent of the Chinese American vote, while the Democratic candidate Al Gore got 82 percent.) The turn is particularly noticeable in comparison to other ethnic and racial groups, whose voting patterns have remained relatively stable throughout the same period.[4] Nevertheless, the commitment of Chinese voters to the Democratic Party can easily be shaken when a Democratic candidate runs against an ethnic Chinese. In the California senate race in 1998, for instance, the Democratic incumbent Barbara Boxer got only 45 percent of the Chinese American vote, as many voters crossed the party line to vote for her ethnic Chinese Republican challenger Matt Fong.

Because of such unpredictable shifts and the lack of a mechanism to deliver the Chinese American vote as a reliable block, mainstream parties have had no incentive to cultivate the Chinese American community politically. Although the Chinese vote can potentially provide a critical margin in a tight local race, the investment the parties must make in order to overcome the language problem and nurture Chinese contacts to gain access is too high when resources can be spent more efficiently elsewhere. Roland Quan, president of the Chinese American Democratic Club in San Francisco, has been quoted as saying, "The Democratic Party has for all practical purposes ignored the Chinese/Asian American . . . communities for over twenty five years."[5]

In San Francisco, where 30 percent of the population is Chinese, there is only one elected Chinese supervisor on the city's eleven-member board. New York has the largest Chinese American community in the country, but no Chinese American was ever elected to a city-wide, state, or national office until John Liu from Queens finally won a seat on the City Council in late 2001.

COMMUNITY DISCORD

For some twenty years Chinese American political activists have been attempting to overcome what they see as institutional barriers that handicap the voting strength of Chinese American communities. Among other things, they have lobbied with some success for the introduction of bilingual ballots in a number of states. They have also argued for the redrawing of voting districts, so that the Chinese could maximize their voting strength. What some of the efforts have unfortunately revealed, however, is that the lack of Chinese American political power is, as often as not, caused by divisions within the community.

This was certainly what came to light during the drive to unite New York's Chinatown into one voting district. Nobody disputed that the city's districting was sapping the power of Chinese voters. As Margaret Fung, executive director of AALDEF, explained: "The voting strength of Chinese Americans has been diluted because Chinatown was divided into two state assembly districts. Moreover, Chinatown has also been split between two community board districts and two school board districts. This . . . has merely reinforced our community's inability to organize and develop a political cohesiveness."[6] But divisive factors came to light when an opportunity for change came in 1989, after a successful lawsuit against New York City found the city in violation of the U.S. Constitution for the racially discriminatory way it had devised to form voting districts. As a result of the ruling, the city established a Districting Commission charged with finding ways to enhance the political representation of minorities by increasing the number of city council districts.

All Chinatown community activists agreed that the principal goal was to unite Chinatown. Unfortunately, the number of Chinatown residents—62,895 according to the census—fell short of the approximately 143,579 needed to form a district. This is where the activists split: in deciding which other community Chinatown would have to join in order to form one district.

One side, led by AAFE, argued that Chinatown should join with the predominantly white, affluent, and fashionable neighborhoods of Soho, Tribeca, and Battery Park City to the west because of their liberal tradition and the likelihood of voters there supporting Chinese American candidates. This faction's goal was to have a Chinese elected to the City Council. In the words of AAFE's Doris Koo: "Our objective is not to look for districts where Asians did well. Our objective is to look for districts where Asians have *won*."[7] AAFE's confidence stemmed from the fact that its leader, Margaret Chin, had been elected twice to the Democratic State Committee in the 1980s with white liberal support. Virginia Kee, president of the Chinese American Planning Council, reinforced this faction's agenda by saying: "As a teacher, I can tell you that our young people must see their own faces in their government."[8]

The other side was led by AALDEF and argued that Chinatown, as a working-class minority community, had more shared interests with the neighboring Puerto Rican community to its north and east. As Elaine Chan, a leader promoting this option under the banner of a "multiracial district" pointed out, "Asians, Latinos, and African Americans have had a historic working relationship on issues of common concern: housing, health care, immigration, day care, bilingual education, affordable commercial space, job training, and general quality of life issues."[9] Working-class multiracial activism on Manhattan's Lower East Side goes as far back as the 1930s, and the long-time Lower East Side community activist Mini Liu best expressed this faction's trust in class as the primary basis for political coalition: "Yes, we want minority representatives. But we want minority representatives who are accountable to the Asians and Latinos on the Lower East Side, not just Asian and Latino faces in the City Council, representing white middle and upper class interests."[10]

As the gentrification of Lower Manhattan progressed at high speed during the early 1990s, the top issue for the area's Chinese as well as Latino residents was affordable housing. Their demands would be heard louder if spoken in a unified voice. But the Districting Commission in the end ruled in favor of Chinatown joining with the white community on the Lower West Side. Its executive director explained: "The Districting Commission opted to craft a district designed to offer the only opportunity in the city to the Asian-American community to elect a candidate of its choice."[11] This has not happened. Two attempts by AAFE's Margaret Chin to win a seat on the City Council have failed, as have all other attempts by Chinese American candidates.

What's worse, the decision not to join Chinatown and the working-class Latino neighborhood into the same voting district weakened the city's anti-gentrification forces. The 1992 redistricting gerrymandering of the East Village and the Lower East Side into one district with the higher-income Gramercy Park and Murray Hill to the north, and of Chinatown with its affluent neighbors to its north- and south-west, left tenement dwellers throughout Lower Manhattan with a weakened and divided political base. As a result, squatters and working-class homesteaders were systematically cleared out, and in less than a decade the developers swallowed much of the East Village, converting tenements in the working-class Latino community to market-rate apartments, new middle-class housing, designer boutiques, art galleries, gourmet restaurants, and night clubs that attract an ever-growing young and trendy crowd. That done, the same gentrification forces are now working to gobble up Chinatown.

The redistricting experience in New York's Chinatown points to a painful failure of vision and a serious lack of a unified political agenda within the Chinese American community.

A NARROW POLITICAL AGENDA

Activists' efforts to energize Chinese American political life through pan-ethnic alliances with other Asian American groups have, similarly, not been effective. The original idea behind the Asian American Movement was the hope that a shared racial experience would bring Asians together to fight against discrimination. To this end, the movement emphasized common histories and shared interests while avoiding issues that caused divisions. The result has been a narrowing of the political agenda to middle-class demands, such as the appointment of Asians to high profile political positions and the dismantling of the "glass ceiling," and the one issue every Asian in the country can agree on: stopping anti-Asian violence that is still quite rampant in the United States.

In 1982 Vincent Chin, a twenty-seven-year-old Chinese American waiter and part-time draftsman from Detroit, went to a bar with two friends to celebrate his upcoming wedding when two white unemployed autoworkers, mistaking him for a Japanese, began blaming him for the recession in the American automobile industry. The exchange turned violent, and Mr. Chin was killed by the two in the parking lot as he was leaving the bar. Chin's mistaken identity became the hallmark of the kind of experience Asian Americans fear the most. The two perpetrators, initially charged with second-degree murder, were allowed to plead guilty to manslaughter. The judge sentenced them to a three-year probation and set them free, explaining: "We're talking about a man who held down a responsible job with the same company for seventeen or eighteen years. . . . These men are not going to go out and harm somebody else." The ruling set off a groundswell of outrage among Asian Americans across the nation, who began forming ad-hoc committees to demand redress and write letters of protest to politicians. The public pressure grew intense enough to force the Justice Department to intervene and convict the two killers of Civil Rights violations. The Vincent Chin incident was a pivotal event in making dissimilar Asians of diverse national origins conscious that they were Asian Americans.

The momentum, however, did not carry over. In 1990 the Congress passed the Hate Crime Statistics Act, requiring the Justice Department to collect data on crimes which "manifest prejudice based on race, religion, sexual orientation, or ethnicity" from law enforcement agencies across the country and to publish an annual summary of the findings. But while the federal government finally took a stand on the problem that has long plagued Asian American communities, local law enforcement authorities often hesitate to classify incidents against Asians as hate crimes—in clear contrast to their response to similar incidents against African Americans and Jews. Asians are treated differently because they lack the political power to influence local politicians, who in turn can put pressure on law enforcement. "Our issues are being ignored because the candidates are not focused on our communities as voters,"[12] comments Karen Narasaki of the National Asian Pacific American Legal Consortium.

Anti-Asian violence continues. Three hundred and thirty five anti-Asian incidents were reported to the Justice Department in 1993, and at least thirty Asian Pacific Americans died as a result of homicide. There were 452 reported incidents in 1994; an increase of 35 percent. In 1995, there were 458; another increase of 17 percent. The 1999 Audit of Violence Against Asian Pacific Americans conducted by National Asian Pacific American Legal Consortium (NAPALC) noted a 13 percent increase in reported anti-Asian incidents between 1998 and 1999. But the number of racially motivated incidents against Asians really skyrocketed after the 9/11 terrorist attacks. A 2002 NAPALC report tracked 243 in just the first three months following the attacks.[13]

Statistics kept by the Department of Education indicate that the number of on-campus racially motivated bias incidents against Asian Pacific Americans is also on the rise. Most go unaddressed. New York City's Department of Education ignored appeals by parents, community leaders, and the United Chinese Association of Brooklyn to look into a series of racially motivated verbal and physical assaults against immigrant Chinese students at Lafayette High School in Brooklyn in 2004. The Justice Department eventually had to step in and force the Department of Education to take measures, finding that New York City school officials remained "deliberately indifferent" to the "extreme and persistent" and "clearly racially-motivated" violence against Asian students.[14] Similar complaints of racial violence have been heard from Asian students all across the nation.

Physical attacks and racial insults directed against Asians, when reported, are at least an issue that the Chinese American community can muster enough goodwill to unite around and address as a group. Other important and seemingly straightforward issues affecting Chinese Americans have, regrettably, caused plenty of disagreement. The quotas set by elite universities to keep down admissions of Asian Americans is one of them.

QUOTAS AGAINST ASIAN AMERICAN STUDENTS

Asians have long suffered from racial discrimination in America, though few would argue that their experience approaches that of African Americans. Consequently, from the very beginning of the Civil Rights Movement, Asian Americans did not demand affirmative action considerations for college admission. (One exception was at the University of California, which until the mid-1980s recognized Filipinos as a disadvantaged population qualified for special consideration.) The Asian American problem with college admissions turned out to be quite the opposite.

In the early 1980s, as children of new immigrants benefiting from the 1965 Immigration Act came of college age and the number of Asian Americans applying for college admission increased dramatically, many with impeccable scholastic records and extracurricular activities found themselves unable to enter top schools, although their performance matched that of admitted white students. There seemed to be a barrier set to keep Asian admissions down. When challenged, schools like Stanford, UCLA, UC Berkeley, and Brown University all denied that this was the case. Their initial response was that Asian students had poor English verbal SAT scores. When challengers pointed out that colleges base admissions on the total number of SAT points, not separate verbal or math scores, the schools said that Asian students had fewer credits in extracurricular activities. Finally, the schools invoked concern for the diversity of the campus environment. They eventually had to admit that they had indeed set a quota for Asians.

The colleges, committed to affirmative action programs for African Americans, could have chosen to treat Asian and white students equally. But as the Asian American population grew and Asian students became increasingly competitive, the number of qualified Asians was causing a decrease in the proportion of admitted white students. When the tolerance for the growing imbalance reached a tipping point, the colleges decided to institute a form of affirmative action for white students by increasing the admission standards for Asians in order to reduce their entrance rates.[15] Media were initially not interested in exposing this travesty. It became the focus of national attention only after UC Berkeley Professor L. Ling-chi Wang went to the *New York Times* with the story, comparing the Asian experience to the quota set against Jewish students during the 1920s and 1930s. College administrators were forced to admit what they were doing. "I wish we were more sensitive to the underlying concerns," UC Berkeley Chancellor Ira Michael Heyman said. "While they did not manifest themselves as neatly as I now see them, Berkeley could have acted more openly and less defensively. I apologize for that."[16]

Others were less apologetic. Some took the opportunity to blame African Americans for taking the spots away from deserving Asians. James Gibney wrote in the *New Republic*: "If Asians are underrepresented based on their grades and test scores, it is largely because of affirmative action for other minority groups. And if blacks and Hispanics are underrepresented based on their fraction of the population, it is increasingly because of the statistical overachievement of Asians. Both complaints can't be just, and the blame can no longer be placed solely on favoritism toward whites."[17] Conservatives used the "suffering" of Asian Americans, who were more likely to be perceived as "victims" in the public's eye than the whites, to attack the affirmative action programs. Their siding with Asians is disingenuous, because affirmative action was meant to give a temporary boost to African American youth, allowing them to catch up to the rest of the society. Affirmative action is a form of payback for the wrongs that white American society had perpetrated against African Americans for centuries. But many white Americans today don't see why they should have to sacrifice for the actions of their ancestors, and elite colleges discretely devised a quota system to shift the burden of past wrongs onto the shoulders of Asians. It was a clever tactic: by pushing Asians into conflict with African Americans, white America could get out of the way and still have its less competitive children enjoy the benefits of white privilege.

Some Chinese Americans took the cue to attack African Americans. Elaine Chao, U.S. Secretary of Labor under George W. Bush, has repeatedly stated her belief that affirmative action quotas hurt Asian Americans. She has called Asian Americans "victims of reverse discrimination."[18] But those who fought against quotas for Asian college admissions never challenged the merits of affirmative action programs. Henry Der, Executive Director of Chinese for Affirmative Action, who was one of the leaders in the fight against Asian quotas, accused opportunistic politicians of using "our issue to try to undo affirmative action for all minority groups, and we can't go along with that."[19] When University of California Regent Ward Connerly remarked, "I would be quite comfortable with only white and Asian students at UC," Der protested: "As a parent, I do not want any of my three children to experience or choose a segregated college education."[20]

Former contributor to *Asianweek*, Arthur Hu, was one of the most outspoken Asian American critics of affirmative action. He thought that the phony truce between Asians and the universities, such as at UC Berkeley, that had dropped the "quota" against Asians, resulted in white under-representation at elite universities and expressed concern that an adverse reaction was merely a question of time. "Whites haven't even noticed, much less cared about it. Maybe it's not a problem yet, but sooner or later, someone else will notice. If our educated leaders don't talk about it soon, some nut with an AK-47 may decide to beat them to it."[21]

Hu's concerns for the suffering of white Americans should be put to rest. They have certainly noticed and cared enough about the situation to set a quota against Asians to begin with. It is the preferential treatment they receive that rarely gets noticed. The federal Office of Civil Rights, for instance, cleared Harvard University of charges that its admissions policy favors white students, although Asian students still need higher scores to be admitted. Harvard gives preferences to athletes and legacy admissions. Legacy admissions allow relatives of alumni, the overwhelming majority of whom are white and well off, to enter the university at lower standards. (President George W. Bush was admitted to Yale as a beneficiary of such policy.) People generally think that "sports admissions" benefit black applicants. Actually, outside football and basketball, most sports slots, such as for swimming, tennis, squash, gymnastics, fencing, volleyball, hockey, field hockey, winter sports, gymnastics, etc., go to white students. When legacy and athletic admissions are added up, the number of white students who get to attend ivy league schools that they do not qualify for academically is far greater than of those who benefit from affirmative action. Yet as soon as Asians raised the quota issue, conservative politicians began to look for ways to get rid of affirmative action programs for African Americans nationwide with no mention of legacy and athletic admissions.

Perverted as the current discourse on the issue may be, the quota conflict is not going away. Many of the best and most popular public high schools across the country are plagued by the problem of "Asian over-representation." Some of these schools have set up racial quotas in order to give a "fair" chance to others in the name of diversity. The most heated debate occurred at Lowell High School in San Francisco, one of the most prestigious high schools in the nation, which counts among its alumni two Nobel Laureates, a former governor, a Supreme Court justice, and a president of Yale University. Based on a consent decree, the San Francisco School District had established caps on the number of any one group attending the school, mandating that it may not exceed 40 percent of the student body. As a result, a Chinese student had to score 61 out of possible 69 points on the entrance exam to enter, while white and other Asian students needed 59, and African American and Hispanic students needed only 53.[22]

Asian American civil rights organizations did not want to challenge the school district, considering that Lowell was already over 50 percent ethnic Chinese and 70 percent Asian American. But a group of disgruntled Chinese parents, with support from conservative organizations, especially the Chinese American Democratic Club (a group that had, interestingly enough, fought to increase the minority share in government contracts through affirmative action), took the school district to court. In the resulting *Ho vs. San Francisco Unified School District* case, the California Ninth Circuit Court of Appeals ruled that the school district had imposed "racial classifications and quotas." However, it also found evidence of segregation of black and Latino students. In view of a long history of discrimination against Chinese American students in California, and particularly in San Francisco, it found it "especially hazardous to adopt racial classifications and racial caps that bear most heavily upon [Chinese American] schoolchildren." Nevertheless, it ruled that a school could use racial classifications if it

proves them necessary to prevent and repair the "vestiges of segregation."[23]

California's famously liberal court decided to favor a quota against
Chinese American students in the name of protecting African American
and Latino students against the "vestiges of segregation," though no
one has ever accused Asians of responsibility for the historical wrongs
committed against African Americans and Latinos. The seeming incon-
gruity of the argument generated immense frustration and confusion
within the Chinese American community. Some Chinese Americans are
able to keep the two issues apart and work to make sure that there are no
quotas set against Asians in competition with white Americans, while at
the same time honoring the affirmative action programs as a commitment to assist historically disadvantaged minorities. Others believe that,
plain and simple, affirmative action harms the opportunities of better-
qualified Chinese Americans.

The small group of parents who would not accept the court's liberal
ruling continued litigation, and finally won a settlement in 1999,
thereby overturning three decades of efforts at integration in the San
Francisco school system. As a result of the settlement, 50 percent fewer
African American and Latino students entered Lowell that year.
African Americans, who make up 16 percent of the school district's student population, accounted for 1.5 percent of Lowell's freshman class;
4.5 percent of the incoming class were Latinos, who comprise 21.5 percent of the district enrollment. Diane Chin of Chinese for Affirmative
Action warned: "Chinese Americans are being used as a proxy of anti-
affirmative action and anti-integration viewpoints, which will ultimately increase discrimination against our community."[24]

THE DISENFRANCHISED IMMIGRANT
WORKING CLASS

When the Chinese American Voter Education Committee surveyed
the position of Chinese voters in San Francisco on admission quotas at
Lowell High School, 45 percent thought it was a bad idea, 32 percent
thought it was a good idea, and 23 percent had no opinion.[25] Chinese
American opinion is at least as divided over the college admissions
quotas and affirmative action. But, if these issues that can be broadly

classified as middle-class discrimination concerns fail to produce a unified position within the Chinese American community, labor issues that afflict the working class often fail to even elicit a response. The consequences are tragic for a good number of working-class Chinese immigrants who continue to flock to America's urban centers in search of jobs.

A study of the five major Chinese urban concentrations in the nation conducted in 2003—in San Francisco, New York, Sacramento, Chicago, and Seattle—has described them as "communities in serious distress."[26] Over 60 percent of Chinese who live in them are foreign born. Over 50 percent of their residents speak only Chinese; 60 percent have less than high school education. These disadvantages force the immigrants into the segregated ethnic labor market, where they receive wages that are well below regional averages (as low as 50 percent of the average wage in the case of New York's Chinatown). As a result, over 20 percent of Chinese residents in all five surveyed communities live in poverty; in Sacramento, the poverty rate is as high as 50 percent.

Because Chinese Americans today rank extraordinarily high in terms of median family income and education, it is easy to overlook the fact that they also comprise a significant percentage of working-class people employed in service industries and unskilled laborers. Since many of them work for co-ethnic employers in segregated Chinese communities, their problems are hidden from public view and easy to ignore. Sweatshops are routinely associated with working conditions in immigrant Chinese communities, yet mainstream America allows them to exist, only periodically expressing outrage—much as it had treated Chinese "coolies" during the nineteenth century. To make matters worse, few Chinese American organizations speak out against the disgrace of labor exploitation in Chinese American communities or condemn as racism the indifferent attitude of the mainstream.

Mission statements of the main Chinese American organizations hardly ever mention labor, preferring to deal with middle-class issues as a way of gaining political visibility and representation in mainstream institutions. On the rare occasions when they do, it is to defer the topic to mainstream labor unions. This is ironic, given the American organized labor movement's long history of discrimination against the Chinese, which was at one time the primary force pushing for exclusionary laws against Chinese laborers. Although no longer openly anti-immigrant, today's bureaucratized unions are run like businesses and are not interested in organizing and protecting powerless immigrant minority groups.

True, there have been attempts by Asian American labor activists to reform mainstream unions. In the early 1990s, Asian American union leaders belonging to the AFL-CIO formed the Asian Pacific American Labor Alliance (APALA) to "combat racism within the union." In practice, however, this meant getting representation for themselves in the union establishment—"diversifying union leadership," as it was called—without changing much in the union's policy toward organizing Asian American workers. Like other union establishments, APALA is based in Washington, D.C., at the apex of national political power, better to influence the federal agenda: to promote civil rights legislation, oppose anti-Asian violence, and ensure fair representation for Asian Pacific Americans at all levels of politics.[27] While such goals are noble, the tragedy of American organized labor is its sole focus on getting the government to enact laws favorable to working people while ignoring the power of grass-roots mass organizing to make the government act. American unions have stayed away from organizing Chinese restaurants, they have provided ineffective representation to Chinese garment workers, and have refused to admit minorities including Chinese into well-paid industries, such as construction.

Without outside scrutiny and intervention, working conditions in the segregated environment of Chinese ethnic enclaves in America have deteriorated to the levels of the nineteenth century–style exploitation. In a 1998 lawsuit against sweatshop Hua Great Procetech Inc. of Sunset Park, Brooklyn, four Chinese immigrant workers accused its manager of making them work 137 hours a week. One said that he worked 130 hours one week and got "several hundred" dollars pay. A machine operator stated that she got $3.50 an hour for a twelve-hour day that included only a brief break for lunch. At the time, the state's minimum wage was $4.25 an hour, but rose to $6.38 for every hour worked in excess of forty hours a week.[28] But overtime pay is nonexistent in Chinatown sweatshops. Sixty-, seventy-, and eighty-hour workweeks have become a norm. "When I first started working here," a presser told a *Daily News* reporter, "we worked about eighty hours a week. But since June last year he forced us to work longer hours. On a normal day, we'd work sixteen hours, and the longest I remember was about thirty hours straight." The few pressers and machine operators who complained were fired.[29]

Abuses of what has become known as the "flexible workforce" are pervasive. Extremely long work hours, lack of basic safety on the job, home-work, child labor, lack of compensation for injuries sustained on the job, and the most dreaded abuse of all—the withholding of back wages—occur not just in non-union Chinatown sweatshops but also in factories whose workers are nominally represented by UNITE (Union of Needletrades, Industrial and Textile Employees). Yet UNITE representatives claim surprise and outrage whenever a particularly egregious case catches public attention—and do nothing to put a stop to the abuses. Only small grass-root groups such as Asian Immigrant Women's Advocates (AIWA) in the San Francisco Bay Area and the Chinese Staff and Workers Association (CSWA) in New York are helping the immigrants fight for their unpaid back wages, worker compensation, and medical benefits if they are injured.

After initial successes in courts—and failure to collect a cent on behalf of the workers from Chinese sweatshop operators who close down their factories and disappear whenever they are seriously challenged—community-based labor organizations have moved their fight to a more visible arena. Rather than targeting only the ethnic subcontractors in the Chinese immigrant community, they have developed a strategy to hold large manufacturers and retailers who subcontract to them equally accountable for sweatshop conditions. Sears, Liberty Apparel, Fashion Bug, Conway's, and Family Dollar stores have all come under attack, and the fight has gained momentum since the Brooklyn-based grass-roots organization National Mobilization Against Sweatshops (NMASS) took the lead in crossing ethnic lines to mobilize shops that include both Chinese and Latino workers. Their most notorious target has been the New York fashion designer, Donna Karan, whose DKNY clothing line was in 2000 sewn at a Chinese-owned factory a few blocks from her Midtown headquarters, where immigrant workers worked seventy to eighty hours a week and complained of being forbidden to drink water and being denied bathroom breaks. The factory bathrooms were, in fact, often padlocked. One worker, Kwan Lai, told of being forbidden to take a phone call when her children were sick.[30]

Donna Karan portrays herself as a champion of the advancement
and empowerment of women and an animal rights activist. The workers who made her DKNY label thought they were treated like animals.
In a class action suit filed in Manhattan Federal Court in 2000, they
blamed her for not coming to their aid.[31] Those who had complained
to UNITE and the Labor Department were fired by the subcontractor.
When NMASS took up the issue on their behalf, the subcontractor
closed down the factory and moved production to another union shop
owned by the same owners. A UNITE official went to the new factory
to warn its workers against following the "troublemakers." But the
Chinese and Latino workers were not scared off by the tactic. Instead,
aided by NMASS, CSWA and AALDEF, they organized protests and
press conferences, in which even many undocumented workers from
Fujian took part, called for a consumer boycott of labels made for the
New York queen of fashion they labeled "the Sweatshop Queen," and
filed a class action lawsuit against Donna Karan International and all
its subcontractors. They won, both against DKI in Federal Court, and
in the suit against the subcontractors filed with the National Labor
Relations Board.

The rank-and-file labor movement that is percolating among seriously abused, often illegal immigrant workers in substandard sweatshops despite all the obstacles flies in the face of the long-standing
accusations by mainstream unions that the new immigrants are not
militant enough to organize. Organized labor, which openly dismisses
immigrant grass-roots organizations as "pre-union formations" that
cannot amount to much, in fact knows that they pose a threat to its
dominant role in the labor movement and therefore frequently sides
with manufacturers in blaming the conditions of Chinese immigrant
workers in America on imports from third world countries like China.

It is small wonder that the Chinese American organizations with an
eye to capturing a spot in the mainstream shrink away from this sort
of agenda. The predicament of the Chinese immigrant laboring class
invariably touches on the issues raised by illegal immigration, and in
the minds of the emerging go-getters in the arena of American partic-
ipatory politics, such issues can only have a negative affect on the image of all Chinese Americans. Insofar as they deal with immigrant
issues at all, they only take positions on legal immigration. By avoiding
the question of illegal immigrants, which is bound to inflame public

sentiment against immigration in general, they hope to ensure that the Chinese American community continues to benefit from the "family preference" type of immigration.

The prevailing silence puts both legal and illegal immigrant workers at an ever-greater risk. Perhaps even more importantly, the silence has allowed one of the most important shifts in American immigration policy in an entire generation to occur without much public notice—a shift that could have devastating racial implications for the whole of American society and that is already affecting minority communities.

THE NEW GUEST-WORKERS PROGRAM: A REPLAY OF CHINESE EXCLUSION?

The 1965 Immigration Act brought an unexpectedly large number of poor, working-class Latino and Asian immigrants to the United States. Since a disproportionate number of them were admitted on the basis of the "family unity" preferences, the critics quickly took to blaming the family-based quotas for allowing too many unskilled and poorly educated people into the country. The public became particularly frustrated by the rising numbers of poorer immigrants during the economic recession of the late 1980s, and pressured Congress to pass a series of immigration reforms to counter this problem.

The clamor against aliens started in earnest after the first attack on the World Trade Center and the Golden Venture incident in 1993. The two events came to symbolize "alien invasion," and set in motion a swell of anti-immigrant sentiment and a suspicion of aliens, whether illegal or legal. During the general election campaign in 1996, the anti-immigrant fever ran so high that even Democratic Party candidates vied among themselves to introduce tougher measures against illegal immigration. The resulting Antiterrorism and Effective Death Penalty Act of 1996 suspended several rights previously granted to all immigrants including the illegals, such as the right to a fair trial and the right to appeal. The Welfare Reform Bill of 1996 cut off all social benefits to illegal immigrants.

Unfortunately, the hostility against illegal aliens turned against legal immigrants as well. The Illegal Immigration and Immigrant Responsibility Act of 1996 (IIRIRA) amended the Immigration and Nationality

Act to require virtually all aliens immigrating through one of the family-based categories to obtain a legally binding affidavit of support as a condition of admission. U.S. citizens who wish to sponsor their relatives by signing such an affidavit must meet an income requirement of at least 125 percent of the federal poverty level. The affidavits are legally enforceable for at least ten years or until the beneficiary has become a U.S. citizen, effectively guaranteeing that no one comes to America to take advantage of its social welfare benefits, such as housing, supplemental security income, Medicaid, and food stamps. Most severely affected are the elderly permanent residents ineligible for social security, because they are barred from receiving welfare assistance. A *Washington Post* editorial called the change in immigration policy "startling and truly mean,"[32] and declared that it was "moving America toward exceptionally ugly results."[33] A report by INS estimated that 25 percent of Chinese Americans fall below the required minimum income standard, and would thus not be able to sponsor further immigration of relatives to this country.[34] Indeed, the new legal provisions have prevented many Chinese working-class U.S. citizens from reuniting with their family members in Hong Kong and China, bringing into question the assumption that American immigration still rests on the humane principle of family reunification.

The introduction of new immigration restrictions and benefit reductions, however, does not mean that the American economy can suddenly do without unskilled immigrants. On the contrary, American society is addicted to cheap immigrant labor—legal and illegal. Recent gains in productivity and profit growth have often been achieved by employing "flexible" immigrant workers, and the government has neither the incentive nor effective means to control illegal immigration. The real consequence of recent laws has been to stigmatize a large sector of the American workforce as an extra-legal entity, while giving employers the power to lower the wages, extend work hours, disregard health and safety regulations, and suppress unionizing efforts.

A gradual consensus among U.S. policy makers has finally emerged that the best way for the country to enjoy the cheap services of undemanding immigrants is to legalize the illegals by giving them guest-worker status without granting them citizenship. The idea of guest workers began to blossom in negotiations between Mexico and the United States, when President Vincente Fox pressured President

George W. Bush to take action on the cross-border migration issue. President Fox characterized Mexicans who have left their country to look for better opportunities in the United States not as illegal immigrants but as people who "are there because the U.S. economy needs them." In a joint news conference President Bush stated: "Every day thousands of Americans and Mexicans cross the border . . . bringing with them optimism and a strong desire to succeed. . . . And in the process, they enrich our nation." He therefore proposed a program of safe, legal, and orderly migration that will "match willing foreign workers with willing American employers. . . . Under this program, undocumented workers currently in the United States will be able to come out of the shadows and establish legal identities."

The joint initiative was stalled because of the 9/11 attacks. Bush reintroduced it during his reelection campaign in 2004, proposing a new program that would offer legal status to the millions who have been offered employment in the United States by issuing them temporary worker cards that would "allow them to travel back and forth between their home and the United States without fear of being denied re-entry into our country." But he emphasized that this was "not amnesty, placing undocumented workers on the automatic path of citizenship." The legal status granted by this program would last three years and be renewable, but it would have an end.[35]

Guest-worker policies are full of contradictions, but they have seduced politicians in many countries. Wherever these programs have been tried, they have never turned out to be temporary, because employers become addicted to the advantages of employing cheap labor. The policies act as a disincentive for investment in labor-saving technologies, because they unnaturally sustain declining industries through low productivity and low wages—as is the case with garment manufacturing in the United States at the moment. In the end, they harm productivity and the growth of the economy as a whole.[36] Above all, immigrant workers are never easily disposable. Germany, which along with other developed Western European nations during their economic expansion in the 1960s imported "guest workers" from Italy, Yugoslavia, Turkey, and North Africa, has not been able to get rid of them when the economy slowed down. Guest workers are not machines. They are people, with social ties, families and children, and their extended "visits" have been the cause of persistent racial and ethnic strife. The second and third generation offspring of Turkish guest workers, born and raised in Germany, have yet to gain legal status and social acceptance. Immigrant specialists Philip Martin and Michael Teitelbaum, who have studied guest-worker programs in other nations, have come to a simple conclusion: there is nothing more permanent than temporary workers.

The United States had its own "guest worker" Bracero Program, instituted in 1942 to bring a stable supply of farm laborers into the country from Mexico to cover wartime shortages of agricultural workers. The program actually accelerated the flow of illegal immigrants across the border, contributing to the hostility of the white population toward Mexican immigrants, including those with proper documentation. This ugly xenophobia led the INS in the 1950s to deport three million undocumented and documented Mexican immigrants and U.S. citizens through a campaign known as "Operation Wetback." It was a campaign of fear and gross violations of human rights, with INS agents declaring war on anyone who "looked Mexican"—stopping them in the street, asking for identification and interrogating them without due process. Longtime residents of the United States and their American-born children were often deported along with the illegals, leaving deep scars in the collective memory of Chicanos.

The real intent of the Bracero Program, however, was to use the special status of Mexican workers to separate them from American workers through a de facto apartheid labor system, which allowed farmers and employers to violate labor laws—sometimes even having workers deported before they got paid. The Labor Department official in charge of the program when it ended, Lee G. Williams, called it "legalized slavery."

This is certainly not a historical experience that ought to be repeated. Similarly, Chinese laborers during the nineteenth century were introduced to this country with a special status. They were recruited and offered work by enthusiastic American employers looking for cheap labor but were never granted citizenship and labor rights. The resulting tragic history of the Chinese in America left wounds that are yet to heal. Unfortunately, Bush's new temporary work program is a replay of this dangerous script. The civil rights of all Chinese Americans could easily come under attack if just one segment among them—the alien "guest workers"—were to be subject to super-exploitation and deportation. But Chinese American organizations are too timid to take a critical position on the issue. The Organization of Chinese Americans in fact went as far as to announce it was "pleased" with Bush's guest workers program. It promotes itself as a civil rights advocacy and education organization with over eighty chapters and affiliates nationwide, but the OCA, it seems, has yet to learn the lessons of the nineteenth-century Chinese exclusion, which is, ironically, one of its favorite topics.

PART VI

Suburban and Symbolic Politics

Chapter 28

The Middle Class
Enters the Fray

NETWORKING

At the entrance to the Princeton branch of the Asian Food Market, half a dozen free Chinese-language newspapers are stacked next to the usual supermarket offerings: one intended for locals of Taiwanese origin (*Global Chinese Times*, printed in traditional Chinese script), two targeting mainland Chinese immigrants (*The American Chinese Times* and *Chinese News Weekly*, both printed in the simplified Chinese characters used on the mainland), a paper published by the religious group Falun Gong (*The Epoch Times*), a Christian publication (*The Graceful Way of the Cross*), and *Duowei Times* (a printed version of a Web newsletter intended for a mixed Chinese American audience). What is surprising is that even though Princeton (where there is a significant presence of professional Chinese) is far away from any major metropolitan Chinese concentration, several of these papers are published locally, aimed specifically at the Chinese-reading suburbanites in the New Jersey and Philadelphia region. The others are local editions of national papers. All contain coverage of major international events with special focus on mainland China, Taiwan, and Hong Kong, as well as local New Jersey community news and analysis. Remaining sections are devoted to family pages—homecare advice, food recipes, and moralistic lectures to parents on the correct way to rear children. Finally, there are consumer, business, and investment tips.

Most important, the papers are full of advertising for every conceivable type of business and service—all offered by Chinese professionals to Chinese-speaking residents of New Jersey's suburban areas: Chinese certified public accountants, lawyers, photo shops, and real estate agents in almost every township; dentists; tile, plumbing, and construction companies conveniently located at expressway exits; Chinese babysitters and home-care providers with good references; piano, violin, and dance teachers; math and physics tutors; Chinese astrologists and fortune tellers; florists; flower arrangement classes; art schools teaching traditional Chinese calligraphy and ink painting, operated by eminent graduates of famous art schools in China; ballroom dancing at a Chinese dance floor in Roselle Park, etc. It goes without saying that there are numerous ads for Chinese restaurants. The papers serve as focal points for Chinese speakers in the geographic areas they cover, and by dispensing information about the needs of their readers and the services and opportunities offered them, they make the otherwise disconnected Chinese immigrants feel that they in fact belong to a community.

Similar kinds of communication networks exist in other Chinese suburban areas as well. The old Chinatown in downtown St. Louis, for instance, was destroyed in 1966 due to urban renewal, but the suburban Chinese population in the Greater St. Louis area has grown from 106 people in 1960 and 3,873 in 1990 to somewhere between 15,000 and 20,000 today. They have their own weekly paper, association, Chinese Culture and Education Foundation, Baptist Church, and numerous Chinese-language schools.

As the earliest Chinese institutions to emerge in American suburbia, Chinese-language schools have long served the function of anchoring widely dispersed suburban Chinese communities. There are more than six hundred of them around the country. Funds to set them up and hire teachers are raised by parents locally, but there are associations with national reach that can assist with such projects, most notably the National Council of Associations of Chinese Language Schools (based in Macon, Georgia), Chinese School Association in the United States, Chinese Language Teachers Association, and Chinese Language Association of Secondary-Elementary Schools.

Typically, the decision regarding which association a school will be affiliated with is political, as both the Nationalist government of Taiwan and the Communist government of mainland China have sought to influence overseas Chinese communities through Chinese-language schools. So important have the two governments deemed this to be that both have Overseas Chinese Affairs Commissions and Cultural Affairs Councils, which occupy themselves with pushing their version of Chinese-language textbooks abroad.[1] At times, they provide the textbooks free of charge, and pay for annual conventions of school teachers, seminars where parents can exchange ideas, and national competitions to select the best students in reading and writing Chinese, calligraphy, Chinese dance, singing, and debate.

Since so much of the parents' time is devoted to their children's schools, the schools have become the center of their own social life. While waiting for their children, parents themselves might take a class or two: tai chi for health or painting for the soul. During the requisite Chinese New Year celebrations, the school turns into a Chinese culture center to showcase its own talent but also to impress non-Chinese neighbors with performances by visiting Peking Opera or Kun Qu Opera troupes, lectures by health gurus of Chinese traditional medicine, and movie screenings. Recently, in some communities, Chinese-language schools turned community centers have also invited stockbrokers to discuss investment and business ventures.

Just as easily, the schools can be converted to serve political purposes. Previously, political debates among immigrant professionals tended to be over disputes between Taiwan and mainland China. Sometimes they got together to speak out on issues that neither government wanted to deal with. In 1971, for instance, foreign students and young professionals from Taiwan took to protesting the Nationalist government's inept handling of a dispute with Japan over oil-rich Diaoyutai Island. Similar protests in Taiwan were silenced by the government, fearful that Japan might retaliate by cutting off aid and trade relations—a move reminiscent of Chiang Kai-shek's earlier decision to fight Chinese Communists rather than Japanese aggression. So it fell to the overseas Chinese, from Hong Kong and Southeast Asia to North America, to carry the torch of public discontent through teach-ins on college campuses and demonstrations in front of the Taiwanese embassy in Washington, D.C., and consular offices in New York and

San Francisco. Many graduate students, research assistants, professors, and engineers took part despite threats of being "exposed as communists" by KMT spies operating in the United States, because here they were free to express their long-felt anger against the dictatorial rule of the Nationalist Party at home.

By speaking out for the interests of all Chinese who could not do so in China, Taiwan, or elsewhere, progressive Chinese in America bridged the gap between the two Chinas, particularly after the U.S.-China rapprochement initiated by Nixon. They launched a protest in 1982, when new Japanese history textbooks depicted the Japanese military aggression in the Asia-Pacific War as an effort to liberate Asian countries from Western colonization, while calling the torture and murder of some two hundred thousand civilian residents of the city of Nanjing in 1937 a "minor incident" and "a story made up by the Chinese . . . a lie." Discussion of the topic was not allowed in either mainland China or Taiwan, both of whom had developed extensive trade and diplomatic relationships with Japan, so it was the overseas Chinese action committees, such as the Alliance for Preserving the Truth of Sino-Japanese War and the Global Alliance for Preserving the History of WWII in Asia, that pressed the Japanese government to apologize for war crimes, pay reparations to victims, and correct the facts in the history textbooks.

When the Nationalist Party lost out as the governing party of Taiwan in the 1990s, originally opposed groups in overseas Chinese communities shifted their attention to local issues and came together to fund-raise for Chinese Americans running for office. Occasionally, they mobilized around international issues, such as the riots against ethnic Chinese in 1998 that accompanied the ouster of Indonesian President Suharto, in which hundreds of Chinese-owned shops and homes were looted and burned, sometimes with their owners and families locked inside, while numerous Chinese were physically attacked, and many women brutally gang-raped. Reminded of the ouster of Indonesia's previous president, Sukarno, in 1967, when some five hundred thousand Chinese and Indonesians were killed, the concerned overseas Chinese took the initiative in raising funds to support the victims and demanding that the international community intervene. Sometimes overseas Chinese even united over a controversial issue, such as the persecution of the Taiwanese-born Chinese American physicist Wen Ho Lee, wrongly accused of being a spy for Communist

China. His case brought together Chinese immigrant scientists and professionals regardless of "which China" they came from.

Other attempts at unifying various Chinese Americans have come from Chinese Christian groups, many of whom organize community activities before or after Chinese-language church services to bring people together, very much as the Chinese-language schools do. For many of the secular Chinese professionals, however, most of the socializing and networking is built around alumni associations. As a rule, Chinese feel great loyalty toward the schools in which they were educated—not just colleges but even high schools. Given the fact that there were and still are relatively few schools in China, Taiwan, and Hong Kong that offer quality education, most immigrant professionals, being a highly preselected group, have graduated from a very small number of top schools, and they are proud of it. They also trust their compatriots who graduated from the same schools because they know exactly what it took to achieve that, making organizations such as the Beijing University Alumni Association, Taiwan University Alumni Association, Tsing Hua Alumni Association, and many others into centers for enjoying social activities, fostering business connections, promoting scholarly exchange, or simply networking.

MASTERING SUBURBAN POLITICS

As the number of Chinese American professionals increases in suburbia and their stake in their new communities becomes more apparent, they have had to organize politically, even if they did not particularly want to, so that they could respond to day-to-day challenges on issues they care about: the right for their children to access quality education, the right to bilingualism, the right to maintain their way of life, and the right to be free from discrimination.

Ethnoburbs, like the one in San Gabriel Valley, are deliberate creations of the immigrants who have moved there. Namely, the Chinese have not slipped into these bedroom communities as passive bystanders; rather, they have picked them as places where they want to make a living, do business through the support of their ethnic networks, speak their mother tongue, and keep close ties to their countries of origin. In doing so, they have seen their suburbs of choice turn into zones of social and racial conflict. In Monterey Park, for instance, when Chinese immigrants began developing the area, longtime residents—mostly white, with a smaller percentage of Latinos, but even the original Asian settlers—felt displaced. University of California at San Diego professor Leland Saito interviewed scores of disgruntled folks, such as the young Japanese American who said, when he came back to visit his childhood home, "Damn it, Dad, where the hell did all these Chinese come from? Shit, this isn't our town anymore." Even an African American, who had once gotten the NAACP involved to demonstrate against racial exclusion so he could move into the neighborhood, now demanded that the city hall adopt regulation to prevent Chinese from moving in. There were getting to be too many of them in Monterey Park, he claimed, and he didn't move from a black ghetto to live in an Oriental ghetto.[2]

The initial reaction of many residents was to accuse the Chinese of "taking over their community" and of ruining the cherished *Leave It to Beaver* dream of a safe, tranquil, and affordable neighborhood.[3] Then, as Monterey Park began to experience traffic gridlocks due to a proliferation of malls and condominiums, the resentment crystallized into a slow-growth movement, seeking control over land use.

Every old resident in the valley, including Latinos and Asian Americans, could recite the same litany of complaints about uncurbed development, but it was the white population that was the most vocal. Only, this confrontation cast white natives in an unfamiliar role, since whites have historically fought the influx of minorities into their neighborhoods on the grounds that it would lead to the devaluation of their property. The Chinese were in fact gentrifying the area, driving real estate values up. As commercial signs with "inscrutable" Chinese characters replaced familiar landmarks and stores, expressions of nativism became quite common. "I feel like I'm in another country," was the most common complaint.[4]

Anti-Chinese feelings were often mixed with a sense of inferiority. The typical American complaint that foreigners can't drive, when applied to the Monterey Park Chinese, acquires a telling twist. "The Chinese people gave us gunpowder, the modern calendar and noodles, giving evidence of their genius as a people. So why can't they drive a car?" a resident wrote to the editor of a local paper. "I saw a Mercedes 450 SL make a U-turn on Atlantic Boulevard at 5:30 P.M., Rolls Royces drive up Crest Vista on the wrong side of the street, and Porsches turn left on red lights from the right lane."[5] On the other side are those—mainly the high-powered developers and land speculators—who reject the criticism as xenophobia of the old-timers maintaining that "slow growth" means "no growth."[6]

The two sides fought fiercely over mayoral and city council elections. The nativists resorted to xenophobic appeals, forcing the city council to pass a resolution declaring English the official language and following up with battles over whether to allow Asian lettering on the storefronts of Asian-owned businesses or Asian-language books in the library. Monterey Park was the first city in California to place an "English Only" issue on the municipal ballot. It was also a leader of the national movement to make English the official language of the United States. As the debates raged, Monterey Park's new immigrants felt victimized. Many other residents, including some whites, Latinos, and other Asians, while not progrowth, were offended by the racist tactics used by the antigrowth faction. Although Asian and Latino Americans constituted over 80 percent of Monterey Park's population in 1988, the city staff and elected officials were predominantly white. Only one nonwhite person, a harmony and managed-growth advocate, Judy Chu, was on the city council, which was headed by the city's most outspoken "official English" movement proponent, Mayor Barry Hatch. In 1990, a multiethnic coalition of Asian Americans, Latinos, and whites, formed to oppose Hatch's divisive leadership and to beat back the old Anglo establishment, ousted him from office. Two Chinese Americans and one Latino won seats on the five-member council. The biggest vote getter was a Chinese immigrant, Samuel Kiang. Judy Chu became the mayor.[7]

The hostility toward new Chinese immigrants in Monterey Park actually forced them to become politically involved, with the effect that they now serve on city councils, commissions, and local school boards. While they are still not a majority of Monterey Park's population, Chinese Americans today make up the majority of the city council.

Fremont, which is approximately 15 percent Chinese, has experienced similar racial hostilities. In 2003, City Councilmember Bill Pease proposed that the city "develop regulations requiring all retail signs [to] contain a majority of English content." He called it a safety issue. Many Chinese denounced the proposition as an act of discrimination, pointing out that no one had ever had a problem with stores bearing only French and Italian names, while Gary Harmon, owner of the *Minuteman Press*, thought the proposal "a waste of everybody's time" since in a free country every business "has right to do what's best for business."[8] After the bill was defeated, Bill Pease got a civics lecture from Mayor Gus Morrison for not realizing that "the community was changing."

The fiercest fight, however, erupted when the Fremont Unified School District announced plans to redraw boundaries for Fremont's top high schools. Under the new plan, students graduating from Fremont's highest-ranking Weibel Elementary School would no longer be guaranteed enrollment in either William Hopkins Junior High School or the district's top-scoring Mission San Jose High School. Students in all three schools are predominately Asian American and white. Many Chinese had moved to the area precisely so their children could attend these schools. Some twenty Asian American families filed a racial discrimination lawsuit against the Fremont School District, alleging that the district's plans to change attendance boundaries were designed to divert high-performing Asian students to mediocre high schools in order to boost those school' scores. The superintendent of schools cited overcrowding, saying the goal was "to get schools to the size that fit their neighborhood." The lawsuit, however, did not focus just on education. It charged that white parents had made disparaging remarks about Asian families during public meetings, mimicked and mocked those who spoke with accents, and accused the Chinese of abusing their children by forcing them to study.[9]

In the exclusive community of Cupertino in Silicon Valley, too, longtime residents complain that they no longer recognize their hometown. A *San Jose Mercury News* poll of Santa Clara County, where almost 30 percent of the population is Asian, found that 37 percent of whites would like to see more restrictions on immigration, and 28 percent think immigration has caused the quality of life in the county to deteriorate.[10] Predictably, the community is swept up in controversies about Chinese-language signs and about whether it is appropriate to feature Chinese dragon dancers in Fourth of July celebrations. Another public debate focuses on "pink palaces"—the hulking, two-story stucco houses painted pink that have mushroomed all over town, dwarfing Cupertino's traditional ranch-style homes—because some residents blame the phenomenon on Taiwanese newcomers.[11]

Taiwanese immigrants attribute such public displays of unease and animosity to the fact that many white people are not used to seeing well-off Chinese professionals. Whites, say the newcomers, still have the notion that immigrants should start out poor and work their way up. But a proposal to add Mandarin classes in Cupertino's public schools really struck a raw nerve. When the school board began to discuss the possibility of a voluntary two-way Mandarin-English program at a local elementary school in 1997, it encountered vehement opposition from some longtime Cupertino residents. "What the hell, Mandarin in the schools? This is the United States," representatives of the old establishment were grumbling. The school board's Taiwanese-born member Barry Chang started receiving hate mail and angry phone calls urging him to "go back to where he came from." "I was at the point of thinking of buying a gun and carrying a gun," he confessed.[12]

Here, too, the attacks have made the Chinese realize that they have to organize politically. Now nine out of the city's twenty-eight elected officials are Asian American. What is most impressive is that they were able to campaign on a wide range of community issues and won appointments by not relying on just Chinese votes (23.8 percent of Cupertino's population is Chinese). Also, since the job of the mayor rotates among members of the city council, Cupertino has already had two Chinese American mayors: Michael Chang, a professor, and Patrick Kwok, a civil engineer.[13]

Elsewhere in Southern California, three Chinese Americans—all of them immigrants—won city council seats in 2003. Laura Lee, born in Taiwan, came to the United States to earn a graduate degree in biology and switched to a career in real estate before winning a seat in Cerritos; Chi Mui and Peter Yao both came from Hong Kong and became the first Asians ever to be elected to the city councils of San Gabriel and Claremont, respectively.[14] Meanwhile, the political progress of American-born Asians has been painfully slow. A few Asian civil rights activists, campaigning as populists, have gotten elected to local school boards and city councils, even to a governor's office (Washington's Gary Locke). But the headway made by the immigrant Chinese is more remarkable, especially since they have traditionally been viewed as basically apolitical, coming from countries not accustomed to democratic practices.

Yet the professionals and entrepreneurs among new Chinese immigrants have a number of advantages, not the least of which are their financial resources. Many of the winning candidates are successful real estate brokers or high-tech entrepreneurs with their own money to put into campaigns, and are capable of tapping into a large pool of willing contributors among their fellow Chinese. In American politics, the importance of mass mobilization pales next to one's ability to fill the campaign chest with money. Chinese American professionals have plenty of that. In addition, these new suburbanites have immigrated to this country with a strong sense of pride and are confident that their affluence can buy them the life they want in a place of their choice. As a group, they have made an effort to build communities that suit their purposes, and when challenged, as was the case in Monterey Park and Cupertino, they have demonstrated that they can convert their strong social and professional ties to political use.

There has also been an effort to create Chinese American political organizations with national reach. Committee of 100 is composed of Chinese Americans in prominent leadership positions in American society and institutions who bring their clout to various issues concerning the Chinese American community and U.S.-China relations. Cause-Vision 21—the Center for Asian Americans United for Self-Empowerment—is dedicated to advancing the political empowerment of Asian Americans through voter registration and education, community outreach, and leadership development. "We aim to motivate young people to take an interest in politics, cajole old politicians to become excited about new ideas, and furnish future historians with a first draft," the center's publication *Cause&Effects* boldly proclaims. It is a prototype for organizations that are trying to bring professional immigrant communities scattered through the suburbs to political activism as well as to train the next generation in politics.

Chapter 29

The Money Trail

IDENTITY POLITICS

The full potential of Chinese Americans in electoral politics remains unrealized, but the well-off among them have found an instant way to engage politically—through campaign contributions.

Ethnic representation is extremely important to many middle-class Chinese Americans, 71 percent of whom, according to a recent survey, would vote for Asian American candidates.[1] If no Chinese American candidate runs in their own district, they are willing to financially support promising Chinese candidates anywhere in the country—if they think that they can help elect the first ethnic Chinese mayor, governor, congressman, or senator. Although the affiliation of Chinese American voters is split among Democratic (with a slight edge), Republican, and no party affiliation at all, there is a clear trend for them to vote for candidates with Asian surnames.[2]

Exit polls in the 1992 U.S. Senate race indicated that Democrat Barbara Boxer got 52 percent of the Asian American vote, while Republican Bruce Herschenson got 48 percent. Six years later, the Chinese American Voters Education Committee found that Chinese voters in San Francisco preferred Matt Fong, a Republican, over Boxer by a more than a three-to-one margin. At the same time, with the exception of voting for Fong, Chinese continued to lean toward the Democratic

Party. The exit poll conducted during the primaries showed that Fong won three-fourths of the Chinese American votes cast in the Senate race, while 81 percent of these same voters chose a Democratic gubernatorial candidate.[3] San Francisco attorney Bruce Quan Jr., who is a Democrat, openly supported the bid of Republican Matt Fong. "Just being there in the Senate will raise the level of consciousness in Congress and the nation of who Asian Americans are," he stated as justification for his decision.

Matt Fong may have gotten the majority of the Chinese vote because of his mother, a Democrat and the former California state secretary March Fong Eu. When she ran for governor in 1988, she entered the race saying, "Chinese Americans . . . identify with me," and claiming that they would "even cross party lines to vote for me." They did more than that. They supported her with substantial contributions. Chinese Consolidated Benevolent Associations (CCBA) in different Chinatowns hosted fifty- to-hundred-table banquets, requiring all the member associations to purchase tables at $500 to $1,000 each. That same year Lily Chen, a Democrat from Southern California and a onetime Monterey Park mayor, entered the race for the U.S. House of Representatives banking on the "we can do it too" sentiment of Chinese Americans nationwide. "I've been receiving support from New York to San Francisco. You know, I have financial contributions from all over the place, just like March Fong Eu and S.B. Woo, and many other Asian American candidates," she explained when asked why it was that the $70,000 in donations she received nearly all came from the East Coast. "The enthusiasm may not be because of me," she also conceded, "but people think that after 120 years [of Chinese presence in this country], it's about time that we have a Chinese American in the House of Representatives."[4]

In 1992, when S.B. Woo, a onetime lieutenant governor of Delaware, decided to run for Senate, about 70 percent of the $250,000 he raised for the effort came from Chinese Americans outside of his home state. Those who gave him money did not know or care what his political positions were. For his part, he was reluctant to take on controversial issues, preferring to appeal to the pride—and pocketbooks—of Chinese Americans nationwide. He refused to get involved with the case of Vincent Chin, a Chinese American engineer who was murdered in Detroit after being mistaken for a Japanese. As Woo said at the time, "I detect among young Asian-Americans the tendency to copy after the . . . action patterns of black Americans. . . . But our educational level is much higher. Financially, we are better off. Our cultural base is that we're patient, we're deep thinkers."[5]

The benchmark for Chinese American candidates' nationwide fundraising was Los Angeles city councilman Michael Woo's 1993 campaign to become Los Angeles mayor. Of the $12 million he collected, more than $6 million came from the Chinese community.[6] By the time Gary Locke ran for governor of the State of Washington in 1996, the fundraising tactics targeting Chinese Americans were substantially refined. In addition to a nationwide tour, his campaign took advantage of the Chinese American print, radio, TV, and Internet media—many of them subsidiaries of major media outlets in Asia. By projecting an image of someone who is able to bring Asian Americans "to the table where discussions are made," although his poor immigrant grandfather once worked as a houseboy less than a mile from the governor's mansion, he stirred a great deal of excitement in places such as Hong Kong, Taiwan, and mainland China.[7] This allowed him to present himself to the domestic audience as an American politician with Pacific Rim ties—a profile that seemed to elevate him into a prominent leader of the Democratic Party, which in turn gained him more support from Chinese Americans, seduced by his great American success story.

It would be naive to think that minorities make financial contributions to politicians simply out of ethnic pride. Like anybody else, Chinese Americans expect to gain access to politicians and influence their policies in a way favorable to themselves in return. Campaign funds being the lifeblood of any politician, all sorts of Pan-Asian and Chinese American lobby groups are willing to donate funds to local, state, and federal officials who might advocate and address their special interests.

Chinese American "generosity" has not been lost on American politicians. As early as the mid-1970s, the Democratic National Committee (DNC) began to focus on identifying potential Asian American financial supporters, and by the 1980s it had established an Asian Pacific Caucus. Ten percent of Los Angeles mayor Tom Bradley's 1982 and 1986 election campaign donations came from Asian Americans. But the Democratic Party really took notice in 1992, when Bill Clinton netted $200,000 at one fund-raiser in Monterey Park. The Republican Party has tried to appeal to Asian Americans for contributions as well.

John Miller, the vice president of the conservative Center for Equal Opportunity, predicted that Asian Americans could turn into the Jews of the twenty-first century; namely, at the end of the twentieth century, they already gave to political campaigns at a higher rate than any other racial or ethnic group except Jews.[8] If they keep up their level of political giving, immigrant historian Louis Winnick said, they could complete their transformation from immigrant pariahs to "America's trophy population." Republican Ron K. Unz, the author of the controversial Proposition 227—the successful California initiative to dismantle bilingual education—thinks that "Asians are similar to Jewish voters, but without the liberal guilt," and suggested that "if Republicans were able to pocket a good share of Asian support right now, they may never stop thanking themselves later."[9]

As American campaigns become more expensive, politicians desperate for cash are increasingly turning to soft money—contributions from corporations, labor unions, and wealthy individuals, which are unregulated by campaign laws if given to candidates indirectly, through partisan political action committees. (This was the case until the McCain-Feingold Campaign Reform Act in 2002, that is. Now soft money contributions are redirected through a loophole to what is called the "527 political groups.") The competition for the few potential donors with serious money is fierce. Those who contribute expect serious returns.

One group that has appeared, seemingly out of nowhere, with a lot of money and a willingness to contribute, is the immigrant entrepreneurs with transpacific connections—the ethnic Chinese from Hong Kong, Taiwan, mainland China, and Southeast Asia who have invested in the United States. UC Berkeley anthropologist Aihwa Ong calls them "flexible citizens."[10] They are the opportunistic global capitalists whose transnational corporations have branch offices on both sides of the Pacific and who maintain residences in California or New York in addition to their homes in Taipei or Hong Kong—the kind of people who, in the words of one investor "based" in San Francisco, "can live anywhere in the world, but it must be near an airport."

Taiwan has been the second largest source of direct investment from Asia into the United States after Japan. In addition to creating a symbiotic relationship between Taiwan and California's Silicon Valley, its latest investment has gone into the plastics, petrochemical, metal, timber, furniture, cable television, and computer industries; the production of medical supplies; transportation; banking; real estate; food and beverage; and import-export, particularly in Texas, but also in Louisiana, Mississippi, New Jersey, Delaware, and Illinois. One of the largest investors is Formosa Plastics Group—a $15 billion global enterprise based in Taiwan, with several subsidiaries in the United States.

Mainland Chinese investment is quickly catching up. In 1999, there were already some six hundred branches and subsidiaries of mainland Chinese companies in the United States, with a total investment of $800 million, including garment and home appliance manufacturing, banking, and insurance.

Much of the overseas Chinese investment has been welcomed by America's de-industrialized states and cash-poor urban centers. With office space in Los Angeles going for one-tenth of the price of its equivalent in Hong Kong, Chinese investors have gobbled up prime office towers from downtown to Santa Monica.[11] They have picked up many of the properties unloaded by earlier Japanese investors on both coasts. Wealthy overseas Chinese own about 10 percent of the real estate in downtown San Francisco, primarily hotels and commercial buildings—a phenomenon the *San Francisco Chronicle* columnist Herb Caen has dubbed the "Hongkongization of San Francisco." Chinese transnational capital is also behind the development of new suburban Chinese landscapes all across the country, resplendent with shopping malls, supermarkets, apartment complexes, and restaurant chains—the Little Taipeis and Chinese Beverly Hills. Henry Cheng, whose Hong Kong–based New World Development Corporation owned the Ramada hotel chain in the United States during the 1990s, was the lead investor in Donald Trump's $3 billion Riverside South apartment building project, built in Manhattan on top of the abandoned rail yards.[12] George Sternlieb, Rutgers University expert in urban development, has been quoted as saying, "There's nothing wrong with New York that a million Chinese couldn't cure."

Municipal officials appreciate the benefits of Chinese investment to the local economy and have welcomed Chinese political contributions. In exchange, Chinese investors receive speedy permits, tax breaks, easements, and relaxed zoning regulations, or, when their contributions are substantial enough, a warm welcome at city halls, governor's mansions, and even the White House. In the 1960s and 1970s civil rights activists spent years to lay the groundwork for Chinese American grassroots political participation by promoting voter registration, naturalization, and bilingual balloting, and by mobilizing the community on issues that mattered to it, but they met with only limited success. The Johnny-come-lately fleeting investors of the decades that followed, however, have made it directly into the inner sanctum of political power and have received appointments to various community outreach and city planning commissions.[13] As the most powerful group among Chinese Americans now, they claim to represent the whole of the community. They say that they care for the well-being of all Chinese Americans, but that it is "money politics," after all, that can gain Chinese Americans recognition and respect.

Some Chinese American community activists have gone along with this logic (AAFE, for instance) and allied themselves with the transnational investors, persuaded that any crack in the system of white old-boys' networks is a step forward. Besides, it is clear that without money in American politics no one gets anywhere. Yet it is these very investors that have been the force of gentrification in Chinese American communities; it is their speculation that has escalated the real estate prices and forced small groceries and restaurants to close, working-class people to move out, and their factory jobs to disappear. Things have only gotten worse now that Chinese American developers and transnational investors in many parts of the country can conspire with local officials to push through development projects over the objections of local residents, and dismiss criticism as an outdated expression of preglobalization provincial mentality.

In 1997, Henry Der, at the time executive director of Chinese for Affirmative Action, publicly questioned whether Chinese donors ever "talk about welfare reform, human rights, bilingual education, student loans, housing and health insurance for the poor with the president? Or is it even realistic to expect Asian Americans who can afford to donate large sums of money to act differently from other well-heeled donors, who, more often than not, pursue private interests?"[14] According to UC Berkeley professor Ling-chi Wang, "The losers in all of this are the idealists in our communities. The original vision of an Asian American movement . . . has been pushed aside in favor of moneyed politics in which opportunists buy instant recognition and influence with cold, hard cash. And since politicians are always hungry for cash, they go along with these opportunists, pretending they are responding to grassroots concerns."[15]

Resentment of these moneyed "outsiders" is not limited to Chinese Americans. Their aggressively opportunistic tactics caused a much stronger reaction when their contributions to President Clinton's re-election campaign developed into a financing scandal, igniting a wave of China bashing and political persecution of Chinese Americans accused of disloyalty.

THE CLINTON CAMPAIGN FINANCING SCANDAL

When Republicans won a majority of Congress in 1994 under Newt Gingrich's aggressive leadership, President Clinton's popularity plunged so ominously that in April 1995 he was reduced to desperately uttering, "The president is relevant here."[16] He launched an expensive, massive TV-ad comeback campaign, although it was well over a year before Election Day, which ended up costing $2 million a week for a total of $85 million. The staggering amount had to be raised quickly, mostly as soft money, and many potential donors were lured by the prospect of a photo op with the president. Mr. Chen, a New York Chinatown garment subcontractor with a factory on Grand Street, went to the Waldorf Astoria and paid $12,500 to have his picture taken with Bill Clinton. He considered it money well spent. He could use it to show off to friends and impress his employees and labor inspectors.

Large contributions could secure a private meeting with the president. Guests were invited to more than one hundred White House coffee sessions, then asked for money afterward. Their contributions totaled $27 million.[17] More prominent contributors, including the chairman of Occidental Petroleum, were overnight guests in the Lincoln bedroom at the White House, and later gave $100,000 to the Democratic National Committee—for a total of $5.2 million, according to the Campaign Study Group.[18] This sleazy operation, marred by sloppy bookkeeping, was a scandal waiting to happen. Sure enough, it took an Asian turn of the screw to blow it into the open.

On October 7, 1996, conservative columnist William Safire of the *New York Times* "blew the cover" on a "sinister plot" by Asian businessmen to influence the policies of the president. Safire had learned that an Asian conglomerate, the Lippo Group, owned by the family of the Sino-Indonesian businessman James Riady, "funneled" $1 million to the Democratic Party using ethnic Chinese holders of a U.S. green card as a conduit. "The Asian Connection," Safire charged, was influencing U.S. policy toward Indonesia as well as mainland China, where Lippo maintained significant investment.

Evidently, the Democratic Party was so pleased with Riady's contribution that it appointed Lippo's onetime executive and by then U.S. immigrant turned citizen John Huang to the Democratic National Committee as its vice chairman for finance. Huang's brief was to continue to tap into Asian and Asian American sources and to raise $7 million for the campaign. Huang eventually did raise nearly $5 million from Asians, but he was careless in drawing a distinction between Chinese contributors from abroad and contributions by American citizens of Chinese or Asian descent. This is not to say that the Republican Party was not involved in shaky fundraising schemes of its own; it's just that its fund-raisers were more experienced in negotiating the very blurry line that divides illegal practices from legal fundraising.[19]

In April 1996, U.S. vice president Al Gore attended a fundraising luncheon at the Hsi Lai Buddhist temple in Hacienda Heights, California, which was organized by John Huang and Maria Hsia and raised $166,750. Of that total, $55,000 was laundered through monks and nuns, who made the contributions in their own names and were then reimbursed by the temple from its general funds—not a pretty picture, given that the temple's tax-exempt status was used for partisan politics. When questioned, Gore insisted that the lunch had been a community outreach event and that he had no idea it would be a fundraiser.

Then there was Yah Lin (Charlie) Trie, friendly with the Clintons since the Little Rock days when they frequented his Chinese restaurant. He received more than $900,000 in wire transfers between 1994 and 1996 from a Chinese developer—a foreign businessman not eligible to contribute to U.S. political campaigns—and then distributed the money to U.S. citizens to make the donations. Among the guests invited through Trie to sip coffee with the president in the White House was the head of a Chinese government-owned company later charged with smuggling two thousand AK-47 automatic rifles into the United States.[20] As a result, the White House was accused of having solicited and laundered millions of dollars from donors that included drug smugglers, illegal arms dealers, and even Chinese Communist officials, prompting the Republicans to launch an attack on Clinton and the DNC not just for breaking the law by taking foreign cash in exchange for favors, but for "treason."

Particularly damning in this respect were the activities of yet another Chinese American fund-raiser, Johnny Chung, who made at least forty-nine visits to the White House despite the fact that a National Security Council official had branded him a "hustler." He purportedly received $300,000 for Democratic campaigns from Liu Chao-ying, an officer in China's People's Liberation Army (PLA) and executive with China Aerospace, Beijing's state-run rocket-manufacturing company. Liu's father happened to be the senior-ranking PLA commander, General Liu Huaqing, who as a vice chairman of China's Central Military Commission and a member of the Standing Committee of the Chinese Communist Party's Politburo—the apex of Chinese political power—was said to be in charge of China's program to acquire modern Western military technology. Thus Liu's contribution to the Democratic Party in the United States—for those wishing to see conspiracy—could certainly be interpreted as China's attempt to break into American national security, even though no one ever gave evidence of such a possibility.

Taking the lead from the *Washington Post*'s Bob Woodward, who reported that the woman who had made the arrangement for Al Gore to visit the Buddhist temple in California was "a Chinese agent doing the bidding of Beijing," the press took free shots at uncovering "sinister Red China plots" and spreading fanciful rumors about the "unlawful activities" of amateurs like John Huang and other easy targets, none of which was ever established for a fact. But the broader thrust of the accusations was that Clinton and Gore sold out our national security interests in exchange for campaign contributions from a foreign power—in this case the Chinese government, with the help of Chinese Americans, whom the press all too readily identified as "Red China spies." William Safire inflamed the situation by throwing around phrases like "Asian connection," "insidious networking," and "penetration by Asian interests." Senator Robert Bennett of Utah decried "classic activities on the part of an Asian who comes out of that culture and who embarks on an activity related to intelligence gathering."[21] Before long the foreign "Asian connection" and "Asian Americans" became synonymous with political corruption and foreign subversion,[22] and the China / Chinese American conspiracy took on a life of its own. Congress was agitated enough to begin numerous investigations. In the midst of it all, a *National Review* cover featured a bucktoothed President Clinton in a coolie hat with first lady Hillary Clinton in a Maoist uniform and Vice President Al Gore in a Buddhist monk's robe, holding a donation cup.

The Chinese American community was stunned. Meanwhile, a large number of donations that the Democratic Party received from other Asian Americans independently of John Huang were erroneously attributed to him, and the unfortunate result was that all Asian American donors were implicated in Huang's indiscretions and became suspected of "foreign influence."

Asian American leaders called the singling out of John Huang racism, and accused the media and the xenophobic Republican Party of using double standards. A foundation controlled by the conservative Republican Senator Jesse Helms, who chairs the Senate Foreign Relations Committee, the critics pointed out, had taken almost a quarter of a million dollars from the government of Taiwan. Moreover, the GOP got plenty of illegal donations from European interest groups, yet its loyalty was never questioned. (Thomas Kramer, a foreign national, was fined $332,600 for illegal contributions using conduits.)[23] Questions were never asked of Jewish fundraisers lobbying for U.S. support of Israel. Unfortunately, most of the media seemed fascinated by the "Yellow Peril" syndrome, although the campaign finance scandal involved much more than the bit part played by Asian American donors.[24] The amount raised by Huang and Trie was about $4.5 million—out of the total of $2.2 billion raised and spent in the 1996 federal election. Tobacco giant Philip Morris alone gave more than $4 million.[25] Most of the soft money came from U.S. citizens, companies, and unions. Foreign money was but a tiny percentage. The *New York Times* columnist Frank Rich denounced the double standard applied to Asian Americans and called them victims of a "drive-by-shooting style of political hyperbole."

Some Asian American leaders suggested that John Huang should be defended as a symbol of the growing financial clout of Asian Americans and their efforts to empower themselves. Keith Umemoto, chair of the DNC Asian Pacific Islander American Caucus, suggested that

John Huang ought to be applauded for leaving the private sector to devote his energy to public service and for "serving as a bridge between influential Asian donors he had access to and the Asian Pacific American community in general."[26] (John Huang himself denied any wrongdoing. The only motive he gave for going to the DNC was the empowerment of Asian Americans, and the only way for their voice to be heard in the United States, he maintained, was through significant contributions to politicians.)

While it is true that China and Chinese Americans were made scapegoats in the all-out attack on President Clinton during a heated national presidential campaign, what Huang and others of his ilk did was still illegal. Bribing politicians is unacceptable if the government is to be made more open, more honest, and more accountable, and John Huang's actions, although he may well have been a victim of racism, undermined American democracy. Rather than defending Huang, responsible Chinese Americans expressed support for campaign financing reform and saw as the most crucial task at hand the rescuing of American politics from being taken over by special, especially moneyed, interests of every kind. "We have to be fools to think that Riady contributed up to $1 million to promote Asian American political power," commented Professor Ling-chi Wang.[27] "The only thing that distinguishes him [Huang] from other influence peddlers in Washington is his race."[28]

In an interview with the FBI during the investigation of his contributions, "the hustler" Johnny Chung admitted that he was trying to "put powder on his face"—trying to look good by inviting big businessmen from Asian companies to the White House, because his access to President Clinton made him and his business look good. "In Asia you need to get close to people in power," he explained.[29] True words, spoken by a person who was clearly not interested in the Asian American community.

In the end, the conflict between Asian American community activists and those willing to go along with the moneyed interests was muted. The community activists could not be too forceful in their criticism, given the pervasiveness of racial attacks on Chinese and Asian Americans. The defenders were lethargic, realizing that they had no grounds for defending Huang's and others' illegal actions. Nevertheless, the fundamental split between the two was instructive in that it showed how community-based activists are concerned with politics in the domestic civil rights arena, while the other side operates from the vantage point of its transnational connections. The community as a whole retreated from public discourse in the hopes of containing the fallout.

After successful reelection, the Clinton administration did not bother to apologize to the Chinese and Asian American communities for the trouble its fundraising schemes had caused them. Nor did the reelected president bother to appoint Asians to prominent political positions. A coalition of Asian Pacific American organizations led by the Congressional Asian Pacific American Caucus Institute tried to push for an Asian American cabinet appointment. Soon after Clinton's reelection in 1996, University of California chancellor Chang-lin Tien seemed poised to receive an appointment as the secretary of energy, but the media frenzy over the "Chinese-Indonesian connection" put an end to any such hopes. Months later, Bill Lann Lee, a longtime director of the NAACP Legal Defense Fund, was named acting assistant attorney general. By installing Lee as a "recess appointment," Bill Clinton, who did not want to expend his political capital on a fight for an Asian American appointment, could bypass an expected nasty Senate confirmation process required for high-ranking administration jobs.

To appease the critics of its campaign fundraising indiscretions, the Democratic Party threw Asian Americans to the wolves. It agreed to an audit of campaign contributions that would focus primarily on Asian American donors, who were subjected to an overzealous investigation by the FBI, were harassed and intimidated, and were treated as "aliens" involved in treasonous activities. Neurologist Suzanne Ahn from Dallas, Texas, who described her family's cumulative donations to both parties as being in the "six figures," was interrogated by the FBI, the Democratic National Committee auditors, and the news media, who obtained her name from the DNC. Los Angeles–based attorney Anthony Ching was told by the DNC investigators that his $5,000 contribution to Clinton's reelection campaign would be "invalidated" if he didn't cooperate. Ching asked the DNC to returned his money instead.[30] The DNC in the end returned $2,825,600 as illegally obtained funds. John Huang pleaded guilty to a felony conspiracy charge for violating campaign finance laws and was sentenced to one year of probation; most of the other offending Asian American fundraisers were also charged and convicted. Their treatment, however, merely signaled the beginning of a new wave of China bashing, which continued to target Chinese Americans and question their loyalties.

PRESUMED GUILTY

Soon after the campaign fundraising scandal, the Chinese American community found itself under media attack again on account of government allegations that a Chinese American research scientist at Los Alamos National Laboratory in New Mexico, Wen Ho Lee, was a spy for the People's Republic of China. It all started with an intelligence report that in 1992 China had tested a bomb suspiciously similar to the Los Alamos–designed W-88, which was considered one of the smallest and most highly optimized nuclear weapons in the world. The question was, Did China steal the design through spying?

Many American weapons experts familiar with the Chinese nuclear program and even FBI agents who had investigated the case believed that the Chinese could have invented in the 1990s the miniaturized warheads that America had developed in the 1950s. Others were quick to point out that most of the details on U.S. missiles were available on a Web site maintained by the Federation of American Scientists. China could have made its own bombs by processing information gathered from magazines and scientific literature obtained legally. But the director of counterintelligence at the Department of Energy, Notra Trulock, refused to believe that the Chinese were capable of developing the weapon on their own. He fixated on the assumption that China would use only an ethnic Chinese to spy for it. So although the spy, if there was one, could have been any of the scientists from a half dozen national nuclear-weapons-design laboratories or an employee of one of the many plants that manufacture the parts, since they all had the blueprints, the list of suspects swiftly shrank from the employees of Los Alamos and Lawrence Livermore research laboratories who had traveled to China to the scientists of Chinese heritage who had worked directly or peripherally on the W-88 design and had had contacts with Chinese scientists. Without investigating anyone else, Wen Ho Lee was identified as the only person who had access to the weapon information and the motivation to leak it to the Chinese.

The choice of Lee as the spy for Communist China was far from logical, as he was a native of Taiwan and had openly expressed his sympathy for Taiwanese independence. During the investigation, he had even admitted to providing unclassified scientific documents to Taiwan's military research center, Chung Shan Institute of Science and Technology, which was involved in developing nuclear weapons. Also, he had in the past been trapped into cooperating with the FBI in an investigation of another Chinese American scientist, while his wife was recruited by the bureau to act as an informant on the activities of visiting Chinese scientists.

But his case came to the attention of California representative Christopher Cox, the head of the House Select Committee on U.S. National Security and Military/Commercial Concerns, just as it was investigating the Clinton administration for being soft on China in exchange for campaign contributions. Cox immediately saw the potential of using an indictment against Wen Ho Lee to help the charges against Clinton stick. Suddenly, although the Department of Energy counterintelligence director's unverified accusations had previously been discarded by the FBI, the CIA, the White House, and the Department of Defense, they became bombshells in Cox's committee report. The Chinese could now be portrayed as stealing not only our political innocence through campaign contributions but our rocket technology and nuclear secrets as well.

The real damage was done when members of the Cox committee leaked the spy story to the ever-hungry-for-a-Clinton-scandal press. A Pulitzer Prize–winning reporter for the *New York Times* published the "information" without corroboration, and soon Congress and the media were locked in a game of one-upmanship, describing Lee's crime in ever more superlative-laden rhetoric. As the storm gathered, Clinton's newly appointed energy secretary, Bill Richardson, weighing the risk of losing his nomination as the vice presidential candidate for the Democratic Party, buckled under and ordered that Wen Ho Lee be summarily dealt with.

Lee was thrown in jail, although the government still had no evidence to convict him as a spy. But since he was prosecuted under the cold war–era Atomic Energy Act, he was put in shackles and locked up in solitary confinement. Members of his immediate family were permitted to visit him for one hour each month but were not allowed to speak to him in Chinese, which was the language they spoke at home. Comparable conditions were rarely experienced by even the most vicious convicted criminals, yet the only wrongdoing the government could charge Lee with, after five years of relentless hounding by at times more than one hundred FBI agents who were working on his case, was his downloading of several weapons codes from the laboratory's secure computer system onto an unsecured one. This is a commonly ignored security infraction. Former CIA director John Deutch, for instance, potentially caused a much graver threat to national security when he downloaded top secret files onto his unsecured home computer (which a family member had been using to surf pornography Web sites), yet he was only disciplined; he did not lose his job, much less end up in jail.

The treatment of Lee was so outrageous that the U.S. District Court judge in New Mexico who was put in charge of the trial ended his sentencing with a personal statement to Lee: "I believe you were terribly wronged by being held in custody pretrial . . . under demeaning, unnecessarily punitive conditions. . . . [The top decision makers in the executive branch] have caused embarrassment by the way this case was handled. They did not embarrass me alone. They have embarrassed our entire nation. . . . I sincerely apologize to you."[31]

The initially cautious Chinese American community, still licking the wounds inflicted by Clinton's campaign fund-raising scandal, picked up Lee's cause as soon as the government began questioning the loyalty of all foreign-born Chinese American scientists and engineers. Those who had for years quietly sweated away in research laboratories and universities, unrecognized, unappreciated, and underpaid, now turned their anger into action and set up the Wen Ho Lee Defense Fund, raising hundreds of thousands of dollars for his legal bills. Other supporters established Web sites and organized rallies and teach-ins around the country, demanding that members of Congress stop the persecution of Lee. A number of eminent non-Chinese scientists and members of the American Physical Society and the American Association for the Advancement of Science took up his cause, and both professional organizations issued statements condemning the government's harsh treatment of their fellow scientist. Brave people were willing to risk their careers to speak out in Lee's favor, seeing how groundless the accusations against him were.

Just how lacking in merit and driven by political agenda the government's case was became obvious when an overzealous member of the House Select Committee on U.S. National Security and Military/Commercial Concerns confused Wen Ho Lee with Bill Lann Lee, who was at the time waiting to be confirmed as assistant attorney general for civil rights. Yet because of the way the government handled Wen Ho Lee's case, many of the more than fifteen thousand Chinese American scientists employed by the defense sector found themselves subjected to innuendo and distressing jokes as their loyalty became questioned by their bosses and colleagues. Numerous security clearances were withdrawn, promotions denied, and people forced into early retirement.

The devastating impact was fully revealed in a survey conducted by the Committee of 100 and the Anti-Defamation League soon after Wen Ho Lee's release from prison: 68 percent of Americans felt negative toward Chinese Americans; 32 percent believed that Chinese Americans were more loyal to China than to the United States; and 46 percent thought that Chinese Americans passing secrets to China was a problem.

As always, the issue had boiled down to this: Because of their hostility toward China, Americans could not trust Chinese Americans. And, once again, Chinese Americans became collateral damage in the conflict between China and the United States.

Chapter 30

The China / Chinese
American Tangle

CHINA BASHING

Before the fall of the Soviet Union, U.S. policy makers had entertained the idea of an alliance between the United States and China. Liberal Democrats and moderate Republicans promoted the policy of "constructive engagement," willing to give China a role in assuring regional and global stability. Since the fall of the Soviet Union, the neoconservatives and the Far Right have considered eventual confrontation with Beijing inevitable. From their prism, Washington's efforts to co-opt China into a Western-dominated global economic system seem dangerously naive.

Instrumental in promoting the Sinophobic view is the "Blue Team" (styling itself so as to rival the "Red Team" of the so-called "panda-huggers" who seek a close and cooperative relationship with Beijing). It is composed of like-minded policy makers, activists, and analysts drawn from among members of Congress, congressional staff, lobby groups, conservative journalists, and think tanks—such as the Heritage Foundation, Gaffney's Center for Security Policy, the William Casey Institute (named for the CIA chief who ran the Contra War), and the U.S. Business and Industry Council, a protectionist group. Some of the roughly forty Blue Team members, who keep in touch via e-mail and sometimes gather for drinks at the American Tavern on

F Street in Washington, D.C., hold critical official positions (Lewis "Scooter" Libby, for instance, is Dick Cheney's top national security adviser, and Douglas Feith is under secretary of defense for policy in Donald Rumsfeld's Pentagon), but many prefer to operate behind the scenes and relish their role as "insurgents."[1] On the whole, the team rejects not only the Clintonian concept of "strategic partnership" with China, but also the mainstream Republican policy of trade-based engagement to encourage reforms.

The team's handiwork was clearly visible in the report issued by the US-China Security Review Commission in 2002, which blamed U.S. policies for helping the Chinese leadership "achieve stunning economic growth and the modernization of their military industrial complex." While China schemes, its authors warned, Washington sleeps. "U.S. Government officials know woefully little about prevailing Chinese perceptions and strategic thinking." The report urged the rethinking of America's policy of "constructive engagement" with Beijing.[2] Instead, it maintained that "raising U.S. military strength in East Asia is the key to coping with the rise of China to great-power status," and that for this reason, "U.S. armed forces must retain their military preeminence."

One of the first issues ripe for rethinking is the trade imbalance between the United States and China. America's record high foreign trade deficit of $489.4 billion recorded in 2003 owed much to the shortfall of $124 billion in trading with China (by far surpassing the $66 billion shortfall with Japan). Critics blame it for the loss of several hundred thousand U.S. jobs, which organized labor attributes to China's "unfair trade advantage." The decline of the U.S. stock market, economic recession, unemployment, and job insecurity, along with the growing trade deficit, have provided American protectionists and labor with a reason to view the outsourcing of jobs to China as the chief problem and the speed of China's economic growth as cause for alarm. According to one study, China accounted for 25 percent of the world's economic growth from 1995 to 2002 (measured by purchasing power)—more than the United States.[3]

However, at this rate of growth, China's economic development is vulnerable itself. China needs to spend heavily on infrastructure, and its demand for raw materials is insatiable. Its share in the world consumption of copper, tin, zinc, platinum, steel, and iron ore rose from less than 5 percent in 1990 to 16 percent in 2002.[4] In 2003, in fact, China became the first country to import more than $1 billion worth of American scrap metal,[5] and surpassed the United States as the world's largest steel importer,[6] pushing up the prices of all raw materials globally in the process. That same year its electric consumption grew by 15 percent[7] and its oil imports by 30 percent (to keep up with auto sales that grew by 70 percent), making China the world's second largest petroleum user after the United States.

By 2030, China is expected to have more cars than the United States and import as much oil as the United States does today. With 60 percent of its oil imports coming from the Middle East, it is bound to emerge as a competitor for influence in the region, which could lead to a collision of interests with the United States.[8] Some scholars, in fact, see America's current adventure in Iraq as a way to control the distribution of oil supply to other nations and a way to have leverage over China's economic growth.[9] Shaping the Middle East oil region under U.S. control has therefore become a crucial national security issue. Sixty-three years ago, the United States blocked Japan's access to Indonesian oil fields to thwart its expansionary policy in the Pacific region, which eventually led to the attack on Pearl Harbor. Hawkish talk at the Pentagon about China as a strategic competitor reinforces the possibility of collision. A stable and powerful China will be constantly challenging the status quo in Asia. An unstable and relatively weak China could be dangerous because its leaders might try to bolster their power with foreign military adventure.[10] This has raised concerns at the Department of Defense about China's development of long-range nuclear and shorter-range missile capabilities, as well as the general "proliferation activities of the Chinese government."[11]

The *Washington Times* and the *Weekly Standard* reliably carry the views of the Blue Team. Both have been promoting containment of China and confrontation with its Communist regime, reminiscent of the methods used on the Soviet Union.[12] Just before the 9/11 crisis hit, the Bush administration was busy planning to build a "missile shield" that would include Japan and Taiwan under its system of protection. The Philippines have a security pact with the United States, Thailand is a major U.S. non-NATO ally, Singapore provides logistical facilities for U.S. forces, and, according to Douglas J. Feith, under secretary of defense for policy at the Pentagon, there are "degrees of cooperation" with Indonesia and Malaysia. The United States has also shown a growing interest in obtaining naval access to Cam Ranh Bay, its former base in Vietnam. Although the Pentagon claims that this new global positioning and realignment are not aimed at any particular country, it is hard for Beijing not to see it otherwise.

That U.S. policy has a confrontational edge was hard to deny when on April 1, 2001, a U.S. surveillance plane got intercepted by Chinese fighter jets over the South China Sea as it was gathering radio and telecommunication signals from China. One of the Chinese fighters collided with the surveillance plane and forced it to land at an airport in China, stoking nationalist sentiment in both countries. Chinese Americans once again became victims of racial profiling and scapegoating in the United States. A local radio talk show host in Springfield, Illinois, said that all Chinese restaurants should be boycotted and all Chinese sent home to "their country."[13] *National Review Online* editor Jonah Goldberg declared, "I will be in favor of apologizing [to the Chinese for the collision incident] the moment they apologize for all those menus they keep leaving outside my front door."[14] Tension between the two nations only eased, at least for the time being, with the 9/11 attacks, which provided the two sides with the shared interest of combating "international terrorists."

CHINA'S CAPITALIST TURN

Bashing the current Chinese regime seems wrongheaded. The Chinese Communist Party has transformed China into a procapitalist market economy, doing exactly what American policy makers had hoped for since the beginning of the Cold War. Since then, the United States has rebuilt Japan and strengthened the stability of Taiwan, South Korea, the Philippines, Thailand, and other countries in the region against the spread of Chinese communism and turned the whole region into an environment friendly to global capital. With the resurgence of the U.S. economy after two decades of relative decline at the end of the 1990s, accompanied by the eclipse of Japan as its competitor, the Pacific has become to a large extent a Great American Lake.

The most impressive accomplishment of American global strategy by far has been the integration of China into the world capitalist marketplace. The combination of plentiful labor, low wages, low taxation, and repression of labor activism has made China into one of the most attractive investment sites for foreign corporations. China has become the most important manufacturing center of the world. Fifty-four percent of the world's DVD players, 28 percent of cellular phones, 13 percent of digital cameras, 30 percent of desktop computers, 12 percent of notebook computers, 27 percent of color televisions, 30 percent of air conditioners, 25 percent of washing machines, and 20 percent of refrigerators are now produced or assembled in China. In addition, multinational companies and their local Chinese contractors also dominate other major exports, such as clothing and textiles.

More important, China is the most popular country for American business investment. Forty percent of "Chinese exports" to the United States are actually produced by and for American multinational companies. This is the case because investment in China has been so profitable that the chief executive officer of Nissan Motor Co., Carlos Ghosn, announced at the annual World Economic Forum meeting in Davos, Switzerland, in 2004, "If your business isn't making money in China, it probably wouldn't make money anywhere else.[15]

At the 2002 Strategic Forum of Transnational Corporations in China, Deputy General Secretary of China's State Economic and Trade Commission Ma Jiantang called attention to the success of American toy manufacturers and retailers, whose original investment in China brought a 54 percent return because the cost of labor and production in China took only 12 percent of the total.[16] Former Premier Zhu Rongji pointed out that China's exports to the United States are "mostly labor-intensive consumer goods with little value added." Sneakers produced for Nike, Adidas, and Puma by factories in China, for instance, retail for $120 in the United States, but the export price from China is only $20 and Chinese workers get a mere $2 out of the whole process.[17]

Chinese Communist Party leadership wants to attract even more investment from foreign banks and corporations and from overseas Chinese, to bring China into the ranks of developed nations. To that end, it has made very major concessions, even sacrificing on the issue of sovereignty. Since joining the World Trade Organization (WTO) in December 2001, China has undertaken to remove most of the remaining barriers to the operation of foreign corporations in China. It will soon allow foreign firms to operate in its stock and financial markets as well as in its highly protected banking, insurance, and securities markets. More than eighty foreign banks and securities houses are already conducting limited operations in China. Foreign ownership will also be allowed, including that by large, flagship industrial corporations in strategic sectors such as energy and natural resources.

Most of the Fortune 500 largest transnational corporations already have operations in China, established through joint ventures with Chinese partners. The arrangement gives transnational companies established production sites, distribution networks, trained personnel, and the patronage of the Beijing regime. Long before the trade tariffs are reduced, they have entrenched their market domination by wiping out less efficient Chinese producers. As China cuts tariffs across the board between 2001 and 2006 from an average of 24.6 percent to 9.4 percent, imports to China are expected to rise exponentially, and with its 1.3 billion people, a $1.2 trillion dollar economy, and a rapidly growing middle-class driving a booming domestic consumption, it promises to finally become the market American and European businesses have coveted for the last two centuries.

It is in this context that, just before the U.S. Congress voted on whether to support China's admission to the WTO, top business executives issued blunt warnings to federal lawmakers. Phil Condit, chairman of Boeing Co., and Robert N. Burt, chairman and chief executive of FMC Corp., said that the vote to facilitate China's entry into the WTO would be a measure of every lawmaker's friendliness to business. "We aim our donations . . . at people who support free enterprise and what we see as the free-enterprise system."

China has received the most foreign direct investment because its government offers preferential tax treatment and other incentives to multinational companies.[18] At the same time, the Chinese government allocates national capital to prop up state-owned companies where Chinese workers produce cheap products for American consumers. In the meantime, to appease protectionist critics in America, it uses foreign earnings to buy U.S. Treasury bonds. China in fact finances the American trade deficit in order to keep American consumers buying imported goods. In the first six months of 2004, China bought a record $41 billion of U.S. Treasuries—less than Japan, but far more than any other foreign country. By the end of 2004, mainland China was the second largest holder of U.S. Treasury bonds, with $195 billion, next to Japan's $701 billion.

Considering that China provides cheap manufactured goods for American consumers, huge profits for American corporations, and loans in the form of Treasury bonds that keep American purchasing power strong, it is not surprising that U.S. Commerce Secretary Donald Evans deems that "China is headed in the right direction . . . and is in good hands," and lavishes praise on the new political route Beijing has taken.

CHINA COMMUNIST?

There are still Americans critical of China because it is a communist country. Yet the Chinese Communist Party has long lost its ideological fervor and its popular support, especially after the Tiananmen Square Massacre in 1989, when it made a Faustian promise to the Chinese people to deliver economic prosperity if its one-party rule remained unchallenged. Chinese leadership clearly depends on robust economic growth to maintain its political legitimacy, and to ensure that, it needs help from the international financial community. It has made a curious bargain: to consolidate the dominant position of the Chinese Communist Party, it has accelerated China's transition to market capitalism.

The Chinese "communist" government has adopted policies to shrink and eventually eradicate all vestiges of socialist public ownership, and as a result private ownership is quickly gaining ground. A report by the International Finance Corporation (IFC), the private-sector arm of the World Bank, says that private businesses generated 33 percent of China's GDP in 1998, compared with 37 percent generated by the state sector.

The labor law passed in 1995 detailed many work provisions, including minimum wage, maximum working hours, and pensions, but its implementation is the responsibility of local governments. Since many provincial officials are in business with foreign and local private manufacturers, they rarely side with the workers. Forced labor, child labor, excessive overtime, and hazardous working conditions have become commonplace. Migrant workers, who number around 100 million and constitute the most significant segment of China's industrial labor force, do not even have the legal right to reside in the urban centers where they work, which would qualify them for legal protection. Workers at state-owned facilities face massive plant closures and layoffs. The unemployment rate in China is estimated at 12 percent.

That the state is more interested in protecting employers is evidenced by persistent labor and safety violations that every year lead to spectacular gas explosions, mine cave-ins, and flooding that kill thousands of people at a time. In 2002, there were an estimated 110,000 deaths in China from industrial accidents and more than 14,000 accidents in the manufacturing and mining industries alone. When an explosion at Baixing Coal Mine in northeastern Heilongjiang Province killed at least thirty-two miners in 2004, the state provided a miserly total of $9,640 to compensate their families.[19] Approximately half the people with pneumoconiosis (a lung disease associated with silica dust) in the world live in China, where more than 15,200 new cases occur each year.[20]

To organize independent unions or strike in China is illegal, and any attempt to protest is severely sanctioned. The leaders of such attempts are regularly jailed and prosecuted as criminals; their families are harassed. For workers, China is hardly a socialist paradise. The Chinese Communist party won its monopoly on power recognizing the working class as the vanguard of the productive forces and promising to free it of the exploitative capitalist system and private ownership. But to maintain that monopoly, it has reneged on everything it stood for. And in the process, it has come up with some ingenious ideas of how to alter the principles of communism to suit its transgressions.

Former party secretary Jiang Zemin, who liked to feature himself next to Marx, Mao, and Deng Xiaoping on party banners and billboards, came up with the theory of Three Representatives. Proclaiming that the Communist Party represents the advanced productive forces, the advanced culture, and the fundamental interests of the majority, he expanded the definition of the "advanced productive forces" to include the capitalist class. According to him, the Communist Party cannot always remain a party of have-nots; it should also become a party of the "rich people," because the "advanced elements" among the rich help others become rich. The party would only benefit by recruiting "outstanding elements" from the "new social strata," because they would enhance the party's mass base and social influence.

"Simply put," in the words of a senior editor at one of the party's leading theoretical journals, "we want to improve our governing capacity, but we don't want to lose political power."[21] In the final analysis, China is "communist" only because the Chinese Communist Party says it is.

CHINESE AMERICAN ROLE IN AMERICAN EXPANSION

Most Chinese Americans couldn't care less what goes on in China. A few do because of family attachments and for sentimental reasons. Those who have professional and business ties do in the interest of American capital expansion in China.

Indeed, Chinese Americans and overseas Chinese have been indispensable agents of change as Asia has transformed into the manufacturing center of the American-led global economy. In much of East Asia, multinational corporations came to rely on Chinese personal contacts, or *guanxi*, to break into new markets. After political rapprochement with the United States, Chinese mainlanders were weary of approaches from American businesses—not so much because they didn't speak the language but because they mistrusted the lack of common references. Chinese Americans jumped in to provide them. Boeing, for instance, made its critical initial approach in China through a Chinese American whose father had been a top KMT official before 1949. His *guanxi* led to billions of dollars in contracts for Boeing, while the Chinese government used him to give substance to the idea of reaching out to the enemy to form a "united front"—its way of trying to win overseas Chinese support for its goal of unifying Taiwan with the motherland.

Because of China's weak legal system and reliance on "strong interpersonal relationships," overseas Chinese became even more important in ensuring smooth sailing once the contacts were made and the agreements signed. "Doing business [in China] means dealing with officials and bureaucrats at all levels and bribing them to leave you alone," explains an overseas Chinese investor in chemical factories in northern China. "The real advantage for the Chinese expatriates is that the officials expect you to understand that. They find it easier to open their mouths to ask for bribes openly."[22] Since law forbids American corporations from paying bribes, using Chinese Americans as "informal agents" to do their dirty work becomes essential.

Larry Wang, who conducted seminars at Harvard Business School and MIT in the early 1990s on doing business in China, founded a human resources firm that recruits American-educated Asian Americans and Asian nationals for multinational companies. "What I'm interested in doing is bringing qualified and motivated people to Asia who can fit in and produce," he has said. "I'm helping Asian Americans develop a presence out there."[23] At the same time, big established agencies, such as Norman Broadbent, Boyden International, and Executive Access, have opened offices in China to recruit among American professionals and managers already there, but with particular interest in Chinese Americans. Multinational corporations are in fact trying to buy Chinese or Asian faces and routinely pay a 30 percent to 50 percent premium to attract Chinese professionals.[24]

Chinese Americans and overseas Chinese actually bring more than faces, contacts, and scientific knowledge to their jobs in China. They also bring the American concept of "modernization"—open markets, free trade, and capitalist economy, framed by the U.S.-dominated global institutions, such as the International Monetary Fund, the World Bank, and the WTO. The Americanization of China involves more than introducing the consumer culture of McDonald's, Coca-Cola, and Hollywood films. It means persuading the Chinese that the American way is the only viable model for economic development, and the overseas Chinese entrepreneurs, scientists, tourists, and educators have carried the message more effectively than anyone else. While the Chinese leadership tends to question the motives of Westerners with interest in China, they are more open to the views of Chinese American scientists and scholars, who are regularly invited to give lectures and seminars on technical matters as well as on political and social issues. The forensic scientist in O.J. Simpson's case, Henry Lee, who is former commissioner of public safety in Connecticut, has been invited to train police officers in both Taiwan and mainland China.[25] "Informal messages" on sensitive issues are often "passed on" to the State

Department by Chinese American scholars after their meetings with top Chinese leaders. Likewise, American side uses Chinese American leaders to transmit messages to China's leadership.

The go-betweens have played a significant role in ensuring that much of China's newly emerging legal, civic, educational, and research institutions are modeled after American prototypes. This group includes Chinese students who returned to China after a period in the United States. China has sent hundreds of thousands of students to the United States. (In 2003 alone, China and Taiwan sent a total of more than a hundred thousand students to the United States, ranking as the countries sending the second and the fifth largest number, respectively.) The majority of them have stayed in the United States after graduation. (The return rate of Chinese students over the period from 1978 to 1999 was only 14.1 percent.[26]) Still, a significant enough number of them did return. With the American economic worldview they brought back, they have become the reformers of China. During a recent trip, a Chinese American scholar was amused to discover that the leading economists at the Academy of Social Science in Beijing were uniformly neoclassical, much like those in the leading U.S. institutions in the field.

With their transnational background and connections, Chinese Americans (and Americanized Chinese) have become an active force in the globalization of the American economy, while shaping the political and economic landscape of Taiwan and mainland China in America's image.

CHINESE AMERICANS' SUSPECT LOYALTY

Although Chinese Americans have been encouraged to play the role of mediator between China and the United States and their services have been eagerly sought, the volatile nature of the relationship between the two countries has often turned their ethnicity into a liability. During the height of the cold war, it was easy to predict how America would determine who was its enemy and who its friend, but with the normalization of U.S.-China diplomatic relations in the late 1970s, those lines began to blur.

For a time, with the USSR understood to be the common enemy, the People's Republic of China was no longer seen as a foe, and American institutions and individuals from all walks of life happily embraced the idea of cultural and scientific exchange. Even nuclear scientists of the two nations visited each other a few times. In testimony before Congress, Deputy Director of the White House Office of Science and Technology John P. McTague emphasized the importance of opening channels of scientific exchange: "We then open up new markets for ourselves and, I think, help stabilize the world situation."[27] The more cynical perspective, of course, is to think of these exchanges as an easy way for both sides to keep up with the latest developments in the other country, better to assess its potential threat. When Chinese American physicist Wen Ho Lee, later accused of espionage for China, and his wife were asked to take part in a number of scientific exchanges between the Los Alamos National Laboratory and its counterpart in China in the late 1980s, they were expected to report on their contacts to the authorities, including the FBI, after each visit.

The cozy relationship with China, however, ended in the early 1990s, soon after the fall of the Soviet Union, when U.S. policy makers, having lost clearly defined targets, began to cast about for a Manichean opponent. China, with its rapidly expanding economy in the 1990s that began to impinge on American interests in Asia, became the most logical choice. The motivations of many Chinese Americans who, like the Lees, had been encouraged to have contact and to develop *guanxi* with their Chinese counterparts and were now caught in a burgeoning conflict between China and the United States and within the American domestic debate of how to relate to the new China, suddenly became suspect.[28]

In a report to Congress in 1999, Representative Cox claimed that as many as three thousand Chinese government-owned firms in the United States could be acting as fronts for the Chinese People's Liberation Army, but, citing security reasons, he refused to divulge which ones.[29] The report created much confusion, because it didn't distinguish between Chinese American– and Chinese government–owned firms in the United States. It also cast an accusatory glance at all Chinese scientists, students, businesspeople, and bureaucrats in the United States. China's own conservatives were in fact accusing the United States of deliberately deploying the tactic to force a "peaceful revolution to capitalism" in China. Worst of all, there were fears that the

Cox report would raise questions about all Chinese Americans. "Do we really want to believe the worst—that they could all be spies?" asked Jonathan Pollack, a onetime East Asia expert at the Rand Corporation. "Is the implication that my Chinese graduate student . . . can be a spy? There is a fine line between prudence and paranoia."[30]

Cox and his committee were never called to account for their demagoguery and its damaging consequences. In an interview with the Associated Press, a senior FBI official charged that China is still the greatest espionage threat to this country over the next decade.[31] Media stories about Chinese theft of sensitive military technologies, commercial secrets, and proprietary corporate data are almost commonplace. Yet the government has not been able to successfully prosecute Chinese spies. Over the past two decades, most cases wilted without a single major conviction.

Katrina Leung, a Chinese American woman from the wealthy suburb of San Marino, who for years used her fluency in English, Mandarin, and Cantonese to orchestrate events honoring Chinese officials on their visits to Southern California, was one such case, whose arrest attracted much media coverage. In 1988, she had helped bring Los Angeles mayor Tom Bradley and the Chinese ambassador to the United States to a dinner of the National Association of Chinese Americans. In 1998, she had traveled to China on a trade mission with Los Angeles mayor Richard Riordan, and later helped put together a fundraiser that raked in $100,000 from the Asian American community for his unsuccessful 2002 gubernatorial campaign. In 1999, she arranged meetings between Los Angeles–area officials and Chinese Premier Zhu Rongji. Leung's China contacts and connections in the U.S. political establishment, combined with her ties to the wealthiest segment of the Asian American community, made her a leading citizen in Los Angeles's Chinese community, but in May 2003 she was indicted on charges of "copying defense-related documents" and "unauthorized possession of documents relating to the national defense." The *New York Times* also reported that Leung compromised a highly sensitive nuclear espionage investigation by exposing the identities of two FBI agents who were working on the case to Beijing, despite the fact that for the past twenty years she had been on the payroll of the FBI, collecting $1.7 million for supplying information on China.

In the media coverage of her case, words such as "spying" and

"Chinagate II" were freely thrown around, although the actual charges against her were the mishandling of official documents. The only thing that sets Leung's experience apart from that of John Huang is that she is a Republican. The wariness of the Chinese American community was well expressed by Christine Chen, the Organization of Chinese Americans executive director who cautioned against "another 'Wen Ho Lee situation,' where a Chinese American was singled out for prosecution despite lack of evidence, because of his ethnicity."

Even Elaine Chao, who as the labor secretary under George W. Bush is the highest-ranking Chinese American official ever appointed, is married to a leading conservative Republican senator from Kentucky and is herself considered a star in the Republican Party, did not escape from suspicion when her name was first presented for the cabinet. John Judis of the *New Republic* and Joe Farah of the conservative *WorldNetDaily* raised the objection that Elaine Chao had "ties to China's President Jiang Zemin," because her father had been a classmate of Jiang's—before the Communist revolution. The Bush administration clearly did not see that as a liability. Chao's *guanxi*, in fact, should be considered an asset for American interests.

Caucasian Americans with close contacts in "communist" China don't cause raised eyebrows. A new sophisticated China lobby, dedicated to unfettered trade with China and spearheaded by Henry Kissinger, who was largely responsible for the Nixon-era thaw in U.S.-China relations in the 1970s and is still able to sell his *guanxi* with Chinese leaders, contributed more than $55 million to U.S. political campaigns in 1995 and 1996. Its chief organ, the U.S.-China Business Council, counts Chase Manhattan Bank, Coca-Cola, American Express, Boeing, Ford, GM, Time Warner, IBM, and other titans of U.S. industry among its more than one thousand members. Prominent foreign policy officials from past U.S. administrations, such as George Shultz, Alexander Haig, Lawrence Eagleburger and Cyrus Vance, have earned tens of thousands of dollars from U.S. companies doing business in China through their involvement with the lobby.[32] But it is Kissinger, one of China's most vigorous advocates, who has turned U.S.-China relations into the cash cow for his milking, often getting money from both sides to expand the trade—sometimes into the most sensitive areas, such as high-tech materials with military applications. He was paid $375,000 by China Ventures, a company engaged in joint ventures with China's state bank, to serve as its chairman, in addition to nearly $1 million in management fees, and has worked for a range of multimillion-dollar joint ventures in China.

Another American whose patriotism has never been questioned is Neil Bush, a younger brother of President George W. Bush, who has a $400,000-a-year contract as a consultant for a computer chip firm, Grace Semiconductor Manufacturing of Shanghai. The company lists Jiang Mianheng, son of former Chinese president Jiang Zemin, as one of its main investors.

With trade volume between the two nations now exceeding $100 billion annually, it is hard to deny that economic interests lie at the heart of China-U.S. relations. The United States has become China's biggest investor, and the largest importer of its goods. The economies of the two countries are integrally tied. The two countries share strategic interests as well. The White House needs China's assistance and influence to handle North Korea and related nonproliferation issues. It also needs China's cooperation in fighting terrorism. No American leader would want to jeopardize that. In this context, one must wonder if bashing Chinese Americans has not been merely a sideshow to distract the attention of the cold warriors. Namely, are Chinese Americans being used as a substitute for China and sacrificed so the overall relationship between the two nations can be maintained?

COMPETITION FOR IMMIGRANTS IN TODAY'S WORLD

Immigrant bashing is certainly not a new phenomenon in America, despite the well-documented contribution immigrants have made to the economic, social, and cultural development of the nation. Their role may well be becoming more important than ever, as America endeavors to maintain its dominance as the only global superpower by importing what it lacks in its seemingly infinite capacity to absorb the best from the rest of the world.

This dependence on foreign talent is especially clear in the realm of science and technology. Roughly one-third of the U.S. Nobel laureates have been naturalized citizens, born and educated elsewhere. American universities have provided the most important channel in recruitment of skilled migrants, absorbing 32 percent of all foreign students who study in the developed world. Forty percent of graduate students at MIT are from outside the United States. More than half of all students enrolled in graduate programs in physics at U.S. schools are foreigners.[33] Many stay on to toil in the nation's research laboratories, universities, and private firms, forming the backbone of American high technology.

America's good fortune is the envy of other developed nations. Germany has recently taken a radical step to alleviate its desperate shortage of high-tech workers: it has overhauled its immigration policy to give skilled foreign workers residence for an unlimited period of time. Not so long ago German chancellor Helmut Kohl had declared that Germany was "not a nation of immigrants," affirming the postwar policy of denying its foreign-born residents, who came as "guest workers" from southern Europe, a permanent status. Germany's experiment may provide a blueprint for other countries in the European Union and Japan, which understand that to keep up with rapidly advancing scientific developments they must be able to tap into the most advanced human resources nurtured elsewhere—currently in India and East Asia. Their long-term economic survival depends on it. As Elspeth Guild of the European Immigration Lawyers Network points out, "The debate [to attract highly skilled immigrants] is no longer about whether, it's about how."

As a country of perpetual immigration, America currently gets the best from the rest of the world in every field of human endeavor. It would be hard to imagine America's classical music scene without Itzhak Perlman or Yo-Yo Ma. Since the spectacular success of the film *Crouching Tiger, Hidden Dragon*, Hollywood producers have signed up a host of Asian stars, including Jet Li, Chow Yun-Fat, and Zhang Ziyi. The aging Jackie Chan has been invited back time and again for a series of *Rush Hour* sequels. The Chinese Gymnastic Association recently complained that as many as sixty of its finest gymnastics coaches have been recruited by the United States and Australia, creating a real threat to China's chances in international competitions. Of the 348 active players in the NBA, 49 are from abroad, and 26 of the 29 teams in the league have at least one non-American player on their roster.[34] It would have been unthinkable just a decade ago for the Chinese player Yao Ming to become the star center for the Houston Rockets.

NATIONAL LOYALTY AND MARKETPLACE
COMPETITION

One of the most vital qualities of America's immigrants is their loyalty to their adoptive country, because it is a prosperous and open society, full of opportunities, that encourages innovation and creativity, and because its political system is democratic and stable, backed by the Bill of Rights. Yet American history has been repeatedly convulsed by spasms of anti-immigrant sentiment whenever this nation has found itself in need of blaming someone—anyone—for the ills that befall it.

During World War I, most of the imprisoned antiwar dissidents were immigrants from Europe, as were the labor activists who were rounded up, beaten, and often deported during the Palmer Raids that followed the war. During World War II, the targets were Japanese Americans, who were put in internment camps because of their ancestry. During the McCarthy era, immigrants from Europe, Asia, and the Caribbean were deported or imprisoned because of the Cold War, and Chinese Americans were singled out for interrogation and harassment during the Korean War, because Hoover believed that all Chinese were potential supporters of Chinese Communists. More recently, Newt Gingrich pushed draconian immigration laws through Congress in reaction to Timothy McVeigh's terrorist attack in Oklahoma City, and as a result INS detentions skyrocketed, making immigrants the fastest growing segment of the population in American jails. After 9/11, the government proceeded with a policy of detention without due process, harassing and intimidating Arab and South Asian Americans in the name of the war against terror. As for Chinese Americans, they can expect once again to be subjected to increased scrutiny and attacks because of the rising economic power of China, just as Japanese Americans were bashed during the 1980s when Japan became an economic powerhouse.

In today's world, characterized by the free movement of capital and goods, however, these sporadic anti-immigrant spasms could be fatal. People could "vote with their feet." Not only could discriminatory and xenophobic antiforeign attitudes take a toll on the desire of new immigrants to come; they could also push those already here to leave. The rapid economic development in Asia, where the growth rate has held at 5 to 10 percent for several decades, is conducive to reverse migration, as has been the case with South Korea, whose rising prosperity coupled with anti-Korean feeling in this country during the early 1990s severely cut down the number of Koreans who decided to come and to stay. Taiwanese nationals still continue to come to the United States for education, but many more are returning home because of the dynamic growth in their homeland. Soon the supply of the best and the brightest from mainland China could dry up as well. After all, just like Americans of their generation, these American-trained MBA holders and technology experts are happy to go wherever they find good jobs and salaries to match. Many who may have contemplated emigrating to the United States are finding opportunities right at home.

The U.S. National Science Foundation warns in its report "Science and Engineering Indicators 2004" that the United States is losing its longstanding scientific and technological hegemony as the rest of the world catches up. The report points to a decline in foreign researchers immigrating to the United States and a decrease in the share of patents granted to U.S. scientists and in the number of U.S. articles in key scientific journals. For instance, while the overall number of patents registered in the U.S. is rising, only 52 percent of them are now issued to U.S. scientists. The European Union's share of U.S. patents has now reached 35 percent, while Asia's rose steeply from less than 2 percent to 12 percent since 1990. "For many years we have benefited from minimal competition in the global science and engineering labor market," says National Science Board chairman Warren M. Washington. "But attractive and competitive alternatives are now expanding around the world."

China is emerging as a leading center in the globalized technology industry and is quickly replacing India as the low-cost home for software development.[35] Both countries are doing their best to bring the foreign-educated expatriates back through special incentive programs. Silicon Valley veterans can get cash grants and office space for free from many city and local governments in China, where they can hire a staff of ten for what it would cost to hire one comparable employee in California. Dennis Wu, managing partner of Deloitte & Touche's Chinese Service Group, calls the trend a "reverse brain-drain," or, when the number of U.S.-trained Chinese professionals returning to China suddenly increased, "a reverse gold rush." Those who return typically earn 10 to 30 percent less than they would in the United

States, but they fall in the top income bracket in China.[36] Their future looks bright, too. Several Japanese companies that act as systems integrators, such as NEC, Fujitsu, and Hitachi, are beginning to sign large outsourcing contracts with China.[37]

In today's marketplace, American policy toward the high-tech immigrants who can easily become global migrants is critical in maintaining its preeminent position in the world. One thing is certain: the Patriot Act has discouraged many people from coming. "It is not just the policies themselves," explains Institute of International Education vice president for education Peggy Blumenthal, "but the understanding and perception of the policies that may have really affected the numbers."[38] Horror stories of student visa holdups and hassles have been widely reported around the world: of PhD candidates flying home for family funerals and being unable to return to their laboratories, and of an Ivy League postdoctoral fellow marooned in Beijing while his $1.5 million U.S. government research grant collected dust.[39]

A Congressional Budget Office study showed that the number of foreign student applications in 2002–2003 at the nation's elite universities declined significantly. At Princeton, the drop was 20 percent for undergraduates and 26 percent for graduate students; the decrease in the number of applications from China was 50 percent. In the spring of 2004, the Washington-based Council of Graduate Schools found that 90 percent of responding U.S. graduate institutions reported a decrease in international applications—a 32 percent plunge across the board, but much higher among students from China and India. Applications from China declined by 76 percent. Understandably, MIT's vice president of research Alice Gast has expressed fears that a continuing decline in foreign student enrollment "may damage our ability to attract the best and the brightest."

In response to the reports on how new policies adopted in 2002 were affecting America's prospects, Secretary of State Colin Powell warned Congress in the spring of 2004 that "people aren't going to take that for very long, and when the word gets out . . . they will start going elsewhere."[40] Indeed, schools overseas appear to be benefiting from the U.S. crackdown. The number of Chinese students enrolling in British institutions rose by more than 36 percent in 2004 (and by 16 percent for students from India). Australia reported an increase in international student enrollment of 16.5 percent. Until just two years ago, foreign students fought to get into American universities. If American policy makers continue to cultivate fear of foreigners and suspicion of immigrants—particularly those of certain nationalities—we may no longer even have the privilege of educating our competitors.

The effect of the latest American polices on Chinese immigration is already visible. Less obvious are their consequences for the future of Chinese in America. In a context in which China is increasingly seen as a competitor and potential threat to American dominance—despite the current climate of close economic partnership between the two countries—it is vital for Chinese Americans to take a clear measure of current developments. They must fully understand the crucial role they may find themselves playing in the ever evolving and always uncertain relationship between China and the United States.

Postscript: Chinese America in the Twenty-first Century

SHADY HORIZON

Bill Clinton, widely accused of pandering to China and Chinese Americans, did not see fit to appoint a single Asian American to his cabinet until the last months of his eight-year term in office. (Norman Y. Mineta served as commerce secretary for six months of Clinton's presidency.) George W. Bush, on the other hand, made sure to appoint a diverse cabinet when he took office—one that would "look more like America," he boasted—and included one Latino, two African Americans, two Asian Americans, and four women. His secretary of labor, Elaine Chao, became the first Chinese American member of a presidential cabinet.

An immigrant from Taiwan, Chao is the wife of Kentuckian Mitch McConnell, one of the most powerful Republicans in the Senate. She was first appointed as deputy secretary of transportation during the Reagan administration and headed the Peace Corps during the Bush senior administration. She later became executive director of the United Way of America. Before the Bush junior appointment, Chao was a senior fellow at the Heritage Foundation, a right-wing think tank founded by Joe Coors of the Coors Beer family, which has fought civil rights laws, minimum wage laws, environmental laws, affirmative action, and arms control. (The foundation, for instance, had substantial input in the writing of Newt Gingrich's "Contract with America.")

Chao sits on four corporate boards: Northwest Airlines, Clorox, C.R. Bard, and Columbia/HCA Healthcare. Her sympathies are clear. In one interview, she declared, "Levi Strauss is going bankrupt, basically, because they pride themselves on being the most worker-enlightened corporation in America." The Department of Labor under Chao has issued a proposal that would deny overtime pay and protection of the forty-hour workweek to millions of workers. Those who make between $22,101 and $65,000 and are now eligible to receive overtime pay would be reclassified as executives or administrative and professional employees and would thus no longer qualify.

Chao is a longtime advisory board member of the Independent Women's Forum—an organization that aggressively counters the notion that sexual harassment, glass ceilings, and wage disparities are real problems for women and chalks them up to "gender correctness." She has also made a career of attacking affirmative action programs and other race-conscious remedies, and had opposed the appointment of the Chinese American Bill Lann Lee to the Department of Justice's Civil Rights Division because he sought to use existing laws to counter racial discrimination. Chao sees no point in the struggle for civil rights, arguing instead that the conservative values of hard work and individualism will result in success regardless of color or ethnicity. She likes to present herself as rising from humble origins—coming to the U.S. from Taiwan on a freighter at the age of eight, unable to speak a word of English. According to the Heritage Foundation, Chao's family arrived with "little more than the clothes on their backs."[1] Her father, James Chao, however, came from a well-connected Chinese family with a successful shipping business. Foremost Shipping started out carrying goods between the United States and Taiwan and later diversified into shipbuilding in Shanghai. James Chao was a schoolmate of Chinese leader Jiang Zemin and used this connection to establish business ties with the Chinese government. When Elaine Chao was still young, her family moved from the New York borough of Queens to the decidedly upper-middle-class suburb of Syosset on Long Island, where she attended high school, and then to the exclusive town of Harrison in New York's affluent Westchester County.[2]

But even though she had little previous contact with the Asian American community, her appointment gave her the leverage to speak on its behalf and represent its interests. Asian Americans, fresh from the distasteful experience of the Clinton administration's anointing of John Huang as their representative, were once again stuck with a bestowed "leader." Yet mainstream Asian American organizations did not complain. Daphne Kwok, executive director of the Organization of Chinese Americans, welcomed Chao's nomination as "a recognition that we are full participating Americans. It shows to the world that America fully embraces its diversity."[3] Matt Fong, the onetime California Republican senatorial candidate, declared that "President-elect Bush deserves our gratitude," for helping Asians to break through a historic ethnic barrier.

The Bush administration clearly understood the eagerness for representation among some minority leaders and wanted to show that conservatives could play the diversity game as well as anybody. It has used Colin Powell, Condoleezza Rice, Elaine Chao, and other minority appointments to demonstrate the degree of progress nonwhite minorities have made. Below the surface, however, the Bush administration has not been particularly friendly to minorities. Unemployment and poverty among African Americans have increased for the first time in a decade, education and health care programs that benefit African Americans have been cut, the administration has declared war on affirmative action, and Bush sees no problem with appointing Charles Pikering, who had defended cross-burning Ku Klux Klan members and questioned minority voting rights, to a federal judgeship.

Elaine Chao certainly did not speak out against the Patriot Act's targeting of Asian Americans of South Asian origin. The U.S. Justice Department swept up hundreds of them after 9/11 and held them in detention without charges, without trial, and without the right of legal representation. Nationals of particular countries have been rounded up for "registration," tracking, and questioning. The act has also used the threat of "domestic terrorism" to subject political organizations to surveillance, wiretapping, harassment, and criminal action for political advocacy. It greatly expands the ability of law enforcement to conduct secret searches, and gives it access to highly personal medical, financial, mental health, and student records with minimal judicial oversight.

To add insult to injury, the author of the Patriot Act is Georgetown University professor of law Viet D. Dinh, who came to the United States as a refugee from Vietnamese communism when he was a child. If there is one issue all Asian Americans ought to be aware of, it is the devastating impact of racial profiling on Asian American communities. The wholesale incarceration of Japanese Americans without trial and due process during World War II was one of the worst violations of human rights in American history. It took decades of hard-fought battles by Asian American activists to finally force the government to admit that it had made a mistake. A congressional investigation revealed that not a single act of espionage or sabotage by a Japanese descendant had been committed on U.S. soil. President Reagan signed the congressionally approved legislation extending an official apology to Japanese American citizens and granting them reparations of $20,000 per survivor. The objective was to teach America a lesson: never again to prey on innocent fellow Americans in the heat of wartime emotions.

Americans are notoriously short on historical memory, but how could Asian Americans so quickly forget the lesson? Dinh has been invited by Asian American groups as an honored guest, a keynote speaker, and an Asian American celebrity. Meanwhile, another Asian American, University of California Law School professor John Yoo, wrote the infamous legal memo for the Department of Justice advising the president that he could detain "enemy combatants" without independent review. The interpretation of that memo, many argue, has led to the prison abuses in Guantanamo Bay, in Abu Ghraib, Iraq, and here in the United States.

Alas, influencing the opinions of minority communities is only one of the roles the "multicultural" conservatives are asked to play. The Bush administration is aggressively utilizing them as assets in matters of foreign affairs. They serve as an effective propaganda tool to show that America is a democratic country where everyone, without regard to race and ethnicity, can prosper. When Elaine Chao was first appointed as labor secretary, newspapers and magazines in Taiwan, Hong Kong, and mainland China ran her picture on their cover pages in a display of obvious pride and celebration. No one asked about or commented on her politics. Chao's accomplishments injected a sense of chauvinistic pride in the potency of Chinese civilization. Her immigrant success fairy tale also implanted envy in the minds of millions of Chinese about opportunity in America.

Asian Americans craving "representation" and eager to be "counted at the table" must look carefully at the current American policies that they will be called to support. With the collapse of the Soviet Union and the end of the cold war, America took upon itself the role of the chief defender of freedom in the world. But the freedom it defends as global free trade is the freedom of finance capital. Since the United States acts as the only guarantor of this "New World Order," its intervention is likely whenever the pro-capital and pro–private property system it is based on is threatened.

No longer justified by the fight against communism, American foreign interventions these days are framed as humanitarian interventions in defense of ethnic and women's minority rights, against oppressive regimes and rogue states. America has become the policeman of the world. With the acquiescence of other major powers, America now claims the right to stop any other nation from acquiring any kind of weapon of mass destruction. Zbigniew Brzezinski, President Carter's national security adviser, formulated this policy as crucial in preventing "the emergence of a dominant and antagonistic Eurasian power," which would cause international chaos. Or as Colin Powell bluntly put it when he addressed the U.S. Congress in 1992 as chairman of the joint chiefs of staff, "I want to be the bully on the block," so all others know "there is no future in trying to challenge the armed forces of the U.S."[4]

At the height of this American-dominated free-trade regime in the 1990s, multinational and financial institutions aggressively pursued profits and expanded ownership by forcing smaller nations to privatize and deregulate: to drop state ownership of public utilities, relax foreign ownership regulations, limit government rules on currency exchange, and reduce tariffs on imports and export taxation. The IMF and the World Bank used their power to force debtor states to cut national budgets, public subsidies, and social welfare services to create favorable conditions for debt repayment to outside investors. Countries unwilling to subject their citizens to extreme belt-tightening measures ended up defaulting, and the management of their economies was put under the dictate of the IMF. This gave opportunities to American and European multinational corporations and financial institutions to acquire bankrupted properties for a song. It is what geographer David Harvey calls "accumulation by dispossession." This is what happened during the 1997 Asian financial crisis, which affected most of the East Asian nations as well as the major emerging economies in Southeast Asia. As a result, American and European ownership in countries such as Korea, Thailand, and Indonesia expanded greatly. The same thing happened in 2001 in Argentina, leading to the privatization and foreign ownership of that country's water, energy, telecommunications, and transportation industries.[5]

Yet, despite its ambition to dominate globally, America's own economy is in crisis. In 2004 the IMF, normally preoccupied with the problems of nations such as Indonesia and Argentina, pointed the finger at the huge imbalance between what the U.S. federal government has promised to pay in future benefits and what it can reasonably expect to collect from future taxes, and warned that the United States is careening toward insolvency. Its long-term structural deficit now exceeds 500 percent of the gross domestic product. Closing the gap would require an immediate and permanent 60 percent hike in the federal income tax. Instead, the Bush administration has made the situation even worse by repeated huge tax cuts, mainly for the rich, and a promise that they would be made permanent.

Adding to the fiscal problem is the nation's chronic trade deficit. Globalization has made the United States abandon manufacturing, which was, along with capital and the military, one of the three pillars of its previous might. Having to import manufactured goods has led to an increasingly large trade imbalance. Since Americans continue to have high-flying consumption habits, the deficit has to be financed by foreign capital through purchase of American stocks, U.S. Treasury bonds, and real estate. American people, with their meager savings, are, in effect, turning to other countries to finance their home mortgages, credit card balances, and business investments, according to former Federal Reserve director Peter G. Peterson.[6]

And this does not even take into account what historian Paul Kennedy has called America's "imperial overstretch"—a situation in which its "global interests and obligations" are far greater than its power. The U.S. military budget for 2004 was $399.1 billion (not counting more than $100 billion in additional supplemental requests). It was as large as the rest of the world's combined, and eight times larger than China's, the second largest at $51 billion. The United States now has about 1.4 million active-duty military personnel, and half a million soldiers, spies, technicians, dependents, and civilian contractors based in other nations on 725 military bases around the world.[7] With its lack of manufacturing strength and questionable financial power, it has come to depend on the military to maintain its dominance in the world. It is for this reason that proponents of the Project for the New American Century, a neoconservative think tank formed in 1997, have been arguing that the United States has to accept its post–Cold War imperial role and not be intimidated by the costs, because "if we shirk our responsibilities," the consequences will be deadly.

Since the 9/11 attacks, the center stage of American policy making has been dominated by neoconservatives. They have abandoned fixed alliances and declared America no longer bound by the views of its allies. But even before 9/11 the United States had scrapped participation in the Kyoto Protocol on global warming and refused to sign on to the international war-crimes tribunal and Biological Weapons Convention. It has unilaterally withdrawn from the Anti-Ballistic Missile Treaty to resume Star Wars research, thus ending the disarmament policy cultivated by all administrations since the late 1950s.

By invading Iraq, the United States has also claimed the right of preemptive strike. It was not a war waged in response to an attack. Its motive was the consolidation of America's hold on the Middle East, this strategically most important region in the U.S. effort to maintain world domination in a period of global economic crisis and capitalist rivalry. The Middle East contains two-thirds of the world's known petroleum supplies. Oil is the lifeblood of all developed economies and is crucial for the exercise of military power. More important, the economies of the European Union and Asia are increasingly dependent on oil imports from the Middle East. Controlling them gives the United States crucial leverage and influence over its capitalist competitors, such as Germany, France, Japan, and China.

At this point, the American government acts largely without allies, without international goodwill, without the funds, and without even the full support of the American people. The Bush administration has already instituted laws against dissent, such as the Patriot Act, endangering the very democracy we claim we want to export to others. Persecution of South Asians and Muslim Americans is the domestic "collateral damage" of the war in Iraq and the war against terrorism. At this most dangerous hour for the American empire, when frustration can easily lead to another desperate venture, one has to wonder who might be the next target. Iran? China? Should a conflict with China occur, Chinese Americans would almost certainly be targeted once again amidst the national hysteria that's bound to erupt.

As a group, Asian Americans have been divided for some time and have been moving farther away from the original principles of the movement that gave us "Asian America." This is not surprising, given the great diversity within the community. But one would expect at least an agreement on the issue of racial and ethnic profiling, since all Asian Americans have been persistently subjected to it. Aside from the Japanese internment, American history is full of attacks against different Asian groups, not because of what they did, but because of what Americans blamed their countries of origin for: the harassment of Chinese Americans during the McCarthy era when the United States was angry with China, especially after the heavy losses it had suffered during the Korean War; the scapegoating of Japanese Americans during the 1970s when Japanese imports were undermining domestic manufacturing; violent crimes against Vietnamese Americans to avenge friends and relatives killed in Southeast Asia; vilification of Asian Americans, particularly Chinese Americans, due to Clinton's campaign financing debacle and its implications of his selling out of national interests to China; the prosecution of Wen Ho Lee and other Chinese Americans because of what many Americans see as the rapidly growing threat from China. Last but not least, there are the current attacks and the violation of the human rights of South Asians and Middle Easterners in this country because of 9/11.

Chinese Americans should defend the rights of all minority groups that suffer from ethnic and racial profiling. They should challenge the government whenever it invokes a national crisis to target select groups of U.S. citizens and immigrants by adopting extra-legal measures, such as the Patriot Act. In doing so they would take their rightful place in the fight for the soul of American liberty. Chinese Americans should also speak out on matters of American foreign policy. Rather than allowing themselves to be used as multicultural makeup that conceals policies of unilateral domination, they should use their role in America's thrust into Asia to stand for globalization that promotes peace and benefit to all— acting as true pioneers in our increasingly interconnected world.

Notes

CHAPTER 1: Pioneers

1. "Guofan," in Hsiang-Lin Lo, *Yuedongzhifeng;* quoted in Yong Chen, *Chinese San Francisco, 1850–1943: A Trans-Pacific Community* (Stanford, CA: Stanford University Press, 2000), p. 40.
2. "Furious Riding," *Alta California,* October 11, 1853.
3. Priscilla Wegars, "From Diaspora to Doctor Ing Hay: Chinese Pioneers in the Western United States," Asian American Comparative Collection (AACC), University of Idaho, Moscow.
4. Robert Joe Stout, "Chinese on the Western Frontier," *Wild West,* 2002, http://americanhistory.about.com/.
5. Liping Zhu, *A Chinaman's Chance: The Chinese on the Rocky Mountain Mining Frontier* (Boulder: University Press of Colorado, 1997), p. 80.
6. Quong Gee Kee's story and all the quotes are taken directly from Ben T. Traywick, "Quong Gee Kee: Tombstone's Last Celestial," in *Legendary Characters of Southeast Arizona* (Tombstone, AZ: Red Marie's Bookstore, 1992), pp. 176–85.
7. Zhu, *A Chinaman's Chance,* p. 146.
8. Ibid.
9. Ibid., p. 148.
10. Ibid.
11. Larry Barsness, "The Heathen Chinese," in *Chinese on the American Frontier,* ed. Arif Dirlik (Lanham, MD: Rowman and Littlefield, 2001), p. 387.
12. Zhu, *A Chinaman's Chance,* p. 151.
13. Ibid., pp. 151–54.
14. Kil Young Zo, "Chinese Emigration into the United States, 1850–1880" (PhD diss., Columbia University, 1971), p. 89.
15. Ibid., p 82.
16. Ibid., p. 89.
17. Zhu, *A Chinaman's Chance,* p. 15.

18. Zo, "Chinese Emigration," p. 83.

19. Chen, *Chinese San Francisco*, p. 36.

20. James O'Meara, "The Chinese in Early Days," *Overland Monthly* 3, 2nd series (May 1884), p. 477; Zo, "Chinese Emigration," p. 84.

21. Ping Chiu, *Chinese Labor in California: An Economic Study* (Madison: State Historical Society of Wisconsin, 1967), p. 12.

22. Zhu, *A Chinaman's Chance*, p. 17.

23. The English translation of the text is found in Xiao-huang Yin, *Chinese American Literature since the 1850s* (Urbana: University of Illinois Press, 2000), p. 14. It reflects the language usage of the time.

24. The first known case is of sixty Chinese hired by a British mining company in Tuolumne County in 1849 (Chiu, *Chinese Labor in California*, pp. 12–15).

25. Mary Roberts Coolidge, *Chinese Immigration* (New York: Henry Holt, 1909), p. 18.

26. Randall E. Rohe, "After the Gold Rush," in Dirlik, *Chinese on the American Frontier*, p. 5.

27. Chew Lee, "The Life Story of a Chinaman," in *The Life Stories of Undistinguished Americans as Told by Themselves*, ed. Hamilton Holt (New York, 1906); quoted in Ronald Takaki, *Strangers from a Different Shore: A History of Asian Americans* (Boston: Little, Brown, 1989), p. 34.

28. Rohe, "After the Gold Rush," p. 6.

29. Loven W. Fessler, *Chinese in America: Stereotyped Past, Changing Present*, comp. China Institute in America (New York: Vantage Press, 1983), p. 43.

30. Victor Purcell, *The Chinese in Malaya* (London: Oxford University Press, 1948), p. 98.

31. Liping Zhu, "No Need to Rush: The Chinese, Placer Mining, and the Western Environment," *Montana: The Magazine of Western History* (Montana Historical Society), autumn 1999, p. 4.

32. Horace Parker, "Just a Relic of Idaho's Romantic Gold Rush Days," *Idaho Statesman*, May 17, 1931, p. 2.

33. Zhu, *A Chinaman's Chance*, p. 28.

34. Rohe, "After the Gold Push," pp. 17–18.

35. Russell M. Magnaghi, "Virginia City's Chinese Community, 1860–1880," in Dirlik, *Chinese on the American Frontier*, p. 125.

36. Ibid., p. 142.

37. Loren B. Chan, "The Chinese in Nevada: An Historical Survey, 1856–1970," in Dirlik, ed., *Chinese on the American Frontier*, p. 88.

38. Fessler, *Chinese in America*, pp. 26–27.

39. Ibid., p. 27.

40. Ibid., pp. 23–24.

41. Frank Soule, *The Annals of San Francisco and History of California* (New York: D. Appleton, 1855), pp. 414–15.

42. Fessler, *Chinese in America*, p. 25.

43. Ibid., p. 42.

44. Madeline Yuan-yin Hsu, *Dreaming of Gold, Dreaming of Home: Transnationalism and Migration Between the United States and South China, 1882–1943* (Stanford, CA: Stanford University Press, 2000), p. 58; Fessler, *Chinese in America*, p. 62.

45. Takaki, *Strangers*, p. 92.

46. Lee, "The Life Story of a Chinaman."

47. John Kuo Wei Tchen, *New York Before Chinatown: Orientalism and the Shaping of American Culture 1776–1882* (Baltimore, MD: Johns Hopkins University Press, 1999), p. 251.

48. Dusanka Miscevic and Peter Kwong, *Chinese Americans: The Immigrant Experience*

(Hugh Lauter Levin Associates, 2000), p. 116; Sandy Lydon, *Chinese Gold: The Chinese in the Monterey Bay Region* (Capitola, CA: Capitola Book Company, 1985), pp. 29–59.

49. Thomas W. Chinn, ed., *A History of the Chinese in California* (San Francisco: Chinese Historical Society of America, 1969), pp. 37–39.

50. Lydon, *Chinese Gold*, p. 77.

51. Lawrence A. Kingsbury, *Chinese Properties Listed on the National Register: A Forest Service Initiative, Cultural Resources Management* 17, no. 2, thematic issue (1994): 23–25.

52. Lawrence A. Kingsbury, *Ah Toy: A Successful 19th Century Chinese Entrepreneur* (Heritage Program, U.S. Department of Agriculture, Forest Service Information), p. 7; Sheila D. Reddy, *Mountain Gardens, Mountain Stew* (Heritage Program, U.S. Department of Agriculture, Forest Service Information), p. 4.

53. Priscilla Wegars, *Polly Bemis: A Chinese American Pioneer* (Cambridge, ID: Backeddy Books, 2003), p. 5; Sheila D. Reddy, *The Color of Deep Water: The Story of Polly Bemis* (Heritage Program, U.S. Department of Agriculture, Forest Service Information), p. 8.

54. Shin-shan Henry Tsai, *The Chinese Experience in America* (Bloomington: Indiana University Press, 1986), p. 20.

55. Fessler, *Chinese in America*, pp. 54–55.

56. Ibid., p. 55.

57. Ibid.

58. Ibid., p. 42.

59. Ibid., p. 162.

60. Takaki, *Strangers*, pp. 79–80.

61. Zhu,"No Need to Rush," p. 6.

62. Jeffery Barlow, and Christine Richardson, *China Doctor of John Day* (Portland, OR: Binford and Mort, 1979), pp. 53, 60.

63. Zhu, *A Chinaman's Chance*, p. 77.

64. Chen, *Chinese San Francisco, 1850–1943*, p. 35.

65. Him Mark Lai, *Cong huaqiao dao huaren (From Overseas Chinese to Chinese Americans)* (Hong Kong: Joint Publishing, 1992), p. 47.

CHAPTER 2: The World They Left Behind

1. Kil Young Zo, "Chinese Emigration into the United States, 1850–1880" (PhD diss., Columbia University, 1971), p. 55.

2. Frederic Evans Wakeman Jr., *Strangers at the Gate: Social Disorder in South China, 1839–1861* (Berkeley, CA: University California Press, 1966), p. 43.

3. Yong Chen, *Chinese San Francisco, 1850–1943: A Trans-Pacific Community* (Stanford, CA: Stanford University Press, 2000), p. 14.

4. Ibid., p. 18.

5. Andre Gunder Frank, *ReOrient: Global Economy in the Asian Age* (Berkeley: University of California Press, 1998), p. 111.

6. Chen, *Chinese San Francisco, 1850–1943*, p. 16.

7. Madeline Hsu, *Dreaming of Gold, Dreaming of Home* (Stanford, CA: Stanford University Press, 2000), p. 23.

8. Lynn Pan, *Sons of the Yellow Emperor: A History of the Chinese Diaspora* (Boston: Little, Brown, 1990), p. 13.

9. Zo, "Chinese Emigration," p. 10.

10. "The Admiral of the Western Seas—Cheng Ho (Zheng He)," planet.time.net.my/CentralMarket/melaka.101/chengho.htm, in Dorothy Hoobler and Thomas

Hoobler, *Images Across the Ages—Chinese Portraits* (Austin, TX: Raintree Steck-Vaughin, 1971), p. 1.

11. Pan, *Sons of the Yellow Emperor*, p. 8.
12. Ibid.
13. Gungwu Wang, *The Chinese Overseas: From Earthbound China to the Quest for Autonomy* (Cambridge, MA: Harvard University Press, 2000), p. 81.
14. Pan, *Sons of the Yellow Emperor*, p. 3.
15. Guanhua Wang, *In Search of Justice: The 1905–1906 Chinese Anti-American Boycott* (Cambridge, MA: Harvard University Press, 2001), pp. 18–19.
16. "A Proposal to Permit Return of Those Who Have Settled Abroad: Memorial to the Throne by Chen Hongmou, Governor of Fujian, 1754," Guoli gugong bowuyuan, *GongZhongdang Qianlong Zouzhe*, 8: 138–40; Da Qing Lichao Shilu, QL, 463, 17–18, trans. Philip Kuhn, The Chinese Overseas (course, Harvard University), document 1.5, p. 14.
17. Wang, *In Search of Justice*, p. 19.
18. Pan, *Sons of the Yellow Emperor*, p. 25.
19. "A Proposal to Reform Imperial Policy: Memorial by Xue Fucheng, Ambassador to England, France, Italy and Belgium, on Treatment of Chinese Returning from Overseas (29 June, 1893)," *Huagong chuguo shihliao huibian* 1: 292–94, trans. Philip Kuhn, The Chinese Overseas (course, Harvard University), document 1.7, p. 21.

CHAPTER 3: The China Trade & Chinese Labor

1. "George Washington to Tench Tilghman, August 29, 1785, in *Writings of George Washington*, ed. John C. Fitzpatrick (Washington, DC, U.S. Govt. Print. Off. [1931–44], 1938), vol. 28, p. 239, quoted in Stuart Creighton Miller, *The Unwelcome Immigrant: The American Image of the Chinese, 1785–1882* (Berkeley: University of California Press, 1969), p. 14.
2. John Kuo Wei Tchen, *New York Before Chinatown: Orientalism and the Shaping of American Culture, 1776–1882* (Baltimore: Johns Hopkins University Press, 1999), p. 4.
3. Dusanka Miscevic and Peter Kwong, *Chinese Americans: The Immigrant Experience* (Hugh Lauter Levin Associates, 2000), p. 21.
4. Tchen, p. 17.
5. Miller, *The Unwelcome Immigrant*, p. 19.
6. Michael Hunt, *The Making of a Special Relationship: The United States and China to 1914* (New York: Columbia University Press, 1983), pp. 12–13.
7. Miller, *The Unwelcome Immigrant*, p. 19.
8. Ibid., p. 36.
9. *Baptist Missionary Magazine*, vol. 17 (1836), p. 57; Miller, *The Unwelcome Immigrant*, p. 74.
10. *Methodist Quarterly Review*, vol. 32 (1850), pp. 593, 602; Miller, *The Unwelcome Immigrant*, p. 74.
11. Edmund Roberts, *Embassy to the Eastern Courts of Cochin-China, Siam, and Muscat* (New York: Harper & Brothers, 1837), p. 152; Miller, *The Unwelcome Immigrant*, p. 54.
12. W.S.W. Ruschenberger, M.D., *A Voyage Round the World; Including an Embassy to Muscat and Siam, in 1835, 1836, and 1837* (Philadelphia, PA: 1838), p. 398; Miller, *The Unwelcome Immigrant*, pp. 55–56.
13. Miller, *The Unwelcome Immigrant*, pp. 42–43.

14. Ibid., pp. 145–46.
15. Andrew Gyory, *Closing the Gate: Race, Politics, and the Chinese Exclusion Act* (Chapel Hill: University of North Carolina Press, 1989), p. 17.
16. Hsin-pao Chang, *Commissioner Lin and the Opium War* (New York: Norton, 1964), p. 31.
17. Tchen, pp. 44–49.
18. Chang, *Commissioner Lin and the Opium War*, p. 40.
19. Ibid., p. 135.
20. Ibid., p. 136.
21. Ibid., p. 137.
22. John Quincy Adams, "Lecture on the War with China," in *Asian Americans in the United States*, ed. Alexander Yamato et al., vol. 1 (Dubuque, IA: San Jose State University, Kendall/Hunt Publishing Company, 1993), p. 40.
23. Miller, *The Unwelcome Immigrant*, p. 95.
24. Adams, "Lecture on the War with China," p. 46.
25. The Treaty of Nanjing was signed on August 29, 1842, and ratified in Hong Kong ten months later, concluding the first round of Western armed hostilities, which lasted from 1839 to 1842 and became known as the First Opium War.
26. Hunt, *The Making of a Special Relationship*, p. 19.
27. Lucy M. Cohen, *Chinese in the Post–Civil War South: A People without a History* (Baton Rouge: Louisiana State University Press, 1984), pp. 22–23. Translated phonetically into Chinese, the word took on a meaning of "bitter labor" (*ku-li*)—a person subjected to the harshest form of menial labor.
28. Kil Young Zo, "Chinese Emigration into the United States, 1850–1880" (PhD diss., Columbia University, 1971), p. 36; Tchen, p. 50.
29. Lynn Pan, *Sons of the Yellow Emperor: A History of the Chinese Diaspora* (Boston: Little, Brown, 1990), p. 47.
30. Tchen, p. 50. Guano droppings were used to fertilize the depleted topsoil of Maryland tobacco plantations.
31. Disposition of Li Zhaochun in "Report of the Commission Sent by China," p. 12, quoted in Frederic Wakeman Jr., "Voyages," his presidential address to the American Historical Association annual meeting, Washington, DC, December 28, 1992, *American Historical Review* 98, no. 1 (February 1993): 7.
32. *Ancestors in the Americas: Part 1, Coolies, Sailors and Settlers*, video documentary produced by Loni Ding, Center for Educational Telecommunications 2000, excerpts, p. 5.
34. *Ancestors in the Americas: Part 1, Coolies, Sailors and Settlers*, excerpts, p. 4.
34. Tony Affigne and Pei-te Lien, "Peoples of Asian Descent in the Americas: Theoretical Implications of Race and Politics," *Amerasia Journal* 28, no. 2 (2002): 5.
35. Robert L. Irick, *Ch'ing Policy Toward the Coolie Trade 1847–1878* (San Francisco: Chinese Materials Center, 1982), p. 27, quoted in Wakeman, "Voyages," p. 10.
36. Lisa Yun, "Under the Hatches: American Coolie Ships and Nineteenth-Century Narratives of the Pacific Passage," *Amerasia Journal* 28, no. 2 (2002): 39–57.
37. Madeline Hsu, *Dreaming of Gold, Dreaming of Home* (Stanford, CA: Stanford University Press, 2000), p. 29.
38. Walton Look Lai, *Indentured Labor, Caribbean Sugar: Chinese and Indian Migrants to the British West Indies, 1838–1918* (Baltimore: Johns Hopkins University Press, 1993), p. 38.

CHAPTER 4: Race

1. For a detailed discussion on racial nativism in early America, see Najia Aarim-Heriot, *Chinese Immigrants, African Americans, and Racial Anxiety in the United States, 1848–82* (Urbana: University of Illinois Press, 2003), pp. 15–29.
2. Oscar Handlin, *The Americans: A New History of the People of the United States* (Boston: Little, Brown, 1963), pp. 16–19.
3. Quoted in Ronald Takaki, *A Different Mirror: A History of Multicultural America* (Boston: Little, Brown, 1993), p. 55.
4. Thirty-nine lashes each, "well layed on," in one Virginia case, quoted in Takaki, *A Different Mirror*, p. 55.
5. Michael Goldfield, *The Color of Politics: Race and the Mainsprings of American Politics* (New York: The New Press, 1997), p. 41.
6. The figure is given by Alden T. Vaughan, "The Origins Debate: Slavery and Racism in Seventeenth-Century Virginia, *Virginia Magazine of History and Biography*, vol. 97, no. 3 (July 1989), p. 354, and quoted in Takaki, *A Different Mirror*, p. 57.
7. John Kuo Wei Tchen, *New York Before Chinatown: Orientalism and the Shaping of American Culture 1776–1882* (Baltimore: John Hopkins University Press, 1999), p. 79; Kil Young Zo, "Chinese Emigration into the United States, 1850–1880" (PhD diss., Columbia University, 1971), p. 82.
8. The concept of the Erie Canal was inspired by the Imperial Grand Canal in China, which was greatly admired by both British and American canal promoters, including New York's mayor and governor De Witt Clinton, for its gigantic geophysical manipulation in the interests of interregional trade. Craig R. Hanyan, "China and the Erie Canal," *Business History Review* 35 (1961): 558–66.
9. *New York Times*, December 26, 1856.
10. Material on the early history of Chinese in New York can be found in several sources: Tchen, *New York Before Chinatown*; Arthur Bonner, "The Chinese in New York, 1800–1950," in *Chinese America: History and Perspectives* (San Francisco: Chinese Historical Society of America, 1993); Lucy M. Cohen, *Chinese in the Post–Civil War South: A People without a History* (Baton Rouge: Louisiana State University Press, 1984), pp. 9–11; John Kuo Wei Tchen, "New York Chinese: The Nineteenth-Century Pre-Chinatown Settlement," in *Chinese America*; Xinyang Wang, *Surviving the City: The Chinese Immigrant Experience in New York City, 1890–1970* (New York: Rowman & Littlefield, 2001), pp. 25–26.
11. This was the initial discovery, which led to the gold rush. The Web site maintained by the Museum of the City of San Francisco has eyewitness accounts, excerpts from John Sutter's diaries, newspaper reports, chronologies, and mining documents. See http://www.sfmuseum.org/hist2/gold.html.
12. Thomas W. Chinn, ed., *A History of the Chinese in California* (San Francisco: Chinese Historical Society of America, 1969), provides useful detail.
13. Aarim-Heriot, *Chinese Immigrants*, pp. 27–28.
14. Ibid., p. 22.
15. Ibid., p. 25.
16. *Daily Alta California*, May 12, 1851, quoted in Aarim-Heriot, *Chinese Immigrants*, p. 30.
17. Mary Roberts Coolidge, *Chinese Immigration* (New York: Henry Holt, 1909), p. 22.
18. Randall E. Rohe gives the numbers of Chinese residents in California as follows: 54 on February 1, 1849; 791 by January 1, 1850; more than 4,000 by the end of 1850. Randall E. Rohe, "After the Gold Rush," in *Chinese on the American Frontier*, ed. Arif Dirlik (Lanham, MD: Rowman and Littlefield, 2001), p. 4. On the riot

see Ping Chiu, *Chinese Labor in California: An Economic Study* (Madison, WI: The State Historical Society of Wisconson, 1967), p. 12.

19. Loren W. Fessler, ed., *Chinese in America: Stereotyped Past, Changing Present* (New York: Vantage Press, 1983), p. 52.

20. Ronald Takaki, *Strangers from a Different Shore: A History of Asian Americans* (Boston: Little, Brown, 1989), p. 81; Takaki, *A Different Mirror*, p. 195.

21. Coolidge, *Chinese Immigration* p. 59.

22. Ian F. Haney López, *White By Law: The Legal Construction of Race* (New York: New York University Press, 1996), pp. 51–52.

23. Neil T. Gotanda, "Citizenship Nullification: The Impossibility of Asian American Politics," in *Asian Americans and Politics: Perspectives, Experiences, Prospects*, ed. Gordon H. Chang (Washington, DC: Woodrow Wilson Press; Stanford, CA: Stanford University Press, 2001), p. 85.

24. Roger Daniels, *Asian America: Chinese and Japanese in the United States Since 1850* (Seattle: University of Washington Press, 1988), p. 34.

25. See Gotanda, "Citizenship Nullification," pp. 79–101; Daniels, *Asian America*, p. 34.

26. Leonard Dinnerstein, Roger L. Nichols, and David M. Reimers, *Natives and Strangers: A Multicultural History of Americans* (London: Oxford University Press, 1996), p. 61.

27. Roger Daniel, "The Triumph of Nativism," chap. 10 in *Coming to America: A History of Immigration and Ethnicity in American Life* (New York: Harper Collins, 1990).

28. Ronald Takaki, *A Different Mirror*, p. 150.

29. Noel Ignatiev, *How the Irish Became White* (New York: Routledge, 1995), p. 41.

30. Ibid., p. 42.

31. John Higham, *Strangers in the Land: Patterns of American Nativism 1860–1925* (New Brunswick, NJ: Rutgers University Press, 1988), p. 4.

32. Dinnerstein, Nichols, and Reimers, *Natives and Strangers*, p. 112.

33. Jack Kuo Wei Tchen, "Quimbo Appo's Fear of Fenians: Anglo-Irish-Chinese Relations in New York City," in *New York Irish, 1625–1990*, ed. Ronald H. Bayor and Tymothy Meagher (Baltimore, MD: John Hopkins University Press, 1996), p. 11.

34. Stuart Creighton Miller, *The Unwelcome Immigrant: The American Image of the Chinese, 1785–1882* (Berkeley: University of California Press, 1969), p. 186.

35. Tchen, "Quimbo Appo's Fear of Fenians," p. 161.

36. Ibid., pp. 106–12. According to records, forty-seven Chinese served in either the Confederate or the Union army during the civil war. See Association to Commemorate the Chinese Serving in the American Civil War (ACCSACW), http://hometown.aol.com/gordonkwok/accsacw.html.

CHAPTER 5: Labor

1. Andrew Gyory, *Closing the Gate: Race, Politics, and the Chinese Exclusion Act* (Chapel Hill: University of North Carolina Press, 1998), p. 19.

2. Ronald Takaki, *A Different Mirror: A History of Multicultural America* (Boston: Little, Brown, 1993), pp. 191–92.

3. Iris Chang, *The Chinese in America: A Narrative History* (New York: Viking, 2003), pp. 55–56.

4. Ping Chiu, *Chinese Labor in California: An Economic Study* (Madison: State Historical Society of Wisconsin, 1967), p. 44.

5. Kil Young Zo, "Chinese Emigration into the United States, 1850–1880" (PhD diss., Columbia University, 1971), pp. 161–62.

6. Alexander Saxton, "The Army of Canton in the High Sierra," in *Chinese on the*

American Frontier, ed. Arif Dirlik (New York: Rowman & Littlefield, 2001), pp. 27–36.

7. Takaki, *Strangers from a Different Shore: A History of Asian Americans* (Boston: Little, Brown, 1989), p. 84.

8. Ibid., p. 85.

9. Ibid., p. 85.

10. Shin-Shan Henry Tsai, *The Chinese Experience in America* (Bloomington: Indiana University Press, 1986), p. 17.

11. Saxton, "The Army of Canton," p. 34.

12. Takaki, *Strangers*, p. 86.

13. Mary Roberts Coolidge, *Chinese Immigration* (New York: Henry Holt, 1909), p. 145.

14. Gyory, *Closing the Gate*, p. 27.

15. Najia Aarim-Heriot, *Chinese Immigrants, African Americans, and Racial Anxiety in the United States, 1848–82* (Urbana: University of Illinois Press, 2003), p. 113.

16. Ibid., p. 115.

17. Ibid., p. 134.

18. Ibid., p. 88.

19. Ibid., p. 89.

20. Ibid., p. 110.

21. Charles J. McClain, *In Search of Equality: The Chinese Struggle against Discrimination in Nineteenth-Century America* (Berkeley: University of California Press, 1994), p. 37.

22. Ian F. Haney López, *White by Law: The Legal Construction of Race* (New York: New York University Press, 1996).

23. Aarim-Heriot, *Chinese Immigrants*, pp. 91–92.

24. Ibid., p. 96.

25. Ibid., p. 144.

26. Roger Daniels, *Asian America: Chinese and Japanese in the United States Since 1850* (Seattle: University of Washington Press, 1988), p. 43.

27. Ibid., pp. 43–44.

28. Daniel Lee, "Hireling Labor and Slave Labor," *Southern Cultivator* 12 (June 1854): 169–80; Lucy M. Cohen, *Chinese in the Post–Civil War South: A People without a History* (Baton Rouge: Louisiana State University Press, 1984), pp. 22–24.

29. Cohen, *Chinese in the Post–Civil War South*, pp. 22–30.

30. Ibid., p. 46.

31. Peter Kwong, *Chinatown, N.Y.: Labor and Politics, 1930–1950* (New York: The New Press, 2001), p. 22.

32. Aarim-Heriot, *Chinese Immigrants*, p. 123.

33. Ibid., p. 121.

34. Stuart Creighton Miller, *The Unwelcome Immigrant: The American Image of the Chinese, 1785–1882* (Berkeley: University of California Press, 1969), p. 174.

35. Cohen, *Chinese in the Post–Civil War South*, pp. 65–67.

36. Ibid., p. 70.

37. Ibid., pp. 68–69.

38. Aarim-Heriot, *Chinese Immigrants*, p. 124.

39. Cohen, *Chinese in the Post–Civil War South*, pp. 96–97.

40. Ibid., p. 98.

41. Ibid., p. 98.

42. Ibid., p. 100.

43. Ibid., p. 89.

44. Ibid., pp. 111–112.

45. Arnold Shankman, "Black on Yellow: Afro-Americans View Chinese-Americans, 1850–1935," *Phylon* 39, no. 1 (Spring 1978): 7.
46. Cohen, *Chinese in the Post–Civil War South*, p. 100.
47. Takaki, *Strangers*, p. 97.
48. Chang, *The Chinese in America*, p. 101.
49. Daniels, *Asian America*, p. 41.
50. Chang, *The Chinese in America*, p. 101.
51. Gyory, *Closing the Gate*, p. 41.
52. Aarim-Heriot, *Chinese Immigrants*, p. 161.
53. Alexander Saxton, *The Indispensable Enemy: Labor and the Anti-Chinese Movement in California* (Berkeley: University of California Press, 1971), pp. 19–45.
54. Ibid., p. 41.
55. Ibid., p. 101.
56. Ibid., p. 264.
57. David R. Roediger, *The Wage of Whiteness: Race and the Making of the American Working Class* (New York: Verso, 1991), p. 12.
58. Ibid., p. 12.
59. Noel Ignatiev, *How the Irish Became White* (New York: Routledge, 1995), p. 111.
60. Ibid.
61. Roediger, *The Wage of Whiteness*, p. 136.
62. Ibid.
63. Miller, *The Unwelcome Immigrant*, p. 186.
64. Gyory, *Closing the Gate*, p. 214.
65. Miller, *The Unwelcome Immigrant*, p. 199.
66. Frank H. Wu, "Where Are You Really From? Asian Americans and the Perpetual Foreigner Syndrome," *Civil Rights Journal* (Winter 2002).

CHAPTER 6: The World of Chinese Immigrants

1. Andrew Gyory, *Closing the Gate: Race, Politics, and the Chinese Exclusion Act* (Chapel Hill: University of North Carolina Press, 1998), p. 42.
2. Kil Young Zo, "Chinese Emigration into the United States, 1850–1880," (PhD diss., Columbia University, 1971), pp. 101–2.
3. Dorothy Hoobler and Thomas Hoobler, *The Chinese American Family Album* (New York: Oxford University Press, 1994), p. 26; Franklin Odo, ed., *The Columbia Documentary History of the Asian American Experience* (New York: Columbia University Press, 2002), p. 17.
4. Zo, "Chinese Emigration," pp. 93–94.
5. Stanford Morris Lyman, *Chinatown and Little Tokyo: Power, Conflict and Community Among Chinese and Japanese Immigrants in America* (Millwood, NY: Associated Faculty Press, 1986), p. 183.
6. Shih-shan Henry Tsai, *The Chinese Experience in America* (Bloomington: Indiana University Press, 1986), p. 19.
7. Gyory, *Closing the Gate*, p. 40.
8. John Kuo Wei Tchen, *New York Before Chinatown: Orientalism and the Shaping of American Culture 1776–1882* (Baltimore: The Johns Hopkins University Press, 1999), p. 177.
9. Lucy M. Cohen, *Chinese in the Post–Civil War South: A People Without a History* (Baton Rouge: Louisiana State University Press, 1984), pp. 74–75.
10. Ibid., p. 76.

11. Tsai, *The Chinese Experience in America*, p. 13.
12. Cohen, *Chinese in the Post–Civil War South*, p. 84.
13. Ibid., pp. 84–85.
14. Ibid., pp. 134–35.
15. June Mei, "Socioeconomic Developments Among the Chinese in San Francisco, 1848–1906," in *Labor Immigration Under Capitalism: Asian Workers in the United States Before World War II*, ed. Lucie Cheng and Edna Bonaclich (Berkeley: University of California Press, 1984), pp. 374–75.
16. Takaki, *Strangers from a Different Shore: A History of Asian Americans* (Boston: Little, Brown, 1989), p. 41.
17. Mei, "Socioeconomic Developments," p. 375.
18. Adam McKeown, *Chinese Migrant Networks and Cultural Changes: Peru, Chicago, Hawaii, 1900–1936* (Chicago, IL: University of Chicago Press, 2001), pp. 76–77.
19. Madeline Hsu, *Dreaming of Gold, Dreaming of Home: Transnationalism and Migration Between the United States and South China, 1882–1943* (Stanford, CA: Stanford University Press, 2000), pp. 34–40.
20. Guanhua Wang, *In Search of Justice: The 1905–1906 Chinese Anti-American Boycott* (Cambridge, MA: Harvard University Press, 2001), pp. 29–30.
21. Lyman, *Chinatown and Little Tokyo*, p. 129.
22. Ibid., pp. 165–72.
23. Him Mark Lai, "Historical Development of the Chinese Consolidated Benevolent Association/*Huiguan* System," in *Chinese America: History and Perspectives 1987* (Chinese Historical Society of America), p. 34.
24. Lyman, *Chinatown and Little Tokyo*, p. 167.
25. Lai, p. 20.
26. Yong Chen, *Chinese San Francisco, 1850–1943: A Trans-Pacific Community* (Standford: Stanford University Press, 2000), p. 104.
27. Lai, "Historical Development," p. 21.
28. Ibid., p. 20.
29. Ibid., p. 20.
30. Chen, Yong, p. 71.
31. Mary Roberts Coolidge, *Chinese Immigration* (New York: Henry Holt, 1909), p. 411.
32. Tsai, *The Chinese Experience*, p. 54.
33. Wang, *In Search of Justice*, p. 58.
34. Peter Kwong, *Forbidden Workers: Chinese Illegal Immigrants and American Labor* (New York: The New Press, 1997), p. 144.
35. Alexander Saxton, *The Indispensable Enemy: Labor and the Anti-Chinese Movement in California* (Berkeley: University of California Press, 1971), p. 104.
36. Gyory, *Closing the Gate*, p. 98.
37. Saxton, *The Indispensable Enemy*, pp. 214–18; Kwong, *Forbidden Workers*, p. 145.

CHAPTER 7: The Anti-Chinese Movement

1. Bruce Levine, Stephen Brier, et al., eds., *Who Built America? Working People and the Nation's Economy, Politics, Culture and Society*, vol. 1 (New York: Pantheon Books, 1989), p. 540.
2. Ibid., p. 541.
3. Kwong, *Forbidden Workers: Chinese Illegal Immigrants and American Labor* (New York: The New Press, 1997), p. 146.
4. Arnold Shankman, "Black on Yellow: Afro-Americans View Chinese-Americans, 1850–1935," *Phylon* 39, no. 1 (Spring 1978): 1–17.

5. Peter Kwong, *Chinatown, N.Y.: Labor and Politics, 1930–1950* (New York: Monthly Review Press, 1979), p. 32.

6. Alexander Saxton, *The Indispensable Enemy: Labor and Anti-Chinese Movement in California* (Berkeley: University of California Press, 1974), pp. 128–29; Najia Aarim-Heriot, *Chinese Immigrants, African Americans and Racial Anxiety in the United States, 1848–82* (Urbana: University of Illinois Press, 2003), pp. 191–92.

7. Kil Young Zo, "Chinese Emigration into the United States 1850–1880," (PhD diss., Columbia University, 1971), p. 179.

8. Aarim-Heriot, *Chinese Immigrants*, pp. 173–75.

9. Michael Hunt, *The Making of a Special Relationship: The United States and China to 1914* (New York: Columbia University Press, 1983), p. 86.

10. Aarim-Heriot, *Chinese Immigrants*, p. 183.

11. Ibid., p. 185.

12. Stuart Creighton Miller, *The Unwelcome Immigrant: The American Image of the Chinese, 1785–1881* (Berkeley: University of California Press, 1969), p. 154.

13. Ibid., pp. 162–163.

14. John Kuo Wei Tchen, *New York Before Chinatown: Orientalism and the Shaping of American Culture, 1776–1882* (Baltimore: The Johns Hopkins University Press, 1999), p. 189.

15. George Anthony Pfeifer, *If They Don't Bring Their Women Here: Chinese Female Immigration Before Exclusion* (Urbana: University of Illinois Press, 1999).

16. Xinyang Wang, *Surviving the City: Chinese Immigrant Experience in New York City, 1890–1970* (New York: Rowman & Littlefield, 2001), p. 39.

17. Mary Roberts Coolidge, *Chinese Immigration* (New York: Henry Holt, 1909), p. 105.

18. Aarim-Heriot, *Chinese Immigrants*, p. 159.

19. Ibid., p. 177.

20. Ibid., p. 187.

21. Judy Yung, *Unbound Feet: A Social History of Chinese Women in San Francisco* (Berkeley: University of California Press, 1995), p. 33.

22. Pfeifer, *If They Don't Bring Their Women Here*, pp. 12–27. Aarim-Heriot, *Chinese Immigrants*, p. 178.

23. Ian F. Haney López, *White By Law: The Legal Construction of Race* (New York: New York University Press, 1996), pp. 5–6, 54–56, 63.

24. Shih-shan Henry Tsai, *China and the Overseas Chinese in the United States, 1868–1911* (Fayetteville: University of Arkansas Press, 1983), pp. 66–67.

25. Hunt, *The Making of a Special Relationship*, pp. 86–87.

26. Zo, "Chinese Emigration," p. 26.

27. Tsai, *China and the Overseas Chinese*, p. 11.

28. Guanhua Wang, *In Search of Justice: The 1905–1906 Chinese Anti-American Boycott* (Cambridge, MA: Harvard University Asia Center, Harvard University Press, 2001), p. 23.

29. Tsai, *China and the Overseas Chinese*, pp. 60–61.

30. Leonard Dinnerstein, Roger L. Nichols, and David Reimers, *Natives and Strangers: A Multicultural History of Americans* (London: Oxford University Press, 1996), p. 224.

31. J. S. Tow, *The Real Chinese in America* (New York: Academy Press, 1923; repr., San Francisco: R and E Research Associates, 1970), p. 153.

32. Erika Lee, "The Chinese Exclusion Example: Race, Immigration, and American Gatekeeping, 1882–1924," *Journal of American Ethnic History* (Spring 2002).

33. Bill Ong Hing, *Making and Remaking of Asian America Through Immigration Policy, 1850–1990* (Stanford, CA: Stanford University Press, 1993), pp. 207–14.

CHAPTER 8: White Dominance at Home & Abroad

1. Alexander Saxton, *The Indispensable Enemy: Labor and the Anti-Chinese Movement in California* (Berkeley: University of California Press, 1971), p. 174.
2. Andrew Gyory, *Closing the Gate: Race, Politics, and the Chinese Exclusion Act* (Chapel Hill: University of North Carolina Press, 1998), pp. 245–46.
3. Saxton, *The Indispensable Enemy*, p. 176.
4. Ibid.
5. Gyory, *Closing the Gate*, p. 253.
6. Saxton, *The Indispensable Enemy*, p. 179.
7. David Montgomery, *The Fall of the House of Labor* (London: Cambridge University Press, 1989), p. 85.
8. Stanford Lyman, *Chinese Americans* (New York: Random House, 1974), p. 74.
9. Shih-shan Henry Tsai, *The Chinese Experience in America* (Bloomington: Indiana University Press, 1986), p. 70. Rob Weir, "Blind in One Eye: Western and Eastern Knights of Labor View the Chinese Question," *Labor History* 41, no. 4 (November 1, 2000): 421.
10. Weir, "Blind in One Eye," p. 421.
11. Tsai, *The Chinese Experience*, p. 70.
12. Sucheng Chan, "Hostility and Conflict," in *Asian American Studies: A Reader*, ed. Jean Yu-wen Shen Wu and Min Song (New Brunswick, NJ: Rutgers University Press, 2000), p. 52.
13. Mark Highberger, "Snake River Massacre," *Old West*, Winter 1997.
14. Charlotte McIver, Wallowa County clerk, interview with the author, Joseph, Oregon, August 2001. Also, "Files in Oregon Detail Slaying of 31 Chinese," *New York Times*, August 21, 1995.
15. Mary Roberts Coolidge, *Chinese Immigration* (New York: Henry Holt, 1909), p. 302.
16. Betty Lee Sung, *Mountain of Gold: The Story of the Chinese in America* (New York: Macmillan, 1967), pp. 44–45.
17. Xinyang Wang, *Surviving the City: The Chinese Immigrant Experience in New York City, 1890–1970* (Boston: Rowman and Littlefield, 2001), p. 136.
18. Tsai, *The Chinese Experience*, p. 73; Franklin Odo, ed., *The Columbia Documentary History of the Asian American Experience* (New York: Columbia University Press, 2002), p. 86.
19. Ira M. Condit, *The Chinaman as We See Him and Fifty Years of Work for Him* (New York, F. H. Revell Company, 1900), pp. 86–87; Tsai, *The Chinese Experience*, p. 74.
20. Tsai, *The Chinese Experience*, p. 74.
21. Montgomery, *The Fall of the House of Labor*, p. 85.
22. Stacy A. Flaherty, "Boycott in Butte: Organized Labor and the Chinese Community, 1896–1897," in *Chinese on the American Frontier*, ed. Arif Dirlik (Boston: Rowman and Littlefield, 2001), pp. 395–96.
23. Flaherty, "Boycott in Butte," p. 396.
24. John R. Wunder, "Law and Chinese in Frontier Montana," *Montana: The Magazine of Western History* 30 (July 1980): 18–31.
25. Flaherty, "Boycott in Butte," p. 397.
26. A. Dudley Gardner, "Chinese Emigrants in Southwest Wyoming, 1868–1885," in Dirlik, *Chinese on the American Frontier*," p. 342.
27. Delber L. McKee, *Chinese Exclusion versus the Open Door Policy, 1900–1906: Clashes Over China Policy in the Roosevelt Era* (Detroit, MI: Wayne State University Press, 1977), pp. 69–70.
28. Ibid., p. 70.

29. Luella Miner, ed., *Two Heroes of Cathay: An Autobiography and a Sketch* (New York, Chicago, Toronto: Fleming H. Revell, 1903), p. 234.
30. Tsai, *The Chinese Experience*, p. 77.
31. McKee, *Chinese Exclusion*, p. 74.
32. Ibid., pp. 66–73.
33. Leonard Dinnerstein, Roger L. Nichols, and David M. Reimers, *Natives and Strangers: A Multicultural History of Americans* (London: Oxford University Press, 1996), p. 223.
34. McKee, *Chinese Exclusion*, p. 105.
35. Howard Zinn, *A People's History of the United States, 1492–Present* (New York: Harper Perennial, 1995), p. 290.
36. Ibid., p. 292.
37. Ibid., p. 293.
38. Ibid., p. 292.
39. Oscar Handlin, *The Americans: A New History of the People of the United States* (Boston: Little, Brown, 1963), p. 307.
40. Ibid., p. 307.

CHAPTER 9: Anglo-Conformity

1. Roger Daniels, *Coming to America: A History of Immigration and Ethnicity in American Life* (New York: HarperCollins, 1990), pp. 124–25.
2. Charles Jaret, "Troubled by Newcomers: Anti-Immigrant Attitudes and Actions During Two Eras of Mass Migration," in *Mass Migration to the United States: Classical and Contemporary Period*, ed. Pyong Gap Min (New York: Altamira Press, 2002), p. 23.
3. Ibid., p. 24.
4. David M. Reimers, *Unwelcome Strangers: American Identity and the Turn Against Immigration* (New York: Columbia University Press, 1998), p. 15.
5. Leonard Dinnerstein, Roger L. Nichols, and David M. Reimers, *Natives and Strangers: A Multicultural History of Americans* (London: Oxford University Press, 1996), p. 234.
6. Reimers, *Unwelcome Strangers*, p. 15.
7. Dinnerstein, Nichols, and Reimers, *Natives and Strangers*, p. 219.
8. Reimers, *Unwelcome Strangers*, p. 13.
9. Daniels, *Coming to America*, p. 283.
10. John Higham, *Strangers in the Land: Patterns of American Nativism, 1860–1925* (New Brunswick, NJ: Rutgers University Press, 1988), p. 300.
11. Daniels, *Coming to America*, p. 284.
12. Gary Gerstle, *American Crucible: Race and Nation in the Twentieth Century* (Princeton: Princeton University Press, 2001), p. 53.
13. Jaret, "Troubled by Newcomers," p. 33.
14. Stephen Steinberg, *The Ethnic Myth: Race, Ethnicity, and Class in America* (Boston: Beacon Press, 1981), p. 241.
15. Higham, *Strangers in the Land*, 1988.
16. Xiaojian Zhao, *Remaking Chinese America: Immigration, Family, and Community, 1940–1965* (New Brunswick, NJ: Rutgers University Press, 2002), p. 12.
17. Judy Yung, *Unbound Feet: A Social History of Chinese Women in San Francisco* (Berkeley: University of California Press, 1995), p. 169.
18. Zhao, *Remaking Chinese America*, p. 37.
19. Yung, *Unbound Feet*, p. 169.
20. Zhao, *Remaking Chinese America*, p. 16.

21. Ibid., pp. 17–20.
22. Ibid., p. 17.
23. Yung, *Unbound Feet*, p. 157.
24. Victor Low, *The Unimpressible Race: A Century of Educational Struggle by the Chinese in San Francisco* (San Francisco: East/West Publishing, 1982), pp. x–xi.
25. Yung, *Unbound Feet*, p. 135.
26. Ibid., pp. 204–5.
27. Gloria Heyung Chun, *Of Orphans and Warriors: Inventing Chinese American Culture and Identity* (New Brunswick, NJ: Rutgers University Press, 2000), p. 18.
28. Quoted in Henry Yu, *Thinking Orientals: Migration, Contact, and Exoticism in Modern America* (New York: Oxford University Press, 2001), pp. 73–74.
29. Robert G. Lee, *Orientals: Asian Americans in Popular Culture* (Philadelphia, PA: Temple University Press, 1999), pp. 113–36.
30. Barbara Gregorich, "Earl Derr Biggers: A Brief Life of a Popular Author: 1844–1933," *Harvard Magazine*, March–April 2000, vol. 102, no. 4, p. 58.
31. Paul Chang Pang Siu, *The Chinese Laundryman: A Study of Social Isolation*, ed. with introduction by John Kuo Wei Chen (New York: New York University Press, 1987), pp. 9–12.
32. Yu, *Thinking Orientals*, p. 41.
33. Ibid., pp. 96–102.
34. Ibid., p. 134.
35. Renqiu Yu, *To Save China, To Save Ourselves: The Chinese Hand Laundry Alliance of New York* (Philadelphia, PA: Temple University Press, 1992), pp. 25–26.
36. Tung Pok Chin with Winifred C. Chin, *Paper Son: One Man's Story* (Philadelphia, PA: Temple University Press, 2000), p. 26.
37. Yu, *To Save China*, p. 27.
38. Iris Chang, *The Chinese in America: A Narrative History* (New York: Viking, 2003), p. 169.
39. Yu, *To Save China*, pp. 29–30.
40. Siu, *The Chinese Laundryman*, p. 116.
41. Yu, *To Save China*, p. 29.
42. Adam McKeown. "The Sojourner as Astronaut: Paul Siu in Global Perspective," in *Re-Collection: Earlier Asian America*, ed. Josephine Lee and Imogene L. Lim (Philadephia, PA: Temple University Press, 2002), p. 134.

CHAPTER 10: The Chinese Build Their Community

1. Diane Mei Lin Mark and Ginger Chin, *A Place Called Chinese America* (Dubuque, IA: Kendall Hunt, 1982), p. 54.
2. Madeline Y. Hsu, *Dreaming of Gold, Dreaming of Home: Transnationalism and Migration Between the United States and South China, 1882–1943* (Stanford, CA: Stanford University Press, 2000), p. 72.
3. U.S. Department of Commerce and Labor, *Annual Report 1904* (Washington, DC, 1905), p. 147; Hsu, *Dreaming of Gold*, p. 75.
4. Hsu, *Dreaming of Gold*, p. 75.
5. Tung Pok Chin, with Winifred C. Chin, *Paper Son: One Man's Story* (Philadelphia: Temple University Press, 2000), p. 13.
6. R. David Arkush and Leo O. Lee, trans. and eds., *Land Without Ghosts: Chinese Impression of America from the Mid-Nineteenth Century to the Present* (Berkeley: University of California Press, 1989), p. 58.

7. Him Mark Lai, Genny Lim, and Judy Yung, *Island: Poetry and History of Chinese Immigrants on Angel Island, 1910–1940* (Seattle: Washington University Press, 1980), pp. 23–28.

8. Xiao-huang Yin, *Chinese American Literature Since the 1850s* (Chicago: University of Illinois Press, 2000), p. 37.

9. Judy Yung, *Unbound Feet: A Social History of Chinese Women in San Francisco* (Berkeley: University of California Press, 1995), pp. 65–66.

10. Hsu, *Dreaming of Gold*, p. 87.

11. Julian Ralph, "The Chinese Leak," *Harper's Monthly* 82 (March 1891), p. 520.

12. "Buffalo's Chinese Residents," *Buffalo Times*, January 18, 1902, p. 5; Erika Lee, "Enforcing the Borders: Chinese Exclusion along the U.S. Borders with Canada and Mexico, 1882–1924," *Journal of American History*, 89: 1 (June, 2002), pp. 54–86.

13. Ibid.

14. Ibid.

15. Alfred Yee, *Shopping at Giant Foods: Chinese American Supermarkets in Northern California* (Seattle: University of Washington Press, 2003), pp. 48–53.

16. Ibid., p. 115.

17. Ibid., pp. 4, 78–81.

18. Him Mark Lai, *From Sojourners to Ethnic Chinese Americans*, in Chinese (Hong Kong: Joint Publishing, 1992), pp. 92–93.

19. Ronald Takaki, *Strangers from a Different Shore: A History of Asian Americans* (Boston: Little, Brown, 1989), pp. 251–52; Mark and Chin, *A Place Called Chinese America*, pp. 58–59. Yee, *Shopping at Giant Foods*, p. 46.

20. L. Eve Armentrout Ma, *Revolutionaries, Monarchists, and Chinatown: Chinese Politics in the Americas and the 1911 Revolution* (Honolulu: University of Hawaii Press, 1990), p. 115.

21. Alexander McLeod, *Pigtails and Gold Dust* (Caldwell, ID: Caxton Printers, 1947), pp. 140–43.

22. Peter Chu, Nadia Laurova, Lois M. Foster, and Steven C. Moy, *Chinese Theaters in America* (Federal Theater Project/Bureau of Research [Division of Works Progress Administration], 1936), p. 27.

23. Ibid., p. 34.

24. Ibid.

25. Ibid., p. 37.

26. Ibid., p. 10.

27. Ibid., pp. 286–93.

28. Ibid., p. 13.

29. Mary Roberts Coolidge, *Chinese Immigration* (New York: Henry Holt, 1909), p. 105.

30. Yong Chen, *Chinese San Francisco, 1850–1943: A Trans-Pacific Community* (Stanford, CA: Standard University Press, 2000), p. 89.

31. Ibid., p. 87.

32. Marlon K. Hom, *Songs of Gold Mountain: Cantonese Rhymes from San Francisco Chinatown* (Berkeley: University of California Press, 1987), p. 294.

33. Paul Siu, *The Chinese Laundryman: A Study of Social Isolation* (New York: New York University Press, 1987), p. 298.

34. Ibid., p. 295.

35. Philip Hurn, "His Tribe Increased," in *Chinese in New York*, Works Progress Administration project, article 5, box 1, folder 39, August 14, 1936, p. 4.

36. Victor G. Nee and Brett De Bary Nee, *Longtime Californ': A Documentary Study of an American Chinatown* (New York: Pantheon, 1972), p. 90.

37. Peter Kwong, *The New Chinatown* (New York: Hill and Wang, 1987), p. 26.
38. Yin, *Chinese American Literature*, p. 29.
39. Hsu, *Dreaming of Gold*, pp. 39–44.
40. Chin and Chin, *Paper Son*, p. 5.
41. Ibid., p. 195.

CHAPTER 11: In Search of Respect

1. Guanhua Wang, *In Search of Justice: The 1905–1906 Chinese Anti-American Boycott* (Cambridge: Harvard University Press, 2001), p. 21.
2. Ibid., p. 33.
3. Ibid., pp. 21–22.
4. Ibid., p. 22.
5. Ibid., pp. 22–23.
6. Ibid., p. 36.
7. Ibid., p. 61.
8. Shih-shan Henry Tsai, *The Chinese Experience in America* (Bloomington: Indiana University Press, 1986), pp. 91–93.
9. L. Eve Armentrout Ma, *Revolutionaries, Monarchists, and Chinatown: Chinese Politics in the America and the 1911 Revolution* (Honolulu: University of Hawaii Press, 1990), p. 109.
10. Tsai, *The Chinese Experience*, p. 77.
11. Judy Yung, *Unbound Feet: A Social History of Chinese Women in San Francisco* (Berkeley: University of California Press, 1995), pp. 63, 325.
12. Wang, *In Search of Justice*, p. 37.
13. Delber L. McKee, *Chinese Exclusion versus the Open Door Policy, 1900–1906: Clashes Over China Policy in the Roosevelt Era* (Detroit, MI: Wayne State University Press, 1977), p. 74.
14. Ibid., p. 89.
15. Shehong Chen, *Being Chinese, Becoming Chinese American* (Chicago: University of Illinois Press, 2002), p. 78.
16. Tsai, *The Chinese Experience*, p. 79.
17. Ibid.
18. *Shaonian Zhongguo* [The Young China], December 30, 1911.
19. Lawrence K. Rosinger, *China's Wartime Politics: 1937–1944* (Princeton, NJ: Princeton University Press, 1945), p. 9.
20. Him Mark Lai, "To Bring Forth a New China, To Build a Better America: The Chinese Left in America to the 1960s" (manuscript, August 5, 2003), a revised version of the article published in *Chinese America: History and Perspectives* (Chinese Historical Society of America, 1992), p. 3.
21. Ibid.
22. Kwong, *Chinatown, New York: Labor and Politics, 1930–1950* (New York: The New Press, 2001), p. 49.
23. Lai, "To Bring Forth a New China," p. 6.
24. Ibid., p. 13.
25. Ibid., p. 16.
26. Ibid.
27. *Chinese Vanguard*, February 15, 1933, p. 4.
28. Kwong, *Chinatown, New York*, pp. 53–54.

CHAPTER 12: American-Born Aliens

1. Gloria Heyung Chun, *Of Orphans and Warriors: Inventing Chinese American Cultural and Identity* (New Brunswick, NJ: Rutgers University Press, 2000), p. 8.
2. Sucheng Chan, "Race, Ethnic Culture, and Gender in the Construction of Identities among Second-Generation Chinese Americans, 1880s to 1930s," in *Claiming America: Constructing Chinese American Identities During the Exclusion Era*, ed. K. Scott Wong and Sucheng Chan (Philadelphia, PA: Temple University Press, 1998), p. 135.
3. Shehong Chen, *Being Chinese, Becoming Chinese American* (Chicago: University of Illinois Press, 2002), p. 169.
4. Chan, "Race, Ethnic Culture, and Gender," in Wong and Chan, *Claiming America*, p. 133.
5. Chun, *Of Orphans and Warriors*, p. 16.
6. Chan, "Race, Ethnic Culture, and Gender," in Wong and Chan, *Claiming America*, p. 133.
7. Judy Yung, *Unbound Feet: A Social History of Chinese Women in San Francisco* (Berkeley: University of California Press, 1995), pp. 158–59.
8. Ronald Takaki, *Double Victory: A Multicultural History of America in World War II* (Boston: Little, Brown, 2000), p. 114.
9. Chan, "Race, Ethnic Culture, and Gender," in Wong and Chan, *Claiming America*, p. 155.
10. Ibid.
11. Yung, *Unbound Feet*, p. 143.
12. Chun, *Of Orphans and Warriors*, p. 26.
13. Haiming Liu, "The Trans-Pacific Family: A Case Study of Sam Chang's Family History," *Amerasia Journal* 18, no. 2 (1992): 1–34.
14. Liping Zhu, *A Chinaman's Chance: The Chinese on the Rocky Mountain Mining Frontier* (Boulder: University Press of Colorado), p. 194.
15. Chen, *Being Chinese*, pp. 169–70.
16. Ibid., pp. 172–73.
17. Ibid., pp. 26–27.
18. Yung, *Unbound Feet*, pp. 201–4.
19. Ibid., p. 202.
20. Chun, *Of Orphans and Warriors*, p. 66.
21. Lorraine Dong, "The Forbidden City Legacy and Its Chinese American Women," in *Chinese American Perspectives* (Los Angeles: Chinese Historical Society of America, 1992), p. 126.

CHAPTER 13: Inroads to American Politics

1. Ronald Takaki, *A Different Mirror: A History of Multicultural America* (Boston: Little, Brown, 1993), p. 367.
2. Ibid., p. 366.
3. *Chinese Journal*, December 12, 1930, p. 7.
4. *New York Times*, April 27, 1931, p. 60.
5. Kwong, *Chinatown, New York: Labor and Politics, 1930–1950* (New York: The New Press, 2001), p. 55.
6. Ibid., pp. 55–56.
7. Judy Yung, *Unbound Feet: A Social History of Chinese Women in San Francisco* (Berkeley: University of California Press, 1995), p. 182.
8. Ibid.

9. Ibid., p. 183.

10. Kwong, *Chinatown, New York*, p. 58.

11. Yung, *Unbound Feet*, p. 183.

12. Sucheng Chan, *Asian Americans: An Interpretive History* (Boston: Twayne, 1991), p. 115.

13. Kwong, *Chinatown, New York*, p. 89.

14. Him Mark Lai, "To Bring Forth a New China, To Build a Better America: The Chinese Left in America to the 1960s" (manuscript, August 5, 2003), revised article published in *Chinese America: History and Perspectives* (Chinese Historical Society of America, 1992), p. 18.

15. Kwong, *Chinatown, New York*, p. 63.

16. Gor Yun Leong, *Chinatown Inside Out* (New York: Barrows Mussey, 1936), p. 33; Kwong, *Chinatown, New York*, p. 66.

17. Kwong, *Chinatown, New York*, pp. 64–65.

18. Renqiu Yu, *To Save China, To Save Ourselves: The Chinese Hand Laundry Alliance* (Philadelphia, PA: Temple University Press, 1922), p. 40.

19. Kwong, *Chinatown, New York*, p. 65.

20. Yu, *To Save China*, p. 40.

21. Kwong, *Chinatown, New York*, p. 73.

22. Yu, *To Save China*, p. 62.

23. Kwong, *Chinatown, New York*, p. 82.

24. Victor Nee, and Brett De Bary Nee, *Longtime Californ': A Documentary Study of an American Chinatown* (New York: Pantheon, 1973), p. 170. Takaki, *Strangers from a Different Shore: A History of Asian Americans* (Boston: Little, Brown, 1989), p. 269.

25. Kwong, *Chinatown, New York*, p. 109.

26. Yung, *Unbound Feet*, p. 207.

27. Ibid., p. 237.

28. Kwong, *Chinatown, New York*, p. 111.

29. Harold R. Isaacs, *Scratches on Our Minds: American Images of China and India* (New York: John Day, 1958), p. 157.

30. T. Christopher Jespersen, *American Images of China, 1931–1949* (Stanford, CA: Stanford University Press, 1998), p. 46.

31. Yung, *Unbound Feet*, p. 240.

CHAPTER 14: A Window of Opportunity

1. Harold R. Isaacs, *Scratches on Our Minds: American Images of China and India* (New York: John Day, 1958).

2. Xiaojian Zhao, *Remaking Chinese America: Immigration, Family, and Community, 1940–1965* (New Brunswick, NJ: Rutgers University Press, 2002), p. 22.

3. Ronald Takaki, *Double Victory: A Multicultural History of America in World War II* (Boston: Little, Brown, 2000), p. 119.

4. Ibid., p. 6.

5. Ibid., p. 119.

6. David M. Reimers, *Still the Golden Door: The Third World Comes to America* (New York: Columbia University Press, 1985), p. 13.

7. T. Christopher Jespersen, *American Images of China, 1931–1949* (Stanford, CA: Stanford University Press, 1996), p. 57.

8. Takaki, *Double Victory*, p. 118.

9. Ibid., p. 119.

10. Roger Daniels, *Coming to America: A History of Immigration and Ethnicity in American Life* (New York: HarperCollins, 1990), p. 304.
11. Ronald Takaki, *A Different Mirror: A History of Multicultural America* (Boston: Little, Brown, 1993), p. 367.
12. Michael L. Levine, *African Americans and Civil Rights: From 1619 to the Present* (Phoenix: Oryx Press, 1996), p. 155; Takaki, *Double Victory*, p. 39.
13. Takaki, *Double Victory*, p. 23.
14. Ibid.
15. Ibid., p. 29.
16. Ibid., p. 30.
17. Ibid., p. 40.
18. Ibid.
19. Ibid., pp. 41–42.
20. Ibid., pp. 116–17; Dusanka Miscevic and Peter Kwong, *Chinese Americans: The Immigrant Experience* (Hugh Lauter Levin Associates, 2000), p. 143.
21. Yen Le Espiritu, "Changing Lives: World War II and The Postwar Years," in *Asian American Studies: A Reader*, ed. Jean Yu-wen Shen Wu and Min Song (New Brunswick, NJ: Rutgers University Press, 2000), p. 149.
22. Takaki, *Double Victory*, p. 117.
23. Zhao, *Remaking Chinese America*, p. 57.
24. *Shanghai Evening Post and Mercury* (New York), March 26, 1943, p. 3.
25. Peter Kwong, *Chinatown, New York: Labor and Politics, 1930–1950*, rev. ed. (New York: The New Press, 2000), p. 114.
26. Takaki, *Double Victory*, p. 115.
27. Tung Pok Chin with Winifred C. Chin, *Paper Son: One Man's Story* (Philadelphia, PA: Temple University Press, 2000), p. 43.
28. Christina M. Lim and Sheldon H. Lim, "In the Shadow of the Tiger: The 407th Air Service Squadron, Fourteenth Air Force, CBI, World War II," in *Chinese America: History and Perspectives 1993* (Chinese Historical Society of America), p. 25.
29. Judy Yung, *Unbound Feet: A Social History of Chinese Women in San Francisco* (Berkeley: University of California Press, 1995), p. 257.
30. Zhao, *Remaking Chinese America*, p. 80.
31. Ruthanne Lum McCunn, *Sole Survivor* (San Francisco: Design Enterprises of San Francisco, 1985), p. 221.

CHAPTER 15: Cold War & Chinese American Community

1. Robert G. Lee, *Orientals: Asian Americans in Popular Culture* (Philadelphia, PA: Temple University Press, 1999), p. 156.
2. John Dower, "Occupied Japan and the American Lake, 1945–50," in *America's Asia: Dissenting Essays on Asian-American Relations*, ed. Edward Friedman and Mark Selden (New York: Pantheon Books, 1969), pp. 146–206.
3. Ibid., p. 157.
4. "Castro Speaks" on *Meet The Press*, FBIS, September 30,1960.
5. Lee, *Orientals*, p. 157.
6. Ibid., p. 154.
7. Peter Kwong, *Chinatown, New York: Labor and Politics, 1930–1950*, rev. ed. (New York: The New Press, 2000), p. 140.
8. John Beatz, *The Iron Curtain over America*, publisher unknown, 1951, p. 28.
9. Kwong, *Chinatown, New York*, p. 137.

10. Iris Chang, *The Chinese in America: A Narrative History* (New York: Viking Press, 2003), pp. 237–42.
11. Kwong, *Chinatown, New York*, p. 136.
12. Ibid., p. 134.
13. T. Christopher Jespersen, *American Images of China, 1931–1949* (Stanford, CA: Stanford University Press, 1996), pp. 160, 176.
14. Ibid., p. 176.
15. Kwong, *Chinatown, New York*, p. 139.
16. Him Mark Lai, "The Chinese Marxist Left, Chinese Students and Scholars in America, and the New China: Mid-1940s to Mid-1950s," unpublished paper, p. 7.
17. Lai, "The Chinese Marxist Left," p. 21.
18. Renqiu Yu, *To Save China, To Save Ourselves: The Chinese Hand Laundry Alliance of New York* (Philadelphia, PA: Temple University Press, 1992), p. 191.
19. Kwong, *Chinatown, New York*, p. 144.
20. Ibid.
21. Everett F. Drumright, *Report on the Problem of Passport Fraud at Hong Kong*, Foreign Service Dispatch 931, U.S. Department of State, December 9, 1955.
22. Kwong, *Chinatown, New York*, p. 145.
23. Xiaojian Zhao, *Remaking Chinese American: Immigration, Family, and Community, 1940–1965* (New Brunswick, NJ: Rutgers University Press, 2002), p. 177.
24. Figures provided in the news release by the Department of Justice on December 31, 1972, quoted in Zhao, *Remaking Chinese America*, p. 183. They revised upward the figures listed in the INS annual reports quoted by Mae M. Ngai, *Impossible Subjects: Illegal Aliens and the Making of Modern America* (Princeton, NJ: Princeton University Press, 2004), p. 222.
25. Lai, "The Chinese Marxist Left," pp. 47–48.
26. Ngai, *Impossible Subjects*, p. 222.
27. Lai, "The Chinese Marxist Left," p. 48.

CHAPTER 16: Chinese Professionals Wanted!

1. Peter Kwong, *The New Chinatown* (New York: Hill and Wang, 1987), p. 16.
2. Harriet Zuckerman, *Scientific Elite: Nobel Laureates in the United States* (New York: Free Press, 1977), pp. 69–71.
3. U.S. Congress, Senate, Committee on the Judiciary, 1950, 450–51, quoted in *The New Asian Immigration in Los Angeles and Global Restructuring*, ed. Paul Ong, Edna Bonacich, and Lucie Cheng (Philadelphia, PA: Temple University Press, 1994), p. 54.
4. U.S. Congress, House, President's Commission on Immigration and Naturalization, 1952, 119–20, quoted in Ong, Bonacich, and Cheng, *The New Asian Immigration*, pp. 54–55.
5. U.S. Congress, House, President's Commission on Immigration and Naturalization, 1952, 457, quoted in Ong, Bonacich, and Cheng, *The New Asian Immigration*, p. 55.
6. Quoted in ibid., p. 55. The McCarran-Walter Immigration and Nationality Act removed the ban on Asian and African immigrants to the United States and permitted spouses and minor children to enter as nonquota immigrants, but at the same time it extended the national origins quota system set up by the Johnson-Reed Act of 1924. Its critics pointed out that while Britain was using only half her quota of 65,000, Italy had a twenty-year waiting list for her quota of 5,500.

The emerging nations of Africa and Asia were given only the token quotas of 100 each.

7. David M. Reimers, *Still the Golden Door: The Third World Comes to America* (New York: Columbia University Press, 1985), p. 33.
8. Ong, Bonacich, and Cheng, *The New Asian Immigration*, pp. 53–59.
9. Stanford M. Lyman, *Chinese Americans* (New York: Random House, 1974), p. 130.
10. Betty Lee Sung, *Mountain of Gold: The Story of the Chinese in America* (New York: Macmillan, 1967), p. 257.
11. Sucheng Chan, *Asian Americans: An Interpretive History* (Boston: Twayne, 1991), p. 168.
12. Vijay Prashad, *The Karma of Brown Folk* (Minneapolis: University of Minnesota Press, 2000), p. 69.
13. Rose Hum Lee, *The Chinese in the United States of America* (Hong Kong: Hong Kong University Press, 1960), p. 86.
14. Lee, *The Chinese in the United States of America*, p. 87; Kwong, *The New Chinatown*, p. 15.
15. Lynn Pan, *Sons of the Yellow Emperor: A History of Chinese Diaspora* (Boston: Little, Brown, 1990), p. 282.
16. Y. K. Chu, *History of the Chinese People in America* (New York: China Times, 1975), chap. 14. Also Lee, *The Chinese in the United States of America*, pp. 88–89.
17. Chih Meng, *A Sixty Year Search* (New York: China Institute in America, 1981), pp. 64–65.
18. Weili Ye, *Seeking Modernity in China's Name: Chinese Students in the United States, 1900–1927* (Stanford, CA: Stanford University Press, 2001), p. 91.
19. Tingfang Wu, *America Through the Spectacles of an Oriental Diplomat* (New York: Frederick Stokes, 1914), pp. 16–17, quoted in *Claiming America: Constructing Chinese American Identities during the Exclusion Era*, ed. K. Scott Wong and Sucheng Chan (Philadelphia, PA: Temple University Press, 1998), p. 11.
20. Lee, *The Chinese in the United States of America*, p. 112.
21. C. N. Yang, *Selected Interviews and Essays* (Taiwan: World Scientific Publishing, 1988), p. 123.
22. Steven C. Lo, *The Incorporation of Eric Chung: A Novel* (Chapel Hill, NC: Algonquin Books, 1989), p. 20.
23. Franklin Ng, *The Taiwanese Americans* (London: Greenwood Press, 1998), p. 15.
24. Alex Salkever, Science section, *Christian Science Monitor,* June 28, 1999.
25. Deborah Woo, *The Glass Ceiling and Asian Americans: A Research Monograph*, report prepared for the U.S. Department of Labor Glass Ceiling Commission Office of the Secretary, July 1994.
26. Deborah Woo, "Is the Glass Ceiling Cracking?" (http://goldsea.com/) January 9, 2003.
27. Winfred Yu, "Asian American Charge Prejudice Slows Climb to Management Ranks," *Wall Street Journal,* September 11, 1985.
28. Vivian Louie, "Parents' Aspirations and Investment: The Role of Social Class in the Education Experiences of 1.5- and Second-Generation Chinese Americans," *Harvard Educational Review* 71, no. 3 (Fall 2001): 454.
29. Chang-tsu Wu, *Chink!* (New York: Meridian Books, 1972), pp. 231–38.
30. Yang, *Selected Interviews and Essays*, p. 99.
31. Thomas Sowell, *The Economics and Politics of Race: An International Perspective* (New York: William Morrow, 1983), p. 197.
32. Bruce Brown, "In Evidence of a Glass-Ceiling for Asian American" (paper prepared for WEAI Conference, Denver, Colorado, July 12, 2003).
33. Brendan A. Maher, "Strangers in a Strange Land," *The Scientist,* October 1, 2001.

CHAPTER 17: American-Born Achievers

1. Vivian S. Louie, *Compelled to Excel: Immigration, Education, and Opportunity among Chinese Americans* (Stanford, CA: Stanford University Press, 2004), p. 50.
2. Ibid., p. 104.
3. Ibid., p. 109.
4. Ibid.
5. Ibid., p. 110.
6. Quoted in Ronald Takaki, *Double Victory: A Multicultural History of America in World War II* (Boston: Little, Brown, 2000), p. 187.
7. Takkai, *Double Victory*, p. 188.
8. Louie, *Compelled to Excel*, pp. 98–99.
9. Vivian Louie, "Parents' Aspirations and Investment: The Role of Social Class in the Educational Experiences of 1.5- and Second-Generation Chinese Americans," *Harvard Educational Review* 71, no. 3 (Fall 2001): pp. 438–74.

CHAPTER 18: The Rise of Asian America

1. Michael Goldfield, *The Color of Politics: Race and the Mainsprings of American Politics* (New York: The New Press, 1997), p. 270.
2. Ibid., p. 271.
3. Ibid., p. 289.
4. Robert G. Lee, *Orientals: Asian Americans in Popular Culture* (Philadelphia, PA: Temple University Press, 1999), p. 157.
5. Michael Omi and Howard Winant, *Racial Formation in the United States: From the 1960s to the 1980s* (New York: Routledge, 1991), p. 95.
6. Charles V. Hamilton and Dona Cooper Hamilton, *The Dual Agenda: Race and Social Welfare Policies of Civil Rights Organizations* (New York: Columbia University Press, 1997), p. 151.
7. Ibid., p. 123.
8. Omi and Winant, *Racial Formation*, p. 98.
9. Lee, *Orientals*, p. 158.
10. Glenn Omatsu, "The 'Four Prisons' and the Movement of Liberation: Asian American Activism from the 1960s to the 1990s," in *Asian American Studies: A Reader*, ed. Jen Yu-wen Shen Wu and Min Song (New Brunswick, NJ: Rutgers University Press, 2000), p. 174.
11. Ibid., p. 167.
12. Yen Le Espiritu, *Asian American Panethnicity: Bridging Institutions and Identities* (Philadelphia, PA: Temple University Press, 1992), pp. 32–33.
13. Ibid., p. 34.
14. Andrew Hsiao, "The Hidden History of Asian-American Activism in New York City," *Social Policy* 23 (Summer 1998): 29.
15. Howard Zinn, *A People's History of the United States: 1492–Present* (New York: HarperPerennial, 1995), p. 475.
16. John T. McCartney, *Ideologies: An Essay in African-American Political Thought* (Philadelphia, PA: Temple University Press, 1992), p. 129.
17. *Wikipedia: The Free Encyclopedia*, s.v. "Winter Soldier Investigation," http://en.wikipedia.org/wiki/Winter_Soldier_Investigation.
18. Espiritu, *Asian American Panethnicity*, p. 43.
19. *Wikipedia*, "Winter Soldier Investigation."
20. Espiritu, *Asian American Panethnicity*, p. 44.

21. C. M. Loo and P. N. Kiang, "Race-Related Stressors and Psychological Trauma: Contributions of Asian American Vietnam Veterans," *Asian Americans: Vulnerable Populations, Model Interventions, and Clarifying Agendas*, ed. L. Zhan (Sudbury, MA: Jones and Bartlett, 2003), pp. 19–42.

22. Gloria Heyung Chun, *Of Orphans and Warriors: Inventing Chinese American Culture and Identity* (New Brunswick, NJ: Rutgers University Press, 2000), p. 103.

23. Ibid., p. 103.

24. "History of the Red Guard Party," *Asian American Revolutionary Movement Ezine* (http://www.aamovement.net/history/red_guard/redguardparty.html).

CHAPTER 19: Struggle for Identity

1. Emma Gee, ed., *Counterpoint: Perspectives on Asian America* (Los Angeles: Asian American Studies Center, University of California, Los Angeles, 1976), pp. 205–6.

2. "Salute to the 60s and 70s: Legacy of the San Francisco State Strike," Commemorative Issue, *Amerasia Journal* 15, no. 1 (1989): 3–37.

3. Gee, *Counterpoint*, p. 217.

4. Frank Chin, Jeffery Paul Chan, Lawson Fusao Inada, and Shawn Wong, eds., *Ai-iieeeee!: An Anthology of Asian-American Writers* (Washington, DC: Howard University Press, 1983), p. vii–viii.

5. Ibid., p. viii.

6. William Wei, *The Asian American Movement* (Philadelphia, PA: Temple University Press, 1993), p. 145.

7. Ibid., p. 140.

8. Ibid., p. 146.

CHAPTER 20: Radicals and Reformers

1. Buck Wong, "Need for Awareness: An Essay on Chinatown, San Francisco," in *Roots: An Asian American Reader*, ed. Amy Tachiki, Eddie Wong, Franklin Odo, Buck Wong (Los Angeles: Asian American Studies Center, University of California, Los Angeles, 1971), pp. 265–72.

2. Gloria Heyung Chun, *Of Orphans and Warriors: Inventing Chinese American Culture and Identity* (New Brunswick, NJ: Rutgers University Press, 2000), pp. 108–9.

3. *Wei Min She Reply to IWK Criticism on May Day Asian Contingent Statement*, pamphlet, 1974.

4. Frances Fox Piven and Richard A. Cloward, *Poor People's Movements: Why They Succeed, How They Fail* (New York: Vintage Books, 1977), p. 265.

5. Karen M. Tani, "Asian Americans for Equality and the Community-based Development Movement: From Grass Roots to Institutions" (Honor's thesis, Dartmouth College, May 2002), p. 24.

6. Ibid., p. 92.

7. Ibid., p. 91.

8. *The Forgotten Minority: Asian Americans in New York City* (New York: New York State Advisory Committee to the U.S. Commission on Civil Rights, 1976), p. 1.

9. L. Ling-Chi Wang, "Lau v. Nichols: History of a Struggle for Equal and Quality Education," in *Counterpoint: Perspectives on Asian America*, ed. Emma Gee (Los Angeles: Asian American Studies Center, University of California, Los Angeles, 1976), p. 241.

10. Ibid., p. 243.
11. Tani, "Asian Americans for Equality," p. 43.
12. Susan Anderson, "Eyes on the Prizes, Not the People," *Nation*, October 16, 1989, pp. 1, 422.
13. William Wei, *The Asian American Movement* (Philadelphia, PA: Temple University Press, 1993), p. 217.
14. Ibid., p. 220.
15. Tani, "Asian Americans for Equality," pp. 104–5.
16. Wei, *The Asian American Movement*, p. 222.
17. Tani, "Asian Americans for Equality," p. 121.
18. Jerry Tung, interview with Peter Kwong, Spring 1983.
19. Richard Brookhiser, "The Resistible Rise of Margaret Chin," *City Journal*, Spring 1991 (http://www.city-journal.org/article02.php?aid=1606), p. 2.
20. Louis Proyect, "Re: Max Elbaum to Speak in Sacramento on Social Movement History," *Mail Archive*, August 11, 2002 (http://archives.econ.utah.edu/archives/a-list/2002w32/msg00012.htm).
21. Tani, "Asian Americans for Equality," p. 130.
22. Ibid., p. 189.

CHAPTER 21: Culture Wars

1. Frank Chin, *Chickencoop Chinaman*, in *Two Plays by Fran Chin* (Seattle: University of Washington Press, 1981), quoted in Frank Chin, Jeffery Paul Chan, Lawson Fusao Inada, and Shawn Wong., eds., *Aiiieeeee!: An Anthology of Asian American Writers* (Washington, DC: Howard University Press, 1983), p. 50.
2. Frank Chin, *The Year of the Dragon* in *Two Plays by Fran Chin* (Seattle: University of Washington Press, 1981), p. 124.
3. Chin, Chan, Inada, and Wong, *Aiiieeeee!*, p. 53.
4. Frank Chin and Jeffrey Paul Chan, "Racist Love," in *Seeing Through Shuck*, ed. Richard Kostelanetz (New York: Ballantine, 1972), p. 65.
5. King-kok Cheung, "The Woman Warrior Versus the Chinaman Pacific," in *Asian American Studies: A Reader*, ed. Jean Yu-wen Shen Wu and Ming Song (New Brunswick, NJ: Rutgers University Press, 2000), p. 309.
6. Xiao-huang Yin, *Chinese American Literature Since the 1850s* (Chicago: University of Illinois Press, 2000), p. 235.
7. Jeffery Paul Chan, Frank Chin, Lawson Fusao Inada, and Shawn Wong, eds., *The Big Aiiieeeee!: An Anthology of Chinese American and Japanese American Literature* (New York: Meridian, 1991), p. xii.
8. Yin, *Chinese American Literature*, p. 241.
9. Frank Chin, "This Is Not an Autobiography," *Genre* 18 (1985): 109–30, 129.
10. Sau-ling C. Wong, "What's in a Name? Defining Chinese American Literature of the Immigrant Generation," in *Frontiers of Asian American Studies: Writing, Research and Commentary*, ed. Gail M. Nomura, Russell Endo, Stephen H. Sumida, and Russell C. Leong (Pullman: Washington State University Press, 1989), p. 162.
11. Translated by Marlon K. Hom in Chan, Chin, Inada, and Wong, *The Big Aiiieeeee!*, p. 165.
12. Wong, "What's in a Name?", p. 163.
13. Yin, *Chinese American Literature*, p. 169.
14. Ibid., p. 171.
15. Ibid., p. 167.

16. *US News & World Report*, December 26, 1966, quoted in *Roots: An Asian American Reader*, ed. Amy Tachiki, Eddie Wong, Franklin Odo and Buck Wong (Los Angeles: Asian American Studies Center, University of California, Los Angeles, 1971), pp. 6–7.

17. Robert G. Lee, *Orientals: Asian Americans in Popular Culture* (Philadelphia, PA: Temple University Press, 1999), p. 187.

18. Peter Kwong and Dusanka Miscevic, "The Chinese Diaspora," in *Race and Ethnic Relations: Annual Editions 1989/99* (New York: McGraw-Hill, 1999; originally published in *World Business* [May/June 1996]), p. 158. Citations are to the McGraw-Hill publication.

19. Pui Yao, "The 'Isolation' of New York City Chinatown: A Geo-Historical Approach to a Chinese Community in the U.S." (PhD thesis, City University of New York, 2003), p. 136.

CHAPTER 22: The Rise and Fall of Chinatowns

1. Wilson Record, *Minority Groups and Intergroup Relations in the San Francisco Bay Area* (Berkeley: Institute of Governmental Studies, University of California Press, 1963), p. 23.

2. Bernard Wong, *Chinatown, Economic Adaptation and Ethnic Identity of the Chinese* (New York: Holt, Rinehart and Winston, 1982), p. 41.

3. Peter Kwong, *The New Chinatown* (New York: Hill and Wang, 1987), p. 37.

4. Paul Ong, "Chinatown Unemployment and the Ethnic Labor Market," *Amerasia Journal* 11, no. 1 (1984): 35–54.

5. Bernard Wong, *Ethnicity and Entrepreneurship: The New Chinese Immigrants in the San Francisco Bay Area* (Boston: Allyn and Bacon, 1998), p. 57.

6. Kwong, *The New Chinatown*, p. 44.

7. Jan Lin, *Reconstructing Chinatown: Ethnic Enclave, Global Change* (Minneapolis: University of Minnesota Press, 1998), p. 85.

8. Joel Kotkin, "Will the Chinese Save L.A.?" in "Fixing America's Schools," special issue, *The American Enterprise*, September–October 1996 (http://www.taemag.com/issues/articleid.16298/article_detail.asp).

9. Wellington K.K. Chan, "Chinese American Business Networks and Trans-Pacific Economic Relations Since the 1970s," in *The Expanding Roles of Chinese Americans in U.S.–China Relations*, ed. Peter H. Koehn and Xiao-huang Yin (Armonk, NY: M.E. Sharpe, 2002), p. 152.

10. Lin, *Reconstructing Chinatown*, p. 88.

11. Chan, "Chinese American Business Networks," p. 151.

12. Lin, *Reconstructing Chinatown*, p. 86.

13. Ibid., p. 88.

14. Kwong, *The New Chinatown*, p. 45.

15. Ibid., p. 52.

16. "History of Chicago's Chinatown," http://www.Chicago-chinatown.com.

17. Kwong, *The New Chinatown*, pp. 53–56.

18. Tarry Hum, "Mapping Global Production in New York City's Garment Industry: The Role of Sunset Park, Brooklyn's Immigrant Economy," *Economic Development Quarterly* 17, no. 3 (August 2003): 294–309.

19. Peter Kwong, *Forbidden Workers: Illegal Chinese and American Labor* (New York: The New Press, 1997), p. 101.

20. Rachel X. Weissman, "Reaping What They Sew," *Brooklyn Bridge* 2, no. 9 (May 1997): 52–53.

CHAPTER 23: Into the Suburbs

1. Tarry Hum, "Mapping Global Production in New York City's Garment Industry: The Role of Sunset-Park, Brooklyn's Immigrant Economy," *Economic Development Quarterly* 17, no. 3 (August 2003): 299.
2. "Chinese Communities Vary Widely," *World Journal*, June 20, 2003; translated from the Chinese by Michael Huang, The Citizen, *Gotham Gazette*, July 2003, http://www.gothamgazette.com/citizen/jul03/.
3. Matthew Ruben, "Suburbanization and Urban Poverty under Neoliberalism," in *The New Poverty Studies: The Ethnography of Power, Politics, and Impoverished People in the United States*, ed. Judith Goode and Jeff Maskovsky (New York: New York University Press), 2001, p. 436.
4. "Chinese Communities Vary Widely," Huang, tr.
5. Timothy P. Fong, *The Contemporary Asian American Experience: Beyond the Model Minority* (Upper Saddle River, NJ: Prentice Hall, 2002), p. 48.
6. Pyong Gap Min, ed., *Asian Americans: Contemporary Trends and Issues* (London: Sage, 1995), p. 24.
7. Julie Shiroishi, "American as Apple Pie," *AsianWeek*, September 27–October 3, 1996.
8. Eric Liu, "Chinatown and the Suburbs," *Becoming American: The Chinese Experience—A Bill Moyers Special, Public Affairs Television*, 2003 (http://www.pbs.org/becoming-american/ce_witness 15.html).
9. Janet Dang, "Learning Limits: How Redrawn School Boundaries Are Pitting Asian American Parents Against One East Bay School District," *Asian Week* 21, no. 29 (March 16, 2000) (http://www.asianweek.com/2000_03_16/feature_learninglim-its.html).
10. Matt Leingang, "Area Diverse but Not Blended," *Democrat and Chronicle*, April 7, 2001 (http://www.democratandchronicle.com/news/extra/census/0407diversity.shtml).

CHAPTER 24: Chinese American Transnationals

1. Wellington K. K. Chan, "Chinese American Business Networks and Trans-Pacific Economic Relations Since the 1970s," in *The Expanding Roles of Chinese Americans in U.S.–China Relations*, ed. Peter H. Koehn and Xiao-huang Yin (Armonk, NY: M.E. Sharpe, 2002), pp. 145–61.
2. Ibid.
3. Yen-Feng Tseng, "The Mobility of Entrepreneurs and Capital: Taiwanese Capital-Linked Migration," *International Migration* 38, no. 2 (2000): 143–66.
4. "The Inside Story: Vinyl Chloride," *Chemical Industry Archives*: A Project of Environmental Working Group (http://www.chemicalindustryarchives.org).
5. Bernard Wong, *Ethnicity and Entrepreneurship: The New Chinese Immigrants in the San Francisco Bay Area* (Boston: Allyn and Bacon, 1998), p. 88.
6. Chan, "Chinese American Business Networks," pp. 147–48.
7. Marian Liu, "Chinese Group Unites High-Tech Minorities," *San Jose Mercury News*, February 1, 2002.
8. "Career Choices of Elite Asian American Grads," *GoldSea Asian Air Forum*, November 12, 2002.
9. Ronald Alsop, "Top Programs Compete for Minority Candidates," College Journal section, *Wall Street Journal Online*, 2003 (http://www.collegejournal.com/bschool03/articles/20020909-alsop-minority.html).

10. Meg Lundstrom, "East Meets West Meets East: Chinese Networking in Silicon Valley: Asian Entrepreneurs' Groups Hobnob Across the Pacific," *Business Week On line/Frontier,* January 12, 2000 (http://www.businessweek.com/).
11. George Koo, "Chinese American Contributions to Silicon Valley," a speech given at the 20ᵗʰ Anniversary Banquet of the Chinese American Forum, August 3, 2002, reproduced in ModelMinority.com: A Guide to Asian American Empowerment.
12. Laura Li, "Silicon Siblings: Taiwan Links up with Silicon Valley," Scott Williams, tr., *Sinorama.com,* 1998/8.
13. "Skilled Immigrants and Silicon Valley: New Study Shows Importance of California-Asia Linkages," report by *Global Competitiveness Project,* a public education project of the American Immigration Law Foundation.
14. Koo, "Chinese American Contributions to Silicon Valley."
15. Liu, "Chinese Group Unites High-Tech Minorities."
16. Li, "Silicon Siblings."
17. Ibid.
18. Ibid.
19. Andrew Tanzer, "Made in Taiwan," *Forbes,* April 2, 2001.
20. Lundstrom, "East Meets West Meets East."
21. Koo, "Chinese American Contribution to Silicon Valley."
22. Henry S. Rowen, "Two-Way Brain Drain: Talented Asian Immigrants Flock to U.S. High Tech Companies," *International Economy,* July 2001.
23. Terence Chea, "Cultural Revolution in the Valley," *Wired News,* April 8, 2000.

CHAPTER 25: Ethnoburbs

1. Janet Dang, "Learning Limits: How Redrawn School Boundaries Are Pitting Asian American Parents Against One East Bay School District," *AsianWeek* 21, no. 29 (March 16, 2000): 4–5 (http://www.asianweek.com/2003_3_16/feature_learninglimits.html).
2. John Horton, *The Politics of Diversity: Immigration, Resistance, and Change in Monterey Park, California* (Philadelphia, PA: Temple University Press, 1995), p. 31.
3. Horton, *The Politics of Diversity,* p. 31.
4. Timothy P. Fong, *The Contemporary Asian American Experience: Beyond the Model Minority* (Upper Saddle River, NJ: Prentice Hall, 2002), p. 49.
5. Min Zhou and Rebecca Kim, "A Tale of Two Metropolises: New Immigrant Chinese Communities in New York and Los Angeles," in *New York and Los Angeles: Politics, Society, and Culture,* ed. David Halle (Chicago, IL: University of Chicago Press, 2003), p. 129.
6. Wei Li, "Anatomy of a New Ethnic Settlement: The Chinese Ethnoburb in Los Angeles," *Urban Studies* 35, no. 2, 1998, pp. 470–501.
7. Dennis Akizuki, "Taiwan Ties Rapid Influx Is Changing Bedroom Community to Business Hub," *Mercury News,* July 31, 1999.
8. Patrick Leigh Brown, "In One Suburb, Asian Americans Gain a Firm Political Foothold," *New York Times,* January 3, 2003, p. A9.
9. Walter Nicholls, "A New Chinatown," *Washington Post,* October 22, 2003, p. F1.
10. Ibid.
11. Patricia Leigh Brown, "The New Chinatown? Try the Asian Mall," Nation section, *New York Times,* March 24, 2003.
12. Ibid.

CHAPTER 26: A Culture of Growing Self-Confidence

1. Two sample letters posted @ http://csaus.org/ap/petition-letter2.doc.
2. Alethea Yip, "Campus Politics, College Students Renew Demands for Ethnic Studies Programs," *AsianWeek*, May 10–16, 1996, p. 1.
3. Jennie Kennedy, "Asian American Studies at the University of Texas," *Daily Texan*, November 27–December 1, 2000, available at *Model Minority: A Guide to Asian American Empowerment* (http://modelminority.com/).
4. Kandice Chuh, *Imagine Otherwise: On Asian Americanist Critique* (Durham, NC: Duke University Press, 2003), p. 61.
5. Susan Koshy, "The Fiction of Asian American Literature," in *Asian American Studies: A Reader*, ed. Jean Yu-wen Shen Wu and Min Song (New Brunswick, NJ: Rutgers University Press, 2000), p. 474.
6. Michael Shields, "Yin Yang: Asian Title Signals Big Asian Mag Bang," *Media Daily News*, Monday, June 14, 2004.
7. Ibid.
8. Vanessa Hua, "*Noodle* Magazine Caters to Gay Asian Americans; New Magazine for Gay Asian Americans *Noodle* Publisher Hopes To Increase Understanding, Visibility," *San Francisco Chronicle*, Sunday, June 30, 2002.
9. Frances Kai-Hwa Wang, "Learning Other APA Cultures: Trials and Tribulations," Asian American Village, *IM Diversity* (http://www.imdiversity.com).
10. William Wei, *The Asian American Movement* (Philadelphia, PA: Temple University Press, 1993), p. 53.
11. H. Y. Nahm, "Manifest Destiny," Personalities: Filmmakers, *GoldSea Asian American Supersite* (http://www.goldsea.com).

CHAPTER 27: The Limits of the Civil Rights Agenda

1. Pei-te Lien, *The Making of Asian America through Political Participation*, Philadelphia: Temple University Press, 2001.
2. Joy Jia, "Chinese Urged to Vote but Turnout Uncertain: Election 2004," UC Berkeley Graduate School of Journalism, November 2, 2004.
3. Pei-te Lien, "Taking a Pulse of Chinese Americans at the Dawn of the 21st Century: Results from the Multi-site Asian American Political Survey," (paper presented at the Global and Local Dimensions of Asian America: An International Conference on Asian Diasporas, May 10–12, 2002, Radisson Miyako Hotel, San Francisco, California), pp. 15–16.
4. Jack S. Vaitayanonta, "Trends in Asian American Political Affiliation and Voting, 1984–1996," *Asian American Policy Review*, Vol. VII, 1997, pp. 183–199.
5. Samson Wong, "How Bipartisan Apathy Hurts Us: Neither the GOP, nor the Demos Bother with S.F.'s Asian Americans," *AsianWeek*, September 6, 1998.
6. Leland T. Saito, "Asian Americans and Multiracial Political Coalitions: New York's Chinatown and Redistricting, 1990–1991," in *Asian Americans and Politics: Perspectives, Experiences, Prospects*, (ed.) Gordon H. Chang (Stanford, CA: Stanford University Press, 2001), p. 389.
7. Saito, p. 391.
8. Saito, p. 390.
9. Saito, p. 392.
10. Saito, p. 392.
11. Saito, p. 394.

12. Lynette Clemetson, "Asian American Notes Issues Central to Them for Elections," *New York Times*, February 13, 2004.

13. Terry Hong, "Collateral Damage: Asian Americans On War & Peace," *AsianWeek*, Sept. 6–Sept. 12, 2002.

14. "City to Help Curb Harassment of Asian Students at High School," *New York Times*, June 2, 2004.

15. Ling-chi Wang, "Asian Americans and Debates about Affirmative Action," in *Major Problems in Asian American History*, (eds.) Lon Kurashige and Alice Yang Murray (New York: Houghton Mifflin Company, 2003), pp. 450–456.

16. Dana Y. Takagi, *The Retreat From Race: Asian American Admissions and Racial Politics* (New Brunswick, NJ: Rutgers University Press, 1992), p. 96.

17. Ibid., p. 115.

18. Ethen Lieser, "Thirty Minutes with Elaine Chao," *AsianWeek*, August 24–30, 2000.

19. Takagi, *The Retreat From Race*, p. 148.

20. Paul Rockwell, "Asian American Voices for Affirmative Action," *In Motion Magazine*, 1997 (http://www.inmotionmagazine.com/rockasn.html).

21. Takagi, *The Retreat From Race*, p. 130.

22. *Capital Ideas*, Pacific Research Institute, Vol. 2, No. 19: May 14, 1997.

23. "S.F. Schools Keep Race Caps for Now: But appeals court wants Chinese Americans' Suit Heard Soon," *AsianWeek*, June 11–17, 1998.

24. Jeff Chang, "On the Wrong Side: Chinese Americans Win Anti-Diversity Settlement—and Lose in the End," *Color Lines*, Summer 1999.

25. Paul M. Ong, "The Affirmative Action Divide," in *Asian American Politics*, (eds.) Don Nakanishi and James S. Lai (New York: Rowman & Littlefield, 2003), p. 392.

26. Douglas Miller and Douglas Houston, "Distressed Asian American Neighborhoods," *AAPI Nexus: Asian American & Pacific Islanders Policy, Practice and Community*, Volume 1, Number 1 Summer/Fall 2003, pp. 67–84.

27. Kent Wong, "Building an Asian Pacific Labor Alliance," in *Asian American Politics*, (eds.) Don Nakanishi and James S. Lai, p. 428.

28. Owen Moritz, "Groundbreaking Sweatshop Suit," *Daily News*, June 12, 1998.

29. Diana Gonzalez, "Fired Garment Workers Hit Shop, Others in Suit," *Daily News*, May 5, 1998.

30. Andrew Hsiao, "Yo' Mama," *The Village Voice*, May 17–23, 2000.

31. Michelle Gotthelf, "Treated Like Dogs," *New York Post*, December 24, 2000.

32. Editorial, *Washington Post*, August 10, 1996, p. A18.

33. A.M. Rosenthal, Opinion Column, *New York Times*, August 8, 1996, p. A27.

34. *World Journal*, October 20, 1997, p. A3.

35. "President Bush Proposes New Temporary Worker Program." Remarks by the President on Immigration Policy, Office of the Press Secretary, January 7, 2004.

36. Philip Martin and Michael Teitelbaum, "The Mirage of Mexican Guest Workers," *Foreign Affairs*, No. 6, p. 117.

CHAPTER 28: The Middle Class Enters the Fray

1. Theresa Hsuchao, "Chinese Heritage Community Language Schools in the United States," *ERIC Digest*, June 1997.

2. Leland T. Saito, *Race and Politics: Asian Americans, Latinos, and Whites in a Los Angeles Suburb* (Chicago: University of Illinois Press, 1998), p. 32.

3. John Horton, *The Politics of Diversity: Immigration, Resistance, and Change in Monterey Park, California* (Philadelphia, PA: Temple University Press, 1995), p. 32.
4. Timothy Fong, *The First Suburban Chinatown: The Remaking of Monterey Park, California* (Philadelphia, PA: Temple University Press, 1994), p. 64.
5. Ibid., p. 71.
6. Horton, *The Politics of Diversity,* p. 71.
7. Ibid., pp. 123–25.
8. Michelle S. Man, "Sign Language: Changing Demographics in the City of Fremont Prompts Reactionary Legislation From the Old Guard to Harass New Residents," pamphlet.
9. Janet Dang, "Learning Limits: How Redrawn School Boundaries Are Pitting Asian American Parents Against One East Bay School District," *AsianWeek* 21, no. 29, March 16, 2000 (http://www.asianweek.com/2000_03_16/ feature_learninglimits.html).
10. Patricia Leigh Brown, "In One Suburb, Asian-Americans Gain a Firm Political Foothold," *New York Times,* January 3, 2004, p. A9.
11. Suzanne Lee, "Cupertino Candidates Discuss Changing Demographics," *AsianWeek,* October 18, 2001.
12. Michelle Ku and Pam Marino, "Asians of Change," News and Issues, *Metroactive,* October 8, 1998, pp. 2–3.
13. Brown, "In One Suburb," p. A9.
14. Teresa Watanabe, "Chinese Immigrants Take to U.S. Politics," *Los Angeles Times,* April 8, 2003.

CHAPTER 29: The Money Trail

1. Pei-te Lien, "Taking a Pulse of Chinese Americans at the Dawn of the 21st Century: Results from the Multi-Site Asian American Political Survey," *Chinese America: History and Perspectives* (Chinese Historical Society of America, 2002), p. 17. (Survey, sponsored by a National Science Foundation grant, conducted on December 16, 2001.)
2. Bill Wong, "Fong Versus Boxer—Identity Politics Could Prove Decisive in California Senate Race," *Pacific News Service,* September 8, 1998, p. 4.
3. Wong, "Fong Versus Boxer," p. 6.
4. Peter Kwong and JoAnn Lum, "Chinese-American Politics: A Silent Minority Tests Its Clout," *Nation,* January 16, 1988, p. 4; Leland T. Saito, *Race and Politics: Asian Americans, Latinos, and Whites in a Los Angeles Suburb* (Chicago: University of Illinois Press, 1998), p. 92.
5. Kwong and Lum, "Chinese-American Politics," pp. 49–52.
6. Judy Yu and Grace T. Yuan, "Lessons Learned from the 'Locke for Governor' Campaign," in *Asian Americans and Politics: Perspectives, Experiences, Prospects,* ed. Gordon Chang (Stanford, CA: Stanford University Press, 2001), pp. 359–60.
7. Yu and Yuan, "Lessons Learned," pp. 363–64.
8. John J. Miller, "Asian Americans Head for Politics: What Horse Will They Ride," *American Enterprise,* March–April 1995.
9. Ibid.
10. Aihwa Ong, *Flexible Citizenship: The Cultural Logics of Transnationality* (Durham, NC: Duke University Press, 1999), p. 6.
11. Joel Kotkin, "Will the Chinese Save L.A.?" in "Fixing America's Schools," special

issue, *The American Enterprise*, September–October 1996 (http://www.taemag.com/issues/articleid.16298/article_detail.asp).

12. Assif Shameen, "Henry's New World: How a Hong Kong Property Group Is Riding Out the Slump," *AsianWeek*, October 20, 1995.

13. Ong, *Flexible Citizenship*, pp. 99–100.

14. Henry Der, "Don't Play the Money Game to Be Heard," *Los Angeles Times*, September 17, 1997.

15. Ling-chi Wang, "Whose Asian Peril? Asian Americans Should Be as Concerned about the Asian Money Connection as Dole and Gingrich Are," *Salon*, March 9, 2004.

16. Brooks Jackson, "Clinton's Re-election Road Paved With Money," *CNN/Times*, February 25, 1997 (http://www.cnn.com/allpolitics/1997/02/24/forsale/).

17. Ibid.

18. Ian Christopher, "Rewards for Contributors: White House Expected to Release 'Lincoln Bedroom' List," *McCaleb/CNN*, September 22, 2000.

19. "Unfair Scrutiny? The Asian-American Community and the US Political System," PBS, March 21, 1997.

20. Jackson, "Clinton's Re-election Road."

21. Helen Zia, *Asian American Dreams: The Emergence of an American People* (New York: Farrar, Straus and Giroux, 2000), p. 298.

22. Ling-chi Wang, "Race, Class, Citizenship, and Extraterritoriality," in *Asian American Politics*, ed. Don Nakanishi and James S. Lai (New York: Rowman and Littlefield, 2003), p. 282.

23. Frank Wu and Francey Lim Youngberg, "People from China Crossing the River: Asian American Political Empowerment and Foreign Influence," in Chang, *Asian Americans and Politics*, pp. 311–53.

24. Bert Eljera, "Opening Session Brings Revelations, Strong Reactions," *AsianWeek*, July 11–17, 1997.

25. Frank Wu, "Money Follows Power: Report Confirms Anti-Asian Bias in Campaign Finance Controversy," *AsianWeek*, December 4–10, 1997.

26. Wang, "Race, Class, Citizenship, and Extraterritoriality," p. 286.

27. Annie Nakao, "Asian Political Image Marred," *San Francisco Examiner*, November 17, 1996.

28. Wang, "Whose Asian Peril?"

29. Charles Smith, "Johnny Chung Tells All: Secret Meetings with Chinese Military, Stonewalling by Justice," *WorldNetDaily*, November 17, 1999 (http://www.worldnetdaily.com/news).

30. Zia, *Asian American Dreams*, p. 299.

31. Dan Stober and Ian Hoffman, *A Convenient Spy: Wen Ho Lee and the Politics of Nuclear Espionage* (New York: Simon and Schuster, 2001), p. 330.

CHAPTER 30: The China/Chinese American Tangle

1. Jim Lobe, "For the New US Right, China Is Wrong," *Asia Times*, March 30, 2001.

2. Jay Branegan, "The Hard-Liners: A 'Blue Team' Blocks Beijing," *Times Asia*, April 16, 2001.

3. Nicholas Kristof, "U.S. and China Appear to Be on an Economic Collision Course," *New York Times*, December 13, 2003.

4. Philip Coggan, "Whatever It Is, It's Sure to Be China's Fault," *Financial Times*, January 31–February 1, 2004, p. 12.

5. Andrew Pollock and Keith Bradsher, "China's Need for Metal Keeps U.S. Scrap Dealers Scrounging," *New York Times*, March 12, 2004, p. C3.

6. Jim Yardley, "China's Economic Engine Needs Power (Lots of It)," Week in Review, *New York Times*, March 14, 2004, p. 3.

7. Ibid.

8. Gal Luft, "U.S.A., China on Collision Course Over Oil," *Los Angeles Times*, February 4, 2004, p. 1.

9. David Harvey, *The New Imperialism* (New York: Oxford University Press, 2003), p. 25.

10. Lee Kim Chew, "US Looks for Deeper Alliances as Focus Shifts to Asia," *Straits Times*, February 21, 2004.

11. "Defense Official Feith on Russia, Missile Defense," transcript, Department of Defense News Briefing, Mr. Douglas J. Feith, Under Secretary of Defense for Policy, September 4, 2001.

12. Jay Branegan, "The Hard-Liners: A 'Blue Team' Blocks Beijing," *Time/Asia*, April 16, 2001, vol. 157, no. 15.

13. Organization of Chinese Americans statement, issued by its president, April 11, 2001.

14. Chisun Lee, "Fun with China: In Media Merriment, Fine Line Between Humor and Hate," *Village Voice*, October 7, 2001.

15. Tim Weber, "Is China a Goldmine or Minefield?" *BBC News*, February 19, 2004.

16. *Shijie Ribao* (The World Journal), December 15, 2002, p. A9.

17. Zhu Rongji (speech at Massachusetts Institute of Technology, Cambridge, MA, April 1999).

18. Hugo Restall, "China's Economy Is a Paper Tiger," Opinion Page, *Wall Street Journal*, August 5, 2003, p. A9.

19. Terry Cook, "Drive for Coal Produces More Deaths in China's Mines," *World Socialist*, March 16, 2004 (http://wsws.org/articles).

20. *China Labor Bulletin*, April 28, 2003.

21. Philip P. Pan, "Chinese Leaders Speak of Reform, But How Quickly?" *Washington Post*, March 14, 2004, p. A19.

22. Dusanka Miscevic and Peter Kwong, "The Overseas Chinese Miracle," *Asian American Policy Review* 7 (1997): 75.

23. Mary Sit, "Company Looks to Cash in on Rush for US-Educated Workers in Asia," *Boston Globe*, November 25, 1994.

24. Brian Johns, "Asian Boom Produces Big Market for 'Bi-ers,'" *Journal of Commerce*, November 14, 1994.

25. James Jinguo Shen, "Communicating Through Conflict, Compromise, and Cooperation: The Strategic Role of Chinese American Scholars in the U.S.–China Relationship," in *The Expanding Role of Chinese Americans in U.S.–China Relations*, ed. Peter H. Koehn and Xiao-huang Yin (Armonk, NY: M. E. Sharpe, 2002), p. 104.

26. B. Xiang, "On Emigration from China," special issue 1, *International Migration* 41, no. 3 (2003).

27. Zuoyue Wang, "Chinese American Scientists and US-China Scientific Relations," in Koehn and Yin, *The Expanding Role of Chinese Americans*, p. 219.

28. Shen, "Communicating Through Conflict," p. 105.

29. Wellington K.K. Chan, "Chinese American Business Networks and Trans-Pacific Economic Relations Since the 1970s," in Koehn and Yin, *The Expanding Roles of Chinese Americans*, p. 158.

30. Tom Plate, "Cox Report Was 'an Exercise in Amateur-Hour Paranoia': The House Report on Chinese Spying Drew Sinister Implications Out of Tenuous Reasoning," *Pacific Prospect*, July 21, 1999.

31. Notra Trulock, "China Targets Another Energy Lab," *Media Monitor*, August 29, 2003.

32. Ian Urbina, "The Corporate PNTR Lobby: How Big Business Is Paying Millions to Gain Billions in China," *Multinational Monitor* 21, no. 5 (May 2000).

33. David Wessel, "Foreign Scholars Throng U.S. Schools," *Asian Wall Street Journal*, March 2–4, 2001.

34. David Shields, "Foreign Guys Can Shoot: That's Why the N.B.A. Is in the Import Business," *New York Times Magazine*, March 3, 2002, pp. 56–57.

35. William J. Holstein, "How a Technology Gap Helped China Win Jobs," *New York Times*, July 18, 2004, p. BU9.

36. Carrie Kirby, "Opportunities in China Entice Overseas Chinese; Tech Professionals Returning to China; Opportunities are Plentiful in Nascent Market," *San Francisco Chronicle*, January 2, 2002.

37. Holstein, "How a Technology Gap Helped China Win Jobs," p. BU9.

38. Theresa Bradley, "Degrees of Discontent: Fewer Chinese Students Seek to Study in U.S.," *Shanghai Star*, June 10, 2004.

39. Ibid.

40. Ibid.

POSTSCRIPT

1. Laura Flanders, "Elaine Chao: Livin' the American Dream: First Daughter for the First Son," *CounterPunch*, April 1, 2004.

2. Ibid.

3. Chisun Lee, "Chao Time," *Village Voice*, January 30–February 6, 2001.

4. Rick Salutin, "The New Post-Imperial Imperialism," *Toronto Globe and Mail*, November 15, 2002.

5. David Harvey, *The New Imperialism* (London: Oxford University Press, 2003), p. 159.

6. Peter G. Peterson, *Running on Empty: How the Democratic and Republican Parties Are Bankrupting Our Future and What Americans Can Do About It* (New York: Farrar, Straus and Giroux, 2004), p. xiii.

7. Chalmers Johnson, *The Sorrows of Empire: Militarism, Secrecy, and the End of the Republic* (New York: Metropolitan Books, 2004), p. 1.

Selected Bibliography

This is a list of the books that were most helpful in writing this book, and that offer a good starting point for further research. More detailed information can be found in the notes section.

GENERAL BOOKS

Chan, Sucheng. *Asian Americans: An Interpretive History.* Boston: Twayne, 1991.

Chang, Iris. *The Chinese in America: A Narrative History.* New York: Viking, 2003.

Chu, Y.K. *History of the Chinese People in America* (in Chinese). New York: China Times, 1975.

Daniels, Roger. *Asian America: Chinese and Japanese in the United States Since 1850.* Seattle: University of Washington Press, 1988.

———. *Coming to America: A History of Immigration and Ethnicity in American Life.* New York: HarperCollins, 1990.

Miscevic, Dusanka, and Peter Kwong. *Chinese Americans: The Immigrant Experience.* Hugh Lauter Levin Associates, 2000.

Nee, Victor G., and Brett de Bary Nee. *Longtime Californ': A Documentary Study of an American Chinatown.* New York: Pantheon, 1972.

Sung, Betty Lee. *Mountain of Gold: The Story of the Chinese in America.* New York: Macmillan, 1967.

Takaki, Ronald. *A Different Mirror: A History of Multicultural America.* Boston: Little, Brown, 1993.

———. *Strangers from a Different Shore: A History of Asian Americans.* Boston: Little, Brown, 1989.

Zinn, Howard. *A People's History of the United States, 1492–Present.* New York: Harper Perennial, 1995.

IMPORTANT PERIODICALS AND WEBSITES

Asian American Empowerment (http://modelminority.com)
Asian American Village (http://www.imdiversity.com)
AsianWeek
Amerasian Journal
China Daily News (in Chinese) for pre–1950 events
The Duowei Times (in Chinese) for current news
World Journal (in Chinese) for current events

PART I: THE CHINESE ENCOUNTER AMERICA (1840–1882)

Aarim-Heriot, Najia. *Chinese Immigrants, African Americans, and Racial Anxiety in the United States, 1848–82.* Urbana: University of Illinois Press, 2003.

Chang, Hsin-pao. *Commissioner Lin and the Opium War.* New York: W.W. Norton & Company, 1964.

Chen, Yong. *Chinese San Francisco, 1850–1943: A Trans-Pacific Community.* Stanford: Stanford University Press, 2000.

Chiu, Ping. *Chinese Labor in California: An Economic Study.* Madison: The State Historical Society of Wisconsin for the Department of History, University of Wisconsin, 1967.

Cohen, Lucy M. *Chinese in the Post–Civil War South: A People Without a History.* Baton Rouge: Louisiana State University Press, 1984.

Coolidge, Mary Roberts. *Chinese Immigration.* New York: Henry Holt, 1909.

Dirlik, Arif, ed. *Chinese on the American Frontier.* New York: Rowman & Littlefield, 2001.

Erick, Robert. *Ch'ing Policy Toward the Coolie Trade, 1847–1878.* Taipei: Chinese Material Center, 1982.

Fessler, Loren W., ed. *Chinese in America: Stereotyped Past, Changing Present.* New York: Vantage Press, 1983.

Goldfield, Michael. *The Color of Politics: Race and the Mainsprings of American Politics.* New York: The New Press, 1997.

Gyory, Andrew. *Closing the Gate: Race, Politics, and the Chinese Exclusion Act.* Chapel Hill: University of North Carolina Press, 1998.

Haney-López, Ian F. *White by Law: The Legal Construction of Race.* New York: New York University Press, 1996.

Ignatiev, Noel. *How the Irish Became White.* New York: Routledge, 1995.

Lydon, Sandy. *Chinese Gold: The Chinese in the Monterey Bay Region.* Capitola, CA.: Capitola Book Company, 1985.

McClain, Charles J. *In Search of Equality: The Chinese Struggle against Discrimination in Nineteenth-Century America.* Berkeley: University of California Press, 1994.

McKeown, Adam. *Chinese Migrant Networks and Cultural Changes: Peru, Chicago, Hawaii, 1900–1936.* Chicago: University of Chicago Press, 2001.

Miller, Stuart Creighton. *The Unwelcome Immigrant: The American Image of the Chinese, 1785–1882.* Berkeley: University of California Press, 1969.

Pan, Lynn. *Sons of the Yellow Emperor: A History of the Chinese Diaspora.* Boston: Little Brown, 1990.

Saxton, Alexander. *The Indispensable Enemy: Labor and the Anti-Chinese Movement in California.* Berkeley: University of California Press, 1971.

Tchen, John Kuo Wei. *New York Before Chinatown: Orientalism and the Shaping of American Culture, 1776–1882.* Baltimore: Johns Hopkins University Press, 1999.

Tsai, Shih-shan Henry. *China and the Overseas Chinese in the United States, 1868–1911.* Fayetteville: University of Arkansas Press, 1983.

———. *The Chinese Experience in America.* Bloomington: Indiana University Press, 1986.

Wang, Gungwu. *China and the Chinese Overseas.* Singapore: Times Academic Press, 1991.

Zhu, Liping. *A Chinaman's Chance: The Chinese on the Rocky Mountain Mining Frontier.* Boulder: University Press of Colorado, 1997.

Zo, Kil Young. "Chinese Emigration into the United States, 1850–1880." PhD diss., Columbia University, 1971.

PART II: THE TRANSNATIONAL GHETTO: LIFE DURING THE EXCLUSION ERA (1882–1945)

Chan, Sucheng. ed. *Entry Denied: Exclusion and the Chinese Community in America, 1882–1943.* Philadelphia: Temple University Press, 1991.

Chen, Shehong. *Being Chinese, Becoming Chinese American.* Chicago: University of Illinois Press, 2002.

Chun, Gloria Heyung. *Of Orphans and Warriors: Inventing Chinese American Culture & Identity.* New Brunswick, NJ: Rutgers University Press, 2000.

Dinnerstein, Leonard, Roger L. Nichols and David M. Reimers. *Natives and Strangers: A Multicultural History of Americans.* London: Oxford University Press, 1996.

Higham, John. *Strangers in the Land: Patterns of American Nativism, 1860–1925.* New Brunswick: Rutgers University Press, 1988.

Hom, Marlon K. *Songs of Gold Mountain: Cantonese Rhymes from San Francisco Chinatown.* Berkeley: University of California Press, 1987.

Hsu, Madeline Y. *Dreaming of Gold, Dreaming of Home: Transnationalism and Migration Between the United States and South China, 1882–1943.* Stanford, CA: Stanford University Press, 2000.

Kwong, Peter. *Chinatown, N.Y.: Labor and Politics, 1930–1950.* New York: The New Press, 2001.

Lai, Him Mark, Genny Lim, and Judy Yung. *Island: Poetry and History of Chinese Immigrants on Angel Island, 1910–1940.* Seattle: Washington University Press, 1980.

Lai, Him Mark. *Becoming Chinese American: A History of Communities and Institutions.* Walnut Creek, CA: AltaMira Press, 2004.

———. *Cong huaqiao dao huaren* (From Sojourners to Ethnic Chinese Americans). Hong Kong: Joint Publishing, 1992.

Leong, Gor Yun. *Chinatown Inside Out.* New York: Barrows Mussey, 1936.

Lyman, Stanford M. *Chinese Americans.* New York: Random House, 1974.

Ma, L. Eve Armentrout. *Revolutionaries, Monarchists, and Chinatown: Chinese Politics in the Americas and the 1911 Revolution.* Honolulu: University of Hawaii Press, 1990.

McKee, Delber L. *Chinese Exclusion versus the Open Door Policy, 1900–1906.* Detroit, MI: Wayne State University Press, 1977.

Siu, Paul Chang Pang. *The Chinese Laundryman: A Study of Social Isolation.* Edited with introduction by John Kuo Wei Tchen. New York: New York University Press, 1987.

Wang, Guanhua. *In Search of Justice: The 1905–1906 Chinese Anti-American Boycott.* Cambridge: Harvard University Press, 2001.

Wang, Xinyang. *Surviving the City: The Chinese Immigrant Experience in New York City, 1890–1970.* New York: Rowman & Littlefield, 2001.

Wong, K. Scott, and Sucheng Chan, eds. *Claiming America: Constructing Chinese American Identities During the Exclusion Era.* Philadelphia: Temple University Press, 1998.

Yee, Alfred. *Shopping at Giant Foods: Chinese American Supermarkets in Northern California*. Seattle: University of Washington Press, 2003.

Yu, Henry. *Thinking Orientals: Migration, Contact, and Exoticism in Modern America*. New York: Oxford University Press, 2001.

Yu, Renqiu. *To Save China, To Save Ourselves: The Chinese Hand Laundry Alliance of New York*. Philadelphia: Temple University Press, 1992.

Yung, Judy. *Unbound Feet: A Social History of Chinese Women in San Francisco*. Berkeley: University of California Press, 1995.

PART III: THE COLD WAR SHAPES CHINESE AMERICA (1946–1965)

Chin, Tung Pok with Winifred C. Chin, *Paper Son: One Man's Story*. Philadelphia: Temple University Press, 2000.

Isaacs, Harold R. *Scratches on our Minds: American Images of China and India*. New York: John Day Co., 1958.

Jespersen, T. Christopher. *American Images of China, 1931–1949*. Stanford: Stanford University Press, 1996.

Kwong, Peter. *Chinatown, N.Y.: Labor and Politics, 1930–1950*. New York: Monthly Review Press, 1979.

Lee, Robert G. *Orientals: Asian Americans in Popular Culture*. Philadelphia: Temple University Press, 1999.

Lee, Rose Hum. *The Chinese in the United States of America*. Hong Kong: Hong Kong University Press, 1960.

Ngai, Mae M. *Impossible Subjects: Illegal Aliens and the Making of Modern America*. Princeton: Princeton University Press, 2004.

Takaki, Ronald. *Double Victory: A Multicultural History of America in World War II*. Boston: Little Brown, 2000.

Zhao, Xiaojian. *Remaking Chinese America: Immigration, Family, and Community, 1940–1965*. New Brunswick, NJ: Rutgers University Press, 2002.

PART IV: FROM CIVIL RIGHTS AND IDENTITY POLITICS (1965–1980s)

Chan, Jeffery Paul, Frank Chin, Lawson Fusao Inada, and Shawn Wong, eds. *The Big Aiiieeeee!: An Anthology of Chinese American and Japanese American Literature*. New York: Meridian, 1991.

Chin, Frank, Jeffery Paul Chan, Lawson Fusao Inada, and Shawn Wong, eds. *Aiiieeeee!: An Anthology of Asian-American Writers*. Washington, DC: Howard University Press, 1983.

Espiritu, Yen Le. *Asian American Panethnicity: Bridging Institutions and Identities*. Philadelphia: Temple University Press, 1992.

Gee, Emma, ed. *Counterpoint: Perspectives on Asian America*. Los Angeles: Asian American Studies Center/University of California, Los Angeles, 1976.

Goldfield, Michael. *The Color of Politics: Race and the Mainsprings of American Politics*. New York: The New Press, 1997.

Lee, Rose Hum. *The Chinese in the United States of America*. Hong Kong: Hong Kong University Press, 1960.

Lowe, Lisa. *Immigrant Acts: On Asian American Cultural Politics*. London: Duke University Press, 1996.

Omi, Michael, and Howard Winant. *Racial Formation in the United States: From the 1960s to the 1980s*. New York: Routledge, 1991.

Piven, Frances Fox and Richard A. Cloward. *Poor People's Movements: Why They Succeed, How They Fail.* New York: Vintage Press, 1977.

Tachiki, Amy, Eddie Wong, Franklin Odo, with Buck Wong, eds. *Roots: An Asian American Reader.* Los Angeles: UCLA Asian American Studies Center, 1971.

Takagi, Dana Y. *The Retreat from Race: Asian-American Admissions and Racial Politics.* New Brunswick, NJ: Rutgers University Press, 1992.

Wei, William. *The Asian American Movement.* Philadelphia: Temple University Press, 1993.

Yin, Xiao-huang. *Chinese American Literature Since the 1850s.* Chicago: University of Illinois Press, 2000.

PART V: CONTEMPORARY CHINESE AMERICA

Bonacich, Edna, Lucie Cheng, Nora Chinchila, Nora Hamilton and Paul Ong, eds. *Global Production: The Apparel Industry in the Pacific Rim.* Philadelphia: Temple University Press, 1994.

Fong, Timothy. *The Contemporary Asian American Experience: Beyond the Model Minority.* Upper Saddle River, NJ: Prentice Hall, 2002.

———. *The First Suburban Chinatown: The Remaking of Monterey Park, California.* Philadelphia: Temple University Press, 1994.

Koehn, Peter H. and Xiao-huang Yin, eds. *The Expanding Roles of Chinese Americans in U.S.–China Relations.* Armonk, NY: M.E. Sharpe, 2002.

Kwong, Peter. *Forbidden Workers: Chinese Illegal Immigrants and American Labor.* New York: The New Press, 1997.

———. *The New Chinatown.* New York: The New Press (revised edition), 2000.

Lin, Jan. *Reconstructing Chinatown: Ethnic Enclave, Global Change.* Minneapolis: University of Minnesota Press, 1998.

Louie, Vivian S. *Compelled to Excel: Immigration, Education, and Opportunity among Chinese Americans.* Stanford: Stanford University Press, 2004.

Ong, Paul, Edna Bonacich, and Lucie Cheng, eds. *The New Asian Immigration in Los Angeles and Global Restructuring.* Philadelphia: Temple University Press, 1994.

Wong, Bernard. *Chinatown, Economic Adaptation and Ethnic Identity of the Chinese.* New York: Holt, Rinehart and Winston, 1982.

———. *Ethnicity and Entrepreneurship: The New Chinese Immigrants in the San Francisco Bay Area.* Boston: Allyn and Bacon, 1998.

PART VI: SUBURBAN AND SYMBOLIC POLITICS

Chang, Gordon H., ed. *Asian Americans and Politics: Perspectives, Experiences, Prospects.* Stanford, CA: Stanford University Press, 2001.

Dillard, Angela D. *Guess Who's Coming to Dinner Now? Multi-cultural Conservatism in America.* New York: New York University Press, 2001.

Harvey, David. *The New Imperialism.* New York: Oxford University Press, 2003.

Horton, John. *The Politics of Diversity: Immigration, Resistance, and Change in Monterey Park, California.* Philadelphia: Temple University Press, 1995.

Johnson, Chalmers. *The Sorrows of Empire: Militarism, Secrecy, and the End of the Republic.* New York: Metropolitan Books, 2004.

Nakanishi, Don, and James S. Lai, eds. *Asian American Politics.* New York: Rowman & Littlefield, 2003.

Ong, Aihwa. *Flexible Citizenship: The Cultural Logics of Transnationality*. Durham, NC: Duke University Press, 1999.

Saito, Leland T. *Race and Politics: Asian Americans, Latinos, and Whites in a Los Angeles Suburb*. Chicago: University of Illinois Press, 1998.

Stober, Dan and Ian Hoffman. *A Convenient Spy: Wen Ho Lee and the Politics of Nuclear Espionage*. New York: Simon and Schuster, 2001.

Zia, Helen. *Asian American Dreams: The Emergence of an American People*. New York: Farrar, Straus and Giroux, 2000.

Index